Including all the features that make this book
A BESTSELLER!

■ **A wealth of pedagogical features** include author boxes, focus boxes, film boxes, a glossary of literary terms, Internet resources, charts, and tables to enhance student learning

■ **Author Boxes** acquaint students with prominent writers and their views on current issues as they relate to literature

■ **Focus Boxes** provide annotated bibliographies of new books on important topics

■ **Film Boxes** suggest ways for teachers to make connections between books and film

■ **Coverage of nonfiction books** is incorporated throughout each chapter and focused on in Chapter 9

■ **Recommended readings** allow students to move beyond the text and further explore concepts and literature presented

Additional resources and materials are available at
www.ablongman.com/donelson7/e

Seventh Edition

Literature for Today's Young Adults

Kenneth L. Donelson
Arizona State University

Alleen Pace Nilsen
Arizona State University

PEARSON

Boston   New York   San Francisco
Mexico City   Montreal   Toronto   London   Madrid   Munich   Paris
Hong Kong   Singapore   Tokyo   Cape Town   Sydney

SERIES EDITOR: Aurora Martínez Ramos
SERIES EDITORIAL ASSISTANT: Erin Beatty
SENIOR MARKETING MANAGER: Elizabeth Fogarty
COMPOSITION BUYER: Linda Cox
MANUFACTURING BUYER: Andrew Turso
SENIOR EDITORIAL-PRODUCTION ADMINISTRATOR AND DESIGNER: Karen Mason
EDITORIAL-PRODUCTION SERVICE: Walsh & Associates, Inc.
ELECTRONIC COMPOSITION: Publishers' Design and Production Services, Inc.
COVER ADMINISTRATOR: Linda Knowles
COVER DESIGNER: Suzanne Harbison

For related titles and support materials, visit our online catalog at www.ablongman.com.

LIBRARY OF CONGRESS CATALOGING-IN-PUBLICATION DATA
Donelson, Kenneth L.
    Literature for today's young adults / Kenneth L. Donelson, Alleen Pace
Nilsen.-- 7th ed.
        p. cm.
    Authors' names appear in reverse order in 6th ed.
    Includes bibliographical references and index.
    ISBN 0-205-41035-9
    1. Teenagers--Books and reading—United States.   2. Young adult
literature--History and criticism.   3. Young adult fiction—History and
criticism.   4. Young adult literature—Bibliography.   5. Young adult
fiction--Bibliography. I. Nilsen, Alleen Pace. II. Title.

    Z1037.A1D578 2004
    028.5'5--dc22

                                                         2004044306

Printed in the United States of America

10 9 8 7 6 5 4 3 2 1   10 09 08 07 06 05 04

To the memory of
our dear friend and teacher,
G. Robert Carlson,
1917–2003

And to our grandchildren
who are happily finding many of these books:

From Ken to
Jason, Devon, Valerie, Amanda, Jo Jo, Jackie, Jacob, and
Kayden (our first great-grandson)

From Alleen to
Taryn, Britton, Kami, Erich, David, Lauren,
Michael, Jenna, Jim, and Luke

Brief Contents

Contents

Part Two
Modern Young Adult Reading   111

Specialized Contents

Author Statements

Tables and Charts

As we have said before, doing another version of our book is both an obligation and an opportunity because the field of young adult books is constantly changing. Since the first edition, defining the nature of the literary canon has become more and more confused, no matter how many of our conservative friends are only too happy to provide a list of what makes up the "true" canon. A few years ago, how many of us could have foreseen the effect of computers—as word processors—on writing programs across the country? How many of us would have foreseen the effect of email or websites on young people? And how many would have foreseen the effect of VCRs or, now, DVDs on the literature curriculum in some schools?

Young adult literature continues to gain attention and respectability as well as support. Where bookstores might have had only a few YA books on their shelves, now there are many, and Amazon has most of the leading YA writers and their books.

The problem, as it has always been, is defining young adult literature so that it is differentiated from adult literature. Some teachers and librarians have argued that Francesca Lia Block's novels, surrealistic and Hollywood-bound as they are, are adult books, partly because of the content and Block's style. Young people know better, but there's nothing new about the issue. Judy Blume's *Forever* was deemed so outside the sphere of YA literature that Bradbury Press created a one-time only adult division that included only one book, *Forever*, to protect itself from the inevitable criticism that the book was sure to receive. The only surprise is that no other publisher has tried the same ploy, though a few have come close by listing a suspect title in both young adult and adult divisions.

Defining young adult literature is not easy. The confusion is illustrated in the Sunday edition of the *New York Times* for September 7, 2003, in Polly Shulman's guide to movies soon to come out, "Crib Sheet: What to Read at the Movies," she writes of *Girl with a Pearl Earring,*

> Although [it] spent most of 2001 on the *New York Times* list of best-selling paperbacks, it has all the hallmarks of a successful young-adult movie: a teenage heroine, an educational setting, a painful run-in with love and a tug-of-war between family responsibilities and the allure of art.

So it goes.

When we sat down to plan this edition of our textbook, we agreed that it should look forward to see what new books and new trends and ideas are coming out but also, just as important, what older books deserved to be brought to our readers' attention. Young adult literature has accomplished much in the 135 years since the publication of Alcott's *Little Women.* To write only of the new is to do little except tell what is hot. To write only of the old is to do little except visit a graveyard.

The field of young adult literature is changing, as was dramatically brought home by the recent deaths of such significant writers as Robert Cormier, Virginia Hamilton, Joan Lowery Nixon, Chaim Potok, and Paul Zindel. These talented individuals deserve much of the credit for bringing respect to our field. We are thankful that the new guard is already hard at work. Michael Cadnum is prolific, consistently entertaining, and brilliant. Vivian Vande Velde writes marvelous stories, usually touched with the supernatural and always touched with humor. Geraldine McCaughrean spins incredible adventure stories set on the high seas or in China or Oklahoma or wherever her fertile imagination takes her.

If you're curious about other newcomers, see Michael Cart's list on page 116 of his *English Journal* column in the September 2003 issue. While you're there, glance at page 7 and read Don Gallo's description of his column, "Bold Books for Innovative Teaching." The first sentence reads:

> More excellent novels, short stories, poems, and nonfiction appealing to high school readers have been published in the past three years than any previous time period in our history.

Whether Gallo is indulging in hyperbole is open to question, but his point—that publishers are producing many quality novels, short stories, poems, and nonfiction today—has merit.

One more time we want to thank Mary Jones, former ASU secretary in English Education. She retired before we started work on this edition, which is how we know what a debt of gratitude we owe her for previous editions. For help and support with this edition, we thank the English Department at ASU and especially our colleague Jim Blasingame. He shared not only his expertise and his books, but also his students, who are frequently pictured in class activities. Also, thanks to Lynn Nelson for his friendly support and to three of our doctoral students. Aaron Levy wrote the plea on behalf of drama teachers on p. 158, while Ann Dutton Ewbank did most of the work in finding and evaluating the various websites that we recommend, and Elizabeth Stolle directed our undergraduate students in the Literature Circles Service Learning Project described in Chapter 11.

And we wish to thank Aurora Martinez, the senior acquisitions editor at Allyn and Bacon, who supported us on this edition, along with the reviewers that she arranged for. We are grateful for the guidance of Dottie Bibbee, West Virginia University at Parkersburg; Cora Dunkley, University of South Florida; Fern Kory, Eastern Illinois University; and Linda Tabers-Kwak, University of Wisconsin at Green Bay.

One of these reviewers wrote, "Of course as the years go by, Nilsen and Donelson learn more and so their textbook keeps getting bigger and more expensive." We took this implied criticism seriously and made the following changes to reverse the trend, while still keeping the kind of comprehensive coverage that users tell us they want as a support for both beginning and graduate level classes:

- We moved most of the film boxes and some of our longer discussions such as the one on Robert Cormier's *The Chocolate War,* to our website: www.ablongman.com/donelson7e
- We invited one-third fewer authors to contribute statements.

- We cut down on the length of transitional materials by moving more books out of paragraphs and into focus boxes or timelines.
- Rather than giving full descriptions of journals, magazines, and organizations, we provided brief identifying comments and URLs.
- We deleted references to many books that we love but that have been out of print so long that even used copies are not being offered on Amazon.com.
- We pretended we were editing the writing of strangers and so conscientiously cut phrases, sentences, and paragraphs—even some that we loved.

On a more positive side, we have tried to provide more help for the many teachers and librarians working with students in junior high and middle schools. Of course we have written about many new books and new trends, and in Chapter 1, we added new materials dealing with questions about gender and literacy. In Chapter 10 we inserted information on graphic novels, while in Chapter 11 we added information on literature circles. Because the world around us changes so fast, we did almost a total rewrite of Chapter 3 dealing with connections between young adult literature, the mass media, and big business. We replaced our discussion of Pokémon, which by now has gone the way of the Hula Hoop, with one on archetypes, which we hope will be relevant to book discussions throughout the semester.

As a good luck talisman, we will end by repeating the quote we started out with when young adult literature was only ninety years old. We agree with its sentiments even more now that it is 115 years old:

> It is no uncommon thing to hear children's literature condemned as wholly bad, and some people are good enough to commiserate with me on having waded through so much ephemeral matter. It may be my fault or my misfortune not to be able to see my loss. I have spent many pleasant and I may say not unprofitable hours in company with the printed thoughts of Mr. Kingston, Mr. Ballantye, Mr. Henry, Jules Verne, Miss Alcott, Miss Meade, Mrs. Molesworth, Miss Doudney, Miss Yonge, and a dozen others, and hope to spend as many more in the time to come as a busy life will permit.*

And that, really, is why we are happy to have been given the privilege of writing—and rewriting—this textbook.

Kenneth L. Donelson

Alleen Pace Nilsen

*Should Children Have a Special Literature?" *The Parents' Review* 1 (June 1890): 339.

CHAPTER

1

Young Adults and Their Reading

"Of all passages, coming of age, or reaching adolescence, is the purest, in that it is the loneliest. In birth one is not truly conscious; in marriage one has a partner; even death is faced with a life's experience by one's side," wrote David Van Biema for a special issue of *Life* magazine devoted to *The Journey of Our Lives.*

He went on to explain that going from boy or girl to man or woman is "a huge leap on the slimmest of information." The person who fails grows older without growing wiser and faces ostracism, insanity, or profound sorrow. Because such a debilitated or warped individual is a "drag on the community," the community bands together with the young person to see that the journey is accomplished.[1]

Life would go more smoothly if young people's aspirations were simply to step into the roles of their parents. The job of growing up, however, is more demanding because, at the same time that young people are trying to become adults, they are also trying to show that they are different from their parents. This leaves each generation scrambling to find its own way to be unique, which is one of the reasons that literature for young adults tends to be a contemporary medium. Each generation wants its own stories.

What Is Young Adult Literature?

We recently heard young adults defined as "those who think they're too old to be children but who others think are too young to be adults." In this book, we use the term to include students in junior high as well as those graduating from high school and still finding their way into adult life. By *young adult literature,* we mean anything that readers between the approximate ages of 12 and 18 choose to read (as opposed to what they may be coerced to read for class assignments). When we talk about *children's literature,* we refer to books released by the juvenile or junior division of a publisher and intended for children from prekindergarten to about sixth grade.

*I*n addition to having young adult rooms and YA librarians, most libraries make an effort through programming and other services to show teenagers that they are no longer considered to be children, as with this invitation to join the Phoenix Public Library Teen Council.

While our definition of *children's literature* is fairly standard, we should caution that not all educators define young adults the same as we do. The Educational Resources Information Clearinghouse (ERIC), for example, defines young adults as those between the ages of 18 and 22, whereas the National Assessment of Educational Progress (NAEP), administered by the Educational Testing Service, refers to "young adults, ages 21 through 25."

We confess to feeling pretentious when referring to a 12- or 13-year-old as a *young adult,* but we shy away from using the term *adolescent literature* because as librarians have confided, "It has the ugly ring of pimples and puberty," and "It suggests *immature* in a derogatory sense." Still, many college courses in English departments are entitled *Adolescent Literature,* and, because of our English teaching backgrounds, we find ourselves using the term for variety, along with *teenage books, teen fiction,* and *YA* or *young adult literature.* The terms *juvenile literature, junior novel, teen novel,* and *juvie* have been used in the past, but they became so weighed down with negative connotations that they are seldom heard today. Even with the newer terms of *young adult* and *YA,* some teenagers feel condescended to, so librarians and teachers are looking for alternatives. David Spritz, writing in *Time* magazine in 1999, used the term *teen fiction* for the genre that he said "used to be called" *young-adult novels.*[2] While some librarians and bookstores have experimented with the term *popular literature,* at least in academic circles chances are that *young adult* is so firmly established that it will continue to be used for the near future. Anyone well acquainted with teenagers realizes that there is a tremendous difference between 12-year-olds and 17-year-olds, or even between 14-year-olds and 16-year-olds. As teenagers are buying more books and publishers have become more interested in developing this market, a subcategory of young adult literature has developed. These are the books aimed primarily at students in junior high or middle school. Most Newbery Award winners are what some people describe as *tweeners;* see the examples in Focus Box. 5.6, p. 166, "Loves and Laughs for Tweeners."

Patty Campbell has described tweener books as fiction "hanging on to the literary coattails" of young adult fiction.[3] Tweener books sell better than "true" young adult fiction because in nearly every geographical area there are more middle school and junior high libraries than high school libraries. Also, this is an age where adults (parents, grandparents, teachers, and librarians) are still purchasing books for young readers or at least having an influence on what they read. The books are, of course, shorter and simpler, and because they are about younger protagonists, the love relationships—and the language—are fairly innocent. This means the books are less likely to be censored.

Tweener books also are better fitted to series books because in most series (the *Harry Potter* books, as well as the *Laura Ingalls Wilder* books, are exceptions) the protagonists resemble those in sitcoms. The story starts with the protagonist in a particular situation, then a complication occurs, which is solved as much through luck or help from outside as through the efforts of the protagonist. By the end, the situation is back to normal so that the protagonist is ready to be picked up and put into a similar, but slightly different, story. This differs from "true" YA fiction because as Patty Campbell explains,

> The central theme of most YA fiction is becoming an adult, finding the answer to the question "Who am I and what am I going to do about it?" No matter what events are going on in the book, accomplishing that task is really what the book is about, and in the climactic moment the resolution of the external conflict is linked to a realization for the protagonist that helps shape an adult identity.[4]

She then cited a Richard Peck statement that "the last page of every YA novel should say not, 'The End' but 'The Beginning'." For some of Campbell's other opinions about YA literature see her statement on p. 4.

It wasn't until the early 1930s that most publishers divided their offerings into adult and juvenile categories. Today it is sometimes little more than chance whether an adult or juvenile editor happens to get a manuscript. Robert Cormier had never thought of himself as a writer for young people, but when his agent submitted *The Chocolate War* (see our website www.ablongman.com/donelson7e for a discussion) to Pantheon, the editor convinced Cormier that, as good as the book was, it would be simply one more in a catalog of adult books. If it were published for teenagers, however, it might sell well, and it certainly would not be just one more in a long string of

PATTY CAMPBELL
On Old Adult versus
Young Adult Books

*I*n the thirty years that I have been having fun being a critic of young adult literature, I've seen an amazing thing happen: Most YA fiction has become better than most adult fiction. This is a secret that only those of us in the club know, but a truth that should be trumpeted from the rooftops.

In 2001, when a gaggle of well-known adult writers flocked to try their hands at writing young adult novels, the media took notice, but only to praise these big names for being so generous as to produce a "children's book." There was no attempt to rank them within the pantheon of big names in young adult literature, no references to great YA writers against which they might be measured. But when all the hoopla died down and the smoke cleared, those of us who know our Bob Cormier and Chris Crutcher and Virginia Euwer Wolff immediately saw that most of these adult interlopers couldn't cut the mustard when it came to the YA novel. Even those one or two who seemed to have an adequate grasp of the parameters of the genre had produced works that were only middling good, compared to

what else was being published for teens that year.

Occasionally, when I give in to a friend's recommendation and read some highly touted new adult novel, I often find it self-indulgent, overwritten, meandering, trivial, unfocused. There is a discipline involved in writing YA fiction that comes from the need to grab those kids' short-lived attention from the first paragraph and keep them turning those pages, a discipline that requires a rigorous economy of words and a taut structure that moves the story with compelling directness to a conclusion that matters. To add subtlety of expression, richness of character development and setting, intricacy of voice and plot, integrity of moral thought, without losing this necessary spareness requires literary art of the highest caliber. If we really care about great writing, instead of encouraging young adults to read adult books, we should be encouraging adults to read young adult books.

Patty Campbell writes "The Sand in the Oyster" column for Horn Book and is the editor of Scarecrow Studies in Young Adult Literature for the Scarecrow Press. *Disturbing the Universe: The Life and Work of Robert Cormier* (tentative title) is forthcoming from Random House.

available adolescent novels. The editor's predictions came true, and Cormier later acknowledged that although his initial reaction to becoming a "young adult" author was one of shock followed by a month-long writer's block, he was grateful for the editorial help, which led to considerable attention from reviewers as well as his first financial success as an author.

People who enjoy reading and talking about books need to feel comfortable in using literary terms efficiently and accurately. The main terms used in this textbook are defined in Appendix A. Before going on to the other chapters in this text, it would probably be a good idea to review those terms to ensure that your understanding of them matches the way they are used throughout this textbook. Being comfortable using literary terms will:

- Give you terminology and techniques to use in sharing your insights with young readers.
- Help you gain insights into authors' working methods so that you get more out of your reading.

- Enable you to evaluate books and assist readers to move forward in developing the skills needed to further appreciate literature.
- Help you read reviews, articles, and critical analyses with greater understanding.

A Brief Unsettled Heritage

The decade of the mid-1970s through the mid-1980s may come to be known as the golden age of young adult literature. An editor told us that in the 1960s and 1970s, he could count on one hand the number of young adult authors who earned their living exclusively by writing (most were teachers or were partially supported by spouses), but by the end of the 1980s he could name thirty authors writing for teenagers who could accurately be described as affluent because of the way their books were selling.

Contributing to the change was the need by television and movie producers for stories that would appeal to a youth-oriented society. Also, in many schools, teachers who had previously scorned teenage books found themselves facing students who simply could not, or would not, read the so-called *classics*. Taking a pragmatic approach, these teachers concluded that it was better to teach adolescent literature than no literature at all. This made schools and libraries a primary market for young adult books, especially paperbacks. When the book industry discovered that teenagers were willing to spend their own money for paperbacks, both financial and critical bases began to change.

This sounds perfectly normal today, but it is a stark contrast to such earlier attitudes as the one expressed in 1965 by J. Donald Adams, editor of the "Speaking of Books" page in *The New York Times Book Review*. He said he had "nothing but respect for the writers of good books for children" because "the greatest books which children can enjoy are read with equal delight by their elders. But what person," he went on to ask, "of mature years and reasonably mature understanding (for there is often a wide disparity) can read without impatience a book written for adolescents."[5]

Twelve years later, in 1977 John Goldthwaite writing in *Harper's* gave as one of his nine suggestions for improving literature for young readers in particular and the world in general the termination of teenage fiction. His reasoning was that any literate 12-year-old could understand most science fiction and fantasy, and "[a]s for all that novelized stuff about alienation, drugs, and pregnancy, the great bulk of it might be more enjoyable presented in comic books."[6] With the recent advent of graphic novels, Goldthwaite may have been twenty-five years ahead of his time.

While we have grounds for rejecting this kind of negative criticism, we need to be aware that it exists. Such a pessimistic view of teenage books is an unfortunate literary heritage that may well influence the attitudes of school boards, library directors, parents, teachers, and anyone else who has had no particular reason to read and examine the best of the new young adult literature. Besides, so many new books for young readers appear each year (approximately 2,000, with about one-fourth of them aimed at teenagers) that people who have already made up their minds can probably find titles to support their beliefs no matter what they are. In an area as new as young adult literature, we can look at much of the disagreement and the conflicting views as inevitable—as signs of a lively and interesting field—a concept that will be further discussed in Chapter 3.

We also need to realize that many educators, while not as negative as these two critics, are nevertheless hesitant to support young adult literature. For example, in a 1998 book promoting a multicultural approach to literature, we were surprised and disappointed to read as part of the summary to a forty-four-page chapter on African American literature:

> Missing from this review are the writings of several African American authors who have tremendous appeal to young adults. Rosa Guy (*The Friends, Ruby, The Ups and Downs of Carl Davis III,* and *The Music of Summer*); Rita Williams-Garcia (*Blue Tights*); and Walter Dean Myers (*Scorpions, Glory Field*). Their writings are not part of the curriculum. The absence of their work in this chapter is not because these authors' voices are unimportant but because their work has yet to enter the mainstream of young adult literature used in schools in grades 9–12.[7]

We were glad to see at least an after-the-fact acknowledgment of these young adult authors but were disappointed that while the writer of the chapter was brave enough to give information about and recommendations for teaching dozens of stories and novels that are not currently part of the curriculum, her courage failed when it came to the young adult books. Perhaps she had not read them and so felt uncomfortable in recommending them, or perhaps she feels that it is hard enough to sell minority literature without also trying to sell young adult literature. Either way, her reluctance to recommend that young adult literature become part of the curriculum illustrates the mixed feelings that people have toward the genre.

Another illustration of the mixed feelings that people have is the current argument in the American Library Association revolving around the Alex Award, which was established in 1998 to honor adult titles that are being recommended for teenagers. The award's stated purpose is "to help librarians encourage young adults ages 12–18 to read by introducing them to high quality books written for adults." The award is named for Margaret Alexander Edwards, who, for her work during the 1940s and 1950s at the Enoch Pratt Free Library in Baltimore, is generally credited with being the first YA librarian. Librarians who voted against the idea of the award question the wisdom of moving teenagers out of YA books and into adult literature as fast as possible. Fans of young adult literature point out that once students start reading adult books, they are unlikely to return to YA books. The situation is similar to that of parents who take pride in sending their fifth and sixth graders to Saturday morning "Great Books" programs where they struggle through some of the greatest and longest classics in the English language. This spoils these books for many students. In our children's literature college classes, we sometimes meet students who have had such an experience, and they are amazed—and often resentful—at how much pleasure they missed. When they could have been reading wonderful children's literature, they were forced into struggling through books that they did not have the life experience to understand and appreciate.

As shown by the fact that throughout the chapters in this book we often include books published for general adult audiences, we do not believe in limiting students to young adult books, but we do believe in letting young people know that some wonderful writers have written books about the very kinds of experiences and emotions they are likely to relate to.

TED HIPPLE
On the Printz and Mock Printz Winners

*E*ver since I became involved with ALAN (the Assembly on Literature for Adolescents of the National Council of Teachers of English), I looked forward to each year's Newbery Award winner from the American Library Association. The winning book would be a topic of conversation at the ALAN events and would be featured in program sessions. Yet some years the Newbery went to books intended for audiences much younger than those normally considered in the young adult sector, a group regarded as about 12 to 17 or so. Thus, it was good news in 2000 when the ALA created the Printz Award for what its committee considered the best book of the past year *for young people 12 years of age and older.* Here was an award that, had it been around earlier, would have permitted such esteemed authors as Robert Cormier and Chris Crutcher to have won with books clearly beyond the reach of the typical Newbery audience.

First winners include *Monster* by Walter Dean Myers in 2000, *Kit's Wilderness* by David Almond in 2001, *A Step from Heaven* by An Na in 2002, *Postcards from No Man's Land* by Aidan Chambers in 2003, and *First Part Last* by Angela Johnson in 2004. Descriptions of these books and the runners up each year can be found on the ALA website.

As I mentioned above, earlier winners might well have included works by Cormier and Crutcher, and this belief probably helped to inspire scholars Sarah Cornish and Patrick Jones to explore that point further. They wondered what books might have won the award had it been around since, say, 1978. To find out, they used the ALA's best books for young adult lists (excepting 1989, when the list was not published because of changes in eligibility) and took the top ten for each year. They then created a ballot that they sent to some 125 leaders in the field of young adult literature, asking them to choose the one book from each set of ten that they would have chosen for the Printz Award, had it been in existence at the time of publication. Their findings, which they called the "Mock Printz Awardees," include many books that, though now perhaps a bit old by usual young adult literature standards, ought not to escape the attention of current teenagers or their teachers and librarians.

Their full report can be found in *Voice of Youth Advocates,* December 2002, but here are the winners for each year: M. E. Kerr's *Gentlehands,* 1978; Robert Cormier's *After the First Death,* 1979; Katherine Paterson's *Jacob Have I Loved,* 1980; Mildred Taylor's *Let the Circle Be Unbroken,* 1981; Nancy Garden's *Annie on My Mind,* 1982; Chris Crutcher's *Running Loose,* 1983; William Sleator's *Interstellar Pig,* 1984; Bruce Brooks's *The Moves Make the Man,* 1985; Cynthia Voigt's *Izzy Willy Nilly,* 1986; Brock Cole's *The Goats,* 1987; Walter Dean Myers's *Fallen Angels,* 1988; Francesca Lia Block's *Weetzie Bat,* 1990; Annette Klause's *The Silver Kiss,* 1991; Robert Cormier's *We All Fall Down,* 1992; Terry Davis's *If Rock and Roll Were a Machine,* 1993; Lois Lowry's *The Giver,* 1994; Karen Cushman's *Catherine, Called Birdy,* 1995; Chris Crutcher's *Ironman,* 1996; Rob Thomas's *Rats Saw God,* 1997; Edward Bloor's *Tangerine,* 1998; and Louis Sachar's *Holes,* 1999.

These current and mock-past winners and the Printz Award itself can enrich our knowledge of fine books.

Professor Ted Hipple, from the University of Tennessee at Knoxville, was elected President of ALAN in 1978. Following his presidency, he served for eighteen years as ALAN Executive Secretary. He edited the three-volume set of *Writers for Young Adults* produced by Scribners in 1997, with a supplement in 2000.

The Abracadabra Kid: A Writer's Life by Sid Fleischman. Greenwillow, 1996. Fleischman's story of his teenage years as a traveling magician is so interesting it was chosen for the Honor List.

All God's Children Need Traveling Shoes and **I Know Why the Caged Bird Sings** by Maya Angelou. Random House, 1986 and 1970. These lyrical and powerful autobiographies remain favorites of both adults and young readers.

Anonymously Yours by Richard Peck. Julian Messner, 1991. Readers can make interesting comparisons between the real-life events in *Anonymously Yours* and the fictional events that Peck writes about in his Newbery winning books: *A Long Way from Chicago* and *A Year Down Yonder.*

Bad Boy: A Memoir by Walter Dean Myers. Amistad Press, 2001. The two strengths of this book are the vivid details that Myers presents about Harlem in the 1940s and the documentation of his development from a street kid into a writer.

Counting Stars by David Almond. Delacorte, 2002. These eighteen stories about Almond's growing up in a large Roman Catholic family are told in the same magical and poetic tones that he has used in *Skellig, Heaven Eyes,* and *Kit's Wilderness.*

Frenchtown Summer by Robert Cormier. Delacorte, 1999. Although Cormier doesn't say this is an autobiography, the thirty narrative poems, all in first person, are told with such feeling that readers feel they are Cormier's own stories.

Hole in My Life by Jack Gantos. Farrar, 2002. Gantos spent a year in jail between high school and college because he helped sail a boatload of hashish from the Caribbean to New York City.

King of the Mild Frontier: An Ill-Advised Autobiography by Chris Crutcher. Greenwillow, 2003. Because Crutcher works as a family counselor, many of us thought his plots came from the kids he counsels, but this forthright memoir shows that he has personally "lived" many of the emotions he writes about.

Knots in My Yo-Yo String by Jerry Spinelli. Knopf, 1998. Spinelli uses the lively style of his fiction to tell about the events he remembers from his first 16 years.

Looking Back: A Book of Memories by Lois Lowry. Walter Lorraine, 1998. Lowry comments on and explains photos from four generations of her family. One reviewer shuddered at the thought of less skilled writers following suit.

ME, ME, ME, ME, ME, Not a Novel by M. E. Kerr. HarperCollins, 1983. Although these eleven short stories are just as much fun to read as are Kerr's novels, she says they are true accounts of the young life of Marijane Meaker, which is Kerr's real name.

My Life in Dog Years by Gary Paulsen. Delacorte, 1997. Paulsen recounts his experiences with ten different dogs—not the ones that went with him on the Iditarod race, which he writes about in his 1990 *Woodsong.*

Oddballs by William Sleator. Dutton, 1993. Kids who dream of getting even with family members by telling the world how strange they are can use Sleator's nine funny stories as a model.

The Pigman and Me by Paul Zindel. HarperCollins, 1992. Readers will both laugh and cry at this true account of a year in the teenage life of Paul Zindel when he was lucky enough to have Nonno Frankie (the model for Zindel's fictional Pigman) as a neighbor and friend.

A Way Out of No Way: Writing about Growing up Black in America, edited by Jacqueline Woodson. Holt, 1996. Woodson writes about the hope and inspiration that she received from reading books by James Baldwin, Ernest J. Gaines, Rosa Guy, and Ntozake Shange.

Fortunately, ever since the 1970s educators' interest in young adult books has continued to increase as shown by the success of such publications as *VOYA* (Voice of Youth Advocates) and *The ALAN Review* (Assembly on Literature for Adolescents of NCTE), the numbers of teachers and librarians attending workshops on contemporary young adult books, the inclusion of YA literature in reading and literature textbooks, and the honoring of YA writers and scholars through the Printz Award (see Ted Hipple's statement on p. 7), the Margaret A. Edwards award, and the National Book Award. See the Yalsa Booklists site (www.ala.org/yalsa/booklists) for a sampling of prizes currently being given in YA literature.

Today's Authors

If we compare the total group of today's young adult authors with those of a generation ago, we have much for which to be thankful. Don Gallo's *Speaking for Ourselves: Autobiographical Sketches by Notable Authors of Books for Young Adults* and its sequel, *Speaking for Ourselves, Too,* have autobiographical statements from nearly 150 active and well-respected authors. As part of a Twentieth-Century Writers Series, the St. James Press features nearly 500 authors in its 1999 *St. James Guide to Young Adult Writers* edited by Tom Pendergast and Sara Pendergast. Charles Scribner's Sons gave fuller writeups to the 125 authors featured in the three-volume set *Writers for Young Adults* edited by Ted Hipple and published in 1996. Another 25 are included in a year 2000 supplement.

We should be encouraged not only by the numbers but also by the variety. Today's writers for young readers include men and women from all socioeconomic levels and from all over the world writing about life experiences of every possible kind. Donna Jo Napoli is chair of the linguistics program at Swarthmore College; Joan Bauer came to writing from the world of advertising; Berlie Doherty wrote her first YA book after interviewing young adults for her job as a BBC telejournalist. At a recent National Council of Teachers of English conference, it was fun to listen to Gary Paulsen, Will Hobbs, and Theodore Taylor swap stories about their childhoods spent in places as varied as the Panama Canal Zone, the Philippines, and Craddock, Virginia. Their adult jobs ranged from wilderness guide to merchant seaman and soldier and from roofer to truck driver and teacher. In the course of gathering the comments for our Author Boxes, we also learned that U.S. fantasy writer Robin McKinley is married to the British fantasy writer Peter Dickinson, and they really do have a garden filled with the beautiful roses that McKinley likes to write about.

It is because we are so eager for you to get acquainted with young adult authors that we chose to make our first Focus Box (see p. 8) "Memoirs by Honor List Authors." We hope you will read at least one of these books and then go on to read one or more of the authors' novels. Also, see if you can find some of these authors' websites for more thorough introductions to some very interesting people.

One of the pleasures of working with contemporary authors of young adult books is that most of them are eager to reach out and communicate with their readers as shown by the snapshots on the following pages.

Since we prepared the last edition of this textbook, death came to five authors who were instrumental in developing young adult literature as we know it today. For all five, full-length obituary articles were nationally published, and a brief look at these obituary articles, listed alphabetically, will serve as both an indication of the diversity of YA authors and the growing respect being given to the field.

Robert Cormier (1925–2000) was identified in the headline as "Author of Enduring Books for Teenagers." "Although several of Mr. Cormier's novels were translated into more than a dozen languages and three were made into movies, he frequently came under attack by individuals and organizations disturbed by his uncompromising realism." When, more than ten years after he published his 1974 *The Chocolate War,* an interviewer for the *New York Times Book Review* asked Cormier if in his books he was sending the "depressing message that even savvy teenagers can't possibly outwit or buck *the system,*" Cormier replied, "They can buck it, but they can't beat it." Then he added, "the terrible thing is not to try."

Cormier began to write when he was only 12, and while he was still a teen had his first poems published in the Leominster town newspaper and a story "The Little Things That Count" in *The Sign,* a national Catholic magazine. In 1948, he began writing for *The Worcester Telegram* and then later for *The Fitchburg Sentinel,* where he stayed until 1978 when he left journalism to work full time on his books. "For decades, Mr. Cormier accepted telephone calls from young readers who felt lonely or distraught.

Chris Crutcher signs autographs for high school students after speaking to the Arizona English Teachers Conference in September 2002.

They discovered he had listed his phone number" in his 1977 *I Am the Cheese.* Before he wrote *The Chocolate War,* he wrote two early novels for adults—*Now and at the Hour* (1960) and *A Little Raw on Monday Mornings* (1963). They were both critical, but not financial, successes. However, they laid the groundwork for him to become " a master of novels for young adults."[8]

Virginia Hamilton (1936–2002) was named in honor of her grandfather's escape from slavery when he managed to leave Virginia by crossing the Ohio River. "Once a year," she wrote, he gathered his children around him, "Set down," he would say, "and I will tell you about slavery and why I ran, so that it will never happen to you." The first line of the obituary identified Hamilton as an "internationally recognized writer for children whose work celebrated the African-American experience as an essential component of American life." Her first book, *Zeely,* appeared in 1967 when the few children's books about black people were mainly "problem" novels, "which threw into sharp relief issues like segregation and poverty. *Zeely* was a rare departure. It was not that race was absent, but that it was so completely unremarkably present." Instead of placing the book in an inner city, Hamilton wrote about Zeely's summer on her uncle's farm where she "is captivated by an enigmatic local woman she believes is a Watusi queen." In 1975, Hamilton won a National Book Award and was the first black writer to be given the Newbery medal for *M. C. Higgins, the Great.* She also won Edgar Allan Poe, Coretta Scott King, and Hans Christian Andersen Medals and was given an honorary doctorate from Ohio State. For her most recent books she "combed dusty archives for early manuscripts with long-forgotten songs, riddles, and stories," which she rewrote "in an accessible vernacular, without the ugly misspellings historically used to render black dialect." Her philosophy was expressed in the subtitle of her *The People Could Fly: American Black*

*K*aren Hesse visits with attendees at one of the ALAN workshops held in conjunction with the annual meeting of the National Council of Teachers of English.

Folktales. Her editor had urged the more conventional wording, "Black American Folktales," but Hamilton said, "No. They're American first and black second."[9]

Joan Lowery Nixon (1927–2003) grew up in Hollywood and published her first poem in a children's magazine when she was 10 and her first short story when she was 17. At college she majored in journalism, which "she later said taught her to streamline her stories and fill them with factual details." All together she wrote more than 100 books, most of them based on newspaper accounts of murders and crimes. Her first book, *Mystery of Hurricane Castle,* was about two girls named after her own daughters, Kathy and Maureen. She sent it to twelve publishers before it was accepted. After this, she averaged two books a year. In 1979, she won her first Edgar Award for *The Kidnapping of Christina Lattimore.* She won subsequent Edgar awards for *The Séance* in 1980, *The Other Side of Dark* in 1986, and *The Name of the Game Was Murder* in 1993. She also wrote historical novels in which enterprising teens overcome personal obstacles.[10]

Chaim Potok (1929–2002) made Hasidic Judaism visible to the rest of the world through his best-selling *The Chosen, My Name Is Asher Lev,* and *The Promise.* The books were published as adult titles, but have probably been enjoyed by as many young readers as adults. He was surprised at their popularity. "I thought 500 people might be interested in reading this story about two Jewish kids," he said about *The Chosen,* which remained on the *New York Times* best seller list for six months and sold more than a million copies. He wrote mostly about young boys agonizing over abandoning Judaism to seek lives in the larger world, a dilemma that Potok lived through when he grew up in a New York Hasidic community, a place he described as "both joyous and oppressive simultaneously."[11]

Paul Zindel (1936–2003) graduated from Wagner College on Staten Island where, even though he was a chemistry major, he took a class from playwright Edward Albee. It was the Albee class that stuck with him during the ten years (1959 to 1969) he was teach-

Christopher Paul Curtis poses with students after speaking to one of our adolescent literature classes at ASU.

ing chemistry to high school students. He moonlighted as a playwright and in 1965 his play *The Effect of Gamma Rays on Man-in-the-Moon Marigolds* opened at the Alley Theatre in Houston. It was about the relationship between a sensitive girl, her epileptic sister, and their bitter and controlling mother. The title refers to the girl's high school science project. The play won the Pulitzer Prize, a New York Drama Critics Circle award, and an Obie, and when in 1970 it opened off-Broadway it played 819 performances. In 1966, a shortened screen version was produced on public television. Harper and Collins editor Charlotte Zolotow saw it and was so impressed at Zindel's skill in creating interesting and believable teenage dialogue that she contacted Zindel and convinced him to try his hand at a book for young adults. His first book, *The Pigman*, is told in alternating chapters by two teenagers who betray their friendship with an elderly man. While the reporter credited the book with introducing a new level of realism to the teen fiction arena, Zindel may be even more responsible for the flip, first-person style of dialogue that is a characteristic of modern young adult fiction. He is also responsible for increasing the respect accorded to YA books. Both Robert Cormier and M. E. Kerr acknowledged that before they entered the field of young adult literature, they read his work and weighed the fact that a Pulitzer Prize–winning playwright seemed happy to put forth his best efforts for teenagers. Zindel alternated between writing YA books and plays and movie scripts (including the 1972 *Up the Sandbox*, the 1973 *Mame*, and the 1986 *Runaway Train*) and YA books. In 2002 he was awarded the Margaret A. Edwards award for lifetime achievement by the Young Adult Library Ser-

William Sleator answers a question from a reader at an NCTE meeting.

vices Association. His most honored novels, besides *The Pigman,* include *My Darling, My Hamburger; I Never Loved Your Mind; Pardon Me, You're Stepping on My Eyeball!; Confessions of a Teenage Baboon;* and *The Pigman's Legacy.*[12]

Characteristics of the Best Young Adult Literature

We did some research to come up with a selection of books that would be representative of what both young adults and professionals working in the field consider the best books. We should caution, however, that books are selected as "the best" on the basis of many different criteria, and one person's best is not necessarily yours or that of the young people with whom you work. We hope that you will read many books so that you can recommend them not because you saw them on a list, but because you enjoyed them and believe they will appeal to a particular student.

In drawing up our list of "best books," we started with 1967 because this seemed to be a milestone year, when writers and publishers turned in new directions. We have compiled this list from several other "Best Book" lists, including yearly lists from the editors of *School Library Journal, Booklist, VOYA,* and *Horn Book* magazine and from such committees as those who choose the winners of the National Book Award and the winners of the Printz Award (see Ted Hipple's statement on p. 7) as well as those who choose the Newbery Awards and the Boston Globe-Horn Book Awards. We also pay special attention to the units of the American Library Association that put together such lists as "Best Books for Young Adults," "Recommended Books for the Reluctant Young Adult Reader," and "Notable Children's Books."

We have also used our own judgment and that of our colleagues and taken into consideration any special, retrospective lists that happen to appear. We have labeled the results of our research our Honor List, but we make no claim that it includes all the good books or even the best books published each year. We guarantee, however, that a number of knowledgeable people—professionals as well as young readers—were favorably impressed with each book that appears on the Honor List.

As the years have gone by, the number of books has made the list so unwieldy that for this edition we deleted some books that are out of print and moved the biographies, nonfiction, and collections of poetry and short stories to Focus Boxes in appropriate chapters. For example, see Focus Box 1.1 for memoirs written by authors whose books have been chosen for the Honor List. Informative nonfiction seems to date more quickly than other books; books still in print and in use are worked into Chapter 9. Occasionally, we add a book to the Honor List when it is growing in respect and popularity, as we did a few years ago with Robert Lipsyte's *The Contender,* Sandra Cisneros's *The House on Mango Street,* and Orson Scott Card's *Ender's Game.*

We used to identify books as coming from either the juvenile division or the adult division of a publishing house, but this no longer seems like crucial information because within the last fifteen years virtually all the Honor books have been published by juvenile divisions. This is partly because the reviewing sources from which we take our list are slanted toward juvenile books, but a second reason is that today's publishers have a kind of freedom they did not have in 1975 when, for example, Bradbury created an "adult" division specifically to publish Judy Blume's *Forever.* They hoped to soften the controversy by having it come out as an "adult" rather than a "children's book." An asterisk indicates that a book has been made into a movie.

Starting here with the Honor List (see Table 1.1), and continuing through this textbook, we have tried to be consistent in listing the original hardback publisher because this is the company who found the author and did the original editorial and publicity work. If the original publisher has released the book and it is being published by someone else, we have listed the new publisher if we knew about it. In previous editions we included a column in the Honor List giving the most recent paperback publisher, but for this edition we have deleted that column because the companies are increasingly the same. We also found that many of the books are published and distributed in paperback by multiple companies. One company will offer a format bound for school use, another a mass-market edition, and another a tape recording or a large-print edition. Today it is fairly easy to go online and find the publishers through such marketers as Amazon.com or Barnes & Noble or through an online version of Bowker's *Books in Print.* However, there is still a challenge in recognizing which subdivisions or imprints belong to which companies. Twice a year when we get a box from Random House, which for its size is unusually heavy, we know before even opening it that it contains the dozen separate catalogs from the various subdivisions of the company. Recently, when we were trying to obtain permission to use a cover photo of Walter Dean Myer's *Bad Boy: A Memoir,* we looked it up on various websites and saw that it was published by Amistad. Only when we got the real book did we recognize the familiar HarperCollins insignia and read the fine print inside to learn that Amistad is a new imprint from HarperCollins.

$\mathcal{T}$ABLE 1.1 HONOR LIST

Year	Title	Author	Publisher	Genre	Protagonist Sex	Age	No. of Pages	Ethnic Group or Unusual Setting
2003	The Canning Season	Polly Harvath	Farrar	Historical Humorous	F	13	208	Upstate Maine
	Fat Kid Rules the World	K. L. Going	Putnam	Realistic	M	Older teens	177	
	The First Part Last	Angela Johnson	Simon & Schuster	Realistic	M	16	144	African American
	A Northern Light	Jennifer Donnelly	Harcourt	Realistic	F	16	396	1906 Adirondacks
	The River Between Us	Richard Peck	Dial	Historical	F	Older teens	164	Illinois Civil War
	True Confessions of a Heartless Girl	Martha Brooks	Kroupa/Farrar	Realistic	F	17	192	Rural Canada
	Big Mouth and Ugly Girl	Joyce Carol Oates	HarperCollins	Realistic Problem Romance	F	17	226	
2002	Feed	M. T. Anderson	Candlewick Press	Science Fiction	M/F teens	Older	236	Dystopia
	The House of the Scorpion	Nancy Farmer	Atheneum	Science Fiction	M	Young teen	380	Dystopia
	The Kite Rider	Geraldine McCaughrean	HarperCollins Adventure	Historical	M teen	Young	272	13th-century China
	My Heartbeat	Garret Freymann-Weyr	Houghton Mifflin	Problem Romance	F	14	154	
	Postcards from No Man's Land	Aidan Chambers	Dutton	Problem	M Historical	17	312	England Holland
2001	Damage	A. M. Jenkins	HarperCollins	Realistic Sports	M/F	17	186	
	The Land	Mildred Taylor	Phyllis Fogelman	Historical	M	YA+	375	African American

*Books that have been made into films

Year	Title	Author	Publisher	Genre	M/F	Age	Pages	Setting
	Lord of the Deep	Graham Salisbury	Delacorte	Realistic	M	13	184	Hawaii
	The Rag and Bone Shop	Robert Cormier	Delacorte	Realistic Mystery	M	12	154	
	Seek	Paul Fleischman	Marcato/Cricket	Realistic	M	17	167	
	The Sisterhood of the Traveling Pants	Ann Brashares	Delacorte	Realistic	F	16	304	
	A Step from Heaven	An Na	Front Street	Realistic	F	17	156	Korean immigrants
	True Believer	Virginia Euwer Wolff	Atheneum	Realistic	F	15	264	African American
	Zazoo	Richard Moser	Houghton Mifflin	Realistic	F	13	248	England
2000	*The Amber Spyglass*	Philip Pullman	Knopf	Fantasy/Myth Sci-Fi	M/F	Young teens	518	
	The Beet Fields: Memories of a 16th Summer	Gary Paulsen	Delacorte	Realistic Memoir	M	16	158	
	Homeless Bird	Gloria Whelan	HarperCollins	Realistic Quest	F	13	216	India
	Hope Was Here	Joan Bauer	Putnam's	Realistic Quest	F	16	190	
	Kit's Wilderness	David Almond	Delacorte	Historical Supernatural	M	13	229	
	Many Stones	Carolyn Coman	Front Street	Realistic Quest	F	Mid-teens	158	South Africa United States
	Stuck in Neutral	Terry Trueman	HarperCollins	Realistic Problem	M	14	114	
	The Wanderer	Sharon Creech	HarperCollins	Realistic	M/F	Young teens	305	
1999	*A Year Down Yonder*	Richard Peck	Dial	Historical Realism	F	16	130	1930s
	Anna of Byzantium	Tracy Barrett	Delacorte	Historical Fiction	F	Older teens	209	11th-century Byzantium
	Frenchtown Summer	Robert Cormier	Delacorte	Realistic Poetry	M	12	113	Early 1920s

continued

TABLE 1.1   HONOR LIST (Continued)

Year	Title	Author	Publisher	Genre	Protagonist Sex	Age	No. of Pages	Ethnic Group or Unusual Setting
	Hard Love	Ellen Wittlinger	Simon & Schuster	Problem Quest	M/F	16	224	
	Monster	Walter Dean Myers	HarperCollins	Problem	M	16	240	African American
	Never Trust a Dead Man	Vivian Vande Velde	Harcourt	Mystery Supernatural	M	17	194	Medieval
	Safe at Second	Scott Johnson	Philomel	Sports Problem	M	17	224	
	The Smugglers	Iain Lawrence	Delacorte	Adventure	M	16	183	19th-century England
	When Zachary Beaver Came to Town	Kimberly Willis Holt	Henry Holt	Realistic	M	13	231	
1998	Clockwork: Or All Wound Up	Philip Pullman	Scholastic	Fantasy Sci-Fi	M/F	Teens	112	
	Go and Come Back	Joan Abelove	DK Ink	Realistic Historical	F	13	177	Peru
	*Holes	Louis Sachar	FS&G	Fanciful Adventure	M	14	233	
	The Killer's Cousin	Nancy Werlin	Delacorte	Psychological Mystery	M	17	228	
	Rules of the Road	Joan Bauer	Putnam's	Realistic	F	16	201	
	Soldier's Heart	Gary Paulsen	Delacorte	Historical	M	15	106	
	Whirligig	Paul Fleischman	Holt	Realistic	M	17	133	
	The Wreckers	Iain Lawrence	Delacorte	Historical Adventure	M	14	191	
1997	Blood and Chocolate	Annette Curtis Klause	Delacorte	Supernatural	F	18	288	
	Buried Onions	Gary Soto	Harcourt Brace	Realistic	M	18	149	Hispanic

Year	Title	Author	Publisher	Genre	Gender	Age	Page	Setting/Topic
	Dancing on the Edge	Han Nolan	Harcourt Brace	Realistic	F	12	244	
	Ella Enchanted	Gale Carson Levine	HarperCollins	Cinderella Parody	F	12	232	
	The Facts Speak for Themselves	Brock Cole	Front Street	Realistic Abuse	F	13	184	
	Out of the Dust	Karen Hesse	Scholastic	Narrative Poetry	F	13	227	Depression
	When She Was Good	Norma Fox Mazer	Scholastic	Realistic Mental Health	F	Early 20s	240	
	Whistle Me Home	Barbara Wersba	Holt	Realistic Homosexuality	M/F	17	108	
1996	After the War	Carol Matas	Simon & Schuster	Historical Realistic	F	15	116	Palestine
	A Girl Named Disaster	Nancy Farmer	Orchard	Realistic	F	14	306	Africa
	The Golden Compass	Philip Pullman	Knopf	Fantasy/SciFi	F	14	396	
	Jip: His Story	Katherine Paterson	Lodestar	Historical Realistic	M	11	181	African American
	Rats Saw God	Rob Thomas	Simon & Schuster	Realistic	M	17	219	
1995	The Eagle Kite	Paula Fox	Orchard	Realistic Death	M	13	127	
	Ironman	Chris Crutcher	Greenwillow	Realistic Sports	M	16	181	
	Like Sisters on the Homefront	Rita Williams-Garcia	Lodestar/Dutton	Realistic	F	14	165	African American
	The Midwife's Apprentice	Karen Cushman	Clarion	Historical	F	13	122	Medieval
	The War of Jenkins' Ear	Michael Morpurgo	Philomel	Realistic/Religious	M	14	171	1951 England
1994	Deliver Us from Evie	M. E. Kerr	HarperCollins	Realistic Lesbianism	F	17	177	

continued

19

TABLE 1.1 HONOR LIST (Continued)

Year	Title	Author	Publisher	Genre	Protagonist Sex	Age	No. of Pages	Ethnic Group or Unusual Setting
	Driver's Ed.	Caroline Cooney	Delacorte	Suspense	M/F	Teens	184	
	Iceman	Chris Lynch	HarperCollins	Realistic Sports	M	14	181	
	Letters from the Inside	John Marsden	Houghton Mifflin	Realistic	F	Teens	146	Australia
	When She Hollers	Cynthia Voigt	Scholastic	Realistic Abuse	F	17	177	
1993	The Giver	Lois Lowry	Houghton Mifflin	Science Fiction	M	Mixed	180	Futuristic Dystopia
	Harris and Me	Gary Paulsen	Harcourt Brace	Realistic Humorous	M	Young teens	157	Rural
	Make Lemonade	Virginia Euwer Wolff	Holt	Realistic Single parent	F	14/17	200	Inner city
	Missing Angel Juan	Francesca Lia Block	HarperCollins	Problem Occult	F	Teens	138	Los Angeles New York
	Shadow Boxer	Chris Lynch	HarperCollins	Realistic Sports	M	Young teens	215	
1992	Dear Nobody	Berlie Doherty	Orchard	Realistic Pregnancy	M/F	Older teens	192	England
	The Harmony Arms	Ron Koertge	Little	Realistic Humorous	M	14	182	Los Angeles
	Missing May	Cynthia Rylant	Orchard	Realistic Death	M/F	Mixed	89	
	Somewhere in the Darkness	Walter Dean Myers	Scholastic	Realistic Family	M	14	224	African American
1991	The Brave	Robert Lipsyte	HarperCollins	Realistic Sports	M	18	195	Native American
	Castle in the Air	Diana Wynne Jones	Greenwillow	Fantasy	M/F	Teens	199	Middle East

continued

Year	Title	Author	Publisher	Genre	Gender	Age	Page	Setting
	Lyddie	Katherine Paterson	Lodestar	Historical mid-1800s	F	13	183	U.S. Northeast
1990	The Man from the Other Side	Uri Orlev	Houghton Mifflin	Historical	M	14	186	Poland WW II
	Nothing But the Truth	Avi	Orchard	Realistic	M	14	177	
	The Shining Company	Rosemary Sutcliff	Farrar	Historical	M	Mixed	296	7th-century England
	The Silver Kiss	Annette Curtis Klause	Bradbury	Occult Romance	F	Teens	198	
	The True Confessions of Charlotte Doyle	Avi	Orchard	Historical Adventure	F	13	215	1800s Trans-Atlantic
	White Peak Farm	Berlie Doherty	Orchard	Realistic Family	F	Older teens	86	England
1989	Blitzcat	Robert Westall	Scholastic	Animal	M	–	230	England WW II
	Celine	Brock Cole	Farrar	Realistic	F	16	216	
	Eva	Peter Dickinson	Delacorte	Science Fiction	F	13	219	Dystopian Future
	No Kidding	Bruce Brooks	HarperCollins	Science Fiction	M	14	207	Dystopian Future
	Shabanu: Daughter of the Wind	Suzanne Fisher Staples	Knopf	Realistic Problem	F	12	140	Pakistan Desert
	Weetzie Bat	Francesca Lia Block	HarperCollins	Realistic Spoof	M/F	Teens	88	Hollywood
1988	Fade	Robert Cormier	Delacorte	Occult	M/F	Mixed	320	
	Fallen Angels	Walter Dean Myers	Scholastic	Realistic	M	Older teens	309	Vietnam War/ethnic mix
	A Kindness	Cynthia Rylant	Orchard	Realistic Family	M	15	117	
	Memory	Margaret Mahy	Macmillan	Realistic Disability	M/F	19 80+	240	New Zealand

TABLE 1.1 HONOR LIST (Continued)

Year	Title	Author	Publisher	Genre	Protagonist Sex	Age	No. of Pages	Ethnic Group or Unusual Setting
	Probably Still Nick Swanson	Virginia Euwer Wolff	Holt	Realistic Disability	M	Teens	144	
	Scorpions	Walter Dean Myers	HarperCollins	Realistic Crime	M	Teens	167	Ethnic mix
	Sex Education	Jenny Davis	Orchard	Realistic Death	F	Teens	150	
1987	After the Rain	Norma Fox Mazer	Morrow	Realistic Death	F	Mid-teens	290	
	The Crazy Horse Electric Game	Chris Crutcher	Greenwillow	Realistic Sports Disability	M	Teens	224	Ethnic mix
	The Goats	Brock Cole	Farrar	Realistic	M/F	Teens	184	
	*Hatchet	Gary Paulsen	Bradbury	Adventure Survival	M	12	195	
	Permanent Connections	Sue Ellen Bridgers	HarperCollins	Realistic Family	M/F	Teens	164	
	Sons from Afar	Cynthia Voigt	Atheneum	Realistic	M	Mid-teens	224	
	The Tricksters	Margaret Mahy	Macmillan	Occult	F	17	266	New Zealand
1986	Cat, Herself	Mollie Hunter	HarperCollins	Historical	F	Teens	279	British nomads
	The Catalogue of the Universe	Margaret Mahy	Macmillan	Realistic	F	17	185	New Zealand
	Izzy, Willy-Nilly	Cynthia Voigt	Atheneum	Realistic Disability	F	15	288	
	Midnight Hour Encores	Bruce Brooks	HarperCollins	Realistic	F	16	288	Ethnic mix
1985	Beyond the Chocolate War	Robert Cormier	Knopf	Realistic	M	17	234	

Year	Title	Author	Publisher	Genre	Gender	Age	Pages	Setting
	Dogsong	Gary Paulsen	Bradbury	Adventure Occult	M	13	177	Alaska Inuit
	Ender's Game	Orson Scott Card	Tor	Science Fiction	M	Young boy	357	Future
	*In Country	Bobbie Ann Mason	HarperCollins	Realistic	F	Teens	247	
	The Moonlight Man	Paula Fox	Bradbury	Realistic Alcoholism	F	Teens	192	Nova Scotia
	Remembering the Good Times	Richard Peck	Delacorte	Realistic Suicide	M/F	Teens	192	
1984	*The Changeover: A Supernatural Romance*	Margaret Mahy	Macmillan	Fantasy	M/F	Teens	214	New Zealand
	*Cold Sassy Tree	Olive Ann Burns	Ticknor & Fields	Realistic	M/F	Mixed	391	1906 rural Georgia
	Downtown	Norma Fox Mazer	Morrow	Realistic	M/F	Young teens	216	
	Interstellar Pig	William Sleator	Dutton	Science Fiction	M	16	197	
	The Moves Make the Man	Bruce Brooks	HarperCollins	Realistic	M	Young teens	280	Ethnic mix
	One-Eyed Cat	Paula Fox	Bradbury	Realistic	M	Young teens	216	
1983	*Beyond the Divide*	Kathryn Lasky	Macmillan	Historical Fiction	F	Teens	254	1800s American West
	The Bumblebee Flies Anyway	Robert Cormier	Pantheon	Futuristic	M	Teens	211	
	The House on Mango Street	Sandra Cisneros	Arte Publico	Realistic	F	Young teens	134	Hispanic
	A Solitary Blue	Cynthia Voigt	Atheneum	Realistic Family	M	Early teens	182	
1982	*Annie on My Mind*	Nancy Garden	Farrar	Realistic Lesbianism	F	Teens	233	
	The Blue Sword	Robin McKinley	Greenwillow	Fantasy	F	Late teens	272	

continued

TABLE 1.1 HONOR LIST (Continued)

Year	Title	Author	Publisher	Genre	Protagonist Sex	Age	No. of Pages	Ethnic Group or Unusual Setting
	A Formal Feeling	Zibby Oneal	Viking	Realistic Death	F	Teens	162	
	*A Midnight Clear	William Wharton	Knopf	Realistic	M	Early 20s	241	World War II
	Sweet Whispers, Brother Rush	Virginia Hamilton	Philomel	Occult	F	Teens	224	African American
1981	Let the Circle Be Unbroken	Mildred D. Taylor	Dial	Historical U.S. South	F	Early teens	166	African American
	Notes for Another Life	Sue Ellen Bridgers	Knopf	Realistic Family	M/F	Teens	252	
	Rainbow Jordan	Alice Childress	Coward McCann	Realistic	F	14	142	African American
	Stranger with My Face	Lois Duncan	Little	Occult	F	17	250	
	Tiger Eyes	Judy Blume	Bradbury	Realistic	F	15	206	New Mexico ethnic mix
	Westmark	Lloyd Alexander	Dutton	Historical Fiction	M	16	184	England
1980	The Beginning Place	Ursula K. Le Guin	HarperCollins	Fantasy	M/F	Early 20s	183	
	*The Hitchhiker's Guide to the Galaxy	Douglas Adams	Crown	Fantasy	M	Adults	224	
	Jacob Have I Loved	Katherine Paterson	Crowell	Realistic Family	F	Teens	216	Chesapeake Bay WW II
1979	After the First Death	Robert Cormier	Pantheon	Realistic Suspense	M/F	Teens	233	
	All Together Now	Sue Ellen Bridgers	Knopf	Realistic Family	M/F	Teens	238	

Year	Title	Author	Publisher	Genre	Gender	Age	Page	Topic
	*Birdy	William Wharton	Knopf	Realistic Insanity	M	Early 20s	310	
	The Last Mission	Harry Mazer	Delacorte	Realistic	M	Late teens	182	World War II
	*Tex	S. E. Hinton	Delacorte	Realistic	M	Teens	194	
	*Words by Heart	Ouida Sebestyen	Little, Brown	Realistic 1920s West	F	Young teens	162	African American
1978	Beauty: A Retelling . . .	Robin McKinley	HarperCollins	Fantasy	F	Teens	247	
	The Book of the Dun Cow	Walter Wangerin, Jr.	HarperCollins	Animal Fantasy Religion	–	–	255	
	Gentlehands	M. E. Kerr	HarperCollins	Realistic	M	Teens	283	
	Killing Mr. Griffin	Lois Duncan	Little, Brown	Realistic Suspense	M/F	Teens	166	
1977	Dragonsinger	Anne McCaffrey	Atheneum	Fantasy	F	Teens	256	
	*I Am the Cheese	Robert Cormier	Knopf	Realistic Suspense	M	Teens	233	
	One Fat Summer	Robert Lipsyte	HarperCollins	Realistic	M	Teens	150	
	Winning	Robin Brancato	Knopf	Realistic Disability	M	Teens	211	
1976	*Are You in the House Alone?	Richard Peck	Viking	Realistic Rape	F	Teens	156	
	Home Before Dark	Sue Ellen Bridgers	Knopf	Realistic	F	Teens	176	Migrant workers
	*Ordinary People	Judith Guest	Viking	Realistic Family	M	Teens	263	
1975	Dragonwings	Laurence Yep	HarperCollins	Historical Fiction	M	Young teens	248	Chinese American
	Forever	Judy Blume	Bradbury	Realistic	F	17	216	
	*Rumble Fish	S. E. Hinton	Delacorte	Realistic	M	Teens	122	
	Z for Zachariah	Robert C. O'Brien	Atheneum	Science Fiction	F	16	249	Postnuclear

TABLE 1.1 HONOR LIST (Continued)

Year	Title	Author	Publisher	Genre	Protagonist Sex	Age	No. of Pages	Ethnic Group or Unusual Setting
1974	*Carrie	Stephen King	Doubleday	Occult	F	Preteen	199	
	*The Chocolate War	Robert Cormier	Pantheon	Realistic	M	14	253	
	House of Stairs	William Sleator	Dutton	Science Fiction	M/F	Teens	166	
	If Beale Street Could Talk	James Baldwin	Dial	Realistic	F	19	197	African American
	M. C. Higgins, the Great	Virginia Hamilton	Macmillan	Realistic	M	13	278	African American
1973	A Day No Pigs Would Die	Robert Newton Peck	Knopf	Historical 1920s	M	13	159	Rural Vermont
	The Friends	Rosa Guy	Holt	Realistic	F	Early teens	203	West Indians in New York
	*A Hero Ain't Nothin' But a Sandwich	Alice Childress	Coward McCann	Realistic Drugs	M	Early teens	126	African American
	The Slave Dancer	Paula Fox	Bradbury	Historical 1800s	M	13	176	Ethnic mix
	*Summer of My German Soldier	Bette Greene	Dial	Historical WW II	F	14	199	U.S. South Jewish
1972	*Deathwatch	Robb White	Doubleday	Realistic Suspense	M	Early 20s	228	
	*Dinky Hocker Shoots Smack!	M. E. Kerr	HarperCollins	Realistic Family	F	14	198	
	*The Man Without a Face	Isabelle Holland	Lippincott	Realistic Homosexuality	M	16	248	
	My Name Is Asher Lev	Chaim Potok	Knopf	Realistic Family	M	Teens	369	Hasidic Jews
	A Teacup Full of Roses	Sharon Bell Mathis	Viking	Realistic Drugs	M	17	125	African American

Year	Title	Author	Publisher	Theme	Gender	Age	Pages	Setting
1971	*The Autobiography of Miss Jane Pittman	Ernest Gaines	Dial	Historical U.S. South	F	Lifetime	245	African American
	*The Bell Jar	Sylvia Plath	HarperCollins	Realistic Suicide	F	19	196	
1970	*Bless the Beasts and Children	Glendon Swarthout	Doubleday	Realistic	M	Early teens	205	American Southwest
1969	My Darling, My Hamburger	Paul Zindel	HarperCollins	Realistic Abortion	M/F	17/18	168	
	*Sounder	William Armstrong	HarperCollins	Historical U.S. South	M	14	116	African American
	*Where the Lilies Bloom	Vera and Bill Cleaver	Lippincott	Realistic	F	14	174	Rural isolated
	The Pigman	Paul Zindel	HarperCollins	Realistic Death	M/F	16	182	
1968	*Red Sky at Morning	Richard Bradford	Lippincott	Realistic	M	17	256	New Mexico ethnic mix
	*The Chosen	Chaim Potok	Simon & Schuster	Realistic	M	Teen	284	Hasidic Jews
1967	The Contender	Robert Lipsyte	HarperCollins	Realistic	M	17	167	African American
	*Mr. and Mrs. Bo Jo Jones	Ann Head	Putnam	Realistic Pregnancy	M/F	18	253	
	*The Outsiders	S. E. Hinton	Viking	Realistic	M	14	156	

If a book is included on this Honor List, obviously it is outstanding in some way, but the reasons might differ considerably. One book may be here because of its originality, another for its popularity, and another for its literary quality. We should warn that just because a book has not found its way to this list, it should not be dismissed as mediocre. The list covers thirty-seven years during which there were many more outstanding books published than the ones included here. Whenever such lists are drawn up, a degree of chance is involved.

Many of these books are described in more detail in the following chapters. Here they are simply cited as evidence to illustrate the following generalizations about the best of modern young adult literature.

Characteristic 1: Young Authors Write from the Viewpoint of Young People

A prerequisite to attracting young readers is to write through the eyes of a young person. One of the ways authors do this is to write in the first person. This brings an immediacy to such a beginning as the one in Norma Fox Mazer's *When She Was Good:*

> I didn't believe Pamela would ever die. She was too big, too mad, too furious for anything so shabby and easy as death. And for a few moments as she lay on the floor that day, I thought it was one of her jokes. The playing-dead joke. I thought that at any moment she would spring up, seize me by the hair, and drag me around the room. It wouldn't be the first time. . . .

Another technique is for authors to have a young narrator even when the story belongs to someone else. For example, Joan Abelove's *Go and Come Back* is the story of two anthropologists who are in their late 20s when they go for a two-year study visit to a mountain tribe in Peru. What readers learn about the anthropologists comes through the eyes of a young Peruvian girl, Alicia, who refers to the anthropologists as "old women." The tribe is fictionally named the Isabos, and Alicia's first-person observations are supplemented by the conversations she has with her friends, with the two "old women," and with her observant and sarcastic mother.

In *Fade,* Robert Cormier uses the technique of having the story told by the protagonist, Paul Moreaux, as long as he is in his youth. When the story gets to his adult years, however, Cormier changes the narrator to Moreaux's young female cousin, who aspires to follow in Moreaux's footsteps as a writer.

The most consistent characteristic of the books on the Honor List is the age of the protagonists. Teenagers like to read about other teenagers as shown by such books as Sandra Cisneros's *The House on Mango Street,* Orson Scott Card's *Ender's Game,* and Bobbie Ann Mason's *In Country.* In spite of being published and marketed to general adult audiences, these books found their way to teen readers because the protagonists were young. With other Honor List books published for adults, young people play important roles even if they aren't the main characters as with the grandson in Olive Ann Burns's *Cold Sassy Tree* and the surviving son in Judith Guest's *Ordinary People.* General adult

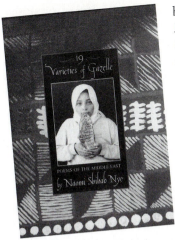

books that do not include teenagers—for example, Douglas Adams's *The Hitchhiker's Guide to the Galaxy* and William Wharton's *A Midnight Clear* and *Birdy*—have protagonists who are only slightly older than teen readers and are involved in activities with which young people identify, such as beginning to live on one's own, finding someone to love, and deciding whether earning money is more important than doing what one wants to do.

The big dividing line—the final rite of passage—between childhood and adulthood used to be having children of one's own so that stories about parenting seldom, if ever, appeared in young adult fiction. With the public acknowledgment of a soaring birthrate to teenaged mothers, however, this is no longer true, as shown by the success of Virginia Euwer Wolff's *Make Lemonade,* the story of 14-year-old Verna LaVaughn who answers a babysitting ad and is surprised to find that it was put up by Jolly, the teenaged mother of 2-year-old Jeremy and a younger "gooey baby" named Jilly. Rita Williams-Garcia's *Like Sisters on the Homefront* is the story of 14-year-old Gayle, whose mother forces her to have an abortion after she gets pregnant a second time and then sends Gayle and her 7-month-old baby boy from Jamaica, New York, to rural Georgia to live "with family."

Characteristic 2: "Please, Mother, I Want the Credit!"

With formula fiction for young readers, one of the first things an author does is to figure out how to get rid of the parents so that the young person is free to take credit for his or her own accomplishments. Although the Honor List is not made up of formula fiction, there is still evidence of the "Please, Mother, I want to get the credit" syndrome. For example, in *Whirligig,* Brent Bishop needs to atone for causing a fatal traffic accident, so author Paul Fleischman contrives to have him travel on a Greyhound bus to the four corners of the United States where he constructs a memorial in remembrance of the girl who was killed. Brent's wealthy father had brought his checkbook to the meeting with the grieving family, but the story is much better because for the first time in Brent's life he must make amends by himself.

Other Honor books in which young people are forced to come to terms with their problems without the help of their parents include Iain Lawrence's *The Wreckers,* Gary Soto's *Buried Onions,* Carol Matas's *After the War,* Nancy Farmer's *A Girl Named Disaster,* Francesca Lia Block's *Weetzie Bat,* Chris Crutcher's *The Crazy Horse Electric Game,* and all of S. E. Hinton's books.

Perhaps because they are both on the edge of—close but not central to—the mainstream of power, young people seem able to relate more comfortably with elderly than with middle-aged adults. In Joan Bauer's *Rules of the Road,* 16-year-old Jenna Louise Boller is happy to leave behind her troublesome parents when she is offered the summer job of driving the "supremely aged" Mrs. Gladstone across country to inspect each of the 172 shoe stores that her company owns. In Han Nolan's *Dancing on the Edge,* Miracle McCloy is at the mercy of some truly bad adults, but at least she knows that her grandfather is there for her.

In keeping with the variety that exists in the Honor List, other books lead young readers to look more realistically at themselves and at parent-child relationships.

Among the books that feature at least one capable parent playing a strong, supportive role for a young protagonist are Louis Sachar's *Holes,* Joan Abelove's *Go and Come Back,* Berlie Doherty's *White Peak Farm,* Peter Dickinson's *Eva,* Virginia Euwer Wolff's *Probably Still Nick Swanson,* Alice Childress's *A Hero Ain't Nothin' But a Sandwich,* and Kathryn Lasky's *Beyond the Divide.* In Robert Newton Peck's *A Day No Pigs Would Die,* the boy desperately loves his father, and in Bobbie Ann Mason's *In Country* and Bruce Brooks's *Midnight Hour Encores,* the young protagonists place great importance on learning about an unknown parent.

Characteristic 3: Young Adult Literature Is Fast-Paced

In July 1999, *Time* reporter David Spitz wrote that, "Teen fiction may, in fact, be the first literary genre born of the Internet. Its fast-paced narratives draw upon the target demographic's kinship with MTV . . . and with the Internet and kids' ease in processing information in unconventional formats."[13] In reality, what Spitz calls "edgy" teen fiction was around long before the Internet, but his point is well taken that many of the most popular books tell their stories at almost the same frantic pace and with the same emphasis on powerful images that viewers have come to expect from MTV. This concept will be further discussed in Chapter 3.

Postindustrial countries have become hurry-up societies, and people want their stories to be presented in the same fashion. Books from the Honor List that come close to being MTV stories because of their pace and their exaggerated and powerful images include Louis Sachar's *Holes,* Annette Curtis Klause's *The Silver Kiss* and *Blood and Chocolate,* and Francesca Lia Block's *Missing Angel Juan* and *Weetzie Bat.* The latter is only 88 pages long. When it was published in 1989, it was a shocking book because people were so accustomed to reading realistic problem novels providing role models for teenagers that they weren't ready for a fairytale spoof of Hollywood and for a writer who was less interested in presenting role models than in presenting vivid images and unforgettable characters.

Not all young adult books are going to have the disjointed punch of music videos or the randomness of the Internet, but there is a relationship because modern mass-media entertainers appeal to the same powerful emotions of adolescence—love, romance, sex, horror, and fear—as do young adult authors. These strong emotions are best shown through a limited number of characters and narrative events and language that flow naturally while still presenting dramatic images. The shorter and more powerful books are among those that have been made into impressive movies; for example, William Armstrong's 1969 *Sounder* with only 116 pages, Alice Childress's 1973 *A Hero Ain't Nothin' But a Sandwich* with only 126 pages, S. E. Hinton's 1975 *Rumble Fish* with only 122 pages, Richard Peck's 1976 *Are You in the House Alone?* with 156 pages, and Ouida Sebestyen's 1979 *Words by Heart* with 162 pages.

The assumption that publishers start with is that teenagers have shorter attention spans than adults and less ability to hold one strand of a plot in mind while reading about another strand. There is a tremendous difference, however, in the reading abilities of young people between the ages of 12 and 18. As students mature and become better readers, they are able to stick with longer, more complex books. Five of the nine books on the Honor List with more than 300 pages were published for general adult audiences. Even though most of the books published for teenagers are fairly short, many of them are complex. Not one of Robert Cormier's books is simple and straightforward. Philip Pullman's fantasies require careful reading and perseverance, and so do Annette Curtis Klause's modern stories of vampires and werewolves. Gary Paulsen's *Dogsong* blends the past and the future with the present, whereas with Ernest Gaines's *A Gathering of Old Men,* William Wharton's *Birdy,* and Alice Childress's *A Hero Ain't Nothin' But a Sandwich* readers must draw together and sort out alternating viewpoints and chronologies. It is obvious from reading Judith Guest's *Ordinary People,* Rosemary Sutcliff's *The Shining Company,* and James Baldwin's *If Beale Street Could Talk* that their appeal is based on something other than easy reading.

Characteristic 4: Young Adult Literature Includes a Variety of Genres and Subjects

Because moving from being a child to being an adult is at the core of most young adult fiction, the "genre" is commonly thought of as featuring a troubled teenager in some kind of rebellion. It is true that young adult writers have created thousands of variations on this theme, but the reason we put *genre* in quotation marks is that there is a tremendous crossover with what are traditionally defined as *genres.* Young protagonists might take important steps toward growing up while in outer space or while challenging nature by climbing a mountain or finding their way home after being lost. It could occur in a courtroom when a young person is either a witness or is on trial; it could occur as part of a love relationship or as part of facing up to a disaster in one's family or one's own life. The taking of such steps is a favorite theme for film producers as shown by the movies listed in Film Box 1.1, The World of Young Adults (p. 33). And the world's great myths often feature young people accepting and overcoming challenges, and as will be shown in the rest of this textbook, the story is an intrinsic part of the archetypal images that reside in the human psyche. This is why we not only have chapters about modern realistic, problem novels, but also about all the other genres including poetry, drama, humor, adventure, sports, the supernatural, mystery, fantasy, science fiction, historical fiction, and both literary and informative nonfiction.

Although we have moved such nonfiction books as poetry, biographies, memoirs, and information books to the appropriate chapters, the books on the Honor List still reflect a tremendous variety of subjects, themes, and genres. Historical fiction includes Gary Paulsen's *Soldier's Heart,* Katherine Paterson's pre-Civil War *Jip: His Story,* Olive Ann Burns's romantic *Cold Sassy Tree,* Kathryn Lasky's pioneer story *Beyond the Divide,* and Rosemary Sutcliff's *The Shining Company,* set in England in A.D. 600. Elements of fantasy and science fiction are as old as the oldest folktales (Gale Carson Levine's *Ella Enchanted* and Walter Wangerin's *The Book of the Dun Cow*) and as new as nuclear war and the latest board game (Robert C. O'Brien's *Z for Zachariah* and William Sleator's *Interstellar Pig*). Occult fiction is filled with romance (Annette Curtis Klause's *The Silver Kiss* and Virginia Hamilton's *Sweet Whispers, Brother Rush*), while futuristic stories thrive on high-tech intrigue (Peter Dickinson's *Eva* and Robert Cormier's *The Bumblebee Flies Anyway*).

American Graffiti (1973, color, 112 min., PG; Director: George Lucas; with Richard Dreyfus, Ron Howard, and Cindy Williams) Here is high school graduation in 1962 and what a few students learn about the real world.

Bend It Like Beckham (2003, color, 112 min., PG-13; Director: Gurindor Chadha; with Parminder Nagra). In this British film, Jess is an Anglo-Indian teenager who has grown up in London and loves soccer, but her traditional Sikh parents don't want her to play.

The Breakfast Club (1985, color, 97 min.; R; Director: John Hughes; with Emilio Estevez, Judd Nelson, Molly Ringwald, Anthony Michael Hall, and Ally Sheedy) Some critics credit Hughes with creating the genre of YA movies in this story about five rebellious teenagers assigned Saturday morning detention.

Fast Times at Ridgemont High (1982, color, 92 min., R; Director: Amy Heckerling; with Sean Penn, Jennifer Jason Leigh, and Judge Reinholdt) California high school students spend most of their time in the mall thinking about drugs and sex.

Finding Forrester (2001, color, 135 min., PG-13; Director: Gus Van Sant; with Sean Connery and Rob Brown) A reclusive writer serves as a friend and mentor to a basketball player on scholarship at an exclusive New York prep school.

Heathers (1989, color, 102 min., R; Director: Michael Lehmann; with Winona Ryder, Christian Slater, and Shannon Doherty) A high school girl hangs out with a friend who bedevils anyone in school at will.

The Last Picture Show (1971, black & white, 114 min., R; Director: Peter Bogdanovich; with Jeff Bridges, Timothy Bottoms, Cybill Shepard, Ben Johnson, and Cloris Leachman). From Larry McMurtry's novel, the death of a movie theatre is a symbol of the dying of a small Texas town.

My Life as a Dog (1985, color, 101 min., NR; Director: Lasse Hallström; with Anton Glanzelius, Tomass von Brömssen, and Anki Liden) A 12-year old boy is sent to live with relatives in 1950s Sweden.

October Sky (1999, color, 107 min., PG; Director: Jake Gyllenhall; with Chris Cooper and Laura Dern) In this film from Homer Hickam's *Rocket Boy,* a boy growing up in a West Virginia coal-mining town sees Sputnik streaking in the skies and determines to build his own rocket.

The Outsiders (1983, color, 91 min., PG; Director: Francis Coppola; with Matt Dillon, Rob Lowe, and Thomas Howell) S. E. Hinton's novel is about two teenage groups in 1960s Oklahoma—the social superiors and the greasers.

Real Women Have Curves (2002, color, 86 min., PG-13; Director: Patricia Cardoso; with America Ferrera and Lupe Ontiveros) A bright young Hispanic girl in Los Angeles wants to go to college, but her mother wants her to work in a dress factory, lose some weight, and get married.

Rushmore (1998, color, 97 min., R; Director: Wes Anderson; with Jason Schwartzmann, Bill Murray, and Olivia Williams) A schoolboy is near expulsion because he is in almost every possible school activity and has no time for his studies. He falls in love with a first-grade teacher.

Slums of Beverly Hills (1998, color, 93 min., R; Director: Tamara Jenkins; with Alan Arkin and Natasha Lyonne) A father moves his motherless family first to this place and then that in Beverly Hills to give them a chance at a good education.

Twist and Shout (1984, color, 99 min., R; Director: Billie August; with Lars Simonson and Adam Tonssberg) Two Danish friends grow up in the early days of the Beatles, one manipulated by his father, one finding love and sadness.

Whale Rider (2002, color, 101 min., PG-13; Director: Niki Caro; with Keisha Castle-Hughes) Filmed in Whangara and Auckland, New Zealand, this is a classic story of a young girl proving her worthiness to be a leader in modern Maori culture.

Although about half the books are contemporary, realistic fiction, they range from tightly plotted suspense stories as in Nancy Werlin's *The Killer's Cousin* and John Marsden's *Letters from the Inside* to serious introspection as in Paula Fox's *One-Eyed Cat.* The theme of alienation and loneliness is seen in William Wharton's *Birdy,* whereas the need for a hero is seen in Robert Newton Peck's *A Day No Pigs Would Die* and Glendon Swarthout's *Bless the Beasts and Children.* Threats to the social order are explored in William Sleator's *House of Stairs* and *Interstellar Pig* and in Lois Lowry's *The Giver.* A search for values is shown in Richard Bradford's *Red Sky at Morning* and Chris Crutcher's *The Crazy Horse Electric Game.* What it means to care for others is examined in Kimberly Holt's *When Zachary Beaver Came to Town,* Han Nolan's *Dancing on the Edge,* Annette Curtis Klause's *The Silver Kiss,* Norma Fox Mazer's *Downtown,* Isabelle Holland's *The Man Without a Face,* Francesca Lia Block's *Missing Angel Juan,* and Gary Paulsen's *Harris and Me.*

Characteristic 5: The Body of Work Includes Stories about Characters from Many Different Ethnic and Cultural Groups

Forty years ago, the novels written specifically for teenagers and sold to schools and public libraries presented the same kind of middle-class, white, picket-fence neighborhoods as the one featured in the *Dick and Jane* readers from which most U.S. children were taught to read. But the mid-1960s witnessed a striking change in attitudes. One by one, taboos on profanity, divorce, sexuality, drinking, racial unrest, abortion, pregnancy, and drugs disappeared. With this change, writers were freed to set their stories in realistic rather than romanticized neighborhoods and to explore the experiences of characters whose stories had not been told before.

This freedom was a primary factor in the coming of age of adolescent literature. Probably because there was such a lack of good books about non–middle-class protagonists, and because this was where interesting things were happening, many writers during the late 1960s and the 1970s focused on minorities and on the kinds of kids that S. E. Hinton called *The Outsiders.* With the conservative swing that the United States took in the 1980s, not as much attention has been paid to minority experiences; nevertheless, several of the most appealing of the new books feature minority characters and will probably be read by large numbers of teenagers of all races. It's also encouraging that we are seeing books with main characters from different ethnic groups relating to each other. In Virginia Euwer Wolff's *Make Lemonade,* there is no overt mention of skin color, but as one reviewer stated, Jolly and LaVaughn are held together by "the race of poverty."

Although most schools and libraries are making a concerted effort to stock and teach books reflecting many different cultures, educators worry that publishers who are now marketing books directly to teenagers are not working as hard to include books about minority characters because less affluent kids, many of whom are from minorities, are not as likely to spend money on books as are white, middle-class teenagers. Also, as publishers try to attract readers by making their books more wishfulfilling, they tend to return to the romanticized beautiful-people view that was characteristic of the old adolescent literature.

Another fear is that, as with most television programming, everything is watered down to suit mass tastes. But there are some crucial differences, because one person at a time reads a book, while television is usually viewed by a group. Even with cable television, the number of channels from which a viewer can choose is limited, but books offer a vast choice. Moreover, advertisers pay for most television programs, while readers pay the production costs of books.

As more and more schools sponsor summer travel and exchange programs, and as the Internet and other mass media continue to shrink national boundaries, teenagers are becoming less parochial in their reading. Joan Abelove's *Go and Come Back* is set in 1970s Peru, Carol Matas's *After the War* is set in 1940s Poland and Palestine, while Nancy Farmer's *A Girl Named Disaster* is set in 1980s Mozambique and Zimbabwe. *Shabanu: Daughter of the Wind,* set in present-day Pakistan, was written by Suzanne Fisher Staples, a UPI news correspondent. She uses the story of a young woman's betrothal to introduce English readers to a culture very different from their own. Mollie Hunter's *Cat, Herself* is a romantic story of a Scottish gypsy; Gary Paulsen's *Dogsong* is about a young Inuit; John Marsden's *Letters from the Inside* is set in Australia; Margaret Mahy's books *Memory* and *The Tricksters* are set in New Zealand; and Berlie Doherty's *White Peak Farm* grew out of her work preparing a BBC documentary in Sheffield, England.

Characteristic 6: Young Adult Books Are Basically Optimistic, with Characters Making Worthy Accomplishments

Ensuring that teenage characters are as smart as, or smarter than, their parents is only one of the devices that authors use to appeal to young readers. They also involve young characters in accomplishments that are challenging enough to earn the reader's respect. In the 1970s, when realism became the vogue and books were written with painful honesty about the frequently cruel world that teenagers face, some critics worried that modern young adult literature had become too pessimistic and cynical. However, even in so-called downer books, authors created characters that readers could admire for the way they faced up to their challenges.

A comparison of E. B. White's beloved *Charlotte's Web* and Robert Newton Peck's *A Day No Pigs Would Die* illustrates one of the differences between children's and adolescent literature. In White's classic children's book, a beloved but useless pig wins a ribbon at the County Fair and is allowed to live a long and happy life, whereas in Peck's young adult book a beloved but useless pig wins a ribbon at the County Fair but must be slaughtered anyway. Nevertheless, rather than being devastated by the death of the pig, readers identify with the boy and take pride in his ability to do what had to be done.

This kind of change and growth is the most common theme appearing in young adult literature, regardless of format. It suggests, either directly or symbolically, the gaining of maturity (i.e., the loss of innocence as part of the passage from childhood to adulthood). Such stories communicate a sense of time and change, a sense of becoming and catching glimpses of possibilities—some that are fearful and others that are awesome, odd, funny, perplexing, or wondrous.

One of the most popular ways to show change and growth is through a quest story (see Chapter 4 for a discussion and Focus Box 4.7 for examples). Avi's *The True Confes-*

sions of Charlotte Doyle is an almost pure example of a quest story camouflaged as a rollicking historical adventure. The intrepid narrator explains on page 1:

> . . . before I begin relating what happened, you must know something about me as I was in the year 1832 when these events transpired. At the time my name *was* Charlotte Doyle. And though I have kept the name, I am not for reasons you will soon discover the *same* Charlotte Doyle.

This captures the psychologically satisfying essence of quest stories, which is that over the course of the story, the protagonist learns something and changes significantly.

Characteristic 7: Successful Young Adult Novels Deal with Emotions That Are Important to Young Adults

Often the difference in the life span between two books that are equally well written from a literary standpoint is that the ephemeral book fails to touch kids where they live, whereas the long-lasting book treats experiences that are psychologically important to young people. Good authors do not peruse psychology books searching for case histories or symptoms of teenage problems they can envision making into good stories. This would be as unlikely and as unproductive as it would be for a writer to study a book on literary devices and make a list: "First, I will use a metaphor and then a bit of alliteration and some imagery, followed by personification."

The psychological aspects of well-written novels are a natural part of the story as protagonists face the same kinds of challenges readers are experiencing, such as the developmental tasks outlined two generations ago by Robert J. Havighurst.

1. Acquiring more mature social skills.
2. Achieving a masculine or feminine sex role.
3. Accepting the changes in one's body, using the body effectively, and accepting one's physique.
4. Achieving emotional independence from parents and other adults.
5. Preparing for sex, marriage, and parenthood.
6. Selecting and preparing for an occupation.
7. Developing a personal ideology and ethical standards.
8. Assuming membership in the larger community.[14]

Some psychologists gather all developmental tasks under the umbrella heading of achieving an identity, which they describe as *the* task of adolescence, and some aspect of this is in practically any piece of teenage fiction, as well as in such other genres as poetry, drama, informative nonfiction, biographies, and self-help books.

Close connections exist between adolescent literature and adolescent psychology, with psychology providing the overall picture and adolescent literature providing individual portraits. Because space in this text is too limited to include more than a hint of what you need to know about adolescent psychology, we suggest that professionals working with young people would profit from reading one or more of the books listed in Focus Box 1.2. Notice how many of the titles are tied into the issue of gender, a

FOCUS BOX 1.2   *Books to Help Adults Understand Teenagers*

Adolescents at School: Perspectives on Youth, Identity, and Education, edited by Michael Sadowski. Harvard Education, 2003. In giving this 182-page book, written by sixteen educators, a positive review in *School Library Journal,* Mary Hofman wrote, "You will have an interesting and well documented read that will support much of what it is hoped you are already doing."

All Grown Up and No Place to Go: Teenagers in Crisis, revised edition by David Elkind. Perseus Press, 1997. Elkind argues against the "hurried teens" and the pressure currently put on many teens to grow up quickly.

Boy V. Girl? How Gender Shapes Who We Are, What We Want and How We Get Along by George Abrahams and Sheila Ahtbrand. Free Spirit Publishing, 2002. The authors based their book on a national survey of 2,000 teenagers. The New York Public Libraries chose it for their 2003 "Books for the Teen Age" best book list.

The Culture of Adolescent Risk-Taking by Cynthia Lightfoot. Guilford Press, 1999. Lightfoot helps adults understand and deal with the pressures that contribute to teen attitudes of invincibility and daring.

A Fine Young Man: What Parents, Mentors, and Educators Can Do to Shape Adolescent Boys into Exceptional Men by Michael Gurian. Tarcher, 1998. Gurian is a psychotherapist who stresses the biological basis for male behavioral traits. The fact that teenage boys are more than four times as likely as teenage girls to attempt suicide relates to their different brain structures and hormones.

Just Girls: Hidden Literacies and Life in Junior High by Margaret J. Finders. Teachers College Press, 1997. Finders challenges the efficacy of the "good-girl" role. She also shows that various kinds of literacies play a big part in the social life and the self-image of girls.

Lost Boys: Why Our Sons Turn Violent and How We Can Save Them by James Garbarino. Free Press, 1999. Garbarino, a psychologist and a professor at Cornell University, has interviewed teenaged perpetrators of violence. He believes adults can provide the spiritual, psychological, and social support that is needed to counteract the effects of a culture that legitimizes violence in movies, television, and video games.

The Men They Will Become: The Nature and Nurture of Male Character by Eli H. Newberger. Perseus, 2000. In this thoughtful exploration of the gradual emotional development of boys, Newberger stresses the need for open communication and for leading by example.

Millennials Rising: The Next Great Generation by Neil Howe and William Strauss. Vintage, 2000. The authors claim that the Millennial Generation (those born between 1980 and 2000) are the grown-up kids of *Barney* rather than *Sesame Street,* of soccer moms rather than working moms, and of such bumper stickers as "Have you hugged your child today?" These "wanted" and loved children are having a different kind of adolescence than did the last generation.

Ophelia Speaks: Adolescent Girls Write about Their Search for Self by Sara Shandler. Harper-Collins, 1999. Shandler sent out 7,000 letters asking junior and senior high school teachers to encourage young women to write their own stories as a rebuttal or a supplement to Mary Pipher's *Reviving Ophelia* (Putnam, 1994). Shandler created her well-received book from 800 responses.

Queen Bees and Wannabes: Helping Your Daughter Survive Cliques, Gossip, Boyfriends, and Other Realities of Adolescents by Rosalind Wiseman. Crown, 2002. Although the intended audience is adults, the writing is accessible to young women who might want to skim or read parts of it.

Raising Cain: Protecting the Emotional Life of Boys by Daniel J. Kindlon, Michael Thompson, et al. Ballantine, 1999. These authors tackle the challenge of enlarging our definition of masculinity without "turning boys into girls." They are worried about the sadness, anger, and fear that boys feel because of growing up under the "tyranny of toughness."

"Reading Don't Fix No Chevys" Literacy in the Lives of Young Men by Michael W. Smith and Jeffrey D. Wilhelm. Heinemann, 2002. The authors studied the literacy habits of 49 boys and found that many boys feel little connection to the kinds of literacies taught in schools. They recommend several alternatives to present practices, but concede that these activities would be equally appealing to girls.

"Real Boys": Rescuing Our Sons from the Myths of Boyhood by William S. Pollack. Random House, 1998. Pollack is a clinical psychologist with the Harvard Medical Center and is asking people to take a second look at "the boy code," which describes boys as tough, cool, rambunctious, and obsessed with sports, cars, and sex. He thinks our major job is to help boys develop empathy and explore their sensitive sides so as to increase their ability to cope with frustrations.

Saving Beauty from the Beast: How to Protect Your Daughter from an Unhealthy Relationship by Vicki Crompton and Ellen Zelda

Kessner. Little, Brown, 2003. Crompton's 15-year-old daughter was killed by her ex-boyfriend, and Crompton vowed to help other families avoid such a tragedy.

To Be a Boy, To Be a Reader by William G. Brozo. International Reading Association, 2002. Of all the authors here, Brozo makes the most specific suggestions for books and classroom activities designed to promote "honorable expressions of masculinity." Not everyone would agree with Brozo's definition of *masculinity*, but that is the Catch-22 of the whole issue.

"Trust Me, Mom—Everyone Else Is Going!" The New Rules for Mothering Adolescent Girls by Roni Cohen-Sandler, Viking, 2002. The author uses the acronym BRAIN to summarize her advice: Be flexible, Respectful, Attuned, Involved, and Noncontrolling.

The War against Boys: How Misguided Feminism Is Harming Our Young Men by Christina Hoff Sommers. Simon & Schuster, 2000. Sommers has a point when she complains that many of the statistics and incidents cited in contemporary books about how girls are disadvantaged in school come from the conditions in schools of twenty years ago.

When We're in Public, Pretend You Don't Know Me: Surviving Your Daughter's Adolescence So You Don't Look Like an Idiot and She Still Talks to You by Susan Borowitz and Ava L. Siegler. Warner Books, 2003. Siegler is a child psychologist and Borowitz is a Hollywood writer and producer, as well as a mother. The book is filled with sensible advice aimed mostly at mothers, but teachers and librarians can learn some things too.

As shown in Focus Box 1.2, Books to Help Adults Understand Teenagers, there is a strong new interest in how gender affects the reading lives of teenagers.

subject that continues to puzzle all of us. Teachers and librarians who understand the psychology of young people are better able to

- Judge the soundness of the books they read.
- Decide which ones are worthy of promotion.
- Predict which ones will last and which will be transitory.
- Make better recommendations to individuals.
- Discuss books with students from their viewpoints.
- Gain more understanding and pleasure from personal reading.

Stages of Literary Appreciation

The development of literary appreciation begins long before children learn to read. Table 1.2, Stages of Literary Appreciation, presents an approximation of how individuals develop the personal attitudes and the reading, watching, and listening skills that are a necessary part of literary appreciation. The table should be read from the bottom up because each level is built on the one below it. People do not go *through* these stages of development; instead they *add on* so that at each level they have all that they had before plus a new way to gain pleasure and understanding (see also the discussion of teaching literature in Chapter 11).

Level 1: Understanding That Pleasure and Profit Come from Literature

Children are fortunate if they have loving adults who share songs and nursery rhymes and who talk with children about the television and the movies they see together. They

Read this chart from the bottom up to trace the stages of development most commonly found in reading the autobiographies of adults who love to read.

Level	Optimal Age	Stage	Sample Literary Materials	Sample Actions
7	Adulthood to death	Aesthetic appreciation	Classics Significant contemporary books Drama Film	Reads constantly Dreams of writing the great American novel Enjoys literary and film criticism Reads 50 books a year Sees plays Revisits favorites
6	College	Reading widely	Best-sellers Acclaimed novels, poems, plays, films, magazines	Talks about books and films with friends Joins a book club Gathers books to take on vacation
5	High school	Venturing beyond self	Science fiction Social issues fiction Forbidden material "Different" stories	Begins buying own books Sees movies with friends Gets reading suggestions from friends Reads beyond school assignments
4	Junior high	Finding oneself in literature	Realistic fiction Contemporary problem novels Wish-fulfilling stories	Hides novels inside textbooks to read during classes Stays up at night reading Uses reading as an escape from social pressures
3	Late elementary	Losing oneself in literature	Series books Fantasies Animal stories Anything one can disappear into	Reads while doing chores Reads while traveling Makes friends with a librarian Checks books out regularly Gets "into" reading a particular genre or author
2	Primary grades	Learning to decode Developing an attention span	School reading texts Easy-to-read books Signs and other real-world messages	Takes pride in reading to parents or others Enjoys reading alone Has favorite authors
1	Birth to kindergarten	Understanding of pleasure and profit from printed words and from visual depictions	Nursery rhymes Folktales Picture books Television programs	Has favorite books for reading aloud "Reads" signs for certain restaurants and food Memorizes favorite stories and pretends to read Enjoys listening to adults read

are also lucky if they get to go to bookstores and libraries for buying and borrowing books and for participating in group story hours. Researchers in reading education are discovering the social nature of reading. Children who seem to get the most from their reading are those who have had opportunities for "talking story" and for having what Ralph Peterson and Maryann Eeds call "grand conversations" both with other children and with adults.[15]

If children are to put forth the intellectual energy required in learning to read, they need to be convinced that it is worthwhile—that pleasure awaits them—or that there are concrete benefits to be gained. In U.S. metropolitan areas, there's hardly a 4-year-old who doesn't recognize the golden arches of a McDonald's restaurant. Toddlers too young to walk around grocery stores reach out from their seats in grocery carts to grab favorite brands of cereal. We know one child who by the time he entered first grade had taught himself to read from *TV Guide*. While its format breaks almost every rule any good textbook writer would follow in designing a primer for clear and easy reading, it had one overpowering advantage. The child could get immediate feedback. If he made a correct guess, he was rewarded by getting to watch the program he wanted. If he made a mistake, he knew immediately that he had to return to the printed page to try again.

Level 2: Learning to Read

Learning the principles of phonics (i.e., to turn the squiggles on a page into meaningful sounds) is the second stage of development. It gets maximum attention during the primary grades, where as much as 70 percent of the school day is devoted to language arts. Developing literacy, however, is more than just decoding; it is a never-ending task for anyone who is intellectually active. Even at a mundane level, adults continue working to develop their reading skills. People tackling new computer programs or rereading tax guides in preparation for an audit exhibit the same symptoms of concentrated effort as do children first learning to read. They point with their fingers, move their lips, return to reread difficult parts, and in frustration slam the offending booklet to the floor. In each case, however, they are motivated by a vision of some benefit to be gained, so they increase their efforts.

Those of us who learned to read with ease may forget to help children who are struggling to find pleasure and enjoyment. Children who learn to read easily—the girl who sits in the backseat of the car and reads all through the family vacation and the boy who reads a book while delivering the neighborhood newspapers—find their own rewards for reading. For these children, the years between 7 and 12 are golden. They can read the great body of literature that the world has saved for them: *Charlotte's Web,* the Little House books, *The Borrowers, The Chronicles of Narnia, The Wizard of Oz, Where the Red Fern Grows,* and books by Beverly Cleary, William Steig, Dr. Seuss, and hundreds of other good writers.

At this stage, children are undemanding. They are in what Margaret Early has described as a stage of unconscious enjoyment.[16] With help, they may enjoy such classics as *Alice in Wonderland, The Wind in the Willows, Treasure Island,* and *Little Women,* but by themselves they are far more likely to turn to less challenging material. Parents worry that their children are wasting time, but nearly 100 percent of our college students who say they love to read went through childhood stages of being addicted for months to one particular kind of book. Apparently, readers find comfort in knowing the characters in a book and what to expect, and this comfort helps them develop speed and skill.

Level 3: Losing Oneself in a Story

Children who read only during the time set aside in school and children who live in homes where the television set is constantly switched from channel to channel and where the exigencies of daily life leave little time for uninterrupted conversations and stories probably have a hard time losing themselves in a good story. There are exceptions, of course, such as Worm (short for bookworm), the 11-year-old in Rod Philbrick's *Max the Mighty,* who escapes the horrors of her everyday life by reading all the time. She even uses a miner's helmet and headlight to read in the dark.

Because of life's complications, many children do not lose themselves in a good story until much later than the third or fourth grades, which is typical of good readers, or it may not happen at all. In this segment quoted from *The Car Thief* by Theodore Weesner, Alex Housman, who is being kept in a detention home, is 17 years old when he first experiences losing himself in a story (i.e., finding what we refer to as "a good read"). Someone has donated a box of books to the detention home, and, because there's nothing else to do, Alex starts to read. He is intimidated by the words because he had never read anything before except school assignments, but because the book is straightforward and written in a style he can understand,

> [he] sat on the floor reading until he grew sleepy. When his eyelids began to slide down and his head began to cloud, he lay over on his side on the floor to sleep awhile, pulling up his knees, resting his head on his arm. When he woke he got up and carried the book with him to the bathroom . . . reading the book again, he became so involved in the story that his legs fell asleep. He kept reading, intending to get up at the end of this page, then at the end of this page, if only because he would feel more comfortable with his pants up and buttoned, but he read on. . . . Something was happening to him, something as pleasantly strange as the feeling he had had for Irene Sheaffer. By now, if he knew a way, he would prolong the book the distance his mind could see, and he rose again, quietly, to sustain the pleasant sensation, the escape he seemed already to have made from the scarred and unlighted corridor. Within this shadowed space there were now other things: war and food and worry over cigarettes and rations, leaving and returning, dying and escaping. The corridor itself, and his own life, was less present.[17]

Level 4: Finding Oneself in a Story

The more experience children have with literature, whether through words or pictures, the more discriminating they become. To receive pleasure they have to respect the story. In reminiscing about his childhood fondness for both *The Hardy Boys* and motorcycles, the late John Gardner remarked that his development as a literary critic took a step forward when he lost patience with the leisurely conversations that the Hardy boys were supposed to have as they roared down country roads side by side on their motorcycles.

Good readers begin developing this critical sense in literature at about the same time they develop it in real life at the end of childhood and the beginning of their teen years. They move away from a simple interest in what happened in a story to ask *why*. They want logical development and are no longer satisfied with stereotypes. They want characters controlled by believable human motives because now their reading has a real purpose to it. They are reading to find out about themselves, not simply to escape into someone else's experiences for a few pleasurable hours. They may read dozens of contemporary teenage novels, looking for lives as much like their own as possible. They read about real people in biographies, personal essays, and journalistic stories. They are also curious about other sides of life, and so they seek out books that present lives totally different from their own. They look for anything bizarre, unbelievable, weird, or grotesque: stories of occult happenings, trivia books, and horror stories. And, of course, for their leisure-time reading and viewing they may revert to level 3 of escaping into a good story. When they are working at the highest level of their capability, however, their purpose is largely one of finding themselves and their places in society. Parents and teachers sometimes worry, when children seem stuck at a particular level or with a particular kind of book. In most instances, as long as there are other choices available as well as time for reading, students sooner or later venture onward in a natural kind of progression.

Level 5: Venturing beyond Themselves

The next stage in literary appreciation comes when people go beyond their egocentrism and look at the larger circle of society. Senior high school English teachers have some of their best teaching experiences with books and stories by such writers as Ernest Hemingway, John Steinbeck, Harper Lee, F. Scott Fitzgerald, Carson McCullers, William Faulkner, Arthur Miller, and Flannery O'Connor. Students respond to the way these books raise questions about conformity, social pressures, justice, and other aspects of human frailties and strengths. Book discussions at this level can have real meat to them because readers make different interpretations as they bring their own experiences into play against those in the books.

Obviously, getting to this level of literary appreciation is more than a matter of developing an advanced set of decoding skills. It is closely tied to intellectual, physical, and emotional development. Teenagers face the tremendous responsibility of assessing the world around them and deciding where they fit in. Reading at this level allows teenagers to focus on their own psychological needs in relation to society. The more directly they can do this, the more efficient they feel, which probably explains the popularity of contemporary problem novels featuring young protagonists, as in the books by Will Hobbs, Brock Cole, M. E. Kerr, Robert Cormier, Jacqueline Woodson, Paula Fox, Sue Ellen Bridgers, Richard Peck, and Virginia Euwer Wolff.

Although many people read fantasy and science fiction at the level of losing themselves in a good story, others may read such books as Nancy Farmer's *The House of The Scorpion,* Neal Shusterman's *The Dark Side of Nowhere,* and Philip Pullman's *The Subtle Knife* and *Clockwork—Or All Wound Up* at a higher level of reflection. Such readers come back from spending a few hours in the imagined society with new ideas about their own society.

Levels 6 and 7: Aesthetic Appreciation

When people have developed the skills and attitudes necessary to enjoy imaginative literary experiences at all the levels described so far, they are ready to embark on a lifetime of aesthetic appreciation. This is the level at which producers, playwrights, authors, critics, talented performers, and literary scholars concentrate their efforts. Even they don't work at this level all the time, however, because it is as demanding as it is rewarding. The professor who teaches Shakespeare goes home at night and relaxes by watching *The Simpsons* or scanning the Internet to see what might turn up on the Drudge Report or on various bulletin boards. The author who writes for hours in the morning might put herself to sleep at night by listening to a tape recording of Ayn Rand's *The Fountainhead,* while the producer of a new play may flip through magazines as a way of relaxing. Teenagers are much the same. Top students take a break from the seriousness of homework by watching *Friends* or *The Simpsons*, listening to music, or playing video games.

In summary, the important points to learn from this discussion of stages of literary appreciation are that teachers, librarians, and parents should meet young people where they are and help them feel comfortable at that stage before trying to move them on. We also need to continue to provide for all the levels below the one on which we are focusing; for example, people at any stage need to experience pleasure and profit from their reading, viewing, and listening. This is especially true with reading, which requires an extra measure of intellectual effort. People who feel they are not being appropriately rewarded for their efforts may grow discouraged and join the millions of adults who no longer read for personal fulfillment and pleasure but only to get the factual information needed to manage the daily requirements of modern living.

Questions about Gender and Literacy

The books listed in Focus Box 1.2, Books to Help Adults Understand Teenagers, illustrate a level of interest in the literacy of boys that is comparable to the panic that ensued in the United States after the Soviet Union successfully launched Sputnik in 1957. At that time, Americans were so afraid that the Russians were getting ahead in the space race that educators and publishers began a lopsided concentration on the education of boys because they envisioned them as the future scientists, engineers, technologists, and soldiers who would save the Western world. The situation became so lopsided that in the 1970s, feminist critics and educators began to notice and demand changes. Over the next twenty-five years, much was done to encourage girls in school, but today the pendulum is swinging the other way and the focus is again on educating boys. The Columbine shootings (along with other acts of violence by young males), plus the September 11th terrorist attacks, have made Americans feel as fearful as they were in the 1960s when the Soviets appeared to be winning the space race. But this time, it is not just Americans who are worried about the issue. If you go to a computer and feed into a search engine something like "Books (or Schooling) for Boys" you will get sites not only from America, but from worried educators in New Zealand, Australia, and England. For example, a BBC report entitled "School 'gender gap' remains a mystery," quoted Schools Minister Estelle Morris saying that "underachievement by boys at school is a major challenge, but there is no simple, single solution." Among the factors cited as playing a part in the "crisis" were:

- An "anti-achievement" culture among some boys.
- Macho peer groups disrupting schoolwork.
- Teaching styles that suit girls rather than boys.
- A loss of motivation brought on by a loss of traditional male jobs.
- The way students are grouped in lessons.
- The choice of books studied including "the need for nonfiction."

Gender differences in schooling was a focus topic on CBS's May 25, 2003, *Sixty Minutes* program. Leslie Stahl led the discussion about how strong males have always had the choice of going out and making good money in a job requiring physical strength, while women have known that to make good money they needed an education. Stahl pointed out that society as a whole is conflicted about what role we imagine for our boys. The athletic male is still the high school "hero," and whole towns will turn out to watch boys play football. "Revenge of the nerds" jokes about computer geeks now being the bosses of their old high school classmates are still "jokes" because they go so against cultural expectations.

A PBS program the same week pointed out that Seattle University is now 61 percent women and that some rigorous colleges are now 75 percent women. The University of Georgia has been hit with a lawsuit for favoring men in admission. Many colleges have increased their budgets for recruiting in business and engineering, assuming that this will guarantee them more men. Some schools are also putting more money into big-time football in hopes of getting male students. An alarmist prediction, obviously thought up for its shock value, was that if women continue to outpace men in college admissions at the same rate as in recent years, by something like 2060, only women will be graduating from colleges.

Leslie Stahl had said something similar, but less dramatically when she said that it is time to start worrying about having a country where women hold the white-collar jobs and men hold the blue-collar jobs. This is especially true with some minority groups. In the last year for which statistics were available, twice as many black women as black men received bachelor's degrees. Stahl went on to ponder whether we are talking about "female success" or "male failure." As education becomes more about reading and writing, boys are opting out.

The PBS program interviewed a white, middle-class brother and sister. They had both enrolled in their local community college, but the brother had dropped out to become an apprentice electrician where he could earn over $20.00 an hour. The girl didn't like her classes any better, but her only option was to become a waitress. This is a job that paid less and had no future, in contrast to her brother's hopes of becoming a journeyman electrician with a substantial salary. However, with the downturn in the economy his apprentice job was growing more irregular and he too was thinking that maybe he should return to school to get trained for something else. The biggest differences in male and female wages occur in the jobs based on physical labor. This is where boys have a "natural" advantage and so many of them hesitate to give up this advantage by going into professions that require long years of schooling.

It is obvious that for the sake of both individuals and society, we need to give serious thought to the matter of how gender affects both teachers and students. However, we should not rush to throw the baby out with the bath water. Many boys are doing just fine in school, and if educators focus their teaching methods only on the dropouts or on those students who are at the lower end of the scale, we might do damage to the very good education that the majority of students are presently receiving. Another caution is that we should think about what we are willing to use to bribe boys into reading. In the post-Sputnik era, educators bribed boys to read by portraying them as smarter, bigger, and more successful than girls. As a way of encouraging boys to read, we could take a video-game approach and bring in books and magazines filled with pornography and violence. However, it is doubtful that such blatant pandering will help boys develop the kind of sensitivity they need to cope with the world. In the sixth edition of this textbook, YA author and sports writer Robert Lipsyte wrote:

> There is a tendency to treat boys as a group—which is where males are at their absolute worst—instead of as individuals who have to be led into reading secretly and one at a time. Boys are afraid of being humiliated, of being hurt, of being hit by the ball, of being made to look dumb or inadequate in front of other boys and in front of girls. . . . Boys need reassurance that their fears of violence and humiliation and competition are shared fears. Books can reassure them. But to be able to read a book properly, you have to be able to sink into a scene, to absorb characters, to care, to empathize. You have to be willing to make yourself vulnerable to a book as surely as you need to make yourself vulnerable to a person. This is not easy for a male in this society to do, particularly an adolescent male who is unsure of his own identity, his sexuality, his future.[18]

We could also let boys be the ones to make the choices for what will be read by the class as a whole, or by the groups they are in. Educators openly advocated such practices in the 1960s and 1970s, but today we are more likely to ask if it is fair to raise boys with the idea that their choices count more than do those of their classmates, who happen to be girls.

Fortunately, we no longer expect all students to read and love a single book. In the best schools, teaching revolves around small groups reading books of their choice and talking about them. Whatever teachers and librarians can do to help kids communicate and cooperate across gender lines will be all for the good. It won't hurt us to bring more nonfiction into classrooms and to welcome the "edgy" humor of such writers as Roald Dahl, Jack Gantos, Ron Koertge, Gordon Korman, Dav Pilkey, Daniel Pinkwater, Louis Sachar, and Jon Scieszka and provide opportunities for lots of different kinds of reading, including magazines, comic books, graphic novels, how-to books, catalogues, Internet browsing, and games.

As we think about this whole matter, we might take to heart the lesson that is implied in Comedian George Carlin's observation: "Whatever Americans think is worth doing, they think is worth overdoing." It is this characteristic that got us into trouble back in the 1960s when we started focusing on the education of boys, and then in the 1980s when we started focusing on the education of girls. Let's hope that this time we can get it right by focusing on the young people we work with as individuals.

Notes

[1]David Van Biema, "The Loneliest—and Purest—Rite of Passage: Adolescence and Initiation," *The Journey of Our Lives, Life* magazine (October 1991): 31.

[2]David Spitz, "Reads Like Teen Spirit," *Time* magazine, July 19, 1999, p. 79.

[3]Patty Campbell, "The Sand in the Oyster: Middle Muddle," *Horn Book* 76 (July–August 2000): 483–485.

[4]Campbell, 486.

[5]J. Donald Adams, *Speaking of Books and Life* (Holt, Rinehart, and Winston, 1965), pp. 251–252.

[6]John Goldthwaite, "Notes on the Children's Book Trade," *Harper's* 254 (January 1977): 84.

[7]Arlette Ingraham Willis, "Celebrating African American Literary Achievements," *Teaching and Using Multicultural Literature in Grades 9–12: Going Beyond the Canon.* (Christopher Gordon, 1998), p. 72.

[8]William H. Honan, "Robert E. Cormier, 75, Author of Enduring Books for Teenagers," *New York Times,* November 5, 2000.

[9]Margalit Fox, "Virginia Hamilton, Writer for Children, Is Dead at 65," *New York Times* February 20, 2002.

[10]Mary Rourke, "Mystery writer Joan Lowery Nixon dies," *Los Angeles Times,* reprinted in the *Arizona Republic,* July 14, 2003.

[11]*New York Times,* July 24, 2002.

[12]Don Shirley, "Author, Pulitzer playwright Paul Zindel, 66, dies of cancer," *Los Angeles Times,* reprinted in the *Arizona Republic,* March 30, 2003.

[13]David Spitz, "Reads Like Teen Spirit," *Time* magazine, July 19, 1999, p. 79.

[14]Robert Havighurst, *Developmental Tasks and Education* (McKay, 1972).

[15]Ralph Peterson and Maryann Eeds, *Grand Conversations: Literature Groups in Action* (Scholastic, 1990).

[16]Margaret Early, "Stages of Growth in Literary Appreciation," *English Journal* 49 (March 1960): 163–166.

[17]First cited by G. Robert Carlsen in an article exploring stages of reading development, "Literature Is," *English Journal* 63 (February 1974): 23–27.

[18]Robert Lipsyte, "On Books for Boys," *Literature for Today's Young Adults* by Alleen Pace Nilsen and Kenneth L. Donelson (Longman 2001), p. 39.

A Brief History of Adolescent Literature

Of course, the best way to know adolescent literature is to read widely in contemporary books, but we also have at least three reasons for believing that professionals ought to know something about the history of the field in which they are working:

1. Knowing our common background gives us a sense of the past and a way of knowing why and how certain kinds of books have consistently proven popular. Too many teachers and librarians think their profession was miraculously born from nothing the day before yesterday.

2. For anyone who cares about the mores and morals of our time, there is no better way to see what adults wanted young people to accept as good and noble than to examine adolescent books of a particular period. The analysis may breed some cynicism as we detect the discrepancies between the lessons taught by a Felsen or an Alger or a Stratemeyer Syndicate author and the truth about the world at the time. However, the lessons are nonetheless important and not necessarily less sincere.

3. Many of the older books are surprisingly fun to read. We are not suggesting that the books deserve to be reprinted and circulated among today's young adults, but that librarians and teachers may profit from discovering that books as different as Mabel Robinson's *Bright Island* (1937), John Tunis's *Go, Team, Go!* (1954), or John Bennett's *Master Skylark* (1897) are fun, or that books such as Ralph Henry Barbour's *The Crimson Sweater* (1906) or Susan Coolidge's *What Katy Did* (1872) or Mary Stolz's *Pray Love, Remember* (1954) are not without their charm.

For the convenience of readers, this chapter is divided into roughly equal parts: 1800–1900, 1900–1940, and 1940–1966, each affected by the conditions and technologies of the day.

1800–1900: A Century of Purity with a Few Passions

Before 1800, literature read by children and young adults alike was largely religious. Such books as John Bunyan's *The Pilgrim's Progress* (1678) reminded young people that they were merely small adults who soon must face the wrath of God. In the 1800s, the attitude of adults toward the young gradually changed. The country expanded, we moved inevitably toward an urban society, medical knowledge rapidly developed, and young people no longer began working so early in their lives. The literature that emerged for young adults remained pious and sober, but it hinted at the possibility of humanity's experiencing a satisfying life here on earth. Books reflected adult values and fashions but of this world, not merely the next.

The American Sunday School Union

Largely forgotten, a spiritual and practical movement that began in 1817 in Philadelphia under the title of the Sunday and Adult School Union changed its title to the American Sunday School Union in 1824. By 1830, it had determined to change the course of U.S. education by offering Sunday School lessons that taught religion at the same time they educated young people in mathematics and grammar and history and all sorts of practical, job-related skills.

For the next forty years, the Union produced millions of books for use in Sunday Schools, which were open from 8:00 A.M. to 10:00 A.M. and from 4:00 P.M. to 6:00 P.M. All titles were approved by a board representing six major religions. Titles varied from *History of Patriarchs; Wild Flowers: or the May Day Walk; The Early Saxons; Curiosities of Egypt; Delaware and Iroquois Indians;* to *Kindness to Animals, or the Sin of Cruelty Exposed and Rebuked.*

The Union was best known, however, for its heavily moralistic fiction, rarely deviating from two basic formulas. First, a young child near death would remind readers of all his virtues, all that they must remember and practice, and then the child would die, to the relief of readers. On page 1 of E. P. Grey's *My Teacher's Present: A Select Biography of the Young,* the author wrote:

> You have in this little volume the biography of six Sunday school pupils, who were early called from this world. They were happy and beloved whilst they lived, and deeply lamented when they died.

Another formula portrayed good children who had temporarily forgotten duties to parents and siblings and who would soon get their come-uppance.

Most of the books were little more than sugar-coated sermons; the titles usually gave away the plot, and the writing was unbelievably mawkish. By the 1870s and 1880s, the Union books lost most of their readership to the almost equally badly written work of Horatio Alger, to the often brilliant prose of Louisa May Alcott, and to various writers of dime novels or domestic novels. At a time when few children had any chance of a formal education in schools, however, the American Sunday School Union books were widely read and did much to advance the cause of literacy in America.

Alcott and Alger

Louisa May Alcott and Horatio Alger, Jr. were the first writers for young adults to gain national attention, but the similarity between the two ends almost as it begins. Alcott wrote of happy family life. Alger wrote about broken homes. Alcott's novels were sometimes harsh but always honest. Alger's novels were romantic fantasies. Alcott's novels are still read for good reason. Alger's novels are rarely read save by the historian or the specialist.

The second daughter of visionary Amos Bronson Alcott, Louisa May Alcott lived her youth near Concord and Boston with a practical mother and a father who was brilliant, generous, improvident, and impractical. The reigning young adult writer of the time was Oliver Optic (the pen name of William T. Adams), and Boston publishers the Roberts Brothers were eager to find a story for young adults that would compete with Optic. Thomas Niles, Roberts's representative, suggested in September 1866 that Louisa May Alcott write a girls' book, and in May 1868 he gently reminded her that she had agreed to try.

She sent a manuscript to Niles, who thought parts of it dull, but other readers at the publisher's office disagreed, and the first part of *Little Women: Meg, Jo, Beth, and Amy. The Story of Their Lives. A Girl's Book* was published September 30, 1868. With three illustrations and a frontispiece for $1.50 a copy, *Little Women* was favorably reviewed, and sales were good, here and in England. By early November 1868, Alcott had begun work on the second part, which was published on April 14, 1869.

Little Women has vitality and joy and real life devoid of the sentimentality common at the time, a wistful portrait of the life and world Alcott must have wished she could have lived. The Civil War background is subtle, expressing the loneliness and never-ending war far better than many adult war novels, for all their suffering, pain, and horror. Aimed at young adults, *Little Women* has maintained steady popularity with them and children. Adults reread it (sometimes repeatedly) to gain a sense of where they were when they were children.

Although *Little Women* is Alcott's best-known book, most of the recent research and criticism on Alcott has been devoted to the thrillers she wrote anonymously to make money for the family. Madeleine Stern has edited several collections of these thrillers (e.g., *Behind a Mask: The Unknown Thrillers of Louisa May Alcott; Plots and Counterplots: More Unknown Thrillers of Louisa May Alcott;* and *The Lost Stories of Louisa May Alcott*). The most recent is edited by Kent Bicknell, *A Long Fatal Love Chase.*

Son of an unctuous Unitarian clergyman, Horatio Alger, Jr. graduated from Harvard at 18. Ordained a Unitarian minister in 1864, he served a Brewster, Massachusetts, church only to leave it two years later under a cloud of scandal and claims of sodomy, all hushed at the time. He moved to New York City and began writing full time.

The same year, he sent *Ragged Dick; or, Street Life in New York* to Oliver Optic's magazine, *Student and Schoolmate,* a popular goody-goody magazine. Optic recognized salable pap when he spotted it, and he bought Alger's book for the January 1867 issue. Published in hardcover in 1867 or 1868, *Ragged Dick* was the first of many successes for Alger and his publishers, and it is still his most readable work, probably because it was the first from a mold that soon became predictably moldy.

*T*oday's high school students are reading many of the same basic stories that teenagers read a hundred years ago. See Focus Box 2.1, Old Stories in New Dress. Also, see Film Box 2.1 for new ways of viewing Shakespeare.

The plot, as in most Alger books, consisted of semiconnected episodes illustrating a boy's first steps toward maturity, respectability, and affluence. Ragged Dick, a young bootblack, is grubby but not dirty, he smokes and gambles occasionally, but even the most casual reader recognizes his essential goodness. Through a series of increasingly difficult-to-believe chapters, Ragged Dick is transformed by the model of a young man and the trust of an older one into respectability. But where the sequence of events was hard to believe, Alger now makes events impossible to believe as he introduces the note that typified his later books. What pluck and hard work had brought to Dick is now cast aside as luck enters in—a little boy falls overboard from a ferry, Dick saves the child, and a grateful father rewards Dick with new clothes and a better job. Some readers label Alger's books "rags to riches" stories, but the hero rarely achieves riches, although at the close of the book he is a rung or two higher on the ladder of success than he has any reason to deserve. "Rags to respectability" is a more accurate statement about Alger's work.

FOCUS BOX 2.1   *Old Stories in New Dress*

The Amazing Maurice and His Educated Rodents by Terry Pratchett. HarperCollins, 2001. Loosely based on the old story of the Pied Piper, Pratchett's book makes readers laugh out loud. The rats will remind readers of those in Robert C. O'Brien's *Mrs. Frisby and the Rats of NIMH* (Atheneum, 1971).

The Ballad of Sir Dinadan by Gerald Morris. Houghton, 2003. Students who have enjoyed this light-hearted Arthurian tale about the younger brother of the famous Sir Tristram will have a head start when they get to college and read *The Faery Queene.*

Ella Enchanted by Gale Carson Levine. HarperCollins, 1997. Levine's charming new telling of Cinderella was chosen as a Newbery Honor Book. Her **Cinderellis and the Glass Hill** (HarperCollins, 2000) is part of a series for readers in middle school.

The Goose Girl by Shannon Hale. Bloomsbury, 2003. The first in a planned trilogy, this 383-page story is based on the Grimm's fairy tale of the same name.

The Magic Flute, retold by Anne Gatti, illustrated by Peter Malone. Chronicle, 1997. A multisensory feast is prepared for readers in this retelling of Mozart's operatic fairy tale, which comes with full-page paintings and a CD.

Othello: A Novel by Julius Lester. Scholastic, 1995. In giving it a starred review, *School Library Journal* praised Lester for "an incredibly skillful blend of his own words and Shakespeare's language into modern English."

Parzival: The Quest of the Grail Knight by Katherine Paterson. Lodestar, 1998. Parzival (or Percevel) is one of the lesser known of King Arthur's knights, which is fine with Paterson because it gave her more freedom to create an 800-year-old character who is both touching and humorous.

Robin of Sherwood by Michael Morpurgo, illustrated by Michael Foreman. Harcourt, 1996. The characters have the same names as in the classic tale,

but they have distinguishing characteristics that make them quite different. The story starts with a contemporary boy finding Robin's skull, fainting, and dreaming of Robin. The team also created *Arthur: High King of Britain* (Harcourt, 1995).

Shadow Spinner by Susan Fletcher. Simon & Schuster/Atheneum, 1998. A young crippled storyteller, Marjan, brings a new story to Queen Shaharazad, who has already been spinning stories for nearly 1,000 nights. Complications ensue when Marjan can't remember the ending.

The Silver Treasure: Myths and Legends of the World by Geraldine McCaughrean, illustrated by Bee Willey. Simon & Schuster, 1997. Among the characters getting new life from McCaughrean's stories are Rip Van Winkle, King Arthur, and Sir Patrick Spens.

Sirena (Scholastic, 1998), **Zel** (Dutton, 1996), and **The Magic Circle** (Dutton, 1993) by Donna Jo Napoli. Scholastic, 1998. Sirena is one of ten sirens (mermaids) intent on luring sailors to their island because of the belief that a man's love will give them immortality. Sirena foregoes such trickery, but as luck would have it she is the one to fall in love with a mortal. **Zel** is a retelling of Rapunzel, focusing on the psychology of the mother who keeps her daughter locked away in a tower, while **The Magic Circle** presents the viewpoint of the witch who imprisons Hansel and Gretel.

Spider's Voice by Gloria Skurzynski. Simon & Schuster/Atheneum, 1999. Skurzynski retells the story of the twelfth-century French lovers Abelard and (H)Eloise through the voice of a fictional servant nicknamed Spider. The plot is as tangled as a spider's web and the characters' lives as easily dismantled.

Spindle's End (Putnam, 2000) and **Rose Daughter** (Greenwillow, 1997) by Robin McKinley. McKinley writes beautifully developed novels based on the characters and plots of ancient stories. These two are taken from "Sleeping Beauty" and "Beauty and the Beast," respectively.

The Two Most Popular Types of Novels: Domestic and Dime Novels

In 1855, Nathaniel Hawthorne wrote his publisher bitterly lamenting the state of American literature:

> America is now wholly given over to a d—d mob of scribbling women, and I should have no chance of success while the public taste is occupied with their trash—and should be ashamed of myself if I did succeed. What is the mystery of these innumerable editions of *The Lamplighter,* and other books neither better nor worse?—worse they could not be, and better they need not be, when they sell by the 10,000?[1]

The trash was the domestic novel. Born out of the belief that humanity was redeemable, the domestic novel preached morality; woman's submission to man; the value of cultural, social, and political conservatism; a religion of the heart and the Bible; and the glories of suffering.

Most domestic novels concerned a young girl, orphaned and placed in the home of a relative or some benefactor, who meets a darkly handsome young man with shadows from his past, a man not to be trusted but worth redeeming and converting. Domestic novels promised some adventure amidst many moral lessons. The heroines differed more in names than characteristics. Uniformly submissive to—yet distrustful of—their betters and men generally, they were self-sacrificing and self-denying beyond belief or common sense and interested in the primacy of the family and marriage as the goal of all decent women. Domestic novels were products of the religious sentiment of

T hese two half-dime novels illustrate the promised action, the purple prose, and the erudite vocabulary of their day.

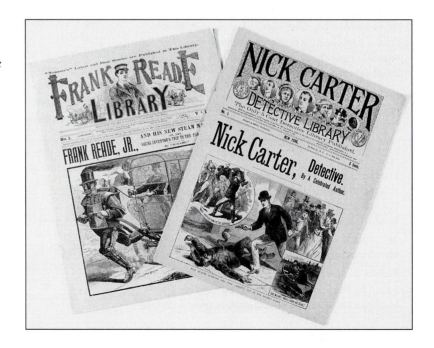

Chimes at Midnight (1966, color, 119 min., NR; Director: Orson Welles; with Welles, Jeanne Moreau, John Gielgud, and Margaret Rutherford) Welles pieces together parts of five Shakespeare plays into a portrait of Falstaff.

Hamlet (1948, black & white, 153 min., NR; Director: Laurence Olivier; with Olivier, Jean Simmons, Felix Aylmer, and Eileen Herlie) This Freudian reading of the play has great music by William Walton.

Henry V (1989, color, 137 min., NR; Director: Kenneth Branagh; with Branagh, Derek Jacobi, Ian Holm, and Richard Briers) A marvelous reading of the "St. Crispin's Day Speech" gives this an edge over Olivier's fine 1945 film.

Looking for Richard (1996, color, 118 min., PG-13; Director: Al Pacino; with Pacino, Kevin Spacey, Aidan Quinn, and Alec Baldwin) Actors play bits from *Richard III* to help Pacino find a way of getting into the play.

Much Ado about Nothing (1993, color, 111 min., PG-13; Director: Kenneth Branagh; with Branagh, Emma Thompson, Denzel Washington, and Richard Briers) Sunny Italy is glorious in this bright and energetic reading of the play.

Ran (1985, color, 161 min., R; Director: Akira Kurosawa; with Tatsuya Nakadai and Akira Terao) Kurosawa's Japanese version of *King Lear* is an interesting contrast.

Richard III (1955, color, 155 min., NR; Director: Laurence Olivier; with Olivier and Claire Bloom) This is Olivier's best film. Ian McKellen's 1995 version is also worth seeing.

Rosencrantz and Guildenstern Are Dead (1990, color, 118 min., NR; Director: Tom Stoppard; with Tim Roth, Gary Oldman, and Richard Dreyfus) Stoppard's play, and the subsequent film, is about two minor characters in *Hamlet* who wander in and out of the story.

Shakespeare Wallah (1965, black & white, 115 min., NR; Director: James Ivory; with Felicity Kendal and Shashi Kapoor) A troupe of Shakespearean actors travel through India giving performances.

Throne of Blood (1957, black & white, 108 min., NR; Director: Akira Kurosawa; with Toshiro Mifune and Isuzu Yamada) Set in the time of Samurai warriors, this Japanese *Macbeth* is one of the greatest of movie experiences.

the time, the espousal of traditional virtues, and the anxieties and frustrations of women trying to find a role in a changing society.

Writing under the pen name of Elizabeth Wetherell, Susan Warner wrote more than twenty novels and the first domestic novel, *The Wide, Wide World* (1850). As much as forty years later, the novel was said to be one of the four most widely read books in the United States, along with the Bible, *The Pilgrim's Progress,* and *Uncle Tom's Cabin.* An abridged edition was published in England in 1950 by the University of London Press, and the Feminist Press republished Warner's book in 1987.

The novel was rejected by several New York publishers. George Putnam was ready to return it but decided to ask his mother to read it. She did, she loved it, she urged her son to publish it, and the book was out in time for the Christmas trade. Sales slowly picked up, and the first edition sold out in four months. Translations into French, German, Swedish, and Italian followed, and by 1852, *The Wide, Wide World* was in its fourteenth printing.

The author's life paralleled that of her heroine, Ellen Montgomery. Warner's father was pathetically and persistently broke, and although the fictional world is not quite so ugly, Ellen's mother died early, and her father was so consumed with family business that he asked Aunt Fortune Emerson to take over Ellen's life. Ellen, to her aunt's irritation, formed a firm friendship with the aunt's intended. Ellen's closest friend—the daughter of the local minister—was doomed to die soon and succeeded in doing just that. In the midst of life, tears flowed. When Ellen and her friends were not crying, they were cooking. Warner's novel taught submission, the dangers of self-righteousness, and the virtues of a steadfast religion. Despite all the weeping, or maybe because of it, the book seemed to have been read by everyone of its time. E. Douglas Branch called it, "The greatest achievement of any of the lady novelists."[2]

Warner's popularity was exceeded only by Augusta Jane Evans Wilson for her *St. Elmo* (1867). Probably no other novel so literally touched the American landscape—thirteen towns were named, or renamed, St. Elmo, as were hotels, railroad coaches, steamboats, one kind of punch, and a brand of cigars. The popularity of Wilson's book may be gauged by a notice in a special edition of *St. Elmo* "limited to 100,000 copies." Only *Uncle Tom's Cabin* had greater sales, and Wilson was more than once called by her admirers the American Brontë.

Ridiculously melodramatic as the plot of *St. Elmo* is, it was so beloved that men and women publicly testified that their lives had been permanently changed for the better by reading it. The plot concerns an orphaned girl befriended by a wealthy woman whose dissolute son is immediately enamored of the young woman, is rejected by her, leaves home for several years, returns to plead for her love, is again rejected, and eventually becomes a minister to win the young woman's hand. They marry, another wicked man reformed by the power of a good woman.

While domestic novels took women by storm, dime novels performed almost the same miracle for men. They began when two brothers, Erastus and Irwin Beadle, republished Ann S. Stephens's *Malaeksa: The Indian Wife of the White Hunter* in June 1860. The story of a hunter and his Indian wife in the Revolutionary War days in upper New York state may be as melodramatic as any domestic novel, but its emphasis is more on thrills and chills than tears, and it apparently satisfied and intrigued male readers. Indeed, 65,000 copies of the 6- by 4-inch book of 128 pages sold in almost record time. The most popular of the early dime novels, also set in the Revolutionary period, appeared in October 1860. *Seth Jones: or, The Captives of the Frontier* sold 60,000 copies the first day; at least 500,000 copies were sold in the United States alone, and it was translated into ten languages.

For several years, dime novels cost ten cents, ran about 100 pages in a 7- by 5-inch format, and were aimed at adults. Some early genius of publishing discovered that many readers were boys who could hardly afford the dime cost. Thereafter, the novels dropped to a nickel, although the genre continued to be called the *dime novel.* The most popular dime novels were set in the West—the West of dime novels increasingly meant Colorado and points west—with wondrous he-men like Deadwood Dick and Diamond Dick. Dime novels developed other forms, such as mysteries and even early forms of science fiction, but none were so popular or so typical as the westerns.

Writers of dime novels never pretended to be writing great literature, but they did write satisfying thrills and chills for the masses. The books were filled with stock characters. Early issues of the *Library Journal,* from 1876 onward for another thirty years, illustrate how many librarians hated dime novels for their immorality; but in truth dime novels were moral. The Beadles sincerely believed that their books should represent sound moral values, and what the librarians objected to in dime novels was nothing more than the unrealistic melodramatic plots and the stereotyped characters, more typical of the time than of just the dime novel.

Development of the American Public Library

The development of the public library was as rocky and slow as it was inevitable. In 1731, Benjamin Franklin suggested that members of the Junto, a middle-class social and literary club in Philadelphia, share their books with other members. That led to the founding of the Philadelphia Library Company, America's first subscription library. Other such libraries followed, most of them dedicated to moral purposes, as the constitution of the Salisbury, Connecticut, Social Library announced: "The promotion of Virtue, Education, and Learning, and . . . the discouragement of Vice and Immorality."[3]

In 1826, the governor of New York urged that school district libraries be established, in effect using school buildings for public libraries. Similar libraries were established in New England by the 1840s and in the Midwest shortly thereafter. Eventually, mayors and governors saw the wisdom of levying state taxes to support public libraries in their own buildings, not the schools, and by 1863, there were 1,000 public libraries spread across the United States.

The first major report on the developing movement came in an 1876 document from the U.S. Bureau of Education. Part I, "Public Libraries in the United States of America, Their History, Condition, and Management," contained 1,187 pages of reports and analyses on 3,649 public libraries with holdings of 300 volumes or more.

That same year marks the beginning of the modern library movement. Melvil Dewey, then assistant librarian in the Amherst College Library, was largely responsible for the October 4, 1876, conference of librarians that formed the American Library Association the third day of the meeting. The first issue of the *American Library Journal* appeared the same year (it was to become the *Library Journal* the following year), the world's first professional journal for librarians. While there had been an abortive meeting in 1853, the 1876 meeting promised continuity the earlier meeting had lacked.[4]

In 1884, Columbia College furthered the public library movement by establishing the first school of Library Economy (later to be called Library Science) under Melvil Dewey's leadership. Excellent as these early public libraries were, they grew immeasurably under the impetus of Andrew Carnegie's philanthropy. A Scottish immigrant, Carnegie left millions of dollars for the creation of public libraries across the United States.

Fiction and Libraries

The growth of public libraries presented opportunities for pleasure and education of the masses, but arguments about the purposes of the public library arose almost as fast as the buildings. William Poole listed three common objections to the public library in the October 1876 *American Library Journal:* the normal dread of taxes; the more

1864: *Frank the Young Naturalist* by Harry Castlemon (really Charles Austin Fosdick) is close to unreadable today, but Castlemon's series books were popular well into the twentieth century.

1867: *Elsie Dinsmore* by Martha Finley (really Martha Farquharson), and the 27 volumes that followed, featured a girl who was nauseatingly docile, pious, virtuous, sweet, humble, timid, ignorant, good, and lachrymose.

1868: *Little Women: Meg, Jo, Beth, and Amy. The Story of Their Lives. A Girl's Book* by Louisa May Alcott is so honest that it is still loved today.

1870: *The Story of a Bad Boy* by Thomas Bailey Aldrich launched a new kind of literature about boys who were imperfect and tough—a refreshing counterbalance to the good-little-boy figures prevalent in too many unrealistic books of the time.

1872: *What Katy Did* by Susan Coolidge (really Sarah Chauncey Woolsey), featured a prankish and fun-loving tomboy and for a time rivaled *Little Women* in popularity.

1876: *Tom Sawyer* by Mark Twain (really Samuel Clemens) and ***Huckleberry Finn*** in 1884 were the culmination of the "bad boy" genre started by Aldrich and continued by George Wilbur Peck with his *Peck's Bad Boy and His Pa*, 1883.

1876: *The Boy Emigrants* by Noah Brooks is a romanticized but fascinating tale of boys traveling across the plains.

1883: *Treasure Island* by Robert Louis Stevenson is filled with the kind of adventure and derring-do that still appeals to boys.

1885: *The Boat Club* by Oliver Optic (really William Taylor Adams) was the first of a six-book series that ran through sixty editions.

1897: *Master Skylark: A Story of Shakespeare's Time* by John Bennett is the witty account of young Nick Attwood, a golden-voiced boy singer involved in more than his share of adventure.

1898: *Pawnee Hero Stories and Folk Tales,* followed in 1929 by ***Cheyenne Campfires*** by George Bird Grinnell, established an honest and generally unsentimentalized portrait of Native American life.

1899: *The Half-Back* by Ralph Henry Barbour was the first of many popular sports books, including ***The Crimson Sweater*** (1906), in which boys at school learn who and what they might become through sports.

1899: *Peggy* by Laura Elizabeth Richards is about a poor girl going to school and becoming a basketball hero.

1902: *The Virginian: A Horseman of the Plains* by Owen Wister provided a mystique of violence and danger mixed with open spaces and freedom, plus a model of colloquial speech and romantic and melodramatic adventures.

1904: *Rebecca of Sunnybrook Farm* by Kate Douglas Wiggin sold more than 1.25 million copies and launched a formula in which a young child (usually a girl) makes life happy for apathetic or depressed adults.

1908: *Anne of Green Gables* by Lucy Maud Montgomery continued the Wiggin formula when an orphan girl is sent by mistake to a childless couple who wanted a boy to help on the farm.

1909: *The Last of the Chiefs,* followed in 1910 by ***The Horsemen of the Plains,*** by Joseph Altsheler helped establish conventions still followed in western adventure stories.

1910: *The Varmint,* followed by ***The Tennessee Shad*** and ***Stover at Yale*** both in 1911, by Owen Johnson attacked snobbery, social clubs, fraternities, and anti-intellectualism.

1912: *The Riders of the Purple Sage* by Zane Grey is still a good read, as well as an illustration of such classic elements as the mysterious hero, the innocent heroine, evil villains, and open land.

1913: *Pollyanna* by Eleanor Porter, the climax (or the finishing blow) to the child-as-savior formula, was a popular adult novel, eighth among best sellers in 1913 and second in 1914.

1926: *Smoky, the Cowhorse* by Will James was originally published as an adult novel but was soon read by thousands of young people and twice filmed for appreciative audiences.

1936: *Tangled Waters,* about a Navajo girl on an Arizona reservation, *Shuttered Windows* (1938) about an African American girl who leaves Minneapolis to live with her grandmother in South Carolina, and *The Moved Outers* (1945) about Japanese Americans forced into a relocation camp during World War II, all by Florence Crannell Means, were the first sympathetic and rich portraits of young protagonists from minority cultures.

1936: *Peggy Covers the News* by Emma Bugbee, a reporter for the *New York Times,* launched a deluge of career books for girls that included Helen Boylston's books about nurse *Sue Barton* and Helen Wells's books about nurse *Cherry Ames* and flight attendant *Vicki Barr.*

1937: *The Great Tradition* by Marjorie Hill Allee intrigued young adults with its mixture of romance, college life, and the spirit of research among five graduate students at the University of Chicago.

1937: *Bright Island* by Mabel Robinson is the story of spunky Thankful Curtis, who was raised on a small island off the coast of Maine and later attends school on the mainland.

1938: *Iron Duke* by John Tunis was the first of several popular books written by an amateur athlete and sports reporter. Other Tunis titles, some of which have been recently reprinted, include *All American* (1942), *Yea Wildcats* (1944), and *Go, Team, Go!* (1954).

1942: *Seventeenth Summer* by Maureen Daly is the story of shy and innocent Angie Morrow and her love for Jack Duluth during the summer between high school and college.

1942: *Adam of the Road* by Elizabeth Janet Gray revealed the color and music of the Middle Ages as young Adam Quartermain became a minstrel.

1943: *The Innocent Wayfaring* by Marchette Chute covers four days in June 1370 when Anne runs away from her convent school to join a band of strolling players.

1945: *Pray Love, Remember* by Mary Stolz is one of the earliest and one of the best of Stolz's many quiet, introspective books; it is a remarkable story of Dody Jenks, a popular but cold young woman who likes neither her family nor herself.

1947: *The Divided Heart* and *A Cup of Courage* (1948) by Mina Lewiton were pioneering problem novels in being, respectively, an honest and groundbreaking study of the effects of divorce on a young woman and of alcoholism and its destruction of a family.

1950: *Swiftwater* by Paul Annixter (really Howard A. Sturzel) mixes animals, ecology, symbolism, and some stereotyped characters into a rousing tale that remains a better than respectable book.

1950: *Amos Fortune, Free Man* by Elizabeth Yates was given the Newbery Award for the way Yates presented the story of a slave who gained his freedom in 1801 and fought the rest of his life for freedom for other African Americans.

1950: *Hot Rod* by Henry Gregor Felsen, followed by *Two and the Town* (1952), *Street Rod* (1953), and *Crash Club* (1958) were incredibly popular, even with boys who had never finished a book on their own.

1957: *Ring Around Her Finger* and *The Limit of Love* (1959) by James Summers, were effective delineations of young people's sexual feelings and actions told from the boys' points of view. Critics feared readers were too young to handle such emotional intricacies.

1957: *Married on Wednesday* by Anne Emery is the best of her many books that while preaching the status quo, especially acceptance of parental rules, still managed to touch on personal concerns.

1958: *South Town, North Town* (1965) and *Whose Town?* (1969) by Lorenz Graham presented realistic African American characters, but because of societal changes the books now seem dated.

1959: *Jennifer* by Zoa Sherburne is an enduring portrait of the effects of alcoholism, but it is not as good as *Too Bad about the Haines Girl* (1967), a superb novel about teenage pregnancy that is honest and straightforward without being preachy.

1961: *A Separate Peace* by John Knowles, the story of two boys whose friendship ends in tragedy, was predicted to be a story that would be taught in high school English classes for generations, but interest in it has faded.

1965: *Jazz Country* by Nat Hentoff is a superb story of a white boy trying to break into the African American world of jazz.

philosophical belief that government had no rights except to protect people and property—that is no right to tax anyone to build and stock a public library; and concern over the kinds of books libraries might buy and circulate.[5] In this last point, Poole touched on a controversy that raged for years, that is, whether a public library is established for scholars or the pleasure of the masses. Poole believed that a library existed for the entire community, or else there was no justification for a general tax. Poole's words did not quiet critics who argued that the library's sole *raison d'etre* was educational. Waving the banner of American purity in his hands, W. M. Stevenson maintained:

> If the public library is not first and foremost an educational institution, it has no right to exist. If it exists for mere pleasure, and for a low order of entertainment at that, it is simply a socialistic institution.[6]

Many librarians of the time agreed. Probably, a few agree even today.

The problem lay almost entirely with fiction. Indeed, the second session of the 1876 American Library Association meeting was devoted to "Novel Reading," mostly but not exclusively about young people's reading. A librarian announced that his rules permitted no fiction in his library. His factory-patrons might ask for novels, but he recommended other books and was able to keep patrons without supplying novels. To laughter, he said that he had never read novels so he "could not say what their effect really was."[7]

Teachers worried almost as much as librarians. A principal of a large endowed academy was approvingly quoted by a librarian for having said:

> The voracious devouring of fiction commonly indulged in by patrons of the public library, especially the young, is extremely pernicious and mentally unwholesome.[8]

That attitude persisted for years and is occasionally heard even today among teachers and librarians.

1900–1940: From the Safety of Romance to the Beginning of Realism

During the first forty years of the twentieth century, the western frontier disappeared, and the United States changed from an agrarian society to an urban one. World War I brought the certainty that it would end all wars. The labor movement grew along with Ford's production lines of cars, cars, cars. President Hoover came along, then the Wall Street crash of 1929 and the Great Depression. By 1938, three million young people from age 16 through 25 were out of school and unemployed, and a quarter of a million boys were on the road. Nazi Germany rose in Eastern Europe, and in the United States, Roosevelt introduced the "New Deal." When the end of the Depression seemed almost in sight, the New York World's Fair of 1939 became an optimistic metaphor for the coming of a newer, better, happier, and more secure life. But World War II lay just over the horizon, apparent to some, ignored by most.

In the decades before the 1929 stock market crash, U.S. high schools developed in their present form, including the establishment of athletic teams as a way of "bribing" boys into reading and writing. Shown here is the 1917 Tempe Public Schools baseball team. (Photo courtesy of the Tempe Historical Museum)

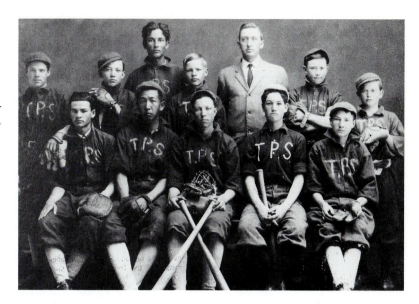

Reading Interests versus Reading Needs

In the high schools, which enrolled only a tiny fraction of eligible students in the United States, teachers faced pressure from colleges to prepare the young for advanced study, which influenced many adults to be more intent on telling young people what to read than in finding out what they wanted to read. Recreational reading seemed vaguely time-wasting, if not downright wicked. Young people nevertheless found and read books, mainly fiction, for recreation. Popular choices were series books from Stratemeyer's Literary Syndicate, including Tom Swift, Nancy Drew, the Hardy Boys, Baseball Joe, and Ruth Fielding. Non-Stratemeyer series books were also popular, as were individual books written specifically for young adults, along with some classics and best sellers selected by the Book-of-the-Month Club when it began in 1926 and the Literary Guild when it began a year later.

Arguments over what students choose to read have raged for years, and the end is unlikely to come soon. In 1926, when Carleton Washburne and Mabel Vogel put together the lengthy *Winnetka Graded Book List,* they explained, "Books that were definitely trashy or unsuitable for children, even though widely read, have not been included in this list."[9] Apparently enough people were curious about the trashy or unsuitable to lead the authors to add two supplements.[10] *Elsie Dinsmore* was among the damned, and so were Edgar Rice Burroughs's *Tarzan of the Apes,* Eleanor Porter's *Pollyanna,* Zane Grey's westerns, books from the Ruth Fielding and Tom Swift series, Mark Twain's *Tom Sawyer Abroad,* and Arthur Conan Doyle's *The Hound of the Baskervilles. The Adventures of Sherlock Holmes,* however, was considered worthy of inclusion.

Representative of the other side of the argument is this statement by English professor William Lyon Phelps:

> I do not believe the majority of these very school teachers and other cultivated mature readers began in early youth by reading great books exclusively; I think they read *Jack*

Harkaway, an Old Sleuth, and the works of Oliver Optic and Horatio Alger. From these enchanters they learned a thing of tremendous importance—the delight of reading. Once a taste for reading is formed, it can be improved. But it is improbable that boys and girls who have never cared to read a good story will later enjoy stories by good artists.[11]

Girls' Books and Boys' Books

Up to the mid–1930s, teachers and librarians frequently commented that girls' books were inferior to boys' books. Franklin T. Baker wrote that with the obvious exception of Alcott, girls' books of 1908 were "painfully weak" and lacking "invention, action, humor."[12] Two years later, Clara Whitehill Hunt agreed that many girls' books were empty, insipid, and mediocre.[13] In 1935, Julia Carter broke into a review of boys' nonfiction with what appeared to be an exasperated *obiter dictum:*

> Will someone please tell me why we expect the *boys* to know these things and still plan for the girls to be mid-Victorian, and consider them hoydens beyond reclaiming, when instead of shrieking and running like true daughters of Eve, they are interested in snakes and can light a fire with two matches?[14]

Such writers as Caroline Dale Snedeker, Cornelia Meigs, Jeanette Eaton, Mabel Robinson, and Elizabeth Forman Lewis responded to these kinds of criticism by writing enough good girls' books that in 1937 Alice M. Jordan wrote as if the difference in quality was a thing of the past:

> There was a time not long ago when the boys had the lion's share in the yearly production of books intended for young people. So writers were urged to give us more stories in which girls could see themselves in recognizable relationship to the world of their own time, forgetting perhaps that human nature does not change and the vital things are universal. Yet, nonetheless, the girls had a real cause to plead and right valiantly the writers have responded.[15]

Critics believed then, as they continued to insist for years, that girls would read boys' books, but boys would never read girls' books. At least part of the problem lay with stereotypes of boys' and girls' roles as expressed by two writers. Clara Vostrovsky, author of the first significant reading interest study, went back to ancient times for her stereotypes, suggesting that it was "probable" that the differences in reading interests between boys and girls lay "in the history of the race."[16] Psychologist G. Stanley Hall predicted reading interests of girls and boys on psychological differences:

> Boys love adventure, girls sentiment. . . . Girls love to read stories about girls which boys eschew, girls, however, caring much more to read about boys than boys to read about girls. Books dealing with domestic life and with young children in them, girls have almost entirely to themselves. Boys, on the other hand, excel in love of humor, rollicking fun, abandon, rough horse-play, and tales of wild escapades. Girls are less averse to reading what boys like than boys are to reading what girls like. A book pop-

ular with boys would attract some girls, while one read by most girls would repel a boy in the middle teens. The reading interests of high-school girls are far more humanistic, cultural and general, and that of boys is more practical, vocational, and even special.[17]

The simple truth, perhaps too obvious and discomforting to be palatable to some parents, English teachers, and librarians, was that boys' books were generally far superior to girls' books. That had nothing to do with the sexual or psychological nature of boys or girls but rather with the way authors treated their audience. Many authors insisted on making their girls good and domestic and dull (if a heroine were allowed some freedom to roam outside the house, she soon regretted it or grew up, whichever came first), perhaps because they thought parents and librarians wanted books that way. Boys were allowed outside the house not only to find work and responsibilities, of course, but also to find adventure and excitement in their books.

Changing English Classroom

By 1900, the library played a significant role in helping young adults find reading materials. Although many librarians reflected the traditional belief that classics should be the major reading of youth, other librarians helped young adults find a variety of materials they liked, not trash, but certainly popular books.

This would rarely have been true of English teachers, saddled as they were with responsibility for preparing young adults for college entrance examinations. At first, these examinations simply required some proof of writing proficiency, but in 1860 and 1870, Harvard began using Milton's *Comus* and Shakespeare's *Julius Caesar* as alternative books for the examination. Four years later, Harvard required a short composition based on a question about one of the following: Shakespeare's *The Tempest, Julius Caesar,* and *The Merchant of Venice,* Goldsmith's *The Vicar of Wakefield,* or Scott's *Ivanhoe* and *The Lay of the Last Minstrel.*

In 1894, the prestigious Committee of Ten on Secondary School Studies presented its report, and English became an accepted discipline in the schools, although not yet as respectable as Latin. Chaired by controversial Harvard president Charles W. Eliot, the committee was appointed by the National Education Association in July 1892 and met later that year to determine the nature, limits, and methods appropriate to many subject matters in secondary school. Samuel Thurber of the Boston Girls' High School was unable to promote his belief that a high school curriculum should consist almost entirely of elective courses, but as chairman of the English Conference, his report liberalized and dignified the study of English. Two important recommendations were that English be studied five hours a week for four years and that uniform college entrance examinations be established throughout the United States.

The result was the publication of book lists, mainly classics, as the basis of entrance examinations. Plays and books such as Shakespeare's *Twelfth Night* and *As You Like It,* Milton's Books I and II from *Paradise Lost,* Scott's *The Abbot* and *Marmion,* or Irving's *Bracebridge Hall* virtually became the English curriculum as teachers, inevitably concerned with their students' entry into college, increasingly adapted the English curriculum to fit the list.

National Council of Teachers of English Begins

Out of the growing protest about college entrance examinations, a group of English teachers attending a national Education Association Table formed a Committee on College Entrance Requirements in English to assess the problem through a national survey of English teachers. The committee uncovered hostility to colleges presumptuous enough to try to control the secondary English curriculum through the guise of entrance examinations. John M. Coulter, a professor at the University of Chicago, tried to sound that alarm to college professors but without much success:

> The high school exists primarily for its own sake; and secondarily as a preparatory school for college. This means that when the high school interest and the college interest comes into conflict, the college interest must yield. It also means that the function of a preparatory school must be performed only in so far as it does not interfere with the more fundamental purpose of the high school itself.[18]

Some irate teachers recognized that the problem of college control would hardly be the last issue to face English teachers and formed the nucleus of the National Council of Teachers of English. The First Annual Meeting in Chicago on December 1 and 2, 1911, was largely devoted to resentment about actions of the National Conference on Uniform Entrance Requirements, particularly because that body had representatives from twelve colleges, two academies, and only two public high schools (principals, not English teachers). Wilbur W. Hatfield, then at Farragut High School in Chicago and soon to edit the *English Journal,* relayed instructions from the Illinois Association of Teachers of English that the new organization should compile a list of comparatively recent books suitable for home reading by students and that they should also recommend some books of the last ten years for study because the "present custom of using only old books in the classroom leaves the pupil with no acquaintance with the literature of the present day," from which students would choose their reading after graduation.[19]

James Fleming Hosic's 1917 report on the *Reorganization of English in Secondary Schools,* part of a larger report published under the aegis of the U.S. Bureau of Education, looked at books and teaching in ways that must have seemed muddle-headed or perverse to traditionalists. Looking at literature for the tenth, eleventh, and twelfth grades, Hosic chose works that pleased many, puzzled others, and alienated some. He explained that English teachers should lead students to read works in which they would, "find their own lives imaged in this larger life," and would gradually attain from the author's "clearer appreciation of human nature, a deeper and truer understanding. . . . It should be the aim of the English teacher to make [reading] an unfailing resource and joy in the lives of all."[20] Hosic's list included classics as well as modern works, such as Helen Hunt Jackson's *Ramona* and Owen Wister's *The Virginian* for the tenth grade, Rudyard Kipling's *The Light That Failed* and Mary Johnston's *To Have and To Hold* for the eleventh grade, and John Synge's *Riders to the Sea* and Margaret Deland's *The Awakening of Helena Richie* for the twelfth grade. Teachers terrified by the contemporary reality reflected in these books—and perhaps equally terrified by the possibility of throwing out age-old lesson plans and tests on classics—had little to fear. In many schools, nothing changed. *Silas Marner, Julius Caesar, Idylls of the King, A Tale of Two Cities,* and *Lady of the Lake* remained the most widely studied books. Most books were taught at interminable length in what was known as the "intensive" method with four to six weeks—sometimes even more—of detailed examination, while horrified or bored students vowed never to read anything once they escaped high school. A 1927 study by Nancy Coryell offered proof that the "intensive" method produced no better test results and considerably more apathy toward literature than the "extensive" method in which students read assigned works faster.[21] Again, however, in many schools nothing changed.

Fortunately, the work of two college professors influenced more English teachers. A 1936 study by Lou LaBrant on the value of free reading at the Ohio State University Laboratory School revealed that students with easy access to different kinds of books and some guidance read more, enjoyed what they read, and moved upward in literary sophistication and taste.[22] Earlier, University of Minnesota professor Dora V. Smith discovered that English teachers knew next to nothing about books written for adolescents. She began the long process of correcting that situation by establishing the first course in adolescent literature. She argued that it was unfair to both young people and their teachers "to send out from our colleges and universities men and women trained alone in Chaucer and Milton and Browning to compete with Zane Grey, Robert W. Chambers, and Ethel M. Dell."[23]

School Libraries

The development of the school library was almost as slow and convoluted as the development of the public library. In 1823, Brooklyn's Apprentice Library Association established a Youth Library where "Boys over twelve were allowed . . . as were girls whose access to the library were limited to one hour an afternoon, once a week." In 1853, Milwaukee School Commissioner Increase A. Lapham provided for a library open Saturday afternoons and recommended that schools spend $10 a year for books. Rules for the Milwaukee library were clear and more than a bit reminiscent of rules in some school and public libraries until the 1940s:

> (1) Only children over ten years old, their parents, teachers, and school commissioner could withdraw books; (2) books might be withdrawn between 2:00 P.M. and sunset on Saturdays and kept for one week; (3) withdrawals were limited to one book per person; and (4) fines were to be assessed for overdue or damaged books.[24]

Writers in the early years of the *Library Journal* encouraged the cultivation of friendly relations between "co-educators."[25] The National Education Association formed a Committee on Relations of Public Libraries to Public Schools, and its 1899 report announced that "The teachers of a town should know the public library, what it contains, and what use the pupils can make of it. The librarian must know the school, its work, its needs, and what he can do to meet them."[26]

A persistent question was whether schools should depend on the public library or establish their own libraries. In 1896, Melvil Dewey recommended to the National Education Association that it form a library department (as it had for other subject disciplines) because the library was as much a part of the educational system as the classroom.

The previous year, a branch of the Cleveland, Ohio, Public Library was established within Central High School, and in 1899, a branch of the Newark, New Jersey, Public Library was placed in a local high school. In 1900, Mary Kingston became the first library school graduate appointed to a high school library (Erasmus High School in Brooklyn). In 1912, Mary E. Hall, librarian at Girls' High School in Brooklyn, argued the need for many more professionally trained librarians in high school libraries:

> (1) The aims and ideals of the new high school mean we must stop pretending that high school is entirely college preparatory. "It realizes that for the great majority of pupils it must be a preparation for life." (2) Modern methods of teaching demand that a textbook is not enough. "The efficient teacher today uses books, magazines, daily papers, pictures, and lantern slides to supplement the textbook." (3) Reading guidance is easier for the school librarian than the public librarian. "The school librarian has the teacher always close at hand and can know the problems of these teachers in their work with pupils."[27]

In 1916, C. C. Certain, as head of National Education Association committee, began standardizing high school libraries across the United States. He discovered conditions so mixed, from deplorable (mostly) to good (rarely) that his committee set to work to establish minimum essentials for high schools of various sizes. Two reports from the U.S. Office of Education indicate the growth of high school libraries. A 1923 report found only 947 school libraries with more than 3,000 volumes, and these were mostly in the northeastern part of the United States. Six years later, the 1929 report found 1,982 school libraries with holdings of more than 3,000 volumes, and the libraries were more equally spread over the country with New York having 211 such libraries and California having 191. The steady growth of high school libraries, however, slowed drastically during the Depression.

Edward Stratemeyer's Literary Syndicate

The Boston publishing firm of Lee and Shepard established *the* format for young adult series, and to the distress of teachers, librarians, and parents, series books became the method of publishing for many young adult novels. If sales were any index, readers delighted in Lee and Shepard's 440 authors and 900 books published in 1887 alone. However, the format became far more sophisticated a few years later when Edward Stratemeyer became the king of series books.

Whatever disagreements librarians and English teachers may have had about books suitable for young adults, they bonded together, although ineffectively, to oppose the books produced by Edward Stratemeyer and his numerous writers. Stratemeyer founded the most successful industry ever built around adolescent reading. In 1866, he took time off from working for his stepbrother and wrote on brown wrapping paper an 18,000-word serial, *Victor Horton's Idea,* and mailed it to a Philadelphia weekly boys' magazine. A check for $75 arrived shortly, and Stratemeyer's success story was under way. By 1893, Stratemeyer was editing *Good News,* Street and Smith's boys' weekly, building circulation to more than 200,000. This brought his name in front of the public, particularly young adults. Even more important, he came to know staff writers such as William T. Adams, Edward S. Ellis, and Horatio Alger, Jr. When Optic and Alger died leaving some uncompleted manuscripts, Stratemeyer was asked to finish the last three Optic novels, and he completed (or possibly wrote from scratch) at least eleven and perhaps as many as eighteen Alger novels.

His first hardback book published under his own name was *Richard Dare's Venture; or, Striking Out for Himself* (1894), first in a series he titled Bound to Succeed. By the close of 1897, Stratemeyer had six series and sixteen hardcover books in print. A major breakthrough came in 1898. After Stratemeyer sent a manuscript about two boys on a battleship to Lothrop and Shepard, one of the most successful publishers of young adult fiction, Admiral Dewey won his great victory in Manila Bay. A Lothrop editor asked Stratemeyer to place the boys at the scene of Dewey's victory. He rewrote and returned the book, and *Under Dewey at Manila; or, The War Fortunes of a Castaway* hit the streets in time to capitalize on all the publicity. Not one to miss an opportunity, Stratemeyer used the same characters in his next books, all published from 1898 to 1901 under the series title Old Glory. Using the same characters in contemporary battles in the Orient, Stratemeyer created another series called Soldiers of Fortune, published from 1900 through 1906.

By this time, Stratemeyer had turned to full-time writing and was being wooed by the major publishers, notably Grossett and Dunlap and Cupples and Leon. For a time he turned to stories of school life and sports, the Lakeport series (1904–1912), the Dave Porter series (1905–1919), and the most successful of his early series, the Rover Boys (30 books published between 1899 and 1926). These books were so popular that somewhere between 5 or 6 million copies were sold worldwide, including translations into German and Czechoslovakian.

Stratemeyer aspired to greater things, however. Between 1906 and 1910, he approached both his publishers, suggesting they reduce the price of his books to 50 cents. The publishers may have been shocked to find an author willing to sell his books for less money, but, as they soon realized, mass production of 50-centers increased their revenue and Stratemeyer's royalties almost geometrically. An even greater breakthrough came at roughly the same time, when he evolved the idea of his Literary Syndicate. Stratemeyer was aware that he could create plots and series faster than he could possibly write them. He advertised for writers who needed money and sent them sketches of settings and characters along with a chapter-by-chapter outline of the plot. Writers had a few weeks to fill in the outlines, and when the copy arrived, Stratemeyer tightened the prose and checked for discrepancies with earlier volumes of the series. Then the manuscript was off to the publisher and checks went out to the authors, from $50 to $100, depending on the writer and the importance of the series.

Attacks on Stratemeyer were soon in coming. Librarian Caroline M. Hewins criticized both Stratemeyer's books and the journals that praised his output:

> Stratemeyer is an author who misuses "would" and "should," has the phraseology of a country newspaper, as when he calls a supper "an elegant affair" and a girl "a fashionable miss," and follows Oliver Optic closely in his plots and conversations.[28]

Most librarians supported Hewins, but their attacks hardly affected Stratemeyer's sales. A far more stinging and effective attack came in 1913 from the Boy Scouts of America. Chief executive James E. West was disturbed by the deluge of inferior books and urged the organization's Library Commission to establish a carefully selected and recommended library to protect young men. Not long afterward, Chief Scout Librarian Franklin K. Mathiews urged Grosset and Dunlap to make better books available in 50-cent editions—to compete with Stratemeyer—and on November 1, 1913, the first list appeared in a Boy Scout publication, "Safety First Week."

Before World War II, books published for teenagers were clearly divided into "boys' books" and "girls' books," with the boys getting the more exciting stories. However, a surprising number of pre-1950s girls' books were designed to make girls think about careers.

But that was not enough to satisfy Mathiews, who in 1914 wrote his most famous article under the sensational title "Blowing Out the Boy's Brains,"[29] a loud and vituperative attack, sometimes accurate but often unfair. Mathiews's attack was mildly successful for the moment, although how much harm it did to Stratemeyer's sales is open to question. Stratemeyer went on to sell more millions of books. When he died in 1930, his two daughters ran the syndicate, which still persists, presumably forever.

Series books were inevitably moral. Whatever parents, teachers, or librarians might have objected to about the unrealistic elements of the books or the poor literary quality, they would have agreed that the books were clearly on the side of good and right, if simplistically so. Series books—and many adult books as well—repeatedly underlined the same themes. Sports produced truly manly men. Foreigners were not to be trusted. School, education, and life should be taken seriously. The outdoor life was healthy, physically and psychologically. Good manners and courtesy were essential for moving ahead. Work in and of itself was a positive good and would advance one in life. Anyone could defeat adversity, any adversity, *if* that person had a good heart and soul. The good side (ours and God's) always won in war. Evil and good were clearly and easily distinguishable. And good always triumphed over evil (at least by the final chapter).

The Coming of the "Junior" or "Juvenile" Novel

Although for years countless books had been published and widely read by young adults, the term *junior* or *juvenile* was first applied to young adult literature during the early 1930s. Rose Wilder Lane's novel *Let the Hurricane Roar* had been marketed by Longmans, Green, and Company as an adult novel. A full-page blurb on the front cover of the February 11, 1933, *Publishers Weekly* bannered THE BOOK THAT MAKES YOU PROUD TO BE AN AMERICAN! and quoted an unnamed reader, presumably an adult, saying, "Honestly, it makes me ashamed of cussing about hard times and taxes." The tenor of the ad and ones to follow suggest an adult novel likely to be popular with young adults as well. It had been the same with the earlier serialization of the novel in the *Saturday Evening Post* and also with the many favorable reviews. Sometime later in 1933, Longmans, Green began to push the novel as the first of their series of "Junior Books," as they termed them.

That the company wanted to attract young adults to Lane's novel is not difficult to understand. Lane wrote of a threatening frontier world she had known in a compelling manner certain to win readers and admirers among young adults. *Let the Hurricane Roar* tells of newly married David and Molly and their life on the hard Dakota plains. David works as a railroad hand for a time, Molly waits for her baby to arrive, and both strive for independence and the security of owning their own fifty-acre homestead. When they realize that dream and the baby is born, all looks well, but David overextends his credit, grasshoppers destroy the wheat crop, and no nearby employment can be found. David heads east to find work and later breaks his leg, leaving Molly isolated on the Dakota plains for a winter. Neighbors flee the area, and Molly battles loneliness, blizzards, and wolves before David returns. In summary, *Let the Hurricane Roar* sounds melodramatic, but it is not. In a short, quiet, and loving work, Lane made readers care about two likable young adults living a tough life in a hostile environment. The book's popularity is attested to by its twenty-six printings between 1933 and 1958 and a recent television production and reissue in paperback under the title *Young Pioneers.*

The development of publishing house divisions to handle books lying in limbo between children's and adults' books grew after *Let the Hurricane Roar,* although authors of the time were sometimes unaware of the "junior" or "juvenile" branches as was John T. Tunis when he tried to market *Iron Duke* in 1934 and 1935. After sending the manuscript to Harcourt, Tunis was invited into the president's office. Mr. Harcourt clearly did not want to talk about the book but instead took the startled author directly to the head of the Juvenile Department. He explained that Harcourt wanted to publish the book as a juvenile, much to Tunis's bewilderment and dismay, since he had no idea what a "juvenile" book was. Thirty years later, he still had no respect for the term, which he called the "odious product of a merchandising age."[30]

1940–1966: From Certainty to Uncertainty

During the 1940s, the United States moved from the Depression into a wartime and then a postwar economy. World War II caused us to move from hatred of Communism to a temporary brotherhood, followed by Yalta, the Iron Curtain, blacklisting, and Senator McCarthy. We went from "Li'l Abner" to "Pogo" and from Bob Hope to Mort Sahl. Problems of the time included school integration, racial unrest, civil rights, and riots in the streets. We were united about World War II, unsure about the Korean War, and divided about Vietnam. We went from violence to more violence and the assassinations of John Kennedy and Malcolm X. The twenty-five years between 1940 and 1965 revealed a country separated by gaps of all kinds: generational, racial, technological, cultural, and economic.

Educators were as divided as anyone else. Reading interest studies had become fixtures in educational journals, but there was little agreement about the results. In 1946, George W. Norvell wrote, "Our data shows clearly that much literary material being used in our schools is too mature, too subtle, too erudite to permit its enjoyment by the majority of secondary-school pupils." Norvell offered the advice that teachers should give priority to the reading interests of young adults in assigning materials that students would enjoy and in letting students select a portion of their own materials based on their individual interests. He thought that three-fourths of the selections currently in use were uninteresting, especially to boys, and that "to increase reading skill, promote the reading habit, and produce a generation of book-lovers, there is no factor so powerful as interest."[31]

Other researchers supported Norvell's contention that young adults' choices of voluntary reading rarely overlapped books widely respected by more traditional English teachers. In 1947, Marie Rankin surveyed eight public libraries in Illinois, Ohio, and New York and discovered that Helen Boylston's *Sue Barton, Student Nurse* was the most consistently popular book.[32] Twelve years later, Stephen Dunning surveyed fourteen school and public libraries and concluded that the ten most popular books were Maureen Daly's *Seventeenth Summer,* Henry Gregor Felsen's *Hot Rod,* Betty Cavanna's *Going On Sixteen,* Rosamund Du Jardin's *Double Date,* Walter Farley's *Black Stallion,* Sally Benson's *Junior Miss,* Mary Stolz's *The Sea Gulls Woke Me,* Rosamund Du Jardin's *Wait for Marcy,* James Summers's *Prom Trouble,* and John Tunis's *All American.*[33]

Near the height of the outpouring of published studies, Jacob W. Getzels assessed the value of reading interest surveys and found most of them wanting in "precision of *definition,* rigor of *theory,* and depth of *analysis.*"[34] He was, of course, right. Most reports were limited to a small sample from a few schools, and little was done except to ask students what they liked to read. The studies at least gave librarians and teachers insight into books young adults liked and brought hope that somewhere out there somebody was reading—a hope that for librarians and teachers needs constant rekindling.

In the mid-1950s, G. Robert Carlsen summarized the findings of published reading interest surveys as showing that young people select their reading first to reassure themselves about their normality and their status as human beings and then for role-playing:

> With the developing of their personality through adolescence, they come to a partially integrated picture of themselves as human beings. They want to test this picture of themselves in the many kinds of roles that it is possible for a human being to play and through testing to see what roles they may fit into and what roles are uncongenial.[35]

Carlsen's observations tied in with those of University of Chicago psychologist Robert J. Havighurst, who outlined the developmental tasks necessary for the healthy growth of individuals. (See Chapter 1, p. 35, for the tasks that Havighurst thought crucial to adolescence.)

An outgrowth of the tying together of reading interests and psychology was an interest in bibliotherapy. In 1929, Dr. G. O. Ireland coined the term while writing about the use of books as part of his treatment for psychiatric patients.[36] By the late 1930s and early 1940s, articles about bibliotherapy became almost commonplace in education journals, and by the 1950s, the idea of using books to help readers come to terms with their psychological problems was firmly entrenched. Philosophically, it was justified by Aristotle's *Poetics* and the theory of emotional release through catharsis, a theory with little support except for unverifiable personal testimonials.

One clear and easy application of bibliotherapy was the free reading program (sometimes too clear and too easy for the inept psychologist/English teacher who, finding a new book in which the protagonist had acne, sought the acne-ridden kid in class saying, "You must read this—it's about you"). Lou LaBrant, popularizer of free reading, sounded both a recommendation and a warning when she wrote:

> Certainly I can make a much wiser selection of offerings if I understand the potential reader. . . . [but] This does not mean, as some have interpreted, that a young reader will enjoy only literature which answers his questions, tells him what is to be done. It is true, however, that young and old tend to choose literature, whether they seek solutions or escape, which offers characters or situations with which they can find a degree of identification.[37]

Rise of Paperbacks

Young adult readers might assume paperbound books have always been with us. Despite the success of dime novels and libraries of paperbacks in the late 1800s,

VIRGINIA EUWER WOLFF
On Wintertime Reading

I was a painfully slow reader in school. As an adult I have a lot of catching up to do, so I read a literary classic each winter. The book takes me months to get through, it is never from the library (I write all over the pages), and it helps me get to know the world, bit by bit.

Sometimes it begins before winter. During the week that Soviet Premier Mikhail Gorbachev disappeared and angry crowds were shouting in Red Square in Moscow, I was reading *War and Peace*, watching crowds swell in the very same Kremlin Square during Napoleon's attack. It was August 1991, but for me the year was 1812, and I was writing brusque complaints in the margins, such as, "Grow up, Natasha!" (Of course, I found out later that she was growing as fast as she could.) Nearly a decade afterward, I saw the St. Petersburg Memorial to the Siege of Leningrad: acres of mass graves of those who died during Hitler's 900-day occupation of the city. Two monstrous men, a century apart, both determined that the Russians should not survive their terrible swift sword. Both men were wrong, and I could not have known that without Tolstoy.

In St. Petersburg I visited the flat where Dostoevsky lived with his wife and young children, where he wrote *The Karamazov Brothers*, and where he died. I returned home and spent months reading that prodigious novel, which takes the prize for Most Odious Dead Father. The photo I took of Dostoevsky's study is beside my desk, 8,000 miles west of his.

One winter when I was a hurried school teacher I read the shortest classic I could find on my bookshelves, Booker T. Washington's *Up from Slavery*. In it I found piercingly smart lessons. Here's one. He "resolved that I would permit no man, no matter what his colour might be, to narrow and degrade my soul by making me hate him." Difficult wisdom for the disturbing twenty-first century.

Just after September 11, 2001, I knew I needed to make an attempt, however futile, to fathom the question of evil. So I read *Paradise Lost.* Of course I still can't explain evil, but I've found how expansive, dramatic, merciless, made-for-the-movies, and at times how hilarious Milton could be.

This past winter I did a re-reading. *David Copperfield* spent the gray months beside my bed, on my desk, in my carry-on bag, propped on hotel room bedspreads. And David became my best friend again as I revisited what may have been the first Young Adult novel of all.

The point seems plain: To grow as a writer I must grow as a reader. Everything I learn in my winters' tales affects what I eventually write for young readers, although I rarely see the connection clearly. Every book teaches me about the lifelong struggle to live with painful ambiguity. Each day I hope to be able to infuse a manuscript page with what Allen Ginsberg called "generous energy." An ambitious goal, but not impossible with a rich mental library.

Virginia Euwer Wolff's books include *True Believer*, Atheneum, 2001; *Make Lemonade*, Holt, 1993; *Bat 6: A Novel,* Scholastic, 1998; and *Probably Still Nick Swanson*, Macmillan, 1988. Copyright © 2004 by Virginia Euwer Wolff.

---

paperbacks as we know them entered the mass market in 1938 when Pocket Books offered Pearl Buck's *The Good Earth* as a sample volume in mail-order tests. In the spring of 1939, a staff artist created the first sketch of Gertrude the Kangaroo with a book in her paws and another in her pouch. It became Pocket Books' trademark. A few months later, the company issued ten titles in 10,000-copy editions, most of them remaining best sellers for years. Avon began publishing in 1941; Penguin entered the U.S. market in 1942; and Bantam, New American Library, Ballantine, Dell, and Popular Library began publishing in 1943. By 1951, sales had reached 230 million paperbacks annually. Phenomenal as the growth was, paperbacks were slow to appear in schools despite an incredible number of titles on appropriate subjects. Librarians complained that paperbacks did not belong in libraries because they were difficult to catalog and easy to steal. School officials maintained that the covers were lurid and the contents little more than pornography. As late as 1969, a New York City high school junior explained, "I'd rather be caught with Lady Chatterley in hardcover than *Hot Rod* in paperback. Hard covers get you one detention, but paperbacks get you two or three."[38]

Regardless of "official" attitudes, by the mid-1960s paperbacks had become a part of young adults' lives. They are easily available, comfortably sized, and inexpensive. Fortunately, not all school personnel were resistant. The creation of Scholastic Book Clubs and widespread distribution of Reader's Choice Catalogs helped paperbacks get accepted in schools and libraries. Eventually, Bantam and Dell's Yearling books became the major suppliers of books written specifically for young adults.

Changes and Growth in Young Adult Literature

From 1941 to 1965, the quality of young adult literature rose steadily, if at times hesitatingly and uncertainly. Series books, so popular from 1900 to the 1940s, died out—except for Stratemeyer Syndicate stalwarts Nancy Drew, the Hardy Boys, and the new Tom Swift, Jr. series. They were killed by increasing reader sophistication combined with the wartime scarcity of paper. Many of the books that replaced the series celebrated those wonderful high school years by focusing on dating, parties, class rings, senior year, the popular crowd, and teen romances devoid of realities such as sex. The books often sounded alike and read alike, but they were unquestionably popular.

Plots were usually simple, with only one or two characters being developed, while others were stock figures or stereotypes. Books dealt almost exclusively with white, middle-class values and morality. The endings were almost uniformly happy and bright, and readers could be certain that neither their morality nor their intelligence would be challenged.

Taboos may never have been written down, but they were clear to readers and writers. Certain things were not to be mentioned—obscenity, profanity, suicide, sexuality, sensuality, homosexuality, protests against anything significant, social or racial injustice, or the ambivalent feelings of cruelty and compassion inherent in young adults and all people. Pregnancy, early marriage, drugs, smoking, alcohol, school dropouts, divorce, and alienation could be introduced only by implication and only as bad examples for thoughtful, decent young adults. Consequently, young adult books were often innocuous and pervaded by a saccharine didacticism.

Despite these unwritten rules, some writers transcended the taboos and limitations and made it possible for Stanley B. Kegler and Stephen Dunning to write in 1961, "Books of acceptable quality have largely replaced poorly written and mediocre books."[39]

Adult Books That Set the Stage for Contemporary YA Novels

Perhaps as a reaction to the realities of war, the most popular series of books for both adults and teenagers during the 1950s and 1960s centered around the fascinating James Bond, Agent 007. Ian Fleming caught the mood of the time with escapist excitement tinted with what appeared to be realities. Kathleen Winsor was also one of a kind, although what one and what kind was widely debated. When her *Forever Amber* (1944) appeared, parents worried, censors paled, and young adults smiled as they ignored the fuss and read the book. The uproar was much the same as that awaiting Grace Metalious and *Peyton Place* when it appeared in 1956.

Well-written romances include Margaret E. Bell's Alaskan story *Love Is Forever* (1954), Vivian Breck's superior study of young marriage in *Maggie* (1954), and Benedict and Nancy Freedom's *Mrs. Mike*, set in the northern Canadian wilderness. Elizabeth Goudge's *Green Dolphin Street* (1944) had everything working for it—a young handsome man in love with one of two sisters. When he leaves and writes home expressing his wishes, the wrong sister accepts. The true love, apparently overwhelmed by his unfaithfulness, becomes a nun. Passion, love, and adventure are all handled well by a first-rate writer.

Young readers, especially in the last year or two of high school, have often been receptive to books about human dilemmas. Between 1940 and 1966, society changed rapidly and drastically with deeply disturbing consequences. There was a growing awareness that the democracy described in our Constitution was more preached than practiced. As the censorship applied to John Steinbeck's *The Grapes of Wrath* (1939) and *Of Mice and Men* (1937) lessened—although it never entirely disappeared—young people read of the plight of migrant workers and learned that all was not well. Many were deeply disturbed by Alan Paton's stories of racial struggles in South Africa, *Cry the Beloved Country* (1948) and *Too Late the Phalarope* (1953). Still more were touched by Harper Lee's *To Kill a Mockingbird* (1960) set in the U.S. South.

Richard Wright and his books *Native Son* (1940) and *Black Boy* (1945) served as bitter prototypes for much African American literature. The greatest African American novel, and one of the greatest novels of any kind in the last fifty years, is Ralph Ellison's *Invisible Man* (1952). Existential in tone, *Invisible Man* is at different times bawdy (the incest scenes remind readers of Faulkner without being derivative), moving, and frightening, but always stunning and breathtaking.

Three African American nonfiction writers are still read. Claude Brown painted a stark picture of African American ghetto life in *Manchild in the Promised Land* (1965), whereas Malcolm X and Alex Haley, the latter better known for *Roots*, painted a no more attractive picture in *The Autobiography of Malcolm X* (1965). The most enduring work may prove to be Eldridge Cleaver's *Soul on Ice* (1968), an impassioned plea by an African American man in prison who wrote to save himself.

The development from this period that has had the most direct effect on young adult literature was the popularization of the *bildungsroman*, a novel about the initiation, maturation, and education of a young adult. Most bildungsroman were originally published for adults but soon read by teenagers. Dan Wickenden's *Walk Like a Mortal* (1940) and Betty Smith's *A Tree Grows in Brooklyn* (1943) were among the first. William

Golding's *Lord of the Flies* (1955) is better known, but none of these books won young adult favor or adult opposition as did J. D. Salinger's *The Catcher in the Rye* (1951). It is still the most widely censored book in U.S. schools and still hated by people who assume that a disliked word (*that* word) corrupts an entire book. Holden Caulfield may indeed be vulgar and cynical and capable of seeing only the phonies around him, but he is also loyal and loving to those he sees as good or innocent. For many young adults, it is the most honest and human story they know about someone they recognize (even in themselves)—a young man caught between childhood and maturity and unsure which way to go. Whether *Catcher* is a masterpiece similar to James Joyce's *A Portrait of the Artist as a Young Man* depends on subjective judgment, but there is no question that Salinger's book captured—and continues to capture—the hearts and minds of countless young adults as has no other book.

Nonfiction was not yet as popular as it would become, but Jim Piersall's *Fear Strikes Out* (1955) and Roy Campanella's *It's Good to Be Alive* (1959) attracted young readers. Popular true stories about battles and survivors included Richard Tregaskis's *Guadalcanal Diary* (1943), Ernie Pyle's *Here Is Your War* (1943) and *Brave Men* (1944), Robert Trumbull's *The Raft* (1942), and Quentin Reynold's *70,000 to One* (1946).

Rise of Criticism of Young Adult Literature

Today we take criticism of young adult literature as discussed in Chapter 10 for granted, but it developed slowly. In the 1940s, journals provided little information on, and less criticism of, young adult literature except for book lists, book reviews, and occasional references in articles on reading interests or improving young people's literary taste. The comments that did appear were often more appreciative than critical, but given the times and the attitude of many teachers and librarians, appreciation or even recognition may have been more important than criticism.

In 1951, Dwight L. Burton wrote the first criticism of young adult novels, injecting judgments along with appreciation as he commented on works by Dan Wickenden, Maureen Daly, Paul Annixter, Betty Cavanna, and Madeleine L'Engle. Concluding his article, Burton identified the qualities of the good young adult novel and prophesied its potential and future:

> The good novel for the adolescent reader has attributes no different from any good novel. It must be technically masterful, and it must present a significant synthesis of human experience. Because of the nature of adolescence itself, the good novel for the adolescent should be full in true invention and imagination. It must free itself of Pollyannaism or the Tarkington–Henry Aldrich–Corliss Archer tradition and maintain a clear vision of the adolescent as a person of complexity, individuality, and dignity. The novel for the adolescent presents a ready field for the mature artist.[40]

In 1955, Richard S. Alm provided greater critical coverage of the young adult novel.[41] He agreed with critics that many writers presented a "sugar-puff story of what adolescents should do and should believe rather than what adolescents may or will do and believe." He cited specific authors and titles he found good and painted their

*T*hese "good girls" of the 1950s, waiting here to shake President Eisenhower's hand at Girls' Nation, were more likely to be reading fiction published in women's magazines and such books as Mrs. Mike, Forever Amber, and Peyton Place *than books published specifically for teenagers.*

strengths and weaknesses in clear strokes. He concluded by offering teachers some questions that might be useful in analyzing the merits of young adult novels.

A year later, Emma L. Patterson began her fine study of the origin of young adult novels showing that "The junior novel has become an established institution."[42] Her command of history, her knowledge of trends in young adult novels, her awareness of shortcomings and virtues of the novels, and her understanding of the place of young adult novels in schools and libraries made her article essential reading for librarians and teachers.

Despite the leadership of Burton, Alm, and Patterson, helpful criticism of young adult literature was slow in arriving, but biting criticism was soon forthcoming. Only a few months after Patterson's article, Frank G. Jennings's "Literature for Adolescents— Pap or Protein?"[43] appeared. The title was ambiguous, but if any reader had doubts about where Jennings stood, the doubt was removed with the first sentence: "The stuff of adolescent literature, for the most part, is mealy-mouthed, gutless, and pointless." The remainder of the article added little to that point, and although Jennings overstated his case, Burton, Alm, Patterson, and other sensible supporters would have agreed that much young adult literature, similar to much adult literature, was second-rate or worse. Jennings's article was not the first broadside attack, and it certainly would not be the last.[44]

Much of the literature written for young adults from 1940 through 1966 goes largely and legitimately ignored today. Some writers are still read, however, and more important than mere longevity is the effect that these authors had on books appearing after 1966. Readers before then could not have anticipated S. E. Hinton's *The Outsiders* or Paul Zindel's *The Pigman,* which were to appear in only a year or two, much less Isabelle Holland's *The Man Without a Face;* Norma Klein's *Mom, The Wolfman and Me;* Rosa Guy's *Ruby;* or Robert Cormier's *The Chocolate War.* These iconoclastic, taboo-breaking novels and others of today would not have been possible had it not been for earlier novels that broke ground and prepared readers, teachers, librarians, and parents for contemporary novels.

Notes

[1]Caroline Ticknor, *Hawthorne and His Publisher* (Houghton Mifflin, 1913), p. 141.

[2]E. Douglas Branch, *The Sentimental Years, 1836–1860* (Appleton, 1934), p. 131.

[3]Jesse H. Shera, *Foundations of the Public Library: The Origins of the Public Library Movement in New England, 1629–1885* (The University of Chicago Press, 1949), p. 238.

[4]A brief summary of the 1853 and 1876 library conventions can be found in Sister Gabriella Margeath, "Library Conventions of 1853, 1876, and 1877," *Journal of Library History* 8 (April 1973): 52–69.

[5]William F. Poole, "Some Popular Objections to Public Libraries," *American Library Journal* 1 (October 1876): 48–49.

[6]W. M. Stevenson, "Weeding Out Fiction in the Carnegie Free Library of Allegheny, Pa.," *Library Journal* 22 (March 1897): 135.

[7]"Novel Reading," *American Library Journal* 1 (October 1876): 98.

[8]"Monthly Reports from Public Librarians upon the Reading of Minors: A Suggestion," *Library Journal* 24 (August 1899): 479.

[9]Carleton Washburne and Mabel Vogel, *Winnetka Graded Book List* (American Library Association, 1926), p. 5.

[10]Carleton Washburne and Mabel Vogel, "Supplement to the Winnetka Graded Book List," *Elementary English Review* 4 (February 1927): 47–52; and 4 (March 1927): 66–73.

[11]William Lyon Phelps, "The Virtues of the Second-Rate," *English Journal* 16 (January 1927): 13–14.

[12]Franklin T. Baker, *A Bibliography of Children's Reading* (Teachers College, Columbia University, 1908), pp. 6–7.

[13]Clara Whitehill Hunt, "Good and Bad Taste in Girls' Reading," *Ladies Home Journal* 27 (April 1910): 52.

[14]Julia Carter, "Let's Talk About Boys and Books," *Wilson Bulletin for Librarians* 9(April 1935): 418.

[15]Alice M. Jordan, "A Gallery of Girls," *Horn Book Magazine* 13 (September 1937): 276.

[16]Clara Vostrovsky, "A Study of Children's Reading Tastes," *Pedagogical Seminary* 6(December, 1899): 535.

[17]G. Stanley Hall, "Children's Reading: As a Factor in Their Education," *Library Journal* 33 (April 1908): 124–125.

[18]J. M. Coulter, "What the University Expects of the Secondary School," *School Review* 17 (February 1909): 73.

[19]Wilbur W. Hatfield, "Modern Literature for High School Use," *English Journal* 1 (January 1912): 52.

[20]*Reorganization of English in Secondary Schools,* Department of the Interior, Bureau of Education, Bulletin 1917, No. 2. (Government Printing Office, 1917), p. 63.

[21]Nancy Gillmore Coryell, *An Evaluation of Extensive and Intensive Teaching of Literature: A Year's Experiment in the Eleventh Grade,* Teachers College, Columbia University, Contributions to Education, No. 275 (Teachers College, Columbia University, 1927).

[22]Lou LaBrant, *An Evaluation of the Free Reading Program in Grades Ten, Eleven, and Twelve for the Class of 1935.* The Ohio State University School, Contributions to Education No. 2 (Ohio State University, 1936). See also Lou LaBrant, "The Content of a Free Reading Program," *Educational Research Bulletin* 16(February 17, 1937): 29–34.

[23]Dora V. Smith, "American Youth and English," *English Journal* 26 (February 1937): 111.

[24]Graham P. Hawks, "A Nineteenth-Century School Library: Early Years in Milwaukee,"*Journal of Library History* 12 (Fall 1977): 361.

[25]S. Swett Green, "Libraries and School," *Library Journal* 16(December 1891): 22. Other representative articles concerned with the relationship include Mellen Chamberlain, "Public Libraries and Public School," *Library Journal* 5 (November–December 1880): 299–302; W. E. Foster, "The School and the Library: Their Mutual Relations," *Library Journal* 4 (September–October 1879): 319–341; and Mrs. J. H. Resor, "The Boy and the Book, or The Public Library a Necessity," *Public Libraries* 2 (June 1897): 282–285.

[26]"The Report of the Committee on Relations of Public Libraries to Public Schools," *NEA Journal of Proceedings and Addresses of the 38th Annual Meeting* (The University of Chicago, Press, 1899), p. 455.

[27]Mary E. Hall, "The Possibilities of the High School Library," *ALA Bulletin* 6 (July 1912): 261–63.

[28]Caroline M. Hewins, "Book Reviews, Book Lists, and Articles on Children's Reading: Are They of Practical Value to the Children's Librarians?" *Library Journal* 26

(August 1901): 58. Attacks on series books, especially Stratemeyer's books, persisted thereafter in library literature. Mary E. S. Root prepared a list of series books not to be circulated by public librarians, "Not to Be Circulated," *Wilson Bulletin for Librarians* 3 (January 1929): 446, including books by Alger, Finley, Castlemon, Ellis, Optic, and others, the others being heavily Stratemeyer. Two months later, Ernest F. Ayers responded, "Not to Be Circulated?" *Wilson Bulletin for Librarians* 3 (March 1929): 528–529, objecting to the cavalier treatment accorded old favorites and sarcastically adding, "Why worry about censorship so long as we have librarians?" Attacks continue today. Some librarians and English teachers to the contrary, the Syndicate clearly is winning, and students seem to be pleased.

[29]Franklin K. Mathiews, "Blowing Out the Boy's Brains," *Outlook* 108 (November 18, 1914): 653.

[30]John Tunis, "What Is a Juvenile Book?" *Horn Book Magazine* 44 (June 1968): 307.

[31]George W. Norvell, "Some Results of a Twelve-Year Study of Children's Reading Interests," *English Journal* 35 (December 1946): 532, 536.

[32]Marie Rankin, *Children's Interests in Library Books of Fiction,* Teachers College, Columbia University, Contributions to Education, No. 906 (Teachers College, Columbia University, 1947).

[33]Stephen Dunning, "The Most Popular Junior Novels," *Junior Libraries* 5 (December 15, 1959): 7–9.

[34]Jacob W. Getzels, "The Nature of Reading Interests: Psy-chological Aspects" in *Developing Permanent Interests in Reading,* ed. Helen M. Robinson, Supplementary Education Monographs, No. 84, December 1956 (University of Chicago Press, 1956), p. 5.

[35]G. Robert Carlsen, "Behind Reading Interests," *English Journal* 43 (January 1954): 7–10.

[36]G. O. Ireland, "Bibliotherapy: The Use of Books as a Form of Treatment in a Neuropsychiatric Hospital," *Library Journal* 54 (December 1, 1929): 972–974.

[37]Lou LaBrant, "Diversifying the Matter," *English Journal* 40 (March 1951): 135.

[38]S. Alan Cohen, "Paperbacks in the Classroom," *Journal of Reading* 12 (January 1969): 295.

[39]Stanley B. Kegler and Stephen Dunning, "Junior Book Roundup—Literature for the Adolescent, 1960," *English Journal* 50 (May 1961): 369.

[40]Dwight L. Burton, "The Novel for the Adolescent," *English Journal* 40 (September 1951): 363–369.

[41]Richard S. Alm, "The Glitter and the Gold," *English Journal* 44 (September 1955): 315.

[42]Emma L. Patterson, "The Junior Novels and How They Grew," *English Journal* 45 (October 1956): 381.

[43]*English Journal* 45 (December 1956): 226–231.

[44]See, for example, Alice Krahn, "Case Against the Junior Novel," *Top of the News* 17 (May 1961): 19–22; Esther Millett, "We Don't Even Call Those Books!" *Top of the News* 20 (October 1963): 45–47; and Harvey R. Granite, "The Uses and Abuses of Junior Literature," *Clearing House* 42 (February 1968): 337–340.

3

Pop Culture, YA Lit, Big Business, and Archetypal Images

As evidenced throughout this textbook, both the literary world and the expectations of young readers have recently undergone significant changes. It would be a mistake, however, to view these changes as having happened overnight simply because of computers and the Internet. Instead, they are continuations of trends that have been developing throughout the twentieth century. Nevertheless, we prepared this chapter and made space for it early in this edition because the influence of the Internet has increased the speed with which these changes are occurring. Those of us who work professionally to encourage young people to read and to develop skills in literary appreciation need to think deeply about how these changes—across genres and across media—affect what we do.

In her book *Radical Change: Books for Youth in a Digital Age,* Eliza T. Dresang points to several ways that computer experiences have influenced the expectations that young people have for print media. The seven characteristics listed here combine some of her observations with some of our own and with those of our graduate students, who are working more closely than we are with teenagers.

1. *Young readers expect changing styles and formats.* See Focus Box 3.1, New Styles and Formats, for an illustration of how today's books differ from those of even a decade ago. After the ease of clicking on a mouse to move to new pages, mostly in color and often supplemented with movement and sound, plain pages of type seem boring. Today's designers of information books create pages that resemble television screens with sidebars and cut lines to provide the equivalent of "time out for commercials." Even in fiction, young readers expect photos, sketches, doodles, different type fonts, and increased amounts of white space.

2. *Various kinds of media play such an important part in the lives of students that authors are putting camcorders, television, zines, and other media into the plots of their books.* See Focus Box 3.2, The Media as the Message in Fiction, for examples. Authors are also including more dialogue, almost as if they are

writing plays, and they are making use of email, journal entries, school assignments, interviews, notes, news clippings, court transcriptions, psychologists' notes, or whatever else they can think of putting between the covers of a book. Today's authors have gone even further by writing in multiple genres. They trick readers of realistic fiction by slipping into magical realism or free verse poetry. They realize that picture books can have sophisticated messages (see Focus Box 3.3, Picture Books for High Schoolers) and that some very good stories can be told through poetry—even poetry that does not rhyme (see Focus Box 5.1, p. 148, Stories in Verse)

3. *The Internet has enlarged perspectives so that young people are more ready to accept stories with multiple points of entry.* They have more tolerance for contrasting points of view and more patience in waiting for authors to bring together all the loose ends of a story, or "to fill in the holes," as Louis Sachar put it. The "other" is being given increased space. As will be shown in Chapters 8 and 9, history is being looked at from new viewpoints, and books are being written to let readers learn the background and the details that are left out of contemporary newscasts and most textbooks.

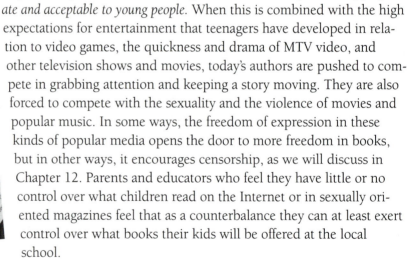

4. *The great freedom of the Internet has changed the boundaries of what is appropriate and acceptable to young people.* When this is combined with the high expectations for entertainment that teenagers have developed in relation to video games, the quickness and drama of MTV video, and other television shows and movies, today's authors are pushed to compete in grabbing attention and keeping a story moving. They are also forced to compete with the sexuality and the violence of movies and popular music. In some ways, the freedom of expression in these kinds of popular media opens the door to more freedom in books, but in other ways, it encourages censorship, as we will discuss in Chapter 12. Parents and educators who feel they have little or no control over what children read on the Internet or in sexually oriented magazines feel that as a counterbalance they can at least exert control over what books their kids will be offered at the local school.

5. *Kids' own thinking and writing is being given more respect.* Whether it is because we have a youth-oriented society with young people taking on more responsibility and power, because schools have changed their approaches to the teaching of writing, or because of the ease with which kids can do desktop or Internet publishing, we are seeing an increase in the numbers of young people whose ideas and thoughts are being published. This is especially true in collections of interviews, essays, and poems circling around topics of concern to teenagers. See Focus Box 3.4 for Teen Voices.

6. *The teen years are not a time for subtlety.* Young people looking for entertainment want real thrills and chills. If something is supposed to be funny, they want to laugh out loud; if it's supposed to be sexy, they want to feel it; and if it's supposed to be informative, they want the exact information they need in a format that is easy to navigate.

7. *The literary canon is expanding.* All of the factors mentioned above contribute to an expansion of what is being offered to young people to read, view, and listen to. As with the question of censorship, however, the diversity of the offerings makes people feel out of control. This is why people keep asking for lists—the 100 best books, the 100 greatest films, the 20 books every high school student should read, etc. Every time such a list appears, however, it is immediately met with heavy criticism and counter suggestions simply because today's society is so diverse. Barring some science fiction-like dystopian future, gone are the days when we could recommend to a class of thirty students exactly what they should all read. Instead, we have to work with each student as an individual.

A Youth-Oriented Culture

In the late 1980s and early 1990s, many of us who loved adolescent literature lamented a cutback by YA publishers who began focusing their attention on junior high and middle school readers because that's where the most students were. We assumed that once this big population bubble (the children of the baby boomers) was in high school, we would have another golden age of books written specifically for young adults. It has not been quite that simple.

Indeed, there was a population bubble whose members are now in high school and early college. English teachers and librarians, however, were not the only ones waiting for these young people, nor were they a generation to stand back and wait for us. Partly because of their sheer numbers and partly because of the eagerness of advertisers to attract this large body of potential lifelong customers, we are now in a youth-oriented (some would say "youth-dominated") era. The competition for the attention of young adults has encouraged—and in some ways, forced—authors and publishers to experiment and to try new forms. It has also encouraged talented authors from other areas to try their hand at writing books for teenagers (see Joyce Carol Oates's statement on "Writing Your Heart Out" on p. 82). In today's university classes and departments, people use such terms as *critical literacy* and *media literacy,* etc.

The best reading instruction has always involved higher order thinking skills, but the term *literacy* stresses the fact that much more than decoding is involved. This concept is treated in such books as *Adolescents and Literacies in a Digital World,*

FOCUS BOX 3.1 *New Styles and New Formats*

Damage by A. M. Jenkins. HarperCollins, 2001. Instead of the typical procedure of telling a story in first person, past tense, golden boy Austin uses second person, present tense to tell his story: "You undo your chinstrap but don't take off your helmet. Instead, you just stand there, staring out at a world framed by rigid plastic edges."

Heaven Eyes by David Almond. Delacorte, 2001. Three "damaged" children run away from an orphanage and end up living in an abandoned print shop with an old man and a young girl with webbed toes and fingers. It is hard to separate reality from dream and imagination from memory in this strange book that says more about love and life than can be revealed in a plot summary.

I Believe in Water: Twelve Brushes with Religion, edited by Marilyn Singer. HarperCollins, 2000. It is the topic that is unusual in this book of short stories written by such noted authors as Jacqueline Woodson, Kyoko Mori, Virginia Euwer Wolff, M. E. Kerr, and Naomi Shihab Nye. Each story evokes a spiritual experience of some kind.

Mind's Eye by Paul Fleischman. Holt, 1999. Readers get the feeling that they are hidden in a closet overhearing the conversations of three women in a nursing home. Sixteen-year-old Courtney was paralyzed in an accident while the other two are elderly. Surprisingly, it is the woman with Alzheimer's who helps Courtney the most.

Mosque by David Macaulay. Houghton Mifflin, 2003. Macaulay is an architect who for years had thought about doing a book on the building of a mosque to go along with his *Cathedral, City, Pyramid,* and *Castle.* Since he didn't know as much about mosques, he kept putting the idea aside until the September 11th attacks. Within four days he had started researching for the new book in hopes of showing that all people are capable of amazing things when they are inspired.

Rats Saw God by Rob Thomas. Simon & Schuster, 1996. Steven Richard York, whose astronaut father named him after Richard Nixon, writes his story to make up for failing a semester of English. He juxtaposes chapters about his senior year in California, where he has come to live with his mother and his sister, with chapters from his sophomore year when he lived in Houston with his father.

A Time to Love: Stories from the Old Testament, told by Walter Dean Myers, illustrated by Christopher Myers. Scholastic, 2003. It was hard to know whether to classify this brilliantly illustrated book as a picture book, a book of short stories, or a book of nonfiction. Each of the 127 standard-sized pages is designed on what looks like fine art paper. There are three or four paintings for each of the six stories.

Truth & Lies: An Anthology of Poems, edited by Patrice Vecchione. Holt, 2001. The idea that today's teens are willing and able to consider a subject from many different perspectives is the philosophy that underlies this collection of over 70 poems (mostly free verse) that explore complex questions about honesty and lying.

Wasteland by Francesca Lia Block. Joanna Cotler/HarperCollins, 2003. In this intense story of the love between a brother and a sister, Block forces readers to slow down and ponder with such sentences as this one that begins a two-page chapter, "I didn't think you were in there. Didn't I?"

You Don't Know Me by David Klass. Farrar/Frances Foster Books, 2001. Klass goes beyond his usual straightforward style and uses magical realism to help readers understand and empathize with John, the 14-year-old protagonist. John receives a terrible beating from "the man who is not my father," but whom his mother describes as her "almost fiancé." Thankfully, the story ends more positively than it begins.

edited by Donna E. Alverman; *Situated Literacies: Reading and Writing in Context,* edited by David Barton; and *Multiliteracies: Literacy Learning and the Design of Social Futures,* edited by Bill Cope and Mary Kalantzis.

Popular culture makes up a big part of today's literacy, and as Jeffrey Passe argued for social studies teachers,

> As educators, we need to know what our students are watching. If we wish to understand their references, their role models and anti-role models—indeed, if we want to know what makes our students tick—we have to be in touch with the popular culture that influences them. We need to understand why everyone is excited after someone is voted off the island. We need to recognize why tests should not be given the morning after the final episode of *Dawson's Creek.*

And more importantly, he argued, we need to be able to build on popular culture "happenings" to help our students understand and empathize with the emotional impact of similar events in history. As English teachers and librarians, we could say much the same for events in literature. Also, we might want to follow Passe's approach of dealing with the demands of popular culture as if it were the kind of assignment he used to love when a teacher would assign the class to watch something on television. He turns on the tube and tries "to grasp the popular boy bands on MTV," he checks out the teen magazines while he waits in line at the supermarket, and he sits through the latest teen flicks at the movies. He also logs "on to eBay, Instant Messenger, and the newest video games," and since he lives in North Carolina, he even watches NASCAR, but not for very long: "After all, I have other things to do. For instance, the Yankee game is on in fifteen minutes."[1]

We used to think of *crossovers* as books being marketed to both children and adults, but with today's crossovers we see connections among different formats and different parts of the entertainment world. We are accustomed to books being made into movies, but today movies spawn books and video games and television programs, and vice versa. When big-budget books come out, excerpts are published in magazines and newspapers, and the authors are interviewed on television so that people take credit for reading—although maybe "not personally"—many books they have never physically touched.

When *Harry Potter and the Order of the Phoenix* was released in June 2003, both the Seattle Mariners and the Baltimore Orioles held special Harry Potter days at their ballparks. A corporate promotions manager explained that they were reaching out to kids as future season-ticket holders and future fans. The same month we read a story in our local newspaper attributing the growing popularity of hip-hop and hard rock music among teens to the fact that kids as young as 6 and 7 listen to hard rock and punk-pop as background music on their video games. This means the millions of teenagers who flocked to see *The Matrix Reloaded* were not surprised that it was pulsating with the rap metal of *Linkin Park* and the horror-inspired drone of *Rob Zombie.*

Another example of a crossover is the www.fanfiction.net website, which encourages teens to write and submit original stories about famous characters from one of eight categories: Anime, Cartoon, Game, Movie, Book, Miscellaneous, Comic, and TV

JOYCE CAROL OATES
On Writing Your Heart Out

*I*f it's your ambiguous destiny to be a writer, you already know that no one can tell you what to do; how to behave; still less how to think, and how to feel about yourself. At the most, you can acquire from others an "external self"—a mode of being that allows you to seem to conform while releasing you, in your imagination, to whatever adventures await you as you. In this, you need to *write your heart out*.

Transcribing visions into language, giving a form and structure to the imagination within, is a self-consuming activity. Each work you create exacts a price from you, in proportion to its worth to you. To be a writer—or any kind of "creative" artist, as opposed to an artist-for-hire (which may be a perfectly honest and legitimate vocation)—is to plunge into the unknown that lies within.

Never be ashamed of your subject and of your passion for your subject. Your "forbidden" passions are likely to be the fuel for your writing. Your struggle with your buried self, or selves, yields your art; these emotions are the fuel that drives your writing and makes possible hours, days, weeks, months, and years of what will appear to others, at a distance, as "work." Without these ill-understood drives, you might be a superficially happier person, and a more involved citizen of your community, but it isn't likely that you will create anything of substance.

What advice can an older writer presume to offer to a younger? Only what he or she might wish to have been told years ago. Don't be discouraged! Don't cast sidelong glances and compare yourself to others among your peers! (Writing is not a race. No one really "wins." The satisfaction is in the effort, and rarely in the consequent rewards, if there are any.)

And again, *write your heart out.*

Read widely, and without apology. Read what you want to read, not what someone tells you you should read (As Hamlet remarks, "I know not *should.*") Immerse yourself in a writer you love, and read everything he or she has written, including the very earliest work. Especially the very earliest work. Before the great writer became great, or even good, he or she was groping for a way, fumbling to acquire a voice, perhaps just like you.

Language is an icy-cool medium, on the page. Unlike performers and athletes, we get to re-imagine, revise, and rewrite completely if we wish. Before our work is set *in print,* as *in stone,* we maintain our power over it. The first draft may be stumbling and exhausting, but the next draft or drafts will be soaring and exhilarating. Have faith: The first sentence can't be written until the last sentence has been written. Only then do you know where you've been and where you're going.

And one final time: *Write your heart out.*

Joyce Carol Oates's young adult titles include *Big Mouth & Ugly Girl,* 2002; *Small Avalanches,* 2003; and *Freaky Green Eyes,* 2003, all from HarperCollins.

Show. The site was created in 1998 by 24-year-old Xing Li, a California computer programmer who devotes roughly 25 hours a week to his "hobby," which has attracted over 150,000 kids to submit stories and/or respond to stories written by others between the ages of 13 and 20.[2] In February 2003, Li added a companion site: www.fictionpress.net, to accept stories about original characters. See Focus Box 11.4, p. 350, for URLs of other sites that publish teen writing.

*T*here is no end to the kinds of popular culture crossovers that enable the same characters to circulate through movies, books (fiction and nonfiction), comic strips, television, video games, and kids' own writing.

YA Lit as Big Business

The news clippings summarized below were all collected in the spring of 2003. They illustrate both how young people are being wooed by big business and the mass media and also how varied are their experiences with out-of-school and crossover literacies.

- "Tonys mirror Broadway's quest for youth" was the headline on a *Christian Science Monitor* story explaining that the theater community was looking to the June 8, 2003, "nationally televised TONY Awards to make its case that the Great White Way is alive and kicking. And one way to do it is to cater to a young audience." The first step was to choose as the show's host the young "Hollywood hunk" Hugh Jackman, star of the film *X-Men 2*. One of the featured performances at the show was the energetic sounding off by the young poets in *Def Poetry Jam*, who, after exiting the theater, did a whole new performance for the benefit of the television audience on a stage set up in Times Square. Although only a cynic would suspect that the 710 Tony voters were influenced by the planned emphasis on interesting a younger generation in Broadway plays, it was a grand moment when Marissa Jaret Winokur, who is barely out of her teens, won the best actress award for a musical and received raucous cheers when she gushed, "If a 4-foot-11, chubby New York girl can be a leading lady in a Broadway show and win a Tony, then anything can happen!"[3]

■ "Read the book, buy the clothes," was the headline on a long feature story about a new series of *Roxy Girl* books aimed at girls between the ages of 8 and 13 who "seem to all want to wear their jeans low and their shirts short, and to shop only in a few trendy stores." Chances are that "a good number of them probably have at least one Roxy Girl item in their closets." The company that specializes in "sweetly sexy, surfer-centric sportswear," has now "come up with the ultimate brand-name accessory: preteen reading with the Roxy Girl label. It's the first time a clothing company has ventured into the literary field." They hired Francess Lantz, a 50-year-old surfer and mother of a 10-year old boy (previous writing credits include *Stepsister from the Planet Weird* and *Someone to Love*) to begin the series, which is being published by HarperEntertaiment, a division of HarperCollins. The books feature five 15-year-old girls who live and surf in the fictional Luna Bay. They are to be promoted on the Roxy Web site and at surfing events, while Roxy merchandise will be offered inside the books' covers. Alissa Quart, 30-year-old author of *Branded: The Buying and Selling of Teenagers,* was quoted as saying, "It's insidious and subversive. . . . There's a multi-billion-dollar industry out there feeding off America's teens. The whole idea is repellent." Daniel Cook, assistant professor at the University of Illinois at Urbana-Champaign, whose specialty is children's consumer culture, said, "No one ever says, 'We're doing this to shake the money out of kids' pockets.' What you hear is, 'We want to educate them, entertain them.'" Los Angeles librarian Albert Johnson, who was also interviewed, predicts that we'll be seeing more of such deals. If the books are high interest and will attract kids to the library, he will be there to "offer readers something better."[4]

■ Johnson's prediction about marketing deals is already coming true according to a story, "Girls who love books get a Web room of their own," which told about *Book Divas* (www.bookdivas.com) a collaboration of *Seventeen* magazine and ElectricArtists, a New York City–based marketing company. Marc Schiller, founder and chief executive officer of ElectricArtists, which launched the Web site in December 2002, acknowledged that it helps market books for his clients, which include HarperCollins and Random House. But the prime goal, he says, is to provide girls, ages 13 to 20, a place to talk about books. "We know there are millions of girls who love Britney Spears, and we know there are millions of girls who love *American Idol*," but "How do teenagers know there are other girls that love Hemingway? They don't. So this puts girls who love Hemingway in a virtual room together to flourish."[5]

■ In a grim story from the Associated Press, reporter Zeina Karam described worries about crossovers from violence in computer games to violence in real life. Her story, "Computer game lets Hezbollah kill Israelis," told about a 3-D computer game, *Special Force,* being sold in Lebanon under the slogan "Fight, resist, destroy your enemy in the game of force and victory." The game, which was described as the "Hezbollah group's latest weapon in its propaganda war on Israel," features a guerrilla armed with a knife, a pistol, hand grenades, and an assault rifle fighting against Israeli soldiers operating from fortified positions protected by land mines, an Apache helicopter, and a Merkava tank. The game is challenging enough that virtual victory is not always assured, and guerrillas are often shot and killed by the Israelis. The game can be played in Arabic, English, French, and Farsi, the language of Iran. The game's creators say they are trying to counter the "invasion" of Arab markets by foreign games. While Jewish groups protest against the "racism" in the game, the creators counter that the game is no different from such Western games as *Conflict: Desert Storm,* an action-packed game depicting the 1991 Gulf War.[6]

■ "The Fresh-Face Factory" is how *Time* magazine billed a story about such young TV stars as Hilary Duff, 15, moving from the Disney Channel and ABC's Saturday mornings to star on the big screen in *Agent Cody Banks* and *The Lizzie McGuire Movie.* Frankie Muniz, 17, from TV's *Malcolm in the Middle,* was her co-star on *Agent Cody Banks* and also the star of *Big Fat Liar.* Amanda Bynes, from Nickelodeon, was a huge success in *What a Girl Wants,* a wish-fulfilling story about a girl finding her "royal" father in London. "The studios, finally acknowledging the power of the *tween* audience, are packaging 10- to 15-year-olds for their own TV shows, then rewrapping them for the big screen." Kids who have watched these stars on TV now want to go see them on the big screen, "And they can't travel alone, so they bring a parent. The tween audience has developed from barely a concept three years ago "to a group that delivers in ratings and box office." *Big Fat Liar* grossed nearly $50 million on a $15 million budget, while *Agent Cody Banks* brought in $36 million in its first three weeks.[7]

■ "3 teens, like, teach FBI to BC (be cool)" was the headline on a *Washington Post* story about three eighth-graders in Maryland who at their graduation from Middle School were presented silver-framed letters of commendation signed by FBI Director Robert Mueller. The girls are part of Operation Innocent Images, an FBI sting operation with the goal of stopping pedophiles from sexually exploiting children. The program has led to the convictions of about 2,200 people across the country for swapping child pornography or arranging to meet minors for sex. In the process of teaching agents to communicate in cyberspace through the voices of young girls, the young teens assigned readings in *Teen People* and *YM* and set down such rules as "Never begin a chat with hello" and "Never use proper grammar in instant messages." They had a hard time convincing one agent that *l2m* means "listen to music," rather than "like to meet," and when they were publicly thanked at the graduation ceremony for letting agents in on the secret that *pos* stands for "parent over shoulder," they worried that their classmates might feel betrayed.[8]

■ "This year, every comic-book collector, every Dungeons & Dragons player, every cloistered worshiper of Elektra or Trinity can sit back and laugh. Hollywood, it seems, is now the province of the *fanboy,*" began a "Fanboys in Paradise" article. *Spider-Man* started the trend in 2002 when it won the box-office crown with a superheroic $400 million, followed closely by *The Lord of the Rings: The Two Towers,* which brought in $330 million. Fantasy films scheduled for 2003 included *Daredevil, X-Men 2, The Matrix: Reloaded, The Hulk, Terminator 3: Rise of the Machines, The League of Extraordinary Gentlemen, The Matrix: Revolutions,* and *The Lord of the Rings: The Return of the King.* Two contributing factors were cited. "For one, baby boomers who collected comics as kids have grown up, and make up a big part of the movie audience," and second, "It's getting to the point that technology can actually manifest our imagination almost completely."[9]

FOCUS BOX 3.2   The Media as the Message in Fiction

Blue Avenger and the Theory of Everything (Marcato/Cricket, 2002), **Blue Avenger Cracks the Code** (Holt, 2001), and **The Adventures of Blue Avenger: A Novel** (Holt, 1999) by Norma Howe. Fifteen-year-old David Schumacher invents a cartoon alter ego, The Blue Avenger, to be "secret champion of the underdog, modest seeker of truth, fearless innovator of the unknown." When he decides to become *Blue Avenger,* the results are even more fun.

The Gospel According to Larry by Janet Tashjian. Holt, 2001. Josh loves Beth, but is too shy to court her in person and so pours all his frustration into creating a website under the name of Larry. His plan works too well because, along with Beth, thousands of other teens begin to adore Larry and the situation gets wonderfully complicated.

Gossip Girl by Cecily von Ziegesar. 17th Street Productions/Little, Brown, 2002. One of our graduate students described this as a YA version of *Bridget Jones' Diary* held together not by a diary but by the protagonist's participation on the *gossipgirl.net* website.

Hard Love by Ellen Wittlinger. Simon & Schuster, 1999. The setting for this unusual novel is the world of *zines* (desktop published magazines) as seen through the eyes of a high school junior who is grateful to find an outlet for his talent and interests. He meets a soulmate in Marisol, another zine writer, but there are too many complications for them to walk happily off into the sunset.

Making Up Megaboy by Virginia Walter, illustrated by Katrina Roeckelein. Dorling Kindersley Ink, 1998. The high-tech graphics, computerized photos, and varied type fonts help tell this story of a 13-year-old boy who refuses to communicate except through the story he writes about Megaboy, his own comic strip superhero.

Monster by Walter Dean Myers, illustrated by Christopher Myers. HarperCollins, 1999. There are no pages of plain type in this story that a boy tells through a movie script he is writing about being

charged as accessory to a crime. Scattered through the script are hand-printed pages from his journal, photos that resemble excerpted freeze frames, and tentative drawings of how he envisions the on-screen credits.

Ruby Electric by Theresa Nelson. S&S/Atheneum, 2003. Ruby lives near the concreted Los Angeles "river" with her mother and her 3-year-old brother. The grimness of Nelson's story is softened by ironic humor and by the dialogues that Ruby creates in her head for the movie scripts she plans to get Steven Spielberg to produce.

Spitting Image by Shutta Crum. Clarion, 2003. When Lyndon Johnson sends VISTA volunteers to the Kentucky hometown of 12-year-old Jessie Bovey, news reporters follow. Jessie thinks she is doing a good thing by assisting reporters and photographers to get their stories, but she learns that publicity is not always a good thing.

Stoner & Spaz by Ron Koertge. Candlewick, 2002. Ben (Spaz) is a lonely teen with cerebral palsy, who whiles away his time sitting in the back of the old Rialto theater watching movies. By the end of the book, a neighbor is helping Ben make movies, but in the meantime Ben (and readers) get treated to one of the most original romances in all of YA literature.

Toning the Sweep by Angela Johnson. Orchard, 1993. Emily's grandmother is terminally ill and is being taken away from the California desert home that she loves. In this three-generational story of African American women, Emily learns about herself and her family when she uses a camcorder to make a record of the people and the places that are important to her grandmother.

Violet and Clare by Francesca Lia Block. HarperCollins, 1999. Violet dresses in "forever black" but dreams in technicolor, while Claire dresses and acts like a real-life Tinkerbell. As with Block's *Weetzie Bat,* the magic of movie making has seeped into Violet's soul and serves as a metaphor for this attractively designed 5-by-7-inch book.

A Survey of Students' Relationships to Popular Media

Because modern media plays such a large part in the lives of teenagers, we devised a two-page questionnaire on the interconnectedness of teenagers and books with comics, computers, magazines, newspapers, popular music, television, and video games. We again leaned on our graduate students to administer the questionnaire to a sampling of students in inner-city, suburban, and rural high schools.

We probably learned the most from an open-ended question where we invited students to tell us anything we should know when we write about teenagers and what they read. Their comments covered the waterfront, ranging from a 15-year-old boy's claim that "books are gay," to the advice from a 14-year-old girl that "most teenagers listen to music in their spare time. You should ask us to comment about that." A 16-year-old girl reminded us that we hadn't asked anything about religion, which is the basis for her reading, while an 18-year-old girl offered the opinion that "teenagers are only interested in teen magazines and the newspaper." A 15-year-old girl observed that many kids her age enjoy reading Anne Rice and Stephen King books. She wondered why teens seem to be so interested in blood and sex and conjectured that we would find Anne Rice to be the Number 1 author among teens. Actually, only one out of our 177 participants listed Anne Rice, but this may relate to the fact that they were filling out the survey in school and so responded as they thought appropriate.

Here are some of the main points spoken to by several students, followed by a sampling of their comments:

1. Don't overgeneralize; teenagers are different from each other.
    - Kids read what they like: drama, horror, or the funnies. It depends on the person, so talk about how they are different. (Girl, age 15)
    - Every teenager is different so it is hard to say what most teens want to read. (Girl, age 18)
    - Teenagers (though they seem to act alike) are completely different from each other. But they all experience love, hate, depression, happiness, and anger, plus a lot of other mixed emotions. The problem adults have when they try to talk— or in this case write—about us is that they see us as totally ignorant. The kids I know are young, but many of us have been through a lot of pain and agony in our few years. In my first two years of high school, my best friend died, my brother temporarily disowned me, my grandparents died, and a whole lot more. (Girl, age 18)
    - I guess it's childish, but I enjoy reading the Harry Potter books. I enjoy Orson Scott Card, but overall I don't do a lot of reading now. (Boy, age 16)
2. We want to read about things that are realistic and true.
    - Teen books should be interesting—or have something to do with life, not totally to do with it, but they should relate. And the books should have GOOD BEGINNINGS. (Girl, 12)
    - Despite most beliefs, teens are focused on what's right and wrong. It's just that some of our visions on the boundaries of "wrong" are different. (Boy, 16)

- I read realistic things (well, besides *Lord of the Rings*) like *Bridget Jones' Diary* and stuff, because I like to see perspectives on other people's lives. (Girl, 16)
- Sometimes in a teenager's life, one of the most important things is social status. Their position of being either the popular guy/girl or the hopeless nerd that no one wants to hang out with can greatly affect how they view their lives and therefore what they want to read. (Girl, 18)
- I read to learn and talk about girls. (Boy, 16)

3. We want to escape from our own lives.
   - I read a lot of romance and my life isn't romantic. (Girl, 16)
   - I read about what interests me, which is action-packed westerns or military/spy books. These kinds of book are very intriguing, e.g., *Flint* by Louis L'Amour or *Hunt for Red October* by Tom Clancy. (Boy, 17)
   - I like to read and have read many books mostly about adventures or exciting experiences such as the book *Hatchet* or Louis L'Amour's westerns. (Boy, 17)
   - My relationship to reading is to escape to another world where it's like watching TV, but I imagine me instead of the real characters. (Boy, 16)
   - I like dark things. I usually read about vampires and stalkers. However, I'm also religious so I read the *Left Behind* series. I think teens read fiction to take their minds off current events. Who wants to know about the people being killed for someone else's country? (Girl, 18)
   - I have loved to read science fiction/fantasy books since I was about 10. If I had a choice between a good book and going to a movie, without a doubt I would choose to read. (Girl, 16)
   - I choose to read fictional novels usually on women characters who struggle in life with either family problems or rapes. This has nothing to do with my real life issues or activities. I'm just interested. (Girl 15)
   - I love all the sci-fi kind of books, actually, more fantasy than anything—portals to different worlds, witches, magic, and that stuff. (Girl, 15)

4. Many teenagers do not consider reading to be entertainment.
   - I love to read, but when someone tells me to read, like a school assignment, it seems like a chore. (Girl, 15)
   - I choose to read for recreation instead of watching television. This has pushed me out of the spectrum of normal teen pop culture. (Girl, 16)
   - Teenagers don't really like to read, they like to be entertained. (Girl, 17)
   - In general, students do not like being forced to read. Having a reading schedule makes kids not want to read. (Girl, 16)
   - Being a kid is too short to be spent inside reading. We need to get outside and have some fun. (Boy, 15)

5. Books need to be really interesting.
   - I read what looks interesting. End of story! (Boy, 16)
   - I like to read action and adventure, not those dull nothing-happens books. (Boy, 16)
   - I read anything deliberately controversial and poignant—unapologetically truthful, sensual, and passionate like my internal life. [I like] anything that's subtly philosophical without being blatant. (Girl, 16)
   - The relationship between myself and what I choose to read is this: For the most part, the books I read never include clear answers. They make me think. I like to figure things out on my own. (Girl, 17)

Answers to More Specific Questions

In answering our more specific questions related to particular media, the students proved their claims that teenagers are different from each other. Not wanting to perpetuate the kinds of stereotyping that inevitably followed from the old custom of teachers and librarians dividing their offerings into "books for boys" and "books for girls," we have usually tried to downplay gender differences. But in light of all the recent discussions relating to gender and literacy, this time we counted the results from boys and girls in two different stacks. Here are some of the things we learned, followed by fuller discussions of key points. In all, 100 girls participated and 77 boys, which means that for the percentages to be equal, the numbers from girls should be approximately one-fourth higher than those from boys.

When we asked, "Where do you get your ideas for leisure reading?" only one out of the 177 students circled *a librarian* (a point we will discuss further in Chapter 10), but 29 students circled *browsing in a library.* Another 29 students circled *browsing in a bookstore,* with all but one of these students being 16 or older. Seventeen students (more than twice as many boys as girls) circled *a teacher.* The overwhelmingly popular choice was *friends,* which was circled by 87 students. On the blank we left for *other,* several boys wrote *parents,* while one wrote *work,* one wrote *movies,* and one wrote *TV.* Six girls wrote *my mom,* while several wrote *sister* and one wrote *TV.*

Where we asked students to list a couple of their favorite entertainment stars or groups, we soon gave up counting because even more than in the last survey, we discovered that we are a deconstructed society with widely ranging differences in who we know and what we enjoy doing. We learned that musical groups are still thinking up surprisingly creative names—e.g., *Slipknot, Stereomud, Mudvayne, Jet Ice,* and *Godsmack,* and that kids are still taking a wonderfully multicultural approach to the stars they like including Jackie Chan, Denzel Washington, Jennifer Lopez, Margaret Cho, and Halle Berry.

Magazines

The question where male and female answers were the most different was the one in which we asked students to list favorite magazines. Here are the ones listed by three or more students.

Boys	Girls
Sports Illustrated (12)	*Seventeen* (26)
Transworld (Skateboarding, Snowboarding, etc.) (8)	*YM* (Young Miss) (20)
Maxim (8)	*Cosmo* (13)
ATV (3)	*Teen Magazine* (11)
Low Rider (3)	*People* (7)
MAD Magazine (3)	*Cosmo Girl* (6)
Playboy (3)	*Teen People* (5)
Play Station Magazine (3)	*Glamour* (4)
Thrasher (3)	
FHM (3)	

Several of the popular boys' magazines relate to sports, while all of the popular girls' magazines are people-oriented. It was mostly the under-16 group that subscribed to *Teen Magazine, Teen People,* and *Cosmo Girl,* while the juniors and seniors preferred *Cosmo* and *People* aimed at a general adult audience.

Sexuality is a common theme for both of these lists. Although only one of the boys who listed *Sports Illustrated* specified "swimsuit issue," other boys probably thought about it. We wouldn't have known what *Maxim* and *FHM* were except for a Joel Stein essay in *Time* magazine that appeared the same month that we were tallying the questionnaires. It was entitled, "For Lad Mags, the Jig Is Up" with a subheading, "If you're going to publish porn, you shouldn't get away with being so coy."[10] Stein was writing in reference to Wal-Mart's decision that it was no longer going to sell *Maxim, Stuff,* and *FHM.* Stein chided Wal-Mart for some of the censorship-related mistakes it has made in the past, but said that "eventually Wal-Mart was going to get one right. *Maxim* is pornography, and finally someone figured it out." The timing may have been affected by a cover-line on the May *FHM,* "SEX RECORDS! ASTONISHING FEATS OF NAKED AMBITION" and a recent *Maxim* cover line, "SEX SCENES: GOOD GIRLS RATE DIRTY MOVIES!" A month after the decision on the "Lad mags," Wal-Mart also announced that it would partly obscure the covers of four women's magazines sold in its checkout aisles. The magazines (*Redbook, Cosmopolitan, Marie Claire,* and *Glamour*) deal with fashion, dating, beauty, sex, and health issues, but in recent years have turned increasingly to sexual titillation in hopes of wooing younger readers. This appears to be working, at least for *Cosmopolitan,* which has long been the leader in sexual frankness. In our 1999 survey, only 5 girls listed it as a favorite compared to 13 in this survey, plus another 6 who listed the junior version of *Cosmo Girl.* Back in 1999, Paul D. Colford explained that such magazines as *Redbook, Marie Claire,* and *Glamour* were following *Cosmopolitan's* lead in doing "what certain men's publications have done effectively for a long time." They are "increasing the amount of sexual information (and titillation), and luring buyers with suggestive cover lines in hopes of boosting their single-copy sales."[11] Newsstand sales are more lucrative than subscription sales, but they have fallen 40 percent within the last decade. Magazines wanting to remain acceptable in "home" environments, while at the same time being intriguing enough to garner attention at the newsstand, now print two covers. The ones being mailed into homes (and now probably to Wal-Mart) use the word *love* on the cover, while the newsstand copy uses the word *sex.* Magazines that do this also send their less daring covers to newsstands in areas of the country judged to be more conservative.

Newspapers   We asked about newspapers because we have heard so many doom and gloom stories about the future of newspapers. One hundred and ten (out of 177) families subscribe to a newspaper, with 93 students answering *YES* and 17 answering *NO* to our question of whether they read the paper.

In answer to what parts they read, more than half the girls, but only about one-fifth of the boys, read the actual news. The favorite page for boys was the sports page, but an even larger percentage of girls also read the sports page. We were surprised that 39 girls, as compared to 12 boys, said they read the comics, with about equal numbers of males and females reading the entertainment section, which includes movie and concert schedules. The next most popular category was local news, read by 8 boys and 25 girls. This is where students can read the non-sports-related news about themselves and their friends. Equal numbers (3) of boys and girls identified the *classifieds* as something they read, but only girls (5) said they read the *advertisements.* Girls also showed more interest in reading their horoscopes (4 girls and 1 boy).

From Comics to Graphic Novels   Even though more girls than boys read newspaper comics, boys seemed more interested in our specific question about comic books and comic book characters. Here are the favorites listed by more than a couple of students in each group:

Boys	*Girls*
Spiderman (25)	*Spiderman* (14)
Superman (12)	*Calvin & Hobbes* (7)
Wolverine X-men (10)	*Garfield* (6)
Batman (8)	*Superman* (5)
Garfield (4)	*Archie* (5)
Dragonball (3)	*Batman* (4)

That Spiderman is at the top of both lists undoubtedly relates to the success of the 2002 movie, more than to the actual comic books. However, Steve Ditko's *Amazing Spider-Man* was a story just waiting to be made for young viewers. In the original comic book, a teenage boy acquires his magic powers through being bitten by a radioactive spider. In spite of his new superhuman status, he is plagued with mundane problems as shown in this line, "If this doesn't take the cake!! I can't go out in public as Spider-Man until my mask is sewn up, and when it comes to sewing, I'm all thumbs!" Some critics have conjectured that the teenage Spider-Man was the forerunner of *Archie* comics, and to take it one step further, of much of today's romanticized adolescent literature.

Comic books can be divided into basically three types: (1) innocent, (2) hero and adventure tales, and (3) underground or "adult" comics that rely on horror and sex. As long as comic strips appeared only in daily newspapers, they were limited to gags, but when in the 1930s comic books were created with original materials focusing on a single character, the door was opened to more complex characters and stories. The current focus on graphic novels may turn out to be an equally significant development.

Our survey showed that while girls enjoy reading the same kinds of "hero" comics as do boys (*Spiderman, Superman,* and *Batman*), they have a greater appreciation for such "innocent" comics as *Calvin & Hobbes, Garfield,* and *Archie.* Nevertheless, 6 girls felt compelled to make such comments as, "I don't ever read comic books or even look at them."

Students in our survey probably listed horror and sex comics, but we failed to recognize them by name. Also, such titles are more varied with only one or two students listing a particular creator or character. When we've gone scouting in comic book stores, we have noticed that some of today's horror comics have such lurid and gruesome covers that it is hard to believe that they are less "offensive" than were the comic

The blockbuster success of the 2002 Spider-Man *not only inspired this 16-year-old to try climbing up the wall of the theater, it also inspired producers in 2003 to make at least a dozen more big-budget films based on comic book heroes.*

books of the early 1950s, which were so shocking that the U.S. Senate appointed a subcommittee headed by Estes Kefauver to investigate Juvenile Delinquency as Encouraged by Comic Books. Even more alarming to the industry was that the British Parliament outlawed the importing of U.S. comic books.

In 1954, to protect themselves from lawsuits and from outside censorship, U.S. comic book publishers formed an association and established the Comic Authority Code to monitor the editorial content and advertising allowed in comic books. An outgrowth of this action was the establishment of *Mad* as a magazine instead of a comic book so that it did not have to follow the guidelines. Another was the establishment of underground comics created and published by individuals or small companies who bypassed industry standards and mainline marketing. In such comics, many of which have worked their way back into general marketing, the topics of drugs, sex, violence, racism, elitism, blasphemy, risqué music, bodily functions, and crude language are made light of rather than preached against. This heritage influences people's acceptance of graphic novels, which we will discuss in Chapter 10.

Computers   When we asked students to identify how much time per week they usually spend on a computer, about 40 percent of the participants said they spent over six hours a week on computers, while another 40 percent spend less than two hours a week on a computer. The other 20 percent identified themselves as spending from two to five hours. Males and females were about the same, except in the category of playing games, which was listed as a primary activity by 31 boys as compared to 13 girls. Here in descending order are what they listed as primary activities.

Doing homework (123)

E-mail (118)

Surfing the net (92)

Chatting (80)

Playing games (44)

Instant messaging (40)

Video Games   In a different survey question, we asked participants to list specific video games they liked. The boys named 73 different games while the girls named 66. Games listed as favorites by more than a couple of the participants are as follows:

Boys	*Girls*
Grand Theft Auto (7)	Mario Brothers Franchise (8)
Halo (6)	Crash Bandicoot (5)
College Football (5)	Donkey Kong (4)
Final Fantasy (4)	Pac-man (4)
James Bond (3)	Harry Potter (3)
Resident Evil (3)	
Final Fantasy (3)	
Mortal Kombat (3)	

We were surprised at how many games the girls listed because we had assumed that it is mostly boys who play video games. At least a few of the girls shared this assumption as shown by the one who left the question blank, but wrote "Yeah, right!" and another one who wrote, "I have never ever touched a video game." Also, we noticed that girls were more likely to list such older and less violent games as *Pac-man* and *Donkey Kong,* which have been in restaurants and theater lobbies for twenty years now. In relation to our earlier discussion of genre crossovers, we were interested to see how many video games were based on books and movies. Tom Clancy was mentioned in all three categories and so were Tolkien's *Lord of the Rings* and J. K. Rowling's *Harry Potter.* The last is ironic, because Rowling campaigns against video games. Remember how in Book One only the obnoxious Dudley had a Play Station? Three girls, but no boys, listed *Harry Potter* as a game they enjoyed.

Television   Favorite television shows are listed as follows:

Boys	*Girls*
The Simpsons (25)	*Friends* (37)
Friends (15)	*The Simpsons* (12)
That 70s Show (7)	*Gilmore Girls* (11)
College Football (5)	*Will & Grace* (11)
Malcolm in the Middle (4)	*American Idol* (10)
Futurama (4)	*Smallville* (7)
Smallville (3)	*That 70s Show* (7)
Southpark (3)	*Everybody Loves Raymond* (4)
Reality TV (2)	*Malcolm in the Middle* (3)
Spongebob Square Pants (3)	

We were amused to notice how at the top of the list, the position of *The Simpsons* and *Friends* are reversed for male and female viewers. All the way through, females showed a greater liking for such people-oriented shows as *The Gilmore Girls* and *Will & Grace*. These are similar to *Friends* in featuring characters older than teenagers but not so old as to be mired in family responsibilities and grim "adult" problems. In our last survey, *Dawson's Creek* and *Buffy the Vampire Slayer* (now out of production) were included in the top five shows. They were created by Warner Brothers for a teenage audience, but surprised everyone by attracting viewers far beyond their teenage years.

In relation to *American Idol* and the 2003 spin-off movie *From Justin to Kelly* (featuring winners Justin Guarini, age 24, and Kelly Clarkson, age 21), Joel Stein marveled at the popularity and the wholesomeness of the show and the fact that when "the children of Wal-Mart" vote they choose talent over "slutted-out model wannabes," as was they case with the British version. After making the snide remark that "Britney may have to buy a whole shirt," he concluded:

> So maybe teenagers really are like . . . they've always been: a little optimistic, a little overexcited and a little into just having a good time. Maybe we took small cultural differences—new slang, new fashions, new music—and, as our parents did, misinterpreted them. The *Idol* team is already planning a Bob Hope–Bing Crosby–style buddy musical comedy for Ruben Studdard and Clay Aiken, the winner and runner-up of the second season of *Idol*. It might turn out that you can't lose money underestimating the niceness of teens.[12]

Animation   That the animated *The Simpsons* received such high ratings reflects a relatively new trend. *The Simpsons,* an animated satire of life in Springfield, a mythical Anytown, U.S.A., was into its fourteenth season when we took the survey. In the 2003–2004 season, it surpassed *Ozzie and Harriet* as the longest-running comedy in TV history. The success of *The Simpsons* has inspired other networks to create animated shows for prime time, several directly aimed at teenagers. Caryn James writing in the *The New York Times* (June 22, 1998) gave as one reason for the trend, "With so little realism on the surface, animated characters can sneak up and irreverently hit plenty of nerves. The dunderheaded fathers of *The Simpsons* or *King of the Hill,* much less the boys of *South Park,* would never get on the air if they were breathing actors." Computer-assisted animation has also helped in the creation of such successful movies as *Toy Story* (1995), *A Bug's Life* (1998), *Shrek* (2001) *Ice Age* (2002), and *Finding Nemo* (2003).

International influences have also brought about a new interest in animation both through video games and imported movies. *Anime Mania: How to Draw Characters for Japanese Animation* by Christopher Hart (Watson-Guptill, 2002) was one of the top ten Quick Pick books recommended for reluctant readers by the Young Adult Library Services Association. In the summer of 2003, the Hamilton Branch library in Chandler, Arizona, held an Anime Movie Fest for patrons between the ages of 12 and 18. They showed two popular animated Japanese movies, *Cowboy Bebop* and *Princess Monoke,* and served Japanese-style snacks. Note that libraries need to get permission from the distributor before showing films in this kind of public setting. For more information read "Showing Anime in the Library" by Kat Kan and Kristin Fletcher-Spear in the April 2002 *VOYA,* pp. 20–23.

A Night Out at the Movies   When in 1985, we saw *The Breakfast Club,* we remember thinking, "This is YA lit!" The film was directed by John Hughes and starred Jud Nelson, Ally Sheedy, Emilio Estevez, Molly Ringwald, and Anthony Michael Hall as teenagers confined to early morning detention because of the various manifestations of teenage angst. Today, people in the movie business look back on *The Breakfast Club* similar to the way we in the book business look back on S. E. Hinton's *The Outsiders*—as the beginning of a movement. Jonathan Bernstein in his book *Pretty in Pink: The Golden Age of Teenage Movies* says that director John Hughes brought depth to what had been "a bubble gum genre." It was the first movie to take teen angst seriously, and it "opened the door for everything that's followed."

The spring 2003 University of Michigan alumni magazine put out by the College of Literature, Science, and the Arts featured work done by the University's Institute for Social Research. One of the studies it reported on was based on the five types of high school characters portrayed in *The Breakfast Club:* Jocks, Princesses, Basket Cases, Criminals, and Brains. The researchers tracked 900 sophomores who categorized themselves as one of these types. They tracked the participants through age 24, periodically collecting information on the participants, including educational attainment, job characteristics, and psychological adjustment. The researcher, University of Michigan psychologist Jacquelynne S. Eccles, reported that "Breakfast Club identity choices often predicted both levels and long-term patterns of substance use and mental health suggesting that the impact of sophomore identity may extend well beyond adolescence." In answer to the question of why tenth-grade identities seem to have such lasting predictive effects, Eccles said:

> To some extent, adolescents choose the crowd they're in, but they are also assigned to a crowd by their peers, as a result of their behavior and personalities. As they go

Baloney (Henry P.) by Jon Scieszka, illustrated by Lane Smith. Viking, 2001. Add this title to Scieszka and Smith's **The Stinky Cheese Man** (Viking, 1993) as fun read-alouds when a class needs a treat or inspiration for students' own writing.

Blues Journey by Walter Dean Myers, illustrated by Christopher Myers. Holiday House, 2003. The second father-and-son creation (following *Harlem*, Scholastic, 1997), *Blues Journey* explores the power of music and color. Each painting is accompanied by a poetic call-and-response; unity is achieved through the artist using the same blue ink, white paint, and brown paper bags on each page.

Building Big by David Macaulay. Houghton/A Walter Lorraine Book, 2000. There is probably too much writing to label this a picture book; nevertheless, it is David Macaulay's drawings that will grab the most attention in this companion book for the PBS series on the building of bridges, tunnels, dams, skyscrapers, and domes. Other Macaulay books that teenagers appreciate include *Mosque*, 2003; *Rome Antics*, 1997; *Black and White*, 1990; *The Way Things Work,* 1988; *Unbuilding*, 1980; and *Motel of the Mysteries*, 1979, all from Houghton Mifflin.

Casey at the Bat: A Ballad of the Republic Sung in the Year 1888 by Ernest L. Thayer, illustrated by Christopher Bing. Handprint, 2000. Made to resemble an old scrapbook, this beautifully illustrated version of Thayer's poem was described in a *School Library Journal* review as "a gold mine for teachers seeking inspiration for period projects." Bing's illustrations in *The Midnight Ride of Paul Revere* by Henry Wadsworth Longfellow (Handprint, 2001) are equally impressive.

Cautionary Tales for Children by Hilaire Belloc, illustrated by Edward Gorey. Harcourt, 2002. Belloc's funny parodies of the goody-good lessons being preached to children of a century ago are made even funnier by Edward Gorey's meticulous drawings. This

72-page book is recommended as a counterbalance for those serious-minded students who take everything at face value.

Doll Baby by Eve Bunting, illustrated by Catherine Stock. Clarion, 2000. The format is one of an easy-to-read children's book, but the story is that of a 15-year-old girl who has a baby and learns that "a real baby is not a doll."

Fireflies in the Dark: The Story of Friedl Dicker-Brandeis and the Children of Terezin by Susan Goldman Rubin. Holiday House, 2000. Two suitcases filled with children's artwork were preserved in a barracks attic at the Terezin (or Theresienstadt) concentration camp in Germany. This is the story of the teacher who packed art supplies instead of personal belongings when she was taken to the camp.

Hiroshima No Pika by Toshi Maruki. Lothrop, Lee and Shepard, 1980. **Faithful Elephants** by Yukio Tsuchiya. Houghton Mifflin, 1988. These two stories look at World War II, including the dropping of the atomic bomb, from a Japanese perspective. American patriots have criticized both books for presenting children who are too young to understand complicated issues with only one side of the story. Because thinking and talking are needed, these are good books for reading aloud and discussing with older students.

The Three Pigs by David Wiesner. Clarion, 2001. This is the kind of creative parody that could well inspire students to create their own retellings of old stories.

The Way a Door Closes by Hope Anita Smith, illustrated by Shane W. Evans. Holt, 2003. Thirteen beautifully illustrated poems tell the story of 13-year-old C. J.'s contentment with his family. But in the last poem, his father leaves and C. J. can tell by the way he holds onto the knob and closes the door with a click, that he isn't coming back.

through high school, and decide—or not—to participate in various activities from sports to performing arts and school government, they consolidate specific skills, attitudes, values, and social networks that together exert a far-ranging impact on the transition to adulthood.[13]

In 2001, Neil Howe and William Strauss, co-authors of *Millennials Rising: America's Next Great Generation,* wrote a piece for the *Los Angeles Times* in which they said that *The Millennial Generation* is still waiting for a movie that will do for them what *The Graduate* did for the baby boomers in 1967, and what *The Breakfast Club* did for Gen-X'ers in 1985. They wrote that,

> Gen-X filmmakers think they're new, hip, out-of-the box thinkers, but it's time they face some facts: When it comes to teen flicks, Gen X is no longer new, its style is post-hip, and the box has moved. Most scriptwriters range in age from their late 20s to their late 30s, which is somewhere on the far side of the moon in the eyes of teenagers. People in that age group seldom have teens as siblings, children or social friends, so when they write, direct or perform these scripts, their frame of reference is dated. They're writing for the teens they were, not the teens of today.[14]

Strauss and Howe began their article talking about the not-so-long-ago successes of *There's Something About Mary, American Pie, Austin Powers: The Spy Who Shagged Me,* and *Scary Movie.* These successes made Hollywood think the formula to attracting teens was simply to pile on "gross-outs and vulgarities." But something happened and teenagers stayed away from *Say It Isn't So, Joe Dirt, The Mexican,* and *Angel Eyes,* and turned instead to tamer PG movies like *Shrek.* They wanted action-oriented movies "with bushels of slapstick fun and uplifting finales . . . plenty of laughs and gasps, but hardly an embarrassed snicker in the bunch."

Our survey results, in which kids listed a movie they really liked, support the point that Strauss and Howe were making.

Boys	Girls
Lord of the Rings (9)	*Lord of the Rings* (8)
The Matrix (8)	*A Walk to Remember* (7)
Dumb & Dumber (5)	*The Matrix* (6)
8-Mile (4)	*Harry Potter* (5)
Old School (4)	*Love and Basketball* (4)
The Breakfast Club (3)	
Chicago (3)	

The fact that there is no great blockbuster winner, as were *Friends* and *The Simpsons* for television, also supports their conclusion that we are still waiting for that fresh and creative film that will be the generation-defining movie for millennials—those born between 1980 and 2000.

Archetypes in Literature and the Pop Culture

Another reason for our including this chapter on pop culture is the circular way in which literature and culture work together to help create archetypal images related to the deepest, most permanent aspects of people's lives (e.g., death, fear, love, the biological family, and the unknown). The kinds of images that Carl Jung, Joseph Campbell, and Northrop Frye have written about play a role in the brief messages that make up a large part of modern communication, including the email and voice-mail messages that we leave for our friends, the 30-second commercials that we watch on television, the cartoons that tell a whole story in one picture and one cut line, and the headlines and cover lines that attract us to newspaper and magazine stories. The "bubbles" from which comic strip characters speak allow for only 15 or 16 words, while the small screens on cell phones that are used for instant messaging encourage the creation of ever more succinct abbreviations. This push toward efficient communication promotes a reliance on archetypal images because just a three- or four-word description or the mention of a name is enough to trigger full-blown images in the minds of readers or listeners.

The concept of archetypal images has itself become a cultural archetype so that critics often rely on pop culture allusions to get their points across. For example, in a full-page farewell to *Buffy the Vampire Slayer,* when it ended its seven-year television run, critic Bill Goodykoontz identified the villains. He said that Faith was like Mae West: "when she's bad, she's terrific." Angelus was "the dark side of Angel. Truly evil, and a lot more fun," while "The Trio" of Warren, Jonathan, and Andrew equaled "revenge of the geeks."[15]

When reviewing *The Matrix Reloaded,* film critic Bill Muller offered five different interpretations, all circling around archetypes. In describing *The Matrix* as a fulfillment of adolescent male fantasy, Muller wrote that "put-upon teens sitting at their computer keyboards" not only get to kick sand in the bully's face, but also "to run off with the head cheerleader (Trinity)." In *The Matrix* as a religious allegory, "Morpheus, Neo, and Trinity represent the Father, Son, and Holy Ghost. Like Christ, Neo is killed but rises again to save mankind." In *The Matrix* as *Star Wars,* think of a combination of "Luke Skywalker and Han Solo, and you've got Neo, with Morpheus as Obi-Wan and Trinity as Princess Leia." In *The Matrix* as Superman, "When he's flying around, Neo looks a lot like that guy from Krypton (the movie even makes note of this), and there's a Lois Lane (Trinity, again) for him to save." And lastly, *The Matrix* as video game, "Well, first of all, there is a video game (*Enter the Matrix*), but *Reloaded* plays like one as well. Neo must visit the Oracle, fight the Smiths, negotiate with Merovingian (Wilson) and free the Keymaker. Extra points for knocking off one of the Twins."[16]

Muller's succinct description of *The Matrix* as video game alludes to the archetypal journey, which is described below, along with some of the other basic archetypes that our college students seem to enjoy finding and talking about, and in turn, leading their high school students to look for. Beth Ricks, one of our doctoral students currently teaching high school in Monroe, Louisiana, wrote to tell us how frustrated she was when trying to get her students to approach literature through a critical lens or perspective. They would lose interest long before she could teach them the backgrounds for Marxism or feminist theory, or even Reader-Response,

But when I used archetype theory as a way to introduce mythology and Homer's *Odyssey,* they were actively involved. And I realized it's because they already have the foundation with archetypes because the archetypes are part of the subconscious and myth is part of who we are. They easily picked up the concept of looking at texts through an archetypal lens. So far, we have applied archetypes to film, music, the newspaper, magazines, and of course, the *Odyssey.* We watched *Shrek* in class, and they saw it through new eyes. . . . With my senior class, we watched an Adam Sandler movie and they wrote essays in which they traced the Innocent's Journey. They loved this exercise and from it realized that many of the books they had previously read included an Innocent embarking on a journey.[17]

In closing, she said the best part was that her students had fun. "My students really enjoyed working with archetypes. For the first time, they understood that they could criticize texts while being positive." Long after the unit is over, class discussions are richer because students are still identifying and arguing about the archetypal roles of particular characters, and in a spillover to real life they take an archetypal approach to current events. One of her students reported on how she tried to calm down her parents by explaining the nature of the archetypal Seeker. They, along with the rest of their congregation, were upset when the popular young minister they had brought to town explained in a sermon that he "needed to find himself at another church." He was looking for something; he was not sure just what, but knew "that it was not in Monroe."[18]

Some people in the Monroe congregation might think of their minister as a Shadow Seeker. Shadow archetypes are characters who have the archetypal characteristics to such an extent that they go beyond reason—for example, the interfering mother-in-law as a Caregiver or the control freak or micromanager as a Leader or Ruler.

In the descriptions given below, notice how many are filled out by names from characters in literature or from real people whose stories are so well known that they have become part of the literature of the world. For example, trigger-happy police officers in Los Angeles have been accused of having a *John Wayne* syndrome, and when the first President Bush was running against Bill Clinton and Al Gore, he referred to them in a speech as "those two Bozos" and was immediately accused of damaging the presidential image. Commentators began talking about *the Bozo factor* and *Bozo politics.* In the same election, John Chancellor accused the wealthy Ross Perot and his supporters of holding a *Daddy Warbucks* theory of presidential qualifications, an allusion to the wealthy but long-absent father of *Little Orphan Annie.* Such eponyms reflect the circularity in the way that literature both reflects and creates the archetypes of a culture.

The Innocent Embarking on a Journey

This is the most archetypal of all stories. It begins with a young person setting out either willingly or through some kind of coercion on a journey or a quest and meeting frightening and terrible challenges. After proving his or her worth, the young person receives help from divine or unexpected sources. Even though a sacrifice is usually demanded, readers rejoice in the success of the young protagonist as when David slays

*W*orking with archetypes at the most basic level simply means dividing characters into antagonists and protagonists. After reminiscing about the images that many people carry around in their heads from children's literature, students in one of our classes took home half sheets of cardstock—either gray on which to draw an antagonist or white on which to draw a protagonist. The protagonists they brought back included Hercules from Greek mythology, Gandalf from Lord of the Rings, Ramona from Beverly Cleary's books, Johnny Appleseed from American folklore, Charlotte from E. B. White's Charlotte's Web, and Alice from Lewis Carroll's Alice in Wonderland. Antagonists included The Twits created by Roald Dahl, The Wicked Witch of the West from The Wizard of Oz, Oscar the Grouch from Sesame Street, Captain Hook from Treasure Island, Miss Wormwood, the teacher in Calvin and Hobbes cartoons, and Professor Snape from the Harry Potter books.

Some weeks later when we had a Harry Potter day, we put up ten blank posters, each labeled as to a particular archetype. Students self-selected which one they wanted to work with. Each group brainstormed and filled in the poster with examples and reasons, which they later presented to the class while we munched on "every-flavored jelly beans" and chocolate-covered frogs.

Goliath, when Cinderella is united with the noble prince and given the fitting role of queen, and when Dorothy and Toto find their way back to Kansas. In every culture, legends, myths, and folk and fairy tales follow the pattern of the adventure/accomplishment romance. They are called romances because they contain exaggeration. The bad parts are like nightmares, while the good parts are like pleasant daydreams. Such romances came to be associated with love because the traditional reward for a successful hero on such a quest was the winning of a beautiful maiden.

The Biblical story of Joseph, celebrated in today's musical *Joseph and the Amazing Technicolor Dreamcoat*, is a prototypical example of a worthy young hero being forced to go on a journey. Early in life, Joseph was chosen and marked as a special person as shown by the prophetic dreams he related to his brothers and by his father's special love demonstrated through the multicolored coat. When Joseph was sold to the Egyptian traders, he embarked on his quest for wisdom and knowledge. Just when all seemed lost, Joseph was blessed with the ability to interpret dreams. This got him out of prison and into the Pharaoh's court. The climax came years later during the famine that brought Joseph's brothers to Egypt and the royal palace. Without recognizing Joseph, they begged for food. His forgiveness and his generosity were final proof of his worthiness.

A distinguishing feature of such romances is the happy ending achieved only after the hero's worth is proven through a crisis or an ordeal. Usually as part of the ordeal the hero must make a sacrifice, be wounded, or leave some part of his or her body, even if it is only sweat or tears. The real loss is that of innocence, but it is usually symbolized by a physical loss, as in Norse mythology when Odin gave one of his eyes to pay for knowledge. J. R. R. Tolkien used a similar theme in *The Lord of the Rings* when Frodo, who has already suffered many wounds, finds that he cannot throw back the ring and so must let Gollum take his finger along with the ring.

Among the world's great stories of journeys are Homer's *The Iliad* and *The Odyssey,* John Bunyan's *The Pilgrim's Progress,* Jonathan Swift's *Gulliver's Travels,* and the Biblical story of Adam and Eve being banished from the Garden of Eden. Modern children's journey stories include William Steig's *Sylvester and the Magic Pebble,* Ezra Jack Keats's *The Snowy Day,* and Maurice Sendak's *Where the Wild Things Are.* See Focus Box 4.7, Literal Journeys/Figurative Quests, for examples of YA stories that follow this archetypal pattern. When Richard Peck was speaking to one of our classes at ASU, he explained that authors like to write journey stories, not just because the archetypal journey is inherently pleasing, but because such plots provide room for interesting developments as protagonists are removed from their old associates and patterns of life and are challenged by meeting new people and new situations.

The Archetypal Seeker

The Archetypal Seeker has much in common with the real lives of young adults because they know that sooner or later they must leave their parents' homes and make a life for themselves. Joseph, in the Bible story, was forced to go on his journey, but in contrast, Moses, who led the Jews in their Exodus from Egypt, comes closer to being a Seeker because he chose to go forth and find a better life. Pharaoh, who wanted the Jews to stay and work for him, represents the part of the human psyche that resists change and wants to preserve the status quo.

An important part of being a Seeker is in knowing when to stop. Shadow seekers—those for whom the grass is always greener on the other side—abound in modern culture. The comedian who quipped that channel-surfing men don't want to know what's on TV, "they want to know *what else* is on TV," was defining the Shadow Seeker. So are social critics who discuss the modern tendency for marriage partners and the owners of cars and houses to continuously "trade up." The boy in Willa Cather's short story "Paul's Case," was a Shadow Seeker in that he wanted to live in the fantasy world of the theater or in the glamorous world that he imagined for the wealthy. He committed suicide rather than face the dreary life he foresaw for himself back on Cordelia Street after his father repaid the money that Paul had stolen from his employer to finance his trip to New York. The parents in Gary Paulsen's *The Island* are also Shadow Seekers. They have such wanderlust that they constantly move from one town to another in search of an idealized sense of community. Because their son has little to say about his parents' moves, he is forced to become a Seeker in his own right.

The Junex versus The Senex

This archetype simply represents another way of talking about the conflict that exists between young and old. From an adult viewpoint, this is the idea of the *Dennis the Menace* cartoons and *The Little Rascals* movie gang. From a child's viewpoint, this is perhaps what is behind referring to someone as a *Scrooge,* with implications of stinginess, to someone as an old *Witch* or a *Grinch,* with implications of mean-spiritedness, or to someone as a *dirty old man,* with implications of sexual exploitation. This archetype is often referred to as the generation gap, but in fact it does not have to cross a whole generation. With teenagers, only a few years can make a difference in one's attitudes and loyalties as when high school seniors "lord" it over freshmen, or when older siblings make life miserable for younger brothers and sisters. Because of where they are on their life journeys, this archetype is an important one in books for teenagers. But in an interesting switch, a reversal is sometimes shown in which young protagonists skip a generation and identify with people of their grandparents' ages. This may relate to the fact that teenagers and elderly people are both living on the edges. They are not really in control of their lives, and so as "outsiders" may join with each other to present a united front against the mainstream adults in the middle. Examples include Jimmy and his grandmother in Walter Dean Myer's *Somewhere in the Darkness,* Miracle McCloy and her grandfather in Han Nolan's *Dancing on the Edge,* and Tree and his grandfather in Joan Bauer's *Stand Tall.*

The Orphan

The Orphan has always been a well-loved character, probably because deep in our subconscious all readers fear being the lost child. Harry Potter is the latest orphan to tug at our heartstrings, but before Harry, we had the orphans in Charles Dickens's *Little Dorrit* and *Oliver Twist,* the children in C. S. Lewis's *The Lion, the Witch, and the Wardrobe,* and the endearing young redhead in Lucy Maud Montgomery's *Anne of Green Gables.* The comic strip character *Little Orphan Annie* was so famous that she inspired a Broadway musical.

To play the literary role of orphan, young protagonists can have lost both of their parents, as in Robert Cormier's *I Am the Cheese,* or only one parent, as in Mark Twain's *Huckleberry Finn.* A child might be a temporary orphan as was the boy in the *Home Alone* movie, or the protagonist might still have one or both parents, but the parents are unable to play their role, as with the mother in Cynthia Voigt's *Homecoming* series. A higher percentage of orphans appear in children's literature than in real life because many authors do what Betsy Byars has confessed to. When planning a book, she says the first thing she does is figure out some way to get rid of the parents so that the children can be free to make decisions and get credit for their own actions.

The Caregiver

This archetype is someone who steps in to help. From the world's bank of great stories, we have such caregivers as *The Good Samaritan, Robin Hood, Snow White, Jiminy Cricket, Mary Poppins, Wendy* from *Peter Pan,* and even *Charlotte* from E. B. White's *Charlotte's Web.* From real life we occasionally hear someone referred to as a *Florence Nightingale* or a *Mother Theresa.* Even preschoolers know about Horton, the wonderfully patient elephant from Dr. Seuss's *Horton Hatches the Egg,* and about the mother duck who magnificently leads her ducklings through Boston traffic in Robert McCloskey's *Make Way for Ducklings.* One of the most touching contemporary stories about a caregiver is Katherine Paterson's *The Great Gilly Hopkins.* Galadriel, shortened to *Gilly,* is in foster care because, as one of our students described the situation, her "flower-child parents went to seed in the garden of motherhood." While searching for her birthmother, Gilly fails to appreciate her larger-than-life foster mother until it is too late.

The Wicked Stepmother is a universally understood archetype of the Shadow Caregiver. Bruno Bettelheim, along with other critics, has suggested that she isn't a step-mother at all. Instead, she's the dark side of everyone's mother—the scapegoat for the resentments that build up as part of the Junex–Senex conflict. The character is portrayed as a wicked stepmother instead of a wicked stepfather because on a daily basis the mother enforces discipline and teaches children a sense of responsibility as well as the skills of daily living. A milder version of a Shadow Caregiver appears in the nursery rhyme about "The Old Woman who lives in a shoe and has so many children she doesn't know what to do."

Sages

Sages offer spiritual and intellectual care as opposed to the physical care that is thought of as being part of the Caregiver role. The Giver in Lois Lowry's book of that name is an archetypal Sage. By holding the community's memories, he shields the members from responsibilities. In his wisdom, he questions this role and leads Jonas, who has been chosen to be his successor, to also question it. The story evolves around the difficult questions of how knowledge differs from wisdom and whether people really want to use the wisdom of the Sage. In more traditional literature, Merlin is a Sage, and it could make an interesting study to compare how authors ranging from C. S. Lewis to T. H. White and from Mary Stewart to Walt Disney's scriptwriters have portrayed this legendary Sage. Jeff's father, at the beginning of Cynthia Voigt's *A Solitary Blue,* is portrayed as a Shadow Sage. In response to his wife's leaving the family, Jeff's father places himself in "an ivory tower," but finally as the book progresses, he is able to come down and relate to his son. A better known example is Darth Vader from *Star Wars.* One of our students characterized him as a Shadow Sage because he was cut off from reality with no feelings about life. He was obsessed with perfection and being right, but at the same time he was cynical and did not want to feel attachments to people. He wanted to obtain wisdom not so he could help others, but so he could feel superior and criticize them.

A true Sage is wise enough to realize that people cannot search for just one truth, but instead must understand a multiplicity of truths. This is the point made in Hisako

Matsubara's *Cranes at Dusk,* set in post–World War II Japan. When a Shinto priest allows his daughter to attend Christian services, the Christian missionaries are disappointed to learn that the daughter and her father are not being "converted." Instead, the father is just putting into practice his belief that "No religion is enough to answer all the questions."

Friends

Friends in literature range from *Robin Hood and His Merry Men* to *Batman and Robin,* and from *Tom Sawyer* and *Huckleberry Finn* to today's *Harry Potter, Ron,* and *Hermione.* One evidence of the importance of friends to teenagers is the popularity with young viewers of the television program *Friends.* This sitcom is about a group of young adults—both males and females—in their 20s, or maybe early 30s, who are old enough to be free from parental supervision, but who have not yet become entangled with responsibilities for their own children or spouses. What is different about the program is that the characters are living life for what it is now, rather than pining away to get married and "settle down." Friendship is the theme of some of the most popular children's books—e.g., Arnold Lobel's *Frog and Toad Are Friends,* Lois Lowry's *Anastasia* books, Barbara Parks's *Junie B. Jones* books, and Beverly Cleary's *Ramona* books. Middle school girls have loved the friendships shown in books by Judy Blume, Ellen Conford, and Paula Danziger. Friendship was also at the root of the success of *The Babysitters' Club* and the *Sweet Valley High* series. (See Focus Box 4.8 for books that explore friendships among contemporary teens.) Since the story of David and Jonathan in the Old Testament, there have been strong stories about friendships between boys as in John Knowles's *A Separate Peace.* The runaway success of Ann Brashares's 2001 *Sisterhood of the Traveling Pants* shows that friendships among girls can also be satisfying, and in a more positive way than the friendship shown in the 1991 film *Thelma and Louise* starring Susan Sarandon and Geena Davis. Thelma and Louise should probably be described as Shadow Friends in that the results were so damaging, but in a different sense than are such slapstick characters as *Punch and Judy, The Three Stooges,* Abbott and Costello, and Dean Martin and Jerry Lewis, both in their real lives and in the days when they worked as a comedy team.

Lovers

Lovers are such popular protagonists that for general readers they have co-opted the whole genre of *romance.* From a literary standpoint, the first *romances* were stories told in the Roman (or Latin) manner, i.e., those told by speakers of Latin, Italian, Spanish, and French. These stories were often about bold adventurers slaying dragons, rescuing princesses from ogres, and defeating the wicked enemies of a righteous king. Love came into the stories because a successful knight was often rewarded by being given the hand of a beloved maiden. Literary lovers are as different as *Adam and Eve, Beauty and the Beast, Jane Eyre and Rochester, Catherine and Heathcliff,* and even *Tarzan and Jane.* Shadow Lovers, those whose love is out of control or damaging, might include *Samson and Delilah, J. Gatsby and Daisy, Humbert Humbert and Lolita,* and perhaps even the real gangsters *Bonnie and Clyde.*

Being rewarded with the love of a respected character is a common theme in YA books. Stories of star-crossed lovers, the most famous of which is Shakespeare's *Romeo and Juliet*, are intrinsically interesting because of the possibility for greater suspense and tension. Such protagonists are a kind of Shadow Lover in that tragic results come about. The possibility for tragedy and conflict is frequently at the heart of YA books about love between characters of the same sex. Only in fairly recent years have YA authors felt they could portray lesbian and gay characters filling the role of Lovers rather than Shadow Lovers.

Warriors, Heroes, and Villains or Destroyers

These archetypes are strong characters; people who will stand up and fight. Those who become Heroes or Superheroes choose to fight on the side of good as with *Superman, Spiderman, Wonder Woman,* and *Batman and Robin.* If warriors make the wrong choice and go the other direction, they become Villains or Destroyers. Female villains are called such names as *Jezebels* or *Witches,* while male villains might be referred to as *Hitlers* or *Devils.* A fairly new eponym for a Destroyer Warrior is a *Rambo,* taken from the name of the lead character in David Morrell's *First Blood,* made famous in the *Rambo* movies starring Sylvester Stallone. The name caught on not only because of Morrell's powerful characterization, but also because it has the connotations of strength that the makers of Dodge Ram trucks rely on in their advertising. Morrell has explained that on the afternoon he was looking for a name for his macho character, his wife brought home some *rambeaux* apples imported from a region of France. A slight alteration in spelling gave him the memorable name. Another reason the name caught on is that society was becoming aware of a new kind of *Destroyer*—young, hostile males, who were not thieves or criminals in the old sense of the word, but instead were *toughs* and *bullies.* Thirty years after Morrell created his *Rambo* character, society is even more puzzled by these kinds of *Destroyers* and the ripple effects of their actions in schools and communities. (See Focus Box 4.3, Bullies and Buddies.)

Rulers

These characters are more likely to be called *leaders* in the United States because of the country's history as a haven for common people and its rejection of the idea of royalty and inherited power. The good ruler is like Aslan in C. S. Lewis's *The Lion, the Witch, and the Wardrobe* or like Simba in Walt Disney's *The Lion King.* Alison Lurie writes that the great appeal of the *Winnie the Pooh* books to young children is that a child (Christopher Robin) gets to play the role of the beneficent dictator in charge of the whole "100 Akre Woods."[19] Great rulers make mistakes, but when this happens, they are mature enough to recognize their folly and to learn from it. This attitude has brought changes in the biographies written for young people. It used to be that authors put in only the positive aspects of leaders' lives, but today authors include both the good and the bad, in the hopes that young people will be even more inspired to see that "imperfect" people, which all of us are, can still make great contributions. *The Pied Piper,* from Robert Browning's poem based on an old legend, is a Shadow Leader who uses his power to entice the village's children away to their doom. The Pied Piper, however, was reacting

FOCUS BOX 3.4   *Teen Voices*

Broken Hearts . . . Healing: Young Poets Speak Out on Divorce, edited by Tom Worthen. Poet Tree Press, 2001. The poems in this book are testament to the power of words in helping both writers and readers heal from hurts in their lives.

The Courage to Change: A Teen Survival Guide, edited by Brenda Proulx. Second Story Press, 2001. The poems, reflections, stories, and photos are the work of teen members of LOVE (Leave Out ViolencE), a Canadian group founded in 1993 by a woman whose husband was stabbed to death by a 14-year-old boy.

Hearing Us Out: Voices from the Gay and Lesbian Community by Roger Sutton, photos by Lisa Ebright. Little, Brown, 1994. M. E. Kerr wrote the preface to this book, which consists of interviews, many with young people. The photos add an air of authenticity and help readers identify with the heartfelt comments of those being interviewed.

Jump: Poetry and Prose by WritersCorps Youth and **Believe Me, I Know: Poetry and Photography by WritersCorps Youth,** edited by Valerie Chow Bush. WritersCorps Books 2001 and 2002, respectively. The San Francisco Arts Commission sponsors the WritersCorp for poets between the ages of 6 and 21. In the introduction to *Believe Me,* poet Jimmy Santiago Baca wrote about the poems, "Some of them move me to tears, others to laughter—all move me to look at life in a different way."

Merlyn's Pen: Fiction, Essays, and Poems by American Teens, Merlyn's Pen. This annual book prints the best of the stories, essays, and poems that have been published in the magazine during the previous year.

More Than a Label: Why What You Wear or Who You're With Doesn't Define Who You Are by Aisha Muharrar. Free Spirit, 2002. The 17-year-old author speaks with a voice of experience and includes statements from teens all over the country. She collected more than a thousand responses to a Teen Labels Survey, which is printed in the preface to the book so readers can measure their own attitudes before they read the book.

My Sisters' Voices: Teenage Girls of Color Speak Out, edited by Iris Jacob. Owl Books/Henry Holt, 2002. The author was 18 when she set out to collect essays and poems that would speak to biracial teens and others of color as *Reviving Ophelia* and *Ophelia Speaks* communicated to a more general audience.

Oh, Freedom! Kids Talk about the Civil Rights Movement with the People Who Made It Happen by Casey King and Linda Barrett Osborne, illustrated by Joe Brooks, foreword by Rosa Parks. Knopf, 1997. Over two dozen young people conducted interviews with family members and other acquaintances who played roles in the Civil Rights movement.

Paint Me Like I Am: Teen Poems from WritersCorps. Harper/Tempest, 2003. "Bodies sprawled along the shelter's floor—/like sloppy cursive writing . . ." and "Alone in a darkness that laughs in your face," are two of the interesting metaphors in this book of poems written by disadvantaged young people. Nikki Giovanni wrote the introduction.

Teen Ink: Love and Relationships, edited by Stephanie H. Meyer and John Meyer. Health Communications, 2002. R. L. Stine wrote the foreword to this best-of-the-best compendium of memoirs, poems, insights, and stories that were originally published in the *Teen Ink* magazine.

Teen People: Faith Stories of Belief and Spirituality, edited by Megan Howard and Jon Barrett. Avon/HarperCollins, 2001. This is part of a series that includes *Real Life Diaries, Love Stories,* and *Sex Files.* Among the fourteen teens who are pictured alongside their stories are young adult celebrities and teens who were involved in public events such as the Columbine shootings.

What Are You? Voices of Mixed-Race Young People by Pearl Fuyo Gaskins. Holt, 1999. Helping Gaskins make her dream of writing this book come true are some eighty young writers who are identified by full or part names, ages, and racial mix. Hometowns and photographs are also included for many.

to the Shadow leaders in the story, the townsmen who cheated him by refusing to pay the fee they had promised him if he would rid their town of rats. From Harriet Beecher Stowe's *Uncle Tom's Cabin* comes the eponym of a *Simon Legree*, for a cruel leader. From the same book comes an *Uncle Tom*, for an Innocent or for someone who will not stand up for himself. In some ways, however, this is an unfair eponym because at the end of the book it is Uncle Tom who stands against Simon Legree, thereby enabling the two women to escape.

Fools and Tricksters

These archetypes appear in American jokes about "The Little Moron," in some of the Muslim stories about Mullah Nasruddin (sometimes he's wise and other times he's foolish), in Jewish tales about the "Fools of Chelm," and in European and American folktales about Foolish Jack. Readers and listeners enjoy the humor that comes from the surprise, incongruity, spontaneity, and violations of social norms that are part and parcel of stories about fools or clowns. While clowns play the role of the Fool, they are really Tricksters, since they are only pretending to be ignorant. Children have an extra reason for enjoying stories about fools—because of their powerlessness and lack of experience, they are often left feeling foolish and so are glad when they find characters even more foolish than they are. Literary Fools include such characters as Sheridan's *Mrs. Malaprop*, who always mixed up her words, and Thurber's *Walter Mitty*, whose mind kept wandering away from real life and into fantasy daydreams.

Tricksters are only pretending to be fools so that they can get by with something, as when Tom Sawyer tricks the neighborhood boys into whitewashing the fence. Ulysses was a Trickster when he managed to escape with most of his men from the cave of the Cyclops. *The Joker* in the *Batman* movies is a Trickster, and so is *Old Sneep* in Robert McCloskey's *Lentil*. Sneep is jealous that everyone is making such a fuss about his old nemesis, the Colonel, coming back to town, and so when the brass band is getting ready to play, Old Sneep sits on top of the train depot sucking a lemon so that all the players' mouths begin to water and they cannot play their instruments. Lentil saves the day by playing his harmonica. The Fool or Trickster motif is seldom this obvious in books for teenagers, many of which have the very serious purpose of teaching young people not to be fools, a point that will be discussed in more detail in relation to realistic problem novels in Chapter 4.

Magicians

Magicians appear in stories of fantasy where authors create a make-believe world with no explanation of how the magic works. Internal consistency is all that is required. Ursula LeGuin's four books about Earthsea are especially good at illustrating the role of the Magician. Ogion is the Magician/Sage, but readers are most interested in the young people who are training to become Magicians. The boy *Sparrowhawk* becomes the archmage *Ged*, the girl *Goha* becomes the wise woman *Tenar*, and in the last book, an abused Orphan becomes *Tehannu*, destined to become the next archmage. The good magician uses his or her powers for good, while Shadow Magicians use their powers for evil or destructive purposes. Some stories about Magicians and Creators are cautionary tales, which warn against humans trying to take the power of the gods for themselves. When Frankenstein created his monster, he unleashed a host of troubles, but it was not all bad when Galatea created Pygmalion and when Geppetto created Pinocchio.

Creators

Creators do not lift a finger to their noses or bring out an array of helpers to make happy endings possible; instead they transform reality by changing the way characters perceive matters, often with long-term effects on the real world. The Wizard in Frank Baum's *Wonderful Wizard of Oz* was this kind of a magician when he convinced Dorothy's companions that he was giving them what they obviously already had: courage for the lion, brains for the scarecrow, and a heart for the tin woodman. In old folk tales, the role of the magical Creator was filled by dwarves, elves, fairy godmothers, fortune tellers, shamans, witches, healers, and priests and priestesses. In modern life, psychiatrists, therapists, religious leaders, politicians, teachers, friends, and parents are more likely to play these roles. Shadow Creators are the con artists and others who exploit people's emotional needs for selfish purposes. Both kinds of Creators are commonly included in YA books where authors explore some fairly subtle differences between Creators who play a positive role and those who play a negative role by killing others' dreams—usually through being overly controlling or overly negative.

Concluding Comments

This chapter has shown that books for teenagers exist alongside, and as part of, the mass media. Today, we have a youth-oriented society, and many of the books, television programs, films, and computer games created for teenage audiences have surprised their producers by becoming popular with adults. Producers have also found that the tastes and interests of teenagers are just as varied as those of adults. They have responded by creating a wealth of literary materials. That so much is available on the Internet as well as in books, magazines, films, popular music, and the newspapers makes our job of selection harder rather than easier. Nevertheless, we can be comforted by the fact that the situation is the mixed blessing covered in the cliche "When much is given, much is expected."

 Notes

[1] Jeffrey Passe, "Like It or Not: Social Educators Must Keep Up with Popular Culture," *Social Education* 66:4 (May/June 2002): 234.

[2] Maryanne Murray Buechner, "Learning Corner: Pop Fiction" *Time* magazine special issue on the family (March 2002): F-14.

[3] Tony Vellela, "Tonys mirror Broadway's quest for youth." printed in *The Arizona Republic* (June 8, 2003): E-4.

[4] Bettijane Levine, "Read the book, buy the clothes,"*Los Angeles Times,* printed in *The Arizona Republic* (May 9, 2003): E-1, E-7.

[5] Janie Magruder, "Girls who love books get a Web room of their own," *The Arizona Republic* (June 11, 2003): E-1.

[6] Zeina Karam, "Computer game lets Hezbollah kill Israelis," Associated Press, printed in *The Arizona Republic* (June 1, 2003): A-26.

[7]Richard Corliss, "The Fresh-Face Factory," *Time* magazine (April 14, 2003): 76–77, 79.

[8]Phuong Ly, "3 teens, like, teach FBI to BC (be cool)," *Washington Post,* printed in *The Arizona Republic* (June 5, 2003): A-14.

[9]Bill Muller, "2003's wave of comic-book, sci-fi films puts Fanboys in Paradise," *The Arizona Republic* (March 9, 2003): E-1, E-11.

[10]Joel Stein, "For Lad Mags, the Jig Is Up," *Time* magazine (May 19, 2003): 90.

[11]Paul D. Colford, "In Women's Magazines, Everybody Seems to Be Doing It," *Newsday,* reprinted in *The Arizona Republic* (June 21, 1999): D-4.

[12]Stein, Joel, "The Singin', Dancin' American Idyll," *Time* magazine (June 23, 2003): 70. Maryanne Murray Buechner, "Learning Corner: Pop Fiction," *Time* magazine special issue on the family (March 2002): F-14.

[13]Jennifer Crocker, "American Adolescents Desperately Seeking Self-Esteem," *LSA Magazine,* University of Michigan College of Literature, Science and the Arts, Spring, 2003, pp. 15–17.

[14]William Strauss and Neil Howe, "Teens Shun Gross-out Movie Genre," *Los Angeles Times,* July 15, 2001, p. M-1, 2.

[15]Bill Goodykoontz, "Farewell to the Hellmouth: As 7-year run ends, Buffy still slays us," *The Arizona Republic* (May 19, 2003): E-1, E-3.

[16]Bill Muller, "A Neo Classic: Keanu & Co. return in groundbreaking sequel," *The Arizona Republic* (May 14, 2003): E-1, E-7.

[17]Beth Ricks, personal e-mail to Alleen Nilsen, April 30, 2002.

[18]Beth Ricks.

[19]Alison Lurie, *Don't Tell the Grown-Ups: Why Kids Love the Books They Do* (Avon, 1991), p. 145.

Part Two
Modern Young Adult Reading

CHAPTER

4

Contemporary Realistic Fiction
From Tragedies to Romances

When critic Northrop Frye used the term *realism* in his *Anatomy of Criticism,* he put it in quotation marks because when it is applied to literature the term does not—or should not—mean the same thing that it does in other contexts. He argued that expecting literature simply to portray real life is a mistaken notion. The artist who can paint grapes so realistically that a bird will fly up and peck at the canvas is not the one most highly acclaimed. Nor would people want to listen to a symphony in which all the instruments imitated "real" sounds from nature—the cooing of doves, the rushing of a waterfall, a clap of thunder, and the wind whistling through trees.

In the early 1990s when Norman Mailer was being interviewed on CNN by Larry King, he also commented on the concept of realism in relation to nonfiction and fiction. He claimed that as soon as a character—whether real or imagined—is written about, fiction results because the character now lives as imagined in people's minds rather than as a real person who can be talked to and touched. G. Robert Carlsen made a similar point when he said that a story exists first in the mind of its creator and then in the minds of its readers. Because it was never anything "real," it cannot be tested against an external reality, as can the plans for a building, a chemical formula, a case study, and so on.

If we evaluate literature by its realism alone, we should be forced to abandon most of the truly great literature of the world: certainly most of tragedy, much of comedy, and all of romance. We would be forced to discard the Greek plays, the great epics, Shakespeare, Molière. They succeed because they go beyond the externals of living and instead reach out and touch the imaginative life deep down inside where we live.[1]

FOCUS BOX 4.1   Dying Is Easy; Surviving Is Hard

The Bell Jar by Sylvia Plath. HarperCollins, 1971. A young woman who has become famous for her poetry commits suicide. Her story continues to fascinate readers.

Both Sides Now by Ruth Pennebaker. Holt, 2000. Fifteen-year-old Liza is shaken to the foundation of her soul when her mother's cancer returns and she chooses not to undergo an experimental treatment that might save her life. Liza is the narrator, but her mother's thoughts (the other side of the story) are presented in italics.

The Dark Light by Mette Newth, translated by Faith Ingwerson. Farrar Straus and Giroux, 1998. In Norway more than a century ago, a 13-year-old girl tries to work out the meaning of life, God, happiness, and revenge as she lies in a bed dying of leprosy.

A Death in the Family by James Agee. McDowell, Obolensky, 1957. Set in Knoxville, Tennessee, back at the turn of the last century, the Follet family with their two children lead a comfortable life until the father is struck down.

Driver's Ed by Caroline B. Cooney. Delacorte, 1994. Remy Marland and her new would-be boyfriend are out for a lark, driving no place in particular and playing the popular game of stealing road signs. A young mother is killed because of their game, and the teenagers are guilt-ridden.

Ghost Girl: A Blue Ridge Mountain Story by Delia Ray. Clarion, 2003. Set during the Depression, this moving book covers four years in the life of young April Sloane, who feels like a ghost, not only because of her pale hair and eyes, but because ever since the death of her younger brother, her mother doesn't seem to see her.

Green Angel by Alice Hoffman. Scholastic, 2003. Mature readers will grieve with the 15-year-old girl who is now ashamed of her sullen behavior when she didn't get to go with her parents and sister to the city. They never came back.

The Lightkeeper's Daughter by Iain Lawrence. Delacorte, 2002. When the lightkeepers' daughter returns home to the island lighthouse with a 3-year-old daughter in tow, she not only has to reestablish relations with her parents, but also has to come to terms with the death of her beloved brother.

The Man Without a Face by Isabelle Holland. HarperCollins, 1972. The 1993 movie starring Mel Gibson gave a new burst of popularity to Holland's story of 14-year-old Charles who is left to adjust to the death of his friend and tutor.

Missing May by Cynthia Rylant. Orchard, 1992. Summer has been tossed from relative to relative. Then Uncle Ob and Aunt May take her into their loving home, and May dies. Uncle Ob is so devastated that Summer is afraid she will lose him too.

My Brother Stealing Second by Jim Naughton. HarperCollins, 1989. While star athlete and favorite son Billy is drunk, he kills himself along with a couple celebrating their wedding anniversary. Billy's family and the daughter of the couple are left to suffer.

Say Goodnight, Gracie by Julie Reece Deaver. HarperCollins, 1988. When Jimmy is killed by a drunk driver, Morgan realizes how much she loved him, then and even more now.

Someone Like You by Sarah Dessen. Viking, 1998. Halley and Scarlett are friends, but their lives are affected when one of the friends gets a boyfriend and becomes pregnant. Then the boyfriend dies.

A Summer to Die by Lois Lowery. Houghton Mifflin, 1977. While her older sister is dying of leukemia, Meg finds comfort and solace in the help of a 70-year-old landlord, handyman, and photographer.

Tunnel Vision by Fran Arrick. Bradbury, 1980. Fifteen-year-old Anthony dies by hanging himself. When the family gathers around, each one is anxious to figure out why, but they are unable to decipher Anthony's reasoning.

Walk Softly, Rachel by Kate Banks. Farrar, 2003. Fourteen-year-old Rachel reads the journal that her brother wrote before he died when she was seven. She is stunned by what she learns, not only about her brother but also about her parents and herself.

Black-Eyed Suzie by Susan Shaw. Boyds Mills, 2002. Twelve-year-old Suzie is falling deeper and deeper into mental illness. An uncle comes for a visit and recognizes the trouble she is in and takes her to a psychiatric hospital where she can start the long road to healing.

Boys Lie by John Neufeld. DK, Ink, 1999. Gina is traumatized by being sexually assaulted in a New York swimming pool. Rumors follow her to California where her family moves to help her start over.

A Corner of the Universe by Ann Martin. Scholastic, 2002. Hattie looks back on her thirteenth summer when Uncle Adam, someone she had never been told about, comes "home" to live with her grandparents because his "school" has closed. In this powerful look at mental illness, tragedy ensues when Hattie invites Uncle Adam to sneak out with her to a carnival.

Cut by Patricia McCormick. Front Street, 2000. This picture of life in a mental-health facility for teenagers is far from pretty with its constant smell of vomit, its lack of privacy, and the hostility and sadness of the patients. Callie, a girl who secretly cuts herself, is the narrator.

Damage by A. M. Jenkins. HarperCollins, 2001. Austin is unable to appreciate the "good life" that is his because he suffers from depression. He mythologizes a childhood relationship with his long-deceased father, and a turning point in the book is when he realizes that he has created false memories.

Dreamland by Sarah Dessen. Viking, 2000. Vivid characterization makes this story of Caitlin's drift into passivity all the more memorable and haunting.

Every Time a Rainbow Dies by Rita Williams-Garcia. HarperCollins, 2001. Thulani's mother died three years ago, and he is a relatively unwelcome "guest" in the apartment of his older brother and the brother's wife. Thulani spends hours with the pigeons he raises on the roof of their apartment house. When he witnesses a brutal rape, he rushes down to "rescue" the girl and takes an important first step toward reentering life.

The Gypsies Never Came by Stephen Roos. Simon & Schuster, 2001. Sixth-grader Augie's left hand is almost nonexistent because of a birth defect, but this is only one of his problems. The title alludes to a promise made to Augie by a new girl in school. She tells Augie that gypsies, who honor such a defect, are coming to rescue him.

Inside Out by Terry Trueman. HarperTempest, 2003. Zach, who is schizophrenic, waits every day for his mother to pick him up in a small restaurant where he gets caught in the midst of a holdup. Although he comes close to being a hero in this particular situation, there is no happy ending.

Memories of Summer by Ruth White. Farrar Straus Giroux, 2000. Thirteen-year-old Lyric tells this sad story from the 1950s when her widowed father moved her and her sister, Summer, from the rural south to Michigan. The adjustment is difficult for the family, but it is made almost unbearable by Summer's descent into madness.

Stuck in Neutral by Terry Trueman. HarperCollins, 2000. Fourteen-year-old Shawn McDaniel thinks his father is planning to kill him, a suspicion that readers gradually grow to share in this story of a boy who is born with cerebral palsy.

Wasteland by Francesca Lia Block. Joanna Cotler/HarperCollins, 2003. People who think YA lit is easy to read and easy to understand need to immerse themselves in this powerful and sad story about Marina and her brother Lex.

You Remind Me of You by Eireann Corrigan. Scholastic, 2002. When her boyfriend tries to kill himself, the protagonist decides to fight her own bulimia and anorexia.

PAUL FLEISCHMAN
On My House of Voices

"*I* grew up in a house of voices," Rob begins his autobiography in *Seek*. Though his was a duplex in San Francisco, it was my own childhood home in Santa Monica, in southern California, that I saw in my mind: 100 years old now, with two stories and fifteen rooms, the source if not the setting for nearly all my books. Let me give you a tour.

You enter the living room—large, with west windows that let in the afternoon breeze off the ocean, ten blocks away. It's here that my father, Sid Fleischman, read his books aloud to the family chapter by chapter, as they were written. His readings were living-room theater, intimate, no-tech, without props or costumes, but riveting nonetheless. Decades later I found myself writing for the same stage—*Bull Run, Seedfolks, Mind's Eye, Seek,* all spoken, all suitable for performance.

In the corner of the room is a baby grand piano. Under it sit two guitar cases. Both my parents played classical guitar for a time. My mother's real instrument, and my own, was the piano. Both my sisters played flute. I grew up hearing guitar duets and flute duets and I loved playing four-hand piano pieces with a partner. It was here that *Joyful Noise* and my other multivoice poems were born—attempts to carry the camaraderie of chamber music into poetry. The stage I had in mind wasn't Carnegie Hall but our living room couch.

Go down the hall into my father's study, where the bookshelves are floor-to-ceiling. When I was young, they seemed twenty feet tall. Over here are the books he used to research his novels set in the west. Over there are the Old Baedeker guides he used for his adult books. I loved their microscopic print and fold-out maps. Little did I know that I'd later build *Mind's Eye* around his 1911 edition of *Baedeker's Italy*.

Go up the stairs and into my bedroom. My short wave radio used to sit on the desk—you can see it in the cover photo on *Seek*. The short wave allowed spirit travel, much as a book does. Listening in on ship-to-shore calls and the police band developed my taste for eavesdropping—an important skill for a writer. Still on my bookshelf are many of my influences from high school: Twain, Gogol, Dylan Thomas, Richard Brautigan, J. D. Salinger, Sophocles, Edward Lear—living voices, no matter how long-dead the writer. I wasn't a reader until high school. Suddenly, I found myself reading three books at once, the chorus of voices ever-enlarging.

My father still lives and writes in that house. I still sleep in that pine-panelled room when I visit. And in my own books I continue to aspire to the power of a voice coming from a radio late at night in a pitch-black room.

Paul Fleischman's books include *Seek,* 2001, Cricket Books; *Seedfolks,* 1997, HarperCollins; *Bull Run,* 1993, HarperCollins; and *Joyful Noise: Poems for Two Voices,* 1988, HarperCollins.

While respected authors and critics argue against realism as a literary concept, we should explain that we are using the term in our chapter title mainly because we can't think of a better one. Besides, so many people use *realism* to describe the kinds of books being discussed in this chapter that we would be at a communication disadvantage if we invented a new term. We are writing about young adult fiction with real-world settings in historical periods not far removed from our own. For the most part, the books feature young protagonists solving problems without the help of magic. The "realism" part relates to "honesty" and to Marc Aronson's observation about judging young adult books: "The term we should be

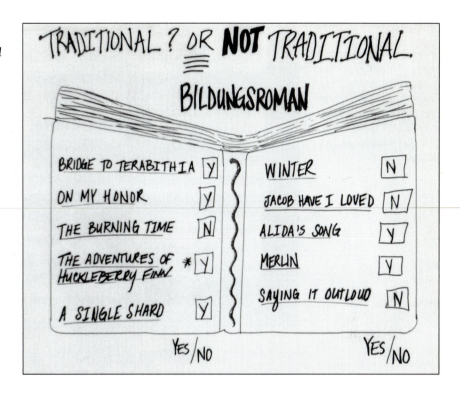

This poster was a visual aid created for a panel presentation in which students in one of our classes compared popular young adult novels with the traditional bildungsroman.

looking for is not popularity but intimacy. Does a book have the potential to touch readers deeply so that, in the struggle with it, they begin to see and to shape themselves?"[2]

In this chapter we will begin with the serious or harsh problem novels, the ones that are commonly referred to as *modern realism, problem novels,* or even *tragedies.* In these books young protagonists are left to deal with the death of a friend or a family member as in Focus Box 4.1 or with such terrible problems as mental illness as in Focus Box 4.2. Then we will move on to *romantic quests* or *accomplishment stories.* In the romantic quests or accomplishment stories, protagonists meet real challenges, which in general they overcome as in Paul Fleischman's *Seek.* These books have happier endings because the young protagonist has at least taken steps toward finding a solution or dealing with the problem. We will end this chapter by talking about books whose main appeal is wish-fulfillment.

The Modern Problem Novel

The general public seems to have an almost subconscious belief that children will model their lives after what they read. Since all of us want our children to be happy, we feel more comfortable when they are reading "happy" books. The problem novel, how-

As shown by these samplings of headlines, today's teenagers do not need the problem novel to let them know that they and their friends have problems and that many adults are less than perfect.

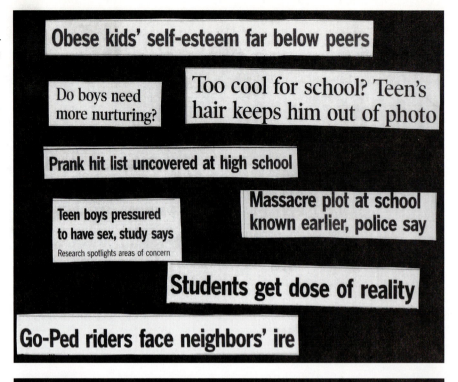

Obese kids' self-esteem far below peers

Do boys need more nurturing?

Too cool for school? Teen's hair keeps him out of photo

Prank hit list uncovered at high school

Teen boys pressured to have sex, study says
Research spotlights areas of concern

Massacre plot at school known earlier, police say

Students get dose of reality

Go-Ped riders face neighbors' ire

Doctor arrested in Tucson sex sting
Arranged meeting with '14-year-old girl' over Internet   spokeswoman for Cigna, which runs the center.

2 parents charged with providing alcohol in school hazing incident

Teacher tricked parents
Ruse covered affair with teen student

Teacher fathered ex-student's child

No charges for coaches in dust-up with umpire

Costa Rica closes school for troubled teens, cites abuse

ever, is based on the philosophy that young people will have a better chance to be happy if they have realistic expectations and if they know both the bad and the good about the society in which they live. This changed attitude is what opened the door to writers of irony and even tragedy for young people. Irony differs from tragedy in that it may be less intense, and, instead of having heroic qualities, the protagonist is an ordinary person, much like the reader. Irony is a "tennis serve that you can't return." You can admire its perfection, its appropriateness, and even the inevitability of the outcome, but you just can't cope with it. There is a refreshing honesty in stories that show readers they are not the only ones who get served that kind of ball and that the human spirit, although totally devastated in this particular set, may rise again to play another match.

When in the late 1960s, societal, education, and business values had changed enough that publishers felt comfortable in encouraging writers to create serious coming-of-age stories to be read by teenagers themselves, they wisely identified the books as *new realism* or as *problem novels* rather than as *bildungsroman*. Publishers were surprisingly successful in creating appealing formats and in marketing them to teen readers through libraries and schools.

In addition to their candor and the selection of subject matter, these new problem novels differed from earlier books in four basic ways. The first difference lies in the choice of *characters.* These protagonists could come from a variety of social and economic levels, which ties in with the second major difference—that of *setting.* Instead of living in idyllic, pleasant suburban homes, the characters in these books mostly come from settings that are harsh, difficult places to live. To get the point across about the characters and where and how they live, authors used colloquial language, which is the third major difference. Authors began to write the way people really talked—for example, creating dialogue filled with profanity and ungrammatical constructions. That the general public allowed this change in language shows that people were drawing away from the idea that the main purpose of fictional books for young readers is to set an example of proper middle-class behavior.

The fourth difference also relates to this change in attitude, and that is the change in *mode.* As people began to think that the educational value of fiction is to provide readers with more vicarious experiences than would be either desirable or possible in real life, the mode of stories for young adults changed. It used to be that most of the books for young readers—at least most of the books approved of by parents and educators—were written in the comic and romantic modes. Statistically, this may still be true, but several of the books that are currently getting critical attention are written in the ironic or tragic modes. For example, *Little Chicago* by Adam Rapp is the grim story of 11-year-old Blacky, who is sexually abused by his mother's boyfriend. Although he is brave enough to tell "all the right people," no one helps him. His best friend makes it even worse by telling kids at school, who cruelly taunt him. He gets a gun and, with no money for ammunition, performs a sexual act to get bullets. His one friend, who suffers almost as much as he does, has told him that if you follow a deer long enough it will lead you to paradise. The book ends with Blacky following a deer into a forest, but only the most optimistic of readers can believe that this is going to make Blacky's life better. Tyrrell Burns closed her *School Library Journal* review with, "The sense of hopelessness in this disturbing novel is almost physically painful."[3] At the end of her review for VOYA, Kathleen Beck wrote that Rapp's books are valuable because of their honest recognition that young people can suffer and face really difficult questions, but "Forget using them as bibliotherapy. . . . There are no solutions here."[4] In the February issue of *VOYA* when the "Top Shelf Fiction for Middle School Readers 2002" (a list of 24 "best books") was published, *Little Chicago* received twice as much space as the other books, but its annotation was in a gray box under the unusual heading "Adult Reader Recommendation." The committee's idea was that adults should read the book to keep such a story from ever happening. Their closing line was "This book is not to be handed to young readers without forethought—not because it is unrealistic but precisely because it shows how heartlessly unprotected they might find themselves to be."[5]

When the problem novel was first developing as *the* genre in young adult literature, it played a relatively unique role in openly acknowledging that many young people lived lives far removed from the happy-go-lucky images shown in television commercials and sitcoms. The books on the Honor List from the 1960s and 1970s were new and interesting because they vividly demonstrated that young people worried about sex, drugs, money, peer pressure, and health problems. However, such information does not come as news today because the mass media does a thorough job of communicating that many adults are less than perfect and that many young people are facing problems ranging from minor to severe. In fact, talk shows, reality shows, courtroom TV, soap operas, and even news programs and magazines make us privy to so many people's problems that we simply do not have the energy to empathize with all the sad stories that we hear. We shrug our shoulders and turn off our tear ducts, which leaves us feeling alienated and dehumanized. Also, most media treatments present a one-shot portrait chosen to tug at the emotions of viewers or readers. To increase the drama, producers make a virtue of suffering and pain by portraying people as victims unable to move beyond their pain. In contrast, in the best of the problem novels authors take the

T he books in this chapter stretch from such somber problem stories as Rita Williams Garcia's Every Time a Rainbow Dies to Meg Cabot's wish-fulfilling All-American Girl.

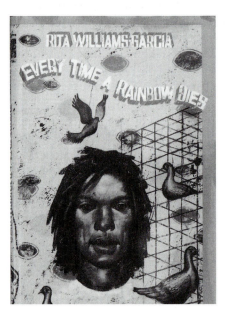

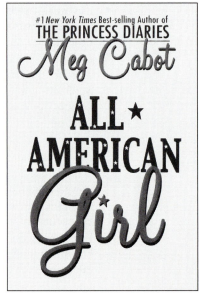

space to develop various strands of their stories and to show differing viewpoints and alternate solutions. This differs from television sitcoms as well as from most series books, which preserve the status quo so that at the end the producer or the author can start all over again with a similar story.

In relation to the term *realism,* it is only fair to mention that some critics have justifiably pointed out that the large majority of high school readers are more likely to experience something akin to a wish-fulfilling romance than to the experiences described in many of the so-called *realistic* novels, as shown in this sampling of recent books:

- One of our students who read E. R. Frank's *America* responded with "grim, grim, grim." A 15-year-old boy named America, born to a drug-addicted woman who abandoned him, nevertheless reappears for terrifying episodes. The boy's best memories are of living with Mrs. Harper and her half-brother. However, the half-brother introduces the preteen America to vodka and sex, and in guilt and rage, America sets the man's blanket on fire and escapes. Years later, a capable therapist is coaxing America's story from a reluctant 15-year-old who is living in a residential treatment center and trying to gain control over his suicidal depression. Readers are left with hope for a boy who, so far, has been a survivor against incredible odds.
- Adam Rapp's *33 Snowfish* is about four kids on the run. One of them has killed his parents and stolen their car. One is a prostitute; one has recently escaped from a pedophile, while the youngest is just a baby, whom the others think they might sell. Reviewer Joel Shoemaker said that the book is bound to be controversial: "The fearsome elements escape the pages like nightmares loosed into daylight, . . . but for those readers who are ready to be challenged by a serious work of shockingly realistic fiction, it invites both an emotional and intellectual response, and begs to be discussed."[6]
- In *Hush,* Jacqueline Woodson uses a similar situation to the one that Robert Cormier used in *I Am the Cheese,* in which a family is uprooted and put into the Federal Witness Protection Program. In Woodson's story, the family is African American, and the protagonist, Evie Thomas (nee Toswiah Green), is 12 years old when her father testifies against other African Americans in a racially motivated murder. Instead of creating the kind of dramatic situation that Cormier created, Woodson shows the tedium and the depression that sets in when a family is torn from its past and has yet to build a future. Evie's mother finds a kind of solace in the Seventh Day Adventist Church, but her father spends his days staring out the front window, while her older sister plots how she can escape from this non-life. Rather than being left with a happy ending, readers are left pondering what is a less-than-perfect solution to a very real family problem.

Such sad books as these are very close to being tragedies. In traditional literary criticism, tragedies have three distinct elements. First, there is a noble character, who no matter what happens, maintains the qualities that the society considers praiseworthy; second, there is an inevitable force that works against the character; and third, there is a struggle and an outcome. The reader of a tragedy is usually filled with pity and fear—pity for the hero and fear for oneself that the same thing might happen. The intensity of this involvement causes the reader to undergo an emotional release as the outcome of the story unfolds. This release, or catharsis, has the effect of draining away dangerous human emotions and filling the reader with a sense of exaltation or amazed pride in what the human spirit is called on to endure.

Rather than writing pure tragedies, most young adult authors soften their stories with hopeful endings. When Virginia Hamilton was awarded the Newbery Medal for *M. C. Higgins the Great,* a reporter asked her if she really thought that the retaining wall that M. C. was building on the mountain above the house would keep the mine tailings from sliding down and ruining the family's home. She responded with something to the effect, that "Probably not, but this is a book for kids. They have to have hope."

Her statement illustrates a long-cherished belief that young readers deserve books with happy endings. These are the kinds of books that serve as a counterbalance to the depressing realism of the "true" problem novel. There is nothing magical in the books, so they are "real" in that sense, but as Richard Peck has observed, teenagers' favorite books are "romances disguised as realism." He was not saying this as a negative, because he was describing his own books along with those of many other well-respected writers. It is understandable that teenagers want both the happy endings and the assurance that happy endings are possible. Actually, most readers prefer happy endings, but it is assumed that adults have had more experience in coping with difficult life experiences so that they might be "turned off" by endings that come across as falsely hopeful. See Table 4.1 for suggestions of how to evaluate problem novels.

Three popular stories about young protagonists that were published as somber adult novels are J. D. Salinger's *The Catcher in the Rye,* Hannah Green's *I Never Promised You a Rose Garden,* and Judith Guest's *Ordinary People.* In all three, worthy young heroes set out to find wisdom and understanding. They make physical sacrifices, including suicide attempts, and even though they receive help from wise and kindly psychiatrists (today's counterpart to the white witches, the wizards, and the helpful gods and goddesses of traditional romances), they must prove their worthiness through hard, painstaking work. This is what Deborah Blau's psychiatrist communicates in the sentence used for the book's title, *I Never Promised You a Rose Garden.* If Green had intended her book for teenagers, she would have been more likely to have ended the book with Deborah leaving the mental institution to "live happily ever after."

It is the details of a story and the author's attitude as much as the plot that determines whether a book is realistic or romanticized. For example, the plot of Joyce Carol Oates's *Freaky Green Eyes* is as somber as any tragedy, but Oates devised several techniques to soften the story of a girl whose father murders her mother and is sent to prison. First, the family is wealthy and the father is a celebrity so that Francesca (aka Franky) lives in a house and goes to the kinds of parties that other kids only dream about. Readers get to see her as a take-charge girl, both for herself and for wild animals that are being kept in cages simply for amusement. At the end she has a loving aunt to provide a new home for her and her sister. And most important of all, she now has Garret as a boyfriend. She met him when she went to visit her mother. They had made arrangements for an informal date, but her enraged father came and took her and her sister away before she could go out with him. She met Garret again only after her mother's death when she came with her aunt to take away her mother's belongings, and Garret wandered over and helped them load the U-Haul trailer. They exchanged email addresses, and at the end of the book she lets readers know that they keep in touch—

TABLE 4.1 SUGGESTIONS FOR EVALUATING THE PROBLEM NOVEL

A good problem novel usually has:	A poor problem novel may have:
A strong, interesting, and believable plot centering around a problem that a young person might really have.	A totally predictable plot with nothing new and interesting to entice the reader.
The power to transport the reader into another person's thoughts and feelings.	Characters who are cardboardlike exaggerations of people and are too good or too bad to be believed.
Rich characterization. The characters "come alive" as believable with a balance of good and negative qualities.	More characters than the reader can keep straight comfortably.
	Many stereotypes.
A setting that enhances the story and is described so that the reader can get the intended picture.	Lengthy chapters or descriptive paragraphs that add bulk but not substance to the book.
A worthwhile theme. The reader is left with something to think about.	A preachy message. The author spells out the attitudes and conclusions with which he or she wants each reader to leave the book.
A smoothness of style that flows steadily and easily, carrying the reader along.	Nothing that stays with the reader after the book has been put down.
A universal appeal so that it speaks to more than a single group of readers.	A subject that is of interest only because it is topical or trendy.
A subtlety that stimulates the reader to think about the various aspects of the story.	Inconsistent points of view. The author's sympathies change with no justification.
A way of dealing with the problems so that the reader is left with insights into either society or individuals or both.	Dialogue that sounds forced or inappropriate to the characters.
	"Facts" that do not jibe with those of the real world.
	Unlikely coincidences or changes in characters' personalities for the sake of the plot.
	Exaggerations that result in sensationalism.

"Sometimes daily." Also his family is going to change their usual plan of skiing at Aspen and going to ski at Taos, where she now lives, so "Garret and I will see each other then."

Devising happy, or at least hopeful, endings for tragic stories is a challenge for authors. Even such a good book as Laurie Halse Anderson's 1999 *Speak,* which was a finalist for the National Book Award and a Printz Honor Book, is marred by its unlikely ending. Fourteen-year-old Melinda is raped at a summer party. When she calls the police who come and break up the party, she becomes a social outcast. No one knows why she called the police, and out of shame she hides behind silence for almost a whole year. Finally, a wonderful art teacher helps her not only to "speak," but to speak about the incident. The boy who raped her is furious and vengeful. He stalks her and after school one day pushes her into a janitor's closet and slams the door. She is saved from a severe beating or another rape—if not from death—by her own efforts and the coincidental arrival of the girls' lacrosse team pounding on the door, "Nicole is there, along with the lacrosse team—sweaty, angry, their sticks held high."

Another challenge for writers of problem novels is that they most often write the books in first person. Thoughtful readers must surely question how these malfunctioning and troubled kids can write so well. In A. M. Jenkins's *Out of Order,* Colt, who is a star baseball player, tells the story of his senior year in high school. The story is beautifully written, but Colt's main problem is that he has little interest and little aptitude for academics. Readers have to enter into a willing suspension of disbelief when they compare the pitiful essay he wrote for his English class with the rest of the beautifully written book.

What Are the Problems?

The best authors treat candidly and with respect problems that belong specifically to young adults in today's world. Many of the problems that go along with modern adolescence did not exist in the nineteenth century, so of course they were not written about. At least in this one area, there is ample justification for books directed specifically to a youthful audience because there is a difference in the kinds of real-

life problems that concern children, teenagers, and adults. If authors have a teaching goal when they are creating problem novels, it is to help young readers develop an internal locus of control through which they assume that their own actions and characteristics will shape their lives. They ask the question, "What am I going to do with my life?" while people with an external locus of control depend on luck, chance, or what others do. Their major life question is "What will happen to me?"

Although we all know adults who blame others for whatever happens to them and take little responsibility for making their own decisions, most of us would agree that we want to help young people feel responsible for their own lives. Books cannot substitute for real-life experiences, and one or two books, no matter how well written, are not enough to change a teenager's view of life. Skilled authors, however, can show what is going on in characters' minds, whereas cameras can show only what is externally visible. The title of Laurie Halse Anderson's *Catalyst* hints at the idea that what happens from outside can trigger changes, but the changes actually come from within. It is the story of Kate Malone, who through her minister father becomes involved with Terri, a classmate who seems to have been touched by all the problems of the world including incest, pregnancy, abuse, and mental illness. Kate is on the track team and the honor roll, and when the book opens her main concern is whether she will be admitted to MIT, the only college she has applied to. Anderson's thought-provoking character study shows how experiences can trigger changes, but it is Kate who is responsible for the growth that allows those changes.

Other examples include Janet McDonald's *Spellbound,* in which a teenage mother who lives in the projects decides to turn her life around by studying for a spelling bee and getting in line for a program that might lead to a college scholarship. Ruth White's *Tadpole* is set in Appalachia in the 1950s. It is the story of a 13-year-old orphan and the effect he has on his four cousins and their mother when he seeks them out as a refuge from an uncle who beats him and uses him as free labor. Sometimes, in spite of all the protagonist does, help is still needed, as in Kimberly Willis Holt's *Keeper of the Night.* When 13-year-old Isabel's mother commits suicide, Isabel struggles to care for her 7-year-old sister and her 12-year-old brother. This story is set in Guam and the father of the family spends long hours on his fishing boat. The family gets help only after the brother collapses.

Peer Groups

Peer groups become increasingly important to teenagers as they move beyond social and emotional dependence on their parents. By becoming part of a group, clique, or gang, teenagers take a step toward emotional independence. Even though they are not making truly independent decisions, as parts of different groups they try out various roles, ranging from conformist to nonconformist and from follower to leader.

All teenagers do not automatically find groups to belong to, and even if they do, they are still curious about other groups. This is where young adult literature comes in. It extends the peer group, giving teenagers a chance to participate vicariously in many more personal relationships than are possible for most youngsters in the relatively short time that they spend in high school. When they were children, making friends was a simple matter of playing with whoever happened to be nearby. Parents were responsible for locating in the "right" neighborhood near "good schools," so that children had no reason to give particular thoughts to differences in social and economic classes or ethnic backgrounds. Then quite suddenly their environments are expanded not only through larger, more diverse schools but also through jobs, extracurricular activities, public entertainment, shopping in malls, and church or community activities.

While high school students have always known that some of their fellow students were truly scary, the Columbine tragedy forced adults to pay attention to a problem that many of us had preferred to ignore. Tackling the problem in 1974 of school bullies and peer pressure was what made Robert Cormier's *The Chocolate War* so unusual for its time. To save space in this text, we have moved our fuller discussion of that book as an example of tragedy to our website (www.ablongman.com/donelson7e), but we hope you will read the book and think about its subtle revelations. When Cormier was asked at a meeting of English teachers about the changing nature of school violence now that kids were bringing guns to school, he sadly admitted that he was as troubled as everyone else. However, one of the teachers in the group pointed out that it is actually the beginnings of the alienation and the hostility that are the most interesting. The simplest of video games can show people getting shot, but it takes great literature to help people understand the intensity of the emotions that might trigger such actions as well as to understand the emotional fallout on victims' families and friends.

Today, virtually everyone is aware that tough kids, mean kids, frightened kids, and plain old nutty kids are "out there," but we are still unsure about what to do. The increased awareness of the problem and the formation of school policies and procedures to deal with incidents may help, but what Michael Cart says, in his book *Necessary Noise,* is needed is something that will help "kids who are living outside the mainstream in radically nontraditional families deal with their circumstances—

circumstances that often result in their being marginalized, rendered invisible, regarded as unacceptably different, or even being persecuted by peers." And equally important is something that will help "mainstream kids begin to comprehend—intellectually and emotionally—the dramatic differences that now define the daily lives of so many *other* teens? Kids need to learn empathy. They need to learn how the *other* can become *us*."[7] One approach, he thinks, "is through reading fiction that captures—artfully, authentically, and unsparingly—the circumstances of kids" whose lives are different. See Focus Box 4.3, Buddies and Bullies, for books whose authors are trying to do this.

Family Relationships

Cart wrote the paragraph just quoted as a partial explanation of why he asked leading YA authors to contribute stories showing how they interpreted *family* "whether light or dark . . . whole or fractured, functional or dysfunctional, traditional or in radical transition." His beautifully stated goal was to illustrate "the abiding importance of dialogue, of discussion, of talking about our circumstances, of leaving room, in short, for some necessary noise."[8] He went on to comment on all the changes in "family" that have come about since he grew up in the 1950s' world of *Ozzie and Harriet, Father Knows Best,* and *Leave It to Beaver.* Well into the 1970s, 45 percent of American households were headed by a husband and a wife living together with their offspring. Today that is true for only 24 percent of U.S. households. Some of the reasons for this massive change in a relatively short time include changing attitudes toward same-sex parents, less restrictive rules on who can be foster parents, and new immigration patterns that have resulted in many partial families or people with different ideas of "family" coming to the United States.

A look at mythology, folklore, and classical and religious literature shows that the subject of family relationships is not what is new about the problem novel. Stories featuring inadequate or absent parents appeal to young readers because they provide opportunities for the protagonists to assert their independence and prove that they can take care of themselves. Nevertheless, in real life, most kids want to be closer to their parents than they are. A news story in July 2003 reported that 75 percent of the nearly 1,500 teenagers contacted in a national survey really liked their parents and wanted to have more to do with them. Still, in most young adult novels, good relationships between teenagers and their parents are the exception. If they are there, the focus is more likely to be on one than on both parents as in Virginia Euwer Wolff's *Make Lemonade* and *True Believer,* in which LaVaugn's mother is a pillar of common sense. In Paul Fleischman's *Seek* (see Author Box on p. 114), Rob puts tremendous importance on the family he has grown up in while still wanting to find the father he has never known. In Carolyn Coman's *Many Stones,* Berry's father is wise and generous as he plans a trip to help both himself and Berry come to terms with the death of older daughter/sister Laura.

Of course, with the problem novel, just as with today's news stories, the focus is going to be on the more dramatic stories about family relationships as in Will Weaver's *Claws.* The story starts with a description of the "perfect" life of Jed Berg, the top player on the school's tennis team. He has a popular girlfriend and is an honors student and the son of adoring and successful parents. His father is an architect and his mother an

Big Mouth and Ugly Girl by Joyce Carol Oates. HarperCollins, 2002. Popular Matt Donaghy says something in the school cafeteria that is interpreted as a threat to school safety. He is ostracized, except by Ugly Girl Ursula Riggs, who knows a thing or two about being on the outside.

The Brimstone Journals by Ron Koertge. Candlewick, 2001. Fifteen students at Branston (aka Brimstone) High reveal themselves and their problems through poetic journal entries. Their problems cover the waterfront, but angry Boyd is the most frightening because he has already made a mental hit-list of students to "get even" with.

Buddha Boy by Kathe Koja. Farrar Straus Giroux, 2003. This book would be way too grim if not for the friendship that develops between Justin and the very different Jinsen, the Buddha Boy of the title, who is victimized by most kids at school.

Fat Kid Rules the World by K. L. Going. Putnam, 2003. Troy Billings weighs nearly 300 pounds and is contemplating jumping off a subway platform. To his surprise, he is stopped by a punk-rock guitarist, and occasional fellow student, from W. T. Watson High School. And so begins a strange friendship.

Friction by E. R. Frank. Simon & Schuster, 2003. Stacy enters the eighth grade at Forest Alternative school and disproves the stereotype that it is always the newcomer who gets bullied. She also demonstrates that bullying can be done through words as well as actions.

Racing the Past by Sis Deans. Holt, 2001. To avoid being picked on by a school-bus bully, 11-year-old Ricky starts walking, and then jogging, and finally running to school. He manages to make a success story out of what could have been a downward slide into the apathy and hopelessness of his alcoholic father.

Rat by Jan Cheripko. Boyds Mills Press, 2002. Fifteen-year-old Jeremy Chandler was called Rat (short for gym rat) because he spent so much time hanging around the gym. He was the basketball team's manager, and for a kid with one useless arm (a birth defect) was a pretty good player himself. His nickname takes on a whole new meaning when he testifies against their popular coach, who molested a cheerleader.

Scorpions by Walter Dean Myers. HarperCollins, 1988. Jamal's brother is in jail, and an old gang leader brings word to Jamal that is to take over as leader of the Scorpions. He also brings Jamal a gun.

Target by Kathleen Jeffrie Johnson. Roaring Brook, 2003. Sixteen-year-old Grady, who has been raped by two men, goes to a new school and with the help of two new friends struggles to view himself as something other than a victim.

Touching Spirit Bear by Ben Mikaelsen. HarperCollins, 2001. Cole Matthews is a street-wise bully who permanently damages a classmate in a beating. He chooses to participate in Circle Justice, an alternative program for Native American offenders because he mistakenly thinks he can outsmart the system.

The Tulip Touch by Anne Fine. Little, Brown, 1997. As Natalie looks back on the intense relationship she shared over the years with a classmate named Tulip, she gains important insights about friendship, accountability, and manipulation.

Who the Man by Chris Lynch. HarperCollins, 2002. An alternate title might be "A Week in the Life of a 13-Year-Old Bully." Lynch does an excellent job of characterization, and by the end even Earl (the 13-year-old bully) has a bit more understanding of what drives him.

The Young Man and the Sea by Rodman Philbrick. Scholastic, 2004. Thankfully, Philbrick's takeoff has a happier ending than the one in Hemingway's classic novelette. But on the way to his success, 12-year-old Skiff not only has to contend with the death of his mother and a father who drowns his depression in beer, but also harassment from the local rich kid.

attorney. Then Jed receives an email from a girl asking Jed to confront his father about the affair he is having with the girl's mother. This is the beginning of what is caustically described as the fun of watching a preppie "in a downward spiral." See Focus Box 4.4, Family Ties, for other examples that prove the old saying that troubled families are all dysfunctional in their own ways.

Living in a Multicultural World

Kids are probably more aware than are their parents of the changing demographics already mentioned in relation to family structures. During the 1970s when the parents of today's teenagers were in school, 4.7 percent of Americans were foreign born. In 1990 the figure was 8.6 percent, while in 2040 it is predicted to be 14.2 percent.[9] Today's immigrants are primarily Asian or Hispanic, with increasing numbers coming from the Middle East. By the year 2020, the fastest-growing segment of the population will be the very old—those over age 80. Marriage is being postponed or not even considered, and over 25 percent of new births are occurring outside of marriage. The population is being divided into extremes with the middle class shrinking and the numbers growing for those in "permanent" poverty and "permanent" affluence. This is especially true for African Americans with many being well-educated professionals whose lives are in sharp contrast with large numbers living under conditions as painful as anything known since the days of slavery.[10]

Many people find these changes threatening. One result has been an increase in incidents of racism on high school and college campuses. While those are the incidents that grab public attention, there have also been many incidents showing the development of friendship and understanding across cultural and ethnic lines. See Focus Box 4.5, Relating across Cultures. These are powerful books because the stories take place at the edges of groups where young people are brushing up against values and practices different from their own.

Among the most critically acclaimed books of the 1960s and early 1970s were Eldridge Cleaver's *Soul on Ice,* William H. Armstrong's *Sounder,* Maya Angelou's *I Know Why the Caged Bird Sings,* Sharon Bell Mathis's *A Teacup Full of Roses,* Alice Childress's *A Hero Ain't Nothin' But a Sandwich,* and Rosa Guy's *The Friends.* As powerful as these books were, they had a grimness to them, and it is refreshing today to have them supplemented by books in which a variety of characters from different backgrounds face problems by working together.

It is expecting too much from any one book to think that its reading will change a bigoted bully into a sensitive and loving individual. However, for the majority of young readers such books can serve as conversation starters and as ways to focus needed attention on the matter of hostility related to racial, ethnic, and class differences. It is a good thing that some authors prefer to focus on the similarities among all people rather than on differences between particular groups. For example, African American author Lorenz Graham is quoted in Anne Commire's *Something About the Author* as saying:

> My personal problem with publishers has been the difference between my image and theirs. Publishers have told me that my characters, African and Negro, are "too much like white people." And I say, "If you look closely, you will see that people are people."[11]

Blind Sighted by Peter Moore. Viking, 2002. The title comes from 16-year-old Kirk's involuntary job of reading to a blind woman. Kirk narrates this story of three very different friendships that help him get through the year in which his alcoholic mother decides it is time for her to get her life together.

Comfort by Carolee Dean. Houghton, 2002. Comfort is the name of the town, not the emotions, in this coming-of-age story about a boy whose mother forces him to lie about his age so he can drive his father to AA meetings when he comes home from the penitentiary.

Dirty Laundry: Stories about Family Secrets, edited by Lisa Rowe Fraustino. Viking, 1998. Among the eleven YA writers who have contributed stories to this collection are Bruce Coville, Chris Crutcher, Richard Peck, Rita Williams-Garcia, and M. E. Kerr. Just as in readers' own families, there are both light-hearted and serious secrets that inspire comparisons and pondering over why particular things are kept secret.

The First Part Last by Angela Johnson. Simon & Schuster, 2003. In this beautifully written story, which won the Printz Award, 16-year-old Bobby is trying to raise his infant daughter. The baby's mother is in an irreversible coma and Bobby is left to cope with this dramatic new addition to his life.

In Spite of Killer Bees by Julie Johnston. Tundra, 2001. The lives of three sisters, age 22, 17, and 14, are suddenly thrown into what many people would think was a dream-come-true. A grandfather they've never met dies and leaves them a fortune, but with strings attached.

Lord of the Deep by Graham Salisbury. Delacorte, 2001. Thirteen-year-old Mikey Donovan helps his stepdad charter his boat to Hawaiian tourists for deep-sea fishing. Mikey feels betrayed when his father lets a customer claim a record he did not really earn. Thoughtful readers will recognize the situation as more complex than Mikey realizes.

Miracle's Boys by Jacqueline Woodson. Putnam, 2000. Two orphaned brothers are holding on as they manage their individual grief; then a third brother is released from a three-year term at a detention center. The boys have to start over in building a tenuous new relationship.

Of Sound Mind by Jean Ferris. Farrar Straus Giroux, 2001. In a family of four, Theo is the only "hearie," which means his main role in the family is translator. Then he meets Ivy and begins to question whether interpreting is to be his lifelong occupation.

Pool Boy by Michael Simmons. Millbrook/Roaring Brook, 2003. Fifteen-year-old Brett has a major lifestyle change when his father is convicted of white-collar crime, and Brett and his mother and sister have to leave their posh neighborhood and move in with a great-aunt. Brett takes a job cleaning swimming pools in his old neighborhood, hence the nickname.

The Same Stuff as Stars by Katherine Paterson. Clarion, 2002. Angel is abandoned, not once but several times, by a father who is in jail and a mother who is drunk and unreliable. It is up to an uncle, himself terribly damaged by life, to convince her of her self-worth through the metaphorical lesson that she is made from "the same stuff as the stars."

Jamake Highwater expresses a counterbalancing view:

In the process of trying to unify the world we must be exceedingly careful not to destroy the diversity of the many cultures of man that give human life meaning, focus, and vitality. . . . Today we are beginning to look into the ideas of groups outside the dominant culture, and we are finding different kinds of "truth" that make the world we

A Publisher's Weekly *reviewer complimented Pam Muñoz Ryan's* Esperanza Rising *by noting that only at the end of the story do readers recognize how carefully* "Abuelita's pearls of wisdom have been strung."

live in far bigger than we ever dreamed it could be—for the greatest distance between people is not geographical space but culture.[12]

Teachers, librarians, and reviewers should not present and discuss any single book as if it represents *the* African American point of view or *the* Asian-American point of view. Adults need to help young readers realize that there are many points of view. This concept is further discussed in Chapter 10, along with the increased willingness of today's teenagers to read about protagonists in countries other than the United States.

The Physical Body

Among the books listed in Focus Box 4.2, Challenges: Physical and Mental, are several relating to sex, but we do not wish to imply that we consider the whole matter of sex to be a problem. We realize that sex also has something to do with the books in Focus Box 4.8, Love and Friendship. In trying to satisfy their curiosity, teenagers seek out and read vivid descriptions of sexual activities, as hinted by the boy who in the Chapter 3 survey said that his reading was for the purpose of "learning about and talking about girls."

Bat 6 by Virginia Euwer Wolff. Scholastic, 1998. World War II has been over for nearly four years, but pockets of prejudice are very much alive in the towns of Barlow and Bear Creek Ridge in rural Oregon. People choose not to notice until the prejudice erupts during the annual Bat 6 girls' softball championship.

The Beast by Walter Dean Myers. Scholastic, 2003. Myers tells two stories—one about Anthony "Spoon" Witherspoon and his leaving Harlem to attend a prep school in Connecticut and the other about his girl-friend, Gabi, who while Spoon is gone loses her foothold on the road of life.

Born Blue by Han Nolan. Harcourt, 2001. Blue-eyed and blonde Janie is abandoned by her heroin-addicted mother. Her one friend is an African American boy who has a set of blues tapes that he and Janie listen to so often and so deeply that Janie decides she is African American.

Born Confused by Tanuja Desai Hidier. Scholastic, 2003. A summer of growing up has some interesting new angles when the protagonist is an Indian American.

Boy Meets Boy by David Levithan. Random, 2003. In the idealized world of this interesting book, all prejudice based on sexual preferences has disappeared.

The Brave by Robert Lipsyte. HarperCollins, 1991. Sonny Bear, an up-and-coming young boxer, leaves the Moscondaga reservation and ends up in Harlem where, fortunately, not all the people he meets are as devious as his self-appointed welcoming committee.

The Cay (Doubleday 1969) and **Timothy of the Cay** (Harcourt, 1993) by Theodore Taylor. A 15-year-old white boy, Philip, and an elderly black man, Timothy, are the only survivors from a shipwreck. They are on an island and Philip, who is blind, must overcome his aversion to blacks before he can accept Timothy's help.

Children of the River by Linda Crew. Delacorte, 1989. Crew's story is about 17-year-old Sundara's life in Oregon after fleeing the Khmer Rouge in Cambodia.

The Circuit: Stories from the Life of a Migrant Child by Francisco Jimenez. University of New Mexico Press, 1997. Even though this collection of auto-biographical stories was published by a university press, which meant it received only limited publicity, within several years it was in its fifth printing.

Esperanza Rising by Pam Muñoz Ryan. Scholastic, 2000. Ryan's engaging novel about how her Mexican family became Americans is both joyous and lyrical. A *Publisher's Weekly* reviewer noted that only by the end of the story do readers recognize how carefully "Abuelita's pearls of wisdom" have been strung.

Jubilee Journey by Carolyn Meyer. Harcourt Brace, 1997. Going on a family trip from Connecticut to a small town in Texas proves to be educational for 13-year-old Emily Rose Chartier, who learns about both racism and her family.

Seedfolks by Paul Fleischman. HarperCollins, 1997. Fleischman traces the sprouting of the Bigg Street community garden in inner city Cleveland through the voices of thirteen young and old neighbors—Mexican, Haitian, Black, Vietnamese, Korean, British, Guatemalan, Rumanian, Indian, and Polish.

Unseen Companions by Denise Orenstein. HarperCollins, 2003. The setting is 1969 in the Alaskan bush. Four teenagers, connected only by having crossed paths with an abused boy, tell their separate stories, which reveal some disturbing facts about humankind.

When the Legends Die by Hal Borland. Harper-Collins, 1963. In one of the first books about a young adult growing up in two cultures, Borland tells about a Ute boy raised by whites after the death of his parents. A 1972 movie starring Richard Widmark and Fredric Forrest was well received.

Zack by William Bell. Simon & Schuster, 1999. It is Zack's senior year in high school and his family (a black mother and a white father) move from the city of Toronto to a small town where, for the first time, Zack stands out because of his color.

In the first edition of this textbook, we wrote that the three sexual issues treated in problem novels were rape, pregnancy, and homosexuality. We stand corrected by a reader who recently wrote to us and made the persuasive point that the problem is *homophobia,* rather than *homosexuality.* In addition to these concerns, we now see problem novels treating disease, incest, and child abuse, and, in a big change, we also see teen protagonists being written about as parents. In the earlier books, pregnant girls had an abortion as in Paul Zindel's *My Darling, My Hamburger;* the baby died as in Ann Head's *Mr. and Mrs. Bo Jo Jones;* or the baby was given up for adoption as in Richard Peck's *Don't Look and It Won't Hurt.* In today's books the babies actually appear as in the highly acclaimed *Make Lemonade* by Virginia Euwer Wolff, *Gypsy Davey* by Chris Lynch, and *Like Sisters on the Home Front* by Rita Williams-Garcia. In *Hanging on to Max* by Margaret Bechard, 17-year-old Sam is a single parent struggling to keep his infant son. An *SLJ* reviewer praised the book because "In a world where much of YA literature is fraught with *noir* plots peopled with dysfunctional characters caught in tragic situations, *Hanging on to Max* is a breath of fresh air."[13] It is a book "peopled with human beings all struggling to make their lives work." One of these people is Sam's father who agrees to support Sam and Max for one year if Sam will stay in high school and graduate.

The reason we refer to the problems that are the topics of the books in Focus Box 4.2 as both physical and mental is that the two usually go together. A few years ago when Paul Zindel was speaking in Arizona, he commented on the fact that next to *The Pigman,* his most popular book was *My Darling, My Hamburger,* which is about pregnancy and abortion. Soon after the book was published in 1969, a Supreme Court decision made most abortions legal, and Zindel thought that would be the end of all sales because his book would seem terribly old-fashioned. It did not turn out that way, however, because rather than settling the issue, the legalization of abortions increased interest in the moral and psychological aspects of the problem. Decision making was passed from the courts to every woman with an unwanted pregnancy. It is not only the woman herself who is involved, but also the father, the grandparents, and the friends.

In any area of life, it is hardly possible for someone to have a severe physical problem without also having an accompanying emotional problem. A vivid example is Priscilla Cumming's *A Face First.* It tells the story of 12-year-old Kelley waking up from her affluent and "beautiful people" world in a Baltimore hospital's burn unit. She has been in a horrific automobile accident and fire, and experts are working to peel off the skin that melted, along with her earrings. Even worse than the pain and the physical therapy is the day when a clear mask is strapped onto her ruined face. In shock and depression, she ceases all human communication. But finally, she starts her long road to emotional recovery when she empathizes with a crying baby who is brought into the burn unit.

More Optimistic Novels

In one sense, all novels are problem stories because the problems provide the tension and the interest; without a problem there would be no plot. The difference in the books we will mention in this section is that the problems are not as grave as are the

Beardance by Will Hobbs. Atheneum/ Simon & Schuster, 1993. Cloyd is a young Native American who risks his own life to guarantee the survival of the last grizzly bears found in the Rocky Mountains.

Bill by Chap Reaver. Delacorte, 1994. The only companion that Jess Gates, the motherless daughter of a moonshiner, has is her loyal dog Bill. When her father is sent to jail, Jess and Bill have to decide where to put their trust.

Brian's Hunt by Gary Paulsen. Random House, 2003. In an afterword, Paulsen admits that he said he wasn't going to write any more books about Brian, the character in *Hatchet* who survived a plane crash in the North Woods. But Brian has become "real" to so many readers that Paulsen changed his mind. In this book, Brian is hunting a bear, but if not for the help of his companion dog, Brian would have been the prey instead of the hunter.

Bull Rider by Marilyn Halvorson. Orca Soundings, 2003. Sixteen-year-old Layne sneaks out to ride rodeo bulls even though his father was killed in a national championship. After Layne comes close to getting seriously injured, his grandfather agrees to help him develop the skills he needs.

California Blue by David Klass. Scholastic, 1994. John discovers a new subspecies of butterfly in one of the old forests of California. He finds himself in conflict with his family and neighbors who work in the lumber business and do not want interference from environmentalists.

Call of the Wild by Jack London. Macmillan, 1903. This coming-of-age classic is set in the excitement of the Alaskan gold rush where both dogs and men were severely tested.

Every Living Thing by Cynthia Rylant. Bradbury, 1985. In these twelve short stories, people's lives are changed by their relationships with animals.

The First Horse I See by Sally M. Keehn. Philomel, 1999. There are no happily-ever-after guarantees in this book, but both humans and horses make progress when Willojean's grandfather lets her choose a horse.

Halsey's Pride by Lynn Hall. Atheneum/Simon & Schuster, 1990. Lynn Hall is a dog lover who wrote this story about a girl coming to live with her father and his prize-winning dog and learning to cope with her imperfections and life in general.

Mariposa Blues by Ron Koertge. Avon/Flare, 1993. Graham's dad is a horse trainer, but Graham decides to make his own decision about when a special horse is ready for competition.

The Music of Dolphins by Karen Hesse. Scholastic, 1996. Hesse has written an intriguing story for middle-schoolers about a girl who has been raised by dolphins after surviving an airplane crash.

Sniper by Theodore Taylor. Harcourt Brace Jovanovich, 1989. When Ben's parents go on a trip, they leave him in charge of their wild animal preserve, never dreaming of the challenges he will face.

A Solitary Blue by Cynthia Voigt. Atheneum, 1983. Jeff Greene, whose mother has left him and his father, feels as alone in the world as a beautiful blue heron that he observes in a Carolina marsh.

Straydog by Kathe Koja. Farrar Straus Giroux, 2002. This novel is told through the voice of Rachel, a smart and angry loner who identifies with a fierce, wild dog brought into the animal shelter where Rachel volunteers.

Taming the Star Runner by S. E. Hinton. Delacorte, 1988. Fifteen-year-old Travis moves from a detention center to his uncle's horse ranch, where everyone hopes he will be rehabilitated.

Under a Different Sky by Deborah Savage. Houghton Mifflin, 1997. Ben Stahler, who dreams of riding his horse in the Olympics, helps take care of horses belonging to the wealthy girls at a nearby boarding school. Other well-written animal stories by Savage include *To Race a Dream* (1994) and *A Rumour of Otters* (1986), both Houghton Mifflin.

ones described earlier, and there is some force or some individual in the story who helps the young person through the experience. Authors frequently use nature or animals as the helper or the catalyst. Many children come to high school already familiar with such stories as Francis Hodgson Burnett's *The Secret Garden* and Kenneth Grahame's *The Wind in the Willows.* Animals play major roles in Allan Eckert's *Incident at Hawk's Hill,* Fred Gipson's *Old Yeller,* Sterling North's *Rascal,* Marjorie Rawlings's *The Yearling,* and Wilson Rawls's *Where the Red Fern Grows.* In many such stories, the animals are sacrificed as a symbol of the loss the young person undergoes in exchange for wisdom. Gordon Korman makes fun of this literary custom in his *No More Dead Dogs,* written for middle school readers, but fortunately some animals in stories live long, happy lives, providing companionship and even inspiration to the humans with whom they share the planet (see Focus Box 4.6, Accomplishment Romances Involving Animals).

A different kind of story is the one in which a young person is helped through a religious experience, as in Cynthia Rylant's *A Fine White Dust.* The book's title comes from the chalklike dust that gets on Pete's fingers when he handles the "little bitty pieces of broken ceramic" that used to be a cross he had painted in Vacation Bible School—back before he got so old that it was not cool to go any more. His best friend is a confirmed atheist, and he has "half-washed Christians for parents." Nevertheless, the summer that Preacher Man comes to town, "something religious" begins itching Pete, something that going to church could not cure.

Rylant's skill in developing Pete's character and revealing the depths of his emotions when he is saved and wooed and then betrayed by the Preacher Man won for her a well-deserved Newbery Honor Award. The twelve short chapters are almost an outline for a traditional quest story beginning with "Dust" and a sense of ennui, moving through "The Joy," "The Wait," and "Hell," and ending with "The Light" and "Amen." In the end, Pete decides that, "The Preacher Man is behind me. But God is still right there, in front."

Books that unabashedly explore religious themes are relatively rare, partly because schools and libraries fear mixing church and state through spending tax dollars for religious books. Also, mainstream publishers fear cutting into potential sales by printing books with protagonists whose religious beliefs may offend some readers and make others uncomfortable. It has been easier for schools to include religious books with historical settings, such as Lloyd Douglas's *The Robe,* Scott O'Dell's *The Hawk That Dare Not Hunt by Day,* Elizabeth George Speare's *The Bronze Bow,* and Jessamyn West's *Friendly Persuasion.* Accepted also are books with contemporary settings that have proved themselves with adult readers—for example, Margaret Craven's *I Heard the Owl Call My Name,* Catherine Marshall's *A Man Called Peter,* and William Barrett's *Lilies of the Field.* In lamenting the shortage of young adult books treating religious themes, author Dean Hughes wrote:

> We need to be careful that, in effect, we do not say to young people that they should be most concerned about pimples and clothes and dates and football games—or even sex. Part of being human is addressing oneself to questions about justice, creation, morality, and the existence of divinity.[14]

Patty Campbell made a similar point when she wrote that although nearly 60 percent of Americans attend some type of religious services, young adult fiction presents a world almost devoid of either personal or corporate religious practices. "Where," she asks, "are the church youth groups, the Hebrew or confirmation classes, the Bible study meetings that are so much a part of middle-class teenage American life? Where, too, is the mainstream liberal Protestant or Catholic practice and sensibility?" Practically the only religious characters developed in young adult books are villains who are "presented as despicable in direct proportion to the degree of their religious involvement."[15]

Examples of the "despicable" characters she was thinking about include the fanatical and unbending parents who make life miserable for their kids in Suzanne Newton's *I Will Call It Georgie's Blues;* Norma Howe's *God, The Universe, and Hot Fudge Sundaes;* and Kathryn Lasky's *Memoirs of a Bookbat.* In Stephanie Tolan's *A Good Courage,* Tie-Dye's hippie mother ends up in a religious commune that forces Tie-Dye to take control of his own future, whereas in M. E. Kerr's *Is That You, Miss Blue?* the hypocritical attitudes of the faculty members at a religious school inspire the students to come to the aid of a teacher who is fired because she "believes." In Bette Greene's *The Drowning of Stephan Jones,* homophobic ministers are at the heart of the evil treatment of two gay men, while in Lois Ruby's *Miriam's Well,* religious leaders do not let Miriam receive medical help. Jane Yolen and Bruce Coville's *Armageddon Summer* is not only about religion gone awry but also about love and survival. Marina and Jed are two teenagers caught up among the 144 "True Believers" chosen by Reverend Beelson to wait with him in an armed camp for the end of the world, predicted to occur on July 27, 2000.

In many ways, the negative portrayal of religion in books for teenagers is similar to the negative portrayal of parents and other authority figures. Such presentations serve as a foil to make the good qualities of the young protagonists shine all the brighter. Authors rely on the general assumption that religious people are good to provide contrast, as when the evil in Robert Cormier's *The Chocolate War* is all the heavier because of the book's setting in a religious school.

Another reason that books for teenagers appear to have so many religious characters portrayed in a negative light is that the good characters go unnoticed. For example, in M. E. Kerr's *Little Little* one of Little Little's suitors is a dishonest evangelical preacher. When Kerr was criticized for this negative portrayal, she pointed out that Little Little's grandfather—the only person in the whole book who approached Little Little's dwarfism with common sense—was also a minister, but few readers noticed because he did his work in the manner expected from a competent clergyman in a mainstream church. Although there are some good books focusing on broad religious themes and questions about whether there is a God and an afterlife (e.g., Aidan Chambers's *NIK: Now I Know,* Iris Rosofsky's *Miriam,* and Phyllis Reynolds Naylor's *A String of Chances*), what is more common is for an author to bring in religion as a small part of a bigger story. In Jim Naughton's *My Brother Stealing Second,* Bobby reminisces about his family's church experiences before his brother was killed, and in Sue Ellen Bridgers's *Permanent Connections,* Rob finds comfort by visiting a little country church. Katherine Paterson, who has attended theological school and served as a missionary in China, includes both implicit and explicit religious references in her books, most directly in *Jacob Have I Loved* and *Bridge to Terabithia.* Her 1999 *Preacher's Boy* is set in rural

Vermont between May 1899 and January 1900. The excitement of a new century is part of the story, but this excitement includes worries about Darwin's theory of evolution and what is predicted to be the end of the world.

Madeleine L'Engle is devout, and along with some other writers of fantasy and science fiction, she includes religious overtones in her books; for example, the struggle between good and evil in *A Wrinkle in Time* and Vicky's hard-won acceptance of her grandfather's dying of leukemia in *A Ring of Endless Light*. Other books that include casual references to religious people and beliefs are Alice Childress's *Rainbow Jordan*, J. D. Salinger's *Franny & Zooey: Two Novellas*, Mary Stolz's *Land's End*, and Jill Paton-Walsh's *Unleaving*. Chaim Potok's *The Chosen, My Name Is Asher Lev*, and *In the Beginning* show what it is to come of age in a Hasidic Jewish community. Cynthia Voigt's *David and Jonathan* asks questions about religious and cultural differences; Marc Talbert's *A Sunburned Prayer* is about 11-year-old Eloy making a seventeen-mile pilgrimage on Good Friday to pray for his grandmother who is dying of cancer.

Of course, religious publishing houses provide books focusing on religious themes, but these are seldom useful in schools because they are aimed so directly at believers of a particular faith, and sometimes in their zeal to convert potential believers, the authors write polemics against other groups. Nevertheless, teachers and librarians are advised to visit local religious bookstores to see what is offered because some students may prefer to fill their independent reading assignments with books from these sources. Today's religious books range from biblical and western romances and adventures to self-help books and inspirational biographies. People who haven't taken a look at religious books over the past few years will probably be surprised at the slick covers and the upscale marketing techniques.

An especially troublesome group of books about religion are the books in which a misguided life is set right by an end-of-the-book conversion. Teachers hesitate to discuss the credibility of such stories because they fear that in the process of building up literary sophistication, they may be tearing down religious faith. Nevertheless, teachers and librarians need to seek out and support those authors and publishers who treat religious motifs with honesty as well as with respect for literary quality. They also must help parents and other critics realize that strong religious feelings, including doubts, are part of the maturation process and that reading about the doubts that others have or about imperfections in organized religion does not necessarily destroy one's own faith.

Kathleen Beck, a young adult librarian in Colorado, wrote an article for *VOYA* in which she recommended "Young Adult Fiction for Questioning Christians."[16] Her article was responding to the comment of one of the members of her ecumenical congregation who had observed about the teen members, "They don't know all the answers, but they sure know all the questions." Among the books she recommended that we have not already mentioned were Bruce Brooks's *Asylum for Nightface* in which a boy develops his own religious faith based on the orderliness of the world and in spite of his "self-indulgent, yuppy parents"; Cynthia Voigt's *Tree by Leaf* in which teenager Clothilde gets help in coming to terms with the wounds her father received fighting in World War I; Neal Shusterman's *What Daddy Did* in which a boy begins to understand the complexities of forgiveness when he goes to live with his grandparents after his father has killed his mother; and Gary Schmidt's *The Sin Eater* in which a boy is aided in understanding his father's suicide by the members of the Albion Grace Church of the

Holy Open Bible, "whose theology is strict but who know the meaning of grace and compassion." In Han Nolan's *Send Me Down a Miracle,* M. E. Kerr's *What I Really Think of You,* and Gary Paulsen's *The Tent,* young people look questioningly at their parents' careers as evangelical preachers.

The Romantic Quest

The archetypal story of The Journey or The Quest has already been mentioned in Chapter 3. Also see Chapter 8, pp. 247, for a discussion of how this archetype relates to the experience of young American soldiers in Vietnam. These stories are especially appealing to young readers because many romantic symbols relate to youthfulness and hope, and many of the protagonists in traditional and classic tales are in their teens. They have reached the age at which they leave home or anticipate leaving to embark on

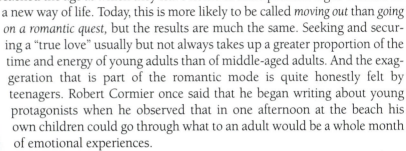

a new way of life. Today, this is more likely to be called *moving out* than *going on a romantic quest,* but the results are much the same. Seeking and securing a "true love" usually but not always takes up a greater proportion of the time and energy of young adults than of middle-aged adults. And the exaggeration that is part of the romantic mode is quite honestly felt by teenagers. Robert Cormier once said that he began writing about young protagonists when he observed that in one afternoon at the beach his own children could go through what to an adult would be a whole month of emotional experiences.

A distinguishing feature of such romances is the happy ending, achieved only after the hero's worth is proven through a crisis or an ordeal. The suffering nearly always purchases some kind of wisdom, even though wisdom is not what the hero set out to find. Authors like to send young people on trips, not just for the symbolism of a quest, but because the trip provides the protagonists with a new environment, new challenges, and new acquaintances, all of which add interest. More than any other author, Sharon Creech has worked with journeys. For the last edition of this text, she wrote:

> I love the way that each book—any book—is its own journey. You open the book, and off you go. You don't know who you're going to meet along the way, nor where you will go, and when you finish a book, you feel as if you've been on a journey. You are changed in some way—large or small—by having traveled with those characters, by having walked in their moccasins a while, by having seen what they've seen, heard what they've heard, felt what they've felt. These journeys echo all of our daily journeys: not knowing who we will meet today, tomorrow; who will affect our lives in small ways and profound ways; where we will go; what we will feel; what will happen to us?[17]

She went on to say that the journey motive extends to her writing process as well as to the way she builds her plots. In *Walk Two Moons,* which won the Newbery Award, 13-year-old Sal takes a car trip with her grandparents from Ohio to Idaho. This is a gift of genuine love as they help Sal come to terms with the terrible question of what happened to her mother. *The Wanderer* is the name of a 45-foot sailboat in which a contemporary "family" crosses the Atlantic. The chapters alternate between Sophie and her cousin Cody. What lifts *The Wanderer* above a simple adventure tale is the subtle way that Creech develops the mystery of Sophie's past and the reason that her reluctant parents viewed this voyage as one of those things that Sophie "just had to do."

As you read the stories in Focus Box 4.7, Literal Journeys/Figurative Quests, make note of the different ways that creative authors have figured out how to adapt ancient literary customs into modern life. For example, in traditional romances the protagonist usually receives the vision or insight in a "high or isolated place like a mountain top, an island, or a tower."[19] In Hamilton's *M. C. Higgins, the Great,* the boy, M. C., comes to his realization about his family and his role while he contemplates the surrounding countryside from a special bicycle seat affixed to the top of a tall steel pole standing in the yard of his mountain home. The unique pole was given to M. C. by his father as a reward for having swum across the Ohio River. Another characteristic is that the young person is shown to be "special," something that Robert Lipsyte communicated in *The Contender* by starting with Mr. Donatelli, the manager of a boxing gym, listening to the confident sound of young Alfred Books climbing the steps to his gym. Donatelli says he can tell who has what it takes to be a contender (readers are to interpret this as meaning a contender in life as well as in the boxing ring) by how they climb those stairs. Young heroes receive unexpected help as did Jerome in Bruce Brooks's *The Moves Make the Man.* Through a wager on his basketball skills, he won a railroad lantern that he named Spin Light. It enabled him to go to a hidden, lonely court and play basketball after dark, but by the end of the book, readers share Jerome's optimism. Spin Light is enabling him to see more than his way around the basketball court.

The idea of a sacrifice is shown in Jean George's *Julie of the Wolves* when Julie learns that her father still lives and that she has arrived at his village. When she learns that he has married a "gussack" and now pilots planes for hunters, the disillusioned Julie grieves for the wolves and the other hunted animals and vows to return and live on the tundra. However, the temperature falls far below zero and the "ice thundered and boomed, roaring like drumbeats across the Arctic." Despite all that Julie does to save him, Tornait, Julie's golden plover, who has been her faithful companion, dies from the cold. Tornait is the last symbol of Julie's innocence, and as she mourns his death, she comes to accept the fact that the lives of both the wolf and the Inuit are changing, and she points her boots toward her father and the life he now leads.

Success is demonstrated in Chris Crutcher's *The Crazy Horse Electric Game,* in which pitching star Willie Weaver is seriously injured in a water skiing accident. He runs away from home when it appears that he is also losing his girlfriend. At first he is only concerned with surviving, but then he gets involved with other people and attends an alternative school where, with help, he recovers many of his motor skills. He returns home strong enough to cope with all the changes that have occurred.

Some critics fear that when authors use such physical changes as Willie Weaver's almost miraculous recovery as a tangible or metaphorical way to communicate emotional or mental accomplishment, young readers interpret the physical achievement literally rather than figuratively. Teenagers are already overly concerned about their bodies and any defects they might have. Many physical challenges, including the common motif of obesity, cannot be totally overcome, so these critics prefer stories in which the protagonist comes to terms with the problem as does Izzy in Cynthia Voigt's

Chasing Redbird by Sharon Creech. HarperCollins, 1997. Zinny does not travel far, only on an old Appalachian trail that she discovers and works to rebuild. Nevertheless, there's plenty to think about in this story of family relationships and young romance. Other Creech books based on journeys include *Bloomability* (HarperCollins, 1998), *Walk Two Moons* (HarperCollins, 1994), and *The Wanderer* (HarperCollins, 2000).

Dunk by David Lubar. Clarion, 2002. Chad's trip is only to the Boardwalk in a Jersey beach town where he takes a summer job running a dunking tank. He learns some subtle lessons about the difference between using humor to insult and recruit potential customers and using a different kind of humor to help his best friend who is seriously ill.

Ghost Boy by Iain Lawrence. Random House, Delacorte. 2000. It is just after WWII and Harold Kline, a partially orphaned albino, becomes friends with three sideshow performers in a traveling circus. He thinks that joining the circus will solve his problems, and in ways it does, but mainly because of the lessons he learns about the difference between outside appearances and inside beauty.

Gingerbread by Rachel Cohn. Simon & Schuster, 2002. Gingerbread is the rag doll that Cyd's biological father, who was almost a stranger, gave her when she was 5. Now as a teenaged "recovering hellion," she is sent from her San Francisco home to New York City to get acquainted with him and his family.

Grasslands by Debra Seely. Holiday House, 2003. In the 1880s, young Thomas lives in Virginia with the wealthy parents of his deceased mother, but he dreams of moving west to live with his father. When, at age 13, Thomas at last receives an invitation to come and live with his father and his new family, he is shocked at the hard work and the lack of glamour and human warmth.

The Great Turkey Walk by Kathleen Karr. Farrar, Straus & Giroux, 1998. In this wish-fulfilling and lively quest story set in 1860, 15-year-old Simon Green becomes partners with his school teacher to buy 1,000 turkeys in Missouri, hoping to sell them to turkey-starved miners in Denver.

Homeless Bird by Gloria Whelan. HarperCollins, 2000. This winner of the National Book Award is set in India and is about 13-year-old Koly, who through an arranged marriage that turns out badly, is forced on a journey toward making a life for herself.

Hope Was Here by Joan Bauer. Putnam's, 2000. Sixteen-year-old Hope and her Aunt Addie leave New York City for promised jobs in Wisconsin—Addie as a cook and Hope as a waitress. They find their jobs—and much more. *Rules of the Road* (Putnam, 1998) and *Backwater* (Putnam, 1999) are also highly recommended Joan Bauer books.

A Long Way from Chicago (1998) and **A Year Down Yonder** (2000) by Richard Peck. Dial/Penguin Putnam. These books, one of which won the Newbery Award, are set during the Great Depression when Mary Alice is sent to live in rural Illinois with her larger-than-life grandmother.

Many Stones by Carolyn Coman. Front Street, 2000. Berry and her father travel to South Africa to attend a memorial service for Berry's older sister who was killed while working at a church school in Cape Town. The title comes from the stones that Berry places on her chest each night, one at a time, to calm her troubled mind.

Olive's Ocean by Kevin Henkes. Greenwillow, 2003. Martha is getting ready to leave for summer vacation at the beach, when Olive's mother brings her a page from the diary that her daughter had kept before she died. In it, Olive mentions some of the things she wanted, including seeing the ocean and making friends with Martha. Olive ponders Martha's kind words during her seaside vacation.

True Confessions of a Heartless Girl by Martha Brooks. Farrar/Melanie Kroupa Books, 2003. A plot summary would make this book seem grimmer than it is. Brooks's main point is to demonstrate the power of community in the process of healing.

Whirligig by Paul Fleischman (Holt, 1998) is a perfect story to show how a journey provides time for reflection and growth. A boy who in a fit of rage causes an automobile accident that kills a girl sets out on a journey to memorialize her in each "corner" of the United States.

Izzy Willy-Nilly, about a young girl who loses her leg, and the young Native American boy in Anne Eliot Compton's historical *The Sorcerer*. The boy is named Lefthand because he was injured by a bear and cannot hunt. In his tribe, this is a serious problem, because hunting is what the men do. There is no miraculous cure for his disability, but he gains both his own and his tribe's respect when he develops enough skill as an artist to draw the pictures of animals needed for the tribe's hunting rituals.

The acceptance of the compromised dream is an element of the romantic quest that is particularly meaningful to young adults. Many of them are just beginning to achieve some of their lifelong goals, and they are discovering the illusory nature of the end of the rainbow, which is a symbolic way of saying such things as, "When I graduate," "When we get married," "When I'm 18," or "When I have my own apartment." Like the characters in the romances, they are not sorry they have ventured, for they have indeed found something worthwhile, but it is seldom the pot of gold they had imagined.

Stories of Friendship and Love

When people hear the term *romance*, their first thought is probably of a love story, which with young readers probably includes friendship as well as love. This is because in the old romances, which were stories coming from such romance languages as Latin, Italian, Spanish, and especially French, the climax of the story was often the uniting of a young couple. A common motif was for successful adventurers to be rewarded with the love of a beautiful maiden. While few of us have the ability or the wherewithall to go on a grand adventure or to compete and win against incredible odds, most of us can imagine finding a true love. Because of the universality of this wish to love and be loved, this element of adventure stories became the feature that many readers, especially females, came to identify with the term *romance*. The challenge or problem is invariably the successful pairing of a likable young couple. An old definition of the love-romance pattern is, "Boy meets girl, boy loses girl, boy wins girl." But with teenage love, the pattern is often reversed because most of the romances are told from the girls' point of view. She is the one who meets, loses, and finally wins a boy.

The tone of most love romances is lighter than that of the adventure romance. Its power lies in its wish fulfillment, although critics worry that we may be setting young girls up for disappointment when we consistently reward girls who have had a disappointment or who have worked their way through a difficult time with a boyfriend who appears out of nowhere. They also worry about the stories in which an ugly duckling girl is suddenly transformed by the love of a boy into a swan. In her new role as swan, she is not only popular and successful but also happy.

For the writer of a love story, probably no talent is more important than the ability to create believable characters. If readers do not feel that they know the boy and girl or the man and woman as individuals, they cannot identify with them, and consequently will not care whether they make it. Another characteristic of the good love story is that it provides something beyond the simple pairing of two individuals. This something extra may be interesting historical facts, introduction to a social issue, glimpses into the complexity of human nature, or any of the understandings and concepts that might be found in quality books or movies. Stories come to life when an author is able to pick out and present the unexpected details that come from close observation.

Although most formula romances are aimed at a female audience, comparable to the way that most pornography is aimed at a male audience, some writers are trying to write romances that will also be read by boys. The most obvious difference between these boy-oriented romances and the larger body of love stories written from a girl's point of view is that their authors, who are mostly men, tend to put less emphasis on courtship and romance and more on sexuality. Rather than relying on discreet fade-outs, they allow their readers to know what happens, which sometimes means sexual intercourse. For the most part, the descriptions are neither pornographic nor lovingly romantic, but in such books as Chris Crutcher's *Running Loose,* Robert Lehrman's *Juggling,* Terry Davis's *Vision Quest,* and Aidan Chambers's *The Toll Bridge,* there is little doubt about the abundance of sexual feelings that the characters experience.

As an antidote to the lopsidedness of books that are either overly romantic or overly sexy, some adult critics suggest offering books in which boys and girls are as much friends as lovers. This is especially true in lighter books read by 11-, 12-, and 13-year-olds. For examples see Focus Box 5.6, Love and Laughs for Tweeners (p. 166). In friendship stories, and in honest love stories, the romantic relationship is only part of a bigger story. Also, there is no indication of either partner exploiting or manipulating the other, as often happens in exaggerated romances or in pornographic or sex-oriented stories. As a ploy to attract male readers (publishers already feel confident that girls will read romances), authors often tell the story through the boy's eyes or perhaps through chapters that alternate back and forth between the boy and the girl, as Paul Zindel did in *The Pigman* and M. E. Kerr did in *I'll Love You When You're More Like Me.* Zindel once told us that he wrote his books for girls to read, but he always kept in mind the fact that lots of girls recommend books to their boyfriends, and he did not want those girls to be disappointed when their boyfriends didn't like the book. He therefore tried to be honest and to never put in anything that would be an automatic turn-off to boys. If more authors followed his example, we would probably have many more "love stories" that could be appreciated by readers of both sexes. See Focus Box 4.8, "Love and Friendship," for examples of books that offer something extra.

Wish-Fulfilling Stories

The most wish-fulfilling stories for males are most likely to be the sports and adventure stories found in Chapter 6, while for females wish-fulfilling stories are usually about friendship or love. In some ways, friendship books are more appealing to young readers than love stories, at least partly because they are free from the complications of sex. It was the friendships that a decade ago kept many girls reading the *Babysitters Club* and the *Sweet Valley High* series. This past year, in one of our classes, Ann Brashares's *The Sisterhood of the Traveling Pants* soon turned into "The Sisterhood of the Traveling Book." While no males borrowed it, the women passed it from friend to friend, even to roommates not taking the class. When we asked for it back, there was always one more student wanting to read it. The book is a coming-of-age story in four parts. Lena, Tibby, Bridget, and Carmen have been "best friends" ever since their mothers took the same aerobics class for pregnant women. By the time the mothers began drifting apart, the girls were old enough to maintain their own close friendships, and the book opens with their getting ready for the first summer they will be apart. Carmen had bought a pair

Cold Sassy Tree by Olive Ann Burns. Tick-nor & Fields, 1984. Teenagers like this book that was published for adults and made into a successful film. It is the story of Will Tweedy's growing up, as well as his grandfather's love story.

Freak the Mighty by Rodman Philbrick. Scholastic, 1993. Opposites attract in this heartwarming but sad story about a "giant" and a "midget" who become the best of friends.

Heart's Delight by Per Nilsson, translated (from Swedish) by Tara Chace. Front Street, 2003. Nilsson's story of a 16-year-old boy reminiscing over the memorabilia from his first love (which includes a bus pass, old movie tickets, unused condoms, and a plant that Ann-Katrin gave him) was chosen for both the *Horn Book* Fan Fare and the YALSA Best Book lists.

If You Come Softly by Jacqueline Woodson. Putnam, 1998. This story of love between a white girl and a black boy was chosen as one of the top ten books of 1998 by the Young Adult Services Association.

Love & Sex: Ten Stories of Truth, edited by Michael Cart. Simon & Schuster, 2001. While living up to their promise of truthfulness, these stories cover the waterfront from light romance to heavy sensuality.

My Heartbeat by Garret Freymann-Weyr. Houghton, 2002. Fourteen-year-old Ellen has a crush on her brother's best friend, but things get complicated when she finds out that her brother and his friend are more than friends. Nevertheless, she and the friend go ahead with their own sexual relationship and readers are left to ponder the difficulties of trying to put people in boxes.

Son of the Mob by Gordon Korman. Hyperion, 2002. Seventeen-year-old Vince Luca, whose father could easily be part of *The Sopranos,* usually manages to stay out of his father's business ventures, but then he falls in love with the daughter of an FBI agent.

True Believer by Virginia Euwer Wolff. Atheneum, 2001. In this sequel to *Make Lemonade,* 15-year-old LaVaughn loves Jody, a boy who comes back into her life from her childhood. Even though this is a love story that can't have the traditional "happy ending," LaVaughn decides she can "live with life the way it is."

The True Meaning of Cleavage by Mariah Fredericks. Atheneum/S & S, 2003. A reviewer for *VOYA* compared Fredericks's book to Judy Blume's *Forever,* but predicted that this one would escape the censor's sword because it is filled with chuckles minus graphic descriptions.

The Unlikely Romance of Kate Bjorkman by Louise Plummer. Delacorte Press, 1995. Kate Bjorkman is a high school senior who is six feet tall and much too smart and too funny to write a typical romance, but that's what makes this first-person story refreshing.

Weetzie Bat by Francesca Lia Block. HarperCollins, 1989. This modern fairy tale is centered around Weetzie and Dirk's off-brand search for love.

When Zachary Beaver Came to Town by Kimberly Willis Holt. Henry Holt, 1999. It is the 1970s and the world is thinking about Vietnam, but 13-year-old Toby is much more interested in Zachary Beaver, a boy billed as the fattest boy in the world, who gets left by his manager in the parking lot of the neighborhood bowling alley.

of jeans at a thrift shop, and as the girls gather to help Carmen pack (she's the first to leave, going to South Carolina to spend the summer with her divorced father), each one playfully tries on the pants. Even though the four friends have different body builds, they are happily surprised to find that the pants "fit" and, in fact, make each girl feel elegantly fashionable. Carmen had offered to give the pants to whoever wanted them, but now everybody wants them and so the girls come up with the idea of taking turns. Each one will have the pants for a few weeks.

Part of the charm of the book is Brashares's writing, which lends credibility and interest to the four stories, but more important are the wish-fulfilling aspects of the supportive friendship. All of the girls experience rough times: Lena in Greece with her grandparents; Bridget at soccer camp in Baja, California; and Tibby staying home with her first real job in a discount store. The supportive friendship of the girls, as symbolized through the traveling pants and shown through their letters, notes, and candid observations, helps them survive and, in some ways, thrive. Ever since the biblical story of David and Jonathan, we have had stories about boys' friendships. It is a refreshing change to read about girls helping each other. And because readers came to know and like the girls, it was to be expected that Brashares would write a sequel, which she did in 2003, *The Second Summer of the Sisterhood.*

Author Meg Cabot came up with the ultimate in wish-fulfilling stories when she created *The Princess Diaries* series about five-foot-nine, flat-chested Mia Thermopolis, who suddenly learns that she is a real princess and is heir to the throne of the small but wealthy European country of Genovia. The books are frivolous and fun "diaries" of Meg's experiences as she trains to be a princess. The books have been bestsellers and led Cabot to also write *All-American Girl,* the story of how Samantha (aka Sam) Madison, the awkward middle daughter in an upper-class family, happens to save the life of the President of the United States and then have his son fall in love with her.

Today most adults are so pleased to see young people reading anything at all that they won't complain at girls who are reading one-sided love stories or such romanticized books as the *Princess Diaries* or *All-American Girl.* But still it requires restraint not to point out that such stories aren't very realistic. If we do that, we are running the risk of insulting the reader because young people are as sensitive as anyone else to hints that they are gullible and lacking in taste and sophistication. Of course they don't really expect to suddenly become real-life princesses or to "go down in history" by having "David + Sam" carved into a windowsill of the White House. It is nevertheless fun to see how many things they have in common with someone who just might do these things. And as shown by the line in a review for *The Princess Diaries* published on Amazon.com by a Toronto teenager, "This book was, I think, one of the cutest little reads I have ever read," young people are aware of the difference between *little reads* and *big reads.*

One of the points we tried to make in Chapter 1, where we outlined the stages of developing literary appreciation, is that throughout life people keep reading at all the different levels. No one wants to read seriously taxing material all the time. It is our job to surround young readers with many books of different types and to give them time and encouragement to read a wide variety. Virtually all of the studies that have been made of people who read widely and with pleasure and understanding show that in their lives they have done a fair amount of "pleasure reading."

Concluding Comments

The books written about in this chapter make up the large body of what the general public views as young adult literature. Such books will undoubtedly continue to be published, but, as we demonstrated in Chapter 3, adolescent literature does not exist in a vacuum separate from the literature of the rest of the world. One reason that the creators of the Printz Award did not specify criterion, other than "the best" book of each year, is that they did not want to limit the creativity of authors for young adults. As producers of realistic books try not to repeat themselves while at the same time plucking psychic strings that remain untouched by superficial media stories, they are pulled in the same directions as writers for adults. Many of them are rejecting boundaries between realism and fantasy. Virginia Hamilton was one of the first to include fantasy in a problem novel when in her 1982 *Sweet Whispers, Brother Rush* she had the ghost of Teresa's uncle help the troubled 14-year-old understand her family's history and its relationship to her dearly beloved brother, who is retarded. Annette Curtis Klause, in her 1990 *The Silver Kiss,* created a vampire ghost to help Zoë adjust to her mother's death. Robert Cormier in his 1988 *Fade* wrote about the struggles of young Paul Moreaux, who through his inherited ability to be invisible begins to understand the difference between good and evil. Francesca Lia Block focuses on such problems as loneliness, alienation, sexual confusion, and love, but she accepts wholeheartedly the deconstructionist idea of creating her own world and then working within it. Readers who are puzzled or troubled by her books are usually those accustomed to looking for a kind of "realism" that can be tested against their own observations or against statistics of probability. This does not work for the many writers who are now experimenting with stretching their readers' imaginations from horror to humor. They are incorporating multiple genres in the same piece and they are leading readers directly from the consideration of serious everyday problems into magical realism.

These various examples of imaginative stories will be further discussed in later chapters. We mention them here to illustrate that the lines between genres are fading, and while we, along with many readers, continue to appreciate well-done realistic books, we are at the same time pleased to realize that the field is not standing still. Many of today's writers are finding new ways to treat old stories.

 Notes

[1]G. Robert Carlsen, "Bait/Rebait: Literature Isn't Supposed to Be Realistic," *English Journal* 70 (January 1981): 8.

[2]Marc Aronson, *Exploding the Myths: The Truth about Teenage Reading* (Scarecrow Press, 2001), p. 20.

[3]Tyrrell Burns, *School Library Journal,* August 2002, p. 197.

[4]Kathleen Beck, *VOYA* 25:3 (August, 2002), p. 197.

[5]*VOYA* 25:6 (February 2003): 437.

[6]Joel Shoemaker, *School Library Journal,* April 2003, p. 166.

[7]Michael Cart, *Necessary Noise: Stories about Our Families as They Really Are* (Joanna Cotler/HarperCollins, 2003) p. x.

[8]Michael Cart, pp. x, xiii.

[9]"Immigrant Impact Grows on U.S. Population," *Wall Street Journal,* March 16, 1992.

[10]George Keller, Director of Strategic Planning for the University of Pennsylvania, outlined these changes in a workshop at Arizona State University, February 24, 1992.

[11]Anne Commire, *Something about the Author,* Vol. 1 (Gale Research, 1971), pp. 122–23.

[12]Jamake Highwater, *Many Smokes, Many Moons* (Lippincott, 1978), pp. 13–14.

[13]*School Library Journal,* May 2002, p. 146.

[14]Dean Hughes, "Bait/Rebait: Books with Religious Themes," *English Journal* 70 (December, 1981): 14–17.

[15]Patty Campbell, "The Sand in the Oyster," *The Horn Book Magazine* (September/October 1994): 619.

[16]Kathleen Beck, "I Believe It, I Doubt It: Young Adult Fiction for Questioning Christians," *VOYA* 21:2 (June 1998): 103–104.

[17]Sharon Creech, "On Journeys in Literature" in *Literature for Today's Young Adults* by Alleen Pace Nilsen and Kenneth L. Donelson (Longman, 2001), pp. 149.

5

Poetry, Drama, and Humor

What the three genres in this chapter have in common is that they are primarily oral and get transferred to paper mainly for safekeeping and preservation. They all existed long before the printing press, and if we want students to enjoy them for their emotional impact, as well as for their intellectual content, we need to do whatever we can to bring them alive through talk and oral presentations.

A New Day for Poetry

One of the surprising best-sellers of the mid-1990s was Lori M. Carlson's *Cool Salsa: Bilingual Poems on Growing Up Latino in the United States*. Writer and editor Marc Aronson gave part of the credit to the fact that Carlson had found hip poems in three languages: English, Spanish, and Spanglish. He then explained:

> Poetry has been out of favor in America for a good long time. It was seen as either incredibly boring, or impossibly difficult to understand. Neither made it a good match for teenagers. But that has changed. The popularity of rap music has made adolescents very conscious of the power of words, rhythm, and rhyme. The revival of the Beat poets as emblems of rebellion, sexuality, and coolness has encouraged teenagers to drink espresso, grow beards, read Kerouac, and recite their own poetry.[1]

The way that poetry has grabbed the attention of teenagers in real life has not gone unnoticed by authors of realistic fiction. Carolee Dean's *Comfort* is about Kenny Roy Willson, a boy whose ambitions exceed those of his controlling mother. At age 14 she falsifies his birth certificate so he can get a driver's license and be ready to drive his father to AA meetings when he gets out of jail. She also makes Kenny give up band and football so he can work in the family's cafe and support her dream of turning her husband into a country-western singer, but Kenny does the books and collects the salary he thinks his mother owes him. He also enters a University Interscholastic League competition in poetry interpretation. It is through this that the author weaves poets and poetry into the story.

A surprising place to find poetry is in A. M. Jenkin's *Out of Order*. Baseball star Colt Trammel struggles in school, especially with the romantic poets. Since it's pretty hard to cheat on essay questions, he condescends to get some tutoring from green-haired Corinne Hecht, who until near the end of the book he calls Chlorophyll (or Chlo if he's

143

feeling good). The book ends with Colt passing his test on Bryon and Shelly and Corinne writing a poem in her journal entitled, "The Pitcher."

Sharon Creech's *Love That Dog* for middle school readers is unusual in that her character reads and enjoys the actual poems of Walter Dean Myers (Creech got Myers's permission before she wrote the story) and then gets inspired to write his own poetry. Nikki Grimes's *Bronx Masquerade* shows students at a Bronx high school writing poems as a reaction to their studying the Harlem Renaissance. In Ron Koertge's *Shakespeare Bats Cleanup*, 14-year-old Kevin Boland's life revolves around baseball, until he gets mono and has to stay home to recover. Out of boredom Kevin starts reading his father's book of poetry and eventually starts writing his own.

Poetry was the focus topic of the April 1999 issue of *VOYA*. Besides a listing of recommended poetry anthologies, articles told about teen poetry events sponsored by several different libraries. By now, poetry slams (or jams) are pretty much a standard part of library offerings. A *Time* magazine article (September 13, 1999)—"Who Are the New Beat Poets? Hint: They're Blue"—told how the Chicago police department began sponsoring poetry readings in local station houses in hopes of establishing better relations with teenagers. While teenagers as well as invited professional poets were the main participants, police officers also began stepping forward to share their thoughts. The article quoted Officer Linda Griffith:

> He allows me to walk the danger,
> He lets me extend help to a stranger,
> My flesh crawls and I miss him when he's not under my wing.
> I don't let people see or touch him, it's a private thing.
> So you should be grateful and understand what I've done.
> If and when I let you touch the butt of my gun.

A standard assignment in our YA literature class has been to ask students to start making their own poetry collections. We ask them to collect at least ten poems that they can imagine using in their own classes, either as part of academic units or simply as a way to enjoy a few minutes of class time. On the day they are to turn in the assignment, we have been asking students to share their favorite poem. But this past year, we got more ambitious and arranged to have a Poetry Slam, and as shown by the photos on p. 145, both the performers and the audience had more fun than in the old days. Sara Holbrook's *Wham! It's a Poetry Jam: Discovering Performance Poetry* and Marc Smith and Mark Eleveld's *The Spoken Word Revolution (Slam, Hip Hop & the Poetry of a New Generation)* may be confidence builders for teachers or other group leaders wanting to get kids interested in performance poetry. But at the time we did ours, we simply followed the pattern we had seen colleague Lynn Nelson do with his Greater Phoenix Area Writing Project. Here is what it required:

- An uninhibited volunteer to act as master of ceremonies.
- Numbered participation tickets on which students wrote their name and the name of their poem. They handed their "tickets" to the MC just before they stepped "on stage." The numbering helped them know when their turn was coming, and the job of the MC was easier because she had the basic information she needed in hand.

Poetry slams, whether held in classes, libraries, parks, or even police stations, are bringing new life to the sharing of poetry.

- Minimal room decorations lent a festive air.
- Simple refreshments added to the coffee-house atmosphere.
- Two sets of double judging cards—the kind used for Olympics scoring—added to the fun and suspense as everyone waited to see if the judges (two uninhibited students seated on opposite sides of the room) would agree.
- For prizes, we gave away pencils and big erasers since it was the week before final exams.

The students had so much fun with the Poetry Slam that we waited until the next class period to share our disappointment as to where they found the poems for their collections: Virtually all the students took their ten poems from Internet sources. This was fine for the Poetry Slam because most of the poems were written in first person and therefore had a kind of drama and urgency to them. However, as we explained when we brought in a cartload of poetry books for them to browse, they had missed out on many of the world's best poems as well as on the appealing designs and organizational structures of the best new books. Obviously, students found enjoyable poetry on the Internet, but as we tried to convince them, they had handicapped themselves because most Internet poems are either too old to be in copyright or too new and too under-valued to be protected with copyrights. Next time we make this assignment we are going to specify that at least half of their poems come from a print source.

Among the books we felt the worst about our students missing are collections put together by Paul Janeczko and more recently by Naomi Shihab Nye. These two wonderful poets and collectors joined forces in 1996 when they went searching for poems from around the world that would present male and female points of view on similar topics. The resulting book is *I Feel a Little Jumpy Around You: A Book of Her Poems and His Poems Collected in Pairs.*

Nye's *19 Varieties of Gazelle: Poems of the Middle East* (see the photo on p. 29) was a finalist for the National Book Award. Nye is an Arab American, who writes,

> I was born in the United States, but my father stared back toward the Middle East whenever he stood outside. Our kitchen smelled like the Middle East—garlic and pine nuts sizzled in olive oil, fried eggplant, hot pita bread. . . . He had been happy as a boy in the Old City of Jerusalem with his Palestinian and Greek and Jewish and Armenian neighbors.[2]

In explaining why she put this book together, Nye writes about her Palestinian grand-mother, who lived to be 106, and now after September 11th has swarmed into her granddaughters' "consciousness, poking my sleep, saying 'It's your job. Speak for me too. Say how much I hate it. Say this is not who we are.' "

Nye's free-verse poems were not written specifically for young readers, and several of them have been previously published. The advantage of the collection is that together the poems present a composite picture. The powerful new poem that serves as part of the introduction to usher readers into the rest of the book is entitled, "Flinn, on the Bus." It tells the story of a young man who happens to be released from jail on September 11th just three hours after the buildings fell. He hasn't heard the news, and "Fresh out of prison, after 24 months," sits down and cheerfully says, "You're my first hello!" The narrator hasn't the heart to tell him how the biggest day in his life has been totally overshadowed by the events of the September 11th morning. "He'd find out/soon enough." Other Nye books include *What Have You Lost?* with photos by Michael Nye, *Come With Me: Poems for a Journey* illustrated by Dan Yaccarino, and *Salting the Ocean: 100 Poems by Young Poets,* illustrated by Ashley Bryan.

In earlier editions of this textbook, we wrote about Paul Janeczko, "He's an American treasure. Buy, rent, borrow, or steal any book he has edited." Several of his more recent books are listed in Focus Box 11.3, Books to Encourage Student Writers. Other collections include *Pocket Poems: Selected for a Journey; Wherever Home Begins; Looking for Your Name: A Collection of Contemporary Poems; The Music of What Happens: Poems That Tell Stories; Postcard Poems: A Collection of Poems for Sharing; Strings: A Gathering of Family Poems;* and *Don't Forget to Fly.* Besides having an uncanny ability to select poems that appeal to teenagers, Janeczko organizes the books so that one poem leads into the next one. He also creates intriguing titles and his publishers are generous with providing spacious and attractive designs. As an explanation of why he collects poems, he says:

Long before I created my first anthology in 1977, I was hooked on poetry, believing the words of James Dickey, "What you have to realize if you love poetry, is that poetry is just naturally the greatest goddamn thing that ever was in the whole universe. If you love it, there's no substitute for it." And if you love it, you have to pass it along.[3]

Readers' appreciation for poetry develops in much the same way as their appreciation for prose. They begin with an unconscious delight in sounds—the repetition and rhythm of nursery rhymes, songs, and television commercials. Then they go on to the fun of riddles, puns, playground chants, and autograph rhymes. Soon they get involved in such simple plots as those found in limericks and the humorous verses of Jack Prelutsky and Shel Silverstein. By the time children are in the middle grades, their favorite poems are those that tell stories, for example, Robert Browning's "The Pied Piper of Hamelin," Henry Wadsworth Longfellow's "Hiawatha's Childhood" and "The Midnight Ride of Paul Revere," Robert Service's "The Cremation of Sam McGee," James Whitcomb Riley's "Little Orphant Annie," and Edgar Allan Poe's "The Raven."

Novels written as prose poetry are a kind of extension of these early stories. Such books are suddenly popular, not just for young readers but for adults as well. David Lehman, series editor of the Best American Poetry series published by Scribner, said in the March/April 2003 issue of *The American Poetry Review* that the genre goes back to the nineteenth-century French poets Charles Baudelaire and Arthur Rimbaud and that English influences are as diverse as the King James Bible, Shakespeare's plays, and John Donne's sermons. However, the new American variant "in all its glorious variety," is keeping its distance from these earlier traditions. It is "saturated" with American culture and vernacular, and while the poets lose much, they also "gain in relaxation, in the possibilities of humor and incongruity, in narrative compression, and in the feeling of escape or release from tradition or expectation."[4]

In writing about the popularity of the new genre, librarian Ed Sullivan stated that the poetry in these books "is not like what most students are forced to study in class—it does not require analysis and explication." They are so different from kids' present idea of poetry that Sullivan catalogs them in his library as fiction so that kids will be more apt to find them. He says the genre is popular because

It is straightforward, but it retains the rhythm and succinctness of traditional poetry. By writing their stories in verse, authors offer readers a voyeuristic perspective not possible with prose. Poetry lends itself well to introspection and intense emotion. There is also a more practical attraction for students—novels in verse are a shorter and faster read. The substantial white space on the pages of these books certainly appeals to reluctant readers.[5]

Mel Glenn is the poet who more than anyone else pioneered this genre for young readers. Back in 1982, he teamed up with fellow teacher and photographer Michael J. Bernstein to publish *Class Dismissed! High School Poems*. He adapted the subjects and the mode of realistic problem novels to individual prose poems. That each one was illustrated with a portrait of a teenager added to the feeling of authenticity. Sequels included *Class Dismissed II: More High School Poems, Back to Class, My Friend's Got This*

FOCUS BOX 5.1 *Stories in Verse*

NOTE: Other examples are scattered through-out this chapter, especially in Focus Box 5.4.

Becoming Joe DiMaggio by Maria Testa. Candlewick Press, 2002. We could have put this in the sports chapter, but we liked the idea of a sports biogra-phy balancing out the stereotypical view of what many people think poetry is all about.

CrashBoomLove by Juan Felipe Herrerra. Univ. of New Mexico, 1999. The story is told through the voice of a pained 16-year-old high school student whose father leaves the family.

Heartbeat by Sharon Creech. HarperCollins, 2004. Twelve-year-old Annie is a runner and the free-verse poems in Creech's book match the rhythm of her pounding feet as well as the feelings she has about her mother's pregnancy and her grandfather's oncoming dementia.

Jinx by Margaret Wild. Walker, 2002. In this sad problem novel, Jen renames herself Jinx after both of her boyfriends die.

Locomotion by Jacqueline Woodson. Putnam's, 2003. Woodson uses a teen voice to create the free verse, the sonnets, and the haiku that tell Lonnie's story as he moves through group and teen homes.

Loose Threads by Lorie Ann Grover. McElderry, 2002. A 12-year-old ponders the meaning of life when she watches her grandmother's struggle with breast cancer.

Make Lemonade by Virginia Euwer Wolff. Holt, 1993, followed by **True Believer** (S & S/Atheneum, 2001, winner of the National Book Award) are highly acclaimed stories of a determined young girl who answers a babysitting ad and finds that the mother is just about her own age. In the second book, LaVaughn's horizons extend beyond her neighbor-hood, but she does not lose her determination. The free verse format adds dignity to what could be just two more problem novels.

Out of the Dust by Karen Hesse. Scholastic, 1996. In diary-like entries, Billie Jo tells how her dreams get lost in the swirling winds of the 1930s Oklahoma dustbowl. The book won the Newbery award.

17: A Novel in Prose Poems by Liz Rosenberg. Cricket, 2002. Stephanie's love story, from beginning to end—and beyond—is told through this collection of rich images.

Split Image by Mel Glenn. Morrow/HarperCollins, 2000. This comes the closest of Glenn's books to being a problem novel in that it is the story of Laura Li, a dutiful Asian daughter, who has a hard time figuring out how to manage her heritage and her new life. The poems come from people who observe Laura as well as from Laura and her family. Glenn's other recent stories in poems include *Foreign Exchange: A Mystery in Poems* (Mor-row/HarperCollins, 1999), *The Taking of Room 114: A Hostage Drama in Poems* (1997), *Jump Ball: A Basket-ball Season in Poems* (1997), and *Who Killed Mr. Chip-pendale* (1996), the last three from Lodestar/Dutton. While Glenn includes dramatic and sometimes violent incidents, the poems are mostly monologues expressing different characters reactions and feelings.

Stepping Out with Grandma Mac by Nikki Grimes, illustrated by Angelo. Scholastic/Orchard, 2001. Twenty poems capture and celebrate the experiences shared by a teenaged girl and her grandmother.

Stop Pretending: What Happened When My Big Sister Went Crazy by Sonya Sones. Harper-Collins, 1999. This powerful story is based on the author's own family experience.

Talkin' about Bessie: The Story of Aviator Elizabeth Coleman by Nikki Grimes, illustrated by E. B. Lewis. Scholastic. This unusual biography is presented through 21 poetic speeches given at a funeral parlor where people have come to mourn the death, at age 34, of the first African American woman to become a licensed pilot.

The Voyage of the Arctic Tern by Hugh Mont-gomery. Candlewick, 2002. Unlike most of the new prose poets who are writing realistic problem stories, Montgomery spins a high-seas adventure story.

Who Will Tell My Brother? by Marlene Carvel. Hyperion, 2002. Carvel's sensitive story treats the issue of offensive Indian mascots used by sports teams.

Problem, Mr. Candler: High School Poems. His more recent books, which tell unified stories through related poems, are included in Focus Box 5.1, Stories in Verse. Also, see Glenn's statement on p. 354, which will be helpful to the sponsors of teen poetry clubs as well as to classroom teachers.

The Teaching of Poetry

Only about half of the prose poetry books we have seen include a cover statement identifying them as poetry. We wonder if some authors and publishers shy away from the word *poetry* because they do not want to remind potential readers of any negative feelings they might have toward poetry. When we ask our college students about their in-school experiences with poetry, on the negative side they tell us about teachers who did not like poetry themselves and so flooded lessons with technical terms or turned poems into guessing games that made students feel stupid. On the positive side, they tell us about teachers who seemed to take genuine pleasure in poems and shared them with students as a gift. Their actions match the advice of Richard W. Beach and James D. Marshall:

- Never teach a poem you don't like.
- Teach poems that you're not certain you understand. Teach poems about which you may have some real doubt.
- Teach poems that are new to you as well as your store of "old standards."
- Become a daily reader of poems, a habitué of used bookstores, a scavenger of old *New Yorkers* and other magazines that contain poetry.
- Give students the freedom to dislike great poetry.[6]

Books about teaching literature inevitably give suggestions on teaching this or that genre, but readers can almost palpably sense the urgency of suggestions for teaching poetry. Recommended books include Louise Rosenblatt's seminal *The Reader, the Text, the Poem: The Transactional Theory of the Literary Work*; Patrick Dias and Michael Hayhoe's *Developing Response to Poetry*; and Stephen Dunning's *Teaching Literature to Adolescents: Poetry* (see Focus Box 11.3 on p. 349 for other helpful books about the writing of poetry).

With the help of these books and poems gleaned from teachers' reading, any teacher can soon have several hundred poems worth reading and using in class. Here we offer some other suggestions.

1. Avoid units on poetry. Poems deserve to be used frequently but not en masse. It is better to use poems in thematic units where they can be tied in with short stories or drama.
2. Drop a funny poem—or a monster poem—into class just for the fun of it.
3. Let students, at least occasionally, help choose the poems that a class will study.
4. Remember that poetry takes time and plan accordingly. This is not to see how many poems you can knock off in one class, but to allow students to hear poems again and again and to talk about them. We saw one teacher who obviously hated poetry set a record by killing thirty-six Emily Dickinson poems in less than one class period. It takes time to recognize kinship with a poet, to find someone who expresses a feeling

FOCUS BOX 5.2 *More Excellent Poetry*

American Sports Poems, edited by R. R. Knudson and May Swenson. Orchard, 1988. Poets as good as Grace Butcher, Tess Gallagher, John Updike, Anne Sexton, and Robert Francis treat both common and unusual sports.

Earth-Shattering Poems, edited by Liz Rosenberg, Holt, 1998. When Rosenberg looked for the poems in this collection, she remembered the intensity of young people's emotions and so looked for poems illustrating emotions on the furthest edges as with supreme joy and darkest anger.

Good Poems, compiled by Garrison Keillor. Viking, 2002. After a light-hearted introduction, Keillor presents 300 poems that he has read on his PBS radio show *A Prairie Home Companion.* They range from the well-known to the obscure, but they are all accessible.

Heart to Heart: New Poems Inspired by Twentieth-Century American Art, edited by Jan Greenberg. Abrams, 2001. In this Printz Honor Book, Greenberg commissioned poets to write in response to some of the greatest twentieth-century American paintings. She arranged the paintings and the poems according to the poet's approach.

I Am the Darker Brother: An Anthology of Modern Poems by African Americans, revised edition, edited by Arnold Adoff, illustrated by Benny Andrews. Simon & Schuster, 1997. Since its publication in 1968, this has been the premier anthology of black poetry. Twenty-one new poems are included with pieces coming from nine women including Rita Dove and Maya Angelou.

I, Too, Sing America: Three Centuries of African American Poetry, edited by Catherine Clinton, illustrated by Stephen Lalcorn. Houghton Mifflin, 1998. This attractive, large-sized book is a good resource for classrooms and libraries.

Love Speaks Its Name: Gay and Lesbian Love Poems, edited by J. D. McClatchy. Knopf, 2001. The 144 poets include Sappho, Walt Whitman, Frank Ohara, and Muriel Rukeyser.

Pierced by a Ray of Sun: Poems about the Times We Feel Alone, selected by Ruth Gordon. Harper-Collins, 1995. These 73 poems all explore human loneliness. Also recommended are Gordon's earlier collections including *Time Is the Longest Distance* (1991), *Under All Silences* (1987), and *Peeling the Onion* (1993), all HarperCollins.

Poetry Speaks: Hear Great Poets Read Their Work from Tennyson to Plath, edited by Elise Pashen and Rebekah Presson Mosby. Source Books, 2001. A bonus to this book are the three CDs presenting many of the 42 poets doing interpretive readings.

Reflections on a Gift of Watermelon Pickle, edited by Stephen Dunning and others. Scott, Foresman, 1967, reissued, 1994. A landmark book, this collection proved that young readers could enjoy modern poetry without the help (or hindrance) of teachers. Its sequel, *Some Haystacks Don't Even Have Any Needles and Other Complete Modern Poems* (Lothrop, 1969) is almost as good.

Step Lightly: Poems for the Journey, collected by Nancy Willard. Harcourt Brace, 1998. Theodore Roethke, D. H. Lawrence, Lucille Clifton, Eleanor Farjeon, Wallace Stevens, and Elizabeth Bishop are among the poets.

A Thousand Peaks: Poems from China by Siyu Liu and Orel Protopopescu. Pacific View, 2002. Each of 35 poems selected from two millennia of Chinese literature is displayed on its own page. Illustrations add interest and so do the prose explanations of the poems, of selected Chinese characters, and of the challenges of translation.

Truth & Lies: An Anthology of Poems, edited by Patrice Vecchione. Holt, 2001. Vecchione adds illuminating notes to help young readers enjoy the poems that she carefully chose from across centuries and across cultures.

Wáchale! Poetry and Prose About Growing Up Latino in America, edited by Ilan Stavans. Cricket Books/Carus Publishing, 2001. A reviewer described the vivid word pictures in this bilingual collection as speaking from the heart and lingering in the mind.

Because humorous poetry is short and easy to keep on hand, it works well as a classroom break between more tedious tasks as in this readers theatre presentation by two "bugs" reading from Paul Fleishman's Joyful Noise: Poems for Two Voices.

    or makes an observation that the reader has come close to but has not quite been able to put into words.

5. Surround your students with as many beautifully designed poetry books as you can borrow from libraries, scrounge from friends and neighbors, or buy. See Focus Box 5.2, More Excellent Poetry, for suggestions.

Understanding and appreciating the skill with which a poet has achieved the desired effect brings extra pleasure. This is why English teachers are interested in helping students arrive at higher levels of poetic appreciation, but the teacher who tries to get there too fast runs the risk of leaving students behind. Because readers come to poetry not so much for information as for a change of pace, a bit of pleasure through wordplay, a sudden recognition or insight, a recollection from childhood, or a time of emotional intensity, the design of a book needs to invite readers in.

    Even though the age range of those who can read and enjoy a particular poem is usually much wider than for prose, there is still a subtle dividing line between children's and young adult books. While teenagers may be amused by the humorous poetry of Shel Silverstein and Jack Prelutsky, they are likely to feel slightly insulted if offered serious children's poetry. Many young adults are ready to read and enjoy the same poetry that educated adults enjoy, especially if teachers smooth the way by first providing access to poets whose allusions they are likely to understand and then gradually leading them into poetry representing cultures and times different from their own. It may help to ease students into appreciating the work of some poets by first offering various kinds of biographical reading as with Neil Baldwin's *To All Gentleness, William Carlos Williams: The Doctor Poet;* Jean Gould's *American Women Poets: Pioneers of Modern Poetry;* or Paul Janeczko's *Poetspeak: In Their Work, About Their Work.* In a similar way, someone who has read Alice Walker's *The Color Purple* will probably be ready to appreciate the poems in her *Good Night Willie Lee, I'll See You in the Morning.* Readers of Ray Bradbury's science fiction may want to read his fifty-plus poems in *When Elephants Last in the Dooryard Bloomed.* Students who have read Maya Angelou's autobiographical *I Know Why the Caged Bird Sings* will probably be interested in her poetry.

One of the delights and challenges of working with modern poetry is that students (and teachers) have no source to turn to for determining the meaning or worth of the poems. Comments on a T. S. Eliot poem are easy to come by, and a glance at criticism tells us whether this poem is major Eliot or minor Eliot. We hardly need to read the poem to comment on it, to determine its place in the canon, or to chase down all those wonderful symbols and allusions. With a modern poem, teachers and students must fall back on honest responses to the poem. Years ago, Luella Cook, one of the great people in English education, warned teachers about the dishonesty of canned responses to literature, and although she referred to students alone, her warning might be extended to teachers as well.

> The problem of teaching literature realistically faced, then, becomes one of widening the range of responses to literature, of guiding reading experience so that reaction to books will be vivid, sharp, compelling, provocative. The great tragedy of the English classroom is not that students may have the "wrong" reactions—that is, veer from accepted judgment—but that they will have no original reaction at all, or only the most obvious ones, or that they will mimic the accepted evaluations of criticism.[7]

Making Drama a Class Act

We used to say that playwrights did not write plays for teenagers because teenagers were not the ones buying tickets to Broadway plays or flying to London on theater tours. That's still true, but as we discussed in Chapter 3, teenagers make up a healthy portion of television and movie audiences, so that talented writers are now writing serious plays designed for young people either to read or to perform. Be warned, however, that these are not the kinds of nondescript plays that were found in books for high school students a generation ago. In an *English Journal* article, "Toward a Young Adult Drama," Rick E. Amidon described them as "works which question fitting in, popularity, sex, drugs, making choices, taking chances." He labeled Jerome McDonough the "father of young adult drama" because of his dozen "powerful, practical-to-produce, and effective plays for the young adult stage."[8] His plays differ from those typically produced at high schools in that they are shorter (50 to 70 minutes long); they deal with topics dear to the hearts of teenagers; most of the casts are flexible, so the plays can be adapted to how many actors are available; and they have contemporary settings. Hindi Brooks, who has been a writer for television's *Fame* and *Eight Is Enough*, has also written plays specifically for young

FOCUS BOX 5.3   *Plays Commonly Read in English Classes*

Children of a Lesser God by Mark Medoff. Dramatists, 1980. Especially since the success of the movie, students appreciate this Tony Award–winning play about a deaf young woman and her relationship with a hearing teacher.

Driving Miss Daisy by Alfred Uhry. Dramatists, 1988. The impressive film serves as a backdrop for reading this play that helps students learn what is involved in a lasting friendship.

The Effect of Gamma Rays on Man-in-the-Moon Marigolds by Paul Zindel. Dramatists, 1970. This moving story of the damaging forms that parent–child love can take brought Paul Zindel to the attention of the literary world.

Fences by August Wilson. Drama Book Shop and New American Library paperback, 1995. Wilson's play won the Pulitzer Prize for the way it shows an African American family losing its dreams in the 1950s.

Inherit the Wind by Jerome Lawrence and Robert E. Lee. Dramatists, 1955. Based on the Scopes trial, this play is especially interesting in relation to current controversies over creationism versus evolution. The lines are easy to read aloud, and there is a good balance between sharp wit and high drama.

Les Miserables by Tim Kelly. Dramatists, 1987. With eleventh and twelfth graders, the boys like action, the girls like romance, and they all like music. So here's a play that answers everyone's needs.

A Man for All Seasons by Robert Bolt, 1960. Baker (also French), 1960. It's good for its portrayal of one of the most famous periods of English history and for its exploration of a hero. Interesting comparisons can be drawn to works treating heroes of noble birth, as in *Antigone* and *Hamlet,* and heroes of ordinary birth, as in *Death of a Salesman* and *The Stranger.*

"Master Harold" and the Boys by Athol Fugard. Penguin, 1982. This powerful one-act play asks students to examine the psychological effects of racism on whites.

The Miracle Worker by William Gibson. Baker (also French), 1951. Students love the poignancy of the story of Helen Keller and Annie Sullivan, but it is also a good illustration of flashbacks, foreshadowing, symbolism, and dramatic license when compared to such biographies as Nella Braddy's *Annie Sullivan Macy* and Helen Keller's *The Story of My Life.* Gibson's *Monday After the Miracle,* a continuation of the story, is also a good read.

Sorry, Wrong Number by Lucille Fletcher in *Fifteen American One-Act Plays,* edited by Paul Kozelka. Pocket Books, 1971. Because it is a radio play written to be heard and not seen, it is ideal for reading aloud.

A Storm in Summer by Rod Serling in *Great Television Plays,* Vol. 2, edited by Ned E. Hoopes and Patricia Neale Gordon. Dell, 1975. Students like the way it relates an encounter between a 10-year-old Harlem boy and a bitter, sarcastic, Jewish delicatessen owner in upstate New York.

The Teahouse of the August Moon by John Patrick. Dramatists, 1953. The way it lightheartedly pokes fun at American customs and values is refreshing.

Visit to a Small Planet by Gore Vidal in *Visit to a Small Planet and Other Television Plays.* Little, Brown, 1956. Because this play was written for television, the action is easy to visualize and the stage directions simple enough to discuss as an important aspect of the drama itself.

What I Did Last Summer by A. R. Gurney, Jr. Dramatists, 1983. As Anna tells 14-year-old Charlie in this play about the last summer of World War II, "All choices are important. They tell you who you are."

adults. (Both McDonough's and Brooks's plays are available from I. E. Clark in Schulenberg, Texas.)

Without encouragement from teachers, few teenagers read drama because it needs to be read aloud with different voices and it is hard to visualize the scenery and the stage directions. One of our graduate students, Alison Babusci, who came to study in Arizona State University's well-known program in Children's Theater, drew up these five suggestions for teachers who are planning to have students read and study such plays as those listed in Focus Box 5.3.

1. *Make students feel like they are "on the inside" of the theatrical world.* To help them visualize the world of the play, bring in books or photocopies of reproductions of sets and costume designs from previous productions. Teach students what stage directions *mean.* It is a simple concept, and it isn't difficult to obtain a stage diagram from any drama textbook. The more students understand about drama, the more interested and excited they will be.

2. *Become "friends" with the cast.* Suggest that students copy down the cast list (dramatis personae) from the beginning of the play, but instead of relying on the dramatist's descriptions of the characters and their relationships, encourage students to write their own. How would *they* describe the character? Jotting down their own observations will help them remain active readers and will add to their visualization of the action and characters.

3. *Convince yourself and students that drama is fun.* Half the excitement of reading dramatic literature is that readers have to form their own opinions and images.

4. *Let students see the play.* Contact theater groups in your area. Almost everyone will have an outreach program designed to include children and the community and to make drama more accessible and affordable. Theaters pick their seasons about a year in advance, so contact them early and see if there will be an appropriate show in their upcoming season for you to teach. Or use one of the many plays available on video.

5. *Rely on improvisation and storytelling.* Instead of always having students read parts aloud, try using improvisation. Start with either a line of dialogue or a situation and let students say what they think they would say if they were one of the characters. You can also use games, storytelling, and interdisciplinary activities that combine drama with music, fine arts, or even dance or other physical activities. People do not fall asleep when their bodies are active.

Her concluding advice was that teachers have to be excited by drama. Students will quickly identify and adopt the teacher's attitude: If the teacher is bored, students will be bored. Because so many students work after school and are involved in extra heavy academic loads, some high schools are trying alternative ways to get drama included. The Community Schools program affiliated with the Catalina Foothills School District in Tucson, Arizona, offers a theatre program in the summer. One of the reasons it is so popular may be that in Tucson it is too hot to do anything outside in the summer, but the fact that students withstood the heat to line up several hours in advance for registration (the first fifty are accepted) speaks well to the kind of enthusiasm that is generated year after year when a program is successful. See the photo on p. 155, which was

One of the "Pink Ladies" relaxes backstage at the Community Schools' presentation of Grease, which in the summer of 2003 played to five full houses.

taken backstage at the 2003 production of *Grease,* which played to five sold-out houses. See Aaron Levy's statement on p. 158.

The criteria for choosing plays for reading aloud are different from those for performing. A favorite is Reginald Rose's three-act television play *Twelve Angry Men,* the story of a jury making a decision on the future of a 19-year-old boy charged with murder. Some classes affectionately refer to the play as "Twelve Angry People" because girls as well as boys are assigned parts. Teachers have offered the following reasons for the play's success, which can serve as guides when predicting the potential of other scripts.

- It calls for twelve continual parts, enough to satisfy all students who like to read aloud.
- It teaches practical lessons of value to students' lives.
- It may serve as a springboard for research and further discussion on how the judicial system works.
- It creates a forum for students to prove the psychology of group dynamics and peer behavior.
- It sparks student excitement from the beginning and sustains it throughout.
- It can be read in two-and-a-half class sessions.
- The "business" is minimal and can be easily carried out as students read from scripts.
- Pertinent questions can be asked when the jury recesses after Acts I and II.
- Students are attracted to the realism, and they can relate to a motherless slum youth of 19.
- The excellent characterization allows students to discover a kaleidoscope of lifelike personalities.

Partnering with a theatre teacher and ordering actual scripts for classroom reading is an easy way to give students a "feel" for theatre.

Play scripts are sold through distributors, most of whom will happily send free catalogues to teachers who request them. A typical script price for a full-length play is $5.00; a typical royalty charge is $50 for the initial production and $25 for each subsequent production. Teachers wanting scripts for in-class reading rather than for production should so note at the time of ordering so that no royalty is charged. If the play is to be produced, whether admission is charged or not, the producer should pay the fee when the scripts are ordered. A royalty contract is mailed along with the scripts. Two of the largest distributors are Samuel French (7623 Sunset Blvd.; Hollywood, CA 90046) and Dramatists Play Service, Inc. (440 Park Avenue S.; New York, NY 10016). Anchorage Press (P.O. Box 8067; New Orleans, LA 70182) is recommended for children's and teenage drama, and Contemporary Drama Service (Box 7710-5; Colorado Springs, CO 80933) is good for spoofs and for television scripts.

Two guides are especially useful. Theodore J. Shank's *A Digest of 500 Plays: Plot Outlines and Production Notes* has brief summaries (e.g., *Godot* is about one-third of a page), but the book is excellent on production matters. The third edition of the National Council of Teachers of English and Bowker's *Guide to Play Selection* has even briefer summaries (*Godot* gets eight lines) but includes many more plays. A good overall book that contains scripts by such writers as Sam Shepard, Caryl Churchill, Athol Fugard, David Henry Hwang, August Wilson, David Mamet, Tony Kushner, and Anna Deavere Smith is *The Bedford Introduction to Drama* edited by Lee A. Jacobus.

But even better than launching yourself on a solitary tour of such guides as these is to go and visit the theatre teacher that Aaron Levy says every English teacher should know. Somewhere in his or her office will be several catalogues that have arrived in the mail. Borrow them. Read the quick plot summaries and order some plays to read with your classes. Perhaps you can share costs with the theatre department, while your students serve as first readers—as scouts—for appealing new scripts. Reading new plays from professionally prepared scripts is one of the simplest ways to follow Alison

Babusci's suggestion that we make students feel "on the inside" of the theatrical world. Another way is to let students create their own plays from such books as those listed in Focus Box 5.4.

Books that are helpful in introducing students to performance with something less daunting than a whole play include *The Actor's Book of Contemporary Stage Monologues,* edited by Nina Shengold, and *100 Monologues: An Audition Sourcebook for New Dramatists,* edited by Laura Harrington. Don Gallo's *Center Stage: One-Act Plays for Teenage Readers and Actors* has worked well for us. Two other books that are helpful are Anita Manley and Cecily O'Neill's *Dreamseekers: Creative Approaches to the African American Heritage* and Patricia Sternberg's *Theatre for Conflict Resolution.*

Humor Matters

Despite what must seem obvious truth to good teachers and librarians—that a sense of humor is essential for the survival of educators and students—some deadly serious people wonder if this (or any other time, presumably) is the time for levity. The answer is, of course, yes. Given their enforced world of school and an ever-demanding society, young people need laughter every bit as much as—maybe even more than—adults. See Helen and Jerry Weiss's statement on p. 163.

What do young people find funny? Lance M. Gentile and Merna M. McMillen's article, "Humor and the Reading Program," offers a starting point. Their stages of children's and young adult's interest in humor, somewhat supplemented, are as follows:

- *Ages 10–11.* Literal humor, slapstick (e.g., The Three Stooges), laughing at accidents (banana-peel humor) and misbehavior, sometimes mildly lewd jokes (usually called "dirty jokes"), and grossness.
- *Ages 12–13.* Practical jokes, teasing, goofs, sarcasm, more lewd jokes, joke-riddles, sick jokes, elephant jokes, grape jokes, tongue twisters, knock-knock jokes, moron jokes, TV blooper shows, and grossness piled on grossness.
- *Ages 14–15.* More and more lewd jokes (some approaching a mature recognition of the humor inherent in sex); humor aimed at schools, parents, and other adults in authority as in television's *Malcolm in the Middle,* and grossness piled on even greater grossness. Young adults may still prefer their own humor to their parents' humor, but they are increasingly catching on to adult humor and may prefer it to their own.
- *Ages 16 and up.* More subtle humor, satire and parody now acceptable and maybe even preferable, witticisms (rather than last year's half-witticisms, which they now detest in their young brothers and sisters). Adult humor is increasingly part of their repertoire, partly because they are anxious to appear sophisticated, partly because they are growing up.[9]

From Chills to Giggles

Something in the human mind encourages crossovers between fear and amusement as shown by how often people who have suffered a fright burst out laughing as soon as the danger is over. Humor about death can be traced back at least as far as the early

AARON LEVY
A Theatre Teacher
Speaks to English Teachers
and Librarians

*O*nce we admit that theatre is an endangered species, we can get to work, especially if we realize that our last shot at creating patrons of the theatre happens at the high school level. The problem isn't that teens prefer movies, malls, and skateboarding over plays; they just prefer these activities over the theatre they currently know. Most have stumbled and fumbled over the language of Shakespeare, misunderstood the romanticism of Tennessee Williams, ho-hummed at Neil Simon's coming of age, and poked fun at the silliness of most musicals. Before us is the eerie reality that once out of high school, our students may choose to never see a piece of live theatre. And with their current history, why should they?

I can identify with their attitude because I have a similar history. In high school, I didn't even know where the theatre was, but then in college I started writing dialogue and so I ventured over to the theatre. On many a night, I was surprised at the magic of a live story unfolding before me. I connected with the actors and the characters they portrayed in a way I've never done with a movie. In the one-woman play by Jane Wagner, *Search for Signs of Intelligent Life in the Universe,* one of the characters played by Lily Tomlin is the bag lady, Trudy, who admits that going crazy and dropping out of corporate America was the best thing she ever did. The play has Trudy taking visiting aliens on tours of *our* universe. They end their visit with a night in the theatre where her charges wind up watching the audience instead of the play because Trudy hadn't thought to tell them otherwise. At the end of the evening one of them shows Trudy his goose bumps. Trudy reflects, "Yeah, to see a group of strangers sitting together in the dark, laughing and crying about the same things . . . that just knocked 'em out. . . . So they're taking goose bumps home with 'em. Goose bumps! Quite a souvenir."

That's a great lesson that the aliens teach us about our own theatre—the audience is the real art, and it's our job to make sure with every production (and every reading in our classrooms) we keep it that way. When I work with students either in class or on the stage, we talk every day about audience. Unlike other literary forms, without an audience, theatre does not exist.

Too often, high school theatre perpetuates archaic notions about theatre with slow-moving dramas, repetitive musicals, and plays that don't speak to the teenage experience. We do not need to acquiesce to the MTV style of telling stories in quick snippets, but we have to be aware of certain trends in the teenage attention span. If we want them to actually turn their cell phones all the way off and sit there for an hour-and-a-half, we best deliver goose bumps or lose them forever.

Before we can deliver the goose bump experience and make it so teenagers leave high school craving theatre, we've got to figure out a way to get them into high school auditoriums in the first place. We also have to make it so that when we read plays in English classes, it feels like something stronger than a requirement. We need to read drama with such fervor that students are actually curious to see it produced.

Here are a few suggestions for ways that English teachers and drama teachers can work together.

- Invite the drama teacher to your very first English Department meeting. Get acquainted and make plans for him or her to come to your class to promote the first play. Some teachers send students around to pitch the play or perform a scene, but I think that's risky because students often feel silly performing without the benefit of a stage. If their performance falls flat, the visit has had adverse effects, and even when it succeeds, it has taken away some of the surprise of the performance.

- Offer extra credit for students to attend the plays. If you don't believe in extra credit, make two assignments for homework, one a textbook type and the other attending the play. Inform students early and often of the play dates so they can get off work and/or make other arrangements. Most productions run three or four performances so students should be able to attend at least one if they plan ahead.

- Attend the performance yourself. This is big. I know (believe me I know) that an English teacher's job, if performed perfectly, would never end. We could grade until our heads drop into our morning cereal. But think of your attendance as a built-in lesson plan. If you attend, your students are twice as likely to attend, and you can use the performance as an actual piece of literature. Your theatre teacher might be able to provide you with some background information, study guides, or quizzes.

- Suggest and support a theatre teacher's opportunity to select some riskier plays that speak closer to the teen experience or tell a story in a nontraditional structure. If you and/or your theatre teacher scout the catalogues, you can order several plays besides the usual ones that are produced over and over, sometimes by schools in the same district during the same academic year.

- As a way of returning the favor of your tireless support of the theatre program, many theatre teachers are willing to work with their students to perform a scene or two from one of the plays in *your* curriculum. After reading and dissecting a play like *Death of a Sales-*

man, wouldn't it be a breath of fresh air to see and hear Willy Loman on his feet?

- Suggest and support library collaboration with theatre productions. When I produce a play, I always visit our librarian and explain the play's plot and themes to see if she can help us set up a promotional display. When I did Jim Leonard's *The Diviners,* a humorous and touching story about a mentally challenged teenager who had a gift for divining, the librarian displayed books about the Depression (that's when the play is set) and about the art of divining.

- Help with press releases for promotion. While newspapers won't write articles on high school plays, they will if you spin it in an interesting way. When we produced my comedy-drama about teen suicide, *Pizza with Shrimp on Top,* we wrote the header for the press release something like, "Valley students reach out to community to fight against teen suicide." Both reporters and photographers showed up at our rehearsals.

- Invite and engage the community. Too often we produce plays whose quality suffers supposedly for the sake of "education." But I wonder if we're teaching our theatre students the right things when we choose boring scripts, produce them at a low level of cost and effort, and then present them in half-filled arenas.

When I am teaching theatre, I try to include my students in every aspect of production, especially marketing. The most important marketing lesson we learn is that if we are going to invite the whole school and the community, our product needs to make patrons want to see our next play.

Aaron Levy has taught both English and theatre. As a prize-winning playwright and director, he specializes in plays for the teen audience. He is currently completing his Ph.D. in English Education at Arizona State University and can be reached with comments and questions at Levycurio@aol.com.

Books Recommended for Reading Aloud or Adapting into Reader's Theatre

Breakout by Paul Fleischman. Cricket, 2003. This finalist for the National Book Award begins with a 17-year-old runaway stuck in a traffic jam on a Los Angeles freeway. Eight years later, she is a playwright and performance artist. The book includes several of her monologues, which, as with other Fleischman books, students can excerpt for oral presentations. Fleischman's *Seek* (see his statement on p. 114) was described by a *Horn Book* reviewer as "A musical blend of rhythmic, almost metered prose that—not surprisingly—begs to be read aloud." Fleischman wrote his *Joyful Noise: Poems for Two Voices* (see the photo on p. 151) as a way of "forcing" readers to approach poetry out loud.

Carver: A Life in Poems by Marilyn Nelson. Nikki Giovanni praised this winner of the 2001 Boston Globe Horn Book Award, by writing, "Oh, Marilyn Nelson, what a magnificent job you have done to bring the past so alive it looks like our future." The individual poems make for an easy way of dividing up this biography of George Washington Carver for a class presentation.

A Gift from Zeus: Sixteen Favorite Myths by Jeanne Steig, pictures by William Steig. Joanna Cotler Books/HarperCollins, 2001. William Steig's drawings as in *Sylvester and the Magic Pebble* and his *Dr. DeSoto* books have always been *brut art.* Now that he is in his 90s, his style is even more succinct and could serve as a model for kids to do their own giant-sized drawings to assist them in doing their own storytelling.

God Went to Beauty School by Cynthia Rylant. HarperCollins, 2003. Rylant explores two themes about God in 23 "down-home" poems. She extols God's presence in everything, while at the same time making him very human.

The Hitchhiker's Guide to the Galazy by Douglas Adams. Ballantine, 1980. Arthur Dent and Ford Prefect are on a perilous and very funny journey through the galaxy. The stories were originally produced in England as radio shows and so work well as read-alouds.

Keesha's House by Helen Frost. Frances Foster Books/FSG, 2003. These first-person accounts from seven teenagers show that kids who are pushed out of their own homes and are dealing with such "heavy" issues as abandonment, racism, addiction, delinquency, and sexual consequences can still come together and help each other.

Short Circuits: Thirteen Shocking Stories by Outstanding Writers for Young Adults, edited by Donald R. Gallo, 1992. Several of these suspenseful and ghostly stories can be used for humorous read-alouds. Alvin Schwartz's *Scary Stories to Tell in the Dark, More Scary Stories to Tell in the Dark,* and *Scary Stories 3: More Tales to Chill Your Bones* (HarperCollins, 1981, 1984, and 1992) are also the kind that will make the hair on listeners' arms stand up straight.

The Song Shoots Out of My Mouth: A Celebration of Music by Jamie Adoff, illustrated by Martin French. Dutton, 2002. Jamie Adoff is the son of Virginia Hamilton and Arnold Adoff and as a musician has put together a poetic tribute to all kinds of music.

What My Mother Doesn't Know by Sonya Sones. Simon & Schuster, 2001. These free verse poems can stand on their own, but when read all together they tell the story of 14-year-old Sophie's longings as well as her adventures.

Witness by Karen Hesse. Scholastic, 2001. It is 1924 and a small town in Vermont is caught up in intrigue and prejudice. Hesse uses carefully constructed free verse to present a little-known piece of U.S. history through the eyes and voices of eleven different townspeople.

Greeks. English speakers refer to this blend of humor and horror as *Gothic* because they associate it with the grotesque gargoyles and other frightening figures in tapestries, paintings, sculptures, and stained glass windows, which were created to represent the devil and to frighten people into "proper" beliefs and behavior. Instead, people coped with their fears by turning such icons into objects of amusement.

People still do this at Halloween with spider webs, skeletons, black cats, bats, rats, ghosts, coffins, tombstones, monsters, and haunted houses. Halloween developed out of the sacred or "hallowed" evening preceding All Saints Day, which falls on November 1. The holiday is now second only to Christmas in the amount of money expended for costumes, parties, and candy to be given to trick-or-treaters.

The world has had great fun with Mary Shelley's 1818 story of *Frankenstein, or the Modern Prometheus,* but when it was written many people viewed it as a cautionary tale against medical experimentation. Shelley's story followed close on the heels of the development of autopsies and of dissection for purposes of medical study. Such practices made people nervous and fearful. One way of calming such fears was by laughing at them. While Shelley's story was itself rich in Gothic details with a complex plot and fully developed characters, hundreds of parodies and imitations are comic in nature.

Gothic novels underwent a similar kind of transformation from scary to funny when the same year that Shelley published *Frankenstein* (1818), Jane Austen published *Northanger Abbey* as a parody of the earlier novels. Later Gothic stories in the mid- and late-1800s included some darkly humorous moments caused by visits from the dead as in Edgar Allan Poe's *The Fall of the House of Usher,* Emily Brontë's *Wuthering Heights,* and Charles Dickens's *A Christmas Carol* with its Ghosts of Christmas Past, Christmas Present, and Christmas Yet to Come. In *Bleak House,* Dickens creates a character who spontaneously combusts; in *Little Dorrit* the prison resembles a haunted castle, and in *Great Expectations,* Pip meets the criminal in a graveyard and has a hallucinatory vision of Miss Havisham's hanged body "with but one shoe to the feet."

Bram Stoker's 1897 *Dracula* is not the first story about a vampire, but it is the one that established such western traditions as a vampire's need for periodically sucking blood, the requirements of a prolonged relationship before a human can be turned into a vampire, vampires sleeping in coffins during the day and arising for actions only after dark, the impossibility of killing vampires with ordinary human weapons, and the use of such conventional techniques for repelling vampires as garlic, a silver crucifix, and a wooden stake through the heart.

Bud Abbott and Lou Costello were among the early film comedians to take advantage of the possibilities of film for stretching viewers' emotions between the frightening and the ridiculous. Their 1948 *Abbott and Costello Meet Frankenstein* still appears on all-time best comedy lists, with such other comedies as *Abbott and Costello Meet the Killer Boris Karloff* (1948), *Abbott and Costello Meet Dr. Jekyll and Mr. Hyde* (1953), and *Abbott and Costello Meet the Mummy* (1955).

In the mid 1960s, *The Munsters* was a popular television show. Also, Charles Addams's ghoulish cartoons, which had been published in *The New Yorker,* were adapted into the pseudoscary *The Addams Family.* A generation later, children who had enjoyed watching these television shows took their own children to theaters to see the feature films *The Addams Family* (1991) and *Addams Family Values* (1993) starring Anjelica Huston, Raul Julia, and Christopher Lloyd. Laughs come mostly from the surprise of seeing ordinary family life conducted in a spooky old mansion by scary-looking individuals with such names as Uncle Fester, Morticia, Gomez, Wednesday, and Pugsley.

Other Gothic movies that made people both shiver and laugh include the 1973 *Rocky Horror Picture Show,* a spoof of a Gothic novel, which originally failed at the box office, but soon developed a cult following. The 1984 *Ghostbusters* starred Bill Murray and Dan Aykroyd, while the 1986 *Little Shop of Horrors* starred Steve Martin, Rick Moranis, and a plant that eats people. Also in 1986, *The Witches of Eastwick,* based on John Updike's novel, starred Jack Nicholson, Cher, Susan Sarandon, Michelle Pfeiffer, and Veronica Cartwright. This fascination with horror led right into the *Batman* movies of the 1990s, in which New York City was renamed Gotham City. Its underground tunnels and sewer systems were made to serve as modern substitutes for the secret passageways, hidden entries, and basement crypts of the castles and mansions in Gothic novels.

In 1975, folklore collector Alvin Schwartz was happily surprised when his 1981 *Scary Stories to Tell in the Dark* and its sequels *More Scary Stories to Tell in the Dark* and *Scary Stories 3: More Tales to Chill Your Bones* started winning state contests where children voted on their favorite books. Today, these books are at the top of the American Library Association's list of books banned during the 1990s. They are nevertheless still favorites. The stories that Schwartz collected are kids' versions of some of the scary urban legends published in such adult books as Jan Harold Brunvand's *The Vanishing Hitchhiker: American Urban Legends and Their Meanings* and Paul Dickson and Joseph C. Goulden's *There Are Alligators in Our Sewers and Other American Credos.* A similar, but newer, book that includes such stories as "The Stolen Kidney," "The Scuba Diver in the Forest Fire," and "Aliens in Roswell, New Mexico," is Thomas Craughwell's *Alligators in the Sewer: And 222 Other Urban Legends.*

In the mid 1980s writer Robert Lawrence Stine, who had written joke books for Scholastic as well as a *How to Be Funny* manual under the pen name of Jovial Bob Stine, created the *Goosebumps* series for 8-, 9-, and 10-year-olds, and the *Fear Street* series for young teens under the pen name of R. L. Stine. Although by now, interest in Gothic humor has peaked, Stine's books became a publishing phenomenon. As of 1996, the books and related merchandise (T-shirts, CD-ROMs, TV shows, videos, and games) had grossed $450 million, and Stine became known as the "best-selling" children's author in history—a title now passed to J. K. Rowling.

Ethnic-Based Humor

Discussions and news stories about *political correctness* have made everyone aware of the fact that ethnic-based humor can be used in negative ways. However, the other side of the coin is that such humor can also be used for positive purposes. Among members of their own groups, people use ethnic-based humor as a way of bonding and as a sign of solidarity and group pride. For example, humorous undertones often run through the *Spanglish* that young Hispanics use and through the exaggerated slang that is part of Black English.

An important point is that positive uses of ethnic humor usually come from within the group itself. This does not mean that all elements of criticism are avoided. Just as individuals sometimes use self-deprecating humor, they also use group-deprecating

HELEN S. WEISS AND M. JERRY WEISS
On the Importance of Humor

*W*hen we were teaching in New Jersey and our four children were young, we participated in an annual event that is unique, we think, to New Jersey. In 14 B.C. when the state came into being, God came down and created a constitution, and it was written that there shall be an educational convention every year regardless of whether the state has money to run its schools. And so every November the schools in New Jersey would close for two days and 60,000 teachers would drive to Atlantic City—the only city large enough to hold all of us.

One year when we were driving down the Garden State Parkway in our station wagon with our four children in the back, we heard them saying, "That's a teacher car," "That's not a teacher car," "Yes, there's a teacher car!" In the front seat, we were saying, "That's a Ford," "Well, that's a Cadillac," and "There's an Edsel." We couldn't break the code or come up with a reason for their conjecturing. Finally, we asked: "How do you know when it's a teacher car?"

Kids being kids, they condescendingly explained, "Isn't it obvious? Look at their faces!" And they were right. Teachers have grim faces. We don't laugh enough. We don't let kids laugh enough. Now we're learning, and it is important to realize that humor is

the one genre that appeals to *non-readers, can't-readers,* and *won't-readers,* as well as to *avid-readers.* That's why in our first two anthologies we focused on humor. It gave us an excuse to read and reread American humor going from Ben Franklin to Woody Allen.

It is wonderful to find humor in literature, but there is also humor in our classrooms. Students will provide it (Paula Danziger was once a student in Jerry's adolescent literature class) and so will we as teachers, as when Jerry accidentally welcomed summer school students to the university's *intercourse session,* instead of to the university's *intersession course.*

Ever since the days of yore when every self-respecting Lord had his own court jester, humorists have been cultural, social, and political commentators. They help us maintain balance and perspective and prevent us from taking ourselves and the world that we live in too seriously. Laughter is therapeutic. Scientists are now proving what our literary geniuses have known forever—comic relief is essential in literature; it's even more essential in life. People of all ages and stages in life can, and do, laugh together. A smile is the international language understood everywhere. It's the safety valve of the psyche.

The Weisses' anthologies include *The American Way of Laughing,* Bantam, 1977; *From One Experience to Another,* TOR, 1997; *Lost and Found,* TOR, 2000, and *Big City Cool,* Persea Books, 2002.

humor. The difference when such humor comes from inside versus outside a group is that the insider is probably chiding the group to change, while the outsider is making fun of, and cementing, old stereotypes.

When ethnic-based joking finds its way into books or films, thoughtful readers or viewers can learn a lot about each other. Henry Spalding has described the way that Jews use self-deprecating humor as "honey-coated barbs" at the people and things Jews love most. He says they "verbally attack their loved ones and their religion—all done with the grandest sense of affection—a kiss with salt on the lips, but a kiss nevertheless."[10]

Sherman Alexie's 1998 movie *Smoke Signals,* based on a short story from his book *The Lone Ranger and Tonto Fistfight in Heaven,* has some of this same kind of humor in it. The story is set on the Coeur d'Alene Indian Reservation in northern Idaho, and

The Arizona Kid by Ron Koertge. Little Brown, 1988. In a *School Library Journal* article, Roger Sutton praised Koertge for being able to treat the subject of homosexuality with humor and respect for both the characters and the reader. Other Koertge books that combine humor and seriousness are *Tiger, Tiger, Burning Bright* (1994) and *Confess-O-Rama* (1996), both Orchard.

The Earth, My Butt, and Other Big Round Things by Carolyn Mackler. Candlewick, 2003. This Printz Honor Book has a serious theme, but there's also some refreshing humor as overweight Virginia Shreves shares the Fat Girl Code of Conduct that allows her to survive in a Manhattan private school.

How Angel Peterson Got His Name: And Other Outrageous Tales about Extreme Sports by Gary Paulsen. Random/Wendy Lamb Books, 2003. Paulsen is at his storytelling best in these entertaining sketches about the extremes to which he and his 13-year-old friends would go as they created their own entertainment. Paulsen's *Harris and Me: A Summer Remembered* (Harcourt Brace, 1993) is an equally funny story about the son of an alcoholic couple being dumped off on a farm with some odd relatives. The boy's cousin greets him with, "We heard your folks was puke drunks is that right?"

If I Love You, Am I Trapped Forever? by M. E. Kerr. HarperCollins, 1973. Alan Bennett, the narrator, describes himself as "The most popular boy at Cayuta High. Very handsome. Very cool. Dynamite," but then Duncan Stein comes to town and Alan's life and world begin to crumble. Among Kerr's other humorous books all from HarperCollins are *Dinky Hocker Shoots Smack* (1972), *Little Little* (1981), *Him She Loves?* (1984), and *I'll Love You When You're More Like Me* (1977).

Martyn Pig by Kevin Brooks. Scholastic, 2002. The humor is pretty dark, but it's here in the story of a boy and the-girl-next door (an aspiring actress) who work to cover up the accidental death of Martyn's drunken and mean father.

The Secret Diary of Adrian Mole, Aged 13¾ and **The Growing Pains of Adrian Mole** by Sue Townsend. First published in England in 1982, reissued as HarperTempest, 2003. These very funny books are taken from Adrian's diaries as he recounts his life struggles, in which no one (especially the BBC) fully appreciates the value of his sensitive writings, in which the beloved Pandora does not long for Adrian's caresses as much as Adrian longs to caress Pandora.

Son of the Mob by Gordon Korman. Hyperion, 2002. Television's Sopranos have nothing on this story about 17-year-old Vince Luca, whose "family" business keeps interfering with his regular life. Things get especially wacky when he falls hard for Kendra, whose father is in the FBI.

Uncle Boris in the Yukon and Other Shaggy Dog Stories by Daniel Pinkwater, illustrations by Jill Pinkwater. Simon & Schuster, 2001. In his usual style, Pinkwater starts with a smidgin of autobiography and then adds large helpings of exaggeration to these stories about dogs he has known. Other funny Pinkwater books include *The Snarkout Boys and the Avocado of Death* (Lothrop, 1982) about nonconformists who do things with vigor. His *Young Adult Novel* (Crowell, 1981) is about the Wild Dada Ducks, five boys determined to upset the routine at Himmler High School.

Weetzie Bat by Francesca Lia Block. HarperCollins, 1989. Weetzie Bat, Dirk, and Slinkster Dog have their sad moments, but overall they are three of the hippest and funniest characters in all of YA literature.

The Wish List by Eoin Colfer. Hyperion, 2003. There's murder (almost) and mayhem in this lighthearted story in which St. Peter and the Devil argue over which one is to get Meg's soul. Computer geeks will be glad to know that Heaven is fully wired, but they might not be so happy to learn that irascible old men and mouthy young girls keep their basic personalities in the afterlife.

while it is about such serious problems as alcoholism, alienation, and broken dreams, it does not shy away from wry humor. When we went to see the film in Scottsdale, Arizona, the audience was almost equally divided between Anglos and Native Americans. Both groups laughed at such parodies as a T-shirt advertising "Fry Bread Power" and at "The miracle of the fry bread" when Victor's mother magically feeds a crowd that is twice as big as she had expected. She simply raises her arms heavenward and solemnly rips each piece of bread in half. Both groups also laughed at the KREZ radio station announcer who sounds like Robin Williams when he shouts, "It's a great day to be indigenous!" Indian viewers seemed more amused by Victor telling Thomas to shut off the television, "There's only one thing more pathetic than Indians on TV and that's Indians watching Indians on TV."

Indian viewers also laughed uninhibitedly at the two gum-chewing, soda-drinking sisters who sat sideways facing each other in the front seat of their old car as they listened to rock music and drove backwards. While white viewers were troubled by such practical questions as, "Is the gear shift broken?" and "Can't they afford to get it fixed?" the Indian viewers appeared to accept the women as genuinely funny versions of contrary clowns.

Several tribes rely for humor on contraries. These are clowns that do the opposite of what is expected. They dress in buffalo robes in the summer and stand naked in winter snow. In Thomas Berger's 1964 *Little Big Man* (based on his 1961 novel *Black Elk Speaks; Being the Life Story of a Holy Man of the Oglala Sioux as Told through John G. Neihardt),* a contrary clown arrives riding backwards on a horse with his body painted in motley colors. He says "Goodbye" for "Hello," "I'm glad I did it!" for "I'm sorry," and cleans himself with sand before striding off by walking through the river.

The point is that humor is a powerful literary technique that can be used for a multitude of purposes as in the books listed in Focus Box 5.5. Because humor is so intimately tied to the culture of particular groups, it will probably be one of the last things that outsiders catch onto. Nevertheless, it is well worth whatever attention we can give to it, whether working with middle-school readers (see Focus Box 5.6) or with older students.

Teaching Literary Humor

Students are sometimes disappointed because an adult recommends a "funny" book. When they read it, they don't feel like laughing all the way through. The fact is that for people to laugh, they have to be surprised, and there is no way that an author can surprise a reader on every page. Instead, authors sprinkle humor throughout their books. The greater the contrast between the rest of the book and the humor, then the bigger the surprise and the more pleasure it will bring to the reader. Our job at school is not just to repeat the same kinds of humor that students get on the Comedy Channel or through lists of jokes on the Internet but to help students mature in their taste and appreciation. We need to educate students to catch onto a multitude of allusions and to have the patience required for reading and appreciating subtle kinds of humor. See Focus Box 5.7, Humorous Essayists Accessible to Teens.

At one of the International Society for Humor Studies meetings, Jacque Hughes, who teaches at Central Oklahoma University in Edmond, presented an example of how

Angus, Thongs, and Full-Frontal Snogging and **On the Bright Side, I'm Now the Girlfriend of a Sex God: Further Confessions of Georgia Nicolson** by Louise Rennison. HarperCollins, 2000 and 2001. There's also a third book in the series, but it doesn't have quite the sparkle of these first two British imports, which are similar in style, except from a girl's point of view, to the truly hilarious *The Secret Diary of Adrian Mole, Aged 13 ¾* by Sue Townsend (Grove Press, 1986).

The Canning Season by Polly Horvath. Farrar, 2003. There is both poignancy and slapstick humor in this story of Ratchet Clark, who unexpectedly finds herself alone on a train going from Florida to a remote part of Maine where she is to spend the summer with two elderly relatives, twins Tilly and Penpen.

Fair Weather by Richard Peck. Dial, 2001. History has never been as funny as this account of three children and their exuberant grandfather enjoying the wonders of the 1893 World's Fair in Chicago.

Flipped by Wendelin Van Draanen. Knopf/Borzoi, 2001. Juli Baker's and Bryce Loski's "romance" is told in alternating chapters. Juli once raised some chickens for a science project and now she can't bear to part with them, so she starts an egg business—a real turn-off to Bryce, who throws away the eggs that Juli lovingly provides for his family.

No More Dead Dogs by Gordon Korman. Hyperion, 2000. Twelve-year-old Wallace Wallace is tired of reading books in which the dog always dies. He's in trouble with his English teacher because he hates reading another such story: *Old Shep, My Pal*. It gets even worse when the drama club decides to put on a play and Wallace Wallace takes steps to keep the fictional Old Shep alive.

Surviving the Applewhites by Stephanie S. Tolan. HarperCollins, 2002. As a last resort, 12-year-old Jake Semple, complete with spiked hair, numerous body piercings, and "attitude," is sent to an extremely loose and creative "academy" run by the Applewhite family. Thank goodness, everyone is too busy to notice, except for E.D., who, in the way she shoulders responsibility, bears some resemblance to Hermione in the *Harry Potter* books.

The Misfits by James Howe. Atheneum/Simon & Schuster, 2001. Can a group of misfits change their school through running for election? Probably not, but it's nevertheless fun to imagine through this exploration of what it means to be "different" in seventh grade.

The Steps by Rachel Cohn. Simon & Schuster, 2003. "The Steps" in this funny, family story are the "bazillion" stepbrothers, stepsisters, and half-siblings that 12-year-old Annabel gets acquainted with when she travels from New York to Australia to visit her divorced father.

What Would Joey Do? by Jack Gantos. Farrar Strauss Giroux, 2002. In these funny books about hyperactive Joey Pigza (*Joey Pigza Swallowed the Key*, 1998, and *Joey Loses Control*, 2000) Gantos manages to walk the fine line between humor and empathy. In the third book, Joey has matured into "Mr. Helpful," and he proves himself quite as capable as—in some ways more capable than—the adults around him.

drawing relationships between raucous humor and more subtle humor can help students move to new levels of appreciation. She was having a hard time getting her 18-year-old freshmen to understand the dark humor in Flannery O'Connor's "A Good Man Is Hard to Find." Then she happened to see *National Lampoon's Vacation* starring Chevy Chase. It was wonderfully funny, and because most of her students had seen the movie, class members were able to compare the personalities and the incidents. When they realized that the similarities were too extensive—and too funny—to be coincidental, they gained a new appreciation for O'Connor's skill to do only with words what cost the movie producers millions of dollars to do with words and film.

It takes skill and practice, along with a broad, cultural background of knowledge, to understand a full range of humor. In *New York Magazine* (July 17, 1995), readers sent in some thoughtful letters as a follow-up to an article on today's depressing state of stand-up comedy. One writer answered his own question of "Why were the Bennys, the Aces, the Allens (Steve and Fred, both), Berles, Benchleys, Parkers, Woollcotts intuitively brilliant and where are their kind now?" with the observation that these earlier comedians "were the products of a literate society, widely read or with extensive cultural experience, which gave them backgrounds upon which to draw. . . . They knew how to think and were well edited, either by erudite editors or by perceptive audiences." Another reader wrote that the place to look for delightful wit today is not in the comedy clubs but "in written form, in comic novels and essays." Most of our students aren't going to find this kind of humor unless we help prepare them.

While few people appreciate having jokes explained to them, analyzing humor can be a good way to entice students into other kinds of literary analysis. Humor is an obvious emotion, and students are genuinely interested in figuring out what causes them to smile or laugh. While philosophers, psychologists, linguists, anthropologists, writers, actors, and comedians have all tried to figure out why people laugh, no one has come up with a proven system. All the reviewers we know, however, have come to agreement that Louis Sachar's *Holes* is a very funny book. It won both the Newbery Award and the National Book Award and was listed on practically every "Best Book" list created for 1998. *Holes* consists of two stories. One is set in the present featuring young Stanley Yelnats, while the other one is set in the past and is about Stanley's ancestors. When the contemporary story would get too grim, Sachar would slip in a chapter from the past.

As explained very early in *Holes,* Stanley and his family seem to have more than their share of bad luck "all because of his no-good-dirty-rotten-pig-stealing-great-great-grandfather!" The very next line says that Stanley smiled when he thought of this because "It was a family joke," but some readers are just like Stanley and his family in forgetting that this is a joke.

Stanley is mistakenly accused of theft, found guilty, and sentenced to Camp Green Lake Juvenile Correction Facility, where every day each of the boys must dig a five-foot by five-foot hole supposedly to strengthen his character. Actually, the warden is forcing the boys to help her (yes, the warden is a woman) look for buried treasure. Stanley figures he'll lose weight or die digging, but his friend and fellow criminal Zero tries another way: He runs off. Stanley sets out after Zero, knowing little about the environment and forgetting to fill up his canteen. Stanley and Zero save themselves, partly through their own devices and partly through a series of coincidences that even Sachar realizes is a bit much. However, he lets readers in on the joke by entitling his denouement "Filling in the Holes."

To illustrate the complexity and the interrelatedness of narrative humor, in Table 5.1 we list several of the features that humor scholars identify as being what people find funny. We illustrate them with examples from Sachar's *Holes.* The chart will, of course, be more meaningful to those who have read the book, so if nothing else, we hope it will encourage you to do just that.

FOCUS BOX 5.7   Humorous Essayists Accessible to Teens

Woody Allen is most famous for his movies, but some critics think that his compilations of stories and essays are wittier and have better one-liners than do his films. Sophisticated students can enjoy *Side Effects* (Random House, 1989), *Getting Even* (Random House, 1971), and *Without Feathers* (Random House, 1975).

Dave Barry is a newspaper columnist who in 1998 won the Pulitzer Prize for commentary. Among his books are *Dave Barry's Greatest Hits* (Columbine/Fawcett, 1998), *Dave Barry Slept Here: A Sort of History of the United States* (Random House, 1988), *Dave Barry's Complete Guide to Guys: A Fairly Short Book* (Fawcett, 1996), and *The World According to Dave Barry* (Random House, 1994).

Henry Beard founded *The National Lampoon* and then resigned to write his own very funny books including several sports "daffynitions" done with Roy McKie. His *Poetry for Cats: The Definitive Anthology of Distinguished Feline Verse* (Villard, 1994) is a favorite, at least with cat-lovers.

Erma Bombeck was still writing her syndicated newspaper column and had 12 books in print at the time of her death in 1996. Teenagers especially like her *I Want to Grow Hair, I Want to Grow Up, I Want to Go to Boise: Children Surviving Cancer* (Harper-Collins, 1989) because it focuses on young people. In 1994, three of her books were gathered into *The Best of Bombeck* (Budget Book Service). They included *At Wit's End, Just Wait Until You Have Children of Your Own,* and *I Lost Everything in the Post-Natal Depression.*

Bill Cosby's *Cosbyology: Essays and Observations from the Doctor of Comedy* (Hyperion, 2001) includes 19 autobiographical essays. YAs will especially appreciate the ones from his youth.

James Herriot was a British veterinarian who wrote four well-loved books about, in the words of the *Atlantic Monthly,* "recalcitrant cows, sinister pigs, neurotic dogs, Yorkshire weather, and pleasantly demented colleagues." His books include *All Creatures Great and Small* (1972), followed by *All Things Bright and Beautiful* (1974), *All Things Wise and Wonderful* (1977), and *The Lord God Made Them All* (1981), St. Martins Press.

Garrison Keillor has been labeled by *Time* magazine "the funniest American writer still open for business." Tapes and CDs are available for several of his books including *Lake Wobegon Days* (1985), *Happy to Be Here: Even More Stories and Comic Pieces* (1983), *Leaving Home: A Collection of Lake Wobegon Stories* (1987), and *Wobegon Boy* (1977), all Viking Penguin.

Richard Lederer's *The Bride of Anguished English: A Bonus of Bloopers, Blunders, Botches, and Boo-Boos* (St. Martin's, 2000) is a sequel to his classic *Anguished English* (Wyrick, 1987, Dell, 1989). They are best read in short chunks to get full pleasure from the funny errors Lederer gleans from unpublished writings.

Dorothy Parker died in 1967, but several relatively new books are available. *The Portable Dorothy Parker,* edited by Brendan Gill, was published in 1991 by Viking, while in 1994 Modern Library published *The Poetry and Short Stories of Dorothy Parker.*

James Thurber's *Fables for Our Time* (Harper & Brothers, 1940) is his most accessible book, but students can also be led to such stories as "The Night the Bed Fell," "University Days," "The Catbird Seat," and "The Secret Life of Walter Mitty." *The Thurber Carnival,* originally printed in 1945, has by now gone into more than thirty printings, and in 1996, Garrison Keillor edited *James Thurber: Writings and Drawings for Library of America.*

It is almost easier to find laugh-out-loud books for middle schoolers than for high school readers.

Evidence of the power of Sachar's humor is the difficulty we had in pulling out succinct examples of humor because a well-developed book differs from stand-up comedy in being more than a series of one-liners. For example, Sachar carried some of his jokes throughout the entire book as when Stanley first gets to camp and the guard tells him, "You're not in the Girl Scouts any more." The guard regularly repeats this idea sometimes by just reminding the boys they aren't Girl Scouts, while at other times he asks, "You Girl Scouts having a good time?" Near the end of the book, when Stanley's lawyer and the Attorney General drive into the camp and the Warden wonders if it's "them," the guard tells her, "It ain't Girl Scouts selling cookies." This all leads up to the ironic denouement when readers are told that the camp is "bought by a national organization dedicated to the well-being of young girls. In a few years, Camp Green Lake will become a Girl Scout camp."

Another difficulty in making the chart was matching specific examples with the designated features because many of Sachar's jokes serve several purposes. At the same time Sachar is surprising readers or making them feel superior to a particular character, he is puzzling them with incongruous details, which he later resolves, thereby bringing more smiles. For example, on first seeing this description of the animals who share the amenities of Camp Green Lake Detention Center, readers probably do not realize they are being let in on a crucial plot element. Instead they just sit back and enjoy a standard three-part joke in which a comedian sets up a pattern and then surprises listeners by breaking the pattern.

TABLE 5.1   SOME FEATURES OF NARRATIVE HUMOR AS ILLUSTRATED BY INCIDENTS IN LOUIS SACHAR'S *HOLES*

Ambiguity	*Stanley Yelnats* is the name of either Stanley, his father, or his grandfather.
	The whole story would have collapsed if *Zero*'s name hadn't been a shortened form of *Zeroni* instead of a reference to the contents of his brain.
	When Stanley finds the gold cap with *K.B.* on it, he thinks it might be the cap to the pen of a famous writer, but readers figure out that the *K.B.* stands for both *Kate Barlow* and the *Kissing Bandit*.
	Upon seeing the name *Mary Lou* on the back of the sunken boat, Stanley and Zero imagine a boy rowing across the lake with a beautiful girlfriend; readers know that *Mary Lou* was a 50-year-old donkey who lived on onions.
Exaggeration	The digging of five-foot-by-five-foot holes every day by every boy was surely an exaggeration.
	The characters are eccentrics, especially those bigger-than-life ones from the 1890s including the Kissing Bandit, Kate Barlow, who "died laughing," the mean sheriff, the too-good-to-be-true "onion man," and the too-bad-to-be-true townspeople including Trout Walker and Linda.
	Equally exaggerated is Stanley's great grandfather who carried his wealth in his suitcase and after losing it to Kate Barlow spent three weeks wandering in the desert. He was saved by the "Thumb of God," and married the nurse who took care of him at the hospital because he thought she was an angel—literally.
Hostility	There is enough hostility to go all around. When Stanley first gets to camp, the guard asks him if he's thirsty and when Stanley gratefully says, "Yes, thanks," the guard tells him to get used to it because "You're going to be thirsty for the next 18 months."
	Stanley fantasizes about his new "friends" coming to his old school and intimidating his nemesis.
	The warden puts rattlesnake venom in her nail polish so when she slaps Mr. Sir and scratches his face, he writhes in pain and his face is swollen for days.
Incongruity	There could hardly be a more incongruous set of characters ranging from Clyde "Sweet Feet" Livingston to Warden Walker and from Madame Zeroni to poor love-sick Elya Yelnats.
	Stanley had thought about becoming an F.B.I. agent, but he realizes the group meeting with Mr. Pendanski is not "the appropriate place to mention that."
	Readers laugh right along with the other boys when Stanley innocently responds to Mr. Pendanski's lecture about there being only one person responsible for Stanley's predicament: "My no-good-dirty-rotten-pig-stealing-great-great-grandfather."
Incongruity Resolution	The whole story revolves around Sachar resolving such incongruities as the boys being covered with the dreaded lizards but not being bitten, why the warden made the boys dig so many holes, why Zero never learned to read, how Zero and Stanley were tied together by "fate," how Stanley's great grandfather was saved in the desert, and why the curse is now lifted.

Irony	Not only is there no lake at Camp Green Lake, there is no greenery except in the two trees whose shade is owned by the warden.
	The townspeople of Green Lake said that God would punish Kate Barlow for kissing a black man, but instead God punishes the town so that no rain falls and the lake dries up so that not only its shape but also its surface is like a frying pan.
	In his search for Zero, when Stanley comes up on the old, wrecked boat, he realizes that someone probably drowned in the very spot where he might die of thirst.
Superiority	Throughout the story kids feel superior to the adults, and well they might, judging by the Warden, Mr. Sir, and Mr. Pendanski.
	The whole adult society is made to look ridiculous so that readers agree with Stanley's "Well, duh!" when he reads the sign at the entrance to the camp declaring it "a violation of the Texas Penal Code to bring guns, explosives, weapons, drugs, or alcohol onto the premises."
	Readers cheer when Zero and Stanley, who are the lowest on the totem pole of the camp, are the ones who get out and become something less—"but not a lot less"—than millionaires.
	Everyone feels superior to the pot-headed Myra who does not have sense enough to choose to marry Stanley's great-great-grandfather.
Surprise or Shock	Readers are as surprised as is Stanley at the sneakers falling from the sky and hitting him on the head. When Zero tells Stanley that he knows he didn't steal Clyde Livingston's sneakers, Stanley shakes his head because when he tells the truth nobody believes him, and now when he lies, he still isn't believed.
	Stanley and Zero's adventure is one surprise after another starting with Stanley finding Zero and Zero finding the "Sploosh" and ending with their finding the trunk with Stanley Yelnats's name on it.
A Trick or a Twist	An intriguing new setting is provided for the old trick of convincing someone that by lifting a calf every day, his strength will increase at the same rate that the animal gains weight.
Word Play	The recreation hall is named the *W–R–E–C–K* room.
	The boys all have descriptive names: *Zigzag, Magnet, Squid, Armpit, Caveman, Barf Bag,* and *Xray.*
	The macho guard is named *Mr. Sir* (he's doubly a man), while the boys call *Mr. Pendanski* ("pen-dance-key") *Mom.*
	Sachar constantly plays with the word *holes* as when Stanley finds the lipstick tube initialed with *K.B.* and "digs that hole into his memory," and Sachar entitles the denouement, "Filling in the Holes."

Here's a good rule to remember about rattlesnakes and scorpions: If you don't bother them, they won't bother you.

Usually.

Being bitten by a scorpion or even a rattlesnake is not the worst thing that can happen to you. You won't die.

Usually. . . .

But you don't want to be bitten by a yellow-spotted lizard. That's the worst thing that can happen to you. You will die a slow and painful death.

Always.

Concluding Comments

Of all the chapters in this book, this is the one that cries out for some kind of out-loud sharing. We hope that in class you can have a poetry slam (or jam) and that selected students will perform an excerpt or an improvised scene from a play or do a humorous readers' theatre presentation. It would also be a good experience for you to go to a local high school production of a play, and by making a few phone calls to the central administration of your local library you might be able to locate a teen poetry slam that you could observe. Newspaper or online announcements might also help you find adult poetry slams that you could attend. Within the last decade, poetry has changed more than any other genre. Thus, it behooves all of us to sit up and pay attention to the poetry that young people are writing and putting on the Internet as well as to the many new novels that are being written in verse both for adults and young people.

 Notes

[1] Marc Aronson, "When Coming of Age Meets the Age That's Coming: One Editor's View of How Young Adult Publishing Developed in America," *VOYA* 21:5 (December 1998): 340–342.

[2] Naomi Shihab Nye, *19 Varieties of Gazelle: Poems of the Middle East* (Greenwillow, 2002), p. xii.

[3] Paul Janeczko, "On Collecting Poems," *Literature for Today's Young Adults* by Kenneth L. Donelson and Alleen Pace Nilsen (Longman, 1997), p. 345.

[4] David Lehman, "The American Prose Poem," from *The American Poetry Review,* March/April 2003, quoted in "This Week's Chronicle" at http://chronicle.com/chronicle, April 18, 2003.

[5] Ed Sullivan, "Up for Discussion: Fiction or Poetry: A Librarian Looks at the Profusion of Novels Written in Verse," *School Library Journal,* August 2003, pp. 44–45.

[6] Richard W. Beach and James D. Marshall, *Teaching Literature in the Secondary School* (Harcourt Brace Jovanovich, 1991), p. 384.

[7] Luella B. Cook, "Reading for Experience," *English Journal* 25 (April 1936): 280.

[8] Rick E. Amidon, "Toward a Young Adult Drama," *English Journal* 76 (September 1987): 59.

[9] Lance M. Gentile and Merna M. McMillan, "Humor and the Reading Program," *Journal of Reading* 21 (January 1978): 343–350.

[10] Henry Spalding, quoted in *Encyclopedia of 20th Century American Humor* by Alleen Pace Nilsen and Don L. F. Nilsen (Oryx Press 2000), p. 173.

Adventure, Sports, Mysteries, and the Supernatural

Remembering English teachers who pleaded with us to "read only the best—the classics," many of us feel vaguely worried when we read books simply to enjoy characters and their adventures. Somewhat defensively, we make claims that are hard to substantiate. For example, we claim that reading about adventures makes us more interesting people, sports books teach us the game of life, mysteries are psychologically helpful to our inner well-being, and horror stories are a substitute for aggression. These claims may have some truth, but they are hard to prove. We would be on safer ground if we simply accepted "Rosenberg's First Law of Reading: Never apologize for your reading tastes,"[1] and promoted the idea that reading for pleasure is a worthy activity and goal, in and of itself. If we, or our students, gain something more than pleasure, we should be grateful that serendipity is still at work in today's complex world.

Adventure Stories

"Once upon a time" is a magical phrase. In one way or another, it opens every adventure tale and suggests actions and excitement. While we may care about the people in these adventures, we care equally—or more—about the actions to come. The greatest of these is implied violence, things we fear that will happen. The pace and tempo force the action to move faster and faster and to speed us into the tale.

Adventure books sell well, for good reason. Antony Brandt in *American Heritage* noted that the country was mad for adventure.

> The whole country seems bent on getting out there and having adventures, and if you can't do it, you can read about it. Magazines like *Mens' Journal* and *Outside* that specialize in the subject are thriving. The staid old National Geographic Society has launched its own magazine, *National Geographic Adventure* to take advantage of what has reached the state of a craze.[2]

The author then added, "A taste for adventure is as old as the human race itself, a function of an evolutionary development that rewards risk takers over the timid and the meek." Readers of adventure tales feel much the same way about taking chances as did Susan Hiscock. For fifty years she and her husband sailed the globe, never letting loose of their wanderlust. She was a fan of Arthur Ransome's books and one of his mottos was painted over their cabin door: "Grab a chance and you won't be sorry for a might-have-been."[3] That's a great motto for either reading or living.

The best adventure tales demand more than plot and a series of actions (see Table 6.1). Good writers provide believable characters, at least a likable and imperfect (and probably young) protagonist and a wily and dangerous antagonist (or villain). Because we are primarily interested in the action, we're likely to be irritated by long descriptive or meditative passages. Writers must reveal characterization through the plot—what could happen, what might happen, and how all the incidents tie together. We want surprises and turns of the screw. Heroes become trapped, and the only way to safety is through even greater jeopardy. Adventure tales usually focus either on person-against-person or on person-against-nature, with person-against-self becoming important only as the tale unfolds and the protagonist faces frustration and possible failure.

The most important literary device found in adventure stories is verisimilitude. With so much emphasis on danger, writers must provide realistic details galore to assure us, despite some inner misgivings, that the tale is possible and believable. We must believe that whatever the hero's frustrations, the cliffhanging scenes are possible.

Robb White's *Deathwatch* epitomizes the elements of adventure novels—person versus person, person versus nature, person versus self, conflicts, tension, thrills, chills, and a hero frustrated at every turn by an inventive, devious, and cruel villain. The first paragraph forces us into the action and introduces the two actors:

> "There he is!" Madec whispered. "Keep still!" There had been a movement up on the ridge of the mountain. For a moment something had appeared between the two rock outcrops.
> "I didn't see any horns," Ben said.
> "Keep quiet!" Madec whispered fiercely.

TABLE 6.1   SUGGESTIONS FOR EVALUATING ADVENTURE STORIES

A good adventure story has most of the positive qualities generally associated with good fiction. In addition it usually has:	A poor adventure story may have the negative qualities generally associated with poor fiction. It is particularly prone to have:
A likable protagonist with whom young readers can identify	A protagonist who is too exaggerated or too stereotyped to be believable
An adventure that readers can imagine happening to themselves	Nothing really exciting about the adventure
Efficient characterization	Only stereotyped characters
An interesting setting that enhances the story without getting in the way of the plot	A long drawn-out conclusion after the climax has been reached
Action that draws readers into the plot within the first page or so of the story	

We know from those few words that *Deathwatch* has something to do with hunting, although we have no reason yet to suspect that hunting will become an ominous metaphor. We recognize that the name Madec sounds harsh and seems vaguely related to the word mad, again without recognizing how prescient we are. Within the next few pages, we learn how carefully White has placed the clues before us. Ben crouches with his little .22 Hornet and watches Madec with his "beautifully made .385 Magnum Mauser action on a Winchester 70 stock with enough power to knock down an elephant—or turn a sleeping Gila monster into a splatter" and remembers that Madec had been willing to shoot anything that moved.

> Madec huddled over his gun. There was an intensity in his eyes far beyond that of just hunting a sheep. It was the look of murder.

And murder is present. Before long, Madec takes a shot at a bighorn sheep, which turns out to be an old desert prospector—now quite dead—and he asks Ben to quash the incident and forget it ever happened. Ben refuses, and the book is off and running. So is Ben, running for his life, without gun, water, or food, amid hostile desert mountains and sand and a killing gun.

Madec personifies the maddened but crafty villain, able to read Ben's mind and forestall his attempts to get clothes, weapons, or water. We are almost certain Ben will win, but we wonder because Madec is an extraordinary opponent. We see Ben change from a calm, rational young man to a frightened, desperate animal and then into a cold, dangerous person who must think as Madec thinks to win out over the villain. Madec begins with all the power on his side—guns, water, food, and wealth. Given reality, we know that Madec must win, but given our sense of rightness and justice, we believe that he cannot be allowed to win. Ben has little interest in right or wrong after the first few pages. His interest is more elemental and believable—simple survival until he can escape.

Part of the charm of adventure stories is their variety of settings—both in time and space. Cornelia Funke's (see her statement on p. 176) *The Thief Lord* and *Inkheart* are set on the watery "streets" of modern Venice. The books are about orphans who flee from cruel relatives and meet a charismatic young man who calls himself the Thief Lord. The reviewer for *School Library Journal* praised Funke for her skill in delineating her characters and the subtle way that she uses puckish humor to reveal changes in their relationships.

In Iain Lawrence's historical *The Wreckers,* a young man who longs for the sea but is denied it by his businessman father becomes involved in the dangerous business of looting wrecked ships. His adventures continue in *The Smugglers* and *The Buccaneers.* Lawrence also used a seaside setting and a similar time frame for *The Lightkeeper's Daughter,* but it focuses a bit more on human emotions than on actions. A couple had moved to an isolated island hoping to provide their children with an idyllic upbringing. But by the time the book opens, their 17-year-old daughter is returning home with a 3-year-old daughter of her own and their beloved and gifted son has apparently died.

Geraldine McCaughrean's *The Pirate's Son,* set in the 1800s and packed with derring-do, opens with the death of Nathan Gull's father. Nathan is forced out of his school because he has no money, but luckily for Nathan, Tamo White, son of a pirate,

CORNELIA FUNKE
On the Miracle of Translation

When I came to America in 2002 to promote my book *The Thief Lord*, both children and adults asked me whether it was my first book. "No," I answered, "I have published about forty books in Germany, but this is the first one translated into English." I started as an illustrator, but I soon started writing because I often had to illustrate stories I didn't like.

It is still a great adventure for me and I believed it couldn't get much better until the summer of 2002 when suddenly I began meeting children on the other side of the ocean, who were not so very different from the ones I already knew in Germany. *The Thief Lord* has now been sold to publishers in almost thirty countries. I have pictures that Japanese children drew of the characters, and I have photographs from Switzerland where children built a snow dragon because of *Dragonrider*. Families who went to Venice because they had read *The Thief Lord* and looked for all the places write, "Cornelia, it is just as you described it."

I wish I could speak all the languages in the world. Well, sadly I can't. I am only able to read Italian, German, and English—so I asked all my translators to read one chapter of the book they have translated for me on tape so I can at least hear how my story sounds in their tongue. Many of my translators write to me. My Japanese translator came all the way to Hamburg to bring me pictures of Japanese children. My Italian translator asks me questions about the names I chose, and my French translator tells me she just did a reading of my book in a French bookstore. As for the translation of *The Thief Lord* into English, my cousin did it. English was his first language, though he is German and was raised in Africa. I still remember the moment he gave me his translation. It felt like I was reading my own story for the first time.

Another language always adds something. Of course it doesn't change the content, but maybe one could say, the story wears another dress. I loved the translation my cousin did, but when *Inkheart*, my newest book, needed to be translated, he was so busy selling my foreign rights to other countries that Anthea Bell, the most reknowned translator from German to English, took over. And once again I sat there reading my own story aloud to myself in a foreign tongue. It resembled the original like a perfectly fitted glove.

So, with the help of many translators and publishers my stories have started traveling to places I've never been. They find their way to people I've never met who choose to spend some of their time walking in my imagination. In a world where borders still cut the world into artificial pieces, where differences are thought to be more important than the things that people share, it is wonderful that writers and readers can travel together for a while in their imaginations. It still feels like a miracle—touching children and their parents with a pile of printed letters that come alive in their heads and hearts. Is there any profession on earth more exciting?

Cornelia Funke's books include The Thief Lord, *which won the 2003 Mildred L. Batchelder Award for outstanding translated book;* Inkheart, *2003; and* The Princess Knight *and* Dragonrider, *forthcoming, all from Scholastic.*

decides to leave school and take Nathan with him. The first half of McCaughrean's *The Kite Rider* is even more action-packed. The setting is thirteenth-century China after the mongols have conquered China, and hatred and distrust between Chinese and Mongols permeate the land. When 12-year-old Haoyou's father takes his son to see his ship, the boy is thrilled until the first mate takes offense when the father insults the Khan's wife. The mate kicks Haoyou off the ship and, worse yet, attaches the father to a kite hoisted over the ship to determine whether the winds are likely to augur a profitable voyage for the ship and the crew. Horrifying as this is, Haoyou is unprepared when his father catches the wind and is lifted high aloft, only to be just as suddenly plummeted to his death. The father has returned, "but his spirit had remained among the birds." It is now up to Haoyou to carry on the duties of the family and the honor of his father. He manages admirably, and a bonus for readers is that they also get to meet Mipeng, a girl cousin, who in clever, funny, and wise ways saves Haoyou from himself.

Two writers who appeal to young adults because they write convincing adventures are Gary Paulsen and Will Hobbs. Paulsen may well be the most popular writer among young people today. His stories are widely admired by both young and adult readers. In *Hatchet*, 13-year-old Brian Robeson is the only passenger in a small plane when the pilot dies from a heart attack. The plane goes down far off course in the Canadian wilderness, and Brian must save himself from starvation and predators with only the help of his hatchet and his wits. In *Brian's Return*, he has found his way back to civilization, yet after two years he dreams of the quiet and happiness of the northern woods compared to the miseries of the rat race and the so-called civilization to which he has returned. In the more recent *Guts*, he tells the real-life events behind the two books. Other Paulsen adventure stories are *Caught by the Sea*, *Voyage of the Frog*, *The Tracker*, and *The Island*.

Hobbs's interest in hiking, white-river rafting, archaeology, and natural history are reflected in his books. *Bearstone*, about a Native American boy sent to live with an old rancher whose wife has died, combines adventure with a story of growth and friendship. His stories are more action-packed than Paulsen's and sometimes less introspective, though in *Downriver* the change that Jessie makes in her life is impressive. In *Far North* and *Jason's Gold*, readers learn what it is like to be really cold. *Jackie's Wild Seattle* is about mountain climbing, while both *Ghost Canoe* and *Down the Yukon* are canoeing adventures.

Hobbs's recent *Wild Man Island* may not wind up precisely as an adventure tale, but it begins with all that makes a book an adventure. Andy Galloway, 14, sneaks off from his kayaking tour group early one morning to find Hidden Falls on Baranof Island, Alaska, where his father had died. He should have been back in plenty of time to join the group, but he hadn't counted on hostile sea lions or a wind that mightily came at him and drove him off course as he headed back to his group. Sea lions wreck his kayak and he swims to the beach, almost dead from exposure.

From there on, Andy has a run-in with a grizzly bear; he hears wolves howling; he sees a dog where none should be; he finds an abandoned cannery; and more frightening—and intriguing—he runs into "a giant of a man overgrown with gray hair." *Wild Man Island* becomes a combination of adventure mixed with Andy's need to justify his father's archeological theories.

Harry Mazer writes great adventure as shown in *Snowbound* and *The Island Keeper*, both unfortunately out of print. His more recent *Boy at War: A Novel of Pearl Harbor* starts with a boy whose father is a naval officer, out for an early morning fishing expedition. He sees the planes fly in and bomb the harbor, including the Arizona, his father's ship. The rest of the story has the boy looking for his father.

In Avi's Newbery-winning *The True Confessions of Charlotte Doyle*, a young girl is forced to overcome circumstances before they overcome her. Charlotte is raised in an upper-class family with a strong father. Even though she is warned not to board the brig

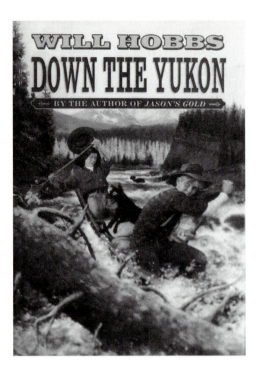

One of the charms of adventure stories is their varied settings as with Will Hobbs's several books set in the far north of the American continent.

Seahawk bound from Liverpool, England, to Providence, Rhode Island, her father has told her to take the ship, and so she goes on board, the only female on a ship commanded by evil and cruel Captain Jaggers. Trapped by the captain, she evades his plan to kill her and watches as the ship tips and plunges in a storm and the captain goes overboard. The crew makes her the ship's new captain—mostly because Charlotte is the daughter of an officer of the ship's company—but also because she has shown courage in facing down the captain and aiding the crew.

While most readers enjoyed Charlotte's adventures, at least one reviewer had qualms. Anne Scott Macleod said, "It's a fine and vicarious adventure story. It is also preposterous."[4] Avi took exception and in the Summer 1999 *Signal,* wrote:

> It is a legitimate task . . . of fiction to re-invent the past, if you will, so as to better define the future . . . Historical fiction—among other things—is about today's possibilities.[5]

Perhaps both Macleod's and Avi's statements illustrate the truth of critic Henry Seidel Canby's words, which are more than seventy years old, "Historical fiction, like history, is more likely to register an exact truth about the writer's present than the exact truth of the past."[6]

Nonfiction adventures in which people set out to challenge nature (see Focus Box 6.1, Real People Challenging Nature) have an extra level of excitement because readers know that human lives are at stake. While young people seldom have what it takes to embark on such purposeful adventures, they can nevertheless read about them. They

Addicted to Danger by Jim Wickwire. Pocketbooks, 1998. Wickwire gives readers a sense of what it means to battle mountains, doing what the human body was never meant to do.

Annapurna: A Woman's Place by Arlene Blum. Sierra Club Books, 1980. Thirteen women climbers tackle one of the world's greatest challenges. Two reached the top, two died.

Annapurna: First Conquest of an 8000-Meter Peak by Maurice Herzog. Dutton, 1952. A French Alpine Club climbs Annapurna (26,493 feet) in 1950 when the mountain had only been poorly surveyed.

Cave Passages: Roaming the Underground Wilderness by Michael Ray Taylor. Scribner, 1996. This takes readers into a number of underground adventures, from a Chinese burial cave to a Mexican sinkhole.

Clouds from Both Sides by Julie Tullis. Sierra Club Books, 1987. This is the biography of a woman who at 47 conquered K2 and died two days later.

Ghosts of Everest: The Search for Mallory and Irvine by Jochen Hemmleb, Larry A. Johnson, and Eric Simonson. The Mountaineers, 1999. Hemmleb and friends set out to find the bodies of two climbers—George Mallory and Andrew Irvine—who perished on Everest on June 6, 1924. They were successful. See also *Last Climb: The Legendary Everest Expeditions of George Mallory* by David Breashears and Audrey Salkeld (National Geographic Society, 2000).

In the Wake of Madness: The Murderous Voyage of the Whaleship Sharon by Joan Druett. Algonquin Books, 2003. In 1841, the sea and the brutal captain of the whale ship Sharon drove his men to mutiny.

Mountains of the Mind by Robert Macfarlane. Pantheon, 2003. This history of the relationship between mountains and humans traces the changing attitudes from when mountains were first considered to be eyesores or obstacles to progress but are now viewed with awe.

Revenge of the Whale: The True Story of the Whaleship Essex by Nathaniel Philbrick. Putnam, 2000. The author did a good job of condensing and adapting his adult title *In the Heart of the Sea* (Viking, 2000) for young readers.

Titanic Adventure by Jennifer Carter and Joel Hirschhorn. New Horizon, 1999. A woman tells how her fascination with the sea and shipwrecks ultimately took her to the Titanic.

can also imagine what they would do if they happen to be forced into such an adventure, as were the young people whose story is told in *Alive* (see the discussion in Chapter 9, pp. 256–257).

Climbing mountains is one of the ways that people face off against nature because, as Reinhold Messner reminds us, "In all true adventure, the path between the summit and the grave is a narrow one indeed."[7] Nowhere is that clearer than in Jon Krakauer's *Into Thin Air: A Personal Account of the Mount Everest Disaster.* In the spring of 1996, fourteen groups of climbers were making their way up Mount Everest. Krakauer reached the summit on May 10, as did five teammates, but five others died, and nineteen others were stranded for a time when a freak storm hit and left them to survive temperatures of 100 degrees below zero.

Ultimately, Everest took twelve lives that spring. Krakauer describes the work that went into planning and setting up the camps, the difficulties of the climb, the heroism shown by many of the climbers—and some incidents that exhibited cowardice or self-ishness—but he cannot explain fully why anyone should take such risks.

Krakauer had agreed to take part as a climber and writer for *Outside Magazine,* but when he delivered his article—on time—he learned how bitter were many of the friends and relatives of those who died. *Into Thin Air* is an attempt to get the story straight and to explain what role Krakauer had in saving a few climbers and in being unable to save others. It is also one more effort to explain why it is that anyone would climb a mountain, specifically Everest.

> People who don't climb mountains—the great majority of humankind, that is to say—tend to assume that the sport is a wreckless, Dionysian pursuit of ever-escalating thrills. But the notion that climbers are merely adrenaline junkies chasing a righteous fix is a fallacy, at least in the case of Everest. What I was doing up there had almost nothing to do with bungee jumping or skydiving or riding a motorcycle at 120 miles per hour.
>
> Above the comforts of Base Camp, the expedition in fact became an almost Calvinistic undertaking. The ratio of misery to pleasure was greater by an order of magnitude than any other mountain I'd been on. I quickly came to understand that climbing Everest was primarily about enduring pain. And in subjecting ourselves to week after week of toil, tedium, and suffering, it struck me that most of us were probably seeking, above all, something like a state of grace.[8]

Adventure stories are popular because boredom chafes at our souls and crowds out of our minds such practical concerns as safety and caution; however, the human body—at least our own—reminds us all too quickly of the risks. This may be why we prefer our adventures to come through books or, even better, through movies in which trick photography and special effects can make it easier for viewers to forget that losing is more common than winning.

Sports and the Game of Life

Because we lack the space to say everything that adults working with young people need to know about sports books, we recommend that interested readers find Chris Crowe's *More Than a Game: Sports Literature for Young Adults.* As shown by the listing in Focus Box 6.2, An Armful of YA Sports Fiction, most sports books, whether fiction or nonfiction, include information about the training that is needed, the expected rewards, tangible or not, and the inevitable disappointments that make the rewards even sweeter. Early sports books in the 1800s and 1900s focused on the character-changing possibilities of sports along with an inning-by-inning or quarter-by-quarter account. The minute-by-minute account was almost never successful. But the excitement of sports—the euphoria that sometimes comes to players—and the potential character development has remained. Occasional nonfiction writers have focused almost exclusively on a player's character flaws, an iconoclastic approach that seems to have had its day.

The excitement of sports is what readers want, just as winning is the only acceptable verdict for fans. Way back on June 5, 1974, the *Los Angeles Times* headlined the

FOCUS BOX 6.2   *An Armful of YA Sports Fiction*

Athletic Shorts by Chris Crutcher. Greenwillow, 1991. These stories may attract readers to Crutcher's sports novels because several of the protagonists make second appearances in the longer pieces.

Baseball in April and Other Stories by Gary Soto. Harcourt Brace Jovanovich, 1990. These eleven fairly simple stories are about everyday events—including neighborhood sports—in the lives of Mexican American kids living in Fresno, California, where Soto grew up.

Becoming Joe DiMaggio by Maria Testa. Candlewick, 2002. While the father is in prison during World War II, an Italian American family struggles to move on, with DiMaggio and radio always in the background.

The Boxer by Kathleen Karr. Farrar Straus & Giroux, 2002. In New York City of the 1880s, John Aloysius Xavier Woods works in a sweatshop, but daily he goes by a saloon soliciting would-be bare-fisted boxers. Because boxing is illegal in New York, he's tossed in jail. When he comes out, he's now Johnny "The Chopper" Woods.

Every Day and All the Time by Sis Deans. Holt, 2003. Emily's life is her dancing, but her dreams, along with her ankle, are shattered by an automobile accident that kills her brother. Nevertheless, she doesn't give up.

Fighting Reuben Wolfe by Markus Zusak. Scholastic, 2001. This story of two brothers joining an illegal fight circuit to earn money for their family received positive votes from all fifteen members of the Best Books for Young Adults committee of ALA.

Friends Till the End by Todd Strasser. Delacorte, 1981. A soccer star agrees reluctantly to visit Howie, who is dying of leukemia. A wonderful friendship develops.

High Heat by Carl Deuker. Houghton, 2003. Baseball pitcher Shane Hunter undergoes an abrupt change in lifestyle when his dad commits suicide over money problems. Shane's anger gets the best of him, and he pitches a fast ball directly at the head of the boy whose family has moved into Shane's former home.

Home of the Braves by David Klass. Farrar Straus & Giroux, 2002. Jo Brickman, captain of the soccer and wrestling teams, faces a Brazilian transfer student who's a whiz at soccer and ready to sweep Jo's would-be girlfriend off her feet.

Horse Thief by Robert Newton Peck. HarperCollins, 2002. During the Depression, a teenage boy searching for a family lives in a rodeo world.

In Lane Three, Alex Archer by Tessa Duder. Houghton Mifflin, 1987. Swimmer Alex (short for Alexandra) trains for the 1960 Olympic Games in Rome.

The Passing Game by Richard Blessing. Little, Brown, 1982. In one of the best YA novels ever, Craig Warren has potential greatness but his play is erratic.

Slot Machine by Chris Lynch. HarperCollins, 1995. Elvin is sent to a summer sports camp as a prelude to entering a private school. He is by turns cynical and amused as he proves that he does not fit into any of the expected slots. Lynch's *Iceman* (1994) explores the common idea among young males that anger is "cool," while *Shadow Boxer* (1993) is similar in being the story of two boys tempted to go into professional boxing, even though their father died from boxing injuries.

Three Clams and an Oyster by Randy Powell, Farrar Straus & Giroux, 2002. Flint is captain of a four-man flag-football team faced with a real problem, namely how to get rid of a teammate who is unreliable.

Ultimate Sports: Short Stories by Outstanding Writers for Young Adults, edited by Don Gallo, Delacorte, 1995. Stories by Robert Lipsyte, Chris Crutcher, Tessa Duder, and Norma Fox Mazer are included.

sports section, "There's Nothing Like the Euphoria of Accomplishment." *The New York Times* for August 11, 1974, headlined its sports section with an article (first published in *Dial* in 1919): "Baseball: A Boys' Game, A Pro Sport and a National Religion." And scholar—and baseball fan—Jacques Barzun had the final say, "Whoever wants to know the heart and mind of America had better learn baseball, the rules and realities of the game.[9]

To deny or even to question the significant place of sports in many American lives is to misunderstand American life or values. In the 1950s and early 1960s such writers as H. D. Francis and John Carson wrote good novels filled with heroes reeking of sweat. Their heroes often examined the price of fame and the temptation to believe—always doomed—that fame would last. Writers as powerful as John Updike killed that dream much as F. Scott Fitzgerald had killed other dreams of society or business and glory and permanence. The sentimental fiction of the 1950s and 1960s was never real, but it had a charm that we have lost, and with it some readers of more innocent sports books.

Two particularly impressive books about baseball that mature high school students can appreciate are about love and friendship and fatherhood. They are Mark Harris's *Bang the Drum Slowly* and Donald Hall's *Fathers Playing Catch with Sons*. Harris's story of a second- or third-string catcher dying of leukemia is touching, just as it is also good baseball. Hall, a major poet, offers a warm and almost sentimental account of his love for sports, particularly baseball. The first two sentences of his introduction tie together the two worlds he loves and needs: writing and baseball.

> Half of my poet-friends think I am insane to waste my time writing about sports and to loiter in the company of professional athletes. The other half would murder to take my place.

Later, he distinguishes between baseball and football to the detriment of the latter.

> Baseball is fathers and sons. Football is brothers beating each other up in the backyard, violent and superficial.

Basketball is today's favorite spectator sport, so we should expect good basketball stories written for young adults. The story that James Bennett tells in *The Squared Circle* focuses on Sonny Youngblood, a high school star basketball player now entering Southern Illinois University as the hope of their athletic department. Whether Sonny even likes the sport is a question he avoids asking himself, mostly out of fear of the answer. His father long ago walked out; Sonny didn't like his high school coach; he is the only non-African American on the squad; he hates the fraternity he is ready to join, and if all that were not bad enough, a cousin who is an art professor wants Sonny to work out what he wants to do with his life. The ending is powerful and disturbing, but Sonny is on his way to somewhere.

Other sports books by young adult authors range from Jerry Spinelli's lighthearted look at wrestling in *There's a Girl in My Hammerlock* to such heavier and highly acclaimed wrestling stories as Rich Wallace's *Wrestling Starbridge* and Terry Davis's *Vision Quest*. In Will Weaver's *Striking Out*, Billy Baggs is a natural baseball player, but

DAN GUTMAN
Confessions of a Reluctant Reader

*O*kay, I admit it. I hated to read when I was a kid. I thought reading was boring and hard to do. My mother was worried about me and used to buy comic books hoping they would get me interested in reading. Because I was a "reluctant reader," I think I might be more sensitive than other authors to kids who don't like to read. I'm thinking of those kids while I'm writing. That's why I don't write deep, serious, descriptive novels. Those types of books bored me when I was a kid. And they still do, to be honest.

Don't bother looking for heavy messages, moral lessons, or deep symbolism in my books. I don't claim to have the intelligence or wisdom to share those messages, and I'm not sure kids want to read them.

I like to keep things short, concise, and to the point. I'm not going to go on for page after page describing what characters look like or what they are wearing. In *The Million Dollar Shot,* I described this girl named Annie with four words: "She shaves her head." That's it. Now the reader knows what she looks like.

I'm not going to have a character walk into a room and describe what the room looks like or walk outside and describe the weather unless the color of the walls or the weather matters to the story.

I don't write beautiful sentences the way a lot of authors do. For one thing, I'm not capable of writing beautiful sentences. For another thing, I don't think most kids want to read them. Some people think there is some merit in having sentences that are so beautiful that it's necessary to read them three or four times to appreciate just how beautiful they are. I don't think these kinds of sentences get kids excited about reading. In fact, I think they turn a lot of kids off to reading. I would like kids to read a sentence once and want to know what the next sentence will be. Any time I am tempted to go into a long description of something, I look at my bulletin board where I have a quote from Anton Chekov in which he compares the clarity of "The man sat on the grass" to a 26-word alternative filled with adjectives and adverbs. Just because a book is serious and has a hundred adjectives per page doesn't mean it's well written. And just because a book is funny and entertaining doesn't mean it's not good writing.

What I try to do is create stories that are easy to read, entertaining, and exciting. I like to take an ordinary kid and put that kid into an extraordinary situation and then put that situation right in the title so that kids can start fantasizing as soon as they pick up the book. If you put in some action, some tension, some humor, and a villain if possible, you can make a kid so captivated that he (I say he because boys are usually the ones who hate to read) will look up two hours later and not even realize he was reading.

Dan Gutman's books include *The Kid Who Ran for President,* Scholastic, 1996; *Honus & Me,* HarperCollins, 1997; *The Million Dollar Shot,* Hyperion, 1997; and *Race for the Sky,* Simon & Schuster, 2003.

Billy's father, a farmer, needs Billy on the farm. The story is continued in *Farm Team* and *Hard Ball.* Dan Gutman grabs younger readers by combining sports, time travel, and historical fiction. In *Mickey and Me,* for example, Joe's father sends his son back to 1951 to stop Mickey Mantle from being hurt in a game. Other Gutman titles that bring smiles, if not laughs, include *Honus and Me, Jackie and Me, Babe and Me,* and *Shoeless Joe and Me.*

Chris Crutcher is one of the most talented YA writers to combine sports and personal development stories. It is obvious that Crutcher knows and loves sports, but this

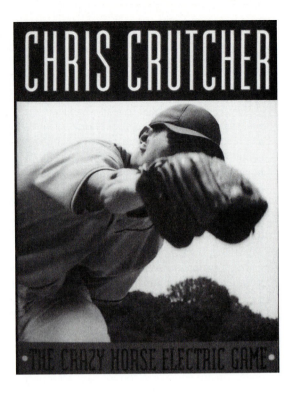

*C*hris Crutcher's sports books are popular with boys as well as girls.

does not keep him from criticizing some of the peripheral elements. In *Whale Talk,* his protagonist is T. J. Jones, a mixed-race swimmer who decides to get revenge on the establishment by inviting "losers" to join the swimming team. In *Running Loose,* Louie Banks wants to play football, but not the way his unethical coach wants it played. Crutcher's *Stotan!* is about swimming and how a team faces up to the serious illness of one of its members. In *The Crazy Horse Electric Game,* a star athlete suffers brain damage from a waterskiing accident. In *Ironman,* Bo Brewster, a bitter high school athlete forced to attend anger-management classes, writes letters to Larry King because he does not feel anyone else will listen.

Three recent and especially fine YA sports novels remind any doubters that sports books are still important to young readers. David Klass's *Home of the Braves* portrays a high school terrorized by football players who force certain students to bow down to them, and a captain of the wrestling and soccer teams trying to figure out who and what he is. *Rat* by Jan Cheripko concerns a 15-year old boy who is the manager of the basketball team and who sees the popular basketball coach molesting a cheerleader. Robert Lipsyte's *Warrior Angel* continues a loosely organized series that goes way back to *The Contender* in 1967. At the beginning of *Warrior Angel,* heavyweight champion Sonny Bear, whom readers already know from *The Brave,* is no longer interested in his Harlem training gym and has substituted the questionable joys of Las Vegas and its crowds.

The best sports book of recent years is a slim work of nonfiction, David Halberstam's *The Teamates: A Portrait of a Friendship.* The only baseball player young people are likely to recognize is Ted Williams, late of the Boston Red Sox. Dom Dimaggio, also late of the Red Sox—Joe's brother but a far more complex and intriguing person—sets out to travel from Massachusetts to see his dying friend and former teammate, Ted Williams. This is the simple story of two road trips by old men who had been something in their youth—and in Halberstam's language—gain a nobility as ballplayers and decent men and, most important, as teammates and friends.

The storylines of two books about athletes who were somebodies, but who as time flies become nobodies, are hardly new, but they come highly recommended by us: Jay Acton's *The Forgettables* and Martin Ralbovsky's *Destiny's Darlings*. Acton's book is about the Pottstown, Pennsylvania, Firebirds, who even in their glory, were rejects of professional football and yet athletes worth watching. The subtitle on Ralbovsky's book spells out the point—"A World Championship Little League Team Twenty Years Later." Growing old happens to all of us, world champions or not, but Ralbovsky's book powerfully reminds us of the evanescence of victory.

Because sports is a subject where high school readers admire adult athletes and look forward to joining their ranks, both YA and adult books are included in Focus Box 6.3, Sports Nonfiction—Real Life Dreams.

Mysteries

Why are mysteries so enduringly popular? Basically they are unrealistic and, as mystery writers cheerfully admit, usually have almost nothing to do with real-life detection by police or private agents. They demand that we suspend most of our disbelief, and we gladly do so. Mysteries are mere games, but we love games. Some of us claim that we want to beat the detective to the murderer, but we rarely do, and when we do succeed, we feel cheated.

The popularity of mystery movies and the number of hotels, ships, and individuals who sponsor parties in which a mock murder takes place, with the partygoers playing detectives, shows the entertainment value of mayhem, murder, and suspense. Because of the high entertainment value of mysteries and their sometimes easy reading level, many mysteries published for a general audience find their way into the hands of young adults. For examples, see Focus Box 6.4, 100 Years of Accessible Adult Mysteries.

Daniel's detection of the guilty Elders in "The Story of Susanna" in the Apocrypha may be the world's first detective story. Critics generally agree, however, that the modern mystery begins with Edgar Allan Poe's "The Murders in the Rue Morgue," although "The Purloined Letter" is more satisfying today. Poe's detective, C. Auguste Dupin, is unquestionably the first criminal investigator.

Writer and critic Hillary Waugh has said that the skeletons on which mysteries hang are "nothing more nor less than a series of ironclad rules." The rules are essential to present the puzzle properly and to ensure fair play. He lists them as follows:

Rule One: All clues discovered by the detective must be made available to the reader.

Rule Two: The murderer must be introduced early.

Rule Three: The crime must be significant.

FOCUS BOX 6.3   *Sports Nonfiction—Real Life Dreams*

Babe Didrikson Zaharias: The Making of a Champion by Russell Freedman. Clarion, 1999. Freedman's biographies are a pleasure to read because of the care he takes with the research and the writing as well as with the design of the book.

Baseball: An Illustrated History by Geoffrey C. Ward and Ken Burns. Knopf, 1994. Maybe it looks like a coffee table book, but it's filled with solid research and is great fun to read.

Basketball: A History of Hoops by Mark Stewart. Watts, 1999. Stewart gives details and general information about the history of basketball and the major players and teams.

Between Boardslides and Burnout: My Notes from the Road by Tony Hawk. HarperCollins, 2002. Full-color photographs add to this realistic journal of a skateboarding champion.

The Boys of October: How the 1975 Boston Red Sox Embodied Baseball's Ideals—and Restored Our Spirits by Doug Hornig. Contemporary Books, 2003. Hornig prepared a hymn to the glories of his favorite team.

Game Time: A Baseball Companion by Roger Angell. Harcourt, Brace, 2003. Angell again proves that he is one of baseball's greatest writers in this book about spring training, the World Series, and lots of other things.

The Greatest: Muhammad Ali by Walter Dean Myers. Scholastic, 2001. Myers brings his skill as a writer to this biography, along with his knowledge of what Muhammad Ali meant to African Americans.

Indian Summer: The Forgotten Story of Louis Sockalexis, the First Native American in Major League Baseball by Brian McDonald. Rodale, 2003. Sockalexis was recruited by the Cleveland Spiders in 1897 and drank himself out of baseball by 1910. A sad story.

Playing for Keeps: Michael Jordan and the World He Made by David Halberstam. Random

House, 1999. Here is a well-written biography of one of today's heroes.

Race across Alaska: First Woman to Win the Iditarod Tells Her Story by Libby Riddels and Tim Jones. Stackpole Books, 1998. Readers who know Gary Paulsen's *Woodsong* (Bradbury, 1990) will enjoy this different perspective on the race.

The Story of Negro League Baseball by William Brashler. Ticknor & Fields, 1994. Brashler takes up the history of Negro baseball and its important players, e.g., Bob Gibson and Smokey Joe Williams. Neil J. Sullivan does something similar in his *The Minors: The Struggles and the Triumphs of Baseball's Poor Relations from 1876 to the Present* (St. Martins, 1990). An introductory book for younger readers is *Biddy Owens: The Negro Leagues,* which is part of the *My Name Is America Series* (Scholastic, 2001).

Triumph and Tragedy in Mudville by Stephen Jay Gould. Norton, 2003. The Harvard scientist takes off on his favorite avocation, baseball, and particular aspects of it that fascinate him, e.g., Joe DiMaggio's 56-game hitting streak.

Wait Till Next Year: A Memoir by Doris Kearns Goodwin. Simon & Schuster, 1997. A historian remembers growing up in Rockville Center, New York, and her passion for the Brooklyn Dodgers. A truly lovely book.

Why Is the Foul Pole Fair? by Vince Staten. Simon and Schuster, 2003. The author takes up an incredible number of questions about baseball and its history and answers them all. For example, why is the distance from the pitching rubber to the plate 60 feet and 6 inches?

Winning Ways: A Photohistory of American Women in Sports by Sue Macy. Holt, 1996. Both in this book and in her *A Whole New Ball Game* (Holt, 1993), Macy presents wonderful photos and intriguing details to show that women have a sports heritage.

Rule Four: There must be detection.

Rule Five: The number of suspects must be known, and the murderer must be among them.

Rule Six: The reader, as part of the game of fair play, has the right to expect that nothing will be included in the book that does not relate to or in some way bear on the puzzle.[10]

Types of Mysteries

The characteristics of the traditional murder mystery are well known and relatively fixed, although devotees are always interested in variations on the theme of murder. A mystery short story may settle for theft, but a novel, of course, demands murder. Accompanying crimes such as blackmail or embezzlement may add to the delights of murder, but they never replace murder. The ultimate crime normally takes place a few chapters into the book, after readers have been introduced to major and minor characters, including the victim and those who might long for his death. The detective appears, clues are scattered, the investigation proceeds, the detective solves the case, the guilty are punished, the innocent are restored to their rightful place, and the world becomes right again.

Shannon Ocork classifies mysteries into these six types.

1. *The amateur detective:* At least in the older stories, the amateur detective was male (e.g., C. August Dupin or Sherlock Holmes and later Rex Stout's Nero Wolfe). These detectives are altruistic and usually optimistic. They are bright and see what others do not. Sometimes called traditional, golden-age, or classic mysteries, these flourished from the 1920s through the 1940s.

2. *The cozy mystery:* These stories are close to the amateur detective stories. They are usually set in a small English village, although New England is increasingly popular. Agatha Christie, who began writing in the 1920s, is the most obvious writer of cozies. She scattered her best books throughout her life. Her 1939 *And Then There Were None* is her best book without a detective. Others include her 1950 *A Murder Is Announced*, a Miss Marple book, and her 1968 *By the Pricking of My Thumbs*, in which the usually tiresome Tommy and Tuppence Beresford stumble into a believable mystery.

3. *The puzzle:* These stories are exercises in ingenuity as we are led into an intricate murder, with the detective daring us to figure out the end of the story. Ellery Queen's early mysteries had a "Challenge to the Reader" about three or four chapters from the end, when the writer announced that we had all the clues Queen had and should be able to solve the mystery. Luckily, we rarely succeeded.

4. *The private detective:* These hard-boiled mysteries differ from other mysteries in significant ways. Private detectives lack altruistic motives. They enter cases for pay rather than for love of the chase or intellectual fondness for the puzzle. Working out of a cheerless office and around even less cheerful people, they are tired and cynical about the courts, the police, class distinctions, and life in general. Many are former police officers who left the force under a cloud. They have seen too much of the seamy world to feel hope for anything or anyone, and they know that detective work is hard and mostly routine and dull. With patience, any bright person could do what they do. Not

The Hound of the Baskervilles by Arthur Conan Doyle. McClure, 1902. More atmospheric than mysterious, this is a fine tale of an escaped convict in inhospitable Dartmoor and a legend of a demented killer-hound.

The Circular Staircase by Mary Roberts Rinehart. Bobbs-Merrill, 1908. The first of the *Had-I-But-Known* genre of mystery, this story of a lonely house, a dead body, and blooming love reads far better today than readers have any right to expect.

The Greek Coffin Mystery by Ellery Queen. Stokes, 1932. Frederic Dannay and Manfred B. Lee, writing under the joint pseudonym of Ellery Queen, find Queen investigating a natural death with a missing will. When the coffin is exhumed, a second body is found and the mystery begins.

The Big Sleep by Raymond Chandler. Knopf, 1939. This study in power and corruption is the first Philip Marlowe mystery with Marlowe trying to determine the truth from two quite different women and a missing man.

Buried for Pleasure by Edmund Crispin (pen name of Bruce Montgomery). Harper and Row, 1949. Gervase Fen, Oxford professor, has been talked into standing for Parliament. After encountering a strange group of small town eccentrics, he also encounters a murder in this very funny mystery.

A Murder Is Announced by Agatha Christie. Dodd, Mead, 1950. A murder to take place in a small town is announced in the local newspaper, and the murder takes place as announced. Miss Marple is both cool and efficient in solving this, her best case.

Death in the Fifth Position by Edgar Box (pen name of Gore Vidal). Dutton, 1952. Press agent Peter Sargeant turns detective to solve the murder of a ballerina.

The Willow Pattern by Robert Van Gulik. Scribner, 1964. Judge Dee is administering a Chinese city in the midst of a plague and a rash of crime. Though here fictionalized, Dee was a real seventh-century judge in the T'ang dynasty.

An Unsuitable Job for a Woman by P. D. James. Scribner, 1972. In this remarkable book, Cordelia Gray learns that her partner has committed suicide, leaving her the business. Although she's a newcomer to the private investigator world, she is hired to find out about another suicide.

Dance Hall of the Dead by Tony Hillerman. Harper and Row, 1973. Reservation policeman Joe Leaphorn investigates the death of a young runner training for a religious ceremony.

Murder on the Yellow Brick Road by Stuart Kaminsky. St. Martins, 1977. In 1940, a munchkin has been murdered on the set of *The Wizard of Oz,* and Judy Garland is frightened. Toby Peters comes to the rescue in the best of the series.

Strike Three, You're Dead by R. D. Rosen. Walker, 1984. Relief pitcher Rudy Furth is killed in the Providence Jewels' clubhouse, and outfielder Harvey Blissberg plays detective.

I Am the Only Running Footman by Martha Grimes. Little, Brown, 1986. The body of a young girl strangled with her own scarf is found near an old pub called I Am the Only Running Footman. Scotland Yard's Richard Jury is reminded of another murder, similar to this one, committed in Devon.

The Ritual Bath by Faye Kellerman. Morrow, 1986. A Yeshiva in the Los Angeles hills is despoiled when a woman leaving the ritual bath is raped. Detective Peter Decker becomes involved.

The Master of the House by Robert Barnard. Scribner, 1994. A mother dies in childbirth, leaving four children and a crazy and ineffectual husband. When townspeople suspect something is wrong, two of the children find a body in the backyard.

O Jerusalem by Laurie R. King. St. Martins, 1999. Mary Russell and her friend Sherlock Holmes come to British-occupied Palestine to investigate a series of murders.

Fatal Voyage by Kathy Reichs. Scribner, 2001. Temperance (Tempe) Brennan learns about the crash of a commercial airplane. She goes to the site, acting in her role of forensic anthropologist, fearful that her own daughter may have been aboard the plane.

only does violence come with the territory, it is the territory. Moreover, we are surprised, even disappointed, if the violence is not there.

5. *The police procedural:* Police procedurals are often the most believable mysteries because the central characters are officers doing their mundane jobs and tracking down murderers with scientific methods and machines available only to the police. The books of Ed McBain are probably the most popular police procedurals today.

6. *The thriller:* These are usually spy thrillers. They may have bits of mystery tucked into them, but as in Ian Fleming's *James Bond* series, the mystery involves not so much who did it as how our hero can escape his latest impossible situation with even more than his usual derring-do.[11]

A Few Popular Mystery Writers

Sue Grafton has been among the hottest mystery writers since 1982 when *"A" Is for Alibi* appeared. Her alphabetical series (e.g., *"J" Is for Judgment, "Q" Is for Quarry,* and *"M" Is for Malice*) shows Kinsey Millhone working as an insurance investigator in Santa Teresa (the name Ross Macdonald gave Santa Barbara in his mysteries). Readers met Kinsey in *"A" Is for Alibi.*

> My name is Kinsey Millhone. I'm a private investigator, licensed by the state of California. I'm thirty-two years old, twice divorced, no kids. The day before yesterday I killed someone and the fact weighs heavily on my mind. I'm a nice person and I have a lot of friends. My apartment is small but I like living in a cramped space. I've lived in trailers most of my life, but lately they've been getting too elaborate for my taste, so now I live in one room, a "bachelorette." I don't have houseplants. I spend a lot of time on the road and I don't like leaving things behind. Aside from the hazards of my profession, my life has always been ordinary, uneventful, and good.
>
> Killing someone feels odd to me and I haven't quite sorted it through. I've already given a statement to the police, which I initialed page by page and then signed. I filled out a similar report for the office files. The language in both documents is neutral, the terminology oblique, and neither says quite enough.

In these relatively brief paragraphs, Grafton lets us know who Kinsey is, not merely the obvious information but details that tell us about the real Kinsey—her taste in apartments, her dislike for stuff she'll have to leave behind, the effect of killing another human being, and her pawky wit as when she says, "The day before yesterday I killed someone and the fact weighs heavily on my mind."

Grafton was following the advice of one of the best writing teachers in history, the Roman poet and critic Horace, who urged writers to begin *in medias res,* that is the middle of the story.

No one writes police procedurals like McBain. Part of his skill lies in his characters' names—Steve Carella, Cotton Hawes (from Cotton Mather), and Meyer Meyer, whose father apparently took delight in duplicating the first and last names. Part of it lies in his knowledge of his imaginary city, Isola, presumably New York City, and anyone and everyone who might want to live there. Two of his recent 87th Precinct novels illustrate the breadth of his city. In *The Last Dance* Detectives Carella and Meyer investigate the killing of an old man, and in *Money, Money, Money* a woman's body is dumped into the lions' cage in the city zoo and a trashcan is stuffed with the body of a book salesman. McBain has been delighting us since 1956, and, logical or not, his books seem to be getting better and better.

In the February 1992 *English Journal,* the editors published responses` to the question, "Who is your favorite writer of detective fiction?" Tony Hillerman won by a margin of ten to one. His books, generally set in the Hopi or Navaho Indian reservations in northeastern Arizona and northwestern New Mexico, breathe of the desert and sand and lonely and quiet places. He gives readers a sense of place. If they've been there, they'll recognize it. If they have not, they will recognize it nonetheless.

. His Navajo police novels began in 1970 with *The Blessing Way,* where we meet Officer Joe Leaphorn and early on recognize his ability at detection and understanding of the Navajo religion. While his later novels have not always maintained the high standard of *The Blessing Way,* they rarely disappoint. In his recent *The Sinister Pig,* Jim Chee and Joe Leaphorn are on the case of an undercover agent murdered while investigating oil pipeline sabotage.

Mysteries Written for Young Adults

While many teenagers have fond memories of such detectives as Encyclopedia Brown and Nancy Drew, and young teens happily read the *Sammy Keyes* books by Wendelin Van Draanen, most teenagers are looking for something a bit "deeper." However, YA authors shy away from doing whole books focused on murder and mayhem, which means that most YA mysteries are concerned with more than the crime. They are also shorter than mysteries for adults, and instead of having professional detectives, the protagonists are likely to be bright and energetic young people, not yet cynical about the world. The violence is more likely to be underplayed, possibly at the edge of the story. The victim is often connected to the protagonist—a family member, a friend, an admired adult, a boyfriend or girlfriend—and the protagonist is virtually forced to enter the game and examine the puzzle.

Robert Cormier's *The Rag and Bone Shop* illustrates most of these characteristics. Seven-year-old Alicia is found murdered only a few hundred yards from her home, and the police have no physical evidence and no suspects. Twelve-year-old Jason, a neighbor and friend, was the last person to see her. To satisfy community pressure, the police arrest him and then bring in an out-of-town interrogator who has a reputation for getting confessions out of suspects. The interrogator, named Trent, works more quickly than did the psychiatrist/interrogator in Cormier's earlier mystery, *I Am the Cheese.* In *The Rag and Bone Shop,* there is some evidence that Jason has antisocial attitudes, but mostly he is just shy. It is because he can't stand up to the neighborhood bullies that he spent so much time with the younger Alicia.

The interrogator is extra motivated because he is hoping that solving this high-profile case will bring him a political appointment. His behavior is all the more repulsive when he keeps pursuing the "confession," even after readers suspect that he knows Jason is innocent. But, thankfully, readers—and Jason—get a reprieve in the very last sentence.

Humor is intrinsic to light-hearted mysteries. YA Lit students at ASU are painting an enlarged cover of Carl Hiaasen's Hoot *in preparation for a skit they were putting on at the Arizona Book Festival.*

Francesca Lia Block's *Wasteland* is a moving but somber story of a sister, a brother, family secrets, love, and death. Block's beautifully enigmatic style of writing heightens the tension and adds to the mystery as Marina (the sister) gets closer and closer to the truth about her brother's death.

Carl Hiaasen's *Hoot* is much lighter in tone, but it still has its share of mystery. Three kids in Florida work through their own mysteries about each other so that they can come together to save a flock of burrowing owls from being covered over by the bulldozers waiting to dig the foundation for a franchise pancake house. People have fun with these kinds of *mystery*-lites, which are, in effect, parodies of the mysteries involving death.

Two young adult mystery writers who stand out are Patricia Windsor and Joan Lowery Nixon. Windsor's *The Christmas Killer* is set in a Connecticut town terrorized by a killer. Rose Potter has a series of dreams in which a murdered girl appears and hints at where her body can be found. The police question whether Rose is believable, or even sane, wonder if she is involved in the murder, and finally realize that Rose is in danger. Sections dealing with Rose alternate with the ramblings of the deranged killer about his need for blood. At one point he says,

> Killing is not a bad thing. Death is easeful, death is kind. I am friends with death. It cools the boiling blood. Blood is as red as a Christmas ribbon. Blood ties a body like a Christmas package. Blood is the color of Christmas berries, baubles, all things of joy. Why shouldn't I find joy in blood?

He finds joy in all things red, and in the last two paragraphs of the book, imprisoned though he is, readers learn that the story may have yet another chapter.

> Let a little time pass. I will send her a letter, tied up in my own blood and sealing wax. She will know me from my work. And she will think of me again.
> And, before long, I will escape this place, and I will be seeing her again.

Here's a fine story, not long on mystery but full of suspense and wonders and fears. It's an eerie and scary book, just right for the night when a reader is home alone with the fierce wind and the blowing shutters and the creaking house.

Joan Lowery Nixon's thrillers are even more popular with young people. *Whispers from the Dead* is about a near-death drowning and a spirit who seems to shadow the protagonist thereafter. *The Dark and Deadly Pool* concerns a young girl who discovers a body floating in a pool, a typical ploy for Nixon, who is eager to grab her readers' attention. Cody Garnett's friend in *Spirit Seeker* is accused of murder, and Cody sets out to find the truth. In *The Kidnapping of Christina Lattimore,* Christina is kidnapped and safely returned, but then she is accused of setting up the whole thing to extract money from her wealthy grandmother.

In Carol Plum-Ucci's *The Body of Christopher Creed,* popular Torey Adams, age 16, is thrown into a whole new life and a new way of looking at people. He is drawn into a mystery when an unpopular classmate disappears after posting a cryptic email message to the school principal in which he mentions Torey and some of his friends. In Elaine Marie Alphin's *Counterfeit Son,* a boy's father (a serial killer himself) is killed by the police, and the boy tries to assume the identity of one of his father's victims. Of course, there are too many complications for such a plan to work.

When we first read Joyce Carol Oates's *Freaky Green Eyes,* we viewed it as an accomplishment story or a problem novel. This made us critical of some of the elements because they seemed to be so romanticized. But now taking a second look and considering the story as a mystery, we can see that Francesca, who prefers to be called Franky, is the bright, young detective who solves the murder. The wealth and glamour of her father, the loving aunt waiting to make a new home for Franky and her sister, and the fortuitous new boyfriend fit perfectly with the conventions of murder mysteries.

Stories of the Supernatural

Fears of death, the unknown, and the supernatural probably go back to prehistoric times, when shadows in a cave and light and dark mystified and frightened humans. We have demanded answers to the unknown but have rarely found them, and so we have settled on myths and legends about superior and unseen beings. Such explanations are satisfying because when we are fighting the inexplicable, they make winning more pleasing and losing more acceptable.

Amidst all of our modern knowledge and sophistication, we hold onto our fascination with the unknowable. We delight in chambers of horrors, tunnels of terror, and haunted houses. We claim to be rational beings, yet we read astrology charts. We mock the superstitions of others yet hold as pets one or two of our own, joking all the time while we toss salt over our shoulder, avoid walking under ladders, and knock on wood. We follow customs without wondering why they came about. Black is assumed to be the appropriate dress for funerals because it is dark and gloomy and demonstrates solemnity. We may not know that black was worn at a time lost in history because spirits, sometimes malignant or perhaps indignant, were thought to linger near a corpse for a year. Wearing black made it more difficult for these evil spirits to see the living. As long as spirits were around, danger lurked; hence, long mourning periods in black dress.

Greek and Roman literature abounds with supernatural elements, but so does Elizabethan literature. Whether Shakespeare believed in ghosts or witches is anyone's guess. Certainly, his audiences often did, and they apparently delighted in or were frightened by incidents in plays such as *Macbeth, Hamlet,* and *The Tempest.*

Few people will admit to believing in supernatural elements, yet they listen eagerly to urban legends and stories about mysterious happenings. Alvin Schwartz was happily surprised when his books *Scary Stories to Tell in the Dark, More Scary Stories to Tell in the Dark,* and *Scary Stories 3: More Tales to Chill Your Bones* began winning statewide contests as kids' favorite books. At the same time, the books also climbed to the top of the American Library Association's list of banned books. Stephen Gammell's creepy illustrations are probably as much to blame as are the stories themselves.

Supernatural novels have well-established ground rules. Settings are usually in an eerie or haunted house or in a place where a mysterious event occurred years ago. Some thrillers occur in more mundane places, perhaps a brownstone in New York City or a hotel shut down for the season, but readers know the mundane remains calm only for a short time before frightening events begin and strange people come out to play. Darkness is usually essential, but not always physical darkness. The protagonist is oblivious to evil for a time but ultimately recognizes the pervasive power of the darkness of the soul. Sometimes the wife or husband sells out to evil and entices the spouse to join in a black mass. Rituals or ceremonies are essential. Family curses or pacts with the devil have become commonplaces of the genre.

Alfred Hitchcock, that master of suspense, reminds us over and over that the most terrifying things can happen in the most commonplace settings. In *North by Northwest,* on a lovely day in the middle of a South Dakota cornfield, Cary Grant is suddenly attacked by a crop-dusting airplane. In *The Birds,* a placid setting alongside the ocean suddenly turns to terror when sweet little birds begin to tear into human flesh.

In the 1989 edition of this textbook, Robert Westall observed that supernatural books break quite naturally into horror stories and ghost stories. The horror stories make the point that "the human organism is a frail thing of flesh subject to an infinity of abuse, and that it is painful and undignified for the human spirit to have to dwell in it." Such a depressing fact may be well worth saying but not over and over again. Even the books by such ingenious and powerful writers as Poe and Lovecraft are not something you would want to read if you were "on the way to build the Taj Mahal, or paint the Sistine Chapel ceiling, or even have a happy love affair."

> On the other hand, the ghost story is about the undying spirit, not the dying flesh. . . . [Ghosts] add an exciting fifth dimension to the often-boring four dimensions of real life. They make it possible for us to escape into the land of the impossible where,

delightfully, anything can happen. They are also a comfort: a reassurance of our own immortality. I would adore to spend my first few years of death as a ghost, drifting round the world painlessly in the company of other friendly ghosts, seeing all the things I never got round to seeing in life because there were other boring earthbound things to be done.

He went on to explain that we need ghost stories:

In terms of love and the passing of time, we are all haunted houses, full of rooms we have shut off because of loss, or fear, or regret. To spend all our time wandering through such rooms would lead to madness. But to wander sometimes can be agonizingly sweet and rich. And never to dare to wander through them can make life a dusty boring hell.[12]

The most promising new star in the firmament of YA supernatural writing would seem to be the prolific Vivian Vande Velde (see her statement on p. 304). Her books cross several genres but always touch base at the supernatural. *Never Trust a Dead Man* presents a young loser. Selwyn has had a terrible week. His girlfriend—or at least the person he'd like to be his girlfriend—has turned him down and plans to marry Farold.

Farold follows this news by beating up Selwyn. And if all that isn't bad enough, Farold is found dead with a knife in his back, and the knife belongs to Selwyn. It is at the point when Selwyn sets out to prove his innocence that the mystery becomes supernatural. In Vande Velde's *Companions of the Night,* a teenage girl is an unwitting accomplice to a vampire, while her *Being Dead* is a compilation of seven creepy stories.

Another rising star is Neil Gaiman, who is already famous for his graphic novels. His 2002 *Coraline* got on nearly a dozen best-book lists and earned endorsements from the likes of Philip Pullman, Orson Scott Card, and Diana Wynne Jones. A girl discovers a door in the house where her family has moved. When she steps through, she is in another house, much like her own, but seemingly newer and better. There's also a new set of parents who want her to stay and be their child. As the *San Francisco Chronicle* wrote, it is a book that is both "creepy and funny" and "bittersweet and playful." It will linger long in the memory, even for readers who rush through it to see what happens.

Annette Curtis Klause's *The Silver Kiss* is a purer illustration of a supernatural story. Nearly every night Zoë comes home to a dark and empty house. Her mother is in the hospital dying of cancer, and as early as page 2 readers get clues about supernatural elements. Zoë is almost as thin as her mother, "a sympathy death perhaps, she wondered half seriously. . . . Wouldn't it be ironic if she died, too, fading out suddenly when her look-alike went?" On page 3, Zoë remembers happier times with her mother, but even here there's a shadow: "You're a dark one," her mother said sometimes with amused wonder. "You're a mystery."

Zoë likes to walk in the neighborhood park and sit in front of the old-fashioned gazebo, where one night "a shadow crept inside, independent of natural shades." Then she saw his face.

> He was young, more boy than man, slight and pale, made elfin by the moon. He noticed her and froze like a deer before the gun. They were trapped in each other's gaze. His eyes were dark, full of wilderness and stars. But his face was ashen. Almost as pale as his silver hair.

In her first meeting with Simon, a 200-year-old vampire from Bristol, England, Zoë recognizes how beautiful he is, he flees, and she cries. The story within a story, in which Simon explains how he became a vampire, is brilliant in its own right, but then so is the book's ending when Zoë and Simon must part.

Klause's *Blood and Chocolate* has also proved itself popular among young people and reviewers. A clan of werewolves, existing since time began, have lost their leader in a fire. They now intend to live in Virginia, led by Vivian, daughter of the late head of the clan. Going to school, she meets a boy who attracts her. She is sure she knows and can trust him, so Vivian shows him who and what she is, and he is frightened and repelled.

Therein lies the dilemma. Can we accept someone disturbingly different even when we mostly admire and trust the person? Are we willing to go below the surface in judging people? That is the essence of much supernatural literature, from Frankenstein to Stephen King.

Leading all the writers in the field is Stephen King, a former high school English teacher who frequently includes likable young people among his characters. The fact

FOCUS BOX 6.5   *The Supernatural in YA Fiction*

Back of Beyond: Stories of the Supernatural by Sarah Ellis. Simon and Schuster, 1997. In each of the stories, ordinary young people go about their daily humdrum lives when something happens that makes them realize things are not so ordinary.

Beware! R. L. Stine Picks His Favorite Scary Stories, edited by R. L. Stine. HarperCollins, 2002. Stine's name is meant to grab young readers who loved his earlier books. He wrote original stories for *Nightmare Hour* and *The Haunting House* (HarperCollins, 1999, 2001).

Fade by Robert Cormier. Delacorte, 1988. Paul Moreaux, a young French Canadian, discovers that he has inherited a family gift/curse that comes to only one person in each generation: the ability to be invisible.

Familiar and Haunting: Collected Stories by Philippa Pearce. Greenwillow, 2002. Not all of these 37 stories are supernatural, but many are, and they are all well-written.

The Ghost Belonged to Me, Ghosts I Have Been, The Dreadful Future of Blossom Culp, and **Blossom Culp and the Sleep of Death** by Richard Peck. Delacorte, 1975, 1977, 1983, 1986. These delightfully funny books for middle school readers are about a boy who finds a charming, although somewhat outspoken, young woman from the past century living in the family barn.

The Great Blue Yonder by Alex Shearer. Clarion, 2002. Once tweeners get over the sadness of 12-year-old Harry being killed on his bicycle, they will love—and laugh—at the story of how he returns home as a ghost.

In Camera and Other Stories by Robert Westall, Scholastic, 1992. Readers who enjoy these stories will want to read Westall's *The Haunting of Chas McGill and Other Stories* (Greenwillow, 1993) and *Rachel and the Angel and Other Stories* (Scholastic, 1988).

The Last Treasure by Janet S. Anderson. Dutton, 2003. Wealthy John Matthew Smith died in 1881, but that doesn't keep his spirit from returning for an annual visit to see how the family is doing and to nudge things along in hopes of helping his descendants appreciate each other.

The Lion Tamer's Daughter: And Other Stories by Peter Dickinson. Delacorte, 1997. In the title story, Keith is drawn into the dark side of the circus when he meets a duplicate of a longtime friend.

The Lovely Bones by Alice Sebold. Little, Brown, 2002. Fourteen-year-old Susie Salmon is on her way to school when she is raped and murdered in a cornfield. She tells her story from Heaven as she watches over her family.

Midnight Magic by Avi. Scholastic, 1999. It's the year before Columbus set sail and 12-year-old Fabrizio is working as a servant to Mangus the Magician in the Kingdom of Pergamontio. Little does he know that he will soon confront a ghost. Avi's *Devil's Race* (Lippincott, 1984) is also recommended.

Skeleton Man by Joseph Bruchac. HarperCollins, 2001. Young teens may get nightmares from this story based on a Mohawk legend about a man so hungry that he eats himself down to the bone. Fortunately, Molly manages to outwit the stranger and save herself and her parents.

Skellig by David Almond. Delacorte, 1999. When Michael goes out to explore new property his family has bought, he discovers Skellig in an old shed. Skellig first appears to be a sick old man, but later he appears to be something more. *Kit's Wilderness* (Delacorte, 2000) also has some intriguing supernatural elements.

Timon's Tide by Charles Butler. Simon and Schuster, 2000. Danile finds something that looks very much like Timon's head in the woods, but Timon has been dead for six years.

Vampires, edited by Jane Yolen. HarperCollins, 1991. This wonderful collection of short stories will make readers shudder and, sometimes, laugh. Yolen's series for Harcourt Brace, *Here There Be Ghosts, . . . Dragons, . . . Unicorns, . . . Angels,* and *. . . Witches* is beautifully put together.

that he writes about them without condescension is not lost on the audience. "The Langoliers" (from *Four Past Midnight*) is the story of a late-night flight from Los Angeles to Boston. The plane goes through a time rip, and the only passengers who survive are the ten who happened to be sleeping. Fortunately, one of them is a pilot; otherwise there wouldn't have been much of a story to tell. There is also the blind Dinah, a young girl on her way to Boston for an operation on her eyes. She has such a super-developed sense of hearing that she is mistaken by the mad Craig Toomy, the ultimate yuppie gone awry, as the chief Langolier. The character most closely filling the role of a young adult hero on a romantic quest is Albert Kaussner, a gifted violinist on his way to enroll in a Boston music conservatory. In his own mind, he's not Albert or Al, but Ace Kaussner, "The Arizona Jew" and "The Fastest Hebrew West of the Mississippi." The journey turns out to be much more difficult than anything faced by Ace's mythical heroes of the Old West, and it even requires him to sacrifice his beloved violin. At the end of the trip, he is rewarded with his first love and the feeling of growth and confidence that comes with having passed a difficult test.

Stephen King's first book, *Carrie*, appeared in 1974 and sold well for a then-unknown writer. From that point on, King maintained his place as *the* writer of the genre. Carrie is a young outsider, the daughter of religious fanatics, and the brunt of cruel jokes. She possesses the power of telekinesis, and she uses it to destroy the school, the students, and the town in a fit of justified rage. *Firestarter* is far better, with its portrait of an 8-year-old girl with the power to start fires merely by looking at an object. A government agency, "The Shop," learns about the child and launches a search for her. King effectively indicts this bureaucracy become evil. *Firestarter* may not be King's best book, but it is his most penetrating study of character and the United States.

Among young adult writers specializing in supernatural themes, Lois Duncan has been consistently popular. In *Summer of Fear*, Rachel Bryant's family is notified that relatives have died in a car crash, leaving 17-year-old Julia behind. The girl, who looks surprisingly mature, arrives and changes the lives of everyone around her. Trickle, the family dog, suspects something is wrong, but Trickle does not live too long, and neither does anyone else who gets in Julia's way. Duncan's *Stranger with My Face* and *The Third Eye* were enjoyable but lacked the power of *Summer of Fear*. See Focus Box 6.5 for other examples of supernatural stories written for teens.

Support for allowing young adults to read supernatural books comes from Jeanine Basinger, chair of film studies at Wesleyan University. While her words were aimed at horror films, they apply equally well to books:

> It never really goes away, this appetite for horror. . . . We have all of these tragedies on our minds. In modern life it's just one damn thing after another, and we seek to explain it to one another. And if there's some experience that gives closure to it, gives an explanation or at least gives us reassurance that we're not the only ones having the scaries, it reassures us.[13]

Concluding Comments

This chapter has been about literature that is sometimes treated as "nonessential," mostly because it tugs at emotional more than intellectual parts of our brains. In today's high-tech world, however, it may be that this is the very kind of reading that serves to remind us of our humanity and our need to reach out and understand the emotions of others.

 Notes

[1] Betty Rosenberg, *Genreflecting: A Guide to the Reading Interests in Genre Fiction* (Libraries Unlimited, 1982), in place of a dedication page.

[2] Anthony Brandt, "The Adventure Craze," *American Heritage* 51 (December 2000/January 2001): 43.

[3] London *Independent,* June 30, 1995, p. 18.

[4] Anne Scott Macleod, "Writing Backward," *Horn Book Magazine* 74 (January/February 1998): 29.

[5] Avi, "Writing Backward but Looking Forward," *Signal* 23 (Summer 1999): 21.

[6] Henry Seidel Canby, "What Is Truth?" *Saturday Review of Literature* 41 (December 31, 1927): 481.

[7] Reinhold Messner, *Everest: Expedition to the Ultimate* (Oxford University Press, 1979), p. 460.

[8] *Into Thin Air* (Villard, 1997), pp. 135–136.

[9] Jacques Barzun, *God's Country and Mine* (Little, Brown, 1954), p. 159.

[10] Hillary Waugh, "What Is a Mystery?" *The Basics of Writing and Selling Mysteries and Suspense: A Writer's Guide* 10 (1991): 6–8.

[11] Shannon Ocork, "What Type of Mystery Are You Writing?" *The Basics of Writing and Selling Mysteries and Suspense* 10 (1991): 10–12.

[12] Robert Westall, "On Nightmares for Money," *Literature for Today's Young Adults* (Scott, Foresman, 1989): 166–167.

[13] Rick Lyman, "The Chills! The Thrills! The Profits," *New York Times,* August 31, 1999, p. B1.

Fantasy, Science Fiction, Utopias, and Dystopias

Fantasy and science fiction are related to each other and to humankind's deepest desires, but it is not always easy to draw a clear-cut line between the two. Ursula K. Le Guin offered this distinction:

> The basic concept of fantasy, of course, is this; you get to make up the rules, but then you've got to follow them. Science fiction refines the canon: You get to make up the rules, but within limits. A science-fiction story must not flout the evidence of science, must not, as Chip Delaney puts it, deny what is known to be known.[1]

Or, as Walter Wangerin, Jr., said in a lecture to a college audience: "Fantasy deals with the 'immeasurable' while science fiction deals with the 'measurable.'"[2]

No matter what the definitions or distinctions, the boundaries between science fiction and fantasy are fuzzy, so that more often than not the two genres are treated together (witness two important journals about these areas—*Science Fiction Chronicle: The Monthly Science Fiction and Fantasy Newsmagazine* and *The Magazine of Fantasy and Science Fiction*). Advertisements for the Science Fiction Book Club often mix choices of science fiction and fantasy with horror, the supernatural, mythology, folklore, and some selections that seem impossible to pigeonhole. Anyone who teaches or is around young people knows that in this area books cross genre lines and age lines. Young adults read what adults read, and books that may have been published for young readers (e.g., Robin McKinley's *Beauty* or Lloyd Alexander's *Prydain* series) are now also read by adults.[3]

What Is Fantasy?

Fantasy comes from a Greek word meaning "a making visible." Perhaps more than any other form of literature, fantasy refuses to accept the world as it is, so readers can see what could have been (and still might be), rather than merely what was or must be.

The appeal of fantasy may be, simply, that it is so elemental. Some see its most comparable form of communication in music, which may be why so many composers have been influenced by it. Fantasy sings of our need for heroes, for the good, and for success in our eternal fight against evil. Composers of works as dissimilar as Stravinsky's *Firebird,* Mahler's *Song of the Earth,* and Strauss's *Thus Sprach Zarathustra* have sung that song. Writers sing similar songs when they tell stories of great heroes, usually of humble means and beginnings, seeking truth, finding ambiguities, and subduing evil, at least temporarily. On its lighter side, musicians sing of beauty, love, and dreams and dreamers, as in Mozart's *The Magic Flute* or Ravel's *Daphnis and Chloë* and Tchaikovsky's *Swan Lake.* Writers sing their lighter tales through stories about Beauty and the Beast, the happier and younger life of Arthur, and many of the old folktales and legends that are childhood favorites.

Ray Bradbury maintains that fantasy is elemental and essential:

> The ability to "fantasize" is the ability to survive. It's wonderful to speak about this subject because there have been so many wrong-headed people dealing with it. We're going through a terrible period of art, in literature and living, in psychiatry and psychology. The so-called realists are trying to drive us insane, and I refuse to be driven insane. . . . We survive by fantasizing. Take that away from us and the whole damned human race goes down the drain.[4]

Fantasy allows us—even forces us—to become greater than we are, greater than we could hope to be. It confronts us with the major ambiguities and dualities of life—good and evil, light and dark, innocence and guilt, reality and appearance, heroism and cowardice, hard work and indolence, determination and vacillation, and order and anarchy. Fantasy presents all these, and it provides the means through which readers can consider both the polarities and the many shadings in between.

Conventions of Fantasy

Jo-Anne Goodwin's comment about the nature of fantasy is worth repeating for its accuracy and succinctness.

> Classic fantasy is centered around quests. The quest may have any number of different motives—spiritual, political, sexual, material—but its presence in the text is essential. The quest expresses the desire to accomplish a thing fraught with difficulty and danger, and seemingly doomed to failure. It also enables fantasy writers to deal with rites of passage; the central figure grows in stature as the quest evolves. Typically, the journey will be full of magical, symbolic and allegorical happenings which allow the hero to externalize his or her internal struggles: thus Odysseus must pass through Charybdis and Scylla and the Knight of Temperance must extricate himself from Acracia and the Bower of Bliss.
>
> Fantasy also deals with flux. The central characters operate in a world turned upside down, amid great wars and events of a cataclysmic nature. The possible outcomes are open and endlessly variable; the responsibility carried by the hero is enormous. In fantasy, the imagined world is always a global village. No action can take place in isolation. Every decision taken by the hero affects someone else, and sometimes the fate of nations. It is a deeply social genre.[5]

Heroes must prove worthy of their quest, although early in the story they may be fumbling or unsure about both themselves and their quests.

The quest may be ordained, required, or, occasionally, self-determined. The hero may briefly confuse good and evil, but the protagonist ultimately recognizes the distinction. When the obligatory battle comes between the powers of good and evil, the struggle may be prolonged and the outcome in doubt. But eventually good prevails, although the victory is always transitory.

John Rowe Townsend, both a fine writer of young adult novels and one of the most perceptive and honored critics of the field, maintained that the quest motif is a powerful analogy of life's pattern:

> Life is a long journey, in the course of which one will assuredly have one's adventures, one's sorrows and joys, one's setbacks and triumphs, and perhaps, with luck and effort, the fulfillment of some major purpose.[6]

We all begin our quest, that long journey, seeking the good and being tempted by the evil that we know we must ultimately fight. We face obstacles and barriers throughout, hoping that we will find satisfaction and meaning during and after the quest. Our quests may not be as earthshaking as those of fantasy heroes, but our emotional and intellectual wrestling can shake our own personal worlds. In the December 1971 *Horn Book Magazine*, Lloyd Alexander wrote about this kind of comparison.

> The fantasy hero is not only a doer of deeds, but he also operates within a framework of morality. His compassion is as great as his courage—greater, in fact. We might consider that his humane qualities, more than any other, are really what the hero is all about. I wonder if this reminds us of the best parts of ourselves?[7]

Tamora Pierce notes an important element of the appeal of fantasy to young people.

> Fantasy, more than any other genre, is a literature of empowerment. In the real world, kids have little say. This is a given; it is the nature of childhood. In fantasy, however short, fat, unbeautiful, weak, dreamy, or unlearned individuals may be, they find a realm in which those things are negated by strength. The catch—there is *always* a catch—is that empowerment brings trials. Good novels in this genre never revolve around heroes who, once they receive the "Spatula of Power," call the rains to fill dry wells, end all war, and clear up all acne. Heroes and heroines contend as much with their granted wishes as readers do in normal life.[8]

Fears of Fantasy

Attacks on fantasy are common and predictable. Fantasy is said to be childishly simple reading. It is true there are simple fantasies, but anyone who has read Walter Wangerin, Jr.'s, *The Book of the Dun Cow* or Evangeline Walton's *Mabinogion* series knows that fantasy need not be childish or simple. Fantasies are often difficult and demand close reading, filled as they are with strange beings and even stranger lands with mystical and moral overtones and ambiguities.

Fantasy has also been labeled escapist literature, and, of course, it is in several ways. Fantasy allows readers to escape the mundane and to revel in glorious adven-

PETER DICKINSON
Sermon against Sermons

*W*hat makes a good novel? *Good* is a tricky word. A novel whose primary aim is to do good, let alone to make people good, is unlikely to be a good book. The more you agree with the overt moral purpose of a book, the more critically you should read it.

This is because the primary aim of fiction is to exercise the imagination. Our imagination is what makes us human, and the exercise of it enlarges and enriches our humanity. We need it, as much as we need food and physical exercise.

It is from a powerful impulse of the imagination that any successful novel must start, and then be followed by a need to let others share it, and be further followed by the need of those others—their hunger of the mind—to do so.

Of course, any good novel must have a moral dimension, as much as it must have some version of the natural dimensions of time and space. Aspects of these can be taught, but they cannot be preached, any more than weather can. I've read novels that read like all-day moral weather channels. I may well have agreed with their viewpoint, but I still wanted to fling them across the room.

For illustration, I'll briefly discuss two of my books. *Eva* began with pure impulse. I was writing a totally different book, which happened to start with a girl coming out of a coma. For plot reasons there'd been chimps in her former life, in a future world. I had done only a few pages when the impulse struck me. I literally leapt in my chair. *I knew what had happened to this girl!* From then on I was telling her story. Imagining her embodiment absorbed all my attention. The trouble was that the power of her predicament meant that one couldn't help taking her side, and I didn't do enough to balance this. As a result, many readers have taken *Eva* to be primarily a tract on animal rights. To that extent I skewed the moral dimension. My fault, alas.

AK sprang from an impulse almost as powerful—a radio program about child guerrillas in Africa and a voice saying, "Even a hardened government soldier may hesitate a fatal half-second before gunning down a child." The hair on my nape prickled, and I knew I had to write about that child and communicate what it is like to live in and try to cope with the chaos of central Africa. But as I wrote I realized that the moral enormity of Africa was such that though the story hinges on the child's gun I couldn't resolve things in a final, heroic burst of gunfire. Though that was where my imagination had been taking me, I had to find a different way. I'd like to think that my solution still springs from the original imaginative impulse, but if it doesn't, too bad.

Imaginative fiction isn't everything.

Peter Dickinson's books include *Eva*, Delacorte, 1989; *AK*, Delacorte, 1992; *A Bone from a Dry Sea*, Delacorte, 1992; *The Ropemaker*, Delacorte, 2001.

tures. For some readers (perhaps for all readers at certain times), escape is all that's demanded. For other readers, venturing on those seemingly endless quests, encountering all those incredible obstacles, and facing all those apparently tireless antagonists to defend the good and defeat the evil lead to more than mere reading to pass time. The escape from reality sends those readers back to their own limited and literal worlds to face many of the same problems they found in fantasy. See Focus Box 7.1 for illustrations. (See also Focus Box 2.1, Old Stories in New Dress, p. 51.)

Fantasy has come under attack because of its use of magic. Therefore, presumably, fantasy justifies young peoples' interest in magic. From that, censors jump to their easy

FOCUS BOX 7.1   *Reality May Not Be Fantasy, but Fantasy Is Reality*

Artemis Fowl: The Eternity Code by Eoin Colfer. Hyperion, 2003. In this third book of the series, Artemis is a 13-year-old mastermind pitted against the billionaire owner of the high-tech firm Fission Chips. The first book in the series was simply named *Artemis Fowl* (Hyperion, 2001) while the second was *Artemis Fowl: The Arctic Incident* (Hyperion, 2002; see photo on p. 209). Colfer combines mystery, sci-fi, and fantasy for young teens.

Believing Is Seeing: Seven Stories by Diana Wynne Jones. Greenwillow, 1999. Fans of Jones's *Dark Lord of Derkholm* will also enjoy these stories.

Circle of Magi: Dajá's Book by Tamora Pierce. Scholastic, 1998. In Pierce's third *Circle* book, Dajá is now an outcast from her people.

Dark Shade by Jane Louise Curry. McElderry, 1998. Time travel back to 1758 reveals some surprising ways in which the past affects the present.

The Eyre Affair by Jasper Fforde. Viking, 2002. In 1985, time travel is common and literature is taken most seriously. Then literary characters are murdered, and Special Operator Thursday Next enters the case when Jane Eyre is taken from Bronte's novel.

Fortress in the Eye of Time by C. J. Cherryh. Prism, 1993. Two men, one a human and the other a Shapeling, must work together to save the land.

A Glory of Unicorns, edited by Bruce Coville. Scholastic, 1998. Coville collected twelve stories about his favorite creature, the unicorn, and how it works with and affects people.

Goose Chase by Patrice Kindl. Houghton Mifflin, 2001. Alexandra's life is suddenly changed when she becomes wildly rich and gorgeous, all because she helped an old woman.

In the Rift by Marion Zimmer Bradley and Holly Lisle. Baen, 1998. Kate must save not only her own world but also the parallel world of Glenraven.

The Sacred Pool by Douglas L. Warren. Baen, 2001. In eighth-century Provence, Pierette learns magic from those who have gone before her in this first book in the *Sorcerer's Tale* trilogy.

Shatterglass by Tamora Pierce. Scholastic, 2003. This concluding volume of Pierce's second quartet of the *Circle Opens* series combines mystery and magic when Keth's glass balls reflect the past, including brutal murders.

Stravaganza: City of Masks by Mary Hoffman. Bloomsbury, 2002. A boy in contemporary England is recovering from an illness and finds himself slipping into a parallel world of intrigue in sixteenth-century Venice.

Summerland by Michael Chabon. Hyperion/Talk Miramax, 2002. In this original story, a Little League player is recruited by an old-timer from the Negro leagues to play in a game that has the potential to save the world.

Sword of the Rightful King: A Novel of King Arthur by Jane Yolen. Harcourt, 2003. Readers not yet acquainted with Yolen could start here and work their way backwards to her *Tartan Magic* series, *The Young Merlin* trilogy, and *The Pit Dragon* trilogy.

The Truth by Terry Pritchett. HarperCollins, 2000. A new journalist, a vampire photographer, and some strange beasts are mixed up in a plot to overthrow the government.

Varjak's Paw by S. F. Said. Random House, 2003. Varjak Paw lives with many other cats in the Countess's walled estate. When she dies and a frightening man moves in with his band of black cats, Varjak is sent outside to save his friends.

Water: Tales of Elemental Spirits by Peter Dickinson and Robin McKinley. Putnam, 2002. These six short stories about mermaids and the Kraken and sea serpents carry themes common to the novels of the authors, who are married to each other.

Wolf Star by Tanith Lee. Dutton, 2001. Claidi is kidnapped and taken to a jungle where she helps to solve a mystery. This is the second in Claidi's Journals series.

Xone of Contention by Piers Anthony. TOR, 1999. To stave off a divorce, a couple visits the planet of Xanith, where magic exists.

conclusion that evil can only come from magic, and since fantasy usually focuses on the struggle between evil and good—and evil is almost always more intriguing than good in fantasy or real life—fantasy clearly attracts young people away from good and surely to evil. Thus goes that circuitous attack.

In the most illogical objection (and more common than we could have predicted only a few years ago), fantasy has been attacked for being unreal, untrue, and imaginative (the term *imaginative* seems to have replaced *secular humanism* as one of today's leading bogeymen). To critics who believe that using imagination leads to unwillingness to face reality, fantasy doubtless seems dangerous. But fantasy is about reality, as Ursula K. Le Guin explained nearly twenty years ago:

> For fantasy is true, of course. It isn't factual, but it is true. Children know that. Adults know it too, and that is precisely why many of them are afraid of fantasy. They know that its truth challenges, even threatens, all that is false, phony, unnecessary, and trivial in the life they have let themselves be forced into living. They are afraid of dragons because they are afraid of freedom.
>
> So I believe we should trust our children. Normal children do not confuse reality with fantasy—they confuse them much less often than we adults do (as a certain great fantasist pointed out in a story called "The Emperor's New Clothes"). Children know perfectly well that unicorns aren't real, but they also know that books about unicorns, if they are good books, are true books.[9]

Or, as Marjorie N. Allen wrote, "Fantasies often have more to do with reality than any so-called realistic fiction. Like poetry, fantasy touches on universal truths."[10]

Seven Significant Writers of Fantasy

While several contemporary authors have produced fantasies that have been critically acclaimed, seven fantasy writers lead all the rest.

J. R. R. Tolkien   For many enthusiasts, J. R. R. Tolkien is the writer against whom all other writers in the field are measured. *The Hobbit, or There and Back Again* began in 1933 as a series of stories that Tolkien told his children at night about a strange being, Bilbo, the Hobbit. His three-part *The Lord of the Rings* is even better known, revealing his love of adventure and his fascination with language.

Alan Garner   Alan Garner is one of the most widely respected writers in the genre and that largely for one book. *The Owl Service* (1968) appeared in the early days of modern adolescent literature in the United States and created something of a sensation among the teachers and librarians who read it. Based on the Mabinogion, a collection of Welsh legends and myths, the three young characters in the story find a set of dishes. As the three get to know each other better, they also find that the pattern reflects a story of love and jealousy and hatred, one of the Mabinogion's tales of a triangular love that ends disastrously.

Ursula K. Le Guin   Best known for her Earthsea books, Ursula K. Le Guin has maintained her popularity with young and adult readers. *A Wizard of Earthsea*, set in a land of vast oceans and multitudinous islands, focuses on a young boy who senses he is capable of becoming a wizard. He is named Ged, and while he generally comports himself satisfactorily, he once showed off his magic and raised an evil spirit who followed him thereafter. Ged appears in *The Tombs of Atuan*, but the chief character is Tenar, dedicated from his youth to the Powers of the Earth. In *The Farthest Shore*, Ged, now an Archmage and the most powerful of wizards, accompanies a young man on a mission to seek out evil.

Readers had long assumed that the Earthsea series was complete, but more than twenty years after the first book, *Tehanu: The Last Book of Earthsea* appeared. Tenar and Ged reappear, but the principal character is a much-abused child, Therru, who is to become the greatest of all opponents of evil. *Tehanu* is a far darker book than the other three and is different in another way as well. While the other three books were told from the perspective of the powerful Ged and Tenar, this is told from the perspective of the—apparently—powerless.

Robin McKinley   Rewriting fairy tales is nothing new, but Robin McKinley's *Beauty: A Retelling of the Story of Beauty and the Beast* and the recent *Rose Daughter* are so amusing and so spirited that in this one narrow niche of fantasy she leads all the rest. McKinley's Beauty is strong and unafraid and loving. When her father steals a rose from the Beast's garden and forfeits his life, Beauty is eager to save her father. She says,

> "He cannot be so bad if he loves roses."
> "But he is a beast," said her father helplessly.
> I saw that he was weakening, and wishing only to comfort him, I said, "Cannot a Beast be Tamed."

The answer to that question, in both *Beauty* and *Rose Daughter* is yes, with time and kindness and love.

Anne McCaffrey   Anne McCaffrey's series of novels about Pern, once a colony of Earth, is required reading for anyone into fantasy. Every 200 years Pern is threatened by shimmering spores, organisms that devour all organic matter. Dragons destroy the threads as they fall. The name Pern comes from *Parallel Earth Resources Negligible*. Beginning with *Dragonflight* in 1968, followed by *Dragonsong*, many of her books have considerable science fiction mixed with the fantasy, not unusual for writers working either genre. McCaffrey has long maintained that she writes science fiction, not fantasy, and in an interview in 1999, McCaffrey was asked again in which genre she wrote. She answered,

> We keep having to settle that question. *I write science fiction.* It may seem fantasy because I use dragons, but mine were biogenetically engineered; ergo, the story is science fiction.[11]

She may protest and she has a point, but most readers are likely to continue to think of her as a writer of fantasy. So it goes.

Philip Pullman   After writing several successful books of mystery and adventure set in Victorian England, Philip Pullman turned even more successfully to fantasy in his three-volume series under the general title "His Dark Materials." *The Golden Compass* introduces readers to Lyra Belacqua and her daemon (an animal companion that reflects both its owner's personality and its own personality) and her education at Oxford. *The Subtle Knife,* the second book, introduces readers to Will Parry, whose father has been lost in the Arctic. Will sets out to find his father and in the journey slides into another universe and meets Lyra. *The Amber Spyglass* concludes the series, not entirely successfully.[12]

These books are filled with adventures and a constant stream of wonders and magic. In the first book, readers learn about the golden compass, which can foretell the future. In the second, the subtle knife, called Aesahaettr, is entrusted to Will. It can cut through anything, real or magical. The significance of the knife and the seriousness of Pullman's book is revealed when a witch remarks that the name of the knife "sounds as if it meant 'god-destroyer.' "

Clockwork—or All Wound Up, Pullman's more recent fantasy, is a brief but powerful tale of an apprentice clockworker who has failed to create a figure to add to the town clock. As he bewails what he has not done, a friend tells a story of the mad sorcerer, Dr. Kalmenius, and soon the doctor appears before the clockworker and the story begins. It's a tale of love and evil and failure and peace.

J. K. Rowling   The most recent addition to the list of significant writers of fantasy is new to the field and to the publishing world, but she may yet surpass all the rest, in sales if nothing else. J. K. Rowling's first five volumes about Harry Potter in a projected seven-volume series have surprised almost everyone in publishing. By October 1999, the first three books had sold almost two million copies in Great Britain alone and had been translated into twenty-eight languages. The story of the fifth volume, *Harry Potter and the Order of the Phoenix,* in 2003, was even more impressive. Advance orders on Amazon came to 760,000 copies, and the number sold across the world was equally impressive. *The Order of the Phoenix* sold more than 1.8 million copies the first day it was available in England—more than 420,000 had been ordered in advance on England's Amazon. The book led best-selling charts for fiction for a number of weeks. *Time Magazine* devoted six pages to the Harry Potter phenomenon in the September 20, 1999, issue. Stephen King[13] gave a rousing review, and adults read the book, much to the disdain of English novelist A. S. Byatt, who wrote an op-ed in the *New York Times* for July 7, 2003, lamenting the number of adults who enjoyed Harry as much as their kids.[14] One young woman, 12, was not amused by Byatt and wrote,

> I see nothing wrong with grown-ups liking J. K. Rowling's books. . . . My parents have both read the Harry Potter books and enjoyed them. I do not appreciate a stranger calling my parents childish for reading (in my opinion) wonderful books that our whole family and many others enjoy.[15]

Why is Harry so popular? Even a cursory reading of the series would suggest some answers. Harry is a remarkable character. He is almost impossible to dislike; he's an incredibly apt student of magic at the Hogwarts School of Witchcraft and Wizardry;

Audiotaping of complete books is now so common that on the first day of the release of Harry Potter and the Order of the Phoenix, people had their choice—many bought both—of the book or the audiotape performed by Jim Dale.

he's athletic in the game played by wizards, Quidditch (played in midair by students on broomsticks); he's clearly a fighter; and he has friends that are attractive to readers.

His parents were murdered by the evil Voldemort, and there are enough reminders of Luke Skywalker and Darth Vader and other aspects of *Star Wars* to fascinate readers for years. In a *School Library Journal* interview, Rowling was asked what young readers are most curious about. She answered, "They were very keen to know whom I'm going to kill." And shortly a related question was posed. "The first two Harry Potter books are very lighthearted. Will the series remain that way?" Rowling answered,

> The books are getting darker, and that's inevitable. If you are writing about Good and Evil, there comes a point where you have to get serious. This is something I really have had to think about.[16]

Other Kinds of Fantasy

Animal Fantasies   Animal stories aimed at instructing humans are as old as Aesop and as recent as yesterday's book review. Many students come to high school having already enjoyed books such as E. B. White's *Charlotte's Web,* Jane Langton's *The Fledgling,* Robert C. O'Brien's *Mrs. Frisby and the Rats of NIMH,* Kenneth Grahame's *The Wind in the Willows,* and Richard Adams's *Watership Down.*

They may be ready to read Walter Wangerin, Jr.'s, *The Book of the Dun Cow,* a delightfully funny theological thriller retelling the story of Chaunticleer the Rooster. Supposedly the leader for good against evil (the half-snake, half-cock—Cockatrice—and the black serpent—Wyrm), Chaunticleer is beset by doubts. He is aided by the humble dog Mondo Cani, some hilariously pouting turkeys, and assorted other barnyard animals. Although this may sound cute, it is not, and the battle scenes are among the bloodiest, ugliest, and most realistic that readers are likely to find in fantasy. *The Book of Sorrows* was a disappointing sequel.

Several other fantasies have focused on animals. Clare Bell sets her *Ratha's Creature* books 25 million years ago. Ratha leads a group of intelligent wild cats who have developed their society and who have learned to herd and keep other animals.

Erin Hunter's *Warriors: Into the Wild* portrays four clans of wild cats living in a loose harmony with each other as they share a forest, but when one clan becomes too powerful, the equilibrium is threatened. *Warriors: Fire and Ice* continues the saga.

Fire Bringer by David Clement-Davies is about intelligent deer who have developed a complex society predicated on their own myths. He later wrote *The Sight* about an intelligent wolf society. The birth of two pups, Fell who is black and Larka who is white, leads to the acceptance of an ancient myth about foreseeing the future.

Eoin Colfer's books about Artemis Fowl go against the old idea that fantasy has to be highly serious. They are playful mysteries, as well as fantasies.

Fantasy and the Mabinogion   The *Mabinogion* is a collection of medieval Welsh tales, first published in English in 1838 to 1849 by Lady Charlotte Guest. The eleven stories fall into three parts: The four branches of the Mabinogi (tales to instruct young bards) deal with Celtic legends and myths of Pywll, prince of Dived; Branwen, daughter of Llyr; Manawyddan, son of Llyr; and Math, son of Mathonwy. There are also four independent tales and four Arthurian romances. Several writers have used the Mabinogi myths and legends as a basis for their books.

Lloyd Alexander's Prydain Chronicles consists of five volumes about Taran, the young Assistant Pig-Keeper. The opening book of this rich fantasy, *The Book of Three,* introduces the main characters, especially Taran, and sends him on his quest to save his land, Prydain, from evil. He seeks his own identity as well, for none know his heritage. Taran's early impatience is understandable but vexing to his master, Dalben, who counsels patience "for the time being."

> "For the time being," Taran burst out. "I think it will always be for the time being, and it will be vegetables and horseshoes all my life."
>
> "Tut," said Dalben, "there are worse things. Do you set yourself to be a glorious hero? Do you believe it is all flashing swords and galloping about on horses? As for being glorious. . . ."
>
> "What of Prince Gwydion?" cried Taran. "Yes, I wish I might be like him."
>
> "I fear," Dalben said, "that is entirely out of the question."
>
> "But why?" Taran sprang to his feet. "I know if I had the chance. . . ."
>
> "Why?" Dalben interrupted. "In some cases," he said, "we learn more by looking for the answer to a question and not finding it than we do from learning the answer itself."

Taran, youthful impetuousness and righteous indignation aglow, is bored by Dalben's thoughts and wants action, and that he finds soon enough in the books that follow: *The Black Cauldron, The Castle of Llyr, Taran Wanderer,* and *The High King.*

Evangeline Walton (real name, Evangeline Walton Ensely) stands out among writers who have used the Mabinogion as a basis for fantasy. Her four-part series, *The Prince of Annwn: The First Branch of the Mabinogion, The Children of Llyr: The Second*

Branch of the Mabinogion, The Song of Rhiannon: The Third Branch of the Mabinogion, and *The Virgin and the Swine: The Fourth Branch of the Mabinogion* (the last volume was reprinted in 1970 as *The Island of the Mighty: The Fourth Branch of the Mabinogion*), is among the best of retellings of the old Welsh legends. Walton's quartet is both mythology and ecology, for the author makes the earth a divinity that must not be despoiled by humanity. In an afterword to the first book, Walton writes,

> When we were superstitious enough to hold the earth sacred and worship her, we did nothing to endanger our future upon her, as we do now.

King Arthur and Other Myths in Fantasy   Arthurian legends have long been staples of fantasy. T. H. White's *The Once and Future King* (a source, for which it can hardly be blamed, for that dismal musical, *Camelot*) is basic to any reading of fantasy. In four parts, *The Sword in the Stone, The Witch in the Wood, The Ill-Made Knight,* and *The Candle in the Wind,* White retells the story of Arthur—his boyhood, his prolonged education at the hands of Merlin, his seduction by Queen Morgause, his love for Guinivere and her affair with Lancelot, and Mordred's revenge and Arthur's fall.

Marion Zimmer Bradley's *The Mists of Avalon* focuses on the conflict between the old religion, the Celtic, represented by Morgan Le Fay (here called Morgaine) and the new religion of Christianity, represented by Guinivere (here called Gwenhyfar).

Young readers curious about the Arthurian world have a choice of several good books. Leading the list, as usual, is Katherine Paterson, whose *Parzival: The Quest of the Grail Knight* complements our knowledge of Arthur's knights and Wagner's *Parsifal.* Nancy Springer's *I Am Mordred* related the sad, even accursed life of Arthur's bastard son.

Two recent Arthurian fantasies should appeal to young readers. Alice Borchardt's *The Dragon Queen: The Tales of Guinevere* shows a powerful and magical Guinevere battling against Merlin to prove she's worthy of being Arthur's queen. In Dianne Wynn Jones's *The Merlin Conspiracy,* Roddy and Grundo wonder if a conspiracy is behind the death of Merlin, but who will believe them, since they are only children?

Fantasy on Other Worlds: Here There Be Dragons   Several other writers have written marvelous tales of dragons and fantastic worlds. Jane Yolen's *Dragon's Blood, Heart's Blood,* and *A Sending of Dragons* comprise a series with two extraordinarily likable young people fighting for their lives and for their dragons. Patricia C. Wrede's *Dealing with Dragons* and *Talking to Dragons* are funny adventure stories. Her best work can be found in *Book of Enchantments.*

Diana Wynne Jones always tells a good story, often peopled with dragons and such. In *Dark Lord of Derkholm,* a world is controlled by dictatorial Mr. Chesney. When Derk, a stumblebum of a wizard, is selected to play a part in an adventure, Chesney's world begins to collapse.

Marion Zimmer Bradley's Darkover books are among the most popular of books set in another world. Colonists from Earth come to the planet Darkover with its one sun and four multicolored moons, but over 2000 years they lose touch with their home planet and evolve new cultures and new myths. *Darkover Landfall* serves as a good introduction, although almost any book in the series will serve equally well. *The Best of Marion Zimmer Bradley's Fantasy Magazine,* a collection of her short fiction along with brief prefaces, serves to remind readers how powerfully Bradley can write.

Three Recent Examples of Fantasy

Peter Dickinson (see his statement on p. 202), one of fantasy's best friends, provides readers with adventures and ideas and an initiation rite in *The Ropemaker.* For twenty generations the Valley has been safe from barbarians to the north and the evil Empire to the south through powerful magic, but now that the magic grows thin, people from the Valley set out to find help. In this fantastic, scary, and satisfying book, they learn of the Ropemaker, a powerful magician who has been protecting their valley. They set out to find him, but in the end, it is not the Ropemaker, but the young girl, Tilja, who becomes responsible for protecting her people.

Paint by Magic by Kathryn Reiss is a time travel fantasy. Connor Chase comes home to a household that lives on fast foods only to discover a mother who is wearing old-fashioned clothes and who is fixing home-cooked food. Later Connor spots an art book that his mother tries to keep hidden; it features his mother as a model for a long-dead painter, Fitzgerald Cotton. Connor is soon sent back in time to 1926 and the era of the art book. Through the help of some relatives, Connor gets himself back to the contemporary world and saves his mother. Interspersed are vignettes of an evil and creepy late fifteenth-century Venetian painter, whose role is basic to the novel.

The best of this small group of successful fantasies is Vivian Vande Velde's (see her statement on p. 304) *Heir Apparent,* an intelligent and suspenseful story that just might be true not all that far into the future. Giannine Bellisario receives a birthday gift certificate from her father to a nearby Rasmussen Gaming Center Virtual Reality Arcade. She decides to play a new game, Heir Apparent. At the same time, organized protesters (read *censors*) under the title of Citizens to Protect Our Children break into the arcade and damage equipment (like some censors today, these misguided adults want to protect young people from fantasy and science fiction, ergo evil and magic and Satanism).

In the game, Giannine chooses to be a young girl, an heir to the throne in medieval England, a world full of dangers and dragons and quests and villains and the supernatural. Unfortunately, the protesters have fouled up the game, and when she dies—and she does eight times—she must start the game anew. If this sounds repetitious, it should be, but the power of Vande Velde's magic is incredible, and dying and starting over again merely increases the delight that readers are certain to take in this book.

Indeed, the ambiguity in this book, which has all the trappings of the genre but mixed with some trappings of science fiction, suggests how close the two genres are. It also suggests how powerful is the appeal of either, or both, genres and how important they are in the world of books today. James Prothero argues for the appeal and the importance of imagination and fantasy and science fiction, especially to teachers:

> Simply put, science fiction and fantasy are present-day forms of mythology and really should be taught as such. The well-written science fiction or fantasy is every bit as *serious* as mainstream fiction. I think most readers and critics stumble over superficial unreality of the tales. Such work cannot be criticized on the realistic level. Our post-industrial indoctrination has taught us that anything not a courtroom or laboratory fact is a lie. That is why myth has come to be synonymous with *falsehood,* a meaning not previously attached to the word. Myth teaches meaning, not by realistic logical exposition but rather by imagination and metaphor, entering the backdoor of the mind through the imagination. We may learn of courage and perseverance from Tolkien's Frodo or Ursula Le Guin's Ged, but not in a lecture followed by a quiz. . . . We tend to teach the facts, not the meaningful content, the web of truth, in which they hang. The result has been a fragmentation of culture and a loss of community. In the past, meaning has been drawn from the myths and rituals of a culture. But our pseudoscientific arrogance has caused us to relegate our mythology, as Tolkien says, to the nursery, as shabby old-fashioned furniture is relegated to the playroom. Reason may answer the question, *What?* but only imagination can answer the question, *Why?* The post-industrial assumption that humankind needs only cold, hard facts and scientific reason is culturally disastrous and psychologically naïve.[17]

What Is Science Fiction?

In 1953, Robert A. Heinlein, asked the question: "But what, under rational definition, is *science fiction?*" He went on to answer the question by defining the genre as speculative fiction based on the real world, with all its "established facts and natural laws." Although the result can be extremely fantastic in content, "it is not fantasy: it is legitimate—and often very tightly reasoned—speculation about the possibilities of the real world."[18] (See Focus Box 7.2.)

There are other conventions, although none are as important as Heinlein's. Characters voyage into space and face all sorts of dangers. (Science fiction is, after all, more

FOCUS BOX 7.2   Science Fiction Tells about Our Future So We Can Know the Present

The Alien Years by Robert Silverberg. Prism, 1998. Aliens landing on the Earth and controlling it may spell the end of humanity.

The Best Alternate History Stories of the 20th Century edited by Harry Turtledove and Martin H. Greenberg. Del Rey, 2001. History is turned on its head in this anthology; e.g., what if the South had won the Civil War; what if the Nazis had won World War II?

Blue Mars by Kim Stanley Robinson. Bantam, 1996. An anti-aging drug used on Mars begins to lose its effect.

The City of Ember by Jeanne DuPrau. Random House, 2003. Middle school readers will probably like the two 12-year-olds, Lina and Doon, who discover the parchment that may provide directions out of the darkness that has befallen their city of Ember.

Coyote by Allen M. Steele. Ace, 2003. Three stories tell about the right-wing government that has overtaken the constitutional government of the United States and a lonely planet called Coyote.

Dune by Fran Herbert. Chilton, 1965. This tale of politics, power, and battles on the planet Arrakis is a science fiction classic.

Dust by Arthur Slade. Random/Wendy Lamb, 2003. The very real setting of a dry and dusty summer during the Great Depression gradually becomes evil and scary when "traders" from the stars begin taking children.

Fire-Us: The Kiln by Jennifer Armstrong and Nancy Butcher. Eos, 2003. The title of this trilogy, which also contains *The Kindling* and *The Keepers of the Flame,* is a pun on the *virus* that has killed almost everyone on earth. The books focus on a small group of kids in Florida, who managed to survive the virus and now must survive other "survivors."

A Matter of Profit by Hilari Bell. HarperCollins, 2001. Star Trek fans will probably relate well to this story of an 18-year-old warrior in the T'Chin Con-

federation. He hates the idea of going off to conquer another planet and so is given a one-year reprieve to figure out who is behind a plot to assassinate the emperor.

Parasite Pig by William Sleator. Dutton, 2002. This sequel to *Interstellar Pig* (Puffin, 1995) opens with Barney playing the game of "Interstellar Pig" with friends, but an alien enters the game and whisks Barney off to a planet to be fattened up and slaughtered.

Phoenix Café by Gwynneth Jones. TOR, 1998. Earth is almost destroyed in the twenty-fourth century, 300 years after an alien invasion.

The Remnant: On the Brink of Armageddon by Tim LaHaye and Jerry Jenkins. Tyndale House, 2002. Tenth in a series about Armageddon, this episode shows Earth as a wasted shell ruled by the Antichrist.

Seize the Night by Dean Koontz. Bantam, 1998. To stop a mad scientist, a man must rescue four kidnapped children.

Singing the Dogstar Blues by Alison Goodman. Viking, 2003. Eighteen-year-old Joss Aaronson is the sarcastic and funny heroine of this Australian novel that combines time travel and alien relationships with the elements of a mystery thriller.

The Sky So Big and Black by John Barnes. TOR, 2002. A young Marswoman wants to become an ecospector who will find ways of releasing gasses and water to make Mars more habitable.

Tomorrowland, edited by Michael Cart. Scholastic, 1999. Prominent YA authors contributed these ten stories about the future.

2041, edited by Jane Yolen. Delacorte, 1991. Yolen collected a dozen short stories about our future world.

Virtual World by Chris Westwood. Viking, 1998. A new virtual reality game makes players into gods.

adventure than philosophy, although the latter is often present.) Other planets have intelligent or frightening life forms, although they may differ drastically from Earth's humans. Contemporary problems are projected hundreds or thousands of years into the future, and those new views of overpopulation, pollution, religious bickering, political machinations, and sexual disharmony often give readers a quite different perspective of our world and our problems today.

Prophecies are not required in science fiction; nevertheless, some of the richest books of Isaac Asimov and Arthur C. Clarke have been prophetic. (Ray Bradbury, conversely, has said, "I don't try to predict the future—I try to prevent it.")

Occasionally a scientifically untenable premise may be used. On the August 15, 1983, *Nightcap* talk show on Arts Cable Television, Isaac Asimov said, "The best kind of sci-fi involves science." Then he agreed that, "Time travel is theoretically impossible, but I wouldn't want to give it up as a plot gimmick." Essentially, he was agreeing with Heinlein but adding that plot and excitement counted even more. The internal consistency and plausibility of a postulated imaginary society creates its own reality.

Ray Bradbury argues that the appeal of science fiction is understandable because science fiction is important literature, not merely popular stuff. Opening his essay on "Science Fiction: Why Bother?" he compares himself to a fourth-rate George Bernard Shaw who makes an outrageous statement and then tries to prove it. Bradbury says, "Science fiction is the most important fiction being written today." He adds that it is not "part of the Main Stream. It *is* the Main Stream."[19]

Carl Sagan, the late Cornell University astronomer/author, added his testimony, writing that it was science fiction that brought him to science. Kurt Vonnegut, Jr., also applauded science fiction through character Eliot Rosewater in *God Bless You, Mr. Rosewater, or Pearls Before Swine*. Stumbling into a conversation of science fiction writers, Rosewater drunkenly tells them that he loves them because they are the only ones who:

> . . . know that life is a space voyage, and not a short one either, but one that'll last billions of years. You're the only ones with guts enough to really care about the future, who really notice what machines do to us, what wars do to us, what cities do to us, what big, simple ideas do to us, what tremendous misunderstanding, mistakes, accidents and catastrophes do to us.

He goes on to praise them for being "zany enough to agonize over time and distances without limit, over mysteries that will never die, over the fact that we are right now determining whether the space voyage for the next billion years or so is going to be Heaven or Hell."

Science fiction writer and scientist Arthur C. Clarke agrees with Rosewater on the admittedly limited but still impressive power of science fiction to scan the future. In his introduction to *Profiles of the Future,* Clarke writes:

> A critical—the adjective is important—reading of science-fiction is essential training for anyone wishing to look more than ten years ahead. The facts of the future can hardly be imagined *ab initio* by those who are unfamiliar with the fantasies of the past.
> This claim may produce indignation, especially among those second-rate scientists who sometimes make fun of science-fiction (I have never known a first-rate one to do

so—and I know several who write it). But the simple fact is that anyone with sufficient imagination to assess the future realistically would inevitably be attracted to this form of literature. I do not for a moment suggest that more than one percent of science-fiction readers would be reliable prophets; but I do suggest that almost a hundred percent of reliable prophets will be science-fiction readers—or writers.[20]

Why does science fiction appeal to young adults and to adults? First and probably most important, it is exciting. Science fiction may have begun with the "rah-rah-we're-off-to-Venus-with-Buck-Rogers" sensational fiction, and although it has gone far beyond that, the thrill of adventure is still there. Science fiction writers do not write down to their audience, and this is recognized and admired. Science fiction allows anyone to read imaginative fiction without feeling the material is kid stuff. Science fiction presents real heroes to readers who find their own world often devoid of anyone worth admiring, of heroes doing something brave, going to the ultimate frontiers, even pushing these frontiers further back, all important at a time when many young people wonder if any new frontiers exist.

Science fiction has a heritage of fine writers and important books. Some critics maintain that the genre began with Mary Wollstonecraft Shelley's *Frankenstein, or The Modern Prometheus* in 1818. Others argue for Swift's *Gulliver's Travels* in 1726 or the much earlier Lucian's *The True History* in the second century A.D. No matter, for nearly everyone agrees that the first major and widely read writer was Jules Verne, whose *Journey to the Center of the Earth* in 1864 and *Twenty Thousand Leagues Under the Sea* in 1870 pleased readers on several continents. The first American science fiction came with Edgar Allan Poe's short story "The Unparalleled Adventures of One Hans Pfaall," which appeared in the June 1835 issue of *Southern Literary Messenger* and was included in *Tales of the Grotesque and Arabesque* in 1840. Hans Pfaall's balloon trip to the moon in a nineteen-day voyage may be a hoax, but the early trappings of science fiction are there. Dime novels occasionally used science fiction, particularly in the "Frank Reade" series, as did some books from the Stratemeyer Literary Syndicate, particularly in the Tom Swift and Great Marvel series.

These books were readable and fun, and they were read over and over by many people who had no idea how good most of the stories were. Most critics, however, were snobs about science fiction. Some fans didn't consider the genre respectable, but the fact that science fiction, or whatever it was called in the early days, was not part of mainstream writing may have made it more attractive to readers who were not seeking literary respectability so much as they were looking for books that were entertaining.

For better or worse, academic respectability came to science fiction in December 1959, when the prestigious and often stuffy Modern Language Association began its science fiction journal, *Extrapolation*. Two other journals, *Foundation* (in England) and *Science-Fiction Studies* (in Canada), began publishing in the early 1970s. Colleges and secondary schools offered courses in the genre, and major publishers and significant magazines recognized and published science fiction.

Four writers are usually regarded as being *the* fathers of science fiction—Isaac Asimov, Arthur C. Clarke, Robert Heinlein, and Ray Bradbury. One writer is often hailed as the writer most likely to become a science fiction master, Orson Scott Card.

*M*any boys like science fiction because it provides an opportunity to read romances without feeling the stigma attached to "girls' love stories."

The prolific Asimov—more than 500 books—wrote so much on so many fields that he comes the closest to being a truly renaissance figure, but whatever his contributions to the study of the Bible or Shakespeare, no one could question his contributions to science fiction. His multivolume *Foundation* series established a basis for a multidimensional society that an incredible number of readers have temporarily inhabited and accepted.

Arthur C. Clarke may be less widely read than Asimov, but few could argue that *Childhood's End* is one of the classics in the field. *2001: A Space Odyssey,* the basis of the movie, is developed from one of Clarke's short stories, perhaps the most widely cited of any work in science fiction.

After several young adult books, Robert A. Heinlein moved on to adult material and never looked back. Books for the young such as *Farmer in the Sky* and *Pokayne of Mars* may be largely forgotten, but for many young people, these books provided a vision of the future new to them. Later books, particularly *The Moon Is a Harsh Mistress* and *Stranger in a Strange Land,* are both better written and far more powerful visions of a deeply troubled universe. Heinlein may have been unable to picture a believable, strong woman, as critics often claim, but he wrote exceptionally fine science fiction.

Ray Bradbury may be less interested in the mechanics of science fiction than any other major writer, but he may have been the most sensitive of them all about humanity's ability to befoul Earth and the rest of the universe. He seemed to have almost no interest in how his characters moved from Earth to Mars, but *The Martian Chronicles* is a marvelous set of semirelated short stories about the problems of being human in a universe that does not treasure our humanity.

Almost anything by Orson Scott Card is magical, but one novel is usually cited as his best novel thus far—with other great ones to come. *Ender's Game* came out of Card's reading of Asimov's first three *Foundation* books and is set in a somewhat vague future time when humans fear another attack from the insectoid Buggers. Seventy years earlier, a military genius in Earth's army saved the world, and the military are now looking for one more military genius who can save Earth again. Peter and Valentine Wiggin have the military genius but the wrong temperament to be the proper choice, but Andrew Wiggin (who wants to be called Ender) has both the temperament and the genius, and he becomes the tactician who can understand and, therefore, defeat the enemy.

Ender's Game is a complex book, as are its sequels through *Children of the Mind. Ender's Shadow* is not another sequel, no matter what the title, because it retells the story of *Ender's Game* with another main character, this time Ender's assistant, Bean. Unquestionably, Card has written the most significant science fiction in the last twenty years. If there are limits to his ability, readers have not found them.

Types of Science Fiction

The most obvious type, and probably the first to be read by many later fans of science fiction, is the simple-minded but effective story of wild adventure, usually with a touch of sociological or environmental concern. Isaac Asimov's "Lucky Starr" series, written under the Paul French pseudonym, begins with *David Starr: Space Ranger* and a story of an overly populated Earth in need of food. It's a poor book, but it's better adventure than most because Asimov simply could not tell a dull story. Robert Heinlein's early juvenile books suffer from the same fate, particularly the episodic but often thrilling *The Rolling Stones.*

H. G. Wells's *The War of the Worlds* spawned many imitations as we read about this group of aliens invading Earth and that group of aliens attacking another threatened outpost of civilization. The visits of the aliens, however, continue to appeal to us, partly because they combine the best of two worlds—science fiction and horror. William Sleator's *Interstellar Pig* may sound like an odd or funny book, but it is not. Sixteen-year-old Barney is intrigued to discover that three different neighbors moved next door. Soon, Barney and the three are playing a board game called Interstellar Pig, and Barney learns fast enough that he stands between the neighbors and the destruction of Earth. *Parasite Pig* is an intelligent sequel. John Wyndham's (pseudonym of John Beynon Harris) *The Midwich Cuckoo* is set in an apparently tranquil small town in England. Suddenly and briefly, the town stops dead, and nine months later a number of children with strange eyes and even stranger attitudes are born.

Time travel has been a theme in science fiction since H. G. Wells's *The Time Machine.* Jack Finney's *Time and Again* and its sequel *From Time to Time* begin with Simon Morley charged with taking part in a government secret mission. He is transported back to New York City of the 1880s along with a sketch book and a camera and a clear mind for taking detailed notes. He meets the usual corrupt officials, but he also meets Julia and he falls in love, and that makes up for what he does not like. He returns to the present only to learn that the government wants him to continue his work and to change history, or as it puts it, "to correct mistakes of the past which have already affected the present for us." *From Time to Time* is, in the minds of some reviewers, one of those rarities, a sequel better than the original.

The wonder and danger of space travel is an obvious theme in much science fiction. In Larry Niven and Jerry Pourelle's *The Mote in God's Eye,* humans have colonized the galaxy. An alien society sends emissaries to work with the humans and the aliens accidentally die. The humans must send representatives dashing through space to ward off disaster and war.

Science frightens most of us some time or other, and the mad scientist or the threat of science gone sour or insane is another theme that runs through science fiction. In a note in Bantam's 1954 revision of Ray Bradbury's *The Martian Chronicles,* Clifton Fadiman describes Bradbury as "a moralist who has caught hold of a simple, obvious but overwhelmingly important moral idea—that we are in the grip of a psychosis, a technology-mania, the final consequences of which can only be universal murder and quite conceivably the destruction of our planet."

William Sleator's *House of Stairs* illustrates how mad psychologists can become to prove a point. Five young people are brought to an experimental house made up almost entirely of stairs madly going everywhere, and the young people learn how cruel scientists can be in attempting to find something adults think is important. Isaac Asimov's *The Ugly Little Boy* is the most touching use of this theme that we know. Scientists have trapped a young Neanderthal boy and have brought him back to our time, all in the name of science. A nurse is hired to take care of him until he is sent back to his own time. The boy is a terrified mess, and the nurse is horrified by him, but her native compassion and his normal need for a friend bring the two together.

The holocaust of a nuclear explosion is a constant fear for all humanity, just as it is for science fiction writers. Robert O'Brien's *Z for Zachariah* begins after the blast. Ann Burden believes that she is the sole survivor because the valley she lives in is protected from fallout. Then she discovers another survivor, and she learns that she is in danger. The book ends somewhat enigmatically with Ann looking for yet more survivors and the hope that decency and compassion survive somewhere out there. Louise Lawrence also writes about the final explosion, and *Andra, Children of the Dust,* and *Moonwind* are powerful stories about survivors.

Perhaps the gloomiest view of the future is in Philip K. Dick's *Do Androids Dream of Electric Sheep?* (reissued as *Blade Runner* in 1982 when the film adaptation came out). A cop/bounty hunter searches for human-created androids who have escaped from another planet to come back to a horribly drizzling and bleak Earth.

Jane Donawerth made some excellent points in her significant and helpful article in the March 1990 *English Journal;* she noted that between 1818 when Mary Wollstonecraft Shelley published *Frankenstein, or the Modern Prometheus* and the 1930s, women were among the most important writers dealing with technological utopias and similar topics that foreshadowed science fiction:

> But the times when such visions were welcomed did not last; at least in *Amazing Stories* and in *Wonder Stories,* the women virtually disappeared by the mid-1930s. I think that

editorial policy, or simply civic pressure on the women, kept their stories from earning money that could go, instead, to a man supporting a family during the Depression.[21]

By the time women returned to science fiction in the 1940s, they used masculine-sounding pen names, for example, Andre Norton and Leigh Brackett. Today, however, science fiction readers have a number of women writers to turn to, notably Ursula K. Le Guin with *The Left Hand of Darkness* and *Dispossessed: An Ambiguous Utopia,* both studies in gender restrictions.

Harry Turtledove's *Worldwar: In the Balance* is another type of science fiction in which the author changes history, a type of "what if" book. In *Worldwar,* the first of four projected volumes, the time is 1942, the Allies are at war with the Axis powers, and an alien force of lizardlike things invades Earth with a technology that far surpasses human knowledge. Turtledove continues his fascination with alternative histories in his and Richard Dreyfuss's *The Two Georges,* with an America in which the Revolutionary War was not fought. In *The Great War: Walk in Hell,* Turtledove announces a new historical lineup of players; the South, which won the Civil War, is now allied with France and England and at war with the thirty-four United States, and, in turn, the United States is now allied with Prussia. Philip K. Dick's *The Man in the High Castle* postulates that Germany and Japan have won World War II, and the Nazis have taken over most of the United States. Robert Harris's *Fatherland* is set in the 1960s, Germany has supposedly won World War II, and the Holocaust has not yet been uncovered.

Cyberpunk is one of the wildest, rampaging kinds of science fiction today. Gene LaFaille defines cyberpunk as:

> A subgenre of science fiction that incorporates our concern about the future impact of advanced technologies, especially cybernetics, bionics, genetic engineering, and the designer drug culture, upon the individual, who is competing with the increasing power and control of the multinational corporations that are extending their stranglehold on the world's supply of information.[22]

Cyberpunk is about technology and the power of communication, particularly power used to manipulate people. Bruce Sterling's *Mirrorshades: The Cyberpunk Anthology* is eighteen years old, but it still has enough variety to give readers opportunity to see what cyberpunk is and what its ramifications can be. William Gibson's *Neuromancer* was the novel that brought cyberpunk to readers' attention. The antihero of *Neuromancer* gives way to far more likable characters in *Virtual Light.* Neal Stephenson's *Snow Crash* is about a strange computer virus that does all kinds of weird and horrible things to computer hackers. David Brin's *Earth* describes the powerful implications of information technology on society at large.

Science fiction was never as popular on radio as it deserved to be, though "Dimension-X" and "X Minus One" had many fans, but science fiction was popular on television. From Rod Serling's *The Twilight Zone* on through the ever-new casts of *Star Trek,* viewers seemed to find TV science fiction irresistible. A more recent entry in the field, *The X-Files,* seemed to have been different enough that it found an audience. N. E. Genge's *The Unofficial X-Files Companion* is a record of the plots and characters along with the serial killers, cults, werewolfs, robots, and other strangenesses that have roamed through *X-Files* episodes.

Humor is not often the strongest feature of science fiction, but Douglas Adams's *The Hitchhiker's Guide to the Galaxy* is rich in humor, a genuinely funny spoof of the genre. The books that follow in the series are not nearly as happily done, but Adams's first book began as a BBC radio script, progressed to a television script, and ultimately became a novel. When Arthur Dent's house is due for demolition to make way for a highway, he finds Ford Prefect, a strange friend, anxiously seeking a drink at a nearby pub. Ford seems totally indifferent to Arthur's plight because, as he explains, the world will soon be destroyed to make way for a new galactic freeway. Soon the pair are safe aboard a Vogon Construction Fleet Battleship, and that is the most easily explained of the many improbabilities that follow. Any reader desperate to know the meaning of life can find a simple answer in this book.

Two other recent books should amuse science fiction fans and possibly others. Christopher Buckley's *Little Green Men* tells of the leader of Majestic Twelve (MJ-12), a group formed to convince cold-war Russia that the United States had UFO technology. Now MJ-12 proposed that because the original purpose for the organization was moot, a new purpose should be found, in this case convincing the American public that an alien invasion was likely, thus assuring that Congress would vote for increased military spending.

Eric Idle, a member of Monty Python's Flying Circus, satirizes science fiction and all sorts of people in *The Road to Mars: A Post-Modern Novel.* Set in the twenty-fifth century, it relates the work of Professor William Reynolds and an android who writes a dissertation on what makes people laugh.

Four recent science fiction books deserve readers today, different as the books are. Tim LaHaye and Jerry Jenkins' *The Remnant: On the Brink of Armageddon* is one of a series of biblical-derived science fiction books that has sold remarkably well. Richard K. Morgan's *Altered Carbon* is a reinvention, via science fiction, or retelling of Raymond Chandler's riveting and confusing mystery *The Big Sleep.* Allen M. Steele's *Coyote* is three related stories in one book. The first is a tale of a right-wing coup that overthrows the government of the United States. The second, and most fascinating, is about the new government sending a spaceship on a 226-year trip to a newly discovered planet, with all the passengers frozen and due to wake up on arrival and not before. One passenger awakens after liftoff and soon learns that his entire life will be spent without human companionship. In the third story, young people on the spaceship play out a series of adventures. All in all, it's a remarkable book.

Last, and the best of the lot, is Ursula K. Le Guin's *Changing Planes,* fifteen short stories about the varieties of people and societies one might meet in space travel. That simple statement belies the complexities and joys of reading Le Guin anytime, particularly in *Changing Planes.*

Utopias and Dystopias

Utopias and dystopias are neither science fiction nor fantasy, but they share characteristics with both. Readers must suspend disbelief and buy into the author's vision, at least for the duration of the story. As with science fiction, utopian and dystopian books are usually set in the future, with technology having played a role in establishing the conditions out of which the story grows. Unlike science fiction and more like fantasy, however, once the situation is established, authors focus less on technology and more on sociological and psychological or emotional aspects of the story. A utopia is a place of happiness and prosperity; a dystopia is the opposite.

Five interesting young adult books are dystopias. One is Nancy Farmer's *The House of the Scorpion*. It is a grim, futuristic novel set along the Southwest border between the United States and Mexico, most of it on an opium farm. Readers meet Matt, the protagonist, when he is 6 years old and is begging Celia to take him to work with her. She is a Hispanic woman who cooks at the "big house," and in secret—at least from most of the people—is raising Matt. The book is in four parts: Youth: 0 to 6; Middle Age: 7 to 11; Old Age: 12 to 14; and *La Vida Nueva* (the new life). The reason Matt's life is on a speeded-up scale is that he is a clone, one of several created from, and for the benefit of, the wealthy Matteo Alacrán (also known as El Patrón), who by the time he dies near the end of the story is nearly 110 years old. El Patrón has been kept alive through the replacement parts furnished by six earlier clones. Most clones on the plantation are surgically brain damaged at birth, so they grow up as something between a human and a machine. However, El Patrón prefers getting his spare parts from "whole" humans, hence Matt is a perfectly normal boy except for the way he lives, especially after he escapes from the farm and is taken into a work camp that is a modern equivalent of the kinds of orphanages that Charles Dickens wrote about.

Peter Dickinson's *Eva* is a fascinating story about the daughter of a famous scientist devoting his life to working with chimpanzees. In this futuristic world, chimpanzees are relatively important because all the big animals have vanished. The scientist, his wife, his 13-year-old daughter Eva, and a chimpanzee named Kelly are driving home from an outing when they get in a horrible wreck. Eva remembers nothing but slowly wakes to a controlled environment. Over several weeks she discovers that her mind has been planted in Kelly's body.

The rest of the book is about the next thirty years of Eva's life. The technology is intriguing to read about, but it's the psychological and the social aspects that leave readers pondering ideas about ecology, parent-child and male-female relationships, mass media advertising, medical ethics, and young adult suicide.

Of these young adult books, Lois Lowry's *The Giver* is the most powerful and disturbing. Jonas lives in an apparently perfect society. At the Ceremony of 12 when the elders assign each young person his career, Jonas is selected to be "our next receiver of memory." Jonas discovers that this job requires him to learn everything that the society has forgotten, in effect things such as color or music or anything else his people have given up for the common good. *The Giver* is brief but gripping, and any reader will be caught up in the story of people who have willingly given up their freedom and their imagination for the supposed "good of the people."

M. T. Anderson's *Feed* satirizes modern life, particularly the corporate world. A group of young people are connected to each other through the "feed," an implant in the brain that provides whatever they want to know. When they arrive on the moon, they receive "feeds" on where to stay and who to know and what to eat and what's hot in styles and more.

Luckily, we took this picture of Nancy Farmer's The House of the Scorpion *before the end of the year when it was covered with stickers because it won the National Book Award for Juvenile Literature and was both a Newbery and Printz Honor Book.*

Francine Prose's *After* begins with a contemporary horror, the threat of a mass killing at a public high school, but in this case, Central High School is not under attack, but "some crazy kids shot up the school gym at Pleasant Valley and killed a bunch of students and teachers." Altogether, five kids and three teachers had been killed and fourteen other students were critically wounded, all by two boys and one girl. That might have been it had the Central High School administration not decided to make sure this never happened at home. Mr. Trent, the principal, announces some changes to come and introduces Dr. Henry Willner, a former professor of clinical psychology "who has generously given up a college teaching career to come down and work in the trenches with high-school kids in crisis."

And the changes begin. Metal detectors are installed and backpacks are inspected daily. No baseball caps can henceforth be worn backward. No more baggy pants or bare midriffs. No wearing anything red (a gang color). Random urine testing of basketball players. Locker searches. And Dr. Willner—the increasingly scary Dr. Willner—confronts a student when he finds "not one but two of those . . . questionable items in your

FOCUS BOX 7.3   *Utopias and Dystopias in Recent Imaginative Fiction*

Cold Tom by Sally Prue. Scholastic, 2003. Tom is an elf who is forced to leave his tribe and enter the dangerous city of the demons (humans). The author bases her story on the old legend of Tam Lin, except from an opposing viewpoint. The biggest danger to Tom is when humans try to "save" him from his tribe.

The Dark Horse by Marcus Sedgwick. Random, 2003. Sigurd belongs to what appears to be an isolated Nordic tribe that fears the marauders known as The Dark Horse. An important part of this mysterious story relates to Sigurd's revelations about his adopted sister, Mouse, who has the ability to communicate with animals.

The Dirt Eaters by Dennis Foon. Annick/Firefly, 2003. In Book One of the Longlight Legacy trilogy, 15-year-old Roan and his younger sister, Stowe, survive the destruction of their village, only to be taken in by a man inappropriately named Saint.

Dust by Arthur Slade. Random, 2003. There's something evil in this beautifully written novel that *Booklist* editors compared to Ray Bradbury's 1962 *Something Wicked This Way Comes*. However, they were reassuring in saying that imperfect hope triumphs over manifest evil.

Eragon by Christopher Paolini. Knopf, 2003. This quest fantasy—a surprise best-seller—is Book One in the Inheritance trilogy. Christopher Paolini, a home-schooled boy living in Montana, was 15 years old when he began writing the book. In 2002, when he was 17, his parents helped him self-publish and sell 10,000 copies of the 500-page book before it was "discovered," edited, and promoted by Knopf.

Flame by Hilari Bell. Simon & Schuster, 2003. First in a proposed The Book of Sorabb Series, *Flame* takes much of its magic and mysticism from ancient Persian poetry and mythology. The lead characters include Jiaan, the illegitimate son of an Army commander, his half-sister Soraya, and Kavi, a traveling merchant. They each have a role to play in saving their country.

Full Tilt by Neal Shusterman. Simon & Schuster, 2003. Readers who have previously viewed carnivals as happy and festive places will come away from this scary story with a sense of foreboding. Shusterman has devised seven carnival rides that take people into their darkest fears.

Heir Apparent by Vivian Vande Velde. Harcourt, 2002. 14-year-old Giannine receives a gift certificate to a futuristic gaming center. The equipment malfunctions and she is trapped inside the game until she finds a way to win.

Hawksong by Amelia Atwater-Rhodes. Delacorte, 2003. Danica's tribe are avian shapeshifters who for generations have been at war with the serpiente, a tribe that shapeshifts into serpents. When Danica and Zane (one of the serpiente) consider marrying in hopes of ending the bloodshed, a reviewer for *School Library Journal* wrote that "the book takes the Romeo and Juliet angle to new heights" dealt with in a "completely original way."

Lyra's Oxford by Philip Pullman, Knopf, 2003. Fans of Pullman's Dark Materials series, will welcome this 49-page gift package that includes a map of Lyra's Oxford and a new story about Lyra and Pantalaimon as they lend help to a witch's daemon named Ragi.

Stravaganza: City of Masks by Mary Hoffman. Bloomsbury, 2002. In this first of a proposed trilogy, 15-year-old Lucien is battling against cancer. As a reward for his heroic efforts, his father gives him a beautiful notebook that transports him into the fantasy world of sixteenth century Bellezza, where he is healthy.

Thorn Ogres of Hagwood by Robin Jarvis. Harcourt, 2002. Younger teens are the ones likely to enjoy this story of a boy starting werling school and getting involved with a dwarf, who has a dangerous secret.

locker during our random locker search." And what are those two sinister items? One is a CD with hip hop and rap music, but it is the other item that most irritates Willner: J. D. Salinger's *The Catcher in the Rye*. Willner announces,

> After much debate, we have decided to remove *The Catcher in the Rye* from our literature curriculum. Studies have proved that it has a terribly deleterious—*destructive*—effect on students too young to realize that Holden Caulfield is a highly negative role model.

And life at Central High School gets worse.

In his *Republic* in the fifth century B.C., Plato presented his vision of the ideal world, offering suggestions for educating the ruling class. With wise philosopher-kings, or so Plato maintains, the people would prosper, intellectual joys would flourish (along with censorship, for Plato would ban poets and dramatists from his perfect society), and the land would be permanently safe.

The centuries-old fascination with utopias is suggested by the Greek origin of the word, which includes two meanings, "no place" and "good place." Most of us, in idle moments, dream of a perfect land, a perfect society, a place that would solve all our personal problems and, if we are altruistic enough, all the world's problems as well. In our nightmares, we also dream of the opposite, the dystopias, which are diseased or bad lands. But few of us do more than dream, which may explain why some people are so intrigued with authors who transfer their dreams to the printed page.

Utopias and dystopias are never likely to be popular with the masses because they usually lack excitement and fast-moving plots. Writers of adventure or fantasy or science fiction begin with a story (the more thrilling the better) and later, if ever, add a message. Writers of utopias and dystopias think first of the message and then devise a story to carry the weight of the message.

The books are usually about dissatisfaction with contemporary society. Readers who do not share the anger or irritation of utopian writers easily miss the allusions needed to follow the story or find the message. For these reasons, utopian literature is likely to appeal only to more thoughtful and intellectual readers. Although these young adults may not share the anger of the writer, given their idealism, they probably share the writer's concerns about society and humanity.

To attract young adult readers, dystopian books have to have something extra because, with a few exceptions, young adults are optimistic and imaginative. Adults might read dystopian books on the premise that misery loves company, but teenagers have not lived long enough to lose their natural curiosity, and they have not been weighed down with adult problems such as failing health, heavy family responsibilities, debt surpassing income, and dreams gone bankrupt. So even when teenagers read dystopian books, they probably wear rose-colored glasses, feeling grateful for the world as it usually is.

Concluding Comments

The books we've talked about in this chapter start with life as we know it and attempt to stretch readers' imaginations. All of us need to dream, not to waste our lives but to enrich them. To dream is to recognize humanity's possibilities. In a world hardly characterized by undue optimism, the genres treated here offer us challenges and hope, not the sappy sentimentalism of "everything always works out for the best" (for it often does not) but realistic hope based on our noblest dreams of surviving. If we go down, we do it knowing that we have cared and dreamed and found something for which we are willing to struggle.

 Notes

[1] Ursula K. Le Guin, "On Teaching Science Fiction" in Jack Williamson, ed., *Teaching Science Fiction: Education for Tomorrow* (Oswick Press, 1980), 22.

[2] Walter Wangerin, Jr., in a lecture, "By Faith, Fantasy," quoted in John H. Timmerman's *Other Worlds: The Fantasy Genre* (Bowling Green University Popular Press, 1983), p. 21.

[3] This point, with many more examples, is made by Leslie E. Owen in "Children's Science Fiction and Fantasy Grow Up," *Publishers Weekly* 232 (October 30, 1987): 32–37.

[4] Mary Harrington Hall, "A Conversation with Ray Bradbury and Chuck Jones," *Psychology Today* 1 (April 1969): 28–29.

[5] Jo-Anne Goodwin, "In Defence of Fantasy," *Independent Magazine,* London, July 25, 1993, p. 32.

[6] John Rowe Townsend, "Heights of Fantasy" in Gerard J. Senick, ed., *Children's Review* 5 (Gale Research, 1983), p. 7.

[7] Lloyd Alexander, "High Fantasy and Heroic Romance," *Horn Book Magazine* 47 (December 1971): 483.

[8] Tamora Pierce, "Fantasy: Why Kids Read It, Why Kids Need It." *School Library Journal* 39 (October 1993).

[9] Ursula K. Le Guin, "Why Are Americans So Afraid of Dragons?" *PNLA* (Pacific Northwest Library Association) *Quarterly* 38 (Winter 1974): 18.

[10] Marjorie N. Allen, *What Are Little Girls Made Of? A Guide to Female Role Models in Children's Books* (Facts on File, 1999), p. 41.

[11] Michael Cart, "Miss M," *School Library Journal* 45 (June 1999): 25.

[12] See Patty Campbell, "A Spyglass on YA 2000," *Horn Book Magazine* 77 (January-February 2001): 125–136.

[13] Steven King, "Potter Gold," *Entertainment Weekly,* July 11, 2003, pp. 80–81.

[14] A. S. Byatt, "Harry Potter and the Childish Adults," *New York Times.* July 7, 2003, p. A-17.

[15] *New York Times,* July 12, 2003, p. A-22.

[16] Roxanne Feldman, "The Truth about Harry." *School Library Journal* 45 (September 1999): 139.

[17] James Prothero, "Fantasy, Science Fiction and the Teaching of English," *English Journal* 79 (March 1990): 33.

[18] Robert Heinlein, "Ray Guns and Rockets Ships," *Library Journal* 78 (July 1953): 1188.

[19] Ray Bradbury, "Science Fiction: Why Bother?" *Teachers' Guide: Science Fiction* (Bantam, n.d.), p. 1.

[20] Arthur Clarke, *Profiles of the Future* (Holt, 1984), p. 9.

[21] Jane Donawerth, "Teaching Science Fiction by Women," *English Journal* 79 (March 1990): 39–40.

[22] Gene LaFaille, "Science Fiction: Top Guns of the 1980s," *Wilson Library Bulletin* 65 (December 1990): 34.

History and History Makers
Of People and Places

The United States has always viewed history in its own way. More than a century ago, Ralph Waldo Emerson described the great American tradition as "trampling on tradition," and Abraham Lincoln said that Americans had a "perfect rage for the new." But by the beginning of the twentieth century, Americans were feeling more confident and began to look back. U.S. history became a standard part of the school curriculum, thousands of towns erected statues of Abraham Lincoln and Ulysses S. Grant, and historical pageants flourished, including in the South, where Confederates began to look back with pride on their role in the Civil War.

We are including both fiction and nonfiction in this chapter because as Chris Crowe shows on p. 226, the two genres complement each other. And especially in relation to war, it is almost impossible to separate memoirs and autobiographical writings from fictional writings. We are also including materials written for both adults and young adults because the reporting of history for a general audience is often done in a manner that is perfectly accessible to young readers. We will first write a general introduction to historical fiction, then move to the settlement of the United States (especially the West) and then look at books about war, with separate sections on the Holocaust and Vietnam. There will be some crossover between the contents of this chapter and the next chapter on informative nonfiction and biographies.

Historical Fiction

Reading historical novels satisfies our curiosity about other times, places, and people, and even more important, it provides adventure, suspense, and mystery. As with any literary form, there are standards for judging historical novels (see Table 8.1). They should be historically accurate and steeped in the sense of time and place. We should recognize totems and taboos, food, clothing, vocations, leisure activities, customs, smells, religions, literature, and all that goes into making one time and one place unique from another. Enthusiasts forgive no anachronism, no matter how slight. Historical novels should give a sense of history's continuity, a feeling for the flow of history from one time into another, which is for good reason different from the period before or after. Historical novels should tell a lively story with a sense of impending danger,

CHRIS CROWE
On Facts Doing Double Duty

When I was working on a book about author Mildred D. Taylor, I learned that she had been profoundly affected by a piece of American history that I had never heard of. In 1955 Emmett Till, a 14-year-old African American kid from Chicago, was murdered by white men in Mississippi. News coverage of his death and the shameful trial of his killers turned the event into one of the biggest media stories of the 1950s. On December 1, 1955, just 69 days after the acquittal of Emmett's murderers, Rosa Parks refused to give up her seat on a segregated city bus in Montgomery, Alabama.

And even I knew what happened after that.

Emmett's death made an impression not only on Mildred Taylor, but on millions of other Americans in the 1950s, especially on African Americans who saw the photograph of Emmett's corpse in the September 15, 1955, issue of *Jet Magazine*. The more I learned about the case and its impact on America, the more I wondered why I did not hear about it until forty years after it happened. A quick survey of history textbooks suggested one reason: The story of Emmett Till was virtually ignored.

I didn't want my own children—or any teenagers—to grow up as I had, ignorant of this vitally important civil rights event, and I decided to find a way to tell Emmett's story to young adults. I continued reading everything I could find about the case, all the time thinking about how to tell this story to teenagers. I eventually decided that historical fiction might be the best approach, and I outlined a novel about a fictional character, Hiram Hillburn, who visits Mississippi at exactly the same time as Emmett Till's visit. In my novel, the murder of Emmett Till and the trial that followed change Hiram forever, just as those same events helped change the racist culture in the United States.

When I finished, I realized that I wasn't through with my work. Though my novel relied heavily on historical facts from the Emmett Till case, including actual statements made in the trial that were stranger than any fiction I could have dreamed up, I had used very little of the historical information I had found. I also worried that some readers might come away from my novel thinking, "Well, it wasn't really *that* bad. This was fiction, the author was just making it up." So I decided to *nonfictionalize* my novel and to use all of the historical data I had gathered to tell Emmett Till's story for young readers.

This was much harder than I expected because in fiction I was able to fudge with dialogue and to create characters and details that suited my story. I had no such freedom in nonfiction. Every fact had to be verified, every detail confirmed. I had to tease the factual historical narrative out of my novel and then supplement it with additional material, including photos that I could not have used in a fictional account.

When I finished both books, I was exhausted but satisfied. I had made the facts of the Emmett Till case serve double duty. They enriched a novel and they documented a work of nonfiction. The two books combined, I hope, will help today's young adults learn the facts of a pivotal event in American history.

Chris Crowe's books include *Presenting Mildred D. Taylor,* Twayne, 1999; *Mississippi Trial, 1955,* Phyllis Fogelman Books, 2002; *Getting Away with Murder: The True Story of the Emmett Till Case,* Phyllis Fogelman Books, 2003; and *More than a Game: Sports Literature for Young Adults,* Scarecrow Press, 2003. His website is www.chriscrowe.com.

TABLE 8.1 SUGGESTIONS FOR EVALUATING HISTORICAL FICTION

A good historical novel usually has	A poor historical novel may have
A setting that is integral to the story	A story that could have happened any time or any place. The historical setting is for visual appeal and to compensate for a weak story
An authentic rendition of the time, place, and people being featured	Anachronisms in which the author illogically mixes up people, events, speaking styles, social values, or technological developments from different time periods
An author who is so thoroughly steeped in the history of the period that he or she can be comfortably creative without making mistakes	Awkward narrations and exposition as the author tries to teach history through characters' conversations
Believable characters with whom young readers can identify	Oversimplification of the historical issues and a stereotyping of the "bad" and the "good" guys
Evidence that even across great time spans people share similar emotions	Characters who fail to come alive as individuals having something in common with the readers. They are just stereotyped representatives of a particular period
References to well-known events or people or other clues through which the reader can place the happenings in their correct historic framework	
Readers who come away with the feeling that they know a time or place better. It is as if they have lived in it for at least a few hours	

mystery, suspense, or romance. Because of the excitement and romance involved, some of the stories that could go in this chapter have already been included in Chapter 6 on Adventure. For example, we almost flipped a coin to decide where to put Geraldine McCaughrean's *The Kite Rider* set in thirteenth-century China and her *Stop the Train* set during the 1890s Oklahoma land rush.

Historical novels allow us—at their best they force us—to make connections and to realize that despair is as old and as new as hope, that loyalty and treachery, love and hatred, compassion and cruelty were and are inherent in humanity, whether it be in ancient Greece, Elizabethan England, or post–World War I Germany. As with most writers, historical novelists may want to teach particular lessons. Christopher Collier, for example, makes no pretense about why he and his brother write about the American Revolution in their fine historical novels:

> The books I write with my brother are written with a didactic purpose to teach about ideals and values that have been important in shaping the course of American history. This is in no way intended to denigrate the importance of the dramatic and literary elements of historical novels. Nothing will be taught, and certainly nothing learned, if no one reads the books.[1]

Collier later added that "there is no better way to teach history than to embrace potential readers and fling them into a living past."[2]

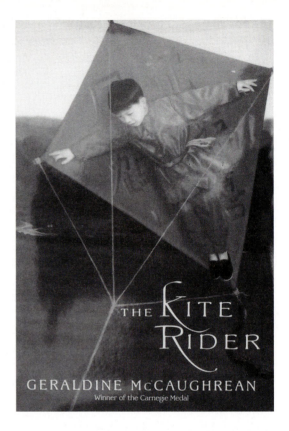

With historical fiction, the setting can be any time in the past and any place in the world. Geraldine McCaughrean chose thirteenth-century China for her exciting The Kite Rider.

Novelist Patricia Lee Gauch has an interesting theory about why the historical novel may appeal to readers. She is talking mostly about adults, but her idea might be worth springing on bright young people at the right time.

> Surely the appeal of historical story has something to do with the ironies of history. Because we know the ending, the twists of fate, the upside downness of history, and the unpredictability, it is particularly poignant. Not only is there craziness . . . but add to the games of history the obvious capriciousness that a long look at historical events reveals.[3]

In our adolescent literature classes, we have students read something like twenty books in a semester spread across various genres. Historical fiction is often one of the last blanks to get filled in, but when students come to us complaining that they cannot find a good piece of historical fiction to read, we ask them which books they've read, and invariably they tell us about two or three that we consider to be historical fiction but that they had not recognized as such. One reason for their surprise is their stereotyped view that historical fictions must be grand and imposing, like a movie spectacle starring Charlton Heston, or exaggerated like a "bodice-ripper" romance. Actually, historical fiction includes mysteries, comedies, adventures, realistic problem stories, and whatever other genres can be listed (see Focus Box 8.1). The only thing they have in common is that they are set in the past. We used to define historical fiction as any story that happened before or during World War II, but as we have grown older and readers

FOCUS BOX 8.1   *Historical Fiction*

The All-True Travels and Adventures of Lidie Newton by Jane Smiley. Knopf, 1998. Lidie marries an abolitionist and moves with him to Kansas where war rages between the northern and southern sympathizers.

The Book of the Lion by Michael Cadnum. Viking, 2000. Seventeen-year-old Edmund goes to the Holy Land as Knight Crusader's squire and takes part in the bloody Battle of Arsuf.

The Burning Road by Ann Benson. Delacorte, 1999. A neurologist seeking a cure for a modern epidemic reads the journal of a fourteenth-century doctor.

Daughter of Venice by Donna Jo Napoli. Random House, 2002. The sheltered life of a girl in sixteenth-century Venice changes as Donata dons boy's clothes and goes exploring.

The Edge on the Sword by Rebecca Tingle. Putnam, 2001. Set in late ninth-century England, this is the imagined story of the teen years of Ethelflaed of Mercia, an extraordinarily accomplished woman noted in the *Anglo-Saxon Chronicle.*

Fever by Laurie Halse Anderson. Simon and Schuster, 2000. An epidemic of yellow fever hits Philadelphia in 1793 and surrounds the world of 16-year-old Matilda.

Frontier Wolf by Rosemary Sutcliff. Dutton, 1980. A young Roman commander of a group of scouts in northern England must begin a retreat from the forces of native tribes.

Frozen Summer by Mary Jane Auch. Holt, 1998. In 1816 in western New York during a year that was known as the year without a summer, Remembrance tries to hold her family together in this sequel to *Journey to Nowhere* (Holt, 1997).

The Horse Thief: A Novel by Robert Newton Peck. HarperCollins, 2002. It is 1938 in Chickalooke, Florida, and 17-year-old Tullis Yoder has a job taking care of the horses in a rodeo. When the owner falls on hard times and decides to sell the horses to a slaughterhouse, Tullis and various "helpers" steal the horses and lead them to life.

Lyddie by Katherine Paterson. Dutton, 1992. When her family goes broke, Lyddie goes to work in a Massachusetts textile mill and finds a cause in a labor movement.

A Murder for Her Majesty by Beth Hilgartner. Houghton Mifflin, 1986. When her father is killed and rumor has it that Queen Elizabeth wanted him dead, Alicia takes refuge as a boy singer in the York Cathedral.

The Queen's Own Fool by Jane Yolen and Robert J. Harris. Putnam/Philomel, 2000. The voice in this unusual coming-of-age story is that of a female court jester serving Mary Queen of Scots.

Search of the Moon King's Daughter by Linda Holeman. Tundra, 2002. The setting is 1830s England and the heroine is 15-year-old Emmaline, whose father dies of cholera and whose mother is injured in a factory job. The mother becomes addicted to laudanum, and it is up to Emmaline to save her brother.

A Single Shard by Linda Sue Park. Clarion, 2001. This winner of the Newbery Award is set in twelfth-century Korea and is a good illustration of the archetypal journey. A young orphan apprentices himself to a master craftsman of celadon pottery and the journey occurs when he must take a sample of his master's work to the royal palace.

The Squire, His Knight, and His Lady by Gerald Morris. Houghton Mifflin, 1999. Along with *The Squire's Tale* (Houghton Mifflin, 1998), this lively and humorous book straddles historical fiction and fantasy.

Susannah by Janet Hickman. Greenwillow, 1998. Susannah is 13 when her mother dies and her father joins the Shaker community on the Ohio frontier.

Thursday's Child by Sonya Hartnett. Candlewick, 2002. This novel makes clear that life in the Australian Depression was no better than that during the American Depression.

of YA fiction seem to have grown younger, we find ourselves using the Vietnam era as the dividing line between "historical" and "contemporary."

Historical novels can take readers any place they want to go—or fear to go—and in any time period they would like. Gary Blackwood's *The Shakespeare Stealer* and its sequel *The Shakespeare Scribe* take us to the Globe Theatre in the sixteenth century. Donna Jo Napoli's *Daughter of Venice* is set in late sixteenth-century Venice with all its sinister intrigues. A trip to King Arthur's time can easily be had through Sarah L. Thomson's *The Dragon's Son,* with its newly created legends about Arthur. An equally easy trip can be made to the Crusades in *The Book of the Lion,* by the prolific and reliable Michael Cadnum, with his portrait of the adventures and horrors experienced in the Holy Land by a 17-year-old knight crusader's squire. Howard Fast's *April Morning* is more than forty years old, but it is still worth reading by anybody who cares about young people and their place in the Revolutionary War. Kathryn Lasky's *Beyond the Burning Time* is a fine novel focusing on the terrors of the Salem witch trials. The most frightening of the new historical fiction, because it is set only half a century ago in our country and at one of our most shameful times, is Chris Crowe's *Mississippi Trial, 1955* about the killing of Emmett Till, a black teenager from the North who had the foolish, or bad, manners to joke with a white Southern girl. (See Crowe's statement on p. 226)

Some Consistently Good Writers of YA Historical Fiction

Christopher and James Lincoln Collier   These two brothers specialize in historical fiction. Their best known book, *My Brother Sam Is Dead,* comes from the time of the Revolutionary War and was a Newbery Honor book. *The Bloody Country* and *The Winter Hero* continue the story. Another trilogy, *War Comes to Willy Freeman, Jump Ship to Freedom,* and *Who Is Carrie?* focuses on African Americans and their role in early American history. Throughout the 1990s, the two produced the *Drama of American History* series for Benchmark Books.

Karen Cushman   As Karen Cushman mentions in her statement, she has chosen to write about girls embarking on journeys to discover themselves. Her first two books are set in medieval Europe. *Catherine Called Birdy* (a Newbery Honor book) is the diary of a 14-year-old daughter of a knight whose feisty and witty observations bring the thirteenth-century to life in ways that few historians could. In *The Midwife's Apprentice,* Cushman looks at the same period, but at a different part of the social scale. She writes about an orphan who manages to get herself apprenticed to a midwife. Her more recent book, *Rodzina,* has a similar plot, except that it is set in the American West in 1881. Rodzina is a large, ungainly Polish American girl (see the photo on p. 232) who is sent west on an ophan train. As the train moves along, she sees the younger and more attractive children adopted. The two invitations she receives are disastrous and she runs away and returns to the train, finally making herself so useful that she becomes an assistant to the woman she calls "Miss Doctor." California's gold rush is the setting for *The Ballad of Lucy Whipple.* Lucy, whose original name was California Morning Whipple, finds herself dragged "like a barrel of lard" from Massachusetts to Lucky Diggings, California. The gold she finds is in pie-baking.

KAREN CUSHMAN
On Gender in Children's Books

*T*he questions I'm most often asked are: "Where do you get your ideas?" "Why are all your books about girls?" and "How old are you anyway?" There is no true answer to the first. The third I ignore. And the second question requires a much longer answer than the asker is usually willing to hear. So I'll talk about it here.

In a way, this career of mine started over fifty years ago with Little Lulu. I loved Little Lulu. She was the only cartoon character who was like me—a girl. All the other cartoon stars were boys—Donald and Mickey and Superman, of course—but even the mice and the robots were boys, I could tell—not to mention the Roadrunner, Foghorn Leghorn, Gerald McBoingBoing, and Mr. McGoo. I wanted to see ordinary girls, girls like me, to see what girls did, said, thought, believed, feared, loved, and hated. Little Lulu, not Tubby.

Many years later, when I began to think about writing for young people, I decided to write about girls, ordinary girls, who are embarking on journeys to discover who they are and where they belong, surviving extraordinary circumstances with courage and grace.

I have been told that boys won't read my books because they are about girls. Teachers choose books about boys because girls will read them. And a number of women writers have taken to writing about boy heroes. But isn't this ignoring the issue? If books about girls who are interesting, active, clever, and curious aren't being read by boys, isn't that the problem? Are we teaching boys somehow to be alienated and offended by female protagonists? Should we writers all give up and just write about boys? Not me. Girls are why I got into this in the first place.

I believe books, like all the media, tell children what they ought to be like. They provide role models for young people constructing their identity. And both genders need role models of both sexes who are strong, independent, determined, and resourceful. We writers can say, "Look. Here are people, all kinds of people, who are worthy of respect and admiration. And this is how they act."

Some say that's imposing an agenda on children. But don't we do that all the time? Kids aren't born religious or polite or cooperative. These are values taught them by adults and the world around them. The world is constantly sending messages about what it means to be lovable, successful, worthy, male, or female. The question is, What do we want those messages to be?

As children are what they eat and hear and experience, so too they are what they read. This is why I write what I do, about strong young women who in some way take responsibility for their own lives with tolerance, thoughtfulness, and caring. Little Lulus, not Tubbys.

Karen Cushman's books include *Catherine Called Birdy*, 1994; *The Midwife's Apprentice*, 1995; *Matilda Bone*, 2000; and *Rodzina*, 2003, all from Clarion.

Leon Garfield   Wit, humor, and liveliness permeate Leon Garfield's books. His world is the eighteenth century, with an occasional detour into early nineteenth-century England. Garfield set a standard for historical writing that few can match. Garfield's eighteenth century is the world of Fielding and Smollett, lusty, squalid, ugly, bustling, and swollen, full of life and adventure and the possibility that being born an orphan may lead you ultimately to fame and fortune. His stories play with reality versus illusion, daylight versus dreams, flesh versus fantasy. His ability to sketch out minor characters in a line or two is impressive. Of a man in *The Sound of Coaches*, he wrote,

*K*aren Cushman's *Rodzina* is a Polish American girl sent west on an orphan train. The offers she received are not the best.

"He was one of those gentlemen who [e]ffect great gallantry to all the fair sex except their wives." Of the protagonist we are told, "although jealousy was ordinarily foreign to Sam's nature, they did, on occasion, talk the same language." The funniest of Garfield's books are *The Strange Affair of Adelaide Harris* and its sequel, *The Night of the Comet.* In *Adelaide,* Bostock and Harris, two nasty pupils in Dr. Bunnion's Academy, become so entranced with stories of Spartan babies abandoned on mountaintops, there to be suckled by wolves, that they borrow Harris's baby sister to determine for themselves the truth of the old tales. Therein begins a wild comedy of errors and an even wilder series of coincidences and near duels and wild threats that hardly let up until the last lines.

Carolyn Meyer   When Carolyn Meyer wrote nonfiction books, she frequently found herself coming up against blank walls where she could find no more information. Because she wanted the stories to continue, she began asking, "What if?" and so began her career as a writer of fiction. Her most highly acclaimed books are probably *White Lilacs,* about the dismantling of a black community in early Texas; *Mary, Bloody Mary,* about the youth of the woman who became one of England's most unpopular rulers; and *Where the Broken Heart Still Beats: The Story of Cynthia Ann Parker,* about a woman who was captured by Comanche Indians at age 9 and unsuccessfully "rescued" by white settlers years later.

Scott O'Dell   *The King's Fifth* is probably Scott O'Dell's most convincing work, with its picture of sixteenth-century Spaniards and the moral strains put on anyone involved in the search for gold and fame. It is convincing, often disturbing, and, like most of O'Dell's historical novels, generally worth pursuing. Students coming to high school with a good reading background probably already know O'Dell from his *Island of the Blue Dolphins* and *Sing Down the Moon,* both of which present original and positive portrayals of young Native American women suffering at the hands of white settlers in the middle to late 1800s. He was a pioneer in featuring strong young women in these two books, and within the last couple of decades several good writers have followed his lead.

Ann Rinaldi   Among Ann Rinaldi's best books are *A Break with Charity: A Story about the Salem Witch Trials* and *Cast Two Shadows,* a Civil War story. She tackled a particularly ambitious subject in *Wolf by the Ears,* a fictional story of Sally Hemmings's family. Sally was a mulatto slave in Thomas Jefferson's household, and some historians believe that Jefferson fathered several of her children. Rinaldi's book implies that this is true, but the question is never clearly answered, even though the protagonist, supposedly Jefferson's daughter, asks it often enough. The book's title comes from Jefferson's statement about slavery: "as it is, we have the wolf by the ears and we can neither hold him, nor safely let him go. Justice is in one scale, and self-preservation the other." Most of Rinaldi's numerous books deal with some aspect of the Revolutionary or the Civil War.

Mildred Taylor   Her own family history provided Mildred Taylor with material for her prize-winning series. The most recent, *The Land,* won the 2002 Coretta Scott King award. It was written as a prequel to the earlier books *Song of the Trees; Roll of Thunder, Hear My Cry; Let the Circle Be Unbroken;* and *The Road to Memphis.* Together, the series chronicles the generations of the Logan family, African American landowners near Vicksburg, Mississippi. *The Land* opens in post–Civil War Georgia when Paul-Edward Logan is about to leave his childhood behind. He is the son of a white plantation owner and a former slave of African American and Native American descent, and he is confused by his station in society. He has always been treated much like his white brothers, but now that he is approaching manhood, his father begins to treat him differently. The father thinks he might save the boy's life by teaching him that his welfare will always be subject to the whims and desires of white men. As reviewer James Blasingame said in *The English Journal,* "The author is fair to her characters, creating good and bad people of all races and genders, while keeping the reality of place and time. Rereading the previously written novels will be even more enjoyable after reading *The Land*."[4]

Rosemary Sutcliff   From her finest early novel in 1954, *The Eagle of the Ninth,* through her 1990 *The Shining Company,* Rosemary Sutcliff has been acclaimed as the finest writer of British historical fiction for young people. We must find ways for librarians and teachers to get her books to the right young readers, those who care about history and a rattling good story, and who are not put off by a period of time they know little about. *The Shining Company* may be harder to sell than her earlier books about the Normans and the Saxons (e.g., *The Shield Ring* and *Dawn Wind*) because it is set in a more obscure time, seventh-century Britain. Sutcliff knew about the cries of men and the screams of stricken horses and the smell of blood and filth, and she cared about people who make history, whether knaves or villains or, in this case, naïve men who trusted their king and themselves beyond common sense.

Frances Temple   *The Ramsay Scallop* is a wonderful book about medieval Europe. In it, Frances Temple describes the apprehension that 13-year-old Eleanor of Ramsay feels as she awaits marriage to 22-year-old Lord Thomas of Thornham. Thomas is no happier about his upcoming marriage because he has become cynical about life and religion after fighting in the Crusades. Father Gregory sends them off on a pilgrimage to the cathedral in Santiago, Spain, and asks that they remain chaste during the trip. Temple's portraits of the people and the time and the friendships they form and the deceit and pain they meet are brilliant. Temple has written several more contemporary books about young refugees as in *Grab Hands and Run* and *A Taste of Salt*.

Westerns

The appeal of the American West is as old as the first explorer who saw it and marveled. Dime novelists of the 1870s and 1880s glorified the wildness and vitality of miners, cowboys, mountain men, soldiers, and outlaws. From the beginning, "Westerns" were written for mass appeal, so they are easily accessible to teen readers.

If anything else were needed to make the West the heartland of adventure, movies provided rootin'–tootin'–shootin' cowboys and rustlers, good guys and bad guys—always easy to spot by who wore white hats versus who wore black. Edwin S. Porter's *The Great Train Robbery,* produced in 1903, even though filmed in New Jersey, helped develop the myth of the West, as did later films like James Cruze's *The Covered Wagon* in 1923 and John Ford's *Stagecoach* in 1939.

Films may not have been needed, at least not at first, because Owen Wister's *The Virginian,* written in 1902, had already established the central characters of too many Westerns. There is the quiet and noble hero, the schoolmarm heroine, the hero's weak friend, the villain, and rustlers, along with such basic plot devices as cattle drives, the inevitable showdown between hero and villain, violence aplenty, and revenge and more revenge. Andy Adams's *Log of a Cowboy: A Narrative of the Old Trail Days* (1903) brought a semblance of honesty to the field, and that was heightened by the fine novels of Eugene Manlove Rhodes, particularly *Paso Por Aqui* (1927). For the most part, realism was rare in Westerns—note the romanticized but highly popular novels of Zane Grey. *The Heritage of the Desert* (1910) and *Riders of the Purple Sage* (1912) are far and away his most popular books.

But an amazing number of fine writers lived and breathed the real West and wrote accurate and non-romanticized novels—for example, Oliver LaFarge with *Laughing Boy* (1929), A. B. Guthrie with *The Way West* (1949), and Charles L. McNichols with *Crazy Weather* (1944). The prototype of the Western came with Jack Schaefer's *Shane* (1949), much overrated but consistently praised by critics and teachers. Frank Waters, one of the best writers of his time, wrote a loving and lyrical novel of a young man caught between two cultures in *The Man Who Killed the Deer* (1942).

Conventions of the Western were so well established by this time that writers knew what was expected. The setting is obviously the West, preferably some time between 1880 and 1895, the high point of cowboy life. Suspense and excitement pervade the novel, as was rarely the case for real cowboys back then—rustlers, lynchings, bank robberies, jailbreaks, crooked lawyers, ladies of the evening, the cavalry riding to the rescue, and on and on. Violence was more likely portrayed than implied. The hero (a marshal, ex-gunman, drifter, wagonmaster) will be moral, though that may have come after a reformation, which he will rarely be willing to talk about save to the heroine and only then in a particularly trying or tender moment. Morality will ultimately triumph as the hero plays a successful Hamlet and puts the world aright.

Fortunately, some Western writers have been able to ignore or work around these conventions. Louis L'Amour continues to sell well, though he has been dead for a number of years. He is a far better writer than most librarians or English teachers realize, hardly a surprise since he has gone almost unread by educators. L'Amour knows the West as a historian, so the West he writes about is accurate. *Down the Long Hills* is one of his best. In it, a 7-year-old goes searching for his horse, which has wandered away. He returns to find his entire wagon train massacred. He and his sister head west, facing starvation, blizzards, and wild animals. It's a remarkable survival tale.

Three writers have focused on gunfighters and violence in small towns. E. L. Doctorow's *Welcome to Hard Times* shows how dismal a dying western town can be when an outlaw sets out to destroy it over and over. Charles O. Locke's *The Hell Bent Kid* is about a man who kills a man in self-defense and then must flee for his life. The best known of the three is Glendon Swarthout's *The Shootist,* about a gunfighter dying of cancer who in his last shootout rids the town of some rough gunfighters. It may be more famous for being the last film made by John Wayne, but its reknown is well deserved either as book or film.

Two great books are about a West that is dead. Robert Flynn's *North to Yesterday* is the story of a group of misfits who gather to ride old cattle drive trails long after they have dried up. Edward Abbey's *The Brave Cowboy* is a portrait of a cowboy who has outlived the wide open plains. He hates barbed wire fences and whatever encloses anything or anyone. He breaks into jail to free a friend, but when the friend indicates he is willing to serve his term, the cowboy breaks himself out and a long and brave manhunt begins.

Westerns are so often serious that it is pleasant to read two books that are genuinely funny—deliberately so. David Wagoner's *The Road to Many a Wonder* is simply one of the funniest books in English. Ike Bender, age 20, leaves home to find gold and is soon followed by his soon-to-be bride. Their struggles to get to Colorado and find the pot at the end of their rainbow are believable, generally, and utterly delightful. Bruce Clements's *I Tell a Lie Every So Often* is about a 14-year-old boy who begins his tale with this long and complex paragraph, which is a reasonably accurate description the book that follows:

> I tell a lie every so often, and almost always nothing happens, but last spring I told a lie that carried me five hundred miles and made a lot of things happen. Somebody got shot because of it, and I had a visit with a beautiful naked girl who stood up in front

of me early in the morning and talked in a foreign tongue, and I saw a ball game with a hundred men on one side and a hundred men and one girl on the other side, and a boat sank, somewhat, under me, and my brother Clayton started acting strangely and sleeping with a loaded rifle, and there were some more things, too.

Kathryn Lasky's *Beyond the Divide* is a YA novel of the western movement. Another good Western written from the perspective of a young person is Marian Calabro's *The Perilous Journey of the Donner Party*. Calabro tells her meticulously researched story of a group of unfortunate western settlers stranded in an early California snowstorm. Her heroine is 12-year-old Virginia Reed, the young survivor who throughout the months of the ordeal hid her rag doll inside her clothes. For other examples, see Focus Box 8.2, Westerns Too Tough to Die.

Books about War

It is increasingly difficult to distinguish between fiction and nonfiction, and that is especially true in memoirs and reminiscences and fiction about war. Struggling to survive in war is not an adventure we would choose, but so many people have been forced into horrible circumstances that books about war—histories, diaries, letters, interviews, fiction—are among the most powerful books young people can read. War is one of the topics treated in the movies, starting with D. W. Griffith's 1915 *The Birth of a Nation* and continuing on to Steven Spielberg's 1998 *Saving Private Ryan*. Newspaper and magazine banner headlines of this or that war and TV assault us with horrible scenes of carnage and tearful scenes of survivors.

Young adults may be conscious of the nearness of war, although they likely know little of the realities of war and even less about the details of past wars. Reading literature about war, fiction or not, acquaints young people with the ambiguous nature of war, on one hand illustrating humanity's evil and horror, on the other hand revealing humanity's decency and heroism.

Civil War literature, once pretty well summarized by Stephen Crane's *The Red Badge of Courage,* has several books worth young people's time. Three of the best are Milton Meltzer's *Voices from the Civil War: A Documentary History of the Great American Conflict,* Annette Tapert's *The Brothers' War: Civil War Letters to Their Loved Ones from the Blue and the Gray,* and Gary Paulsen's *Soldier's Heart: Being the Story of the Enlistment and Due Service of the Boy Charley Goddard in the First Minnesota Volunteers.*

Meltzer's book combines his own voice with voices of those alive during the war—in journals, public records, ballads, and letters. It brilliantly covers virtually everything about the war, for example, slavery, politics, songs, battles, death, and civilians. Tapert's collection of letters is even more personal and touching. David Ash served with the 37th Illinois Volunteer Infantry. On March 11, 1862, three days after the Union victory at the Battle of Pea Ridge in Arkansas, Ash wrote about the aftermath of the battle.

It is the hardest sight a person could behold to see the dead lying round after they bring them in. They lay them in a pile until they get time to bury them. There was twenty-

American Massacre by Sally Denton. Knopf, 2003. Based on the Mountain Meadows Massacre of September 1857, this novel tells the story of a group of pioneers who were misled and then killed by Utah settlers who wanted to discourage travel through their state. The book has the power to raise voices in support of—and opposed to—her interpretation.

Borderlands by Peter Carter. Farrar Straus & Giroux, 1990. Ben Curtis joins a cattle drive in 1871, meets an African American he learns to respect, and loses his brother in a gunfight.

Clem's Chances by Sonia Levitin. Orchard, 2001. With his father chasing gold in California, his mother dead, and Clem being cheated by another family, Clem Fontayne decides his best option is to go west.

I Should Be Extremely Happy in Your Company: A Novel of Lewis and Clark by Brian Hall. Viking, 2003. Brian tells the story of the famous expedition from the viewpoints of Lewis, Clark, Sacagawea, and her interpreter husband. Jealousy erupts when Clark learns that President Jefferson had clearly chosen Lewis as the expedition's leader.

The Last Picture Show by Larry McMurtry. Dial, 1966. The end of the West comes to dusty and drying up Thalia, Texas, where even the movie house shuts down.

Little Big Man by Thomas Berger. Dial, 1964. An old-timer tells of his life in the Old West, his capture by the Cheyennes, his work as a scout for General Custer, and other realities and myths.

North to Yesterday by Robert Flynn. Knopf, 1967. A band of misfits are determined to drive cattle on the old trails—shut down ten years. It's a western adventure with touches of Don Quixote.

The Professor's House by Willa Cather. Knopf, 1925. The most intriguing part of the novel is about Tom Outland and the discovery of what we now call Mesa Verde National Park.

Stop the Train by Geraldine McCaughrean. HarperCollins, 2001. In this rollicking adventure about the Oklahoma Land Rush in 1893, city slickers try to steal land from settlers.

Wagons West by Frank McLynn. Grove, 2002. McLynn describes the first overland wagon train to California in 1841 (and later ones as well) along with all the irritations and terrors of the journey across America.

Walking Up a Rainbow by Theodore Taylor. Harcourt, Brace, 1994. In the 1850s, 14-year-old Susan Darden Carlisle is left an orphan in Iowa. To save her family home, she sets out to drive several thousand sheep from Iowa to California.

West of Everything: The Inner Life of Westerns by Jane Tompkins. Oxford University Press, 1992. Tompkins writes about western literature, films, and everything in between or around or near. It is a wonderful book of scholarship—readable and enlightening.

Wounded Knee by Neil Waldman. Atheneum, 2001. Waldman gives different viewpoints about the events that led up to the infamous slaughter of Native Americans.

one killed out of one regiment and one hundred and nineteen wounded. Albert Hilliard was laying alongside of me when he was shot, says he, "Oh, Dave, I am shot." It was the hardest thing I have done to call the roll the first time after the battle, so many of our boys killed or wounded.

Paulsen's work is an almost understated account of 15-year-old Charley, who enlists and is acclaimed by women and young boys for his bravery and rides in trains and wonders if he will ever get into battle. At his first battle at Manassas he learns what carnage can be with bullets whispering of death and a cannon ball neatly removing the head of a soldier next to him. Charley lived through the war, but he came out physically and mentally wounded and died in his mid-twenties.

World War I inspired some honest and realistic novels. Rudolph Frank's *No Hero for the Kaiser* was so powerful that Hitler banned it in Nazi Germany in the 1930s. Fourteen-year-old Jan and his dog are the only survivors when German troops take his Russian village. The troops befriend him and save him from being sent to a prison camp. He helps them, and they talk of the Kaiser's making him a German citizen. At a great ceremony, the soldiers learn what he thinks of war, and they are deeply troubled.

The most frequently cited book about World War I is again told from the German point of view. Erich Maria Remarque's *All Quiet on the Western Front* is a bitter account of a young German student Paul and his friends and fellow students who are persuaded to join the army by their teacher Kantorek, who fills them with nationalistic propaganda and patriotic fervor. They march off, find what war is really like, and die, one by one.

Pat Barker's award-winning British trilogy—*Regeneration, The Eye in the Door,* and *The Ghost Road*—convey the spirit of the times that led men to enlist for King and country and the inevitable horror and insanity that followed. Lt. Billy Prior is the center of the books, a bright young man from the wrong side of the railroad tracks, a man ordinarily unlikely to be allowed to move up in society. The books are about both the war and the apparently eternal social order before the war and the changing society after it.

During World War II, Ernie Pyle was the American soldier's favorite war correspondent, partly because he preferred talking to soldiers in the ranks rather than to officers, and partly because he reported honestly what he saw, not what was good for the morale of soldiers or civilians. For example, in *Ernie's War: The Best of Ernie Pyle's World War II Dispatches* (edited by David Nichols) he writes about the death of Captain Henry T. Waskow, one of the most "beloved" men Pyle found in the war. He told of Waskow's men coming in, gently, to see and honor the body. Pyle ended his account this way:

> Then a soldier came and stood beside the officer, and bent over, and he spoke to the dead captain, not in a whisper but awfully tenderly, and he said: "I sure am sorry, sir." Then the first man squatted down, and he reached down and took the dead hand, and he sat there for a full five minutes, holding the dead hand in his own and looking intently into the dead face, and he never uttered a sound all the time he sat there.
>
> And finally he put the hand down, and then reached up and gently straightened the points of the captain's shirt collar, and then he sort of rearranged the tattered edges of his uniform around the wound. And then he got up and walked away down the road in the moonlight, all alone.
>
> After that the rest of us went back into the cowshed, leaving the five dead men lying in a line, end to end, in the shadow of the low stone wall. We lay down on the straw in the cowshed, and pretty soon we were all asleep.

Few books about World War II, or any other war, succeed so well in creating a revulsion to the blood and messiness as does Farley Mowat's *And No Birds Sang*. After Mowat's company encountered and killed six truckloads of German soldiers, Mowat said,

It was not the dead that distressed me most—it was the German wounded. There were a great many of these, and most seemed to have been hard hit.

One ghastly vignette from that shambles haunts me still: the driver of a truck hanging over his steering wheel and hiccuping great gouts of cherry-pink foam through a smashed windscreen, to the accompaniment of a sound like a slush pump sucking air as his perforated lungs labored to expel his own heart's blood . . . in which he was slowly drowning.

Mowat's book is hardly the only honest account, but it reeks of death and lost dreams, and anyone wanting to know what war is like should not miss it.

Several novels about World War II are especially worth reading. William Wharton's *A Midnight Clear* is about six high-IQ American soldiers in an intelligence and reconnaissance platoon sent to determine whether there are German troops near a French chateau. The six play bridge and chess and word games and begin to believe they have nothing to do with the war. Then the Germans show up, and instead of warfare, everyone engages in a snowball fight. They sing Christmas carols and set up a Christmas tree and wonderful peace reigns. Then war starts again and the killing resumes, and what had been warm is now bloody.

English novelist Robert Westall writes about young people who refuse to stay outside the war in *The Machine Gunners* and the sequel, *Fathom Five*. The first novel begins in an English coastal town during 1940 and 1941. Rumors of a German invasion are rife, and Chas McGill wants to help win the war. Chas and his friends locate a downed German plane, find the machine gun in working order, and hide it. When a school is hit by a German plane somewhat later, Chas steals sandbags to create a fortress, a safe place to display the machine gun. The rear gunner of the downed plane stumbles into their fortress and becomes the boys' prisoner. All this childish innocence dies when adults discover the fortress, the German is shot, and the young people are rounded up by their parents. *Fathom Five* is a rousing spy story set later in the war and the story of Chas's lost love and lost innocence. Westall had an amazing ability to portray the ambivalence of young people and the alienation they feel, mixed with love and duty.

Harry Mazer's *The Last Mission* is set near the end of World War II. Jack Raab uses his older brother's identification to lie his way into the Air Force to destroy Hitler and to save democracy, all by himself; that dream lasts only a short time before Jack learns that the Air Force involves more training and boredom than fighting. When Jack does go to war, his first twenty-four bombing raids go well, but on the last mission, his plane is hit, all his buddies die, and he is captured. When he returns home, the principal at his old high school asks him to talk.

"I'm glad we won," he said. "We couldn't let Hitler keep going. We had to stop him. But most of all, I'm glad it's over." Had he said enough? There was a silence . . . a waiting silence. There was something more he had to say.

"I don't like war. I thought I'd like it before. But war is stupid. War is one stupid thing after another. I saw my best friend killed. His name was Chuckie O'Brien. My whole crew was killed." Now he was talking, it was coming out, all the things he'd thought about for so long. "A lot of people were killed. Millions of people. Ordinary people. Not only by Hitler. Not only on our side. War isn't like the movies. It's not fun and songs. It's not about heroes. It's about awful, sad things, like my friend Chuckie that I'm never going to see again." His voice faltered.

"I hope war never happens again," he said after a moment. "That's all I've got to say."

He sat down. He hardly heard the applause. The floor of the radio room was still slippery with Chuckie's blood . . . Dave was still fumbling with his chute . . . the plane was still falling through the sky.

Aidan Chambers's *Postcards from No Man's Land* (winner of the 2002 Printz Award) has reminded young people of the ugliness of World War II, and particularly the long-term effects war can have on us. Chambers tells his story in alternating chapters set in 1944 and 1995. In the latter year, 17-year-old Jacob Todd travels to Holland to visit his grandfather's grave on the fifty-first anniversary of the Battle of Arnheim and to see Geertrui Wesseling, the last person to see his grandfather alive. Jacob has no presumption that this trip will be at all interesting, but a Dutch saying he hears early on in Amsterdam—"Nothing in Amsterdam is what it appears to be"—should have alerted him to all he would find out about his grandfather, the war, and Jacob himself.

James Forman's finest work, too little known, is *Ceremony of Innocence*. Hans and Sophie Scholl, brother and sister in Nazi Germany, print and distribute literature attacking Hitler. Arrested by the Gestapo, they are urged by friends to escape. A lawyer, who Hans suspects is a Nazi, encourages them to plead insanity. They refuse, endure the mock trial, are found guilty, and are taken away to be executed. Hans is the last to die by the guillotine.

Hans heard the sound of rollers, and at last there burst from his throat a cry, uttered in a great voice, a voice that combined anger, reproof, and an overwhelming conviction for which he was willing to die.

"Long live freedom!"

Then the greased blade fell. His teeth met through his tongue, and it was over.

Readers curious about the White Rose, a German movement to end the war, can find information in Richard Hanser's *A Noble Treason: The Revolt of the Munich Students Against Hitler;* Hermann Vinke's *The Short Life of Sophie Scholl;* Annette E. Dumbach and Jud Newborn's *Shattering the German Night: The Story of the White Rose;* and Inge Jens's *At the Heart of the White Rose: Letters and Diaries of Hans and Sophie Scholl*. Sebastian Haffner's memoirs of his life in Germany during World War II, *Defying Hitler,* reveals a young man at first enthusiastic about German nationalism and later growing disillusioned about what Hitler represented. At one point, he lies about being a Jew and is horribly shocked by his lie. That leads to his leaving Germany in 1938.

A short book by John Wilson may have the most effect on young readers. *And in the Morning* is a simple and direct story about young John Hay, who thinks war must be a glorious romp, but when his father is killed in World War I and his mother has a mental breakdown, John goes into the service and soon learns in the trenches of France how dismally wrong he was. The remainder of the book is about the death of almost everyone around him that he cares for, and worse yet, after another bombardment and the death of yet another friend, John walks off and is captured by his own side and

FOCUS BOX 8.3   *War's Effect on Young People*

Ain't Gonna Study War No More by Milton Meltzer. Harper and Row, 1985. Meltzer traces pacifism in the United States starting with the Quakers.

Bull Run by Paul Fleischman. HarperCollins, 1993. The first battle of the Civil War is told from multiple points of view by all sorts of participants and onlookers.

Farewell to Manzanar by Jeanne Wakatsuki Houston and James D. Houston. Houghton Mifflin, 1993. The first author describes the three years after 1942 when she and her Japanese American family lived in a camp with open latrines, barbed wire, and guard towers.[5]

Hiroshima: A Novella by Laurence Yep. Scholastic, 1995. Though the story is centered around Hiroshima residents, Yep also tells the story of the bomb itself.

Johnny Got His Gun by Dalton Trumbo. Lippincott, 1939. Filled with patriotic fervor, Joe enlists, but after the battle, he has no arms or legs, and he is blind, deaf, and mute.

Lord of the Nutcracker by Iain Lawrence. Delacorte, 2001. It is 1914 and a 10-year-old London boy is sent, for safety, to live with his aunt in the country. He lives the war, first its patriotism and then its horror, through tin soldiers that his toymaker father sends to him.

Manzanar by John Armor and Peter Wright. Time Books, 1989. The two authors use Ansel Adams photographs and a commentary by John Hersey to create a record of this Japanese internment camp.

Or Give Me Death: A Novel of Patrick Henry's Family by Ann Rinaldi. Harcourt, 2003. Patsy and Anne, the daughters of Patrick Henry and his mentally ill wife, tell their moving story in this book that found a place on *VOYA's* Top Shelf Fiction for Middle School Readers.

Red Scarf Girl: A Memoir of the Cultural Revolution by Ji Li Jiang. HarperCollins, 1997. A young girl tells how she was asked to betray her Chinese family.

Slap Your Sides by M. E. Kerr. HarperCollins, 2002. Jubal Shoemaker is a Quaker who, in the midst of the patriotism of World War II, has mixed feelings about his brother's being a conscientious objector. See also Kerr's *Linger* (HarperCollins, 1993) about patriotism during the Persian Gulf War.

Soldier Boys by Dean Hughes. Atheneum, 2001. Parallel stories of two young soldiers, American Spencer Morgan and German Dieter Hedrick, who enter their country's service full of idealism, only to learn how hellish war is.

A Stone in My Hand by Cathryn Clinton. Candlewick, 2002. After her father is killed in a bus bombing on the Gaza strip, 11-year-old Malaak speaks only to the dove that her father had given her.

Under the Blood-Red Sun by Graham Salisbury. Delacorte, 1994. The bombing of Pearl Harbor on December 7, 1941, changes the life of a young Japanese American as he searches for his father and grandfather.

When My Name Was Keoko: A Novel of Korea in World War II by Linda Sue Park. Clarion, 2002. A brother and a sister use the loss of their Korean names as the focus of their memories of the 1940s when Japan occupied Korea.

The Winter People by Joseph Bruchac. Dial, 2002. Based on a true incident in the fall of 1759, Bruchac's coming-of-age story is about 14-year-old Saxso, an Abenaki boy, who is trying to rescue his mother and sisters who have been taken by the English.

Zlata's Diary: A Child's Life in Sarajevo by Zlata Filipovic. Penguin, 1994. A fifth-grade girl kept a diary of the horrors, the friendships, and the love and the blood that she saw during the Serbian-Croatian war.

taken for a deserter. His court martial is brief, John is found guilty and sentenced to die before a firing squad. In a letter to his wife, John writes:

Sunday, July 9, Bouzincourt

Dear Anne: The decision of the court martial has been confirmed by General Haig. He said that soldiers who avoid their comrades' dangers cannot be tolerated. What nonsense—all my comrades are dead—I avoid their dangers simply by living. But not for long. I am to be shot tomorrow.

John Devaney and Peter Arnett have both written straightforward books about war. Devaney's *America Storms the Beaches: 1944* is an account of the period between September and December of 1944, which was a turning point. In Arnett's *Live from the Battlefield: From Vietnam to Baghdad, 35 Years in the World's War Zones,* a respected reporter gives his up-close view of war and soldiers and politics.

Of all the many books on war, none has a more horrible indictment of the absurdity and cruelty of war than Roger Rosenblatt's *Children of War.* Rosenblatt circled the globe seeking out children in Belfast, Israel, Cambodia, Hong Kong, and Lebanon whom he asked about themselves and what war had done to them. A 9-year-old girl in Cambodia had made a drawing, and after a year of help by an American psychologist, she was able to explain how the instrument in the drawing worked. Rosenblatt writes:

The children harvesting rice include Peov. She is the largest of the three. Whenever a child refused to work, he was punished with the circular device. The soldiers would place it over the child's head. Three people would hold it steady by means of ropes. . . . A fourth would grab hold of the ring at the end of the other rope. . . . When the rope with the ring was pulled . . . the child would be decapitated. A portable guillotine.

But it wasn't the soldiers who worked the device. It was the children.

For other powerful books about war see Focus Box 8.3, War's Effect on Young People.

Literature of the Holocaust

Not many years ago, anyone wishing to read about the Holocaust would read Anne Frank's *The Diary of a Young Girl.* Today an outpouring of films and books about the Holocaust means that no one can pretend not to know about the happenings and the evils that went with it.

One part of that outpouring is the 1995 definitive edition of *Anne Frank's Diary,* in which Anne becomes far more human and far less saintly. A number of passages touch on Anne's interest in sex and love, and Anne's entry for March 24, 1944, is sexual and analytical. The definitive edition should please readers who want to read about a human being with all her faults. It should almost equally please censors, who will have new reasons to find fault with a nearly perfect book. Miep Gies's *Anne Frank Remembered,* the autobiography of the woman who helped hide the Frank family, adds more detail and should be read alongside Anne's *Diary.*

*P*rops as simple as a European sweater, a jacket, a hat, and Stars of David made this readers' theater class presentation more fun for eighth graders at Gilbert Junior High School in Arizona.

Most young adults seek out books about young people caught in the Holocaust because they are better able to identify with people their own age or slightly older. A book that is similar to Anne Frank's Diary is Etty Hillesum's *An Interrupted Life: The Diaries of Etty Hillesum, 1941–1943.* Being 27 years old, Hillesum probably knew precisely what her fate was to be. Her diary begins, "Here goes, then," and she writes of her love affairs, her graduate study at the University of Amsterdam, and her friends and ideas. She seems to have had little interest in politics until Jews were required to wear the yellow star. That jolted her, but she never sought to escape. In her last days, she volunteered to go with a group of condemned Jews to Westerbork Camp. She must have known that Westerbork was the usual first step to Auschwitz. Her journal complements Anne's *Diary;* Etty's irony and sophistication neatly counterpoint Anne's simplicity and innocence. *An Interrupted Life* is completed in *Letters from Westerbork.*

Students continue to read and love Johanna Reiss's *The Upstairs Room* and its sequel *The Journey Back.* The first book is a true story of the author and her sister, two young Jewish girls in Holland, kept safely in hiding by a gentile family for over two years during the Nazi occupation. The girls detest having to stay inside all the time, but when they learn from an underground newspaper what is happening to Jews across Europe, they realize how precarious is their life. The second book is about their trip back to their hiding place after the war. Karen Ray's *To Cross a Line* is about Egon Katz, a 17-year-old Jewish baker's apprentice who was certain that if he followed all the rules, he'd be safe. Then the Gestapo shows up with a warrant for him. Kati David's *A Child's War: World War II Through the Eyes of Children* is an account of World War II through the eyes of eight girls and seven boys, who saw fear and death and every horror that war brings about.

Thomas Keneally's *Schindler's List* should be read alongside any work about the Holocaust. But then so should the accounts of inmates of the concentration camps in Sylvia Rothchild's *Voices from the Holocaust.* Hazel Rochman and Darlene Z. McCampbell's *Bearing Witness: Stories of the Holocaust* is a marvelous collection of material that

After the Holocaust by Howard Greenfield. Greenwillow, 2001. Eight survivors of the Holocaust share their experiences on what happened to them after the defeat of Hitler.

Auschwitz: The Story of a Nazi Death Camp by Clive A. Lawton. Candlewick, 2002. Lawton has written a good introductory book with two-page chapters, which are arranged chronologically so that the book moves from mundane facts about building and organization to horrendous information about medical experiments and the disposing of bodies.

The Beautiful Days of My Youth: My Six Months in Auschwitz and Plaszow by Ana Novac. Holt, 1997. As Nazis kill and cremate concentration camp victims, Novac keeps a dairy of the horrors.

Dancing on the Bridge of Avignon by Ida Vox. Houghton Mifflin, 1995. In Nazi-occupied Holland, Rosa finds solace in her violin while being Jewish becomes more and more dangerous. Read also *Anna Is Still Here* (Houghton Mifflin, 1993) and *Hide and Seek* (Houghton Mifflin, 1991).

Hiding to Survive: Stories of Jewish Children Rescued from the Holocaust by Maxine B. Rosenberg. Clarion, 1994. Fourteen Americans now in their fifties and sixties remember what they can of being hidden

The Key Is Lost by Ida Vos, translated by Terese Eddelstein. HarperCollins, 2000. The author writes from her own childhood memories when she and her sister were separated from their parents and forced into hiding during the Nazi occupation of Holland.

In Kindling Flame: The Story of Hannah Senesh, 1921–1944 by Linda Atkinson. Lothrop, Lee and Shepard, 1985. Senesh, a Hungarian Jew, was a resistance fighter. See also *Hannah Senesh: Her Life and Diary* (Schocken, 1972)

Milkweed by Jerry Spinelli. Knopf, 2003. The VOYA reviewer of this prize-winning book described it as a

war story to be put alongside J. G. Ballard's *Empire of the Sun* and Robert Benigni's film *Life Is Beautiful*. The tragic hero is a homeless boy living on the streets and in the stables of Warsaw before the Nazi occupation.

One, by One, by One: Facing the Holocaust by Judith Miller. Simon and Schuster, 1990. A journalist examines how West Germany, Austria, France, the Netherlands, Russia, and the United States each handled its responsibility for the Holocaust.

Return to Auschwitz by Kitty Hart. Atheneum, 1982. Thirty years after surviving the Holocaust, Hart returns to the camp to help make an English documentary.

Stella by Peter Wyden. Simon and Schuster, 1992. A Jewish boy attends a Jewish school in Berlin. He falls in love with Stella and finds out much later that she was one of the Nazi's chief informants against Jews.

Stories in Water by Donna Jo Napoli. Dutton, 1997. Roberto lives in Vienna during World War II and sneaks into a theatre to see an American Western. German soldiers arrive to round up all the young males, including Roberto and his Jewish friends.

Surviving Hitler: A Boy in the Nazi Death Camps by Andrea Warren. HarperColllins, 2001. The many photographs will help middle school students relate to this account of a boy's experiences in one of the death camps.

Torn Thread by Anne Isaacs. New York: Scholastic, 2000. Two Polish teenagers survive a Czechoslovakian work camp.

Witnesses to War: Eight True-Life Stories of Nazi Persecution by Michael Leapman. Viking, 1998. A British journalist became intrigued by what had happened to the thousands of children of all races who were stolen from their families and raised by German families.

will shock readers just as other selections will give them pictures of real heroes. Hanna Volavkova's *I Never Saw Another Butterfly: Children's Drawings and Poems from Terezin Concentration Camp, 1941–1944* and Chana Byers Abells's *The Children We Remember* are unquestionably the most painful reading because they detail the massacre of the innocent.

Milton Meltzer does his usual fine job of collection and reporting in *Never to Forget: The Jews of the Holocaust.* Ten years later, he wrote a book about a much smaller number of people, *Rescue: The Story of How Gentiles Saved Jews in the Holocaust.* As he explained in the introduction:

> Now I have come to realize the great importance of recording not just the evidence of evil, but also the evidence of human nobility. Love, not hatred, is what the world needs. Rescue, not destruction. The stories in the book offer reason to hope. And hope is what we need, the way plants need sunlight.

Two other books deserve to be read alongside Meltzer—Eva Fogelman's *Conscience and Courage: Rescuers of Jews During the Holocaust* and Maxine B. Rosenberg's *Hiding to Survive: Stories of Jewish Children Rescued from the Holocaust.* Ina R. Friedman's *The Other Victims: First Person Stories of Non-Jews Persecuted by the Nazis* is a worthy addition to Holocaust literature.

Anyone considering a unit or a project on the Holocaust ought to be aware of two movies, a short film that is generally well known and a feature-length film considerably less known. *Night and Fog* (31 minutes, color and black and white, 1955, not rated, Director: Alain Resnais) is a documentary on Nazi concentration camps with color scenes of present-day ruins of Auschwitz played against German black-and-white footage when the camps were active, prisoners arrived, and smoke and death reigned and footage shot by Allied soldiers as they freed the camps and all their prisoners. The voice-over commentary by Jean Cayrol, himself once an inmate, is wonderfully quiet, allowing the film to shock the viewer. One can only guess why so much explicit film was shot by the Germans, but presumably they assumed they would win the war, and the film was a historic record of their work on the home front during World War II.

Night and Fog is a tough film to watch, even nearly fifty years after it was made and sixty years after the events it captures on film. Decapitated heads, mounds of prisoners' hair, huge piles of dead nude bodies being pushed into a long earthen grave—but the horror is intrinsic to the film and necessary for our reactions to the horrors of these concentration camps and the horrors that people do to each other. We'd hate to think that students could view the film dispassionately—though we've seen that happen.

We know from first-hand experience that some students get sick or begin to cry— we've seen that as well. Teachers who consider using the film should see it before showing it and then, judging the film and the sophistication of the students, determine their course of action.

The longer film is even quieter, but it is also the record of the cold-blooded decision of a small group of Nazis about what to do with Jews in Europe, the so-called "final solution." *Conspiracy* (95 minutes, color, 2001, not rated, Director: Frank Pierson) shows how on January 20, 1942, fifteen highly ranked Nazis met at Wannsee on the outskirts of Berlin to determine the future of Jews. The meeting was organized by S.S.

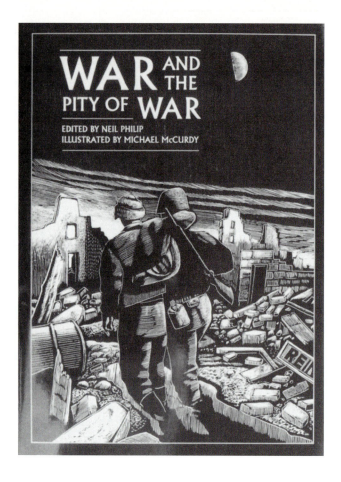

Neil Philip's collection of poetry, War and the Pity of War, *can lend variety to a class reading either memoirs or informative nonfiction.*

WAR AND THE PITY OF WAR

EDITED BY NEIL PHILIP
ILLUSTRATED BY MICHAEL McCURDY

Major Adolf Eichmann and directed by Chief of Security Reinhard Heydrich. It was a civilized meeting with food and wine and lots of talk, but the meeting had only one item on its agenda, the extermination of six million European Jews. The text for the film was taken from minutes at the meeting and found after the end of the war.

Kenneth Branagh, who played Heydrich, described his role as the most difficult and abhorrent of any he had played. It's a distinguished cast with Stanley Tucci, Colin Firth, and David Threlfall. The same topic is covered in a German film, *The Wannsee Conference* (87 minutes, color, 1984, Director: Heinz Schirk).

Some recent YA novels have focused on the obvious fact that bigotry endures. In Lois Ruby's *Skin Deep,* Dan comes from a fatherless home. When multiethnic quotas keep him off the swimming team and from getting a job at the University of Colorado, he turns to the local skinheads for support, adopting their dress code but never quite accepting their racism. Han Nolan's *If I Should Die Before I Wake* portrays a young girl, a neo-Nazi initiate, who is in a coma from a motorcycle accident. In her dreams in the hospital, she becomes a young Jewish girl whose family lives in a ghetto and then Auschwitz. *The Wave* by Morton Rhue (pen name of Todd Strasser) has proved incredibly popular with many young people. In a high school history class, students wonder why the non-Nazi Germans let the Holocaust happen. The teacher responds by introducing students to a new movement, The Wave, which captures the imaginations and the hearts of students apparently longing for indoctrination and belief in certainties.

The best of these books is Fran Arrick's *Chernowitz!* Bob Cherno, 15, looked back on his fights with Emmett Sundback, a bigot who ridiculed Bob's Jewishness. When Bob's school shows a film about the concentration camps, some students who have ridiculed Bob leave in tears because they understand the horrors of the Nazis' treatment of Jews and other minorities. To Arrick's credit, Sundback does not change and remains the horrible creep that he was. See Focus Box 8.4, Experiencing the Holocaust to Keep It from Happening Again (p. 244) for further examples.

Books about Vietnam

Two YA novels about Vietnam stand out. Valerie Hobbs's *Sonny's War* is about a garage mechanic who ignores his younger sister's advice to flee to Canada and ignore the draft; he is subsequently sent to Vietnam. What makes this novel different is the author's attention to the antiwar movement as it is preached by a local history teacher. The other outstanding YA novel is Walter Dean Myer's *Fallen Angels.* Harlem is hard on Richie Perry, so he flees Harlem and joins the army. To his surprise, Richie finds himself dreaming of Harlem and wanting to get back to a world he thought he wanted to forget.

Larry R. Johannessen, a Vietnam veteran, who came home to teach high school in suburban Chicago and now prepares teachers at Northern Illinois University in DeKalb, has been teaching nonfiction from the Vietnam War since the early 1980s. He is the author of *Illumination Rounds: Teaching the Literature of the Vietnam War* and in an article for the *English Journal,* "When History Talks Back: Teaching Nonfiction Literature of the Vietnam War,"[6] he explained that this material appeals to mature high school students because:

1. The Vietnam War was a "teenage" war. The average age of soldiers was 19, as compared to 26 for World War II. Because "many of these young people were not mentally prepared for the carnage and terror that marked the Vietnam experience . . . they describe the idealism, loneliness, homesickness, fear, terror, isolation, abandonment, and betrayal in ways that speak directly to students."
2. The oral histories are especially powerful because the speakers establish "a confidential, intimate relationship with readers in a voice that seems to be speaking directly to them."
3. Many students have relatives, teachers, or family friends who were in Vietnam, and so they have a personal interest in understanding what these people experienced.
4. The experience that in a year-and-a-half turned young, idealistic men and women into disillusioned "old kids," was in many ways the archetypal journey that we described in Chapter 4 as the romantic quest. Johannessen identified the stages as
   - The mystique of preinduction or the John Wayne syndrome.
   - The initiation into the military culture during training.

FOCUS BOX 8.5 *Nonfiction Books about Vietnam*

American Daughter Gone to War: On the Front Lines with an Army Nurse in Vietnam by Winnie Smith. Pocket Books, 1994. As an idealistic 21-year-old, Smith requested assignment as a combat nurse. She went on duty in an intensive care unit in Saigon caring for soldiers flown directly in from the battlefield.

Bloods: An Oral History of the Vietnam War by Black Veterans by Wallace Terry. Ballantine, 1984. As a reporter in Vietnam, Terry began interviewing African American soldiers. He continued the practice when he returned home and has arranged the interviews in a book that speaks to such issues as race relations and media manipulation.

Born on the Fourth of July by Ron Kovic. Pocket Books, 1976. Because of the powerful 1989 movie made by Oliver Stone (starring Tom Cruise) students will already be aware of how Kovic came home from Vietnam in a wheelchair, how he was embittered by the way the Veteran's Administration treated him, and how he became involved in the antiwar movement.

Dispatches by Michael Herr. Vintage, 1991. Larry Johannessen says that of all the books he has taught, this is the one that does the best job of capturing the *feel* of Vietnam.

Everything We Had: An Oral History of the Vietnam War by Thirty-Three American Soldiers Who Fought It by Al Santoli. Ballantine, 1981. Santoli's interviews with men and women take readers through the war from 1962 until the fall of Saigon in 1971.

Homecoming: When the Soldiers Returned from Vietnam by Bob Greene. Ballantine, 1990. Greene is a syndicated columnist who solicited letters from soldiers asking them to tell about their coming-home experiences. The letters document the double war that the veterans had to fight—the one in Asia and the one at home.

If I Die in a Combat Zone by Tim O'Brien. Dell, 1987. O'Brien's book will help students see how Vietnam literature fits into the bigger body of war literature because it starts with O'Brien's going to war identifying with the hero of Ernest Hemingway's *A Farewell to Arms*.

In the Combat Zone: An Oral History of American Women in Vietnam by Kathryn Marshall. Little Brown, 1987. Marshall interviewed twenty women veterans and lets their diverse experiences and the way they tell them speak to an often overlooked part of the war.

- The dislocation of arrival in Vietnam—culture shock.
- The confrontation with mortality in the first firefight.
- The confrontation with moral dilemmas, moving from innocence to experience and consideration, or from innocence to numbness and madness.
- The phenomenon of coming home and learning to live with the legacies of the war, with the guilt and the loss of faith and innocence.
- Putting it together by finding a central meaning.

See Focus Box 8.5, Nonfiction Books about Vietnam, for some of the books that Johannessen recommends, along with our own recommendations. There are enough different books that when a class works on this subject, students can choose which book(s) they want to read, and chances are they can check them out from libraries. There are also good films that can provide common experiences for the whole class. Besides such

Nam: The Vietnam War in the Words of the Men and Women Who Fought There by Mark Baker. Morrow, 1981 Berkley paperback. The interviewees come from a wide spectrum, and the interviews are so well done that many people feel this is the "classic" answer to the question of "What was Vietnam really like?"

Offerings at the Wall: Artifacts from the Vietnam Veterans Memorial Collection by Thomas B. Allen. Times Publishing, 1995. Allen took colored pictures of items left at the Wall and wrote the accompanying text.

Patriots: The Vietnam War Remembered from All Sides by Christian G. Appy. Viking, 2003. A collection of 135 interviews from generals down (or up) to rag-tag soldiers allows readers to come to their own conclusions on what the war was or was not.

A Rumor of War by Philip Caputo. Ballantine, 1977. Caputo went to Vietnam as a young Marine infantry officer in 1965. His book documents his descent from innocence and idealism to disillusionment and despair, all within sixteen months.

Shrapnel in the Heart: Letters and Remembrances from the Vietnam Veterans Memorial by Laura Palmer, Random House, 1987. Palmer was a journalist who covered the war. Afterwards, she gathered 100 letters left at the Vietnam Memorial, traced down the writers, and then interviewed them for her book.

365 Days by Ronald J. Glasser, M. D. Bantam, 1971. Glasser was an Army doctor whose indictment of the war is built on elements of memoir, oral history, and fiction.

Voices from Vietnam by Barry Denenberg. Scholastic, 1995. Anecdotes and horror stories all from Vietnam during the longest war in our history.

What Should We Tell Our Children about Vietnam? by Bill McCloud. University of Oklahoma Press, 1989. McCloud is a junior high social studies teacher who wrote letters to military leaders, ordinary and extraordinary veterans, politicians, protesters, and journalists, asking them to help him decide what to tell his students about Vietnam. The 128 published letters form one of the most readable records of the war.

When I Was a Young Man by Bob Kerry. Harcourt, 2002. An innocent young man sees the Vietnam War as good and patriotic, until on February 25, 1969, he leads his Navy Seal team on a raid into a Vietnamese village and kills thirteen women and children. In the process, he becomes someone he can no longer recognize.

famous films as those directed by Oliver Stone (*Platoon* in 1986 and *Born on the Fourth of July* in 1989), HBO produced a film version of *Dear America: Letters Home from Vietnam* by Bernard Edelman that works well in class. So does the 1999 *Regret to Inform*, a 72-minute film directed by Barbara Sonneborn. In 1968 her husband was killed in Vietnam. In 1992 she went to Vietnam to document what other war widows—American and Vietnamese—suffered.

Concluding Comments

In historical books, fiction and nonfiction are often so intertwined that it is hard to tell the difference. And rather than naming a discrete genre, *historical fiction* is an umbrella concept covering genres as different as romance, adventure, mystery, humor, and biography. What the writing has in common is that it is set in the past, but this could be as long ago as Jean M. Auel's prehistorical *Clan of the Cave Bear* or as recent as the Vietnam War, as with Walter Dean Myers's *Fallen Angels*. A common topic for historical fiction is that of war; however, in relation to recent wars, readers seem to prefer memoirs and nonfiction accounts, much like the material seen on the History Channel. Another recent trend is for authors to look past the movers and shakers involved in big dramatic events and to focus instead on ordinary people and show how their lives have been affected by natural disasters and by developments and changes in society.

Notes

[1] Christopher Collier, "Criteria for Historical Novels," *School Library Journal* 27 (August 1982): 32.

[2] Christopher Collier, "Fact, Fiction, and History: The Role of the Historian, Writer, Teacher, and Reader," *ALAN Review* 14 (Winter 1987): 5.

[3] Patricia Lee Gauch, "Why Writers Write of War: Looking into the Eye of Historical Fiction," *ALAN Review* 21 (Fall 1993): 13.

[4] James Blasingame, "2001 Honor List: A Vote for Diversity," *English Journal* 92.2 (November, 2001): 128–134.

[5] A helpful article to understand the internment of Japanese Americans during World War II is Judith Miller's "Wartime Internment of Japanese Was Grave Injustice, Panel Says," *New York Times*, February 25, 1983, p. 1. For more details, see Roger Daniels, "Incarcerating Japanese Americans," *Magazine of History* 16 (Spring 2002): 19–23, and "Incarceration of Japanese Americans: A Sixty-Year Perspective," *The History Teacher* 35 (May 2002): 297–310. Two helpful books on the subject are Roger Daniels's *Prisoners without Trial: Japanese Americans in World War II* (Hill and Wang, 1993) and Sarah C. Taylor's *Jewel of the Desert: Japanese Internment at Topaz* (University of California Press, 1993). Two articles by Eugene V. Rostow at the time of the internment are worth reading for background: "The Japanese American Cases—A Disaster," *Yale Law Journal* 54 (July 1945): 480–533, and "Our Worst Wartime Mistake," *Harpers* 191 (August 1945): 193–201.

[6] Larry Johannessen's *Illumination Rounds: Teaching the Literature of the Vietnam War* (NCTE, 1992) is an uncommonly helpful source of information on teaching or using material in secondary schools. So are Johannessen's articles "When History Talks Back: Teaching Nonfiction Literature of the Vietnam War," *English Journal* 91:4 (March, 2002) 39–48; and "Young Adult Literature and the Vietnam War," *English Journal* 82 (September 1993): 43–49. Other good articles are by Perry Oldham, "Some Further Thoughts on Teaching Vietnam Literature," *English Journal* 82 (September 1993): 65–67; Christie N. Bradley, "Teaching Our Longest War: Constructive Views from Vietnam," *English Journal* 78 (April 1989): 35–38; and Frank A. Wilcox, "Pedagogical Implications of Teaching Literature of the Vietnam War," *Social Education* 52 (January 1988): 39–40.

Nonfiction
Information, Literary Nonfiction, Biographies, and Self-Help Books

If you are studying this textbook in the order that it is written, then you have already come in contact with several kinds of nonfiction. In the first chapter, Focus Box 1.1 lists memoirs by authors whose books, or memoirs, have found their way to our Honor List. And in Chapter 3, many of the books listed as coming from "Teen Voices" are first-person accounts of young people's experiences and feelings. And in a technical sense, the poetry and drama discussed in Chapter 5, along with much of the humor, is nonfiction, as are many of the historical books and the memoirs discussed in Chapter 8. In this chapter, we will look at four major categories of nonfiction: information books, literary nonfiction, biographies, and self-help books.

While fiction usually gets the lion's share of attention when it comes to reviewing and recommending books for teenagers, in libraries and schools, non-fiction gets the lion's share of the budget. Many teenagers, as well as many adults, go for years without reading a novel or even a short story, but virtually everyone reads nonfiction whether in newspapers, magazines, on the Internet, or on a cereal box. The March 2002 issue of *English Journal* had as its theme "The Truth about Nonfiction." Paul Hirth wrote the introductory piece in which he defended what Louise Rosenblatt labels *efferent* reading as compared to *aesthetic* reading. English teachers usually feel more inspired or more challenged when they focus on aesthetics, but he thinks it can be just as satisfying to help students revel in the "joy of facts" and the "poetry of prose." Teachers scoff, he says, because they think students "are already versed in reading for the literal." But he knows that students need help in reading for irony, in recognizing the subtleties of an argument, and applying facts and details to the development and interpretation of thought.

Hirth likes to pair nonfiction pieces with fiction. For example, Julius Lester's essay "Huckleberry Finn" from *Falling Pieces of the Broken Sky* is a good way to help students understand the controversial nature of Twain's book. Rollo May's *The Cry for Myth* has a wonderful section on *The Great Gatsby*. Other writers whose nonfiction he likes to bring to his students include Annie Dillard, Stephen J. Gould, Anne Morrow Lindbergh, Neil Postman, Richard Selzer, Susan Sontag, George Will, and Gary Wills, along with that of major columnists in magazines and newspapers. "Too

With "fun facts," the illustrations and the layout have to be appealing enough to attract browsers as well as readers.

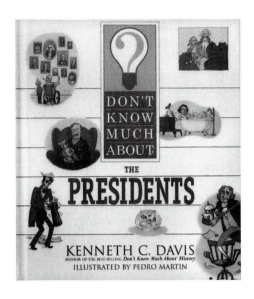

often," Hirth says, teachers "begin with the assumption that students can't or won't read anything with a text more demanding than a billboard, yet they seem to devour the Internet with ease." He concluded that "[j]ust as the study of fiction, drama, and poetry help students explore their thoughts and feelings, nonfiction can offer a reality check—a second opinion, if you will," with which students, and their teachers, can measure their individual responses.[1]

Information Books

When the American Library Association made history by awarding its coveted 1988 Newbery Medal to Russell Freedman's *Lincoln: A Photobiography,* Milton Meltzer, who has long championed the cause of nonfiction, applauded by saying,

> It was a terrific thing to do, but it took fifty years to do it. The few books they gave prizes to before, that were called nonfiction, really were not. Instead, they were books written in the outmoded vein of biography that was highly fictionalized, had invented dialogue, and sometimes concocted scenes. That's all changed today, but it took a long time.[2]

In their 1990 *Nonfiction for Young Adults: From Delight to Wisdom,* Betty Carter and Richard F. Abrahamson cited 22 research studies. Among the reported findings:

- An interest in reading nonfiction emerges at about the fourth grade and grows during adolescence.
- Interest in reading nonfiction crosses ability levels; one study showed that nonfiction made up 34 percent of the leisure reading of academically able teenagers and 54 percent of the control group's leisure reading.

FOCUS BOX 9.1   Fun Facts

Behind the Mask of Spider-Man: The Secrets of the Movie by Mark Cotta Vaz. Ballantine, 2002. Photos and production drawings add interest to this intriguing look at both the human and the technological challenges faced by the producers and the actors of the blockbuster movie.

Body Marks: Tattooing, Piercing, and Scarification by Kathlyn Gay and Christine Whittington. Twenty-First Century, 2002. One of the most interesting parts of this 112-page book is its explanation of how body markings both separate and unite cultures and generations.

Chewing the Cud by Dick King-Smith, illustrated by Harry Horse. Knopf, 2002. This is a personal memoir in which the author focuses on both human and animal characters who have enriched his life.

Do You See What I See? The Art of Illusion by Angela Wenzel, translated from German by Rosie Jackson. Prestel (Adventures in Art Series), 2001. Information is included on such artists as M. C. Escher, Salvado Dalí, Josef Albers, and Tiepolo. Each of the 29 pages includes examples of hidden pictures, coded messages, or tricks to fool the eye.

Food Rules: The Stuff You Munch, Its Crunch, Its Punch, and Why You Sometimes Lose Your Lunch by Bill Haduch, illustrated by Rick Stromoski. Dutton, 2001. Going from funny to gross, *Food Rules* lets readers in on more information than they even thought they wanted to know.

Nibbling on Einstein's Brain: The Good, the Bad, & the Bogus in Science by Diane Swanson, illustrated by Warren Clark. Annick Press, 2001. Reading this book is a much easier way to learn about "scientific" frauds than to be a victim of a scheme or a fraud.

Q is for Quark: A Science Alphabet Book by David Schwartz, illustrated by Kim Doner. Doner, 2001. Schwartz writes folksy and humorous defini-

tions for approximately 30 key science terms. He did something similar for math in his *G Is for Googol* (Tricycle, 1998).

Quotations for Kids, edited and compiled by J. A. Senn, illustrated by Steve Pica. Millbrook, 1999. Humorous full-color cartoons add interest to the over 2,000 quotations in this 256-page book.

So You Want to Be President by Judith St. George, illustrated by David Small. Philomel, 2000. Humorously drawn caricatures add to the light touch. St. George is skilled at hunting out curious tidbits and facts about the men in the White House. David Small puts them together in new ways as when he shows the tailor Andrew Johnson fitting a suit on the actor Ronald Reagan, while the haberdasher Harry Truman stands behind a counter ready to assist in the sale.

There Goes the Neighborhood: Ten Buildings People Loved to Hate by Susan Goldman Rubin. Holiday House, 2001. Local controversies over building permits and city restrictions on people's "freedom of expression" will take on new meaning to students who have read about initial reactions to The Eiffel Tower in Paris, the Guggenheim Museum in New York, and Philip Johnson's glass house in Connecticut.

They Saw the Future: Oracles, Psychics, Scientists, Great Thinkers, and Pretty Good Guessers by Kathleen Krull. Simon & Schuster, 1999. Krull is skilled at finding fascinating tidbits of information about famous people. With Harcourt Brace, she has also published *Lives of the Musicians: Good Times, Bad Times (and What the Neighbors Thought)*, 1993; *Lives of the Artists: Masterpieces, Messes (and What the Neighbors Thought)*, 1995; and *Lives of the Athletes: Thrills, Spills (and What the Neighbors Thought)*, 1999. Kathryn Hewitt did the clever illustrations.

- Nonfiction makes up a much larger proportion of boys' reading than of girls' reading.
- One study categorized the seven most popular types of nonfiction as cartoon and comic books, weird but true stories, rock stars, ghosts, magic, stories about famous people, and explorations of the unknown.
- Remedial readers prefer informative nonfiction and read "primarily to learn new things."
- Students choose nonfiction for a variety of reasons often unrelated to school curricular matters, as shown by the fact that computer-related books are popular in schools with no computers and books on the Ku Klux Klan are frequently checked out in junior highs in which recent U.S. history is not studied.
- When students gave reasons for reading particular books, it became clear that the purpose of the reading is guided more by the student than by the type of book. One boy read books on subjects he already knew about because it made him feel smart; others preferred how-to books so that they could interact with the author while learning to draw, care for a pet, program a computer, make a paper airplane, and so on; and still others preferred *The Guinness Book of World Records*. Even here purposes differed. Some read the book to discover amazing facts, but others read it to imagine themselves undergoing strange experiences.

Students are sometimes seeking answers to specific questions. But other times they are seeking pleasure or change of pace. See Focus Box 9.1 for Fun Facts.

Narrative or Storytelling in Nonfiction

When Thomas Keneally's 1982 *Schindler's List* won a Pulitzer Prize in fiction, there was considerable controversy over whether the book was eligible because it was supposedly a journalistic account of a true event. E. L. Doctorow spoke to the same issue when he said in his acceptance speech for the National Book Critics Circle Award for *Ragtime*, "There is no more fiction or nonfiction, only narrative."

Three hundred English teachers who responded to a survey asking for ten adolescent novels and ten adult novels worthy of recommendation to teenagers gave further evidence that in people's minds fiction and nonfiction are blending together. Among twenty nonfiction titles recommended as novels were Piers Paul Read's *Alive*, James Herriot's *All Creatures Great and Small*, Robin Graham's *Dove*, Peter Maas's *Serpico*, Doris Lund's *Eric*, Alvin Toffler's *Future Shock*, Maya Angelou's *I Know Why the Caged Bird Sings*, Dee Brown's *Bury My Heart at Wounded Knee*, Claude Brown's *Manchild in the Promised Land*, Eldridge Cleaver's *Soul on Ice*, and John H. Griffin's *Black Like Me*.

The blending of fiction and nonfiction has occurred from both directions. On one side are the nonfiction writers who use the techniques of fiction, including suspense, careful plotting and characterization, and literary devices, such as symbolism and metaphor. At the beginning of *Izzy, Willy-Nilly*, Cynthia Voigt acknowledged help from medical personnel who taught her about physical and mental aspects of amputation. And in *A Single Shard*, it is obvious that Linda Sue Park has done extensive research on celadon pottery.

Good novels are fiction in the sense that fictional names are used and they combine bits and pieces of many individual stories. Nevertheless, in another sense, these stories are more real and actually present a more honest portrayal than some pieces labeled nonfiction that are true accounts of bizarre or strange happenings.

Literature—fiction and nonfiction—is more than a simple recounting or replaying of the life that surrounds the writer. It is a distillation and a crystallization. Only when an author skillfully chooses descriptive details and develops believable dialogue does an account of an actual event become real to the reader. Alex Haley's *Roots* became real to millions of television viewers as well as to millions of readers, yet the book contains many fictional elements in both subject matter and presentation. Part of Haley's success comes from his ability to select powerful incidents and details. Good writers of non-fiction do not simply record everything they know or can uncover. With Haley's book, readers' imaginations were captured by the fact that on September 29, 1967, he "stood on the dock in Annapolis where his great-great-great-great-great-grandfather was taken ashore on September 29, 1767," and sold as a slave to a Virginia plantation owner. From this point, Haley set out to trace backward the six generations that connected him to a 16-year-old "prince" newly arrived from Africa. What the public might not stop to consider as they read about this dramatic incident is that it is setting the stage for only a small portion of Haley's "roots." In the generation in which Haley started his story with the young couple, Omoro and Binta Kinte, and the birth of their first son, Kunta, there were 256 parents giving birth to 128 children, each one of whom is also a great-great-great-great-great-grandfather or grandmother to Alex Haley. The point is that even though Haley was writing nonfiction, he had an almost unlimited range of possibilities from which to choose, and he made his choices with the instinct of a storyteller rather than a clerk, who might have put together a more complete but less interesting family history.

New Journalism

Roots is part of the genre sometimes labelled *new journalism.* Truman Capote called it the "most avant-garde form of writing existent today" and coined the term *nonfiction novel* for *In Cold Blood,* an account of an especially brutal murder and the subsequent trial. Other terms that are used include *creative nonfiction, literary journalism, journalistic fiction,* and *advocacy journalism.* Although its roots were growing right along with journalism in general, it did not begin to flower until the 1950s and 1960s. Part of the reason for its development is the increased educational level of the American public. Newspaper readers and television viewers, including young adults, are not satisfied with simplistic explanations. They want enough background information that they can feel confident in coming to their own conclusions.

Affluence, combined with modern technology, helps make the new journalism possible. Compare similar incidents that happened 126 years apart. In 1846, a group of travelers who came to be known as the Donner party were trapped in the high Sierras by an early snow. They had to stay there all winter without food except for the flesh of their dead companions. After they were rescued, word of their ordeal gradually trickled back east, so that for years afterward sensationalized accounts were made up by writers who had no chance to come to the scene or interview the survivors.

JACK GANTOS
On Writing in Journals

Adolescence was a bad time for a lot of things, but especially for my writing. I had faithfully kept diaries all my young life, then during adolescence the diary writing waned, largely because diary writing and personal narratives were never considered anything of educational importance in school. We were instructed to write research papers and commanded not to reach any *personal conclusions.* That was no fun. After all, what was the purpose of knowing anything if it didn't help shape your *personal* opinion?

To make matters worse the word, *diary,* was a word that was fine in elementary school, or around the house, but in middle school and high school the word *diary* was definitely female, and guys at my school in South Florida did not keep diaries, or do anything that could be misconstrued as gender-bending or girlish. So I kept my diary at home, and when I wrote I felt as if I were hiding from people because I was doing something so flagrantly female—as if I were at home in my locked bedroom wearing my sister's undergarments and tweezing my eyebrows. It was a very peculiar feeling to be uncomfortable with myself even when no one else was around. Granted, no one specifically told me not to write, but no one was around to support writing, either. There were no teachers who championed the effort, no clubs or groups. My dad never came home from work and asked, "How's the diary writing coming, son?" Nor did my mother seem interested in the practice.

So in order to continue my diary writing without being too self-conscious, I came up with a simple solution that worked for me. I had a collection of Matchbox cars, which were miniatures of real full size cars. One day I got the idea to make matchbox diaries. I took a box of matches from a restaurant where my parents had dined, pulled out the drawer, threw away the matches then cut slips of paper to fit the little drawer. When finished, the matchbox slipped neatly into my pocket. From then on I'd keep a box in my pants pocket, and when I had an idea at school I could quickly open my matchbox and write it down (as a consequence, I have very small handwriting). To most of the kids, the matchbox diaries looked like matches, which was okay because it appeared to them that either I smoked cigarettes or I was crazy enough to burn the school down.

Now I use the non-gender-specific term *journal* to describe my diaries. Every time I begin a new novel I start a new journal. On each page I draw a vertical line down the middle. In the left-hand column I write my novel. In the right-hand column I keep my daily "diary" notes on my life. Not only do I enjoy discovering the way my real life influences my creative life, but I find it particularly interesting when some fiction I've been writing ends up influencing something I say, or how I make decisions. After I've been working on a novel for quite some time, I can follow how I begin to bend my real life to imitate the fictive life. And when I finish a book, it is quite alarming when I snap back from being the fictive character to being myself again.

Then after some free time has evened me out, I start a new book.

Jack Gantos's books include *Hole in My Life* (2002), *What Would Joey Do?* (2002), *Joey Pigza Loses Control* (2000), and *Jack's Black Book* (1997), all from Farrar Straus Giroux. His website can be found on www.FSGKIDSBOOKS.COM.

In 1972, a planeload of Uruguayan travelers crashed in the Andes mountains. As in the Donner party, some people knew each other before the trip, but others were strangers. During the terrible weeks of waiting to be rescued, they all got to know each other and to develop intense relationships revolving around leadership roles and roles of rebellion or giving up. They endured unspeakable hardships. Many died; those who lived did so because they ate the flesh of those who died. In this situation, however, the people were rescued by helicopters after two of the men made their way out of the mountains. Word of their 2 1/2-month ordeal was flashed around the world, and by the time the sixteen survivors, mostly members of a rugby team, had been flown back to Uruguay, reporters from many nations were there. A press conference was held, and the journalists were told about the cannibalism.

This was the second surprise in the story. The first had been their survival. The drama of the situation naturally fired imaginations all around the world. Lippincott suggested to author Piers Paul Read that this was the kind of story that would make a good book. He went to Uruguay, where he stayed for several months interviewing survivors, rescuers, family, and friends of both the deceased and the survivors, and the government officials who had been in charge of the search. More than a year later, Lippincott published *Alive: The Story of the Andes Survivors,* which was on the *New York Times* best-seller list for seven months, was made into a movie, and will probably continue to be read by young adults for the next several years, both in and out of school.

The fact that the survivors were in their early twenties undoubtedly helps teenagers to identify with the story, but so do the literary techniques that Read used. He focused on certain individuals, presenting miniature character sketches of some and fully developed portraits of others. The setting was crucial to the story, and he described it vividly. He was also careful to write so that the natural suspense of the situation came through. His tone was consistent throughout the book. He admired the survivors but did not shy away from showing the negative aspects of human nature when it is sorely tried. In a preface he said that the only liberty he allowed himself was the creation of dialogue between the characters, although, whenever possible, he relied on diaries and remembered comments and quarrels as well as his acquaintance with the speaking styles of the survivors.

"New journalism" combines factual information with emotional appeal. Such books might be classified as biography, history, drama, essay, or personal experience, but regardless of classification, they serve as a bridge between childhood and adult reading because of the straightforward, noncondescending style that is characteristic of good journalism.

Nonfiction best sellers often outsell fiction best sellers, and television producers have learned the appeal of "reality" shows and they know they can add millions of viewers if they advertise a program as "a documentary" rather than "a drama."

Even the success of the tabloids depends on their nonfiction format. The majority of readers do not really believe all those stories about Elvis Presley still being alive or about women giving birth to aliens or apricot pits curing cancer; yet, for the fun of it they are willing to give themselves over to a momentary suspension of disbelief, something we used to talk about mainly in relation to fantasy and science fiction.

Evaluation of Nonfiction

Evaluating nonfiction for young readers is more complicated than evaluating fiction because

1. People select informational books primarily on the basis of the subject matter, and because there is such a variety in subjects, people's choices vary tremendously, resulting in a lack of consensus on what is "the best."

2. Informative books on such topics as computers and car repair become dated more quickly than fiction books. Students preparing to take the SAT tests, wanting advice on handling money, or planning for a career need the most recent information. The constant turnover of informative books leaves us with few touchstone examples.

3. The transitory nature of informative nonfiction books discourages teachers and critics from giving them serious consideration as instructional materials. Although well-written personal experience narratives have longer life spans, people who have made up their minds that they are not interested in nonfiction find it easy to ignore all nonfiction.

4. Reviewers and prize givers may not feel competent to judge the technical or other specialized information presented in many informative books. Also, many reviewers, especially those working with educational journals, come from an English-teaching tradition, and they tend to focus on books that would be used in conjunction with literature rather than biology, home economics, social studies, industrial arts, history, or business classes.

5. In evaluating nonfiction, there is no generally agreed-upon theory of criticism or criteria for judgment.

We suggest that the evaluation situation can be improved by readers looking at the intended audience and the content of the book. (What is it about? What information does it present?) Then look at the appropriateness and success with which each of the following is established. Examining a nonfiction book carefully enough to be able to describe the setting or scope and the theme, tone, and style will give you insights into how well it is written and packaged. Also, for information books, look at the more specific suggestions in Table 9.1.

Setting/Scope Informative books may be historical, restricted to regional interests, or have a limited scope. In evaluating these, one needs to ask whether the author set realistic goals, considering the reading level of the intended audience and the amount of space and backup graphics available.

Theme Informational books also have themes or purposes that are closely tied to the author's point of view. Authors may write in hopes of persuading someone to a particular belief or to inspire thoughtfulness, respect, or even curiosity. Some authors shout out their themes; others are more subtle. You need to consider consistency as you evaluate the theme. Did the author build on a consistent theme throughout the book?

Tone The manner in which an author achieves a desired goal—whether it is to persuade, inform, inspire, or amuse—sets the tone of a book. Is it hard-sell, strident, one-sided, humorous, loving, sympathetic, adulatory, scholarly, pedantic, energetic, or leisurely? Authors of informative books for children used to take a leisurely approach as they tried to entice children into becoming interested in their subject. Today's young readers, however, are just as busy as their parents and most likely go to informative books for quick information rather than leisure time entertainment. A boy or girl who wants to repair a bicycle does not want to read the history of the Wright brothers and their bicycle shop before getting to the part on slipped gears.

Style The best informative books also have style. As author Jane Langton said when she was asked to serve as a judge, the good books "exude some kind of passion or love or caring . . . and they have the potential for leaving a mark on the readers, changing them

TABLE 9.1 SUGGESTIONS FOR EVALUATING INFORMATIVE NONFICTION

A good piece of informative writing usually has:	A poor piece of informative writing may have:
A subject of interest to young readers, written about with zest. Information that is up-to-date and accurate.	Obsolete or inaccurate information or illustrations. Even one such occurrence causes the reader to lose faith in the rest of the book.
New information or information organized in such a way as to present a different point of view than in previously available books.	Evidence of cutting-and-pasting in which the author merely reorganized previously prepared material without developing anything new in content or viewpoint.
A reading level, vocabulary, and tone of writing that are at a constant level appropriate to the intended audience.	Inconsistencies in style or content, for example, college-level vocabulary but a childish or cute style of writing.
An organization in which basic information is presented first so that chapters and sections build on each other.	An awkward mix of fiction and nonfiction techniques through which the author unsuccessfully tries to slip information in as an unnoticed part of the story.
An index and other aids to help readers look up facts if they want to return to the book for specific information or to glean ideas and facts without reading the entire book.	A reflection of out-of-date or socially unfair attitudes, for example, a history book that presents only the history of white upper-class men with a title and introduction that give the impression that it is a comprehensive history of the time period being covered.
Adequate documentation of the sources of information, including some original sources.	A biased presentation in which only one side of a controversial issue is presented with little or no acknowledgment that many people hold different viewpoints.
Information to help interested students locate further readings on the subject.	
In how-to-books, clear and accurate directions including complete lists of the equipment and supplies needed in a project.	In how-to books, frustrating directions that oversimplify or set up unrealistic expectations so that the reader is disappointed in the result.
Illustrations that add interest as well as clarity to the text.	
A competent author with expertise in the subject matter.	

in some way."[3] George A. Woods, former children's editor of the *New York Times Book Review*, said that he selected the informational books to be featured in his review mostly on his own "gut-level" reactions to what was "new or far better than what we have had before." He looked for a majesty of language and uniqueness and for books that would add to children's understanding by making them eyewitnesses to history.[4] A problem in examining an author's style is that each book must be judged according to the purpose the author had in mind. From book to book, purposes are so different that it is like the old problem of comparing apples and oranges. Some books are successful simply because they are different—more like a mango than an apple or an orange.

Contemporary Influences on the Publishing of Informational Books

Before the 1950s, what was published for young readers was in the main fiction (novels or short stories), poetry, or textbook material to be used in school. Few publishers thought that young readers would be interested in factual books unless they were forced to study them as part of their schoolwork. Then the Russians launched Sputnik, and Americans were sincerely frightened that Russia was scientifically and technologically ahead. In 1961, Congress passed the National Defense Education Act, which gave millions of dollars to school libraries for the purchase of science and math books (later expanded to include all books). Publishers competed to create informative books that would qualify for purchase under the Act and would attract young readers.

The rise in the popularity of nonfiction has paralleled the information explosion and the rise in the power and influence of the mass media. Today there is simply more information to be shared between reader and writer. Television, radio, movies, newspapers, magazines, and now the Internet all communicate the same kinds of information as do books, but people expect more from books because the other media are limited in the amount of space and time that they can devote to information on any one topic. Moreover, whatever is produced by the mass media must be of interest to a *mass* audience, whereas individual readers select books. Of course, publishers want masses of individual readers to select their books. Nevertheless, there is more room for experimentation and the development of minority viewpoints in books than in the kinds of media that are supported by advertisers and that, therefore, must aim to attract the largest possible audience.

Many writers take the same subjects that are treated on television and write about them in more detail or from unexpected viewpoints. They try to answer the questions that cursory news reports do not have time or space to probe (see Focus Box 9.2, Current Events: Going beyond the Headlines). Readers also have more faith in books than in news stories that are necessarily put together overnight or in Internet stories for which it is often impossible to check the sources.

Need for Scientific Literacy

At a meeting of the Conference on College Composition and Communication in St. Louis, science writer Jon Franklin spoke on a panel entitled "Nonfiction: The Genre of a Technological Age." Formerly a science writer for the *Evening Sun* in Baltimore and now a teacher of journalism at the University of Maryland in College Park, Franklin's topic was "Literary Structure: A Growing Force in Science Journalism." He pointed out how in the past decade, more than half the winners of the Pulitzer Prize in nonfiction had been science books and how the increasingly important role of scientific writing in newspapers and magazines is changing basic concepts of journalism. The upside-down pyramid, in which the key points are stated first with the details being filled in later so an editor can cut the story whenever the available space is filled, does not work for science writing because it results in oversimplification. Science stories have to be written inductively, building from the small to the large points because most scientific developments and concepts are too complex for readers to understand unless they get the supporting details first.

Franklin worries about the development of a new kind of elitism based on scientific literacy. He says that if people feel uncomfortable with scientific writing, they are likely to resent and reject scientific concepts. He gives as an example the censorship battles that have developed over beliefs in creationism versus evolution. He proposes a two-pronged approach to keep the gap from widening between the scientifically

FOCUS BOX 9.2   Current Events: Going beyond the Headlines

Alone across the Arctic: One Woman's Epic Journey by Dog Team by Pam Flowers and Ann Dixon. Alaska Northwest, 2001. Pam Flowers retraced in reverse the arctic dogsled journey taken in a 1923–1924 expedition by Norwegian explorer Knud Rasmussen and two Inuit companions. Well-told and beautifully documented, this is both an exciting survival story and a lesson in gaining self-respect.

America's Great Disasters by Martin W. Sandler. HarperCollins, 2003. The dramatic photos and illustrations, along with the clear writing about such tragedies as the Oklahoma Dust Bowl, the Galveston Hurricane, the 1918–1919 influenza epidemic, and the Mt. St. Helens volcanic eruption will help middle school readers put current events into perspective.

The Book of Help: Authors Respond to the Tragedy, edited by Michael Cart. Cricket Books, 2002. Cart used his reputation for careful work and his acquaintance with many of the best authors for young adults to entice such writers as Katherine Paterson, Walter Dean Myers, Russell Freedman, Marion Dane Bauer, James Cross Giblin, and Naomi Shihab Nye to share their thoughts and experiences related to the September 11th tragedy.

A Dinosaur Named Sue: The Story of the Colossal Fossil: The World's Most Complete T. Rex by Pat Relf. Scholastic, 2000. Relf brings to life the 1990 discovery of a magnificent dinosaur and all the human feuding that took place before the dinosaur was finally placed in Chicago's Field Museum.

The Elephant Book for the Elefriends Campaign by Ian Redmond. Candlewick, 2001. The layout and the beautiful photos in this 48-page book are unabashedly meant to bring home the point that "[W]e can replant forests, and even reclaim deserts in time, but no one, when the last elephant has gone, can make another."

Four to the Pole! The American Women's Expedition to Antarctica, 1992–93 by Nancy Loewen and Ann Bancroft. Linnet, 2001. In 1992, four women, including Ann Bancroft, watched a small airplane fly away after dropping them and their 200-pound pack sleds on the ice in Antarctica. Sixty-seven days later they became the first women to walk to the South Pole.

Getting Away with Murder: The True Story of the Emmett Till Case by Chris Crowe. Penguin/Putnam, 2003. Although Emmett Till was murdered early in the 1950s, the story is coming back into the news as its impact on the beginnings of the Civil Rights movement is reassessed. (See Crowe's statement on p. 226.)

Meltdown: A Race against Nuclear Disaster at Three Mile Island: A Reporter's Story by Wilborn Hampton. Candlewick, 2001. One of the reporters who in 1979 rushed to the Three-Mile Island nuclear plant near Harrisburg, Pennsylvania, returned to use what he learned in writing this dramatic and well-balanced book about nuclear power.

A Nation Challenged: A Visual History of 9/11 and Its Aftermath: Young Reader's Edition, edited by Mitchel Levitas. Scholastic, 2002. The contents were pulled from the *New York Times* prize-winning section, "A Nation Challenged." Howell Raines, executive editor, introduces the book, whose generous layout and variety make the information intriguing, but not too grim to be read.

To the Top: The Story of Everest by Stephen Venables. Candlewick, 2003. People who saw televised accounts of the fiftieth anniversary celebration of Sir Edmund Hilary's climbing of Mt. Everest will have an extra appreciation of this beautifully designed book. The author has himself climbed the mountain and includes a section on what its popularity as a climbing destination has done to the Tibetan/Nepalese culture.

When Objects Talk: Solving Crime with Science by Mark P. Friedlander and Terry M. Phillips. Lerner, 2001. Students who have read this book will have a leg up in understanding news stories about crimes and trials. Brief writeups and case histories illustrate the forensic tests that are explained.

literate and those who reject all science. On the one hand, science writers have to work harder to find organizational patterns and literary techniques that make their material understandable and interesting. On the other hand, schools must bring the reading of technological and scientific information into the curriculum with the goal of preparing students to balance their lifetime reading. See Focus Box 9.3, Science and Technology, for recommended titles.

Books to Support and Extend the School Curriculum

Informational books purchased by school libraries are usually referred to as "books to support the curriculum," but a more accurate description would probably be "books to extend the curriculum." These books seldom help students who are doing poorly in class. Instead, they provide challenges for successful students to go further than their classmates. They also serve as models for research, and they go beyond the obvious facts to present information that is too complicated, too detailed, too obscure, or too controversial to be included in textbooks. A legitimate complaint often voiced about history books is that they focus on war and violence and leave out life as it was lived by most people. Another complaint is that they leave out the experiences of women and minorities. For example, school history textbooks do not mention contraception, but nothing has changed women's lives more than the birth control pill. Well-written and well-illustrated trade books serve as a counterbalance to these omissions.

Teenagers are especially interested in books that present the extremes of life's experiences, which is why various editions and adaptations of *The Guinness Book of World Records* remain popular. Whatever is the biggest, the best, or the most unusual is of interest.

A good example is the *Junior Chronicle of the 20th Century.* In 336 oversized pages, each including several full-color photographs, the editors give the major events of each year. They were clever in finding at least one youth-oriented photo for each double-page spread.

Succinctness and easy accessibility are also selling points when encouraging teenagers to dip into collections of essays as opposed to books that need to be read in their entirety. Students who have enjoyed Robert Cormier's fiction might look on his *I Have Words to Spend: Reflections of a Small-Town Editor* as a chance to share thoughts with the kind of uncle or grandfather they wish they had been lucky enough to have. Teenagers can also enjoy Russell Baker's, Erma Bombeck's, and Andy Rooney's collections of newspaper columns.

Space in this text allows us to present only a sample of the many books available as companion reading, or even replacement reading, for typical textbooks (see Focus Boxes 9.3, 9.4, and 9.5 for some suggestions). When selecting such books, librarians and teachers should remember that teenagers most often pick them up to find specific information. Because young readers lack the kind of background knowledge that most adults have, it is especially important that informative books be well organized and indexed in such a way that readers can look up facts without reading the whole book. Unclear references or confusing directions are especially troublesome in how-to books, which range from books as practical and personal as Ron Volpe's *The Lady Mechanic's*

By the Sword: A History of Gladiators, Musketeers, Samurai, Swashbucklers, and Olympic Champions by Richard Cohen. Random House, 2002. This history of the sword and its uses goes back to the early Greeks and up to the most recent Olympic Games. The sword is shown as a weapon in war, as a way of keeping one's honor in duels, and as an instrument for competition in games between nations.

Global Warming: The Threat of Earth's Changing Climate by Laurence Pringle. North-South/SeaStar, 2001. Pringle did a complete revision of this highly acclaimed book, first published in 1991. The illustrations, photos, and maps add interest to Pringle's smooth writing about such topics as El Niño, smog, eroding beaches, and nuclear power.

The Kid Who Invented the Trampoline: More Surprising Stories about Inventions by Don L. Wulffson. Dutton 2001. Short articles about the ups and down—the frustrations and the exhilaration—of inventors make this a fun book for skimming as well as reading.

Looking for Life in the Universe: The Search for Extraterrestrial Intelligence by Ellen Jackson, photos by Nic Bishop. Houghton Scientists in the Field Series, 2002. The author gives this area of science a personal touch by focusing on Astrophysicist Jill Tarter, who directs the Phoenix Project of the Search for Extraterrestrial Intelligence. She is the real-life model for the protagonist in Carl Sagan's best-selling *Contact.*

Rats! The Good, the Bad, and the Ugly by Richard Conniff. Crown, 2002. This cleverly designed

and beautifully written book will give even squeamish readers new respect for these amazingly talented animals.

Sure-to-Win Science Fair Projects by Joe Rhatigan and Heather Smith. Sterling/Lark, 2001. If someone waits until the night before the project is due, this book will not help because the fifty or so suggested projects require thoughtfulness as well as time and care.

Swimming with Hammerhead Sharks by Kenneth Mallory. Houghton, 2001. Part of a well-done series (*Scientists in the Field*), Mallory's book chronicles an expedition of an IMAX film team led by marine biologist Pete Klimley working off Cocos Island in the Pacific Ocean to study the migratory patterns of some of the earth's most fascinating creatures.

The Way Science Works: Discover the Secrets of Science with Exciting, Accessible Experiments by Robin Kerrod and Dr. Sharon Ann Holgate. Dorling Kindersley, 2002. With beautiful layouts and photos, the authors lead young people through six areas: Looking at Matter, Atoms and Elements, Forces and Energy, Heat and Sound, Light and Color, and Electricity and Magnetism.

What a Great Idea! Inventions That Changed the World by Stephen M. Tomecek, illustrated by Dan Stuckenschneider. Scholastic, 2003. History is divided into five time periods, and for each period Tomecek writes about what he considers the most important advances.

Total Car Care for the Clueless to such an ambitious social action book as Arlene Hirschfelder's *Kick Butts! A Kid's Action Guide to a Tobacco-Free America.*

How-to books are seldom best sellers, simply because they are so specialized that they appeal to fairly limited audiences. The challenge for the teacher or librarian is to let students know about their availability. Once students find their way into the library to check out a book that helps them accomplish a particular goal, they are likely to return for other books. If they are disappointed by ambiguous or hard-to-understand

*J*im Murphy's An American Plague *takes on added interest because of people's fears of biological terrorism.*

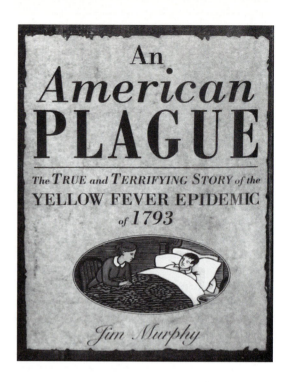

directions or come-on statements that make projects look easier than they are, they may lose interest in both the project and the library.

With sports books, obviously the first thing a reader looks for is the particular sport; consequently, authors choose titles that practically shout to potential readers. The sports books that stand out from the crowd, as with those discussed in Chapter 6, usually have a believable and likable personality behind them. Many such books are inspirational as much as instructive, but one thing to watch for in a how-to sports book is whether costs are mentioned. It is almost cruel for an author to write a glowing account of a child star in tennis, gymnastics, skating, swimming, or dancing and leave young readers with the impression that all it takes is hard work. Those readers whose parents do not have time or money for transportation, lessons, entry fees, equipment, and clothes should be let in on the secret that there's more to how you play the game than meets the eye. A similar warning needs to be given about books telling kids how to establish their own businesses or how to get into show business. Such wish-fulfilling books about unusual successes are likely to set the stage for disappointment among the thousands of more typical kids who find themselves working in fast-food restaurants or as grocery store courtesy clerks for minimum wages. There's a need for more books about these less glamorous jobs as well as for the kind of commonsense guidance found in Neale S. Godfrey's *Godfrey's Ultimate Kid's Money Book*.

For academically inclined high school students, it is important to bring books about college to their attention early on because the actual application process takes eighteen months, and its success or failure may depend on what classes a student took as a freshman. High school libraries should have recent editions of such books as *The Fiske Guide*

FOCUS BOX 9.4   History from New Angles

Black Potatoes: The Story of the Great Irish Famine, 1845–1850 by Susan Campbell Bartoletti. Houghton Mifflin, 2002. One out of five Americans has Irish ancestry and this well-done and well-illustrated book shows why. During the five dreadful years in which the potato crop failed, people had to leave Ireland or die of starvation.

Bury the Dead: Tombs, Corpses, Mummies, Skeletons & Rituals by Christopher Sloan. National Geographic, 2002. Sloan starts with prehistory and works his way up to present-day conflicts over the "unburying" of ancient people.

Countdown to Independence: A Revolution of Ideas in England and Her American Colonies 1760–1776 by Natalie S. Bober. Atheneum, 2001. What's different about this history is that it shows how close the Americans and the British were. In 342 pages, she has room to explore many incidents and personalities that in other accounts have been glossed over.

Hurry Freedom: African Americans in Gold Rush California by Jerry Stanley. Crown, 2000. While being clear to explain that Asian Americans and other minority groups also suffered, Stanley's book focuses on two African Americans, Mifflin Gibbs and Peter Lester, to illustrate the kinds of challenges minorities faced.

The Making of America: The History of the United States from 1492 to the Present by Robert D. Johnson. National Geographic, 2002. In 240 pages and eight chapters, each of which begins with eight pictures of key events, Johnson presents an overview so smoothly written that students can either skim or read the whole thing.

No More! Stories and Songs of Slave Resistance by Doreen Rappaport, illustrated by Shane W. Evans. Candlewick, 2002. After reading these accounts and viewing Evans's dramatic illustrations, readers will know better than to believe the old idea that African American slaves were happy with their lot.

Pearl Harbor: American and Japanese Survivors Tell Their Stories by Thomas B. Allen. National Geographic, 2001. This 57-page book is based on oral histories, supplemented by powerful photographs, maps, and timelines. Postscripts bringing new information about the lives of several of the people whose stories are told help to humanize participants from both sides.

Photo Odyssey: Solomon Carvalho's Remarkable Western Adventure 1853–54 by Arlene B. Hirschfelder. Clarion, 2000. Because Carvalho was a pioneer photographer, the illustrations are especially interesting.

The Shaman's Nephew: A Life in the Far North by Simon Tookoome and Sheldon Oberman, illustrated by Simon Tookoome. Stoddart, 2000. Tookoome was "one of the last of the Inuit to live the traditional nomadic life in the Far North." Over a ten-year period he told his stories to Sheldon Oberman, who translated them and put them into perspective. Oberman describes Tookoome's many illustrations as having the "primal beauty of a cave painting" and the "imagination of a modern Miro or Chagall."

Songs and Stories of the Civil War by Jerry Silverman. Twenty-First Century, 2002. In 96 pages, Silverman gives the history behind twelve of the most popular songs and ballads of the Civil War.

Tell All the Children Our Story: Memories and Mementos of Being Young and Black in America by Tonya Bolden. Abrams, 2002. With the help of photos and reproductions (many in color), Bolden does a good job of communicating the look and the feel of events over the past 300 years.

We Were There, Too! Young People in U.S. History by Phillip Hoose. Farrar, 2001. Nearly seventy stories are arranged chronologically, starting with 12-year-old Diego Bermúdez who sailed with Columbus. Photographs, maps, quotes, and drawings add interest.

FOCUS BOX 9.5   *Humanities and the Arts*

Bibles and Bestiaries: A Guide to Illuminated Manuscripts by Elizabeth B. Wilson. Farrar Straus & Giroux, 1994. Illuminated manuscripts—medieval handmade books illustrated with gold, silver, and various paints—were made by both Christians and Muslims prior to the invention of printing. Examples from the Pierpont Morgan Library in New York City are illustrated in gorgeous color.

Creation by Gerald McDermott. Dutton, 2003. McDermott's picture book for thoughtful people of all ages is itself a testament to the human instinct to answer hard questions with beauty in words and art.

Don't Hold Me Back: My Life and Art by Winfred Rembert. Cricket, 2003. This 40-page autobiography is a combination of the author's words and his vivid paintings of scenes he remembers from growing up in the segregated South.

Harlem Stomp! A Cultural History of the Harlem Renaissance by Laban Carrick Hill. Little, 2003. Hill makes a good case for considering the Harlem Renaissance to be the most significant cultural movement in the nation's history. The book is packed with vivid examples of art, photography, song lyrics, poetry, and prose.

Leonardo's Horse by Jean Fritz, illustrated by Hudson Talbott. Putnam, 2001. Jean Fritz is the author who revolutionized the way biographies were written for children. Here she applies her creativity to tell the story of how in 1999 Leonardo DaVinci's dream of a bronze horse 24-feet-high was realized in the city of Milan.

The Magical Worlds of Harry Potter: A Treasury of Myths, Legends, and Fascinating Facts by David Colbert. Berkley, 2001. Through questions and answers, Colbert reveals the Greek and Latin roots of many of the words Rowling uses. He also shows how much of the magic and many of the characters are based in old legends and myths.

Runaway Girl: The Artist Louise Bourgeois by Jan Greenberg and Sandra Jordan. Abrams, 2003. The authors not only tell about a great woman sculptor, they also introduce readers to a field of art and teach them how to get more out of the experience of viewing sculpture.

Shakespeare: His Work and His World by Michael Rosen, illustrated by Rert Ingpen. Candlewick, 2001. The information may not be new, but the lively writing style, the pencil and watercolor illustrations, and the generous format will attract readers and browsers.

Shoes: Their History in Words and Pictures by Charlotte and David Yue. Houghton Mifflin, 1997. The only really new shoe design of the last century is the sneaker, but that doesn't keep readers from being fascinated by the wealth of shoes in this fascinating history.

Turandot by Marianna Mayer, illustrated by Winslow Pel. Morrow, 1996. In this retelling of Puccini's opera of the same name, a beautiful and proud Chinese princess is told by her father to take a husband, but only if the prospective suitor correctly answers three riddles. His failure will result in a beheading.

Women Artists of the West: Five Portraits in Creativity and Courage by Julie Danneberg. Fulcrum, 2002. The photos in this 84-page book help Danneberg make her point about how artists are influenced by the geography and the culture that surrounds them.

A Young Dancer's Apprenticeship: On Tour with the Moscow Ballet by Olympia Dowd. Twenty-First Century, 2002. Dowd shares her own experience of being accepted as an apprentice with the Moscow City Ballet.

The Young Person's Guide to Music by Neil Ardley and Poul Ruders. Dorling Kindersley, 1995. The essentials of classical music-making and music history make this a helpful introduction. It is accompanied by a CD created for the book.

The Young Person's Guide to Shakespeare by Anita Ganeri. Harcourt, Brace, 1999. Details about Shakespeare's life, his plays at the Globe Theatre, and the actors he used, along with synopses of several of his plays, are accompanied by striking photographs. A CD with speeches from the plays accompanies the book.

to *Colleges* and the Princeton Review's guide to *Visiting College Campuses* as well as various practice books designed to help students do well on admissions examinations.

Books helping students plan their future careers are equally important. As with sports-related books, the ones that are the most fun to read are biographical or personal experience accounts, such as those written by James Herriot on his veterinary practice or by Farley Mowat on being a naturalist. For more complete information on a wider range of jobs, see the *Careers without College* series from Peterson's Guides, the *Career Horizons* books from VGM, and the *Careers and Opportunities* series from Rosen.

Memoirs and Personal Experiences

The best memoir that we have read in the last few years is Jack Gantos's *Hole in My Life* (see the photo on p. 28), which was a runner-up for the 2002 Printz Award. As shown by the smoothness and the power of the writing, Gantos (see his statement on p. 256) has written this story probably dozens of times, if not on paper, at least in his head. It is an account of the fifteen months he spent in a federal prison between high school and college. He had helped to sail a boatload of hashish from the Virgin Islands to New York City, where he used a shopping cart to make the deliveries that his employers, Ken and Hamilton, had set up. As Jack explains one morning after the ritual headcount at the prison,

> I was in. Counted in. After breakfast I was counted. Before dinner I was counted. After dinner. Before lights out. Then while I slept. And even then I turned that phrase over and over in my mind: "Count me in." Those were three words I'd take back if I could. They were my words to Ken and Hamilton. "Count me in." Now I was counted in my cell every day, and I was counted on to be there morning, noon, and night.

The first time Jack wrote this story, he squeezed it in between the lines of a prison library copy of Dostoyevsky's *The Brothers Karamazov* (journals were not allowed). When he was released, the prison guard who searched his suitcase took out the book for return to the library. Although he never saw it again, it is likely that his memories are more vivid because he wrote them down. When he received an early release from prison because of good behavior and because he had gotten himself accepted at a junior college, he began writing "brutal stories about prison, about New York street life, about the men I knew who had hard lives and hard hearts." Then one day he grew "tired of all the blood and guts and hard lives and hard hearts and began to write more stories" about his childhood. Middle school readers know him best for *Joey Pigza Swallowed the Key* and *Joey Pigza Loses Control* (a 2001 Newbery Honor Book).

In recommending this book to readers, adults need to realize that it is written for mature high school students, not the kids who read the Joey Pigza books. When Gantos came and spoke to our students at Arizona State, he said that the book was as much a cautionary tale for adults as for kids. He wants adults to get the message that we should not give up on kids who are in trouble. With the right help, and a lot of luck, they may survive and go on to become the kind of adult who can make the world a better place.

Most personal experience stories are about adventures, successes, and experiences that the writers feel so strongly about that they wish to share their feelings with readers. Some are career stories; for example, former surgeon-general C. Everett Koop's *Koop: The Memoirs of America's Family Doctor*. Partly because of their fondness for animals, many readers appreciate Jane Goodall's *My Life with the Chimpanzees*. Animal lovers might also like Anne E. Neimark's *Wild Heart: The Story of Joy Adamson* and Diane Ackerman's *The Moon by Whale Light: And Other Adventures Among Bats, Penguins, Crocodilians, and Whales,* and Candace Savage's *Wolves*.

Although Farley Mowat's books are not as upbeat, they make fascinating reading. In *A Whale for the Killing,* he thought he had found the perfect place to live until he discovered his neighbors were savages who took pleasure in killing a trapped whale. His angry prose also typifies *Never Cry Wolf* and *Sea of Slaughter*. He's less angry in his earlier *The Dog Who Wouldn't Be* and *Owls in the Family*. *Born Naked* is Mowat's childhood memories of the 1920s and 1930s in Canada. Given Mowat's irritation with people in most of his books, *Born Naked* is a relatively quiet and gentle book.

Some authors tell their own quite ordinary stories of growing up in ways that make young readers feel privileged to get acquainted with a new friend. Annie Dillard's *An American Childhood* tells about growing up in the 1950s and 1960s. Tobias Wolff's *This Boy's Life* is set at about the same time, in Seattle, where he grew up longing to be a "boy of dignity."

Sometimes memories are incredibly funny to readers, although just how amusing the events were to the writer early in his life is open to question. The first paragraph in Mark Salzman's *Lost in Place: Growing Up Absurd in Suburbia* is witty and certainly likely to grab the attention of most readers:

> When I was thirteen years old I saw my first kung fu movie, and before it ended I decided that the life of a wandering Zen monk was the life for me. I announced my willingness to leave East Ridge Junior High School immediately and give up all material things, but my parents did not share my enthusiasm. They made it clear that I was not to become a wandering Zen monk until I had finished high school. In the meantime I could practice kung fu and meditate down in the basement. So I immersed myself in the study of Chinese boxing and philosophy with the kind of dedication that is possible only when you don't yet have to make a living, when you are too young to drive and when you don't have a girlfriend.

The success of personal experience books, as well as autobiographies, depends largely on the quality of the writing because there isn't a plot for readers to get excited about, and honest accounts lack the kinds of literary exaggeration that make for intriguing villains and heroes. One aspect of personal experience books that makes them attractive to young readers is that they are by people looking back on experiences they had when they were young. For example, Robin Graham, author of *Dove,* was only 16 when he set sail on his own boat to go around the world. Steven Callahan, author of *Adrift: Seventy-Six Days Lost at Sea,* was 29 when he set sail. Bruce Feiler in *Under the Big Top* is an adult, but he remembers back to his childhood when he learned to juggle with a handful of oranges and when he first developed his love affair with the circus.

In the personal experience books about adult protagonists that teenagers enjoy, the adults are likely to be unencumbered by family responsibilities. For example, mature young readers enjoy such travel books as Peter Matthiessen's *African Silences,* Charles Kuralt's *A Life on the Road,* and Bruce Chatwin's *What Am I Doing Here?*

Whether to consider a book a personal experience or an autobiography is often up to the reader. For example, Maya Angelou's *I Know Why the Caged Bird Sings* and its three sequels are usually considered to be autobiographies because they move chronologically through Angelou's life, but it might be argued that they are personal experience stories because each book is about only a part of her life.

Biographies

The Greeks enjoyed stories about the gods of Mount Olympus and hero tales about the mortal descendants of the gods. Hero tales, however, had an added feature that helped listeners identify with the protagonists. Unlike the gods, who live forever, heroes had one human parent, which meant that they were mortal. The most that the gods could risk in any undertaking was their pride, but heroes could lose their lives.

When we're reading modern fiction, we know that the author can always bring the protagonist out alive; however, in true hero tales—biographies—protagonists risk their lives, just as readers would in the same situation. This adds credibility and intensity because the reader thinks, "If this happened to someone else, then it might happen to me."

John Dryden introduced the word *biography* to English readers in his 1683 edition of Plutarch's *Parallel Lives.* While the term may have been new, the form was well known to readers who had long read the lives of famous generals and politicians and religious leaders. People today remain fascinated by biographies. Where else can we see the uniqueness and authenticity of one person's life and, at the same time, emotions and problems that all human beings face.

Today's biographies for young adults are likely to provide a balance of both strengths and weaknesses. They demonstrate how the subject and the reader share similar emotions. Both have fears and insecurities, and both succumb to temptations and vanities. After reading a good biography, the reader feels a kinship with the subject, not so much in spite of as because of the character's human frailties.

To say that a biography is written "objectively" does not mean that it is written without feeling. For biographies to ring true, the author must become immersed in the subject's life so that he or she can write with passion and commitment. This implies a point of view, not one imposed by an author who set out to prove a preconceived idea but a unifying force that guided the person's life and was discovered by the author through his or her research.

Few of us admit to selecting the biographies we are going to purchase and promote on the basis of how we feel about the subject, but that's like the old cliché, "Never judge a book by its cover," which is honored more in word than in deed. Someone could write a Ph.D. dissertation on how American values have changed over the last thirty years as reflected by whose biographies were put on the shelves of libraries.

In the early 1960s, readers at almost any library would find a predominance of biographies about white men who were inventors, statesmen, soldiers, and business leaders. During the 1970s, the imbalance became so obvious, particularly in school libraries, that educators and publishers took steps to correct the situation by preparing biographies about previously unsung heroes, including members of minority groups, women, handicapped individuals, and people whose contributions were not in military, political, or business spheres. Of course, there is still room for good books presenting new information on both traditional and nontraditional heroes.

Young readers who have particular favorite authors should enjoy biographies about those favorites. Many teens remember Roald Dahl's *Charlie and the Chocolate Factory* with fondness, but whether they will enjoy Jeremy Treglown's *Roald Dahl: A Biography,* learning that he was not a nice person, may be questionable. Almost certainly, fans of Dr. Seuss will love Judith Morgan and Neil Morgan's *Dr. Seuss and Mr. Geisel: A Biography.* Fans of *The Little Prince*—and they are legion—who read Stacy Schiff's *Saint-Exupery: A Biography* will get a picture of a man of action, a lover of flying, and a man who wrote some exceptional books. With Daniel Dyer's *Jack London: A Biography,* there's bound to be a circular effect with its readers searching out London's fiction and readers of his fiction getting extra pleasure from the biography. Whether Jay Parini's *John Steinbeck: A Biography* convinces readers that Steinbeck is a major writer is unclear, but young adults who love *Of Mice and Men* and *The Grapes of Wrath* will surely enjoy Parini's book. Catherine Reef has also written a biography, *John Steinbeck,* which is a large-size book with plenty of photos and brief excerpts from Steinbeck's writing. Sharon O'Brien's *Willa Cather,* published as part of Chelsea House's *Lives of Notable Gay Men and Lesbians* series, is a solid study of Cather's life and work, not just her sex life.

There is always a place for biographies about women and men who have changed the world. Patricia C. McKissack and Fredrick McKissack's *Sojourner Truth: Ain't I a Woman?* is a compelling life story of a woman who began as a slave and ultimately emerged as a powerful African American voice in the United States. Ellen Chesler's *Woman of Valor: Margaret Sanger and the Birth Control Movement in America* recounts the life of a nurse who became a militant socialist and ultimately saved many other women's lives. Carolyn G. Heilbrun's *The Education of a Woman: The Life of Gloria Steinem* portrays the woman who may have had more power in the women's movement than any other. See Focus Box 9.6, Some Recent Biographies, for other examples.

Collective Biographies

Collective biographies (i.e., one book presenting the stories of several individuals) have become increasingly popular because authors can write about individuals whose lives may not have been chronicled fully enough to provide information for an entire book. Collective biographies are also an efficient way to get information about previously ignored individuals into a library. Authors usually bring together the stories of people who have something in common. This development of a unifying theme may be the best way to show trends and connections among various subjects. For example, Russell Freedman's *Indian Chiefs,* the biographies of six western Indian chiefs during the 1800s, is a stronger condemnation of Anglo treatment of Native Americans than it would have been had he told only one of the stories. In a similar way readers get a broader picture than if they were reading about only one first lady when they read *The Smithsonian Book of the First Ladies: Their Lives, Times, and Issues,* edited by Edith P. Mayo, curator of the Division of Political History in the American part of the Smithsonian Institution. Ruth Ashby and Deborah Gore Ohrn's

FOCUS BOX 9.6   *Some Recent Biographies*

All Shook Up: The Life and Death of Elvis Presley by Barry Denenberg. Scholastic, 2001. Kids who wonder what the music world was like for their parents (or grandparents?) might enjoy this book. Denenberg also wrote *An American Hero: The True Story of Charles A. Lindbergh* (Scholastic, 1996).

Behind the Mask: The Life of Queen Elizabeth I by Jane Resh Thomas. Clarion, 1998. Thomas's highly acclaimed biography needs to be in every high school library, not only for background reading when studying British literature, but also to entice students into looking at women in history.

Ben Franklin's Almanac: Being a True Account of the Good Gentleman's Life by Candace Fleming. Simon and Schuster, 2003. Fleming's book resembles one of Franklin's own almanacs because she found his life and his interests too far-ranging to capture in typical chronological order, so she made such chapters as "Tokens of a Well Lived Life" and "Boyhood Memories."

Carl Sandburg: Adventures of a Poet by Penelope Niven, illustrated by Marc Nadel. Harcourt, 2003. The design makes this an especially appealing book. On facing pages, Niven presents details from Sandburg's life and a related poem.

Fight On! Mary Church Terrell's Battle for Integration by Dennis Fradin Brindell and Judith Bloom Fradin. Clarion, 2003. Mollie Terrell was born to former slaves in 1863, but she went to Oberlin College and was the first black woman appointed to the Washington, DC, Board of Education. When she was 90 years old, she won a case at the Supreme Court that ended segregation in the District of Columbia's restaurants and theaters.

Heroine of the Titanic: The Real Unsinkable Molly Brown by Elaine Landau. Clarion, 2001. Philanthropist and social leader Margaret Brown never went by the name of Molly during her lifetime; it was a nickname that grew along with her reputation as a woman of many talents and lives.

The Ingenious Mr. Peale: Painter, Patriot, and Man of Science by Janet Wilson. Simon & Schuster/ Atheneum, 1996. This lively biography shows an early American balancing three different careers.

Leonardo da Vinci for Kids: His Life and Ideas by Janis Herbert. Chicago Review, 1998. Herbert writes not just about da Vinci's art but about his interests in science and technology as shown through his designs for diving suits and hang gliders.

One More Valley, One More Hill: The Story of Aunt Clara Brown by Linda Lowery. Random House Landmark Books, 2003. Besides being the story of a remarkable woman who rose from being a slave to being a successful businesswoman and Western pioneer, Lowery's book reveals much about U.S. history after the Civil War.

Samuel Adams: Son of Liberty, Father of Revolution by Benjamin Irvin. Oxford University Press, 2003. One of the interesting facts in this well-written biography is that when the 14-year-old Samuel Adams enrolled at Harvard, his tuition was paid in flour.

Shadow Catcher: The Life and Work of Edward S. Curtis by Laurie Lawlor. Walker, 1994. Curtis spent thirty years taking pictures of Native Americans. Lawlor continues Curtis's work by documenting and bringing to people's attention the plight of Native Americans in the early 1900s.

This Land Was Made for You and Me: The Life and Songs of Woody Guthrie by Elizabeth Partridge. Viking, 2002. Joan Baez, Bob Dylan, Ramblin' Jack Elliott, and Odetta are just some of the musicians who in the 1960s (Guthrie was already hospitalized with Huntington's disease) led the world to love Guthrie's music.

The Wright Sister: Katharine Wright and Her Famous Brothers by Richard Maurer. Millbrook/Roaring Brook, 2003. Maurer tells the story of the woman sometimes called "the third member of the team," but she also had accomplishments quite apart from her brothers' flying. A good companion book would be the 32-page *First to Fly: How Wilbur & Orville Wright Invented the Airplane* by Peter Busby, illustrated by David Craig. Crown, 2003.

Herstory: Women Who Changed the World is a marvelous collection of brief comments (1–3 pages) about women from Queen Hatshepsut in the fifteenth century B.C. to Rigoberta Menchú of contemporary Guatemala. Two collective biographies of writers by Rebecca Carroll should attract young people. *I Know What the Red Clay Looks Like: The Voice and Vision of Black Women Writers* has excerpts from fifteen black authors, including Rita Dove, Gloria Naylor, Lorene Cary, and Nikki Giovanni. *Swing Low: Black Men Writing* has works by sixteen authors, including Henry Louis Gates, Jr., Ishmael Reed, and August Wilson.

Gold Rush Women by Claire Rudolf Murphy and Jane G. Haigh takes a look at the women who flocked to Alaska in the 1890s, when gold was discovered. One-tenth of the adventurers looking for riches were women. The authors give short biographies of twenty-three women, including two native women who helped discover the gold and then taught survival skills to newcomers, two sisters who opened a bank, an African American woman who gave birth on the trail, and a woman who panned gold by lantern light and became one of the first millionaires. Ina Chang's *A Separate Battle: Women and the Civil War* looks beyond Scarlett O'Hara to show what real women did during the Civil War.

In *The Greatest Generation,* newscaster Tom Brokaw tells the stories of some fifty Americans who came of age during the Depression and World War II. Their stories are grouped into such categories as Ordinary People; Women in Uniform and Out; Heroes; Shame; and Love, Marriage, and Commitment. While the book was printed for an adult audience, it is accessible to older teens who might be interested in learning about their grandparents' generation. Studs Terkel's *Coming of Age: The Story of Our Century by Those Who've Lived It* includes the voices of more than seventy people, the youngest of whom is 70 and the oldest 99. Similar to all of Terkel's collective biographies, this one ranges from charming chitchat to resounding ideas. A more specific group is looked at in *Hell Fighters: African American Soldiers in World War I* by Michael L. Cooper. In 1916, when the Fifteenth New York Voluntary Infantry of the National Guard went to serve in France, it was segregated from other soldiers, deprived of basic uniforms and equipment, and controlled by white officers. General John J. Pershing intervened on their behalf, and in May 1918, they were renamed the 369th Regiment and, because of the soldiers' bravery in combat, came home to a hero's welcome in Harlem.

We rarely think about young people changing the course of the world, but Ellen Levine's *Freedom's Children: Young Civil Rights Activists Tell Their Own Stories* should make young people proud of other young people. Joseph Berger's *The Young Scientists: America's Future and the Winning of the Westinghouse* tells of Berger's study of the winners of the annual national Westinghouse Science Talent Search. Berger becomes excited, and so will readers, as they learn how dedicated these young scientists are and how they have developed their own research.

Debunking versus Fawning Biographies

We need to keep our wits about us as we read biographies because the authors may have agendas not immediately clear to readers. We used to worry about fawning biographies filled with hero worship, but today's authors are more likely to write debunking books. They may want subtly to poison the reader or to vent their spleens about any number of things, from the subject of the biography to an institution or anything at all.

In the debunking biography, a popular hero or an institution or anything treasured by many people is taken down from a pedestal. Although such books are certainly "antihero," they differ from true examples of the literary meaning of the term in that the subject of a debunking biography is not written about with sympathy. Among the most famous are Kitty Kelley's *Nancy Reagan: The Unauthorized Biography* and Christina Crawford's *Mommie Dearest,* which debunked actress Joan Crawford for the way she played her real-life role of mother.

Borrowing a phrase from Freud, Joyce Carol Oates has called this disturbing new subgenre "pathography." Michiko Kakutani says that the motifs are "dysfunction and disaster, illnesses and pratfalls, failed marriages and failed careers, alcoholism and breakdowns and outrageous conduct." She went on to describe how sensationalized some of these books are "wallowing in squalor and foolishness," playing with the "shrill theme" of "failed promise," if not outright "tragedy."[5]

Autobiographies

Autobiographies have an immediate and obvious appeal to readers. "Who," we ask ourselves, "would know more about this person than the person? Who could better tell us this person's story?" The truth may be that almost any other good writer could have been more honest and could have written a better story. Even a tiny bit of thought might suggest to us that most people are poor witnesses of their lives. Most of us want to look good to others. Most of us might even leave out a significant piece of our lives that still embarrasses us or humiliates us or leaves us feeling unsure of ourselves and our motives. Most of us know friends who are incapable of telling us precisely, much less accurately, what happened at certain turns in their lives.

This is not to say that autobiographies are automatically untrustworthy, only that they may not tell the whole story or that certain parts may be left out, possibly for good reason, possibly not. Writers of autobiographies are not necessarily out to con us, but they may be. Worse yet, they may even con themselves. In today's media-oriented world, autobiographies may simply be business ventures designed to promote a celebrity's fame. In the introduction to comedian Tim Allen's *Don't Stand Too Close to a Naked Man,* he jokingly explained that he was practically forced to write his book because:

> Hyperion [his publisher] is owned by Disney, which also owns my television show. Disney owns Disneyland and Disney World. Disney also owns Euro-Disney, Tokyo-Disney, and a Disney store in every city, town, and hamlet in the world. *They also have my cat.*

He ended his introductory chapter with, "And if all goes well and you buy lots and lots of copies, maybe Disney will give me back my cat."

It's probably a good idea for adults to discuss with students the whole concept of celebrity biographies and autobiographies and the role of ghost writers or "book doctors." An article in the *New York Times Book Review* (January 5, 1997) mentioned that Charles Barkley and O. J. Simpson, both "claimed to have been misquoted in their ghostwritten autobiographies—thus inviting jeers, catcalls and obloquy." John Callahan, the disabled cartoonist who shocks the sensibilities of the politically correct, was more than candid in acknowledging the help he received on his *Don't Worry, He Won't Get Far on Foot.* In his thank yous, he wrote,

> Finally, David Kelly, working from hundreds of hours of my tapes, drafted each chapter and then rewrote it again and again and again and *again* until no trace of his own voice remained. "We're not going to have one of those goddam *as-told-to* books," he would snarl. And we don't.

While celebrity autobiographies and biographies are the ones that get in the news and are likely to be requested from libraries, some of them present problems for educators. One such problem comes from Andy Warhol's statement that each of us will have "15 minutes of fame." The problem is that it takes more than 15 minutes for a book to be written, published, and purchased, so schools and libraries are usually a step behind. By the time a biography or autobiography of some new celebrity has gone through a rigorous selection procedure, the subject may no longer be of interest.

Many of the books also present questionable or outright immoral concepts. For example, Wilt Chamberlain's *A View from Above* has a chapter, "On Sex and Love: What Rules the World," which makes clear that he believes he is lucky because he has had sexual relations with nearly 20,000 women. That may impress Chamberlain, but it is likely to bother most adults. Adults have also been bothered by the popularity of Vincent Bugliosi's *Helter Skelter: The True Story of the Manson Murders,* which is still read by young people as Charles Manson periodically pops up in the news.

With questionable books, it's usually better that teenagers have a chance to read the whole book rather than just get the smatterings of sexual or violent titillation that appear in the media. One thing we can feel confident in suggesting is that when it comes to selecting books about which you are unsure, check out your initial reaction with others. Talk to colleagues, parents, and students, especially students, because unless someone starts young people along such a line of thinking, they may never understand that reading about someone's life does not necessarily mean emulating everything about that person. As librarian Mary Mueller observed:

> Our past and present are full of personages who lived outside traditional rules. They often used poor judgment or acted in a less-than-exemplary fashion. . . . How can we expect our students to really see the personality of Harry Truman without letting them see the tenacity, salty language, and temper that so characterized him?[6]

Nonfiction to Help Teenagers Learn Who They Are and Where They Fit

When young adult specialist Patty Campbell spoke at an American Library Association annual meeting, she pointed out that teenagers are so wrapped up in what the psychologists have labeled the "adolescent identity crisis" that they have neither the time for nor the interest in sitting down and reading about the world in general.

What they are looking for are books that help them decide who they are and where they fit into the scheme of things. Informative books they judge to be helpful include sex education books, some physical and mental health books, selected how-to books, and biographies or true accounts of experiences teenagers can imagine themselves or their acquaintances having. Nearly all the other information books published for teenagers are read under duress—only because teachers assign reports and research papers.

Teenagers especially appreciate books that give advice on managing one's life and being successful right now. Marie Hardenbrook, former librarian at McClintock High School in Tempe, Arizona, says that over the last few years her "Inspirational" display and booklist has been consistently popular. She includes such sports-related books as Richard E. Peck's *Something for Joey,* William Blinn's *Brian's Song,* Steve Cameron's *Brett Favre: Huck Finn Grows Up,* and Shannon Miller's *Winning Every Day: Gold Medal Advice for a Happy, Healthy Life.* The runaway best loaners, however, are Jack Canfield's books including two volumes of *Chicken Soup for the Teenage Soul: 101 Stories of Life, Love, and Learning; Chicken Soup for the Pet Lover's Soul: Stories about Pets as Teachers, Healers, Heroes, and Friends;* and *Chicken Soup for the Woman's Soul: 101 Stories to Open the Hearts and Rekindle the Spirits of Women.* See Focus Box 9.7, Information about Bodies and Minds, for books that answer the more specific kinds of questions that kids ask about both themselves and each other; for example,

Can I get AIDS from French kissing?

Do I have diabetes?

Why do I feel like crying all the time?

How serious is herpes?

What's the difference between just trying a drug and becoming addicted?

If I'm pregnant, what are my options?

What's an STD?

Is being fat really unhealthy?

What causes pimples?

What happens if someone has Hodgkin's disease?

My mother has breast cancer. Is she going to die?

Is anorexia nervosa just in a person's head?

Why does my grandfather say such strange things? Will I be like that when I'm old?

What will happen if I have venereal disease and don't go to the doctor?

The best books offering answers to such questions have good indexing, clear writing, suggestions for further reading, and, where appropriate, information about Web pages, telephone numbers, and support groups. The *Need to Know Library,* put out by Rosen publishers, is a dependable series of self-help books. Each book is 64 pages and includes a glossary, index, photos, and suggestions for further reading. Titles on *VOYA's* 2001 "Honor List" include Alagna Magdalena's *Everything You Need to Know about the Dangers of Binge Drinking,* Sheldon Brooks's *Everything You Need to Know about Romance*

Changing Bodies, Changing Lives: Expanded Third Edition by Ruth Bell et al. Times Books, 1998. Comments from teenagers, along with photos and drawings, are scattered throughout this large, 410-page book, which was created under the philosophy that the more young people know about themselves and their bodies, the better able they will be to manage their lives. Chapters on "Emotional Health Care," "Eating Disorders," "Substance Abuse," and "Living with Violence" supplement the information on sex in this book that is now considered a classic.

For Teens Only: Quotes, Notes & Advice You Can Use by Carol Weston. HarperTrophy, 2003. Each page starts with an intriguing quote from people as different as Homer Simpson and Edna St. Vincent Millay. Weston expounds on the quotes and concludes with a boldfaced little moral, almost like those at the ends of fables. She did an earlier *Private and Personal: Questions and Answers for Girls Only* (HarperTrophy, 2000) based on letters and answers in her "Help" column in *Girls' Life.*

The Girls' Guide to Friends by Julie Taylor. Three Rivers Press, 2002. The subtitle is "Straight talk on making close pals, creating lasting ties, and being an all-around great friend." For older readers, Taylor wrote *The Girls' Guide to Guys: Straight Talk for Teens on Flirting, Dating, Breaking Up, Making Up & Finding True Love* (Three Rivers Press, 2000).

Is It a Choice? Answers to 300 of the Most Frequently Asked Questions about Gays and Lesbians. Harper-San Francisco, 1999. Questions range from what to call same-sex parents to how do people know if they are gay. Dating, telling parents, socializing, and political activism are all treated.

It's Okay to Say No: Choosing Sexual Abstinence by Eleanor Ayer. Rosen, 1997. Both physical and emotional health are touted as benefits of abstinence. While the message fits in with many religious teachings, the author does not focus on religion but instead on self-respect and preparing for a healthy marriage.

It's Perfectly Normal: Changing Bodies, Growing Up, Sex and Sexual Health by Robie H. Harris, illustrated by Michael Emberley. Candlewick, 1994. Of the books in this focus box, *It's Perfectly Normal* is the most light-hearted and most appropriate for tweeners.

The Latina's Bible: The Nueva Latina's Guide to Love, Spirituality, Family, and La Vida by Sandra Guzmán. Three Rivers Press, 2002. While there is a wealth of information here, at least one of our Latina students was offended by what she viewed as overgeneralizations about sexual beliefs and practices.

101 Questions about Sex and Sexuality: With Answers for the Curious, Cautious, and Confused by Faith Hickman Brynie. 21st Century Books, 2003. While emphasizing that abstinence is the only sure way to avoid STDs and pregnancies, Brynie also provides contraceptive information. The questions were collected from middle school and high school students.

Sari Says: The Real Dirt on Everything from Sex to School by Sari Locker. HarperCollins, 2001. Locker is a *Teen People* online advice columnist. She

and the Internet: How to Stay Safe, Cherie Turner's *Everything You Need to Know about the Riot Grrl Movement: The Feminism of a New Generation,* and Katherine White's *Everything You Need to Know about Relationship Violence.* They also have a *Sports Girl* series with books on such subjects as competitive volleyball, track, figure skating, and soccer.

The exploration of sexual matters in books for young readers is an especially sensitive area for the following reasons:

has organized some of her best correspondence into this 321-page book.

The Shared Heart: Portraits and Stories Celebrating Lesbian, Gay, and Bisexual Young People by Adam Mastoon. HarperCollins, 1997. Photographer Mastoon took the thirty-nine pictures of the young people whose stories make up this book. Each is accompanied by a handwritten statement, plus a typeset page or two telling about their experiences relative to being gay.

Stay Strong: Simple Life Lessons for Teens by Terrie Williams with an introduction by Queen Latifah. Scholastic, 2001. Chapters include "Life Isn't Fair and Nothing You Do Matters," "How I Talk Is My Business," and "It's the 'In-Crowd' That Matters."

Staying Safe on Dates by Donna Chaiet. Rosen, 1996. Chaiet's goal is to help girls, starting with those in middle school, develop safety skills. She shows girls the wisdom of setting and maintaining verbal, emotional, and physical boundaries.

Straight Talk about Teenage Pregnancy by Paula Edelson. Facts on File, 1998. If readers wait until they are pregnant to buy this book, they won't get their money's worth because a good portion of it focuses on how to avoid pregnancy. However, there's still plenty of straight talk about parenting, adoption, and abortion.

Teen Fathers Today by Ted Gottfried. 21st Century Books, 2001. At last here is a book that acknowledges the contradictory feelings, the long-term implications, and the complexities of dealing with the baby's grandparents (both paternal and maternal). Contrary to the common notion that teen boys who father babies are interested only in casual sex, studies show that many have a continuing relationship with both the mother and the baby.

Teen People Sex Files, edited by Barbara O'Dair, Managing Editor of *Teen People.* Avon paperback, 2001. Most of the chapters are first-person as-told-to accounts in which teenagers tell about various sexual experiences. Concluding chapters include questions and answers and a glossary.

Teen Pregnancy, edited by Myra H. Immell. Gale/Greenhaven, 2001. Pregnant teens, health-care workers, educators, and professional writers for scientific journals are among the contributors to this book, which works well for both skimming and reading.

The Teenage Body Book, revised edition by Kathy McCoy and Charles Wibbelsman. Perigree, 1999. A new edition adds information on alternative medicine and on ethnic differences. In addition to the chapters on sex and sexuality, chapters that have proven their usefulness in earlier editions include ones on drugs, drinking, smoking, peer pressure, depression, stress, body image anxiety, fad diets, sports medicine, and how counseling can sometimes help.

The What's Happening to My Body? Book for Boys: A Growing-Up Guide for Parents and Sons and **The What's Happening to My Body? Book for Girls: A Growing-Up Guide for Parents and Daughters** by Lynda Madaras with Area Madaras. Newmarket, 2000. The prefaces encourage parents by giving them tips in how to talk to preteens and teens about their developing bodies and their changing emotions. These books are accessible to middle schoolers, while still acceptable to high schoolers. An especially good section in the book for girls talks about dealing with the kind of unwanted attention that is often given to girls who develop early.

1. Young adults are physically mature, but they probably have had little intellectual and emotional preparation for making sex-related decisions.
2. Parents are anxious to protect their children from making sex-related decisions that might prove harmful.
3. Old restraints and patterns of behavior and attitudes are being questioned, so that there is no clear-cut model to follow.

*I*nformation about STDs (Sexually Transmitted Diseases) is now included in virtually every sex-education book. But what teens seem to want even more than this kind of basic information is help in sorting out their emotions and relationships.

4. Sex is such an important part of American culture and the mass media that young people are forced to think about and take stands on such controversial issues as homosexuality, premarital sex, violence in relation to sex, and the role of sex in love and family relationships.

5. Talking about sexual attitudes and beliefs with their teenage children may make parents uncomfortable, especially if the father and the mother have different views. This means that many young people must get their information outside of the home.

While some books focus specifically on a problem such as AIDS or pregnancy, it is more common for books to cover emotional as well as physical aspects of sexual activity. No single book can satisfy all readers, and this is true of those dealing with sex education. An entire collection must be evaluated and books provided for a wide range of interests, attitudes, beliefs, and lifestyles. Those who criticize libraries for including books that present teenage sexual activity as the norm have a justified complaint if the library does not also have sex education books that present, or even promote, absti-nence as a normal route for young people.

Materials dealing with sex are judged quite differently from those on less contro-versial topics. For example, in most subject areas, books are given plus marks if they succeed in getting the reader emotionally involved, but with books about sex, some adults feel that it is better for young readers to be presented with straightforward, "plumbing manuals"—the less emotional involvement the better. Other adults argue that it is the emotional part that young people need to learn. Coming to agreement is not at all easy because adults have such varying attitudes and experiences.

Well-planned and well-written books can present information about different viewpoints, and teachers and librarians are performing a worthwhile service if they bring such books to the attention of young people. As we mentioned in Chapter 3, a new trend in women's magazines is to use sex-related articles as a selling point. In mag-azines for young women, many of the articles are written as though their purpose is sex education, when in fact they border on what *Playboy* editors once described as "pious pornography." Women who have inhibitions or feel guilty about sex can think and talk about sexuality as long as they are doing it to learn something, especially if they are made to feel that they are being unselfish in learning to "please their man." We were talking about this in one of our summer school classes, which had an unusually large number of parents in it, and casually remarked that maybe there was no longer a need for sex-education books because kids could get all the information they wanted from the Internet. There was an immediate uproar with the parents in the class saying there was a greater need than ever for well-thought-out and well-designed books, if for noth-ing more than warning kids against entering into sex-related conversations on web chat rooms, etc. The consensus from the parents was that they wanted their children to have nothing at all to do with sexual information posted on the Internet.

When helping young adults make reading decisions in this area, we need to con-sider the reader's purpose. If the reader wants basic information, nonfiction is far supe-rior because it can present a wider range of information in a clear, unambiguous way. But if the reader desires to understand the emotional and physical aspects of a partic-ular relationship, an honest piece of fiction usually does a better job.

The important thing for adults to remember is that they should provide both kinds of material in conjunction with a listening ear and a willingness to discuss questions. Schools and libraries need to seek community help in exchanging ideas and develop-ing policies. Family values must be respected, but honest, accurate information must also be available for those who seek it. Charting a course along this delicate line is more than any one individual should be expected to do, which is why people need to com-municate with each other. Professionals working with books are also obligated to find and study the latest, most authentic information and to bring that information to those who are helping to shape policies and practices. The general public may get away with objecting to or endorsing ideas and books that they have never explored or read. Not so for the professional charged with leading a group to consensus or compromise. The more you know about the materials, and the more you understand about individual and group differences, the better able you are to participate in book selection, discus-sion, and, sometimes, defense.

Outstanding Authors of Nonfiction for Young Adults

As the role of nonfiction has become increasingly recognized in the young adult market, a group of significant authors has emerged. Brent Ashabranner, Janet Bode, Rhoda Blumberg, Howard and Margery Facklam, William Loren Katz, Michael Kronenwetter, Susan Kuklin, and Patricia Lauber are writers whose names frequently appear on lists of recommended nonfiction. Frederick L. McKissack and Patricia C. McKissack's *Rebels Against Slavery: American Slave Revolts* was a 1997 Coretta Scott King Award Honor Book, while their *Let My People Go: Bible Stories Told by a Freeman of Color* and their *Young, Black, and Determined: A Biography of Lorrain Hansberry* were praised for the way they allowed readers to "drink in the whole civil rights history."

Catherine Reef's *This Our Dark Country: The American Settlers of Liberia* is of current interest at the time we are writing because the United States is being asked to play a peace-keeping role in Liberia. Her earlier books *Walt Whitman* and *Sigmund Freud: Pioneer of the Mind* were both praised for making complicated stories accessible to readers from middle school and up.

Marc Aronson's *Sir Walter Ralegh and the Quest for El Dorado* won the 2000 Boston Globe–Horn Book Award. It was praised for exploring a contradictory and complex Elizabethan figure who had a kind of passion that enabled him to be both a poet and a

*C*atherine Reef's book about Liberia could answer many of the questions people were asking in the spring of 2003, when Liberia was asking the United States to come and help settle the Civil War.

soldier. Aronson's *Art Attack: A Short Cultural History of the Avant-Garde* did an excellent job of tying together art, music, and literature with available Internet resources.

In addition to these authors, the ones described next can usually be trusted to provide the something extra that comes when a writer is truly involved in the subject and puts heart and soul into a book. We are not claiming that the following authors (introduced in alphabetical order and with only a sampling of their books) are the only ones about whom this could be said, but we are willing to say that they are among a growing body of nonfiction writers who prepare their books with the same kind of care and feeling that goes into the best fiction writing. As a side note, we were interested to notice that this listing of prolific and respected writers of informative nonfiction includes only men. In recent years, as people have begun paying more attention to relationships between gender and literacy (a subject discussed in Chapter 1), many people have observed that males are more attracted to nonfiction while females are attracted to fiction. This listing lends support to that observation.

Russell Freedman

Nearly thirty years elapsed between the time that Russell Freedman wrote his first book *Teenagers Who Made History* in 1961 and when he won the Newbery Award in 1988 for *Lincoln: A Photobiography.* Since then he has been honored with the Laura Ingalls Wilder Award, given every five years to honor a lifetime contribution. Among his most recent books are *Confucius: The Gold Rule, Martha Graham: A Dancer's Life,* and *Babe Didrikson Zaharias: The Making of a Champion.* These have between 175 and 200 pages and as such are longer than his earlier books. Freedman began his career by focusing mostly on books about animals for primary and middle grade readers. A turning point came when he attended an exhibition of historical photographs and found himself "communicating" with the young faces that stared out at him from the old photos. He searched out these and other pictures for a book *Immigrant Kids.* Since then he has made a specialty out of finding evocative photographs to use not as decoration but as an integral part of his books. He won the Orbis Pictus Award and the Boston Globe/Honor Book award for his 1990 *Franklin Delano Roosevelt.* His 1991 *The Wright Brothers* was a Newbery Honor Book and so was his 1993 *Eleanor Roosevelt: A Life of Discovery.* In his 1994 *Kids at Work: Lewis Hine and the Crusade Against Child Labor,* he wrote directly about the power of photography to document social conditions under which U.S. children labored. His *In Defense of Freedom: The Story of the Bill of Rights* was praised for its timeliness in 2003.

James Cross Giblin

Giblin's background as an editor of children's books stands him in good stead when he writes informational books. He chooses unlikely topics and then does enough research and careful planning and writing so that his readers find new and interesting information. His *The Life and Death of Adolf Hitler,* with over 80 archival photographs, won the Robert E. Silbert award for distinguished informational book. Its 246 pages are focused directly on Hitler, whom he describes as an "extraordinary villain." *The Riddle of the Rosetta Stone: Key to Ancient Egypt* is a fascinating detective story about how a large stone slab covered with writing in three different languages enabled linguists to decipher one of the world's first writing systems. *The Truth About Unicorns* serves as an excellent model for research as it traces the history of beliefs, superstitions, stories, and art about this mythical creature. His *Charles A. Lindbergh, A Human Hero* was chosen for several best-book lists based on Giblin's meticulous research and the skillful way that he balanced information about "an all-too-human-hero."

James (Jim) Haskins

As with many other authors of nonfiction, James Haskins writes both for children and for young adults. His main contribution has been to recognize the need for biographies and other books about minorities and to do something about it. Since the mid-1970s, he has consistently prepared books on African American heroes and African American history as well as on such topics as rights for people with disabilities, the U.S. labor movement, and women leaders in other countries (e.g., Corazon Aquino and Indira Gandhi). Among his most recent books are *Spike Lee: By Any Means Necessary; Bound for America: The Forced Migration of Africans to the New World,* illustrated by Floyd Cooper; *Get on Board: The Story of the Underground Railroad; I Have a Dream: The Life and Words of Martin Luther King, Jr.; Thurgood Marshall: A Life for Justice;* and *I Am Somebody! A Biography of Jesse Jackson.*

Albert Marrin

Albert Marrin earned a Ph.D. in history from Columbia University in 1968 and shortly thereafter began publishing history-related books. In 1985 his *1812: The War Nobody Won* was chosen as a Boston Globe–Horn Book Honor Book for Nonfiction. Since then, he has written well-received biographies on historical figures ranging from Abraham Lincoln to Adolph Hitler and from Sir Francis Drake to General Robert E. Lee. His *Dr. Jenner and the Speckled Monster: The Search for the Smallpox Vaccine* is a timely book because of new fears about vials of frozen virus preserved in laboratories around the world. His *Secrets from the Rocks: Dinosaur Hunting with Roy Chapman Andrews* is the story of a pioneering paleontologist who led five expeditions into China between 1922 and 1930. Less thoughtful writers would have been satisfied to focus on the excitement and danger of traveling into the Gobi Desert of Mongolia, but Marrin goes further and shows how the expeditions would have been different under today's sensibilities. For example, women were excluded from the expeditions, and he had no compunction about shooting rare animals or loading up treasures and bringing them out of the host countries he visited. A *School Library Journal* reviewer praised Marrin's *The Spanish-American War* for delineating "how American jingoists, expansionists, 'big navy' advocates, yellow journalists, and filibusters maneuvered the nation into taking part in what politicians called 'A splendid little war!'"

Milton Meltzer

Of all the nonfiction writers for young adults, Milton Meltzer is the one most consistently recognized as a spokesperson and champion of the genre. He focuses on social issues and for the third edition of this textbook wrote that except for inventing facts, he uses almost all the same techniques as do writers of fiction. Literary devices help him draw readers into the situation and the story that he is telling, and they help to enrich and deepen readers' feelings for people whose lives may be far different. He believes that it is not so much a question of fiction versus fact, but of truth versus falseness. His conclusion was that both fiction and nonfiction can lie about reality; but they can also tell the truth.

His 1998 *Food: How We Hunt and Gather It, How We Grow and Eat It, How We Buy and Sell It, How We Preserve and Waste It, and How Some Have Too Much and Others Have Too Little of It* grabbed attention for the length of its title as well as for its subject matter. Meltzer pioneered an in-their-own-words technique using historical journals, diaries, letters, and news accounts to bring out the personalities of such subjects as Abraham Lincoln, Frederick Douglass, and Andrew Carnegie. His recent books include *In the Days of the Pharaohs: A Look at Ancient Egypt, Piracy & Plunder: A Murderous Business, Ferdinand Magellan: First to Sail around the World,* and two beautifully illustrated companion books, *Ten Queens: Portraits of Power* and *Ten Kings and the Worlds They Ruled.*

Jim Murphy

Murphy's *Blizzard!* (the story of the great storm of 1888) was described by reviewers as not only humorous, jaw-dropping, and thought-provoking, but also *chilling.* Just as in *The Great Fire,* he blended history and adventure through focusing on the stories of individuals. His well-done *An American Plague: The True and Terrifying Story of the Yellow Fever Epidemic of 1793* (see the photo on p. 264) takes on more interest now that people are worried about the possibilities of biological terrorism. A good companion book would be Laurie Halse Anderson's novel *Fever,* which is set during the same epidemic. Murphy's *Inside the Alamo* was praised for the way it models the sorting out of historical information between folklore and true history, while *Pick & Shovel Poet: The Journeys of Pascal D'Angelo* was praised especially for the photographs, which were taken by D'Angelo after he migrated to American from Italy in 1910.

Laurence Pringle

Laurence Pringle is a respected and prolific writer of science-related books for young readers. For an earlier edition of this text, he discussed the challenge of being "fair" when writing about decision making that involves both social and scientific knowledge and attitudes. Because idealistic young readers may be especially vulnerable to one-sided arguments, he says that writers have a responsibility to present all sides of an issue and to show the gray as well as the black and white. He quickly adds, however, that being fair is not the same as being objective, "anyone who is well informed on an issue is not neutral," but that does not mean that he or she cannot work "to help kids understand the issues so they can make their own decisions."[7] Among Pringle's recent well-received books are *Drinking, A Risky Business* and *Jackal Woman: Exploring the World of Jackals,* in which he introduces middle school readers to the life of a behavioral ecologist, Patricia Moehlman. She was trained by Jane Goodall and is doing for jackals what Goodall did for chimpanzees. Other titles include *Chemical and Biological*

Warfare: The Cruelest Weapons; Oil Spills: Damage, Recovery and Prevention; Living Treasure: Saving Earth's Threatened Biodiversity; Global Warming; and *Rain of Trouble: The Science and Politics of Acid Rain.*

Concluding Comments

We will simply repeat the plea that we made at the beginning of this chapter where we said that in the real world nonfiction gets a greater share of people's money and attention than does fiction. Because there is so much of it, adults working with young readers have an even greater responsibility to help to winnow the wheat from the chaff and to bring to students' attention the books that they are likely to want and need. We also have the obligation that Mary E. Mueller pointed out in an Up for Discussion piece, "History and History Makers" that she wrote for the November 1991 *School Library Journal.* With shrinking budgets, all of us know that we need to buy new computer books, but we hesitate to spend money on new historical and informative books and on new biographies. But, she wrote, that with changing attitudes and outlooks—which, we add, is even more true for self-help books—these sections of a library need just as much loving care and attention, including weeding, replacing, and promoting, as do any other sections of a library.

 Notes

[1] Paul Hirth, "What's the Truth about Nonfiction?" *English Journal* 91:4 (March 2002): 20–22.

[2] "A Conversation with Milton Meltzer," in *Nonfiction for Young Adults: From Delight to Wisdom* by Betty Carter and Richard F. Abrahamson (Orxy Press, 1990), pp. 53–54.

[3] Milton Meltzer, "Where Do All the Prizes Go? The Case for Nonfiction," *Horn Book Magazine* 52 (February 1975): 23.

[4] George A. Woods, personal correspondence to Alleen Pace Nilsen, Summer 1978.

[5] Michiko Kakutani, "Biography as a Blood Sport," *New York Times,* May 20, 1994, pp. B1, B6.

[6] Mary E. Mueller, "Up for Discussion: History and History Makers: Give YAs the Whole Picture," *School Library Journal* 37 (November 1991): 55–56.

[7] Laurence Pringle, "Laurence Pringle on Trying to Be Fair," *Literature for Today's Young Adults,* 4th Edition by Alleen Pace Nilsen and Kenneth L. Donelson. (HarperCollins, 1993), p. 314.

CHAPTER

10

Evaluating, Promoting, and Using Young Adult Books

Chances are that you are studying adolescent literature because you expect to work, or are already working, in a situation that calls for you to bring young adults in touch with books. This chapter begins with a section on evaluation, including the evaluation of literature for and about minorities, followed by discussions centered around common professional roles for adults who work with books and young readers: librarians, reading teachers, social studies teachers, parents, and counselors or youth workers. (See Chapter 11 for specific information for English teachers.) These areas were chosen to give focus and organization to the information, but there is considerable overlap.

Everyone working with young readers and books needs to be skilled in suggesting the right book for the right student or at least pointing someone in the right direction. When two people are talking about a book they both enjoyed, there is no way to divide the conversation into such discrete categories as literary analysis, personal feelings, sociological implications, and evaluation of potential popularity. Librarians find themselves discussing books as if they were classroom teachers. Teachers can adopt some of the promotional techniques that librarians use, and librarians can use some book discussion tactics that teachers use. In short, the organization of this chapter may make it appear that librarians work with young readers and books quite differently from teachers or counselors. In reality, nearly all adults who work with young readers and books have much the same goals and share many of the same approaches.

All of us meet wide-ranging differences in abilities and personalities, which implies great differences in interests. Those interests demand an alert and prepared adult who is aware of them, who can uncover them, and who is familiar with an enormous number of titles to meet them. To an inexperienced person, the information about books that a librarian or teacher can call forth seems magical, but developing that repertoire takes time, patience, and hard work. Reading many young adult books comes with the territory for the professional, but so does reading professional books, magazines of all sorts, several newspapers, adult books, and much, much more. The professional likes to read (or would not be working with books), so that makes the job easier and more fun, but the professional reads beyond the areas that are personally enjoyable. For example, whether a professional likes science fiction or not, he or she must know titles of new science fiction. When young adults ask a teacher or librarian for another book like *The Martian Chronicles* (or the *Redwall* books or *The Hitchhiker's Guide to the Galaxy* or *The Perks of Being a Wallflower* or *The Color Purple*), they pay that person a sublime compliment. Woe unto the teacher or librarian who says, "I'm sorry, but I don't know anything about science fiction," or "Why don't you broaden your reading background just a bit?" Such a response kills interest and will probably turn kids away from reading.

Evaluating Young Adult Literature

The role of the evaluator of books for young adults is more important than ever because more books are being published and publishers are opting for shorter life spans for all books. With so many ephemeral books around, there's a greater need for knowledgeable people to find and promote the excellent ones. It is ironic that when there are more books to choose from, most schools and libraries have less money to spend. Also, book prices have increased more than budgets, so that if a purchasing mistake is made, especially with a series or a set of books, a proportionately larger bite is taken out of school, library, and personal budgets.

Writing about Books

If you devote your professional life to working with young people and books, chances are that at some level you will be involved in evaluating books and helping to decide which ones will receive prizes and get starred reviews and which ones should be ignored or receive "Not Recommended" labels. Teachers and librarians working with books for young people have more opportunity to be among the decision makers than do those working with books for adults because fewer than two dozen people in the United States are full-time reviewers of juvenile books. The bulk of the reviewing is done by teachers and librarians who evaluate books both as part of their assigned workloads and as a professionally related hobby. Regardless of whether you wish to be one of these reviewers, you need to know what is involved, so that you will understand how the work of these people can help you in selecting the books that are best for your purposes. The sheer number of books published each year makes it necessary that book lovers share the reading responsibilities and pool their information through written evaluations.

Evaluation underlies nearly all writing about books. Even when someone is simply making notes to serve as a reminder of the contents of a book, that person is making an evaluation and concluding that the book is worth remembering. Three concerns run throughout the evaluation of young adult literature:

1. What different types of writing meet specific needs, and how can they do it best?
2. Should reviews of young adult books be less promotional and more critical?
3. Is the writing and scholarship in the field aimed too much at the uses of literature rather than at the analysis of the literature itself?

Keeping a Record of Your Reading

The type of writing most often done by teachers and librarians is the making of note cards or, in this day of word processors, typing paragraph-length descriptions filed according to whatever organization is most helpful to the writer. This might be alphabetical or by subject matter, age level, or genre. The advantage to the computerized annotations is that they can be pulled out and reorganized for many different purposes, including booktalking, creating a display, or making a bibliography tailored to a teacher's request for books on the Holocaust, for example, or books about Native Americans. Regularly going over your write-ups jogs your memory about the books you have read and can personally recommend, and when a title or author slips your mind, you can probably find what you need by doing word searches through your write-ups.

Comments vary according to the needs of the writer but should include at least the following:

Author's name and complete book title.

Publisher (both hardback and paperback) with original publication date.

A short summary of the story, including the characters' names and other details that make this book different.

A brief evaluation and any ideas about how you might make special use of the book.

Librarians sometimes write their descriptions in the form of a booktalk identifying a page they could read aloud, while reading teachers note the level of reading difficulty, and English teachers may mention how the book might illustrate a particular literary

---

Shipwreck at the Bottom of the World: The Extraordinary True Story of Shackleton and the Endurance by Jennifer Armstrong. Crown, 1998.

134 pp. 40 B&W photos. Ages 12 and up.

From August 1914 until August 1916, British explorer Sir Ernest Shackleton and his crew of 27 men, which included two doctors, several scientists, and one stowaway, made an incredible journey. They planned to be the first men to cross Antarctica, the most hostile place on earth. Instead, their ship was caught in ice when they were still 100 miles from land. Pressure from the ice gradually crushed the ship and during the next 19 months they set new records for human endurance and bravery as they worked to save themselves. Not one man died. The amazingly clear photographs and diary entries are available because from the beginning the plan was to document the trip for the patrons who financed it. On the night they had to leave the camp they had made by the frozen-in ship, Shackleton set an example for his men by dumping onto the snow the gold coins from his pockets as well as the inscribed Bible which the Queen had given him. He kept only a page from the Book of Job about the hoary frost of Heaven. **Bottom of pp. 51–52 is good for reading aloud.**

---

principle. A youth worker might make a note about the potential of the book as a catalyst to get kids talking along certain lines, whereas a teacher who anticipates that the book could be controversial is wise to note positive reviews and honors.

Even if you prepare your notes on a computer, teachers and librarians tell us it is also a good idea to do a printout on card stock. Of course it makes sense to have a hard copy backup to your computer files, but more important is the fact that a box of cards on your desk is a constant reminder. It is also more accessible and easier to use on the spur of the moment. The sample card above is for a beautifully designed book that grabs readers' attention for either leisure-time reading or for filling assignments related to history and biographies or even photography and journalism.

Writing Annotations

Annotations are similar to note cards, but they are usually written for someone else to see rather than for the writer's own use. Because they are usually part of an annotated bibliography or list in which space is at a premium, as in the Focus Boxes throughout this text, writers must make efficient use of every word. Communicating the plot and tone of a book as well as a recommendation in only one or two interesting sentences is challenging, but no one wants to read lists of characters and plot summaries all starting with "This book . . . ." That annotations can be intriguing as well as communicative is shown by the following two samples for Garret Freymann-Weyr's *My Heartbeat*. To save space, the bibliographical information given on the lists is not reprinted here. These annotations both appeared as part of end-of-the-year best-book lists, so there is already an assumption that the book is well written. However, it is a good idea to add information if a book has won a prize as did the *Booklist* writer who referred to the journal's best book list.

> Three sophisticated Manhattan teens struggle with their shifting relationships and uncertainty about the future. This tightly constructed, smart novel speaks volumes about love, friendship, and sexual identity.
>
> *School Library Journal*, December 2002

> The family dynamics are as compelling as the love and friendship drama, as 14-year-old Ellen discovers she loves her brother's best friend, who loves her brother, who is scared that he's gay. A beautiful, frank, upbeat story of teen bisexual love in all its uncertainty, pain, and joy. (Top of the List Winner-Youth Fiction.)
>
> *Booklist*, January 1 & 15, 2003.

Notice how efficiently both writers communicated the complicated plot, and without making the book sound salacious—which it is not—got across the point that homosexuality was involved. The *SLJ* reviewer communicated the tone of the book by describing it as a *smart novel* and the protagonists as *sophisticated Manhattan teens,* while the *Booklist* reviewer achieved a similar effect with such adjectives as *beautiful, frank,* and *upbeat. Uncertainty* is a good one-word description of the book's theme as reflected in the fact that both reviewers chose to use it.

See Appendix B for magazines and journals devoted to the evaluation and promotion of literature for young readers.

How much you put in an annotation depends on its purpose. If you are recommending titles on a book mark, space is so limited that you will probably want to use just descriptive phrases and key words rather than whole sentences, and for that purpose the most important part might be the library's call number. Several of the journals (shown in the photograph above) print cumulative booklists showing the best books of a particular year or in a particular genre. A key sentence is excerpted or adapted from the original review, and the date of the review is given for those who want to go back and get a fuller picture.

Writing Reviews

A problem in reviewing juvenile books is that more books are published than can be reviewed in the media. (See Appendix B for major reviewing sources for young adult books.) In addition to these, dozens of national publications carry occasional review articles, and many library systems sponsor reviewing groups whose work is published either locally or through such nationally distributed publications as *Book Waves,* from the Bay Area (northern California) Young Adult Librarians, and *Books for the Teen Age,* from the Young Adult Services Office of the New York Public Library. Also, some teachers of children's and young adult literature work with their students to write regular review columns for local newspapers.

The field of juvenile reviewing is sometimes criticized for being too laudatory because the reviews are written by book lovers who are anxious to "sell" literature. One reason is that it's the publishers of well-established authors who can afford to send out review copies. Also, those editors who have room for only a limited number of reviews devote their space to the books they think are the best, so of course the reviews are usually positive.

The fact that juvenile books are reviewed mostly by librarians and teachers working on a part-time basis slows down the reviewing process, especially if they take time to incorporate the opinions of young readers. With adult books, reviews often come out before or simultaneously with the publication of the book, but with juvenile titles it is not uncommon to see reviews appearing a full year or more after the book was released. Once young adult books are launched, however, they are likely to stay afloat much longer than adult bestsellers because teachers work them into classroom units, librarians promote them, and paperback book clubs keep selling them for years. Children continue to grow older and to advance in their reading skill and taste, so that every year a whole new set of students is ready to read *A Separate Peace, The Catcher in the Rye,* and *The Outsiders.* As a result, reviews, articles, and papers continue to cover particular titles years after their original publication dates.

People generally evaluate books based on literary quality, reader interest, potential popularity, or what the book is teaching (i.e., its social and political philosophy). Evaluators should make clear their primary emphasis lest readers misunderstand them. For example, a critic may review a book positively because of its literary quality, but a reader will interpret the positive review as a prediction of popularity. The book is purchased and put on the shelf, where it is ignored by teenagers. Consequently, the purchaser feels cheated and loses confidence in the reviewing source.

In an attempt to resolve that kind of conflict, when Mary K. Chelton and Dorothy M. Broderick founded *VOYA (Voice of Youth Advocates),* they devised the evaluation code shown in Table 10.1. Each review is preceded by a Q number, indicating *quality,* and a P number, indicating *popularity.* They suggest that a fringe benefit to using such a clearly outlined code is that it helps librarians analyze their buying patterns. Those who lean heavily toward either quality or popularity see their biases and are able to strike a more appropriate balance.

A quite different set of criteria from either popularity or literary quality is that of social or political values. Most reviewers—whether or not they realize it—are influenced by their personal feelings toward how a book treats social issues. For example, Sue Ellen Bridgers's *Notes for Another Life* was highly recommended and praised in *Horn Book Magazine,* the *New York Times Book Review,* and the *Bulletin of the Center for Children's Books,* but when Janet French reviewed the book for *School Library Journal* she wrote:

> The blurb suggests that this is "a family chronicle for all ages." It would have been more accurate to describe it as a propaganda vehicle for female domesticity. Good women subordinate their talents and yearnings to the home and their children; all other paths lead to havoc. For a riveting story of four deserted children, lead readers instead to Cynthia Voigt's marvelous upbeat *Homecoming.*[1]

This review was written in such a way that readers can easily recognize that the reviewer's opinion was shaped by her disagreement with the plot. For a reviewer to use this as the basis for a negative recommendation is perfectly justifiable *if* the situation is made clear. The problem comes when reviewers reject books based on such social issues but don't admit to themselves, much less to their readers, that their feelings have

TABLE 10.1   VOYA EVALUATION CODE

Quality	Popularity
5Q: Hard to imagine it being better written	5P: Every young adult was dying to read it yesterday
4Q: Better than most, marred only by occasional lapses	4P: Broad general young adult interest
3Q: Readable without serious defects	3P: Will appeal without pushing
2Q: A little better editing or work by the author would have made it 3Q	2P: For the young adult reader with a special interest in the subject
1Q: Hard to understand how it got published	1P: No young adult will read unless forced to for assignments

been influenced by whether a story sharpens or dulls whatever personal ax they happen to be grinding.

There are as many reviewing styles as there are journals and individual reviewers. Nearly all reviews contain complete bibliographical information, including number of pages and prices, perhaps a cataloguing number, the intended age level, a summary statement of the contents, and some hint of the quality of the book as evaluated by the reviewer. A few years ago, an issue of *Top of the News* (the ALA publication now evolved into *YALS* (Young Adult Library Services) had as its feature topic "Reviews, Reviewing, and the Review Media." Editor Audrey Eaglen solicited answers to the question, "What makes a good review?"[2] Here are excerpts from some of the responses:

> An intelligent review . . . is never obsequious, if it is favorable. It is never flip, if it is unfavorable. It never quotes from the front flap.
>
> Rosemary Wells, author

> Are there any clever devices or intriguing aspects of the book which could be used to pique the interest of a group and "sell" the book? Also I need to be alerted to potentially controversial issues, be it strong language, explicit sex, violence, or whatever, not so I can avoid buying the book, but so I can plan and prepare and thereby deal with a conflict should it arise.
>
> Katherine Haylman, school librarian

> How attractive is the cover? While we might feel that no one should judge a book by its cover, the truth is that everyone does.
>
> Dorothy Broderick, editor and educator

> I want a clear-cut commitment as to recommendation or nonrecommendation. I don't have the time to read every book published, and I'm hoping that some literate person will help me decide where to invest my reading hours.
>
> Walter Dean Myers, author

Does the book have magic for YA's? Are there format faults, for example, does the size and shape make it look like a baby book? Is the word *children* used anywhere on the dust jacket? And if there is going to be a film or television tie-in, who are the stars and when will it be released?

Patty Campbell, author and critic

Writing reviews is a skill that improves with practice and effort. A good way to begin developing this skill is to study several reviews of the same book as they appear in different publications. Note the essentials that seem to be the same in each review and then compare the information that is different. See if you can explain the differences in light of the source's reading audience.

For the person reading reviews, one of the biggest problems is that they all run together and begin to sound the same. To keep this from happening, reviewers need to approach their task with the same creative spirit with which authors write books. They need to think of new ways of putting across the point that a book is highly recommended or that it has some unique quality that readers should watch for, as in these two excerpts of reviews that were written by authors reviewing books written by other authors. Granted, authors probably have had more practice in working with words, and therefore their skill is greater than that of most reviewers, but they probably also try harder because they know how important it is to do something to make a review stand out, to give the reader something by which to remember the book.

The first excerpt is taken from a review of Alice Childress's *Rainbow Jordan,* written by Anne Tyler for the *New York Times Book Review:*

Rainbow is so appealing that she could carry this book on her own, but she doesn't have to. There's Miss Josie, who gives us her clearer view to balance what Rainbow tells us. . . . And there's the mother herself—short-tempered, inconsistent, sometimes physically abusive, not much of a mother at all, really. Seen through Rainbow's adoring eyes, she's at least someone we can understand ("Life is complicated," Rainbow says, "I love her even now while I'm putting her down."). In fact, Rainbow's story moves us not because of her random beatings or financial hardships, but because Rainbow needs her mother so desperately that she will endlessly rationalize, condone, overlook, forgive. She is a heartbreakingly sturdy character, and *Rainbow Jordan* is a beautiful book.[3]

Katherine Paterson made these comments about Virginia Hamilton's *Sweet Whispers, Brother Rush* as part of an article she wrote for the *New York Times Book Review:*

There are those who say that Virginia Hamilton is a great writer but that her books are hard to get into. This one is not. It fairly reaches off the first page to grab you, and once it's got you, it sets you spinning deeper into its story. Needless to say, this is not a conventional ghost story. In fact, the function of the ghost in this book is to provide 14-year-old Tree Pratt with a place from which to view her world. . . . In this book everyone we meet, including the ghost, is wonderfully human. . . . The language too is of Miss Hamilton's own special kind, which uses the speech forms of the young to enhance rather than restrict the music of the book.[4]

NANCY FARMER
On Learning to Write

I came to writing after age 40 and my success has cheered up a great many older people. They feel they missed opportunities when they were young. Now it's too late. But my career shows that simply isn't true. I get asked all the time how I trained myself to write, and now I'm going to give you the answers.

I started out in Zimbabwe about 4,000 miles from the nearest creative writing department. It was clear any instructions would have to come from books. The problem was, there weren't many books in central Africa. Luckily, the British Council had a library. I started my studies with Joan Aiken's *How to Write for Children* and John Braine's *How to Write a Novel.* I read Raymond Chandler for creative language, Stephen King to learn how to build suspense, Ruth Rendell and P. D. James for plot.

This is what I discovered: You learn how a novel is put together by reading one of your favorites three times in a row. The first time you're carried away by the story. By the third reading, you begin to pick up how it's put together. You can also learn by *typing* a novel. Plot, scene, and character can be learned physically, like swimming or riding a bicycle. Try it if you don't believe me. You write the first draft of your own book without stopping. No rewrites. No agonizing over the perfect jeweled sentence. This preserves the excitement. *Then* you make an outline and rewrite.

Everyone should have a good literary background, but train your ear for writing *by reading books that have been published in the past ten years.* I can't tell you how important that is. Most people start out writing like their grandparents. It's probably influenced by what they studied in school. I had no up-to-date children's books and so I studied P. L. Travers and C. S. Lewis. I had many *Gentle Reader, I fear our hero was in for a rude surprise when—* kind of lines. Worse, I'd been in Africa so long I'd lost touch with U.S. speech patterns. I hope no one *ever* gets hold of my earlier works and that all the copies get devoured by termites. Really.

Fortunately, a set of Newbery and Caldecott books was donated to a school. I sweet-talked the school into letting me read them. This was tremendously valuable training, because the next lesson I learned was this: Measure yourself against the best in the field. Any lower standard is a waste of time.

I approached writing the same way I approached getting a college degree. You work full-time for four years and then you get a diploma, only for a writer your diploma is a book contract.

Now that you've learned everything I know, you can go out there and write, write, write. My method, by the way, works for people under 40, too.

Nancy Farmer's books include *The House of the Scorpion,* Atheneum, 2002; *A Girl Named Disaster,* Orchard, 1996; *The Warm Place,* Orchard, 1996; and *The Ear, The Eye, and the Arm,* Orchard, 1994.

Writing Scholarly and Pedagogical Articles

A fourth kind of writing about young adult books is made up of articles or papers that go into more depth than is possible in reviews. Because most reviewers of juvenile books have little hope of coming out with a "scoop" or of being the first one to pass judgment on a new book, they focus on deeper treatments or on tying several books together. Dorothy Mathews analyzed the writing about adolescent literature that appeared in professional journals over a five-year period.[5] She categorized the writing into three types. First were those articles that focus on the subjective responses of readers to particular books, such as reader surveys, lists of popular titles, and reviews written from the point of view of how the book is likely to affect young readers. Articles of this kind are primarily descriptive.

The second type was also descriptive and consisted of pedagogical articles giving teachers lists of books that fit together for teaching units; ideas for book promotion; and techniques for teaching reading, social studies, or English. They may include brief comments on the literary qualities of the novels, but, again, the writer's primary intention is to be informative.

The third kind of writing was that restricted to the books themselves. It is in this group that Matthews thinks hope lies for developing a body of lasting scholarly knowledge that will be taken seriously by the academic community. These papers include discussions of adolescent literature as a genre, historical background of the field, relationships between authors and their work, patterns that appear in young adult novels, and themes and underlying issues. More of this kind of literary analysis is being done as authors write books serious enough to support it. Examples of some of these articles are included in Appendix C, "Some Outstanding Books and Articles about Young Adult Literature."

Twayne Publishers paved the way for some serious extended criticism of young adult literature when they inaugurated a Young Adult Authors subset in their *United States Authors* series. More than a dozen books were completed under such titles as *Presenting Judy Blume, Presenting Sue Ellen Bridgers, Presenting Robert Cormier,* and so on. Rosa Guy, S. E. Hinton, M. E. Kerr, Norma Klein, Kathryn Lasky, Norma Fox Mazer, Walter Dean Myers, Zibby Oneal, Richard Peck, William Sleator, Mildred Taylor, Barbara Wersba, and Paul Zindel are among the featured authors.

When Twayne ceased publishing, editor Patty Campbell moved to the Scarecrow Press, which inaugurated *Scarecrow Studies in Young Adult Literature.* Books on individual authors include Jeanne M. McGlinn's *Ann Rinaldi: Historian and Storyteller,* Pamela Sissi Carroll's *Caroline Cooney: Faith and Fiction,* Lois Thomas Stover's *Jacqueline Woodson: "The Real Thing,"* Arthea J. S. Reed's *Norma Fox Mazer: A Writer's World,* Edith S. Tyson's *Orson Scott Card: Writer of the Terrible Choice,* Walter Hogan's *The Agony and the Eggplant: Daniel Pinkwater's Heroic Struggles in the Name of YA Literature,* and Suzanne Elizabeth Reid's *Virginia Euwer Wolff: Capturing the Music of Young Voices.* Even more interesting are books in the series that explore ideas or genres as with Chris Crowe's *More Than a Game: Sports Literature for Young Adults,* Marc Aronson's *Beyond the Pale: New Essays for a New Era,* Connie S. Zitlow's *Lost Masterworks of Young Adult Literature,* and Joanne Brown and Nancy St. Clair's *Declarations of Independence: Empowered Girls in Young Adult Literature, 1990–2001.*

Also, a look into a recent edition of *Dissertation Abstracts International* shows an increasing number of dissertations being written on young adult literature. The majority of topics, however, deal more with social or pedagogical issues than with literary ones.

To summarize, writing about young adult books falls into four categories: descriptions for personal use, annotations, reviews, and scholarly or pedagogical writing. Most of you will be involved in the first kind, that is, making note cards for your own use. But some of you will also be making annotations, writing reviews, and doing scholarly or pedagogical analyses. This latter kind of writing and critiquing can be especially intriguing because significant changes have occurred within recent years and relatively few scholars have worked with young adult literature. This means there is ample opportunity for original research and observation, whether from the viewpoint of a literary scholar, a teacher, a librarian, or a counselor or youth worker. The field as a whole will grow strong as a result of serious and competent criticism and analysis.

Deciding on the Literary Canon

Educators are finding themselves in the midst of a lively debate over what books should be taught in U.S. classrooms. An oversimplification of the issue is to say that on one side are those who believe in acculturation or assimilation. They think that if we all read approximately the same books, we will come away with similar values and attitudes and, hence, be a more united society. On the other side are those who believe in diversity and want individuals and groups to find their own values, attitudes, and ways of life reflected in the literature they read. This latter group views the traditional literary canon as racist and sexist, with its promotion in schools serving to keep minorities and women "in their place."

Katha Pollitt, contributing editor of *The Nation*, made some interesting observations when she wrote that, "In a country of real readers a debate like the current one over the canon would not be taking place." She described an imaginary country where children grow up watching their parents read and going with them to well-supported public libraries where they all borrow books and read and read and read. At the heart of every school is an attractive and well-used library, and in classrooms children have lively discussions about books they have read together, but they also read lots of books on their own, so that years later they don't remember whether "they read *Jane Eyre* at home and Judy Blume in class, or the other way around."

Pollitt wrote that in her imaginary country of "real readers—voluntary, active, self-determined readers," a discussion of which books should be studied in school would be nothing more than a parlor game. It might even add to the aura of writers not to be included on school-assigned reading lists because this would mean that their books were "in one way or another too heady, too daring, too exciting to be ground up into institutional fodder for teenagers." The alternative would be millions of readers freely choosing millions of books, each book becoming just a tiny part of a lifetime of reading. Pollitt concluded her piece with the sad statement that at the root of the current debate over the canon is the assumption that the only books that will be read are those that are assigned in school: "Becoming a textbook is a book's only chance: all sides take that for granted." She wonders why those educated scholars and critics who are currently debating this issue and must be readers themselves have conspired to keep secret two facts that they surely must know:

> . . . if you read only twenty-five, or fifty, or a hundred books, you can't understand them, however well chosen they are. And . . . if you don't have an independent reading life—and very few students do—you won't *like* reading the books on the list and will forget them the minute you finish them.[6]

Pollitt's argument puts even more of a burden on those of us who have as our professional responsibility the development of lifelong readers. We are the ones who should be raising our voices to explain the limitations of expecting children to read just what is assigned in class. We are also the ones with the responsibility of helping students develop into the kinds of committed and enthusiastic readers that Pollitt described in her imaginary country.

In the meantime, we also have an obligation to become knowledgeable about the issues that underlie the current debate over the literary canon and to assist schools and libraries in making informed choices with the resources they have. We, as authors of this textbook, have already committed ourselves to the idea of an expanded canon. Some of the harshest critics of adolescent literature are those in favor of promoting only the traditional canon; others tolerate adolescent literature only because they view it as a means to the desired end of leading students to appreciate "real" literature.

At the 1991 National Council of Teachers of English convention in Seattle, Washington, Rudolfo Anaya, author of *Bless Me, Ultima* and a professor of creative writing at the University of New Mexico, talked about the incorporation of minority literature

National Council of Teachers of English, 1997. Fifteen educators contributed chapters with such titles as "Negotiating the Meaning of Difference: Talking Back to Multicultural Literature," "Out of the Closet and onto the Bookshelves: Images of Gays and Lesbians in Young Adult Literature," and "Reader Response Theory and the Politics of Multicultural Literature."

Roots and Branches: A Resource of Native American Literature—Themes, Lessons, and Bibliographies by Dorothea M. Susag, foreword by Joseph Bruchac. National Council of Teachers of English, 1998. An especially interesting chapter is the one on Non-Native Authors and Their Stories about Native Americans. Helpful appendices include information on geographical, spiritual, cultural, and historical contexts; stereotypes; and regional publications from the North Central U.S. where the author teaches.

Teaching and Learning about Multicultural Literature: Students Reading Outside Their Culture in a Middle School Classroom by Janice Hartwick Dressel. International Reading Association, 2003. Dressel worked with a teacher of 123 eighth graders, mostly from the dominant culture. They

were reading a variety of multicultural literature and Dressel studied their responses, which focused as much on differences in power as on differences in color.

Teaching the Short Story: A Guide to Using Stories from Around the World, edited by Bonnie H. Neumann and Helen M. McDonnell. National Council of Teachers of English, 1996. A page or more is devoted to each of 175 stories by outstanding writers from dozens of different countries. While the underlying premise is that people should know about other cultures, the message is taught inductively rather than through overt preaching.

Teaching and Using Multicultural Literature in Grades 9–12: Moving Beyond the Canon, edited by Arlette Willis. Christopher-Gordan, 1998. Ten contributors wrote chapters on literature from such specific groups as African Americans, Puerto Ricans, Asian and Pacific Americans, Native Americans, Mexican Americans, and Caribbean Americans. Introductory and concluding chapters discuss both philosophy and methods.

into the mainstream. He did not mean just the inclusion on booklists of the names of authors who are members of minority groups but also the incorporation of new styles and ideas into the writing of nonminority authors.

One example is the incorporation into mainstream literature of the kinds of magical realism that for a long time has been common in Hispanic literature. Another way is through the desegregation of characters. See Focus Box 4.5, Relating across Cultures, on p. 129 for examples. Also see Focus Box 10.1, Books to Help Adults with Multicultural Materials.

Anaya went on to explain that Mexican Americans have a different worldview. When he was in college, he loved literature and read the standard literary canon with enthusiasm and respect, but when he went to write his own stories, he couldn't use Hemingway or Milton as models. He could create plots like theirs, but then he was at a standstill because nowhere in the literary canon did he find people like the ones he knew. His Spanish-speaking family has lived in eastern New Mexico for more than 100 years. The harsh but strangely beautiful landscape and the spirit of the Pecos River had permeated his life, as had stories of *La Grande*, the wise old woman who had safely pulled him from his mother's body even though the umbilical cord was wrapped around his neck. There were also stories of *La Llorona,* a woman who had gone insane and murdered her children and whose tortured cries traveled on the wind around the corners of his childhood home. All his life, such dramatic dreams and stories were woven in and out of reality, but nowhere in the literature that he studied in school did he find such stories.

Anaya worked on *Bless Me, Ultima* for seven years, during which he felt he was "writing in a vacuum. I had no Chicano models to read and follow, no fellow writers to turn to for help. Even Faulkner, with his penchant for the fantastic world of the South, could not help me in Mexican/Indian New Mexico. I would have to build from what I knew best." He went on to explain:

> I began to discover that the lyric talent I possessed, as the poet I once aspired to be, could be used in writing fiction. The oral tradition which so enriched my imagination as a child could lend its rhythm to my narrative. Plot techniques learned in Saturday afternoon movies and comic books could help as much as the grand design of the classics I had read. Everything was valuable, nothing was lost.[7]

Anaya's observations about not having models to follow and being forced to create a new narrative style to tell a story coming from his own experience relates to the frustration that teachers and librarians often express when they go to look for young adult novels about minority characters. They look for the same kinds of coming-of-age stories that are typical in mainstream young adult literature except they want the characters to have brown skin and "different" names. The absence of such books, especially such books written by Native American authors, is in itself part of the cultural difference. We've noticed that the more closely a book with a Native American protagonist resembles what we described in Chapter 1 as a typical young adult book, the greater the chance that the author is not a Native American and that the protagonist is of mixed parentage or is living apart from the native culture.

Young adult books containing mystical elements tied in with Native American themes are another example of how Anaya's prediction that ethnic writing will become incorporated into the mainstream is coming true. Not everyone, however, is pleased to see this kind of incorporation because they view the books as contaminated or impure. The authors have used old legends and beliefs for their own purposes, interweaving them with contemporary situations and ideas. Also, several of the authors are not Native Americans.

Being in the blood line of a particular group, however, does not guarantee acceptance by the group. For example, most high school teachers think they are contributing to an awareness of cultural diversity and the enlargement of the literary canon by leading students to read Maxine Hong Kingston's *Woman Warrior.* But noted Chinese writer Frank Chin criticizes Kingston, along with Amy Tan for *The Joy Luck Club* and David Henry Hwang for his plays, *F. O. B.* and *M. Butterfly.* He accuses these writers of "boldly faking" Chinese fairy tales and childhood literature. Then he goes on to ask and answer the question of why the most popular "Chinese" works in the United States are consistent with each other but inconsistent with Chinese culture and beliefs:

That's easy: (1) All the authors are Christian, (2) the only form of literature written by Chinese Americans that major publishers will publish (other than the cookbook) is autobiography, an exclusively Christian form [based on confession]; and (3) they all write to the specifications of the Christian stereotype of Asia being as opposite morally from the West as it is geographically.[8]

Chin's comments are in an essay, "Come All Ye Asian American Writers," that is used as an introduction to an anthology entitled *The Big Aiiieeeee!,* apparently put together for use in college classes. The 619-page book is too intimidating for most high school students, but they could appreciate many of the individual stories, poems, and essays. The book's title comes from the sound in movies, television, radio, and comic books assigned to "the yellow man" who "when wounded, sad, or angry, or swearing, or wondering" either "whined, shouted, or screamed, 'Aiieeeee!'"

Chin's introductory essay illustrates the complexities involved in the whole matter of ethnic differences. As Chin goes on to state his case, he brings in religion and gender differences as well as differences caused by race, history, social class, and politics. In answer to the kind of criticism he offers, Kingston has explained:

> Sinologists have criticized me for not knowing myths and for distorting them; pirates [those who illegally translate her books for publication in Taiwan and China] correct my myths, revising them to make them conform to some traditional Chinese version. They don't understand that myths have to change, be useful or be forgotten. Like the people who carry them across oceans, the myths become American. The myths I write are new, American. That's why they often appear as cartoons and Kung Fu movies. I take the power I need from whatever myth. Thus Fa Mu Lan has the words cut into her back; in traditional story, it is the man, Ngak Fei the Patriot, whose parents cut vows on his back. I mean to take his power for women.[9]

Knowledge of these opposing viewpoints should not frighten teachers back into the comforts of the established canon; instead, it should help teachers prepare for meeting the challenges involved in going beyond the "tried and true."

Teaching Ethnic Literature

Most educators feel a duty to bring ethnic-based literature to young people in hopes of increasing general understanding. Besides that lofty goal, here are some additional reasons for making special efforts to bring ethnic books to young people:

- Young readers can identify with characters who straddle two worlds because they have similar experiences in going between the worlds of adulthood and childhood.
- Motifs that commonly appear in ethnic-based stories—including loneliness, fear of rejection, generational differences, and troubles in fitting into the larger society—are meaningful to teenagers.

- Nearly all teenagers feel that their families are somehow different, and so they can identify with the theme of family "differentness" that often finds its way into stories about immigrant families.
- Living in harmony with nature is a common theme, especially in Native American literature, and this theme appeals to today's ecology-minded youth.
- As movies, television programs, mass media books, and magazines inundate teens with stories and photos of people who are "all alike," readers find it refreshing to read about people who have their own individuality.
- Myths and legends that are often brought into ethnic-based literature satisfy some deep-down psychological and aesthetic needs that are not met with contemporary realism or with the romanticism masked as realism that currently makes up the main body of fiction provided for young adults.

One of the most important concepts that needs to be taught is that there are large differences among people typically identified as a group. When Europeans first came to the American continent, there were more than thirty distinct nations speaking perhaps 1,000 different languages. During the past 500 years, these people have had such common experiences as losing their lands, being forced to move to reservations, and having to adapt their beliefs and lifestyles to a technological society. These experiences may have affected their attitudes in similar ways, but still it is a gross overgeneralization to write about Native Americans as if they were one people holding the same religious and cultural views. Although in a single class it would be impossible to study dozens of different Native American tribes, a compromise solution might be to study the history and folklore of those tribes who lived, or are living, in the same geographical area as the students. With this approach, it is important for students to realize that they are looking at only one small part of a bigger group, and that if they studied a different group they would learn equally interesting but different facts.

Similar points could be made about the thoughtlessness of talking about Africa as if it were one country and as if one set of folktales could represent a continent that contains nearly 12 million square miles and over forty independent countries.

Asian Americans also resent being lumped together. The Chinese and Japanese, the two groups who have been in the United States the longest, come from countries with a long history of hostility toward each other. A refugee from Vietnam or Cambodia has very little in common with someone whose ancestors came to California in the 1850s. Likewise, Puerto Ricans in New York have quite a different background from southwestern Mexican Americans. Even in the Southwest, people whose families have lived there from the days before Anglo settlers arrived resent being grouped with people who just came over the border from Mexico.

We need to teach about the histories of groups whose literature is being read to help readers understand the bitterness that finds its way into some ethnic literature. Readers who get impatient with Hispanic authors for including words and phrases in Spanish will probably be a little more tolerant if they realize that today's generation of Mexican American authors went to school in the days before bilingual education. In their childhoods, many of them heard nothing but Spanish and were amazed to arrive at English-speaking schools where they would be punished for speaking the only language they had ever known.

While Rudolfo Anaya broke new literary ground with his *Bless Me, Ultima,* many other minority writers are breaking new ground by changing the format of stories and translating them from an oral tradition into a written form. Before printing presses, typewriters, word processors, movies, radio, and television, people had more of an incentive to remember and tell the stories that communicated the traditions and values of a society. Even today, oral traditions play an important role, as seen on television talk shows as well as with kids telling stories at slumber parties and summer camp and workers and travelers whiling away long, boring hours. Many minority writers are experimenting in translating oral stories into written and printed formats, which means that some of the first publications to come from particular groups are more likely to be poetry and short stories than novels.

There are many beautifully designed collections (see Focus Box 10.2, Anthologies of Multicultural Materials) presenting art, poetry, photographs, essays, observations, interviews, and short stories. Besides the obvious advantage that anthologies present a variety of pieces short enough for classroom and library use, the differences in the statements demonstrate that members of groups are first and foremost individuals. They have their own thoughts, feelings, and values, just as do the members of one's own family, one's own church, and one's own neighborhood.

This is probably a lesson that works better through demonstration than through lecturing. Jim Burke in *The English Teacher's Companion* gives two examples of ways that teachers might introduce Sandra Cisneros's *The House on Mango Street.*

Scenario One

"Okay guys, today we're going to be getting a new book called *The House on Mango Street* by a Latina author. I thought it was really important that we read an author from a different culture since so many students here are Latino."

Scenario Two

(after reading a brief section from Cisneros's book) "So, we've been talking about this whole idea of growing up, about creating an identity for oneself, what it means, how and when it happens. *Huck Finn* allowed us to talk about some important aspects of that whole experience. And Nathan McCall's book told us what it was like for him to grow up as a young black man in the sixties. I thought it would be interesting to see what this other book has to say about the experience since unlike Huck she didn't take off but stayed on Mango Street. I love this book a lot. It took her five years to write this 120-page book. It's like a poem almost, the language and images are so intense.[10]

As Burke explains, the second scenario is clearly better in that the teacher grabbed students' interest by reading an excerpt and then linked the book to what the class had been doing. By emphasizing the book's literary quality, the teacher helped students see why they were reading the book. The teacher in the first scenario left students with the idea that they were reading *The House on Mango Street* to be politically correct.

We'll conclude this section with a plea for all those working with books and young adults to continue seeking out and promoting the use of minority literature. Educators have shied away from working with minority literature because:

FOCUS BOX 10.2 *Anthologies of Multicultural Materials*

American Dragons: Twenty-five Asian American Voices, edited by Laurence Yep. HarperCollins 1993. The metaphor in the title relates to the old belief that dragons appear in many guises and are always adaptable. These stories proving the adaptability of Asian Americans are grouped under Identity, In the Shadow of Giants, The Wise Child, World War Two, Love, and Guides.

American Eyes: New Asian-American Short Stories for Young Adults, edited by Lori M. Carlson. Holt, 1994. These well-written stories about immigrants from Japan, China, Vietnam, Korea, and the Philippines are an antidote to readers thinking of all Asians as the same.

American Indian Trickster Tales, selected and edited by Richard Erdoes and Alfonso Ortiz. Viking Penguin, 1998. In Native American folklore, trickster stories take center stage. In this rich collection, two highly respected scholars have collected dozens of stories clearly documented and identified as to their sources. A useful appendix describes the fifty-four groups from which the stories come.

The Big Aiiieeeee! An Anthology of Chinese American and Japanese American Literature, edited by Jeffery Paul Chan, Frank Chin, Lawson Fusao Inada, and Shawn Wong. Meridian, 1991. The editors are on a campaign to get more of what they view as "authentic" Asian literature before the American public.

The Girl Who Dreamed Only Geese: And Other Tales of the Far North, retold by Howard Norman, illustrated by Leo and Diane Dillon. Harcourt/Gulliver, 1997. These lively tales from the Arctic will bring smiles while also letting readers or listeners learn about Inuit cultures and beliefs.

Her Stories: African American Folktales, Fairy Tales, and True Tales by Virginia Hamilton, illustrated by Leo and Diane Dillon. Scholastic, 1995. Hamilton carefully documents these stories collected from African American women. Hamilton's other well-done anthologies illustrated by the Dillons include *Many Thousand Gone: African Americans from Slavery to Freedom* (Knopf, 1993) and *The People Could Fly* (Knopf, 1985).

Las Christmas: Favorite Latino Authors Share Their Holiday Memories, edited by Esmeralda Santiago and Joie Davidow. Random House, 1998. The twenty-five contributions are organized under "Stories," "Poems and Songs," and "Menu." Jose Ortega did the illustrations, which are well placed to provide white space and variety.

Latino Voices, edited by Frances R. Arparicio. Millbrook Press, 1994. The poetry and the short stories, along with excerpts from fiction and biographies, do a good job of illustrating the variety that exists among and within the groups that make up America's fastest growing minority.

Navajo: Visions and Voices across the Mesa by Shonto Begay. Scholastic, 1995. Begay is an artist living on the Navajo reservation in Arizona. While his paintings are the core of the book, he includes chants, poems, stories, and first-person observations to help readers understand a unique community.

The Space Between Our Footsteps: Poems and Paintings from the Middle East, selected by Naomi Shihab Nye. Simon & Schuster, 1998. Nearly forty paintings are spaced throughout this attractive 144-page book of poems celebrating the Middle East by showing deep feelings for such universal topics as school, childhood, love, fear, and family.

Talking Leaves: Contemporary Native American Short Stories, edited by Craig Lesley. Laurel, 1991. Short stories from thirty-five authors are arranged alphabetically. While some are too complex for most high school students, several are short enough for reading out loud.

Where Angels Glide at Dawn: Stories from Latin America, edited by Lori M. Carlson and Cynthia L. Ventura. HarperCollins, 1990. These ten stories do a good job of reflecting the pride that individuals feel about their home countries including Argentina, Chile, El Salvador, Mexico, Panama, Peru, and Puerto Rico. Several include strands of magical realism.

- They didn't study it when they were in school and so they feel less prepared than when teaching mainstream literature.
- They fear censorship both because of prejudice against minorities and because of the fact that some minority writers use language considered inappropriate for schoolbooks.
- Minority literature is harder to find, especially minority literature that has been given a "seal of approval" by the education establishment (i.e., positive reviews and suggestions for teaching).
- Ethnic identification is such a sensitive topic that teachers fear that when they are discussing a piece of literature either they or their students may say something that will offend some students or hurt their feelings.

Being a professional means that you do not shy away from responsibilities just because they are challenging. Instead, you prepare, so that you can be successful—at least most of the time—in the work you have chosen for your career.

Using Young Adult Literature in the Library

When discussing public libraries, we used to assume that every library has a young adult librarian and a special section serving teenagers. Although this may be the ideal arrangement, there are certainly many libraries where this has never been the practice and many others where shrinking budgets are making young adult librarians an endangered species. A fairly common approach is for libraries to enlarge their children's sections to "Youth Sections" serving readers up to age 15 or 16, while sending everyone else to the adult division. Some of the problems with such an arrangement, cited in a *Voice of Youth Advocates* article ("Whose Job Is It Anyway?"[11]), are the following:

- Teenagers enter a children's section reluctantly, and their size, voices, and active natures intimidate the children who are there.
- The purpose of young adult services is to provide a transition from the children's collection to the resources of the total library, and when a librarian accompanies a teenager looking for something into the larger adult collection there's no one left to serve the children.
- It is difficult for the same person who runs programs for preschoolers, prepares story hours for older children, and reviews hundreds of children's books to switch gears to the fads and multiple interests of teenagers.
- Young adult librarians deal not only with "safe" young adult books, but also with adult materials of interest to young adults. These are often controversial and are likely to prove more problematic to a children's librarian whose training has engendered different perceptions and attitudes.
- Without "sponsorship" by knowledgeable young adult librarians, there may not be enough circulation for serious, high-quality books, which results in a greater reliance on popular taste (e.g., formula romances and series books).

Certainly these worries are valid, and we all need to do what we can to persuade decision makers that young adult librarians serve an important role. If the choice is

VIVIAN VANDE VELDE
On "Dear Cranky Author . . ."

I was shocked the first time I heard an author complain about fan letters. If a reader was touched enough by my stories to take the time to write to me (I thought in my just-published naiveté), I would be honored to write back.

Dear Vivian Vande Valda, I like wrestling and X-Men but I don't care much for books, but as part of my writing project . . .
      School assignment letters fall into three categories:

1. The "I-don't-have-time-to-read-your-book/Please-send-me-a-list-of-important-events" category (Not much anybody can do here; the whole purpose of this letter is for the teacher *not* to know about it.)

2. The "author/dog groomer—same difference" category. *Tell why you are an important person. What are your accomplishments? Have you won any major awards in your field? Do you enjoy your work?* (Picture yourself answering these questions. Now picture answering them without getting sarcastic.)

3. The "friendly-advice" category, including: . . . *These are three things I liked about your story . . . These are three things I didn't like . . . This is something I inferred . . .* (I know evaluating a story hones analytical ability. Noting what parts kept you interested vs. when your mind wandered, questioning what makes you want to spend time with certain characters—these kinds of observations are valid and, in fact, could be the first step toward becoming a writer. But why send that report to the author? An author is no more likely to enjoy hearing three things you didn't like about her story than a teacher would relish hearing three things you don't like about her teaching techniques.)

      If learning to write—and send—a letter is part of the assignment, shouldn't the teacher *read* that letter? Some of my mail is almost illegible from erasures and spelling errors, with students asking for copies of my books (no, I don't get them free), or for me to visit their out-of-state school. Then they tell me their project mark depends on getting an answer from me. (. . . *No offense, but what took you so long to get back to me? I sent my email yesterday . . .*)

      My suggestions? A teacher could, without stifling students' creativity, point out there's no need to ask an author for information that can be easily found elsewhere, such as what else she's written. Instead, this could be a chance to ask where she got the idea for the story or—if the students didn't like something, such as the ending—why she chose to do things the way she did.

      On the other hand, if the student is unhappy with unpleasant characters and tense situations, this might be an opening for classroom discussion about conflict in a story and how boring it would be to read about an attractive, popular, healthy, happy child to whom only good things happen.

      I cherish the heartfelt letters from students who say my books made them laugh, made them think, got them through a difficult time: the letters born from enthusiasm. *Those* are letters worth reading—long after the end of the marking period.

NOTE: All excerpts are from real letters.

Vivian Vande Velde's books include *Heir Apparent,* Harcourt, 2002; *Witch's Wishes,* Holiday House, 2003; *The Rumpelstilskin Problem,* Houghton Mifflin, 2000; and *Ghost of a Hanged Man,* Marshall Cavendish, 1998.

between having a library open only four days a week and having separate librarians for children and teenagers, however, most library boards vote to keep the library open. This dictates more flexibility and more challenge for the librarian who serves both age groups. Parents who have both teenagers and young children vouch for the differences between the two, yet they manage somehow. Many librarians have to do the same. We hope this textbook helps.

Matching Books with Readers

Most people working with books and young readers have come to accept the idea that there is no such thing as one sacred list of books that every student should read. The best that can be hoped for are agreeable matches between particular books and particular students. To bring such matches about, adults need to be acquainted with a wide range of books and with individual students. A commonly used technique in getting to know students is to ask them what books they have previously enjoyed and then to suggest something similar or something by the same author. An alternative is to ask young readers to describe the book they would most like if an author were going to write just for them and then to suggest three or four books that contain elements they have mentioned.

Other people use written forms or reader interest surveys in which students write down their hobbies, the kinds of classes they are taking, what they want to do for a career, what books they have read, and the kinds of stories they most enjoy. The problem with such forms is that they are usually filled out and then stored in a drawer. No one has time to interpret them. One of our students who is a junior high librarian, however, designed a reader interest survey for her students. She added their reading test scores and programmed her library computer with 100 of the best books she had read. All her students received individual computer printouts suggesting six books that they would probably like and that would be within their reading level.

Similar commercial programs are becoming available, but what made this program successful was that the librarian had read and personally reacted to each book that she listed in the program. The individualized printouts served as conversation starters from which one-to-one relationships developed. Although she worked hard to initiate the project, she considered it worth the effort because once the machinery was set in order, it could be done for hundreds of students almost as easily as for thirty, and she could continue to update it with the new books she was reading.

Commercial programs and CD-ROMs allow students to search for books using key words. Many YA authors have their own Web sites (see our website for links, www.ablongman.com/donelson7e), and clever booksellers do on an international level the same kind of promotional work that teachers and librarians have for years been doing locally.

Many teachers encourage students to write letters directly to authors, which is all well and good, but before you do this, read what author Vivian Vande Velde has to say.

Perhaps reading an author's Web page could be as effective, or for a special occasion, a teacher might arrange through a publisher to have an online or email conversation with an author.

Electronic aids are wonderful, but nothing can substitute for a large and varied reading background and the ability to draw relationships between what students tell or

FOCUS BOX 10.3   Good Internet Resources for Teachers and Librarians

Assembly on Literature for Adolescents: www.alan-ya.org: The National Council of Teachers of English's Assembly on Literature for Adolescents website offers activities, links to related websites, as well as online access to *The ALAN Review*. ALAN's webmaster is David Gill.

Authors 4 Teens

www.authors4teens.com: This subscription site by noted YA short story editor Don Gallo contains interviews and up-to-date author information.

Carol Hurst's Children's Literature Site

www.carolhurst.com: Professional educator Carol Hurst offers reviews, annotations, and lesson plans in this comprehensive site, featuring books geared toward the younger adolescent.

Children's Book Council

www.cbcbooks.org/: An association of publishers presents classroom ideas, previews of new books, discussions about current issues and trends, links to authors' websites, bibliographies, and news about the publishing business and available promotional materials.

Children's Literature Web Guide

www.ucalgary.ca/~dkbrown: David Brown of the University of Calgary provides information on author resources, reader's theatre, illustrators, and publishers.

Cynthia Leitich Smith

www.cynthialeitichsmith.com: This site contains articles, interviews, reading recommendations, publishing news, and annotated links from the noted author.

Database of Award-Winning Children's Literature

www.dawcl.com: This useful site has many search options and includes YA lit. Frequently updated, it is maintained by Lisa R. Bartle, reference librarian at California State University, San Bernardino.

Florida State English Education WebQuests

www.fsu.edu/~Candl/ENGLISH/web.htm: At this site, teachers and librarians can find YA lit WebQuests created by the students at Florida State University, under the direction of Dr. Pamela S. Carroll.

Lesson Plans and Resources for Adolescent and Young Adult Literature

www.cloudnet.com/~edrbsass/edadolescentlit .htm: This site features a collection of YA lit lesson plans and resources by Dr. Ed Sass, professor at the College of St. Benedict/St. John's University.

Notes from the Windowsill

www.armory.com/~web/notes.html: This e-magazine that reviews children's and YA lit is edited by Wendy Betts, librarian.

Vandergrift's YA Literature Page

www.scils.rutgers.edu/~kvander/YoungAdult: Kay Vandergrift's comprehensive site includes an overview of YA lit, a "top 100" list, bibliographies, and more.

What to Read

www.people.virginia.edu/%7Ejkb3y/project: Produced by YA lit students at the University of Virginia, this site is a resource for students, teachers, and librarians. *What to Read* is maintained by Jane Butler, graduate student at the Curry School of Education at the University of Virginia.

The WebQuest Page

webquest.sdsu.edu/webquest.html: Maintained by Bernie Dodge, this is the definitive site for WebQuests (an online, process oriented lesson). *The WebQuest Page* includes lessons for many YA books.

YALSA Booklists

www.ala.org/yalsa/booklists: This site contains book lists from the Young Adult Library Services Association of the ALA. It includes picks for reluctant readers and the college bound, as well as award-winning books.

ask and what the librarian remembers about particular books. Experience sharpens this skill, and those librarians who make a consistent effort to read a few new books every month rapidly increase their repertoire of books.

Booktalks

With all their other responsibilities, few librarians have as much opportunity as they would like to guide individual reading on a one-to-one basis. The next best thing is to give presentations or booktalks to groups. A booktalk is a short introduction to a book, which usually includes one or two paragraphs read from the book. Booktalks are comparable to movie previews or teasers in presenting the characters and a hint of the plot, but they never reveal the ending. Joni Bodart has described booktalking as a kind of storytelling that resembles an unfinished murder mystery in being "enticing. It is a come-on. It is entertaining. And it is fun, for both the listener and the booktalker."[12]

The simplest kind of booktalk may last only sixty seconds. In giving it, the booktalker must let listeners know what to expect. For example, it would be unfair to present only the funniest moments in a serious book—a reader might check it out expecting a comedy. If a book is a love story, some clue should be given, but care needs to be taken because emotional scenes read out loud and out of context can sound silly. The cover of a book often reveals its tone, which is one of the reasons for holding up a book while it is being discussed or for showing slides or color overheads if a presentation is being given to a large audience.

Booktalks need to be carefully prepared ahead of time. It takes both concentration and skill to select the "heart" of a story. People who try to ad-lib have the advantage of sounding spontaneous, but they also run the risk of using up all their time telling about one or two books or of getting bogged down in telling the whole story, which would defeat the purpose. Most young readers do not want to hear a 10- or 15-minute talk on one book, unless it is dramatic and used as a change of pace along with several shorter booktalks. Even with short booktalks, people's minds begin to wander after they've listened for 10 or 15 minutes. The ideal approach is for the teacher or librarian to give booktalks frequently but in short chunks.

This may not be practical, however, if the person giving the booktalk is a visitor (e.g., a public librarian coming to a school to encourage students to sign up for library cards and begin to use the public library). In situations such as this, the librarian can arrive in class with a cart full of books ready to be checked out. A half-hour or so can be devoted to the booktalks, with the rest of the time saved for questions and answers, browsing, signup, and checkout. In cases like this, it's good to have a printed bibliography or bookmark to leave with students for later use in the library.

This kind of group presentation has the advantage of introducing students to the librarian, which is especially important for helping students feel at ease in public libraries. Students who already feel acquainted are more likely to initiate a one-to-one relationship, a valuable part of reading guidance. Group presentations also give students more freedom in choosing books that appeal to them. When a student asks a librarian to recommend a good book, the librarian has time to tell the student about only two or three titles, and the student probably feels obligated to take one of these books regardless of whether it sounds appealing. But when the librarian presents ten to fifteen different titles, students can choose from a much larger offering. This also enables students to learn about and to select books that might cause them embarrassment if they were recommended on a personal basis. For example, if a girl is suspected of having lesbian leanings, it may not help the situation for the librarian to hand her Nancy Garden's *Annie on My Mind*. But if this were included among several books introduced to the class and the student chose it herself, it might fill a real need. The fact that the librarian talks about it, showing that she has read it, opens the door for the girl to initiate a conversation if she so desires.

Another advantage to group presentations is that they are efficient. If a social studies class is beginning a unit on World War II in which everyone in the class is required to read a novel having something to do with the war and also write a small research paper, it makes sense for the librarian to give the basic information in one group presentation. Being efficient in the beginning enables the librarian to spend time with individual students who have specific questions rather than making an almost identical presentation to thirty individuals. Table 10.2 gives some suggestions adapted from an article by Mary K. Chelton, "Booktalking: You Can Do It" (*School Library Journal,* April 1976). Other sources of information include an American Library Association book and videotape featuring Hazel Rochman and entitled "Tales of Love and Terror: Booktalking the Classics, Old and New," and Joni Richard Bodart's *Booktalk! Booktalking and School Visiting for Young Adult Audiences.*

Displays

Making displays is another effective way to promote books. Most young adults have some common needs, although they might not admit them or even be aware of them. The sensitive adult who knows books can quietly alert students to titles and authors that might prove worthwhile. It can be done simply; indeed, the simpler and less obvious, the better—perhaps nothing more than a sign that says "Like to watch Oprah Winfrey?—You'll Love These" (personal experiences and social issues books, although not identified in just that way), or "Did You Cry Over *Gone with the Wind?*" (books about love problems and divorce). None of these simple gimmicks involves much work, but what's more important is that they do their job without the librarian seeming pushy or nosy. No book report is required and no one will know whether John checks out Howard Fast's *April Morning* because his father recently died, because he likes U.S. history, or because the cover picture appealed to him.

When it comes to promoting books, librarians should not be ashamed to borrow ideas from the world of commerce. After all, we are competing directly for students' time and interest and indirectly for a share of the library budget and the taxpayers' dollars. Attractive, professional-looking displays and bulletin boards give evidence that things are happening in the library (or the classroom), and they help patrons develop positive attitudes toward books and reading. Even if there is no artwork connected with a display, it can encourage reading simply by showing the front covers of books.

Preparing displays can bring the same kind of personal satisfaction that comes from creatively decorating a room or painting a picture. People who have negative feelings about making displays have probably had experiences in which the results did not adequately compensate for the amount of time and effort expended. One way to cor-

TABLE 10.2 DOs AND DON'Ts FOR BOOKTALKING

Do	Don't
1. Prepare well. Either memorize your talks or practice them so much that you can easily maintain eye contact.	1. Don't introduce books that you haven't read or books that you wouldn't personally recommend to a good friend as interesting.
2. Organize your books so that you can show them as you talk. To keep from getting confused, you might clip a note card with your talk on it to the back of each book.	2. Don't "gush" over a book. If it's a good book and you have done an adequate job of selecting what to tell, it will sell itself.
3. When presenting excerpts, make sure they are representative of the tone and style of the book.	3. Don't tell the whole story. When listeners beg for the ending, hand them the book. Your purpose is to get them to read.
4. Even though you might sometimes like to focus on one or two themes, be sure, over the months you meet with any group, that you present a wide variety of books. Include informative books that young readers would probably like to know about but might be too embarrassed to ask for.	4. Don't categorize books as to who should read them, example, "This is a book you girls will like"; or show by the books you have brought to a particular school that you expect only Asian Americans to read about Asian Americans and only Native Americans to read about Native Americans, and so forth.
5. Experiment with different formats, for example, a short movie, some poetry, or one longer presentation along with your regular booktalks.	5. Don't give literary criticisms. You have already evaluated the books for your own purposes, and if you do not think they are good, do not present them.
6. Keep a record of which books you have introduced to which groups. This can be part of your evaluation when you compare before and after circulation figures on the titles you have talked about. Also, good record keeping helps you not repeat yourself with a group.	
7. Be assertive in letting teachers know what you will and will not do. Perhaps distribute a printed policy statement explaining such things as how much lead time you need, the fact that the teacher is to remain with the group, and how willing you are to make the necessary preparation to do booktalks on requested themes or topics.	

rect this imbalance is to follow some general principles that help to increase the returns on a display while cutting down on the work.

1. Go window shopping in the best stores—the ones that appeal to the young adults that you are wooing—and when you see a display that you like, adapt its features to your own purposes.
2. Promote more than one book and have multiple copies available. Enthusiasm wanes if people have to put their names on a list and wait. Use color photocopies of the book jackets, so that as the books are checked out, your display won't look skimpy.
3. Tie the displays into current happenings. Connect them with popular movies, the school play, a neighborhood controversy, or various anniversary celebrations.
4. Use displays to get people into the library. Offer free bibliographies and announce their availability through local media.

5. Put your displays in high-traffic areas where everyone, not just those who already use the young adult collection, will see them.
6. Use interchangeable parts, so that it isn't necessary to start from scratch each time. To get variety and height into a display, use wood-stained fruit baskets and crates, leaning boards with screwed-in hooks for holding books, or cardboard boxes covered with drapes. To focus attention on the books, plain backgrounds are better than figured ones.
7. Take advantage of modern technology. Buy stick-on letters and use your computer and your desktop publishing skills to prepare attractive bibliographies and signs.

The changing location of portable displays is in itself an attention getter. A portable display can be as small as a foot-square board set in the middle of a table or as large as a camper's tent set up in the middle of a room and surrounded by books about camping, hiking, backpacking, ecology, and nature foods. If space is a problem, small bulletin boards can be hung from the ceiling or stood against pillars or walls. They can do double duty (e.g., dividing the children's section from the young adult section or separating a reading corner with its casual furniture from the desks and tables set aside for study). Give students a sense of ownership over the displays by involving them as much as possible. Art teachers are usually happy to work with librarians to have a place where student work can be attractively displayed alongside such art-related books as Louise Plummer's *My Name is Sus5an Smith. The 5 Is Silent;* Gary Paulsen's *The Monument;* Brock Cole's *Celine;* and Zibby Oneal's *In Summer Light.* When you do a display of books about animals, include snapshots of students under the headings of "The Comforts and Delights of Owning a Dog," or "The Comforts and Delights of Being Owned by a Cat."

Occasionally, students working as library interns or helpers enjoy the challenge of doing displays all by themselves. Whatever is interesting and different is the key to tying books in with real life. An ordinary object—a kitchen sink, a pan full of dirty dishes, or a torn and dirty football jersey—is out of the ordinary when it appears as part of a display. Also, don't overlook the possibility of putting up posters such as those offered by the American Library Association or tying commercial posters in with books. Remember the part that the poster message, "Don't disturb the universe," played in Cormier's *The Chocolate War.*

Programs

Stores have special sales and events to get people into the marketplace, where they will be tempted to buy something. In the same way, ambitious librarians put on young adult programs to do something special for those who regularly use the library and, at the same time, to bring nonusers into the library. Advice from people whose libraries have been especially active in arranging programs includes:

1. Take a survey, or better, talk with your teenage clientele to see what their interests and desires are.
2. Avoid duplicating the kinds of activities that students do in school and in conjunction with other community agencies.

*I*t is efficient to make a few interesting signs that can be stored (or hung) flat and then brought out for use with various sets of books.

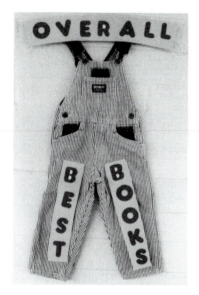

3. Include young adults in planning and putting on programs so that the library can be a showcase for young adult talent.

4. Work with existing youth service agencies to cosponsor events, or plan them in conjunction with school programs so as to have the beginning of an audience and the nucleus of a support group.

5. Do a good job of publicizing the event. The publicity may influence people unable to come so they will feel more inclined to visit the library at some other time.

6. Have a casual setting planned for a relatively small group, with extra chairs available in case more people come than you expect. Bustling around at the last minute to set up extra chairs gives an aura of success that is more desirable than having row on row of empty chairs.

Program possibilities include outdoor music concerts featuring local teenage bands, teenage poetry readings in a coffeehouse setting, chess tournaments, and showings of original movies or videos. Workshops are held in computer programming, photography, creative writing, bicycle repair, and crafts. Guest speakers are often invited to discuss subjects that schools tend to shy away from, such as self-defense and rape prevention, drug and birth control information, and introductions to various hotlines and other agencies that help young adults.

Large-scale workshops are sometimes held in libraries to which various schools bring their students. For example, in a town with three high schools, one big day on choosing careers may be planned at the community library. Guest speakers who could not give up three days of their time may be willing to make a single appearance, and special exhibits and displays can be set up once rather than three times.

Regardless of the topic or format of a program, librarians should view programs as opportunities to encourage library visitors to become regular book users. The following practices help:

1. Hold the program so that it is in or near the young adult book section. If this is impractical, try routing traffic past the young adult area or past displays of young adult books.
2. Pass out miniature bibliographies, perhaps printed on a bookmark or in some other easy-to-carry format.
3. Schedule the program to end at least a half-hour before the library closes, so that participants can browse and sign up for library cards.
4. Place paperback book racks where they are as tempting as the displays that grocery and discount stores crowd into checkout areas.
5. For ten minutes at the start of the program, while waiting for latecomers to straggle in, do a welcome and warmup by giving a few booktalks related to the subject of the evening.

Some libraries have had success with book discussion groups in which teenagers serve as readers and critics. These usually work best if their evaluations can be shared, for example, on a bulletin board, in a teen opinion magazine, through a display of recommended books, in a monthly column in a local newspaper, through the periodic printing and distribution of annotated lists of favorites, or on a library website.

When an author is invited to speak, the host librarian needs to begin publicity several weeks in advance to be sure that people are reading the author's books. English and reading teachers should be notified so that they can devote some class time to the author's work. A panel of students who especially enjoyed the author's work might be set up to interact with the author at the end of the formal presentation. Another way to involve students, and perhaps teachers, would be to invite three or four to have lunch or dinner with the guest author. (Check this out first because some speakers prefer to be left alone to gather their thoughts before making a presentation.) If you are setting up an author's visit, it is usually best that you first write the publisher of the author's most recent book. State how much money, if any, you have available. Sometimes publishers pay for an author's transportation, but you will usually need to pay at least for food and housing and, if possible, to offer an honorarium. If you have no money, say so immediately, and then be patient, flexible, and grateful for whomever you get. An author might be scheduled to speak in or near your area and might then come to you as an extra. Also, it is highly possible that there are young adult authors living in your own state. The Children's Book Council has a helpful site on its web page under "Author & Illustrator Visits."

Magazines

As discussed in Chapter 3, magazines and their place in the reading habits of Americans have changed considerably. There are now magazines for every taste and inter-

*R*egardless of why kids come to a public library, use their presence as an opportunity for making them feel at home by routing traffic past displays and the young adult area and by distributing bookmarks or other information about YA books and activities.

est—even a few that please teachers. The vast number from which to choose makes librarians' jobs harder rather than easier. See Focus Box 10.4 for recommendations of magazines published directly for teens. It was prepared in the fall of 2003 by Diane Tuccillo, youth services librarian for the Mesa, Arizona, Public Library.

Educators must realize that many students who won't pick up books are eager to read the latest magazines in their areas of interest. With many of the teen magazines, poor readers can feel their first success with the printed word because much of the information is communicated through easy-to-read layouts and photographs. Also, the material, which is presented in short, digestible chunks, is of prime interest to teens. Some of the magazines are read by both boys and girls, but because of the abundance of advertising money for cosmetics and fashions, many magazines are purposely designed to appeal only to girls. Others are financed by advertisements for products usually purchased by boys.

There's no limit to the information that good students can find in magazines. A much higher percentage of adult Americans read magazines rather than books, and yet in school we give people little help in introducing them to magazines or in picking out the ones they will get the most from. It is almost as if kids find magazines despite teachers, not because of them. We would do well to change our attitudes and look on magazines as taking up where books leave off in presenting up-to-date information on a wide variety of topics chosen to be especially interesting to young adults.

Graphic Novels

One of the defenses mounted for comic books, which we hear today in the defense of graphic novels, was that they teach children to read. The pictures and the balloons coming from characters' mouths help children comprehend higher-level stories than what they can read in straight type. Art Spiegelman goes a step further and says that "one of the reasons comics are effective is that they mimic the way the brain works. One doesn't think in holograms of reality. One thinks in cartoon signs of reality. You remember a loved one or a friend on the basis of very abstracted information rather than a three-dimensional film in your head."[13]

In 1986 many people were shocked when Spiegelman won a Pulitzer Prize for *Maus: A Survivor's Tale,* in which he used a comic book format to retell his father's Holocaust memories through humanized mice. Spiegelman's success encouraged several mainstream publishers to take a new look at the genre and to publish other graphic novels. At first, sales were disappointing but by now graphic novels are a well-established part of the book world, mostly because of companies who had a headstart doing comic books. College classes are taught on graphic novels, and people are beginning to realize that when talking about comic books and graphic novels, the term *format* is more accurate than *genre* because the stories range from science fiction and fantasy to mysteries, historical fiction, love stories, and whatever else a creative person or team might think of. Librarians vouch for the popularity of graphic novels, not only with teenage boys, but also with teenage girls and increasingly with adult readers. However, the heritage of comic books, as written about in Chapter 3, often leads to resistance, or at least skepticism, from parents and administrators, as well as from other teachers. Because of the way graphic novels are produced and distributed, they come half-way between magazines and books. Because of this, and because the cover and the "tone" need to fit in with the environment in which you will be displaying and using them, we are not providing a Focus Box of recommended graphic novels. They change too quickly and are too different for us to feel comfortable in recommending a dozen key purchases. However, we will offer the following hints, as well as Focus Box 10.5, which lists sources where you can find further information.

- If you aren't brave enough to take "real" graphic novels into your classroom, you can start by bringing in the *Little Lit* books (*Folklore & Fairy Tale Funnies, Strange Stories for Strange Kids,* and *It Was a Dark and Silly Night*). These Joanna Cotler/HarperCollins books are edited by Art Spiegelman and Francoise Mouly and are made from children's stories illustrated in comic book style by well-known artists.
- As an alternative to book reports, let students follow the format of a graphic novel to retell an event or a scene. To do this, they will have to ponder and absorb the thoughts and the pictures in the minds of the original authors.
- Take care in selecting the graphic novels that you and your students bring into your classroom. Stories of superheroes are probably going to be fine, but you may be courting trouble with such genres as horror, the supernatural, crime and punishment, satire, and dark humor.
- While you don't have to personally read every graphic novel that you bring in, you need to read reviews written by people who are knowledgeable about kids and schools. It might be a good idea to keep reviews and feature articles from mainstream magazines posted on a nearby bulletin board or in a folder so that students, parents, colleagues, and other visitors to your room will understand that you have pedagogical support for including graphic novels as one of many choices for student reading.

FOCUS BOX 10.5 Sources of Information about Graphic Novels

The websites in this box were accurate as of September 1, 2003. While some of them may no longer be functioning, the ones that are listed will probably provide other new links.

100 Graphic Novels for Public Libraries (Northhampton, MA: Kitchen Sink Press, 1996) and **The 101 Best Graphic Novels** (New York: NBM Publishers, 2001) both by Stephen Weiner. Weiner is a librarian and a self-taught graphic novel specialist who provides a guide to starting a collection as well as to keeping it in circulation.

Publishers Weekly has a quarterly "Comics" column, which includes reviews and information on new releases.

School Library Journal regularly includes a "Graphic Novel" section in its reviews of "Adult Books for High School Students." It also publishes occasional articles. Worth looking up are two cover stories: "What Teens Want: Thirty Graphic Novels You Can't Live Without" by Michele Gorman in the August 2002 issue, and "'Zap! Whoosh! Kerplow!' Build High-Quality Graphic Novel Collections with Impact," by Lora Bruggeman in the January 1997 issue.

VOYA (Voice of Youth Advocates), which is published bimonthly, includes a "Graphically Speaking" column written by librarian Katharine L. Kan. The column consists mostly of reviews organized around themes—e.g., graphic novels appropriate for younger readers or graphic novels of a particular genre.

YALSA (Young Adult Library Services Association) sponsored a *Getting Graphic@Your Library Preconference* on June 14, 2002 in Atlanta, Georgia. Speeches, interviews, and other "happenings" from the event are presented in the October and December 2002 issues of VOYA including a condensed version of Neil Gaiman's speech and an interview with Art Spiegelman.

ALA's Reference on the Web: Graphic Novels www.ala.org/Content/NavigationMenu/Products_ and_Publications/Periodicals/Booklist/Special_Lists_ and_Features7/Special_Lists_and_Features3/ Reference_on_the_Web/Graphic_Novels_.htm: Produced for the American Library Association's Teen Read Week, this site offers a great introduction to comics and graphic novels for adolescents.

Artbomb.net www.artbomb.net/home.jsp: Artbomb contains reviews, artwork, and author interviews. Edited by Peter Siegel, the site features contributions by noted authors in the graphic novel field.

Comic Books for Young Adults ublib.buffalo. edu/lml/comics/pages: This site explores the question, "Do comic books belong in libraries?" Geared toward comics for young adults, the site is maintained by Michael R. Lavin of the Lockwood Memorial Library at the University at Buffalo.

The Fourth Rail www.thefourthrail.com: Updated weekly, this site contains contributed reviews as well as staff reviews and is maintained by Don MacPherson and Randy Lander.

Graphic Novels www.graphicnovels.brodart.com: Brodart, a supplier of books to libraries, sponsors this commercial site, which includes core lists of "must have" graphic novels as well as a monthly evaluation of "the best, most appropriate new materials."

No Flying, No Tights www.noflyingnotights.com: This website reviews graphic novels especially for teens and is maintained by Robin Brenner, a library technician and graphic novel enthusiast at Cary Memorial Library in Lexington, Massachusetts.

Rational Magic www.rationalmagic.com/Comics/ Comics.html: D. Aviva Rothschild, who put together a noted 1995 bibliography of graphic novels, maintains this site.

Magazines have outgrown their revolving displays and now take up whole walls in Young Adult rooms. See Focus Box 10.4 on page 314 for magazines that are popular with young adults in the Mesa, Arizona, public library.

Using Young Adult Books in the Reading Classroom

Including a section on reading in this text is in some sense superfluous because this whole book is devoted to teaching and promoting reading, but the interests and responsibilities of teachers of reading differ in some ways from those of English teachers or of librarians. One difference is that except for remedial programs, teaching reading as an academic discipline in the high schools is a fairly recent development. The assumption used to be that normal students had received enough formal instruction in reading by the time they completed elementary school. They were then turned over to English teachers who taught mostly literature, grammar, and composition. Certainly English teachers worked with reading skills, but they were not the primary focus. Today more and more states are passing laws setting minimal reading standards for high school graduation, and this has meant that reading has become almost a regular part of the high school curriculum. In some schools, all ninth-graders now take a reading class; in other schools, such a class is reserved for those who test one or two years below grade level. Depending on how long it takes them to pass the test, students may take basic reading classes for several semesters.

In the teaching profession, the reluctant reader is nearly always stereotyped as a boy from the wrong side of town, someone S. E. Hinton would describe as an outsider, a greaser. Actually, reluctant readers come in both male and female varieties and from all social and IQ levels. Many of them have fairly good reading skills; they simply don't like to read. Others are poor readers partly because they get so little practice. What these students have in common is that they have been disappointed in their past reading. The rewards of reading—what they received either emotionally or intellectually—have not come up to their expectations, which were based on how hard they worked to read the material. They have therefore come away feeling cheated. The reading profession has recognized this problem and has attempted to solve it by lowering the price the student has to pay (i.e., by devising reading materials that demand less effort from the student). These are the controlled vocabulary books commonly known as "high-low books," meaning high interest, low vocabulary. They are only moderately successful because the authors are rarely creative artists; they are educators who have many priorities that come before telling a good story. An alternative approach is making the rewards greater rather than reducing the effort. This is where the best adolescent literature comes into the picture. It has a good chance of succeeding with reluctant readers for the following reasons:

1. It is written specifically to be interesting to teenagers. It is geared to their age level and their interests.
2. It is usually shorter and more simply written than adult material, yet it has no stigma attached to it. It isn't written down to anyone, nor does it look like a reading textbook.
3. There is so much of it (almost 800 new books published every year) that individual readers have a good chance of finding books that appeal to them.
4. As would be expected, because the best young adult books are the creations of some good contemporary authors, the stories are more dramatic, better written, and easier to get involved in than the controlled vocabulary books.
5. The language used in good adolescent literature is more like the language that students are accustomed to hearing. In this day of mass media communication, a student who does not read widely may still have a fairly high degree of literary and language sophistication gained from watching television and movies.

Taking all this into account, some types of adolescent literature will still be enjoyed more than others by reluctant readers. In general, reluctant readers want the same things from the books they read that the rest of us want, but they want them faster and in less space. If it's information they are looking for, they want it to be right there. If they are reading a book for thrills and chills, they want it to be really scary. If they're reading for humor, they want it to be really funny. And if they're not sure about committing themselves for a large chunk of time, they want books in which they can get a feeling of accomplishment from reading short sections, paragraphs, or even sentences, as with various kinds of trivia books.

The Young Adult Library Services Association (YALSA) puts together an annual list, "Quick Picks for Reluctant Young Adult Readers." Selection criteria for the "Quick Picks" list includes short sentences, short paragraphs, simplicity of plot, uncomplicated dialogue, a sense of timeliness, maturity of format, and appeal of content. Fiction must include "believability of character and plot as well as realistic dialogue." This list, along with another YALSA list, "Popular Paperbacks for Young Adults," can prove helpful for reading teachers. The lists are available on the American Library Association's (ALA) Web site, www.ala.org/yalsa. The ALA also publishes a yearly book *ALA's Guide to Great Reading,* which includes all of their "Best Book" lists ready for photocopying.

Guided Reading Classes

The push for higher reading scores has opened the high school curriculum to reading classes for all students, not just those with low reading scores. Most high schools offer study skills courses in which skimming, speed reading, and selecting main ideas are taught. Some high schools also offer classes in what used to be called "free reading," but with the back-to-the-basics swing that occurred in the 1980s today are called *individualized* or *guided reading.* Rather than being a semester-long course, such programs are more likely to be incorporated into a six-week unit or a twice-a-week program as part of regular English or reading classes.

One of the chief reasons for providing kids time to read in class is to prevent the dropoff in reading that usually occurs when students begin high school and their social and work schedules leave little time for reading. A classroom library is provided containing multiple copies of popular young adult and adult titles from which students make their own selections. It is wise for teachers to send a note of explanation to parents that includes the statement that the choice of books is up to the student and his or her parents. It helps at the beginning for either the teacher or the librarian to give booktalks; once the class is started, students can recommend "good books" to each other.

When students finish a book, they hold a conference with the teacher, who preferably has also read the book. The purpose is not to test the student as much as it is to encourage thinking about the book and the author's intentions and to give teachers an opportunity to suggest other books that will help the student progress. Teachers need to show that they respect the reading of popular young adult books by being familiar with many of them and by being genuinely interested in what students have to say about them. The class is doomed to failure if teachers view it as a kind of focused study hall in which their job is to do little more than keep control and keep kids reading. It's also doomed to failure if students view it as a "cake" class, and for this reason successful teachers are fairly stringent as they devise various systems for giving credit. Students keep records of the number of books (or number of pages) read, they assist the teacher in judging the difficulty of the material, they mark their improvement over the semester (perhaps shown by a test score or by the number of pages the student reads in a class period), and they receive grades on their preparation for the individual conferences.

Various studies summarized by Dick Abrahamson and Eleanor Tyson in "What Every English Teacher Should Know About Free Reading"[14] have shown:

- Free reading is enjoyed by both students and teachers.
- Over a semester, students pick a variety of books, ranging from easy to difficult and from recent to classic.
- Reading skills improve, with some of this improvement undoubtedly related to attitude change.

- Students taught through free reading are more likely to read as adults and to foster reading activities with their children.
- Individual conferences help literature come alive for students.
- The conferences also help to break down barriers between students and teachers.
- Good teachers employ the concept of reading ladders (e.g., helping a girl move from a *Sweet Dreams* romance to a Norma Fox Mazer or an M. E. Kerr book and on to *Gone with the Wind* and *Jane Eyre*).

With so many benefits, why isn't the course taught more often? Part of the reason is an image problem. *Free reading* smacks of "free love" and the permissiveness of the 1970s. Although the connotations of such a course title might attract students, these same connotations fly in the face of those who believe "You get what you pay for." Besides, the course is already suspect because of its avowal of quantity over quality; i.e., "reading by the pound," and its emphasis on pleasure for students. More people than we care to think about are sure that if students are having a good time they can't also be learning.

Another problem is that the teacher's role is practically invisible. Being able to listen to students while working ever so subtly to suggest books that will raise levels of reading and improve skills without discouraging young readers takes a knowledge of hundreds of books plus tact and considerable talent in communication. Yet this teaching occurs in private sessions between two people. One of our favorite graduate students is a high school reading teacher who teaches an individualized reading class along with some of the more traditional remedial reading classes. She laughs in frustration about her principal's visits to her individualized reading class. After popping his head into her room on several different occasions and seeing the kids reading and her talking with a student at her desk, he sent her a note requesting that she let him know "when you are going to be teaching," so that he could come and observe.

She's still trying to educate him about the type of class she's teaching. It is not for the dysfunctional or disabled reader. It is for the average, or above-average, student who simply needs a chance to read and discuss books. In effect, it is one last try on the part of the school to instill in young people the habit of reading for pleasure. An alternative discussed in Chapter 11 is the organization of literature circles.

Using Young Adult Books in the Social Studies Class

Turning facts into believable stories that touch readers' emotions is the biggest contribution of fiction to the social studies class. It is important for readers to realize, however, that many different books need to be read because each book presents a limited perspective. Stereotypes exist in people's minds for two reasons. One is that the same attitudes are repeated over and over, so that they become a predominant image. Another is that an individual may have had only one exposure to a particular race, group, or country. For example, readers of Chaim Potok's *The Chosen* don't learn everything about Hasidic Jews, but they know a lot more than they did before they read the

FOCUS BOX 10.6   *Teens Outside the Continental United States*

City of the Beasts by Isabel Allende, translated (from Spanish) by Margeret Sayers Peden. HarperCollins, 2003. Allende's first novel for young readers is part magical realism and part contemporary politics. A 15-year-old boy accompanies his journalist grandmother on an expedition into an Amazon jungle in search of a legendary beast that is perhaps human.

A Girl Named Disaster by Nancy Farmer. Orchard Books, 1996, Orchard Classics edition, 2003. The author worked as a water technician for many years (see her statement on p. 293) in Zimbabwe and Mozambique. She used her knowledge of the area and the people to write the story of a girl who in 1981 flees across the border in hopes of gaining her father's help in escaping from a forced marriage to a cruel man.

Haveli by Suzanne Fisher Staples. Knopf, 1993. In this sequel to the well-received *Shabanu: Daughter of the Wind* (Knopf, 1989), Staples continues the story of the strong-willed young woman who because of custom and family needs becomes the fourth wife of a powerful landowner in the Cholistan desert of Pakistan.

Island Boyz: Short Stories by Graham Salisbury. Wendy Lamb/Random House, 2002. The preface to these ten stories is a free-verse poem in which Salisbury establishes what it takes to qualify as "island boyz/not boys/boyz," and adds about his own years of growing up in Hawaii, "I would not have traded places with anyone/not even God."

Letters from the Inside by John Marsden. Houghton Mifflin, 1994. Two Australian girls are penpals, each thinking that the other one has a wonderful life, but their letters gradually reveal that one is incarcerated and the other one is in her own kind of prison.

The Long Season of Rain by Helen Kim. Holt, 1996. The year is 1969 and the country is South Korea. When an orphaned boy is taken in by a family with several daughters, the group dynamics are drastically changed.

One Bird by Kyoko Mori. Holt, 1995. A contemporary Japanese girl gradually learns to defy tradition and her father's demands as she welcomes and accepts her mother who had left the household because of her father's unfaithfulness. In Mori's earlier *Shizuko's Daughter* (Holt, 1993), a daughter comes to terms with her mother's suicide.

The Other Side of Truth by Beverley Naidoo. HarperCollins, 2001. This winner of the Carnegie Award in England is the story of two children smuggled out of Nigeria after their mother's murder. Abandoned in London, they exemplify the courage and the fear of young refugees caught up in a never-ending variety of tragic situations. Naidoo has also written *Out of Bounds: Seven Stories of Conflict and Hope* (2003), *No Turning Back: A Novel of South Africa* (1997), *Journey to Jo'Burg: A South African Story* (1986), and *Chain of Fire* (1990), all HarperCollins.

Purple Hibiscus by Chimamanda Ngozi Adichie. Algonquin, 2003. Marketed as an adult book, this powerful story of a Nigerian brother and sister will be appreciated by older readers. The teenagers are held to horribly strict standards by their overly religious father, but they get a whole new look at life when they visit other members of his family.

Tonight by Sea by Frances Temple. Orchard, 1995. Paulie's uncle builds a boat planning for the family to escape from their troubled Haitian community, but before this comes about, Paulie is off on a journey of her own. Temple also wrote *Taste of Salt: A Story of Modern Haiti* (Orchard, 1992) and *Grab Hands and Run* (Orchard, 1993), which is about a family fleeing El Salvador.

A Walk in My World: International Short Stories about Youth, edited by Anne Mazer. Persea, 1998. While these stories by highly respected authors from around the world feature young protagonists, they were not necessarily written for teenage readers so they may require more sophistication than does the typical collection of young adult stories.

book, and their interest may have been piqued, so that they will continue to watch for information and to read other books.

Nearly everyone agrees that by reading widely and sharing their findings, social studies class members can lead each other to go beyond stereotypes. For this to happen on more than an ad hoc or serendipitous basis, however, the teacher needs to identify clear-cut goals and then seek help from professional sources and other teachers and librarians in drawing up a selective list of books to be offered to students.

Social studies teachers have always recognized the importance of biographies and of the kind of historical books featured in Chapter 8, but they may not be as aware of the many books, both fiction and nonfiction, that are available to help them teach students about contemporary social issues. See Chapter 9 for nonfiction books treating topics of interest to teenagers, such as ecology; issues related to pornography, rape, abuse, abortion, and prostitution; and medicine and health care, including questions about transplants, surrogate parenting, euthanasia, animal rights, cloning, stem cell research, and experiments on humans. Books on government ask questions about individual rights as opposed to the welfare of the group. Such questions range from whether the state has a right to require motorcycle helmets and seatbelts to whether it should legislate drugs and sexual preference.

Social studies teachers also miss a powerful resource if they fail to bring in the kind of fiction discussed in Focus Box 10.6, Teens Outside the Continental United States, when they talk about current social problems. Movies, television, and photographs allow people to see other places, but literature has the added dimension of allowing the reader to share the thoughts of another person. One never feels like a stranger in a country whose literature one has read, and as today's jet age shrinks the distances between countries and cultures, it is more important than ever that people realize that members of the human race, regardless of where or how they live, have more similarities than differences.

Parents and Young Adult Literature

"Tell me a story."

"Read just one more!"

"Can we go to the library today?"

Such requests are among the pleasant memories that parents have of their young children. These memories become even more cherished when parents look at these same children, now teenagers rushing off to part-time jobs or after-school sports or spending so much time with friends that they no longer seem to have time to do required school assignments, much less read a book. When parents ask us what they can do to encourage their teenage children to read, we find it easier to tell them what *not* to do because we've observed at least three clear-cut roads to failure.

1. Don't nag. There's simply no way to force young adults to read, much less to enjoy it.
2. If you choose to read the books your teenagers are reading, don't do it as a censor or with the intent of checking up on your child or your child's school.

3. Don't suggest books to your teenager with the only purpose being to teach moral lessons.

Lest we appear unduly pessimistic, we hasten to add that we have also seen some genuinely rewarding reading partnerships between teenagers and their parents. These successful partnerships have resembled the kind of reading-based friendships that adults have with each other. Mutual respect is involved, and the partners take turns making suggestions of what will be good to read. Conversations about characters, plots, authors, and subject matter come up naturally, with no one asking teacher-type questions and no one feeling pressured to talk about what he or she has just read.

Teenagers enjoy being in a helping role (i.e., being experts whose opinions are valued). Some of the best partnerships we've seen have been between our students whose teenage children have volunteered to read and share their opinions on the books they've seen their mothers reading (sorry we can't remember any fathers in this role, although we have known fathers who do read and serve as examples). A key to enticing young people to read is simply to have lots of books and magazines available. But they need to be available for genuine browsing and reading by everyone in the family, not purchased and planted in a manner that will appear phony to the teenager. A teenager who has never seen his or her parents read for pleasure will surely be suspicious when parents suddenly become avid readers on the day after parent-teacher conferences.

Perhaps a more important benefit than modeling behavior is that when parents read some of the best new books (the Honor List is a good starting place), they gain an understanding of what is involved in being a teenager today. Parents who have read some of the realistic problem novels have things to discuss with their children regardless of whether the children have read the books. Even when children are not interested in heart-to-heart discussions, parents are more understanding if they've read about the kinds of turmoil that teenagers face in struggling to become emotionally independent. In our own classes, and we understand the same is true for others teaching young adult literature, we are getting an increasing number of adult students who are there simply because they enjoy reading and talking about the young adult fiction that was not being written when they were teenagers. Those who are parents of teenagers consider it serendipitous if their teenagers also get interested and begin reading the same books.

A more structured approach is for parents to work with youth groups and church groups or to volunteer as a friend of either the public library or the school library. These kinds of activities provide parents with extra opportunities to involve young people in sharing reading experiences. In such situations, it is often a benefit to have other young people involved and for parents to trade off, so that they aren't always the leader for the particular group in which their child is a member.

Clarifying Human Relations and Values

Workers with church and civic youth groups, teachers of classes in human relations, and professional counselors working with young adults have all found that reading and discussing short stories or books can be useful. When we talk about using books to

Mary Wong, librarian at Explorer Middle School in suburban Phoenix, uses snapshots that she has taken of visiting authors as a conversation starter with students. She encourages students to find a picture of someone who looks interesting. When they come to her, she tells them something about the visit and helps the students find the author's books.

help students understand their own and other people's feelings and behavior, we sometimes use the term *bibliotherapy*. It is a word that goes in and out of fashion, at least in reference to the informal kind of work that most teachers and librarians do with young adults. Its technical meaning is the use of books by professionally trained psychologists and psychiatrists in working with people who are mentally ill. Because of this association with illness, many "book" people reject the term. They reason that if a young adult is mentally ill and in need of some kind of therapy, the therapy should come from someone trained in that field rather than from someone trained in the book business or in teaching and guiding normal and healthy young adults.

Most people agree, however, that normal and healthy young adults can benefit psychologically from reading and talking about the problems of fictional characters. All teenagers have problems of one type or another, and simply finding out that other people have them too provides some comfort. We are reassured to know that our fears and doubts have been experienced by others. David A. Williams, a communications professor at the University of Arizona, said in a newspaper interview that he would die happy if he could "prove that a positive correlation exists between the rise in anxiety in the country and the decline of pleasure reading." Research done during the 1950s and 1960s showed that anxiety is directly related to a poor concept of oneself. "It seems to me," he said, "that the human being's major concern in life is to determine what it means to be a human being." The paradox is that before people can see themselves, they have to get outside of themselves and look at the whole spectrum of human experience to see where they fit in. "When we are feeling anxious it is usually because we have a narrow perspective which sees only what it wants to see." Someone who is anxiety-ridden, paranoiac, or resentful selects experiences from life to validate those feelings. For people like this, reading can put things back into perspective. "When we read about others who have suffered similar anxieties, we don't feel so cut off and, although the world doesn't change, we change the way we look at it."[15]

As books put things back into perspective, they open up avenues of communication that successful discussion leaders tap into. It is important, however, for adults to be careful in guiding students to read and talk about personal problems. No one should be forced to participate in such a discussion, and a special effort should not be made to relate stories to the exact problem that a group member is having. In fact, it would probably be best to avoid matching up particular problems with particular students. When someone is in the midst of a crisis, chances are that he or she does not want to read and talk about someone else in a similar predicament. As a general rule, one would probably get the most from such a discussion before or after—rather than during—a time of actual crisis.

Such discussions are usually held in clubs, church groups, classes on preparation for marriage and human relations, and counseling and support group meetings at crisis centers and various institutions to which young people are sent. Because membership in these groups changes from meeting to meeting and there are no pressures for participants to do outside reading as "homework," a leader will probably be disappointed or frustrated if the discussion is planned around the expectation that everyone will have read the book. A more realistic plan is for the leader to use a short story or to give a summary of the book and a 10- to 20-minute prepared reading of the part that best delineates the problem or the topic for discussion. Using fairly well-known books, including ones that have been made into movies, increases the chances of participation. Using popular books also makes it easier for students whose appetites have been whetted to find the book and read it on their own.

In an adult group of professionals, the same purpose would be accomplished by reading a case study that would then be discussed. But case studies are written for trained adults who know how to fill in the missing details and how to interpret the symptoms. Teenagers are not psychologists, and they are not social workers or philosophers. Literature may be as close as they will ever come to discussing the kinds of problems dealt with in these fields. What follows the oral presentation can be extremely varied, depending on the nature of the group, the leader's personality, and what the purpose or the goal of the discussion is. The literature provides the group—both teenagers and adults—with a common experience that can serve as the focus for discussion. Pressures and tensions are relieved because everyone is talking in the third person about the characters in the book, although in reality many of the comments will be about first-person problems.

TABLE 10.3   THE POWERS AND LIMITATIONS OF YOUNG ADULT LITERATURE

What literature can do:	What literature cannot do:
1. It can provide a common experience or a way in which a teenager and an adult can focus their attention on the same subject.	1. It cannot cure someone's emotional illness.
2. It can serve as a discussion topic and a way to relieve embarrassment by enabling people to talk in the third person about problems with which they are concerned.	2. It cannot guarantee that readers will behave in socially approved ways.
3. It can give young readers confidence that, should they meet particular problems, they will be able to solve them.	3. It cannot directly solve readers' problems.
4. It can increase a young person's understanding of the world and the many ways that individuals find their places in it.	
5. It can comfort and reassure young adult readers by showing them that they are not the only ones who have fears and doubts.	
6. It can give adults as well as teenagers insights into adolescent psychology and values.	

In 1999, Greenwood Press launched a series of professional books edited by Joan F. Kaywell under the heading "Using Literature to Help Troubled Teenagers." Published titles include one on family issues edited by Kaywell, one on identity issues edited by Jeffrey S. Kaplan, one on societal issues edited by Pamela S. Carroll, one on health issues edited by Cynthia Ann Bowman, and one on end-of-life issues edited by Janet Allen. Chapters, which focus on the characters in specific YA books, are co-authored by specialists in young adult literature and mental health workers whose practices include teenagers.

Reading and discussing books can in no way cure mental illness, but reading widely about all kinds of problems and all kinds of solutions helps keep young people involved in thinking about moral issues. As shown in Table 10.3, about what young adult literature can and cannot do when it is used as a tool to teach about human relations and values, the positives outweigh the negatives.

Concluding Comments

This chapter highlights the fact that using and promoting books with young readers is a shared opportunity and responsibility. It belongs not only to librarians and English and reading teachers but also to everyone who works closely with young people and wants to understand them better. It can serve as a medium through which to open communication with young adults about their concerns.

Notes

[1] Janet French, "Review of *Homecoming,*" *School Library Journal* 28 (September 1981): 133.

[2] Audrey Eaglen, "What Makes a Good Review," *Top of the News* 35 (Winter 1979): 146–152.

[3] Anne Tyler, "Looking for Mom," *New York Times Book Review,* April 26, 1981, p. 52.

[4] Katherine Paterson, "Family Visions," *New York Times Book Review,* November 14, 1982, p. 41.

[5] Dorothy Mathews, "Writing about Adolescent Literature: Current Approaches and Future Directions," *Arizona English Bulletin* 18 (April 1976): 216–19.

[6] Katha Pollitt, "Why We Read: Canon to the Right of Me. . . ," *The Nation,* September 23, 1991, reprinted in *The Chronicle of Higher Education,* October 23, 1991.

[7] *Rudolfo Anaya Autobiography as Written in 1985,* copyright 1991 Rudolfo Anaya (TQS Publications; P.O. Box 9275; Berkeley, CA 94709), pp. 16–17.

[8] *The Big Aiiieeeee!: An Anthology of Chinese American and Japanese American Literature,* edited by Jeffery Paul Chan, Frank Chin, Lawson Fusao Inada, and Shawn Wong (New American Library, 1991), p. 8.

[9] Maxine Hong Kingston, "Personal Statement," in *Approaches to Teaching Kingston's THE WOMAN WARRIOR,* edited by Shirley Geok-lin Lim (Modern Language Association, 1991), p. 24.

[10] Jim Burke, *The English Teacher's Companion: A Complete Guide to Classroom, Curriculum and the Profession* (Boynton Cook, 1999), p. 252.

[11] Dorothy M. Broderick, "Whose Job Is It Anyway?" *VOYA* 6 (February 1984): 320–26.

[12] Joni Bodart, *Booktalk! Booktalking and School Visiting for Young Adult Audiences* (H. W. Wilson, 1980), pp. 2–3.

[13] Francisca Goldsmith, "What Comics Do When They Do It Right: An Interview with Art Spiegelman, *VOYA* 25:5 (December, 2002): 362.

[14] Dick Abrahamson and Eleanor Tyson, "What Every English Teacher Should Know About Free Reading," *The ALAN Review* 14 (Fall 1986): 54–58, 69.

[15] "Feeling Uptight, Anxious? Try Reading, UA Prof Says," *Tempe Daily News,* December 15, 1977.

Literature in the English Class
Short Stories, Novels, Creative Writing, Film, and Thematic Units

In response to requests from previous users of this textbook, we devote this chapter to a discussion of standard approaches to the teaching of literature in high school. Although we recognize that there is no single best way to teach and that schools, classes, students, and goals vary from school to school, from teacher to teacher, and from parent to parent, the methods of teaching literature to young people discussed here have proved their worth for large numbers of teachers and their students.

Principles of Teaching English

We believe in five principles about English teachers and the teaching of literature. We have developed these principles from our own experiences and from the writings and thoughts of many others in both books and journals. See Appendix C for a listing.

1. *English teachers must never forget that literature should be both entertaining and challenging.* Teachers must alert students to literature that the students will find challenging and satisfying through talking about individual works in many genres, perhaps in a genre unit, a thematic unit, or free reading. Is this easy to do? No, not always, but it might convince a few students that teachers care about reading and kids. If the literature does not provide entertainment and challenge, English teachers have failed.

2. *English teachers must know a wide range of literature.* Teachers should know classics of English and American literature, of course; they should also know American popular literature and young adult literature and something about Asian and European literature (e.g., Asian folktales, Norwegian drama, French short stories, or Russian novels). They should know women writers and ethnic writers, especially, but not exclusively from the United States, and what they do not know about literature, they should learn. That demands that English teachers read all sorts of literature—the great, the new, the popular, the demanding, and the puzzling. Why do they read? Because they are readers themselves and because they are always looking for books that might work with students. One of life's joys for English teachers, and maybe its greatest annoyance, is that they view every poem, every film, every newspaper article, every football game, every everything for its potential use in class.

3. *English teachers ought to know enough about dramatic techniques and oral interpretation to be comfortable reading aloud to students.* We need teachers eager and able to read material to students that just might interest, intrigue, amuse, or excite them, material that

might make young people aware of new or old books or writers or techniques or ideas. Outside of speech or drama, no classes require so much oral performance from teachers as English classes. Poetry must be read aloud. So must drama. Reading fiction aloud is half the fun of teaching short stories. If students are to learn how to read poetry or drama, it will come from English teachers comfortable with their own oral reading. One added benefit is that common devices in literature, such as metaphor or irony or ambiguity, are often more apparent when heard rather than read. Obviously, the availability of poetry or fiction on tapes or CDs means other voices can be heard, but that does not mean the teacher's voice should be silent. Granted, Ian McKellen's reading of Shakespeare exceeds the grasp of us mortals, but McKellen is not there to explain why he read a passage from *Richard III* or *Macbeth* or *Othello* as he did. English teachers are there to explain why they chose to read a particular passage and why they read it as they did.

4. *English teachers must remember the distance in education and sophistication between them and their students.* No matter what the rapport between them, it is almost equally easy for teachers to overestimate as to underestimate their students, although experienced teachers would surely prefer the first error to the second. Choosing material for an entire class is never easy and often seems impossible. Some materials—say a *New Yorker* short story or a T. S. Eliot poem or a Harold Pinter play—assume a sophistication that high school students often do not have, although sometimes their glibness in class temporarily fools a neophyte. On some occasions, a class is ready for the Pinter, but while waiting for that class, it's tempting for teachers to choose material that challenges no one and that no one greatly enjoys. Selecting literature for 15, 35, or 45 students is almost inevitably an exercise in frustration and failure. That comes with the territory, but it is no excuse for not trying to meet all students' needs with that one fabulous, never-to-be-forgotten classroom novel, poem, short story, or play. Experienced English teachers know this, but most parents and other citizens do not. Teachers should try to let others in on the secret.

5. *Finally, English teachers should teach and use only literature they enjoy.* Teachers should not be expected to fake enthusiasm or interest. If a teacher doesn't like Robert Frost's poetry or Stephen Crane's *The Red Badge of Courage,* the teacher has no business using Frost or Crane. It is permissible for both teachers and young people not to like a work or an author, assuming, of course, the teacher has read and responsibly considered the author or work in question (we can be a bit more charitable toward students on this point). If teachers do not like highly regarded modern works such as Raymond Carver's short stories or Athol Fugard's "*Master Harold*" . . . *and the Boys* or Sharon Olds's poetry, they shouldn't teach them. There are too many stories, plays, and poems out there about which teachers are presumably enthusiastic. (Obviously, this point follows our second point, that teachers are incurable, wide readers.)

None of this implies that teachers cannot change their minds about literature or writers, just as teachers know that occasionally it is great fun and profitable to work with literature about which they feel ambivalent. Nor does this imply that students should be discouraged from reading and talking about works for which the teacher has no great enthusiasm.

Our five principles for teaching literature extend to works in the curriculum guide as well as the literary canon of great books. We are not being unduly critical of the manner in which many literature curriculum guides are developed by noting that they are created by human beings with certain strengths and weaknesses, and they are fallible. As long as they are taken as guides, teachers may be helped, particularly beginning teachers, but when curriculum guides are taken as biblical edicts, absurdity reigns, and any value disappears.

Assuming teachers have a wide knowledge of literature, they can find a variety of works of equal quality to teach. What is gained from a bored teacher presenting Poe's poetry to an equally bored class? It is much better to assume that in the four years of high school these students will have one English teacher who likes Poe. And if it doesn't happen? There are worse disasters. What if no teacher wants to teach Shakespeare? We cannot imagine an English department so devoid of taste or ability, but if one exists, it is surely preferable that students leave school ignorant of Shakespeare than that they be bored by him.

Forcing teachers to teach something they do not like encourages classroom dishonesty. Teachers spout trite and obvious interpretations of literature taken from the teacher's guide, and students regurgitate on tests what they neither care about nor understand. Such dishonesty inevitably breeds boredom with literature and contempt for learning.

Literature that a teacher thinks worth teaching, however defined, ought to encourage honest teaching and honest responses from kids. As Louise Rosenblatt has pointed out again and again:

> No one else can read a literary work for us. The benefits of literature can emerge only from creative activity on the part of the reader himself. He responds to the little black marks on the page, or to the sounds of the words in his ear, and he "makes something of them." The verbal symbols enable him to draw on his past experiences with what the words point to in life and literature.[1]

Allowing young people to respond to literature slows down the teacher and the lesson because thinking takes time and brainpower. Time is required to build trust, especially for students accustomed to memorizing and spitting back whatever the teacher has said. Some students simply do not believe that a teacher wants their opinions, sometimes for good reason. Students have to be convinced that responding honestly to literature is worth the trouble and hard work. An invitation to what appears to be an intellectual coup d'état does not come easily from a teacher, and the acceptance does not come easily from students.

Using Young Adult Literature in English Classes

One of the reasons we endorse young adult literature for English classes is that students can believe a teacher who asks for their honest response to a book that features a contemporary young person facing a problem that students are more likely to face than their teacher. Young adult literature is often recommended as a bridge to appreciating literary techniques, but its role in developing the trust needed for a response-centered approach to literature may be even more important.

Teachers who believe in the value of young adult literature for either of these purposes sometimes forget that many English teachers still make fun of young adult books. To us, the criticisms often seem irrational and defensive, almost as if the books threaten teachers and their worlds. Nevertheless, young adult converts must be aware of the following protestations. We could not resist offering some counterarguments, even though we realize we're preaching to the choir.

1. *No one around here knows anything about it. If it was really worth knowing, we'd have heard about it.* It's been around quite a long time now, and since the publication of books by S. E. Hinton, Paul Zindel, Robert Lipsyte, Norma Fox Mazer, Harry Mazer, Robert Cormier, Rosa Guy, Gary Paulsen, and many more, lots of people have heard about it. In any case, the statement is a rationalization for learning nothing new. Ignorance is not an impressive justification for anything.

2. *Adolescent literature has no heritage and no respectability.* It has a heritage going back more than 130 years. Some people respect it, but few respect something they have not read.

3. *We teach only the greatest of literature, and that automatically eliminates adolescent literature from our consideration. Why should we demean ourselves or our students—and their parents—by stooping to something inferior?* We wonder how the greatest of literature was chosen for this curriculum. Were these great books chosen from a list supplied by a college teacher or by some independent body? How great are they for high school students? How long has it been since the teacher read any adolescent books? Some students—and not just the slowest—get little pleasure from reading. We believe it is the English teacher's responsibility to help students find pleasure in reading. We wonder if only the greatest will do that.

4. *We can't afford thirty or forty copies of something we don't know. That's why we don't use adolescent books.* Maybe you ought to read some of the books. That may tell you whether you'd want to use a class set, and it might suggest that individual titles are better than a set of anything.

5. *Kids have to grow up and take themselves and their work seriously. I do. We expect them to. That takes care of adolescent literature as far as my school is concerned.* We take our work and our kids seriously, too. We'd also like them to enjoy some of their reading. Bruce Brooks's and Sue Ellen Bridgers' books contain plenty of serious stuff, but they also provide the joy of discovering similarities between readers and characters.

6. *Adolescent literature has no permanence. Something is popular today, and something else is popular tomorrow. Great literature is timeless and unchanging. How can we be expected to keep track of ephemera?* What a wonderful justification for reading nothing new. Yes, new books come out all the time. Some new books have a chance to escape the dustheap. Some don't. Most adolescent books don't last, but Alcott's *Little Women* and Twain's *Huckleberry Finn* have been around a long time. Also, consider that S. E. Hinton's *The Outsiders,* Robert Lipsyte's *The Contender,* and Paul Zindel's *The Pigman* are over thirty years old. Will they last? That's anyone's guess. We would put money on a bet that some of Robert Cormier's and Katherine Paterson's books will last. For that matter, we can think of a dozen other young adult writers who seem likely to last.

7. *Why have kids spend time in class reading something they can easily read on their own? Shouldn't class time be spent on books that are challenging, books that kids won't find on their own, books that will make kids stretch intellectually?* Some of those kids may not find those

books as challenging as Cormier's *After the First Death* or Alan Garner's *The Owl Service* or Alice Childress's *A Hero Ain't Nothin' But a Sandwich,* and these three titles, among many more, are challenging emotionally and intellectually. Besides, what is there about *The Pearl* or *Silas Marner* or *The Old Man and the Sea* that makes their difficulties worth stretching for? The painful truth is that many young people do not find reading enjoyable, and even though they may not find *Silas Marner* on their own, they also won't find Lowry's *The Giver* or Voigt's *Homecoming,* which might come closer to reaching them.

8. *Isn't adolescent literature formula literature?* Yes, sometimes, but not always. *Formula* is a dirty word—*archetype* has more positive connotations. We are impressed to hear someone talk about Dostoyevsky's grand inevitability in *Crime and Punishment.* We are not impressed to hear someone talk about the total predictability of a Nancy Drew mystery. There's nevertheless an uncomfortable similarity between the two comments, if not the two books. Then we must not forget that there is young adult literature and there is young adult literature. Surely a teacher could be justified in using Cormier's *I Am the Cheese* or Paula Fox's *One-Eyed Cat* in a discussion of archetypes.

9. *Isn't it silly and simple-minded stuff about dating and trivia like that?* Sometimes, yes. Most of the time, no. How long has it been since you read Virginia Hamilton, Jill Paton-Walsh, Cynthia Voigt, or Zibby Oneal?

10. *Isn't it mostly about depressing problems—like suicide, death, abortion, pregnancy? Hasn't it been censored a lot?* Yes, it can be serious, and some of it has been censored, but see the thoughtful comments that follow.

Observations by Elaine Simpson and Dorothy Broderick speak more effectively than we can to the last three objections. Simpson addresses her remarks to those librarians and others who for years criticized junior novels for their innocence and their pat answers that instilled false conceptions and failed to deal with fundamental problems.

Then juvenile authors and editors began giving us such books as *Go Ask Alice; Run Softly, Go Fast; Admission to the Feast; Run, Shelley, Run; The Chocolate War.* I could go on and on naming both fiction and nonfiction.

And what happened? All too many of these same people who had been asking for an honest story about serious teenage problems began protesting: language like *that* in a book for young people? Are rape, abortion, homosexuality, unwed mothers, suicide, drugs, unsympathetic portrayals of parents, and violence appropriate for junior novels? Are young people ready for such explicit realism? Would you want your daughter to read one?[2]

Dorothy Broderick focused on the charge most often expressed by ultraconservatives, "namely, that young adult books are not uplifting. Why, oh why, cry these critics, do the authors have to deal with such depressing subjects. Why can't we go back to the good old days?" Broderick's answer:

As one who has spent six decades on this planet, let me tell you an important fact: *There were no good old days.* Every problem confronted in a young adult novel today not only existed during my childhood and adolescence, but was known to most of us. There were drunks in families, there were wife abusers, there were child molesters, divorce, certainly death and dying, mental illness, pre-marital pregnancy, and, yes, abortions if you were among the elite. In high school, one of my classmates went home one day to find his father had hung himself in the garage; a couple of weeks later he went home to find his mother had done the same thing.[3]

Adolescent literature has a place in the literature program because it appeals to young people. Why? Young adult novels are short or at least shorter than most modern novels or classics studied in schools. Young adult books are easier to read (or so they seem at first reading) than most adult or classic novels. They are about young people the age of the readers and concerned with real issues and problems facing adolescents, particularly the readers (and that's often not true of adult books or classics). The photos or paintings on young adult paperbacks are calculated to grab readers. There is also a blurb showing, for example, that the book is about a kid who has this wonderful brother who's dying of AIDS, or it is about a girl whose grandmother is senile, or it is about a boy and a girl enmeshed in a love affair against their parents' wishes. With such come-ons, who is surprised when young people grab young adult titles. The last reason for their popularity with many young people is that the books are often perceived to be unacceptable to traditional teachers; that is, they're forbidden fruit.

What makes young adult books so unattractive to some teachers? Besides the reasons listed earlier, Robert C. Small, Jr., adds an unpleasant final reason. He writes that the goal of most literature programs is to designate the teacher as literary expert and translator of books to lowly students who seem to have no role at all, other than to be recipients of the largesse of the expert-translator-teacher.[4] When young people read adolescent books, they are the experts, and they may need to serve as translators to adults who wish to understand the adolescent books.

What makes young adult books so attractive to other English teachers is the fact that for an imaginative teacher, young adult books have so many uses. An individual title can be studied by the whole class, although that's comparatively rare. They can be paired with adult books, classics or not, as recommended by some of the books in Appendix C. And they work beautifully in free reading and thematic units. Their possibilities extend as far as the teachers' imaginations because they provide what other good novels do along with an almost guaranteed adolescent interest. Richard Jackson, when he was editor-in-chief at Bradbury Press, explained that YA literature should illuminate rather than educate, raise questions rather than trot out answers. And it should entertain. Though society changes from one generation to another, its rites of passage remain quite fixed. Literature for young adults will endure because the impulse to record and reconsider those rites strikes us all. We can't resist it—and though they may not admit the fact, adolescents do hear us.[5]

Using Short Stories in English Class

Short story author Tim Wynne-Jones, who has been described as "the master of the glimpse," wrote for the sixth edition of this textbook,

> A good short isn't a lot of things. It isn't long, it isn't preachy, and it certainly isn't a novel wannabe. It isn't a sketch, it's a miniature. Not the whole season, just the big

game. Not the whole sunset, just one straggler on the beach. It does not presume to grandeur. It is happy to invoke a gasp of surprise, a belly laugh, a single tear.[6]

For all of these reasons, short stories work well in classrooms where students can read fifteen short stories in the time it takes to read one or two novels. Through reading the larger number of short stories, they can meet a greater variety of viewpoints and representatives of different ethnic groups and cultures. Because the best of modern American authors have written short stories, students can experience high-quality writing in pieces that are short enough for comfortable reading.

If students are to enjoy and profit from reading short stories (Focus Box 11.1), some preparation is necessary. Kids are not born with genes labeled "How to Read Short Stories Perceptively." Teachers must help students develop the skills to enter imaginative works. Tempting as simple solutions have been to curriculum designers, students should not be required to master a vocabulary list of "Thirty Magic Literary Terms That Will Change Your Life and Make You the Reader You Have Always Longed to Be." There's a place for learning about *verisimilitude, point of view, unreliable narrator, sprung rhythm, synecdoche, foreshadowing, Petrarchan sonnet,* and *carpe diem* if and when the terms enlighten students but never as a series of terms in a pedagogical vacuum.

Finding out about the codes that make one piece of literature succeed while another one fails forces teachers to consider how they went about getting into a short story, for example, and how they get into a story that's new to them. There is no single way of getting at any literary work, and several approaches may need to be tried. Students may come to class already knowing how to listen, to take assiduous notes on what the teacher says is important, and to play all this back at test time, but none of that has much to do with reading. In many ways, a careful reading of a work by student A produces a different work from an equally careful reading by student B or student C because readers base their feelings on past experiences and present morality to yield a slightly different story with each reader, and sometimes a greatly different story. These steps may help a class break the code in reading a short story.

1. Read the first sentence carefully (and the first paragraph). What do they tell you about the setting, characters, or tension?
2. Predict from the first paragraph what's likely to follow.
3. Speed-read the story to get some sense of what it's about and who the characters are (probably the only part that can be done outside of class).
4. Isolate the problems in reading the story (e.g., dialect, structure, conflicting characters).
5. Reread the story, doing parts or all of it aloud.

Going through this with students should help them learn how literary codes can be broken through careful reading. What can we safely say to our classes about virtually all short stories? We can tell students that all fiction is based on conflict, and we might begin by exploring with them different kinds of conflict. We can say, with some confidence, that the title of the story usually is significant.

We can tell students that first-person narrators are similar to readers in many ways—fallible mortals likely to make mistakes in judging people or letting their emo-

FOCUS BOX 11.1   *Teaching Short Stories*

American Short Story Masterpieces, edited by Raymond Carver and Tom Jenks. Dell, 1987. Included are Flannery O'Connor's "A Good Man Is Hard to Find," Bernard Malamud's "The Magic Barrel," and Joyce Carol Oates's "Where Are You Going, Where Have You Been?"

Do You Like It Here? edited by Robert Benard. Dell, 1989. Included are stories about school by Sue Kaufman, Maureen Daly, John O'Hara, Tobias Wolff, and Gore Vidal.

Fifty Great American Short Stories, edited by Milton Crane. Bantam, 1980. Included are Mary E. Freeman's "A New England Nun," Conrad Aiken's "Silent Snow, Secret Snow," James Agee's "A Mother's Tale," William Carlos Williams's "The Use of Force," Jack London's "To Build a Fire," Ambrose Bierce's "The Damned Thing," and Stephen Vincent Benet's "By the Waters of Babylon." Crane has also done *Fifty Great Short Stories* (Bantam, 1981).

Great American Short Stories, edited by Wallace and Mary Stegner. Dell, 1957. This fine and safe collection includes William Daniel Steele's "The Man Who Saw Through Heaven," Henry James's "The Real Thing," and Walter Van Tilburg Clark's "The Wind and the Snow of Winter."

Leaving Home: 15 Distinguished Authors Explore Personal Journeys, selected by Hazel Rochman and Darlene Z. McCampbell. HarperCollins, 1997. Allan Sherman, Tim O'Brien, David St. John, Norma Fox Mazer, Gary Soto, and Toni Morrison are among the authors represented.

Points of View, edited by James Moffett and Kenneth R. McElheny. Mentor/NAL, 1965. Included are William Carlos Williams's "The Use of Force," Nikolai Gogol's "The Diary of a Madman," Joseph Conrad's "The Idiots," Daniel Keyes's "Flowers for Algernon," John Updike's "A & P," and Anton Chekhov's "Enemies."

Short Stories in the Classroom, edited by Carole L. Hamilton and Peter Kratzke. National Council of Teachers of English, 1999. Essays offer advice on teaching the works of such writers as Toni Cade Bambara, Armistead Maupin, Tim O'Brien, and Sherman Alexie.

Short Story Masterpieces, edited by Robert Penn Warren and Albert Erskine. Dell, 1954. Included are Joseph Conrad's "An Outpost of Progress," F. Scott Fitzgerald's "Winter Dreams," D. H. Lawrence's "The Horse Dealer's Daughter," Saki's "The Open Window," Somerset Maugham's "The Outstation," Sherwood Anderson's "The Egg," and William Faulkner's "Barn Burning."

Teaching the Short Story: A Guide to Using Stories from Around the World, edited by Bonnie H. Neumann and Helen M. McDonnell. National Council of Teachers of English, 1996. Annotations provide basic information, while indexes suggest thematic and literary comparisons for 175 highly teachable short stories from fifty countries.

---

tions get in the way. Students are sometimes puzzled when we raise this point, but it's essential because readers tend to take the narrator's word for almost anything.

We can also tell students how important those first words are in most short stories. It is the author's opportunity to grab the audience, and some readers (at least outside school) may decide to drop the story and the author based on those words. Most students rush through the first lines. In class we can force them to slow down by reading aloud the first lines over and over.

The questions English teachers pose for students should be carefully thought out and played with. Beginning teachers need to develop and practice the questions before class, while more experienced teachers can rely on mental notes of what makes the discussion worthwhile rather than mere chitchat to take up 55 minutes of class.

Many teachers ask students to keep journals and to respond to a question or a comment written on the board for the first 5 or 10 minutes of class. This activity serves several purposes, including quieting students, turning their attention to the story, and focusing on an issue in the story (probably a key aspect). It allows or forces students to consider what they will say later in class when the question or comment is posed again. Journals also provide an opportunity for students to outline preliminary ideas for papers that may be developed later.

The first few moments of class discussion are often taken up with simple recall questions, reassuring to students and setting up details in the story that may have significance later on. One schema developed and recommended by Edward J. Gordon and Dwight L. Burton[7] suggests how teachers can move from concrete to abstract, as in the following example based on questions our students devised for teaching Nadine Gordimer's "A Company of Laughing Faces." Gordimer's short story is set at a beach resort in South Africa. A young girl has been brought there by her demanding mother to spend Christmas holidays with "nice" people. The girl is almost raped, finds the nice people dull and not all that nice, and finds a friend in a little boy who later drowns.

1. *Questions requiring students to remember facts:*
   a. Describe the setting of the story.
   b. Describe the protagonist and the other major characters.
   c. What new things had Kathy's mother bought for her?
   d. List the major events in the story.
2. *Questions requiring students to prove or disprove a generalization made by someone else:*
   a. Although the story is set in a South African resort, I think it could have happened at any resort frequented by the upper middle class. Do you agree or disagree? What differences were there between this holiday and that of American college students going to Florida beaches during spring break? Are these differences crucial to the story?
   b. Some readers have interpreted this story as saying that Kathy was a conformist. Do you agree? In what ways was she a conformist? In what ways was she different?
   c. One interpretation is that the nameless young man in the story represents the anonymous crowds of young people at the resort. Do you agree or disagree? On what evidence?
   d. When Kathy put on her new clothes, the author said that the "disguise worked perfectly." Was Kathy in "disguise" any more than the others? Support your answer with evidence from the story as well as from your own experiences.
3. *Questions requiring students to derive their own generalizations:*
   a. What kind of relationship did Mrs. Hack and Kathy have?
   b. What is Kathy's perception of being young? Who has shaped that perception? Do the events in the story change her perception?
   c. Why doesn't the author give the "young man" a name?
   d. Why does the author contrast the constant activity of the other young people with Kathy's stillness?

4. *Questions requiring students to generalize about the relation of the total work to human experience:*

    a. What did Kathy mean when she said that the sight in the lagoon was the "one truth and the one beauty" in her holiday?

    b. Compare Kathy's relationship with the nameless young man to that of the Bute boy. What is the author saying by showing these two different relationships?

    c. Relate the different parts of the story to Kathy's development in life.

    d. What is the significance of the statement "The only need she [Kathy] had these days, it seemed, was to be where the gang was; then the question of what to do and how to feel solved itself." Is Kathy satisfied with the answer the gang provides for her? Why or why not?

5. *Questions requiring students to carry generalizations derived from the work into their own lives:*

    a. Have you been in a situation similar to the one experienced by Kathy? How did it make you feel?

    b. What kinds of security do you get from a group? How hard is it to break away?

    c. Have you seen parents like Kathy's mother? What are some ways that young people defend themselves from well-meaning parents who don't understand the situation?

While teachers should enter their classrooms having thought enough about a story to devise such questions and to have anticipated possible answers, they should not fire off the questions as if they are giving a spelling test, but instead should use them to inspire thinking and comments from the class. Observers of good literary discussions have found that students circle back around to all these levels and that while students seldom pose questions, they frequently make observations that stimulate other students to comment and add their own opinions.

Probably the most important part of a discussion—and unfortunately the most often ignored—is the summing up. In too many classes, the bell rings in the midst of a discussion and students rush away without gathering their thoughts. Such "fly-away" endings cause students to lose respect for class discussions. If they think the teacher is just filling in time until the bell rings, they won't put forth their best efforts. The successful teacher keeps an eye on the clock and saves at least a couple of minutes to draw things together before students are distracted from the topic at hand. Good teachers continually work to develop skill in summarizing throughout a discussion. They draw attention to those points that the class basically agrees on, they praise insightful comments that help the rest of the class see something they might have missed, they search out reasons for disagreement, and they lead students to see connections between the present discussion and previous ones about similar themes or topics.

Determining what short stories (or poems or plays) belong in what grades is one of life's puzzles. Probably the most important thing to consider is whether the teacher likes the story and wants to teach it. More objective considerations are the age of the protagonist, how quickly the author "grabs" the readers, the complexity of both plot and characterization, and how well the story fits in with what else the class is doing.

Useful reference tools for finding publication information about particular short stories are the *Chicorel Index to Short Stories in Anthologies and Collections,* which includes information on publications up until 1977, and the *Short Story Index,* published at frequent

With the help of stick-on letters and two pairs of thrift-shop shorts, this teacher let her students know that she valued her short story collection enough to treat it as special.

intervals by the H. W. Wilson Company. The Wilson *Index* includes information on magazine publications from 1953 to the present.

Within the last fifteen years, publishers have produced several attractive collections of short stories written by young adult authors (Focus Box 11.2). Many of these are designed for independent reading, but they can also be brought into classrooms for various purposes. Genres include realistic fiction, science fiction, fantasy, humor, animal stories, folklore, and myth. Students who are hung up on a particular kind of book can usually be enticed to try at least a short story in another genre. See the photos above and on p. 340 for two teachers' approaches. Within the same genre, students can be encouraged to select more challenging books. While warning teachers not to overanalyze short stories, we suggest reading them aloud in class to introduce a topic for discussion or writing, to illustrate a point, fill out a thematic unit, provide material for readers' theater and dramatization, and give students enough experience with literary concepts that they can learn the meanings of literary terms from actual experience rather than from memorizing definitions.

Using Novels in English Class

Assigning one novel to be read by an entire class is a popular practice with teachers, partly because it is reassuring to know what's on the agenda for the next few days or, in some classes, the next few weeks. After struggling with grammar and composition, in which class members' abilities are obviously at great distances from each other, it should be a treat for teachers and the students all to join in reading the same book,

FOCUS BOX 11.2   *Recommended Short Story Collections by YA Authors*

Note: Other short story collections are listed elsewhere based on subject matter or genre.

Am I Blue? Coming Out from the Silence, edited by Marion Dane Bauer. HarperCollins, 1994. Several popular writers contributed stories centering on coming to terms with homosexuality.

Athletic Shorts: Six Short Stories by Chris Crutcher. Greenwillow, 1991. The athletes in these stories may attract readers to Crutcher's sports novels because several of the protagonists are the same.

Baseball in April and Other Stories by Gary Soto. Harcourt Brace Jovanovich, 1990. These eleven fairly simple stories are about everyday events in lives of Mexican American kids living in the Fresno, California, neighborhood where Soto grew up.

First French Kiss and Other Traumas by Adam Bagdasarian. Melanie Kroupa Books/FSG, 2002. Bagdasarian arranges these mostly funny autobiographical stories not chronologically but as they clump in his memory. They take him from about age 10 into his early twenties.

Girl Goddess #9 by Francesca Lia Block. HarperCollins, 1996. From reading this collection of nine short stories, readers come away feeling acquainted with some young Los Angeles residents who are a lot more interesting than "the girl next door."

Half-Human, compiled and edited by Bruce Coville. Scholastic, 2001. Each of these ten stories is appropriately illustrated with a surrealistic photograph. Coville's own story ends the collection. Earlier short story collections written by Coville include his *Odder Than Ever,* 1999, and *Oddly Enough,* 1994, both from Harcourt Brace Jovanovich.

Heartbeats and Other Stories by Peter D. Sieruta. HarperCollins, 1989. A mix of the romantic and funny, several come from boys' viewpoints.

Kissing Tennessee: And Other Stories from the Stardust Dance by Kathi Appelt. Harcourt, 2000. The magic in these stories all takes place in the Dogwood Junior High School cafeteria on the "most extraordinary night of the year." Even the night janitor loves it because she gets paid for overtime.

The Leaving by Budge Wilson. Philomel, 1992. Winner of the 1991 Canadian Young Adult Book Award, these nine coming-of-age stories are written in first person from the viewpoint of young women. Wilson's 1995 collection, *The Dandelion Garden* (Philomel), was also well received.

Lord of the Fries: And Other Stories by Tim Wynne-Jones. Dorling Kindersley Ink, 1999. Junior high and middle school readers will enjoy meeting the characters in these seven contemporary stories, each with an intriguing plot.

Sixteen: Short Stories by Outstanding Writers for Young Adults, edited by Donald R. Gallo. Delacorte, 1984. Gallo's first collection in which he invited YA authors to contribute short stories was followed by several others, all from Delacorte: *Visions* (1987), *Connections* (1989), *Short Circuits* (1992), *Join In: Multiethnic Short Stories* (1993), *Within Reach* (1993), *Ultimate Sports* (1995), *No Easy Answers* (1997), and *Time Capsule* (1999).

Small Avalanches and Other Stories by Joyce Carol Oates. HarperTrophy, 2003. Collected from Oates's lifetime of writing, these stories are about teenagers although not necessarily written with a teenage audience in mind.

Tomorrowland: 10 Stories about the Future edited by Michael Cart. Scholastic, 1999. Cart collected these stories from top YA authors as a tribute to the new millennium. They hold up well long after the celebration has faded. A plus is that the authors appended comments on their creative processes.

Traveling on into the Light and Other Stories by Martha Brooks by Martha Brooks. Orchard, 1994. Each story presents a moment that matters, a time that stands out from the "insane jumble" of life experiences.

Working Days: Short Stories about Teenagers at Work, edited by Anne Mazer. Persea, 1997. Mazer's collection helps to counterbalance the way authors have mostly ignored the importance of jobs in the life of teenagers.

A class at Gilbert Junior High enjoyed reporting on the short stories they read through creating tryptychs. A square sheet of paper is folded diagonally both directions. Students use one quarter for writing about the story and two quarters for drawing an illustration. When the fourth quarter is folded underneath and taped, the tryptychs are ready to be tacked or taped to a wall for an interesting three-dimensional display.

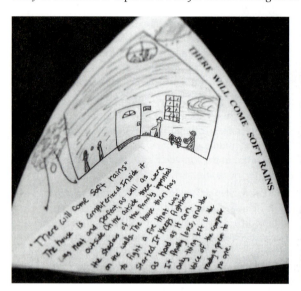

some in class and some at home. For students with reading difficulties, teachers might suggest that they try checking out an audiotape of the novel from a library. A surprisingly large number of books have been recorded. Students can read along with the tape or just listen to the tape. Some are condensations, while others are full readings, but either way the listening experience will be better than resorting to *Cliff's Notes*.

Although many teachers assume that having specific novels read by the entire class has always been a standard part of the English curriculum, the practice is not universally accepted. Some teachers argue that whatever can be learned by studying a common novel can be just as easily learned by studying several short stories. Others say that short stories neither allow for a long-term immersion in a created world nor provide complex character development taking place over a period of a character's lifetime.

One of the problems in using novels is the expense of acquiring a set of novels of your choice (e.g., Bernard Malamud's *The Assistant*, Robin McKinley's *The Hero and the Crown*, or Mary Shelley's *Frankenstein or the Modern Prometheus*) rather than inheriting whatever is left in the English department closet. Another problem is the length of time it takes for students to read the novel (rarely less than a week and more likely two or more). Adults have been known to stop reading when boredom sets in, but no such benediction comes to kids when they're reading a book for a class. More than sixty years ago, Howard Francis Seely wondered about our attraction to novels.

> Just why is it deemed imperative that a whole class read the same novels at the same time, anyway? I haven't heard a sound answer yet. . . . The burden of most of these

answers can be recapitulated briefly. A frequent one is that reading one book permits class discussion (which discussion, however, more often than not turns out to be the answering of factual questions chiefly of a trifling nature). . . . A third answer indicates reading this one particular book in this particular class will enlighten the pupils to the structure of the novel as a literary form (which it won't, and which would be of doubtful immediate or ultimate value even if it did). . . . Perhaps the most frequent (and likely the most futile) argument of all is this: If Johnny hasn't read *The Talisman* in the ninth grade with his group, what will happen to him when he comes to *The Spy* in the tenth? That question is generally hurled at me with an air of utter, crushing finality. I can only faintly ask, "Well, just what *would?*" With that I'm given up as hopeless.[8]

A few years later, a teacher from England worried about teaching the novel on other grounds.

Once the novelty has worn off a book, the child's interest in it can very easily flag. . . . Even the best novel rarely occupies us more than a few evenings. It is curious that teachers . . . should so often expect the restless mind of the child to possess a greater staying power in this respect than they possess themselves.[9]

English teachers who wish to use novels for common reading should choose books they believe will appeal to young people. Never choose something because it is reputedly a classic and, therefore, will somehow be magically good for students. Do not choose a book solely because it has won an award. Some teachers and librarians assume that an award-winning book is quality literature. Generally, there's merit in that, but winners are chosen by human beings, not gods, and human beings make mistakes, some of them wondrous to behold. Anyone who has been part of a committee charged with choosing a book award knows that books are removed from final consideration for reasons having nothing to do with literary merit or adolescent appeal. Controversial books, such as those with more than marginal profanity or mild sex, frighten committees, and compromise is inevitable.[10] This is as true of awards for adults as for young people; Pulitzer and Nobel winners have frequently been controversial and debated for years.

Some teachers do not have to worry about selection because choices are established by school or district curricula. Among the most widely used titles are John Steinbeck's *Of Mice and Men,* Harper Lee's *To Kill a Mockingbird,* Mark Twain's *Adventures of Huckleberry Finn,* William Golding's *Lord of the Flies,* and Robert Cormier's *The Chocolate War.* All five are understandably popular with teachers and students, and all five are among the most widely censored books in public schools.

Those interested in finding suggestions on what novels work well in classrooms should skim through back issues of the *English Journal* or their state NCTE affiliate journals, such as New York's *English Record,* the *Arizona English Bulletin, California English,* the *Connecticut English Journal,* and the *Virginia English Bulletin.* Successful English teachers understandably love to tell about the ones that didn't get away.

Author and former teacher Richard Peck devised the following ten questions[11] to help teachers move students past their *I-liked-it* vs. *I-didn't-like-it* reactions. Each question is followed by his UM (Ulterior Motive):

1. What would this story be like if the main character were of the opposite sex?

UM: To approach the thinking of the author, who must decide what kind of protagonist or narrator will best embody or express the viewpoint. Could the protagonist of *The Member of the Wedding* be a boy instead of a girl? Could Jerry Renault in *The Chocolate War* be a female victim of a female gang? Certainly, though each book would seem different in many superficial ways. Such a question might even temporarily defuse the sexual polarization rampant in junior high.

2. Why is this story set where it is (not *what* is the setting)?

UM: To point out the setting as an author's device to draw the reader into the action by means of recognizable trappings. The isolated setting of *Lord of the Flies* is a clear, if negative, example. But why is a soap opera almost always placed in an upper middle class suburban setting? Why do so few YA novels occur in historic or exotic settings?

3. If you were to film this story, what characters would you eliminate if you couldn't use them all?

UM: To contrast the human richness of a novel with the necessary simplification of a TV show. Confronted with the need to eliminate some of the characters who add texture, some readers may rise up in defense of their favorites.

4. Would you film this story in black and white or in color?

UM: To consider *tone*. The initial reaction in this florid age is to opt for color in everything. But some young readers may remember that the most chilling Dracula films are in black and white, perhaps in part because dark shadows are always darkest and black blood is more menacing than red.

5. How is the main character different from you?

UM: To relent for once in our attempts to get the young readers to identify on their own limited terms. Protagonists regularly embody traits for the reader to aspire to. In YA books, they typically have powers, insights, and surmountable drawbacks that readers will often respond to without processing.

6. Why or why not would this story make a good TV series?

UM: To contrast the shaping of a book's sequential chapters in the larger shape of the plot to the episodes of a TV series that repeat narrowly but do not rise from their formula to a central conclusion.

7. What's one thing in this story that's happened to you?

UM: To elicit an anecdotal response that draws the reader into the book. YA novels typically deal in the shock of recognition in their depicting of highly realistic school, social, and personal situations. Science fiction and fantasy use very human situations to balance their more fabulous elements and to make room for the earthbound reader.

8. Reread the first paragraph of Chapter 1. What's in it that makes you read on?

UM: To begin a book where the author must, in assessing the need for immediate involvement in an age not known for its patient attention span. An even more wistful motive is to suggest that young people include in their own writing immediately attractive devices for gaining the attention of the reader, if only the poor teacher.

9. If you had to design a new cover for this book, what would it look like?

UM: To consider the often deceptive packaging of the book in this visual era, particularly the paperback cover, and to encourage a more skeptical eye among those who were being bombarded by packaging and commercial claims long before they could read.

10. What does the title tell you about the book? Does it tell the truth?

UM: To remind readers that the title may well be the most important words the author writes and to encourage their defenses against titles that titillate and oversell.

Literature Circles

Literature circles are one of the ways that teachers try to initiate students into participating in conversations about books. An obvious benefit of dividing classes into "circles" of five or six students is that in the same amount of time many more students will be able to make observations and comments than in the traditional approach in which one teacher leads thirty students in a discussion. Another advantage is that each group can be reading a book, at least partially of its own choosing. In a college class such as the one you are probably in, students could do all of the reading outside of class and spend only an hour in a discussion with perhaps an extra half-period for group sharing. In high schools, the experience is usually spaced out over two weeks so that the students have time for reading both in and outside of class. Three or four days are spent in discussions, with the final discussion day being devoted to brief presentations by each group to the whole class.

This means that in the six weeks that is usually devoted to a common reading of a single book, students can read and discuss two or three books. The law of averages, plus the fact that the readers help select the books they read, means that participants have a good chance of appreciating their reading experience. Also, when the program succeeds, students often choose to read on their own one or two of the books that their classmates appear to have enjoyed.

The biggest resistance to this approach comes from teachers who feel that if a book is so simple that kids can read and discuss it on their own, there is no use in wasting class time on it. We hear less of this attitude than we used to because more and more teachers are beginning to worry that if they do not lead students to enjoy reading books in school, these students will go through life getting both their enjoyment and their enlightenment from whatever their acquaintances happen to say, or from whatever snippets they happen to find on the Internet or hear through other mass media.

The fact that the teacher cannot be involved in all the groups at once puts greater responsibility on the shoulders of students. This can be good in that students know that the success of the discussion depends on them, but it can also be bad in that students are tempted to talk about other things. To keep the most verbal students from taking over every discussion as well as to encourage involvement from everyone, a common practice is to make a list of jobs that students either volunteer for or receive by assignment on a rotating basis. When setting up literature circles, you can choose from the following list of jobs or devise additional jobs of your own. While you will probably always want someone to fill the first three categories, be flexible with the others and make sure that over the course of a semester students are assigned to different responsibilities. Students get bored with *same-old-same-old,* plus different books lend themselves to different possibilities.

1. *The Discussion Leader* helps the members decide how far the participants should read before their next meeting, keeps the group "on task," and makes sure that all students have a chance to participate. These leaders are encouraged to start with the "seeds" provided by other students and are cautioned against asking simple "fact" questions or questions that can be answered with a *yes* or *no*.

2. *The Recorder* takes notes and is responsible for summarizing the group's observations either for the group itself or in a report to the whole class.

3. *Initiators* (probably two or three) make *seed* cards, on which they write questions or ideas for the group to begin discussion. They give these seeds to the discussion leader and stand ready to explain what they meant or what kinds of ideas they were hoping to elicit.

4. *Character Guides* come ready to describe the personality and the physical characteristics of the main characters and to lead the group in figuring out how and why these characters change throughout the story.

5. *A Word Detective* watches for unusual words or ordinary words used in different senses. This person jots down the words and the page numbers and comes ready to lead the other students in seeing why these words are "special."

6. *A Plot Guide* starts each day's discussion by summarizing the events that have happened in the course of the day's reading. He or she invites other group members to speculate on the importance of the events and helps group members become comfortable with such words as *exposition, rising action, climax,* and *denouement.*

7. *Future Authors* select three or four passages that they wish they had written. They come ready to read the passages and to explain what they like about them. Are there interesting allusions or metaphors? Are they particularly surprising in how much information they present in so few words? Do they have underlying humor or foreshadowing, or do they inspire the reader to thoughtfulness?

8. *A Drama Director* suggests how the group might present the sense of their book to their classmates through a readers' theater presentation, a television talk show, or a short skit. If there is time for such class presentations, the Director is in charge of soliciting help from the other students.

9. *A Graphic Designer* figures out and brings the needed supplies for the group to make some kind of a chart or poster that will help explain the idea of their book.

This past semester at Arizona State University we conducted a service-learning class in which students who are taking, or have taken, the class in young adult literature traveled to a local high school to conduct literature circles with eleventh-grade "reluctant" readers. Everyone involved was pleased to have had the experience, but we need to confess that even with the literature circles being led by seven enthusiastic college students, under the direction of doctoral student Elizabeth Petroelje Stolle, they did not succeed 100 percent of the time. The students went to the high school on Tuesday and Thursday afternoons. They came to the first class with multiple copies of several books including Glendon Swarthout's *Bless the Beasts and Children;* Rudolfo Anaya's *Bless Me, Ultima;* David Almond's *Kit's Wilderness;* Joan Bauer's *Rules of the Road;* Louis Sachar's *Holes;* S. E. Hinton's *The Outsiders;* Gary Soto's *Buried Onions;* and Paul Zindel's *My Darling, My Hamburger* and *The Pigman.* The college students gave book talks, and the high school students then "bid" on which books they wanted to read. The ability to choose which books they read was important to the students, and the circles got off to a rocky start in the few instances in which students were assigned books other than their first choice.

Once the literature circles were organized, the procedures were explained and students were assigned the roles they would take for the first discussion. They were also asked to write down their feelings and ideas in a reading journal and to put sticky notes wherever they had a question or came to a word they did not know.

At the end of the semester students wrote evaluation comments. Nearly all of them expressed positive attitudes about working with the college interns—e.g., "They were fun to talk to" and "They should come three or four times a week." However, it is hard to know how to classify such comments as "The circles took time away from the period, so the day went by faster," and "I finished all the books I read—even when they sucked!" Clearly positive comments included:

- You can learn things that you wouldn't learn if you read a book alone.
- Working together like this showed the differences in our reactions.
- If I missed something, then most likely we would talk about it in our group.
- It's nice talking about the books with the group because when you read a book on your own you can enjoy it, but if you talk about it, it's like a movie.

In answer to a question on how they felt themselves "improving as readers," students wrote:

- I can read for a longer period of time without getting a headache!
- I actually read the books now.
- Since I have been reading more, I'm much faster than before.
- I find myself underlining words I don't know.

In answer to what they liked least about the literature circles, answers varied from "I'd rather read on my own" to "Some of my fellow students bugged me no end." Aspects that were mentioned by several students focused on the formal structure of the circles. Several mentioned that they did not like being assigned particular jobs, especially having to make sticky notes and thinking about "seeds" for discussion. One described the writing parts as "annoying," while another objected to writing in a journal since "We all talk about the book later on anyways." One student candidly confessed, "I'm tired of work around 6th hour because I have just come from lunch," while another objected to having to do "Homework—nobody likes homework!"

When asked to comment on their favorite book, three students listed *Bless Me, Ultima* because "It's a good book with mystery," "It's different from the books I'm used to reading," and "It had some intense stuff that kept me reading." Five students listed *Holes* as their favorite" "It was interesting," "It kept my attention," "The intern made it fun," and "It was easy." *The Outsiders* kept one reader "on my toes the whole time," while *My Darling, My Hamburger* was a favorite because "It's about people and I like books like that," "I like love stories," and "It's about teens."

As might be expected, the evaluative comments from the college interns were more fully developed as shown by these excerpts:

- I know one of the goals is to get the students to talk, but I found it easier to discuss the books when they didn't "realize" they were talking about the book because we shadowed it with something else. I would love to see more possibilities for activities.

- I would improve the choice of books. I overhead one student say, "There aren't any good books to choose." I felt the same way—sorry!
- In my first group we read *Bless the Beasts and Children.* Group members seemed to have done their reading, but they were relatively quiet and didn't speak up unless I prodded them or let the discussion get off topic. Jimmy mostly slept with his head on the desk, Michael either chatted with Jimmy or looked around the room. Robert and Karina paid attention and answered questions, but nothing more, while Michelle did most of the talking. On the third day, after the first couple of minutes, Jimmy had to leave and was gone the rest of class. The others in the group started to talk freely and confidently about what they read. It was the first time that the students initiated ideas and kept the discussion going without either Michelle or me feeding them questions. Looking back, I think it was not a coincidence that the change took place when Jimmy left. This is not to say that Jimmy did anything intentionally. In fact, he may not have even realized the extent of his influence, but even his friend Michael, who gave no appearance of feeling intimidated, still felt he had to "play it cool" in front of Jimmy.
- The one thing that surprised me in my experience was the way all the students interacted with each other. Although once in a while I heard someone say something negative about another student, most of the time I felt the students were working as a team and helping each other out. I personally benefited from this because at first I felt shy and nervous in front of the students. However, I soon felt a connection with them, which allowed me to be more open. I never expected to lose my shyness so quickly. It may be that as a teenager I was more vulnerable to feelings of segregation than I am now, or maybe the students really are closer together here. Because the school is in a more affluent area, maybe the students, even though they come from different racial groups, have had similar experiences and so they are on a more equal footing. I am curious to see if it will be different in a classroom where there is a mixture of upper- and lower-class students.

In conclusion, literature circles are one more technique to use with students, but as with everything else suggested in this book, they do not come with a 100 percent guarantee and there is no exact recipe to follow. You will want to devise your own approach after considering our suggestions as well as those to be found in such books as *Literature Circles: Voice and Choice in the Student-Centered Classroom* by Harvey Daniels and *Literature Circles and Response,* edited by Bonnie Campbell Hill, Nancy J. Johnson, and Katherine L. Schlick. In response to the interns' request for more activities, we drew up the following list:

1. Do a costumed presentation of your book. Dress either as the author or one of the characters.
2. Write a letter from one character to another character.
3. Outline a sequel.
4. Write a new conclusion or a new beginning.
5. If a journey was involved, draw a map with explanatory notes of significant places.
6. Make a diorama and explain what it shows.
7. Write a book review for a class publication.
8. Make and laminate a new book jacket with an original blurb.

9. Use email to tell a reading pal about the book.
10. Participate with three or four classmates in a television talk show about the book.
11. With another student, do a pretend interview with the author or with one of the characters.
12. Use a journalistic style and write a news story about something that happened to one of the characters.
13. For fun, exaggerate either characteristics or events and write a tabloid-style news story related to your book.
14. Cut out magazine pictures to make a collage or a poster illustrating the idea of the book.
15. Draft a letter to a television or movie producer suggesting that your book be considered for a mass-media production. (*Note:* S. E. Hinton's *The Outsiders* was made into a movie as the result of a letter written to Francis Ford Coppola by students at the Lone Star school in Fresno, California.)
16. With two or three other students, do a readers' theater presentation or act out a scene from the book.
17. Lead a small group discussion with other readers of the same book. Focus on a specific topic and report your group's conclusions to the class.
18. Keep a reading journal and record your thoughts at the end of each period of reading.
19. Find a song or a poem that relates to the theme of your book. Explain the similarities.
20. Draw a comic strip about an incident in your book or make a graphic novel by working with a section of the book.

Using Young Adult Literature in Creative Writing

In an "Up for Discussion" article in *School Library Journal,* contemporary author and creative writing teacher Jack Gantos (see his statement on p. 256) told how on the first day of class when he asks his college students about a book they've recently enjoyed, they try to impress him by citing *War and Peace, Crime and Punishment, Wuthering Heights,* and *The Sound and the Fury.* Gantos appreciates and teaches these books in his literature classes, but because not one of his creative writing students "was with Tolstoy when Napoleon retreated from Moscow, or spent part of their youth in a Siberian prison with Dostoyevsky, or wandered the imaginary moors with Emily Brönte while stuck in a parsonage, or sorted mail with Faulkner in Mississippi," he marches his students to the library where he takes them through the stacks and hands them young adult books to read "not for comprehension or analysis, but for inspiration." He wants them to "revel in the juicy details of life" that will help them value their own experiences "with family and friends, in their own communities, observing or participating in the human dramas of the moment."[12]

Language is a social phenomenon, and just as we learned to speak through imitation and trial and error, we learn to write in much the same way. Young adult literature can provide creative teens with inspiration and models to follow because:

- The problems in the books are likely to be ones that readers or their friends have experienced or thought about.
- A variety of ethnic backgrounds and settings enlarges the chances of students finding stories with which they can identify.
- Characters' conversations can serve as models for the writing of dialogue because the speech patterns come close to the everyday, spoken language of teenagers and to the *I-wish-I-had-said-that* kind of rejoinder.
- Even in historical fiction or in fantasy or science fiction, the protagonists are young, which means that their intellectual and emotional development is similar to that of teenage readers.
- Most YA authors write in a succinct and straightforward style so that readers can "get" the story and still have some intellectual energy to expend in looking at the author's techniques.
- The intriguing details that professional writers include in their stories are the same kinds of details that clever and witty teenagers observe and relate to each other, which means they have a head start when it comes to incorporating such details into stories.

While it may be as hard as ever to get teenagers to write scholarly papers, today's teachers have several helps in getting young people to write poetry and to share their personal feelings through prose. See Focus Box 3.4, Teen Voices, p. 107, for examples of published teen writing. Focus Boxes 11.3, Books to Encourage Student Writers, and 11.4, Online Publication Opportunities for Young Writers, should also be useful. Mel Glenn's statement on p. 354, along with Gail Carson Levine's statement on p. 352, should also help to lead students to satisfying writing experiences.

Some teachers of creative writing have found that it works well to use a collection of YA short stories for the text. One that has worked for us is Don Gallo's *Sixteen: Short Stories by Outstanding Writers for Young Adults*. Gallo grouped the stories under the categories of friendships, turmoils, loves, decisions, and families, but for creative writing purposes, we regrouped them into types starting with what we judged to be the easiest for students to imitate, then moved on up to the hardest. We started with wish-fulfilling stories so that students could have fun thinking, talking, and then writing about their daydreams and fantasies. We next looked at stories filled with incongruity and surprise, followed by those showing contrasting points of view. The most sophisticated category of the stories, which we left until last, were the realistic explorations of human emotions.

How much work young writers do depends on their motivation as well as on the setting. Students in a semester- or year-long class probably have more time to put into their writing than those in a six-week unit or in an after-school writing club sponsored by a library or other community organization. Those in extra-curricular writing groups, however, may be more motivated and may be together over several years rather than just for a few months.

While an obvious goal may be the writing of a short story, less ambitious tasks can provide practice as well as feelings of success along the way. For example, students can work in small groups to improvise dialogue for a scene that *might* have occurred in one of the stories, or they can rework a story into a one-act play or a readers' theater production.

FOCUS BOX 11.3   *Books to Encourage Student Writers*

Blood on the Forehead: What I Know about Writing by M. E. Kerr. HarperCollins, 1998. The title comes from the framed quotation that Kerr keeps above her desk, "Writing is easy: All you do is sit staring at a blank sheet of paper until the drops of blood form on your forehead."

From One Experience to Another: Stories about Turning Points, edited by M. Jerry Weiss and Helen S. Weiss. Forge, 1997. Top YA writers (e.g., Joan Bauer, Gordon Korman, Suzanne Fisher Staples, Walter Dean Myers) contributed stories accompanied by introductory remarks tracing the routes their minds took in changing a real life event into a fictional story.

Getting the Knack: 20 Poetry Writing Exercises by Stephen Dunning and William Stafford. National Council of Teachers of English, 1992. The book does exactly what it sets out to do, which is to give young writers specific details about different ways to write poems.

I Am Writing a Poem About . . . A Game of Poetry, edited by Myra Cohn Livingston. Simon & Schuster, 1997. Livingston had so much fun with a gift of magnetic strips of words designed for poets in a hurry that she designed this book to pass the fun onto others. An earlier Livingston book, *Poem-Making: Ways to Begin Writing Poetry* (HarperCollins, 1991), may also be useful.

The Making of a Writer by Joan Lowery Nixon. Delacorte, 2002. This popular author of mysteries for young readers aimed her memoir at fans in junior high and middle school. All the way through she shares advice and tidbits, ending up with her "top ten" tips.

Our Stories: A Fiction Workshop for Young Authors by Marion Dane Bauer. Clarion, 1996. In each of twelve chapters, Bauer includes sample sto-ries and essays from young people who are identified at the back of the book.

Poems from Homeroom: A Writer's Place to Start by Kathi Appelt. Henry Holt, 2002. Appelt is a successful writer for children and middle school students and uses her same fresh style in this encouraging new book.

Poetry Matters: Writing a Poem from the Inside Out by Ralph Fletcher. HarperCollins, 2002. Fletcher describes poems as "emotional x-rays," and then sets out to equip readers with what they need to create the x-rays of their feelings and observations. Interviews with poets are inspiring as well as instructive.

Seeing the Blue Between: Advice and Inspiration for Young Poets, compiled by Paul B. Janeczko. Candlewick, 2002. Janeczko collected advice and models from 32 successful poets and put it all together with the same care that he has used in such previous books as *How to Write Poetry* (Scholastic, 1999), *The Place My Words Are Looking For* (Bradbury, 1990), and *Poetspeak: In Their Work, About Their Work* (Bradbury, 1983).

Teaching Poetry Writing to Adolescents by Joseph I. Tsujimoto. National Council of Teachers of English, 1988. Excellent examples of student poetry are included in this book about getting kids to write better poetry and become better readers of poetry.

Wishes, Lies, and Dreams: Teaching Children to Write Poetry, reprint edition by Kenneth Koch and Ron Padgett. Perennial Press, 2000. Originally published in 1980, this book is a continuation of the philosophies in *Rose, Where Did You Get That Red?* (Random House, 1974), which recounts Koch's experiences and the techniques he used in the New York Public Schools where he was a poet in residence.

FOCUS BOX 11.4   Online Publications Opportunities for Young Writers

Amazon.com

www.amazon.com: Amazon is one of the original places on the Web where teens can submit book reviews. The Listmania! Feature allows users to create personalized book lists and suggestions on any topic.

Bookbrowse.com

www.bookbrowse.com/teens.cfm: Teens can write and submit reviews about their favorite books at this site edited and owned by Davina Morgan-Witts.

Book Crossing

www.bookcrossing.com: This innovative site allows teens to write and publish reviews and, more importantly, to share books with each other! Books are given an ID number and then "released into the wild." If you find a BookCrossing book, you can read it and comment on it using the website. The site is maintained and edited by Ron Hornbaker.

Book Divas

www.bookdivas.com: A collaboration between *Seventeen* magazine and Electric Artists, BookDivas encourages girls to read, review, and discuss books or whatever strikes their fancy.

Book Raps

www.rite.ed.qut.edu.au/oz-teachernet/ projects/book-rap: At this site, teens can discuss books that are nominated by teachers and librarians. "Book Raps" are scheduled on a monthly calendar and anyone can participate. Book Raps is part of the Oz-Teacher Net of Australia and is maintained by Bronwyn Stuckey.

Favorite Teenage Angst Books

www.grouchy.com/angst/: At this appealing site, teens can discuss books related to classic coming-of-age issues, such as relationships, drugs and alcohol, self-esteem, and family problems. The website author, Cathy Young, recently edited an anthology of stories called *One Hot Second: Stories of Desire*.

Guys Read

www.penguinputnam.com/static/packages/us/ yreaders/guysread: Guys Read is an initiative to improve literacy in boys, created by Jon Scieszka. This site features booklists and tips to help improve literacy among boys.

Merlyn's Pen

www.merlynspen.com/home.html: Established long before the days of Internet printing, Merlyn's Pen publishes a yearly collection as well as more frequent issues featuring teenage writing.

Read! Literacy and Education for Life

www.weread.org/teens/Index.asp: Teens can read and submit stories and book reviews at this site. WE READ is an acronym for "World Enterprise for Reading, Education and Academic Development" and is in the process of obtaining its nonprofit status.

Reading Rants!

www.tln.lib.mi.us/~amutch/jen/riot.htm: Maintained by Jennifer Hubert, middle school librarian at the Little Red School House and Elisabeth Irwin High School in Greenwich Village, Manhattan, Reading Rants focuses on books geared toward girls.

Teen Central at Phoenix Public Library

www.phoenixteencentral.org/: Teens can read and write book reviews in this well-organized library site from the Phoenix, Arizona, library system.

TeenInk Magazine

TeenInk.com/Books/: A monthly print magazine and website written by teens for teens. The website accepts original poetry, fiction, and book reviews from teens.

TeensPoint.org

www.teenspoint.org/reviews/index.asp: At this library site teens have opportunities to read and write book reviews. It is maintained by the Central Rappahannock Regional Library in Fredericksburg, Virginia.

WordSmiths

www2.nypl.org/home/branch/teen/Word Smiths-About.html: Sponsored by the New York Public Library, WordSmiths is a site where teens can publish their own creative writing.

See Focus Box 11.4 for places where kids can share their creative writing with others.

Students love to write scenes for movies or television, and now that there are so many teen-centered television shows, they might practice turning a short story into a TV script.

Keeping a response journal helps students focus on a story. Prompts to help readers think of themselves as authors include:

- The part of this story that comes the closest to something I might write is . . .
- If I had written this story I would have . . .
- If I were to write a sequel . . .
- This author is especially skilled at (choose one) developing characters, writing conversations, describing settings, or creating interesting plots as shown by . . .

In anticipation of creating their own story titles, help students examine the titles in a collection. Which are the most intriguing? The most memorable? For example, in Gallo's *Sixteen* collection, what are the extra meanings in Brancato's "Fourth of July" and Lipsyte's "Future Tense"? Which titles help establish setting by hinting at time and place? Which establish a light tone? How about a dark or serious tone? What is the effect of an author asking a question? Does Cormier's "In the Heat" remind readers of the oxymoronic "In the heat of the night," while Major's "Three People and Two Seats" reminds them of the cliché "Two's company, three's a crowd"?

GAIL CARSON LEVINE
On Revising

My favorite part of writing is revising. When I'm working on a first draft, I feel like I'm locked in an iron cell. The walls are iron. The ceiling is iron. The floor is iron. There are no windows and no doors.

Every so often a bit of moisture condenses on a wall. The condensation is an idea. I scrape it off the wall and put it into my novel, writing happily but all too briefly. The idea runs out and I wait again, cold and lonely, for more condensation, which, thank goodness, always comes—has always come, so far anyway.

After a year or two my first draft is done. Hooray! The walls come down. The sun shines. The story is complete. All I have to do is make it better. And that's pure fun.

When I revise, mostly I cut. Why did I think I needed that? Out with a paragraph, out with a page, a sentence, a word.

I also add stuff.

A character needs more history.

The beginning needs more background.

The setting in this spot is vague. How does the castle (or room or forest or whatever) look? Sound? Feel? Smell?

I work on revisions for my critique buddy, the great YA writer Joan Abelove. The book becomes clearer, sharper. I send it to my editor. I act on her edits, which can be substantial, and the book gets stronger. The copyeditor chimes in, and I revise again.

Then I'm done. More hoorays!

Boo! Hiss! I crawl back into my iron cell and wait for condensation.

Gail Carson Levine's books include *Ella Enchanted*, 1997; *Dave at Night*, 1999; *The Wish*, 2000; and *The Two Princesses of Bamarre*, 2001, all from HarperCollins. Her website is gailcarson-levinebooks.com.

As part of talking about the individual stories, lead students to devise alternate titles and to discuss the effects. The point in relation to students' own writing is to illustrate how much thought authors put into creating titles that honestly convey the sense of their stories while arousing a reader's interest.

In examining characters' names, talk about what Rosa Guy reveals in her story "She," when the girl refuses to call her stepmother by her name. In "Midnight Snack," what does it signal when Jerry quits calling his friend *Frogface, Froggy, Froggo,* and *Frog* and calls her *Beth*? What is Richard Peck communicating when he has characters call the bully Monk Klutter *Mighty Monk* and when Monk's gang wears the name *Klutter's Kobras* in silver nailheads on their black, plastic windbreakers?

In "I, Hungry Hannah Cassandra Glen," Glen calls David *Crow,* and he calls her *Hanny,* but at the funeral they sign the condolence book as *David James Alpern* and *Hannah C. Glen.* Students probably won't know about Cassandra, the Greek goddess who makes prophecies that no one will believe, but they might be intrigued by the connection between the mythical Cassandra and Hannah Cassandra's extravagant promises of food with which she entices the reluctant David to crash the family gathering after the funeral.

To give students practice in choosing or creating names that serve multiple purposes, write out two or three obvious plot lines and let students work in small groups to come up with names that are memorable because of alliteration, rhyme, assonance, or a special meaning. It is fine if they exaggerate and have fun while creating puns like the name of cartoon character *Wile E. Coyote* or connotative pseudonyms such as those of performers *Ice-T, Madonna,* and *Magic Johnson.* Once students get the idea that names do more than identify people, teachers can talk about subtlety and how the best writers create names that influence readers at an almost subconscious level.

Picking out figurative language from contemporary short stories is less intimidating than doing the same thing from Elizabethan drama or early American literature. For example, after the funeral hungry Hannah Cassandra describes the widow and her sister as looking "like two swollen black balloons," and in Sebestyen's "Welcome," Tina says when her aunt revealed her reaction to learning that her retarded son "was never going to be right," the effect on Tina's emotions was like taking "the bottom piece of fruit out of the pyramid at the market and everything began to tumble."

Teaching Film in the English Class

Thanks to VCRs and DVDs, English teachers can now have at their fingertips many of the great movies of the world to use with novels, plays, and other materials, as well as in thematic units. See our website for film suggestions matching each chapter of this textbook, along with information about films made from novels and short stories that are frequently taught. You might also check with the library or media center at nearby universities to see what short films are available. Also, see Appendix D for a bibliography of materials on film and for a translation of the coding to the Film Boxes presented on our website. In the meantime, here are a few warnings or comments about using films in classrooms.

1. As with books, especially paperback books, films have a depressingly speedy ability to disappear from catalogues and stores. Don't count on using a film until you have it in your hands.
2. Even if you've seen the film years ago or on TV, see it again before you consider using it in class. Films on TV are often edited for time and content, and your memory may be faulty. There's little so embarrassing—or potentially so dangerous to your career—as watching an orgy of sex or drugs onscreen, which you do not recall, but which your students are pleasantly surprised to see in your class.
3. Ratings are, as George Gershwin's song would have it, a sometime thing, and how they are applied or misapplied to a film may defy logic. An R-rated and sensitive film may seem incorrectly rated, and a PG-13 you take your son to see may seem gross, phony, and worse. A scene included or cut often makes all the difference. Unhappily, some administrators and school boards make a nice, if silly, distinction between PG-13 (allowed in school) and R (not allowed). The distinction ignores the worth of films like *Glory* or *The Red Violin,* but the distinction usually ends the discussion. So it goes.
4. Films deserve to be taken as seriously as the literature you use in class. At the least that means you should think through why you're considering a film for class use. What do you think the film will bring to the class? Are there problems you need to work through? How will you present the film and tie it to what you've been doing in class and what you'll be doing next? Are your students mature and sophisticated enough to

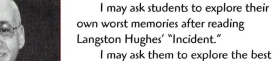

MEL GLENN
On Being Nudgers and Inspirers

Some say the highest goal of the current crop of teenagers is "to chill" and that school represents a minor pit stop on the road to the GAP at the local mall.

I don't believe that at all.

After thirty-plus years of high school teaching, I can say with assurance that behind every defiant look, rebellious stance, and laughing face is a voice waiting to be heard, waiting to say to the universe, "I exist," and waiting for an acknowledgment of that existence.

I am less a teacher of poetry than a provider of poetry. Sure, I can teach meter and rhyme, metaphor and simile, but it's more than that. It's my responsibility to provide a secure, nonthreatening environment where kids will feel comfortable to express what is in their hearts.

There is no magic formula for teaching poetry. I once had a wise professor who said, "You teach who you are." If I can communicate my passions, a favorite poem here, an arresting photograph there, my students might be encouraged to relate their own passions and concerns.

Take, for example, photography. Behind every photo or painting I might show there is a story and I ask my students to speculate on what that story might be. Who is lonely? Who is joyous? Who has a dream and whose dream has been crushed? It's an old adage, you don't know a person until you walk around in his shoes, but that walk can be done mentally through imagination when you put yourself in someone's shoes—or even, thoughtfully, in your own shoes.

Though many adults might feel that teenage emotions run the gamut from A to A, we, who are involved with teens every day, know there is no crisis too small, no problem too big that it does not provoke a dramatic response. Whatever the wound or the triumph, it can be written about. The bright light of words can illuminate the dark corners of the human heart. Writing can help teens find a clearer image of themselves. And we teachers are the ones who can foster that clarity.

I may ask students to explore their own worst memories after reading Langston Hughes' "Incident."

I may ask them to explore the best day of their life.

I may ask them to imagine their own futures.

In short, I may ask them to photograph themselves, their passions, and their loves and hates all in the pursuit of finding out who they are, and what they believe. It's almost irrelevant what "topic" I present. They present themselves. They will announce loudly and clearly that they exist.

Lest the above seems too general, I can offer specifics on teaching poetry. This is by no means the last word on such lists.

1. Use details.
2. Don't rhyme unless it flows naturally. (I positively scream at moon/June rhyming.)
3. Rely on memory, a rich treasure trove.
4. Use specific language: *Car* is OK, *Corvette* better.
5. Good writing is the product of rewriting.
6. Keep a journal with you always. You never know when the Muse will strike. I call her Zelda.
7. Avoid big concepts like Love, Friendship; again get specific.
8. Use vivid verbs.
9. Read what you have written. How does it strike your ear?
10. Give your poem a snappy title.

As teacher Frank McCourt said, "You can teach biology and origami, but I don't think you can teach creative writing. You can hint and nudge, inspire and encourage."

As teachers, be the best "nudgers and inspirers" you can be.

Mel Glenn's books include *Split Image,* Harper Collins, 2000; *Foreign Exchange,* Morrow Junior Books, 1999; *Jump Ball,* Lodestar/Dutton, 1997, and *Who Killed Mr. Chippendale?* Lodestar/Dutton, 1996.

enjoy the film and get something important from it? Before you show the film, it is a good idea to pose questions about significant details or themes to give students something to watch for.

5. Students sometimes argue that films are meant to be fun and nothing more, but most films aren't that simple, certainly not ones we're likely to use in class. The entertainment argument is, in part, a way of staving the claim of teachers that films are worth studying. To study implies work, unlike being entertained—one is active, one passive. Seeing *The Grapes of Wrath* and considering what it has to say demands at a minimum that students watch the film rather than looking its way occasionally. The notion that film is intended to be fun and fun alone takes care of the likelihood of showing challenging work.

6. Never use a film in place of a book for students who cannot or will not read a book. Instead, suggest another book that is simpler or shorter, or encourage the student to listen to an unabridged tape recording. We should not pretend that a book is a film or a film is a book. Film producers often change scenes or settings or characters. It is a good idea in class to talk about the reasons behind such changes, but students who have seen only the movie will be unable to follow such discussions.

7. Perhaps the most irritating student term to describe something not easily understood, certainly not enjoyed, is *boring,* which has apparently replaced *dumb* as the ultimate term of disparagement. *Boring* can be applied to *Walden,* most of Shakespeare, almost all black-and-white films or any film made before 1996, and all world culture and history before 1990. *Boring* means it (whatever *it* is) and you (whoever *you* are) are "not with it," and cannot "relate" to your student or their world. People raised on the comic subtleties of *Police Academy* or *There's Something about Mary* may find much of the world boring.

8. It may be difficult to accept, but many of the greatest films and filmmakers are unlikely to make it into your room, even if your students are brilliant, mature, sophisticated, and more, and that's tough for anyone who loves great film. A glance at the list of 100 greatest films chosen by the American Film Institute—headlined in most newspapers in June 1998—reveals some (or many) titles not likely to be considered "appropriate" for young adults.

If you are curious about how other teachers use and/or teach film, the books in Appendix D may help.

Using Thematic Units in the English Class

Part of the reason that thematic units have become popular in English classes is that they provide a way to bind together a number of apparently dissimilar elements, including literature, language, media, and popular culture. First, however, we need to distinguish the *thematic unit* from two other kinds of units. The *project unit* has a clear end product, with all the steps that lead up to that end. For example, the production of a class play ends when the play is put on, a class-published slang dictionary ends when the booklet is put together and handed out, and reading and talking about a novel ends with the last discussion and the test. A *subject-centered* unit consists of a body of information the teacher feels is important for the class. For example, units on the history of the language, the rise of drama to Shakespeare's time, or "Our Friend, the Introductory Adverbial Clause" (the last is not made up—we saw it in action, if that's the right word). These units have no clear-cut ending, barring a test, but they do have generally clear limits of what is to be included.

The *thematic unit* is different in that it binds together many elements of English while centering on a theme or motif that runs through a body of literature. For example, a question most of us have asked ourselves is, "Why do some people want to manipulate others?" This question is also asked in Aldous Huxley's *Brave New World,* George Orwell's *1984,* Shakespeare's *Othello* and *King Lear,* F. Scott Fitzgerald's *The Great Gatsby,* Henrik Ibsen's *An Enemy of the People,* Robert Cormier's *Fade,* M. E. Kerr's *If I Love You, Am I Trapped Forever?* and Sophocles's *Antigone.* Is this a theme deserving the four or five weeks' time that the usual thematic unit takes? Here are four criteria against which to stack such a question:

1. The theme needs to appeal to kids. If it is too easy, too hard, or too boring, the teacher will lose the students' interest and attention.
2. The theme needs to be worth doing—in other words, intellectually and emotionally respectable for these particular kids at this particular time of their development and at this particular time of the year.
3. There must be lots of easily located literature on the theme.
4. The theme needs to appeal to the teacher; if the teacher is not excited about it, the kids won't be either.

Assuming that the theme meets these four requirements, the teacher must begin a search for literature on the theme that will challenge the students and that they will enjoy, composition topics (written and spoken) worth using and related to the theme, films (short and feature-length) related to the theme and worth viewing, and spelling and vocabulary lists related to the theme. That means the teacher must determine the following:

1. A list of sensible objectives (or learning outcomes, if you prefer) for this *specific* unit (not English classwork in general) that both kids and their parents can understand.
2. A work of some length (usually a short novel or a play) to open the unit and make clear to students what the unit is aiming at. Such a work is not essential, but it's customary and usually helpful.
3. A body of short works (poetry and short stories and essays) to be used throughout the unit because they are related to the theme.
4. A series of composition assignments (usually two or three written assignments and two or three oral assignments) on the theme.
5. A list of vocabulary words related to the unit topic, perhaps twenty to thirty or so, to be talked about and tested five at a time.
6. A list of spelling words related to the unit topic, perhaps twenty to thirty or so, to be talked about and tested about five at a time.
7. A way of beginning the unit that grabs students' attention and interest while focusing on the theme. Obviously, teachers can (and do) begin thematic units with a "Hey, kids,

*N*ow *that it is so easy to download photos, book jackets, and other information from the Internet, both teachers and students enjoy making posters to use in telling other people about their favorite authors.*

how would you like to talk about _____?" or a "Hey, kids, we're going to turn to something entirely different now, a unit on _____," but surely there's a slightly more fascinating way. A short film or the teacher reading aloud a short story (or a recent news clipping) might work.

8. A way of wrapping up the unit that ties all the strands together. Tests, the all-American way to wrap anything up, are always possible. Some classes find panel discussions useful, some might profit from a student evaluation of the unit and the literature read, and others might benefit from some creative art project or a dramatization.

9. The problems that the unit—and students—may encounter and how the teacher works through them. Perhaps it's time to incorporate peer editing into the class, and if this unit is as good a time as any other to introduce kids to peer evaluation and editing, the teacher needs to plan on preparing class members to work in small groups. Perhaps the short book chosen to get the unit started (e.g., Monica Hughes's *Hunter in the Dark*) has some vocabulary problems, or Nathaniel Hawthorne's short story "Young Goodman Brown" may present problems getting the kids to understand colonial life and religion. These and similar problems need to be worked through and solutions found.

Two exceptionally helpful articles on developing thematic units are Richard S. Alm's "What Is a Good Unit?"[13] and John H. Bushman and Sandra K. Jones's "Getting

It All Together . . . Thematically."[14] Thematic units can range from complex and sophisticated topics for college-bound kids to simple topics that are appropriate for junior high. For example, a thematic unit on "Our Ability to Endure," which centers on the theme of survival and power, is a topic of immediate interest to eighth- and ninth-graders. It could open with words from William Faulkner's much-anthologized Nobel Award speech and move to one of these as common reading and the remainder as supplementary reading: Avi's *The True Confessions of Charlotte Doyle,* Alice Childress's *Rainbow Jordan,* Robert Cormier's *After the First Death,* James Forman's *Ceremony of Innocence,* Anne Frank's *The Diary of a Young Girl,* Harry Mazer's *The Last Mission,* or Robb White's *Deathwatch.*

A more intellectually and emotionally complex thematic unit on "Redemption" might begin with reading and discussing Katherine Mansfield's "The Garden Party" or Nadine Gordimer's "A Company of Laughing Faces." This might be followed by the class reading Bernard Malamud's *The Assistant,* and sometime during the unit each student might be asked to read at least one supplementary work on some phase of redemption, for example, classics such as Dante's *The Divine Comedy,* Dostoevsky's *Crime and Punishment,* Goethe's *Faust,* Shakespeare's *King Lear* or *Hamlet,* Sophocles's *Oedipus Rex* or *Antigone,* and almost any other Greek drama or major work of Joseph Conrad, Thomas Hardy, Nathaniel Hawthorne, or Herman Melville. Modern fiction applicable to the same theme includes Hal Borland's *When the Legends Die,* F. Scott Fitzgerald's *The Great Gatsby,* Ursula K. Le Guin's *A Wizard of Earthsea,* Peter Matthiessen's *At Play in the Fields of the Lord,* John Steinbeck's *Of Mice and Men,* Frank Waters's *The Man Who Killed the Deer,* and major works of Arthur Miller, Graham Greene, and Thornton Wilder. Young adult fiction that could fit into the unit includes Fran Arrick's *Tunnel Vision,* Judy Blume's *Tiger Eyes,* Robert Cormier's *The Chocolate War,* Robert Lipsyte's *The Contender,* Margaret Mahy's *Memory,* Paul Zindel's *The Pigman,* and the novels of S. E. Hinton.

Concluding Comments

We once had a student come to our office and announce that he wanted to learn everything that a good high school English teacher needed to know. He wondered where he should begin, and we suggested he start with literature. He agreed and wondered yet again where he should begin. We mentioned that good English teachers know the classics. After we cleared up the confusion that we weren't talking about Steinbeck, not yet, we turned to Aeschylus, Sophocles, Euripides, and Aristophanes, none of whom he knew. Because he begged that we move on to the eighteenth century, where he claimed he knew the novel, we moved onward and upward only to hear his complaint when we brought up writers like John Gay, William Blake, or Richard Brinsley Sheridan. A day or so later, we pointed out that good English teachers not only know English and American literature, of course, but also know third-world literature and German, Japanese, Norwegian, and Russian literature, and more.

Somewhere as we rounded Russian literature, our earnest student gave up. After this catalogue of what he needed to know, he asked one last question before he disappeared from the office: "How can anyone learn all that?"

The answer, which he obviously did not want to hear, was that thousands of good people do it all the time, not in a few hasty weeks but in a lifetime. They are called English teachers.

Notes

[1]Louise M. Rosenblatt. *Literature As Exploration,* 4th ed. (Modern Language Association, 1983), pp. 278–279.

[2]Elaine Simpson, "Reason, Not Emotion," *Top of the News* 31 (April 1975): 302.

[3]Dorothy Broderick, "Serving Young Adults: Why We Do What We Do," *Voice of Youth Advocates* 12 (October 1989): 204.

[4]Robert C. Small, "Teaching the Junior Novel," *English Journal* 61 (February 1972): 222.

[5]Richard W. Jackson, *CBC Features* 39 (October 1984–July 1985): 5. A publication of the Children's Book Council.

[6]Tim Wynne Jones "On Short Stories," *Literature for Today's Young Adults,* 6th edition by Alleen Pace Nilsen and Kenneth L. Donelson (Longman, 2001), p. 364.

[7]Edward J. Gordon, "Levels of Teaching and Testing," *English Journal* 44 (September 1955): 330–334; Dwight L. Burton, "Well, Where Are We in Teaching Literature?" *English Journal* 63 (February 1974): 28–33.

[8]Howard Francis Seely, "Our Novel Stock-in-Trade," *English Journal* 18 (November 1929): 724–725.

[9]G. F. Lamb, "The Reading Habit," *Tomorrow* (England) 2 (July 1934): 10.

[10]Three informative articles that comment on books that did not win awards (or were not nominated), although the books are popular today and deserve careful attention: Joni Bodart's "The Also-Rans; or 'What Happened to the Ones That Didn't Get Eight Votes?'" *Top of the News* 38 (Fall 1981): 70–73; and Pam Spencer's "Winners in Their Own Right," *School Library Journal* 36 (July 1990): 23–27, and "Part II," *School Library Journal* 38 (March 1992): 163–167.

[11]Richard Peck, "Ten Questions to Ask About a Novel," ALAN *Newsletter* 5 (Spring 1978): 1, 7.

[12]Jack Gantos, "Up for Discussion: Warts and All," *School Library Journal* 42:3 (March, 1996): 128–128.

[13]Richard S. Alm, "What Is a Good Unit in English?" *English Journal* 49 (September 1960): 395–399.

[14]John H. Bushman and Sandra K. Jones, "Getting It All Together . . . Thematically," *English Journal* 64 (May 1975): 54–60.

CHAPTER

Censorship
Of Worrying and Wondering

In public schools and libraries, nothing is more constant than censorship. Parents complain about the immorality of characters in books assigned, or books not assigned, or books that someday might be assigned. Violence in literature is unacceptable as is profanity and obscenity, both rarely defined. Books as different as Robert Cormier's *The Chocolate War* or *After the First Death;* Judy Blume's *Forever* or *Are You There God, It's Me, Margaret;* John Steinbeck's *The Grapes of Wrath* or *Of Mice and Men;* Mark Twain's *Tom Sawyer* or *The Adventures of Huckleberry Finn;* and Katherine Paterson's *Jacob Have I Loved* or *Bridge to Terabithia* easily and frequently come under attack. The *Harry Potter* series consistently is challenged supposedly for its attention to wizardry and magic, but what may be even more frightening is its popularity with young people and adults.

A Censorial Spirit

Teachers and librarians know that attacks on books are here to stay and are often deadly serious, increasingly so in the last decade or two. Colin Campbell's words from 1981 still ring true.

> A censorial spirit is at work in the United States, and for the past year or so it has focused more and more on books. Efforts to remove certain titles from school and public libraries, from paperback racks and bookstores, from the eyes of adults as well as children, have increased measurably.[1]

It is difficult for teachers and librarians not to overreact when another censorship incident hits the newspaper. On September 3, 1999, a story in the *Arizona Republic* revealed that at Carson Junior High School in Mesa, a suburb of Phoenix, a few parents had decided that a musical production of *Tom Sawyer* should close before it opened. One parent said, "The script was culturally insensitive." Why? Because *Tom* was clearly a product of another time and place, and it simply did not fit our politically correct time. Parents listed these objections. Injun Joe was a slam at Native Americans. Three female characters were described, respectively, as "extremely feminine," "an outrageous flirt," and "a large, warm, homey woman." Equally offensive, the constable was referred to as "a typical redneck." Also, several references to religion were impolite.

Four school board members supported the ban, although none had received a complaint from parents. Worse yet, the district's associate superintendent announced her view of drama:

A play in which the content and characterization becomes the focus steals the spotlight from the students. A play is entertainment. It's not in an instructional setting.[2]

That's not quite what Aristotle wrote in the *Poetics*. It's not the view that Henrik Ibsen, Eugene O'Neill, and Tennessee Williams and their plays espouse. Maybe Arthur Miller and Tom Stoppard should reconsider what drama is all about and ensure that entertainment is all that drama should be.

While the reasoning of censors and the gibberish they produce frightens us, sometimes it is impossible to fathom the arguments underlying the censorship, as in these three episodes.

In May 1993, the Oskaloosa, Kansas, School Board voted 4 to 2 to enact a new policy requiring teachers to examine their required material for profanities. They are expected to list each profanity and the number of times it's used in the book. They will forward this count to parents who will give permission for children to read the material. Alternate materials must be available for parents who choose not to allow their child to read the required material.[3]

In July 1996, the East Stroudsburg, Pennsylvania, School Board approved 8 to 0 to drop Robert Cormier's *The Chocolate War* and several other books from a new English curriculum. The assistant superintendent for curriculum announced that the book was eliminated because of scheduling conflicts, not because of the furor it had caused the previous school year.[4]

In 1997 in Marysville, California, when the superintendent removed J. D. Salinger's *The Catcher in the Rye* from the required reading list of the district, he announced, "This is not an issue of book banning. Rather it is an opportunity for parents with varied viewpoints to come together, listen to each other, and define common values."[5]

Obviously, not everyone who questions or objects to a book is a censor. Most parents are concerned about the welfare of their children, but being forced to go to school to make a complaint may make them resentful or nervous or angry. If taking time from work were not enough reason to feel irritated, many parents have a built-in love-hate ambivalence toward schools. They may not have fond memories of English teachers when they were young. They may worry about being talked down to by a much younger teacher or librarian. They may wonder if anyone will take them or their complaints seriously. When parents arrive at the school or the library, it is hardly surprising that they may feel hostile. That's easily misread by equally nervous teachers, who may see aggressive censors where there are only concerned parents.

Keeping this possibility of mistaken identity in mind, educators need to be considerate and reasonable and to listen more than they talk, at least for the first few minutes. Once objectors calm down and recognize that the teacher or librarian might possibly be human, then the educator may learn what is really troubling the parents.

Teenagers come in daily contact with various kinds of censorship related to their age as with the ESRB (Entertainment Software Rating Board) identification system when they buy tapes and CDs and with the vagaries of being carded when they go to the movies.

Everyone may learn, sometimes to the listener's surprise, that no one wants to ban anything, but parents do wonder why the teacher is using the book or why the librarian recommended it to their children. They may want their children to read something else, but agree that they have no wish to control the reading of anyone else. This problem is easier to handle (not always easy, but certainly *easier*).

In such cases, teachers and librarians should remember that the announced objection may not always be the real objection. Censors might attack Huxley's *Brave New World* or Orwell's *1984* for their sexual references when the real objection is to the frightening political attitudes the authors displayed (or were thought to display). It is human nature to fear things we do not understand; hence the discomfort that many parents feel over the recent popularity of scary, supernatural books. An attack on the language in John Howard Griffin's *Black Like Me* may be only a subterfuge for a censor's hatred of African Americans (or any minority group), whereas an attack on an oblique reference to masturbation in Judy Blume's *Deenie* may in reality be a protest against the liberal attitudes that parents sometimes believe pervade her books.

The underlying reasons for objections to particular books often are more significant than teachers or librarians may suspect. Sometimes the complaining parents do not even realize why a particular author or book makes them feel uncomfortable. This is why it's so important for parents to talk and for educators to listen. Parents who are worried about the moral climate facing their children are painfully aware that they have little power to change the material on television, and they cannot successfully fight the movies offered by local theaters or do away with local "adult" bookstores. Whom, then, can they fight? What can they change? An easy answer is to go to school and protect at least that little corner of their children's lives.

Thoughts of inflation and recession, fears of sexually transmitted diseases, threats of global warming and the depletion of the earth's resources, and faltering communication and affection among family members depress many of us most of the time, and sometimes these parental fears and worries are exploited for political gain. Parents are courted and brought into political action groups advocating censorship. The selling point of such groups is that there is little we can do to attack the gigantic problems spurred on by who knows what or whom. Either we give up or, in the case of censors, we strike back at the only vulnerable element in most communities, the schools. And why not attack schools, what with the rising militancy of teachers and the massive public criticism of schools' performances on SAT or ACT tests? And so the censors attack. (See the statement by Judy Blume on p. 380.)

These individuals and groups—as opposed to sincere parents wanting what's best for their own children—are the objectors we define as censors. Their desire is not to talk and reason but to condemn, and as educators we feel a strong obligation to uncover their motives and to counter their claims.

The American Library Association has been on record against censorship since the 1920s, but its strongest statement first appeared in 1939 as the Library Bill of Rights. The document has periodically been tightened and strengthened, and the latest version can be found in the *Intellectual Freedom Manual,* 6th ed. The entire *Intellectual Freedom Manual* is filled with provocative ideas and helpful suggestions and should be required reading for librarians and English teachers alike.

In 1962, the National Council of Teachers of English (NCTE) published the first edition of *The Students' Right to Read,* setting forth NCTE's position and containing a widely used form for complaints, "Citizen's Request for Reconsideration of a Book." The 1972 edition expanded and updated the earlier edition, while in 1982, the complaint form was amended to apply to more than books. A complementary publication, *The Students' Right to Know* by Lee Burress and Edward B. Jenkinson, elaborated on NCTE's position toward education and censorship.

A Sampling of Early Attitudes toward Censorship

5th Century B.C.: In *The Republic,* Plato argued that banishing poets and dramatists was essential for the moral good of the young because writers often told lies about the gods or made the gods appear responsible for the evils and misfortunes of mortals. Plato's argument that fiction could be emotionally disturbing to the young is echoed by many censors today.

211 B.C.: In China, the Emperor Chi Huang Ti burned Confucius's *Analects*.

38–37 B.C.: Julius Caesar burned much of the Library of Alexandria.

1525 A.D.: English officials publicly burned copies of William Tyndale's translation of the Bible.

1555: The Catholic Index of Forbidden Works was first published.

1737: Prime Minister Walpole forced passage of a Licensing Act in 1737, which required that every English play be examined and approved before production.

1864: This was the first year that Oberlin College allowed Shakespeare to be studied in mixed classes.

1860s: The Mormons, under the direction of Brigham Young in Utah, created the Deseret Alphabet, a phonetic system that they planned to use for all writing. One reason was to make it easier to teach English to their converts from other countries. However, historians believe that an equally important reason was to keep Mormons from reading "outside" literature and to keep "outsiders" from reading Mormon communications. This was consistent with Brigham Young's request that church members burn copies of a book written by Joseph Smith's widow and destroy copies of a pamphlet written by Orson Pratt (another early leader) on the Holy Spirit. The ambitious program died from neglect after the railroad and the telegraph made such isolation impossible.[6]

*H*istorians believe that one of the reasons that Utah Mormons devised their own alphabet in the 1860s was to keep Mormons from reading "outside" literature and to keep "outsiders" from being privy to church communications.

1872: In the United States, reformer Anthony Comstock founded the Society for the Suppression of Vice in New York. The next year he went to Washington, DC, to urge passage of a federal statute against obscenity, abortion, and contraceptive devices. He got himself appointed as a Special Agent of the Postmaster General and by 1914 had caused the arraignment of 3,697 people with 2,740 convictions. He raised $237,134.30 in fines, which helped somewhat to pay for the prison sentences totaling over 565 years. Even in his last year of life (1915) he remained active with 176 arrests and 140 convictions. In 1883 he published *Traps for the Young,* which defined light literature, newspaper advertisements, saloons, literature obtained through the mail, artistic works, and much more as dooming young people to hell and a life of crime and degradation.[7]

1877: William Kite, librarian at the Friend Free Library in Germantown, Pennsylvania, worried about the influence of novels. He wrote, "I could tell of one young woman of my acquaintance, of fine education, who gratified a vitiated taste for novel-reading till her reason was overthrown, and she has, in consequence, been for several years an inmate of an insane asylum . . . Instances could be furnished by the records of such institutions in too sad frequency, but we need not seek them. Have we the moral right to expose the young to such cancer?"[8]

1890: An editorial writer who was in favor of censorship announced that he was purposely not mentioning the "thoroughly bad books chosen by our young friends" because he remembered hearing the principal of a young ladies' seminary tell how she impulsively said to the students, "I think I should expel a girl if I found her reading such a work." Within the week three copies were being surreptitiously circulated among the students.[9]

1893: Another editorial writer praised students at Oakland High School who objected to studying an unexpurgated edition of *Hamlet.* The newspaper writer praised "the modest and sensible youths and maidens" for their revolt because "The indecencies of Shakespeare in the complete edition are brutal. They are more than indelicacies, they are indecencies. They are no part of Shakespeare's thought, have no connection with the play, and can be eliminated with as little jar as could the oaths of a modern slugger."[10]

1894: An article in the *Library Journal,* which began publication in 1876, quoted a librarian at the Newton Free Public Library who was sympathizing with a primary teacher who said to her, "Encourage my pupils to read? I only wish I knew of some means of stopping their reading. They read too much."[11] Whatever else that comment implies, it is not one likely to be widely repeated among teachers today.

1896: While Mark Twain was coming under widespread attack for his less-than-genteel characters, Stephen Crane's *The Red Badge of Courage* was heavily criticized for its profanity. On a panel at the annual meeting of the American Library Association, A. L. Peck said about Crane's book, "I never could see why it should be given into the hands of a boy." G. M. Jones questioned the praise that the book was receiving in the "literary papers" and surmised that the reviews were being "written by young men who know nothing about war, just as Mr. Crane himself knows nothing about war. Gen. McClurg, of Chicago, and Col. Nourse, of Massachusetts, both say that the story is not true to the life of the soldier. An article in the *Independent,* or perhaps the *Outlook,* says that no such profanity as given in the book was common in the army among the soldiers. Mr. Crane has since published two other books on New York life which are simply vulgar books. I consider *The Red Badge of Courage* a vulgar book, and nothing but vulgar."[12]

1897: Richard Jones announced the moral and literary duty of librarians when he wrote, "The duty of the librarian is to elevate the standard of taste in a town. His function is an educational function . . . He is to elevate as rapidly as possible the standard of taste of the town."[13]

1899: A principal of an academy launched an attack on public libraries by writing in a report of public librarians, "The voracious devouring of fiction commonly indulged in by patrons of the public library, especially the young, is extremely pernicious and mentally unwholesome."[14]

1903: At the first Library Institute of the State of New Jersey, Father McMahoon, director of the Catholic library, spoke of "the idea of children browsing among books as an educational fad, susceptible of nothing but evil."[15]

1910: Arthur E. Bostwick, in a book for librarians, brought up the question of censorship vs. selection, an issue still talked about today: "In the exercise of his duties in book selection it is unavoidable that the librarian should act in some degree as a censor of literature. It has been pointed out that no library can buy every title that is published, and that we should discriminate by picking out what is best instead of by excluding what is bad."[16]

1920: In the *English Journal,* which had been founded in 1912, a teacher discussed her junior high students' reaction to *Treasure Island.* While one girl thought it should be read because "it is considered a classic," a boy wrote "I like a cleaner story. In this story there is too much bloodshed, drinking, and swearing." A girl wrote, "This story full of murder, fighting, and wiping blood off of knives is not suitable for boys and girls to read and if these kinds of books were not written there would not be so many boys go wrong. I don't think there should be any more books written like it, because it don't learn you anything and nowadays we should read books that do us some good."[17]

1932: At a library meeting in Michigan, Mary Silverthorn recommended ten criteria for fiction if it were to be allowed in a library. Among them, "1. It was written in good English . . . 3. It depicted experiences of life worthwhile for others to enter in vicariously . . . 5. It was stimulating to right thinking and action . . . 6. It satisfied natural desires and curiosities in a normal, wholesome way . . . 10. The line between right and wrong was clear-cut and distinct, or there was called forth a judgment on the part of the reader when the issues were blurred."[18]

The State of Classroom and Library Censorship Today

Before World War II, paperback books seemed to offer little of intellectual or pedagogical value to teachers. Even after the war many teachers blithely assumed that paperbacks had not changed, and given the often-lurid covers, teachers seemed to have a point, although it was more superficial than real. Administrators and parents continued to object even after the Bible, Plato's *Dialogues,* and *Four Tragedies of Shakespeare* proved to teachers and librarians that paperbacks had merit. Students discovered even earlier that paperbacks were handy to stick in a purse or back pocket, and paperback titles were appealing, not stodgy, as were most textbooks. So paperbacks came to schools, censors notwithstanding, and these cheap and ubiquitous books created problems galore for teachers.

Perhaps almost as important, young adult books before the late 1960s were generally safe, pure, and simplistic, devoid of the reality that younger people daily faced. Sports, going to the prom, and getting the car for the big Friday night date loomed large as the major problems of young adult life in too many of these novels. Young people read them for fun, knowing that they were nothing more than escape reading with little relationship to reality or to anything of significance. Then in 1967, Ann Head's *Mr. and Mrs. Bo Jo Jones* and S. E. Hinton's *The Outsiders* appeared, and young adult literature changed and rarely returned to the good old days. Paul Zindel's *The Pigman* followed in 1968, and although all young adult books that followed were hardly great or honest, a surprising number were. English teachers and librarians who had accepted the possibility of censorship with adult authors popular with the young—Steinbeck, Fitzgerald, Heller, Hemingway, for example—now learned that the once safe young adult novel was no longer safe, and censorship attacks soon began. Head's, Hinton's, and Zindel's books were denounced, but so were young adult novels as good as Robert Lipsyte's *The Contender* (1967), A. E. Johnson's *A Blues I Can Whistle* (1969), John Donovan's *I'll Get There. It Better Be Worth the Trip* (1969), and Jean Renvoize's *A Wild Thing* (1971)—and that was only the beginning.

Surveys of the state of censorship since 1963 reveal that censorship is either getting worse or fewer teachers and librarians are willing to lie quietly while the censor walks over them. Lee Burress's pioneer study "How Censorship Affects the School," in October 1963, was only the first of these surveys. Nyla H. Ahrens's doctoral study in 1965 was the first national survey. State surveys of Arizona censorship conditions appeared in the February 1969 and February 1975 *Arizona English Bulletin.* National studies appeared ever more often: L. B. Woods's "The Most Censored Materials in the U.S.," in the November 1, 1978, *Library Journal;* Burress's "A Brief Report of the 1977 NCTE Survey," in James Davis's *Dealing with Censorship;* and the much anticipated but disappointing *Limiting What Students Shall Read* (ALA, ASCD), in 1981. The 1982 survey of high school librarians by Burress found that 34 percent of the librarians reported a challenge to at least one book compared to 30 percent in his 1977 survey. A survey of Canadian censorship by David Jenkinson published in the February 1986 *Canadian Library Journal* provided no optimism about censors. Two surveys by Ken Donelson— one in the March 1985 *School Library Journal* of censorship for the previous thirteen years and comparing conclusions from six previous surveys and another in the October–November 1990 *High School Journal* summarizing the censorship incidents in the *Newsletter on Intellectual Freedom* from 1952 through 1989—provide little comfort to teachers or librarians. Don Melichar's comparative study of surveys of Arizona classroom censorship in 1985 and 1994 is the most recent state or national survey that we know of.

Some Assumptions about Censorship and Censors

Given the censorship attacks of the last twenty-plus years, we can safely make the following assumptions about censorship.

1. Any work is potentially censorable by someone, someplace, sometime, for some reason. Nothing is permanently safe from censorship, not even books most teachers and librarians would regard as far removed from censorial eyes—not *Hamlet, Julius Caesar, Silas Marner, Treasure Island,* or anything else.

2. The newer the work, the more likely it is to come under attack.

3. Censorship is capricious and arbitrary. Two teachers bearing much the same reputation and credentials and years of experience and using the same work will not necessarily be equally free from attack (or equally likely to be attacked). Some schools in conservative areas go free from censorship problems even though teachers may use controversial books. Other schools in relatively liberal areas may come under the censor's gun.

4. Censorship spreads a ripple of fear. The closer the censorship, the greater the likelihood of its effect on other teachers. If the newspaper coverage of the incident has been extensive, the greater the likelihood that schools many miles away will feel the effect. Administrators may gently (or loudly) let their teachers know it is time to be traditional or safe in whatever the teachers choose for the coming year.

5. Censorship does not come only from people outside the school. Administrators, other teachers or librarians, or the school board may initiate an incident. That often surprises some English teachers or librarians. It should not.

6. Censorship is, for too many educators, like cancer or a highway accident. It happens only to other people. Most incidents happen to people who know "it couldn't happen to me." It did and it will.

7. Schools without clear, established, school board–approved policies and procedures for handling censorship are accidents waiting to happen. Every school should develop a policy and a procedure that helps both educators and objectors when an incident arises. The aim of both policy and procedures should be to ensure that everyone has a fair hearing, not to stall or frustrate anyone.

8. If one book is removed from a classroom or library, no book is safe any longer. If a censor succeeds in getting one book out, every other person in the community who objects to another book should, in courtesy, be granted the same privilege. When everyone has walked out of the library carrying all those objectionable books, nothing of any consequence will be left no matter how many books remain. Some books are certain to offend some people and be ardently defended by others. Indeed, every library has books offensive to someone, maybe everyone. After all, ideas do offend many people.

9. Educators and parents should, ideally, coexist to help each other for the good of the young, but the clash of parents with some educators appears to be sadly inevitable. Some people would prefer to see young adults *educated,* which means allowing them to think and wonder about ideas and to consider the consequences of those ideas. Others would prefer to see young people *indoctrinated* into certain community or family values or beliefs or traditions and to eschew anything controversial. With so little in

common between these two philosophies of schooling, disagreement is not only natural but certain.

Censors seem unwilling to accept the fact that the more they attack a book, the greater the publicity and likelihood that more young adults will read the offensive book. In their drive to eliminate a book, censors create a wider circle of readers. In some cases with older or more obscure works, they revive something that has been virtually dead for years.

Censors do not believe that in trying desperately to keep young people pure and innocent they often expose those young people to the very thing the censors abhor. Several years ago, in the Phoenix area, a group violently objected to a scholarly dictionary that contained some "offensive" words. Worried that others might not believe all those degrading, evil, pernicious words could be so easily found in one work, censors compiled a sort of digest of "The Best Dirty Words in _____," duplicated the list, and disseminated it to anyone curious, including the very students censors claimed to be protecting. More than one censor has read parts of a book that would "warp any young person's mind" aloud at a school board meeting to prove the point while young students raptly listened.

Censors often have a simplistic belief that there is an easily established and absolute relationship between books and deeds. A bad book, however defined, produces bad actions. What one reads, one immediately imitates. To read profane language automatically leads young people to swear. Presumably, nonreading youngsters who swear must eagerly await more literate fellows to instruct them in the art of the profane. To read about seduction is to wish to seduce or to be seduced (although it is possible the wish may precede the book). To read about crime is to wish to commit that crime or at least something vaguely antisocial. Anthony Comstock loved to visit boys in jail because when he asked what led them into the world of crime, they told him exactly what he wanted to hear (as they knew full well), that dime novels and drinking and shooting pool were *the* sources of all their present misery.

Censors seem to have limited faith in the ability of young adults to read and think. Censors wonder if young people can handle controversial books such as Huxley's *Brave New World* or Salinger's *The Catcher in the Rye* because the young are so innocent and pure and untainted by contact with reality. That may have been what caused one censor who objected to Ann Head's *Mr. and Mrs. Bo Jo Jones* and Paul Zindel's *The Pigman* to announce to an audience, "Teenagers are too young to learn about pregnancy."

Censors alternately love and hate English teachers and librarians. Censors would appear to hate what educators use, but censors would also appear to approve of great literature, particularly the classics. Being essentially nonreaders, they know little about literature but that it must be uplifting and noble and fine. They may claim to have read the uplifting when they were young, "back when schools knew what they were doing," but they often cannot remember titles; when they do their comments suggest the book was read in an emasculated child's edition. Censors assume that classics have no objectionable words or actions or ideas. So much for *Crime and Punishment, Oedipus Rex, Hamlet, Madame Bovary, Anna Karenina,* and most other classics. For censors, the real virtue of great literature is that it is old, dusty, and hard to read, in other words, good for young people.

Finally, censors use language carelessly or sloppily. Sometimes they cannot possibly mean what they say. The administrator who said, "We don't wish to have any controversial books in the bookstore or the library," either did not understand what the word *controversial* meant or was speaking gibberish (the native tongue of embarrassed administrators talking to reporters).

Three adjectives are likely to pop up in the censor's description of objectionable works—*filthy, obscene,* and *vulgar*—along with favored intensifiers such as *unbelievably, unquestionably,* and *hopelessly,* although a few censors favor oxymoronic expressions like *pure garbage* or *pure evil.* Not one of the adjectives is likely to be defined operationally by censors who assume that *filth* is *unquestionably filth,* and everyone shares their definition. Talking with censors is, thus, often difficult, which may disturb others, although it is often a matter of sublime indifference to the censors. If talking is difficult, communicating with them is usually nigh unto impossible.

Attacks on Materials

Who Are the Censors?

There are three reasonably distinct kinds of censors and pressure groups: (1) those from the right, the conservatives; (2) those from the left, the liberals; and (3) an amorphous band of educators, publishers, editors, and distributors who we might assume would be opposed to censorship. The first two groups operate from different guiding principles, or so one would assume. But it is sometimes easy for educators to be confused—whether the attack stems from the right or the left, the coercive methods, the censorial rhetoric, and the messianic fervor seem so similar. The third group is unorganized and functions on a personal, ad hoc, case-by-case approach, although people in the group are more likely than not to feel sympathetic to the conservative case for censorship.

An incredible number of tiny censorship or pressure groups on the right continue to *worry* educators (worry in the sense of alarm *and* harass). Many are better known for their acronyms, which often sound folksy or clever—for example, Save Our Schools (SOS); People of America Responding to Educational Needs of Today's Society (PARENTS); Citizens United for Responsible Education (CURE); Let's Improve Today's Education (LITE); American Christians in Education (ACE); and everyone's favorite, Let Our Values Emerge (LOVE). Chapter 9 in Ed Jenkinson's *Censors in the Classroom: The Mind Benders* summarizes quite well the major groups, big or small.

With few exceptions, these groups seem united in wishing to protect young people from insidious forces that threaten the schools, to remove any vestiges of sex education and secular humanism from classes or libraries, to put God back into public schools, and to restore traditional values to education. Few announce openly that they favor censorship of books or teaching materials, although individual members of the groups may so proclaim. Indeed, what is particularly heartening about the groups is that many of them maintain that they are anti-censorship, although occasionally a public slip occurs. The president of the Utah chapter of Citizens for Decency was quoted as saying:

I am opposed to censorship. We are not a censorship organization. But there are limits to the First Amendment. People have the right to see what they want on television, but that has nothing to do with the right to exhibit pornography on television. We're not stopping anyone from buying books and magazines or going to the movies they want. They just can't do it in Utah. Let them go to Nevada. Nobody there cares.[19]

Whether anyone from Nevada with a similar anti-censorial attitude responded with a suggestion that people from Nevada seeking cheap thrills should go to Utah is unknown. Something similar to the preceding comment came from the Rev. Ricky Pfeil. Wheeler, Texas, apparently has its moral problems with objectionable movies like *Porky's, Flashdance,* and *E.T.* (Pfeil's argument against the last-mentioned film was, "The film's an attempt to show something supernatural and it's not God. There's only one other power that's supernatural and that's Satan.") The good minister also is against censorship, as he said:

You know, I am not for censorship. People have a right to see what they want or read what they want, but I'd just as soon they go to Los Angeles to get a copy of *Playboy* magazine. I'm responsible for here. Evil left unchecked will go rampant. God tells me what to do.[20]

Given the doublespeak of the Utah president and the Rev. Pfeil, readers will admire the honest and the original constitutional interpretation of the Rev. Vincent Strigas, co-leader of the Mesa (Arizona) Decency Coalition. Slashing merrily away at magazines that threatened the "moral fiber" of residents, the Rev. Strigas answered complaints about his approach:

Some people are saying that we are in violation of First Amendment rights. I do not think that the First Amendment protects people [who sell] pornographic materials. The Constitution protects only the freedom to do what's right.[21]

Surely there is no ambiguity in that message.

Whatever else conservative groups may agree or disagree on, they seem united in opposing secular humanism, the New Age Movement, and the teaching of evolution. Secular humanism is both too large and too fuzzy to handle adequately in a few paragraphs (or even a short chapter). Briefly, if inexactly, conservatives appear to define secular humanism as any teaching material that denies the existence of (or ridicules the worth of) absolute values of right and wrong. Secular humanism is said to be negative, anti-God, anti-American, anti-phonics, and anti-afterlife and pro-permissive, pro–sexual freedom, pro–situation ethics, pro-socialism, and pro–one worldism. Conservatives hopelessly intolerant about secular humanism often have problems explaining what the term means to outsiders, or even insiders, usually defining the presumably philosophical term operationally and offering little more than additional examples of the horror that secular humanism implies.

The third kind of censorship or pressure group comes from within the schools: teachers, librarians, or school officials who either censor materials themselves or support others who do. Sometimes these educators do so fearing reprisals if they do not.

Sometimes they do so because they fear being noticed, preferring anonymity at all costs. Sometimes they are fearful of dealing with reality in literature. Sometimes they regard themselves as highly moral and opposed to whatever they label immoral in literature. Sometimes they prize (or so claim) literary merit and the classics above all other literature and refuse to consider teaching or recommending anything recent or second-rate, however they define those terms. Fear permeates many of these people. A survey of late 1960s Arizona censorship conditions among teachers uncovered three marvelous specimens:

> I would not recommend any book any parent might object to.

> The Board of Education knows what parents in our area want their children to read. If teachers don't feel they can teach what the parents approve, they should move on.

> The English teacher is hired by the school board, which represents the public. The public, therefore, has the right to ask any English teacher to avoid using any material repugnant to any parent or student.[22]

Lest readers assume that Arizona is unique in certifying these nonprofessionals, note these two Connecticut English Department Chairs quoted in Diane Shugert's "Censorship in Connecticut" in the Spring 1978 *Connecticut English Journal:*

> At this level, I don't feel it's [censorship] a problem. We don't deal with controversial material, at least not in English class.

> We have no problems at all in my department. The teachers order books directly and don't clear them with me or with a committee. But *I* receive the shipments. Copies of books that I think to be inappropriate simply disappear from the book room.[23]

So much for the good old days.

Publishers, too, have been guilty of rewriting texts or asking authors to delete certain words to make books or texts more palatable to highly moral librarians or communities. "Expurgation Practices of School Book Clubs" in the December 1983 *Voice of Youth Advocates* and Gayle Keresey's "School Book Club Expurgation Practices" in the Winter 1984 *Top of the News* uncovered censorship practices in Scholastic Book Club selections, as titles were changed and deletions of offensive words or ideas occurred between the hardback edition and its publication in a paperback club edition.

What Do the Censors Censor?

The answer to the question of what censors censor is easy—almost anything. Books, films,[24] magazines, anything that might be enjoyed by someone is likely to feel some censor's scorn and moral wrath.

Some works, however, are more likely to be attacked.

A nearly ten-year survey of books listed as under attack in the *Newsletter on Intellectual Freedom* between May 1986 and September 1995 revealed that several books

Even though on June 23, 2003, the Supreme Court upheld CIPA (Children's Internet Protection Act), which says that all libraries receiving federal support must install filters, controversies in regard to online pornography and hate speech are far from over.

IF YOU ARE VIEWING PORNOGRAPHY YOU WILL BE ASKED TO LEAVE

were repeatedly questioned. The most obvious was John Steinbeck's *Of Mice and Men*, but a few others were also frequently listed. Mark Twain's *Adventures of Huckleberry Finn*, J. D. Salinger's *The Catcher in the Rye*, Maya Angelou's *I Know Why the Caged Bird Sings*, Judy Blume's *Forever*, and Robert Cormier's *The Chocolate War* were all listed at least ten times. Nancy Garden's *Annie on My Mind*, Alice Walker's *The Color Purple*, Kurt Vonnegut's *Slaughterhouse-Five*, Robert Newton Peck's *A Day No Pigs Would Die*, John Gardner's *Grendel*, and the anonymous *Go Ask Alice* followed soon thereafter.

Don Melichar's "Objections to Books in Arizona High School Classes" in the Fall 1994 *Arizona English Bulletin* revealed that the most widely attacked book was *Adventures of Huckleberry Finn*, but Steinbeck's *Of Mice and Men* and Harper Lee's *To Kill a Mockingbird* were also popular with the censors.

The most frequently challenged books in People for the American Way's *Attacks on the Freedom to Learn, 1994–1995* were these: Alvin Schwartz's *Scary Stories to Tell in the Dark, More Scary Stories to Tell in the Dark,* and *Scary Stories 3: More Tales to Chill your Bones*; Maya Angelou's *I Know Why the Caged Bird Sings*; Lois Lowry's *The Giver*; Eve Merriam's *Halloween ABC*; Katherine Paterson's *Bridge to Terabithia*; Robert Cormier's *The Chocolate War*; Christopher and James Lincoln Collier's *My Brother Sam Is Dead*; and John Steinbeck's *Of Mice and Men*.

While there's no guarantee that any one of these golden-goodies on the censor's hit list will come under attack soon, clearly some books are beloved of censors. There was a time when Salinger's *The Catcher in the Rye* led every list of censored books. *Go Ask Alice* occasionally threatened *Catcher*, but more and more *Of Mice and Men* and *Adventures of Huckleberry Finn* lead almost every list of censored works.

Racism raises its ugly head on censorship lists, with titles such as Claude Brown's *Manchild in the Promised Land* and Gordon Parks's *The Learning Tree* and Harper Lee's *To Kill A Mockingbird* appearing with nauseating regularity. There are the usual suspects on every list of censored books—Joseph Heller's *Catch-22*, Aldous Huxley's *Brave New World*, George Orwell's *Animal Farm* and *1984*, and William Golding's *Lord of the Flies*.

There are other inevitable censorial favorites such as *The American Heritage Dictionary* or the much-hated story by Shirley Jackson, "The Lottery." Or modern plays such as Tennessee Williams's *The Glass Menagerie* or *Summer and Smoke* or Arthur Miller's *All My Sons* or *Death of a Salesman*.

Readers curious as to why a commonly censored title is not listed here should feel free to add whatever they wish. Anyone who wishes to expand the list could glance casually through any issue of the *Newsletter on Intellectual Freedom*.

Although most of the titles on these lists were published for adults, today's censors seem quite happy to attack books published for adolescents. Titles such as these now frequently appear on lists of censored books, rarely near the top but still disturbingly present:

Judy Blume: *Deenie, Forever*

Brock Cole: *The Goats*

Robert Cormier: *After the First Death, The Chocolate War, Fade, I Am the Cheese*

Chris Crutcher: *Athletic Shorts, Running Loose*

Lois Duncan: *Killing Mr. Griffin*

Paula Fox: *The Slave Dancer*

Rosa Guy: *Ruby*

Nat Hentoff: *The Day They Came to Arrest the Book*

S. E. Hinton: *The Outsiders; Rumble Fish; That Was Then, This Is Now*

Ron Koertge: *The Arizona Kid*

Ursula K. LeGuin: *A Wizard of Earthsea*

Robert Lipsyte: *The Contender*

Lois Lowry: *The Giver*

Harry Mazer: *The Last Mission*

Walter Dean Myers: *Fallen Angels*

Katherine Paterson: *Bridge to Terabithia*

Robert Newton Peck: *A Day No Pigs Would Die*

Jerry Spinelli: *Space Station Seventh Grade*

Todd Stasser: *Angel Dust Blues*

Mildred Taylor: *Roll of Thunder, Hear My Cry*

Paul Zindel: *My Darling, My Hamburger; The Pigman*

And, of course, any of the *Harry Potter* series.

Why Do the Censors Censor What They Do?

Why censors censor what they do is far more important and far more complex than what they censor. Unfortunately, for readers who want simple answers and an easy-to-remember list of reasons, the next paragraphs may be disappointing.

In "Censorship in the 1970s: Some Ways to Handle It When It Comes (and It Will)" in early 1974, Donelson listed eight different kinds of materials that get censored, those that censors:

1. Deem offensive because of sex (usually calling it "filth" or "risqué" or "indecent").
2. See as an attack on the American dream or the country ("un-American" or "pro-commie").
3. Label peacenik or pacifistic (remember the Vietnam War had not yet become unpopular with the masses).
4. Consider irreligious or against religion or, specifically, un-Christian.
5. Believe promote racial harmony or stress civil rights or the civil rights movement ("biased on social issues" or "Do young people have to see all that ugliness?").
6. Regard as offensive in language ("profane" or "unfit for human ears").
7. Identify as drug books, pro or con ("kids wouldn't hear about or use drugs if it weren't for these books").
8. Regard as presenting inappropriate adolescent behavior and, therefore, likely to cause other young people to act inappropriately.[25]

In an article entitled "Dirty Dictionaries, Obscene Nursery Rhymes and Burned Books," published in James E. Davis's 1979 *Dealing with Censorship,* Ed Jenkinson added fourteen more likely targets, including young adult novels, works of "questionable" writers, literature about or by homosexuals, role playing, texts using improper grammar, sexist stereotypes, and sex education. In a *Publishers Weekly* article the same year,[26] Jenkinson listed forty targets, with new ones being sociology, anthropology, the humanities generally (if secular humanism is bad, so then must be humanism or anything that sounds like humanism, and that easily extends to humanities), ecology, world government, world history that mentions the United Nations, basal readers lacking phonics, basal readers with many pictures or drawings, situation ethics, violence, and books that do not promote the Protestant ethic or do not promote patriotism.

A year later, Jenkinson had expanded his list to sixty-seven, with additions including "Soviet propaganda," citizenship classes, African American dialects, uncaptioned pictures in history texts, concrete poetry, magazines that have ads for alcohol or contraceptives, songs and cartoons in textbooks, and "depressing thoughts."[27] The last of the objections is truly depressing, apparently for censors and educators alike.

For the last edition of this textbook, M. E. Kerr wrote about what happens when she goes to speak at schools. In the early 1990s, prior to the publication of her critically acclaimed *Deliver Us from Evie,* she came out publicly as a gay woman. At about the same time, publishers, as part of a marketing technique to take advantage of the large numbers of children in middle schools, began labeling YA literature "age 10-up" or "Junior High-up." This means that Kerr was often invited to speak to children in sixth, seventh, and eighth grades. In these situations, it was common for teachers to let her know they did not want her to talk about her gay novels. One principal met her in the parking lot and said, "We like your books a lot, Ms. Kerr, but these children are too young for *Night Kites, Deliver Us from Evie,* or *Hello, I Lied.*" Her response to this kind of censorship is:

Of course kids know about gays; any kid who watches TV does. There are gay characters in sitcoms now, on soaps, on talk shows and featured in movies and made-for-TV dramas. Gay performers are on MTV, and there are gay rock stars, singers, and composers. The failure to mention us to children, and to discuss books about us, puts us in a special category. Kids know we're there, but they sense that somehow we're reprehensible. Educators are not protecting the child with this blackout, they are protecting the prejudice.[28]

Some Court Decisions Worth Knowing

Legal battles and court decisions often seem abstract and dull and irrelevant to practical matters for too many educators, but several court decisions have been significant and have affected thousands of educators who hardly knew the battles had taken place, much less their disposition. A brief run-through of two kinds of decisions, those involving attempts to define obscenity and its supposed influence on readers and viewers and those directly involving schools and school libraries, may be helpful to readers.

Court Decisions about Obscenity and Attempting to Define Obscenity

Because censors frequently bandy the word *obscene* in attacking books, teachers and librarians should know something about the history of courts vainly attempting to define the term.

Although it was hardly the first decision involving obscenity, the first decision announcing a definition of and a test for obscenity came about in an English case in 1868. *The Queen v. Hicklin* (L.R. 3Q.B. 360) concerned an ironmonger who was also an ardent antipapist. He sold copies of *The Confessional Unmasked: Showing the Depravity of the Romish Priesthood, the Iniquity of the Confessional and the Questions Put to Females in Confession,* and although the Court agreed that his heart was pure, his publication was not. Judge Cockburn announced a test of obscenity that was to persist in British law for nearly a century and in American law until the 1930s:

I think the test of obscenity is this, whether the tendency of the matter charged as obscenity is to deprave and corrupt those whose minds are open to such immoral influences, and into whose hands a publication of this sort may fall.

Clearly, but not exclusively, Cockburn was attempting to protect young people.

In 1913 in *United States v. Kennerly* (209 F. 119), Judge Learned Hand ruled against the defendant because his publication clearly fell under the limits of the Hicklin test, but he added:

I hope it is not improper for me to say that the rule as laid down, however consonant it may be with mid-Victorian morals, does not seem to me to answer to the understanding and morality of the present time, as conveyed by the words, "obscene, lewd, or lascivious." I question whether in the end men will regard that as obscene which is honestly relevant to the adequate expression of innocent ideas, and whether they will not believe that truth and beauty are too precious to society at large to be mutilated in the interest of those most likely to pervert them to base uses.

Then in 1933 and 1934, two decisions (5 F. supp. 182 and 72 F. 2d 705) overturned much of the Hicklin test. James Joyce's *Ulysses* had been regarded as obscene by most legal authorities since its publication, largely for Molly Bloom's soliloquy. The novel was stopped by Customs officials and tried before Judge John M. Woolsey of the Federal District Court for Southern New York. Woolsey found the book "sincere and honest" and "not dirt for dirt's sake" and ruled that in matters determining what is obscene, the work *must* be judged as a whole, not on the basis of its parts. An appeal to the Federal Circuit Court of Appeals in 1934 led to Judge Learned Hand's upholding Woolsey's decision.

In 1957 in *Butler v. Michigan* (352 U.S. 380), Butler challenged a Michigan statute that tested obscenity in terms of its effect on young people, arguing that this restricted adult reading to that fit only for children. Justice Felix Frankfurter agreed, and wrote:

> The State insists that, by thus quarantining the general reading public against books not too rugged for grown men and women in order to shield juvenile innocence, it is exercising its power to promote the general welfare. Surely, this is to burn the house to roast the pig. . . . The incidence of this enactment [the Michigan statute] is to reduce the adult population of Michigan to reading only what is fit for children.

Frankfurter agreed with Butler and declared the Michigan statute unconstitutional.

Later in 1957, in *Roth v. United States* (354 U.S. 476), the U.S. Supreme Court announced that obscenity was not protected by the Constitution, for "implicit in the history of the First Amendment is the rejection of obscenity as utterly without redeeming social importance." (That phrase, "without redeeming social importance" was to cause problems for several years thereafter.) Reading for the majority, Justice Brennan added a new definition of obscenity:

> Obscene material is material which deals with sex in a manner appealing to prurient interest.

And a new test:

> Whether to the average person, applying contemporary community standards, the dominant theme of the material taken as a whole appeals to prurient interest.

Roth rejected the Hicklin test (already in patches) as "unconstitutionally restrictive of the freedoms of speech and press."

Jacobellis v. Ohio (84 S. Ct. 1676) in 1964 further refined the *Roth* test when Justice Brennan announced that the "contemporary community" standard referred to national standards, not local standards, although Chief Justice Warren angrily dissented, arguing that community standards meant local and nothing more.

In 1966, in *Memoirs v. Attorney General of Massachusetts* (86 S. Ct. 975), Justice Brennan further elaborated on the *Roth* test:

> Under this definition, as elaborated in subsequent cases, three elements must coalesce: it must be established that (a) the dominant theme of the material taken as a whole appeals to prurient interest in sex; (b) the material is patently offensive because it affronts contemporary community standards relating to the description or representation of sexual matters; and (c) the material is utterly without redeeming social value.

The *Ginsberg v. New York* (390 U.S. 692) decision in 1968 did not develop or alter the definition of obscenity, but it did introduce the concepts of variable obscenity and caused some concern for librarians and English teachers. Ginsberg, who operated a stationery store and luncheonette, had sold "girlie" magazines to a 16-year-old boy in violation of a New York statute that declared illegal the sale of anything "which depicts nudity" and "was harmful" to anyone under 17 years of age. Ginsberg maintained that New York State was without power to draw the line at the age of 17. The Court dismissed his argument, sustained the New York statute, and wrote:

> The well-being of its children is of course a subject within the State's constitutional power to regulate.

The Court further noted, in lines that proved worrisome to anyone dealing in literature, classic, or modern or what-have-you:

> To be sure, there is no lack of "studies" which purport to demonstrate that obscenity is or is not "a basic factor in impairing the ethical and moral development of . . . youth and a clear and present danger to the people of the state." But the growing consensus of commentators is that "while these studies all agree that a causal link has not been demonstrated, they are equally agreed that a causal link has not been disproved either."

Those words were lovingly quoted by censors across the United States, although few of them bothered to read the citations in the decision that suggested the dangers of assuming too much either way about the matter.

Five U.S. Supreme Court decisions in 1973 brought forth a new test of obscenity. The most important, *Miller v. California* (413 U.S. 15) and *Paris Adult Theatre II v. Slaton* (413 U.S. 49), contained the refined test, one presumably designed to remove all ambiguities from past tests. That the test proved as ambiguous and as difficult to enforce and understand as previous tests should come as no surprise to readers. After attacking the 1957 *Roth* test, the majority decision read by Chief Justice Burger in *Miller* provided this three-pronged test of obscenity:

> The basic guidelines for the trier of fact must be: (a) whether "the average person, applying contemporary community standards" would find that the work, taken as a whole, appeals to the prurient interest; (b) whether the work depicts or describes in a patently offensive way, sexual conduct specifically defined by the applicable state law;

and (c) whether the work taken as a whole lacks serious literary, artistic, political or scientific value.

To guide state legislatures with "a few plain examples of what a state statute could define for regulation under the second part (b) of the standard announced in this opinion," the Court provided these:

(a) Patently offensive representations or descriptions of ultimate sexual acts, normal or perverted, actual or simulated.

(b) Patently offensive representations or descriptions of masturbation, excretory functions, and lewd exhibition of the genitals.

After this so-called Miller catalogue, Burger announced that "contemporary community standards" meant state standards, not national standards.

Paris Adult Theatre II underscored *Miller* and added more worrisome words about the dangers of obscenity and what it can lead to. Chief Justice Burger, again, for the majority:

But, it is argued, there is no scientific data which conclusively demonstrated that exposure to obscene material adversely affects men and women or their society. It is urged on behalf of the petitioner that, absent such a demonstration, any kind of state regulation is "impermissible." We reject this argument. It is not for us to resolve empirical uncertainties underlying state legislation, save in the exceptional case where that legislation plainly impinges upon rights protected by the Constitution itself. . . . Although there is no conclusive proof of any connection between antisocial behavior and obscene material, the legislature of Georgia could quite reasonably determine that such a connection does or might exist.

In other words, no proof exists that obscenity does (or does not) lead to antisocial actions (or nonactions), yet state legislatures can assume or guess that such a relationship may exist and pass legislation to that effect.

Justice Brennan dissented, noting that the dangers to "protected speech are very grave" and added that the decision would not halt further cases before the Court:

The problem is that one cannot say with certainty that material is obscene until at least five members of this Court, applying inevitably obscure standards, have pronounced it so.

To few observers' surprise, Brennan's prophecy proved correct. On January 13, 1972, police in Albany, Georgia, seized the film *Carnal Knowledge* (starring Jack Nicholson) and charged the manager with violating a state statute against distributing obscene material. He was convicted in the Superior Court, and the decision was affirmed by a divided vote in the Georgia State Supreme Court. In 1974, the U.S. Supreme Court announced its decision in *Jenkins v. the State of Georgia* (94 S. Ct. 2750), Justice Rehnquist reading the unanimous decision to reverse the Georgia Supreme Court opinion. Although *Carnal Knowledge* had been declared obscene by state standards and although it had a scene showing simulated masturbation, Rehnquist stated that "juries do not

JUDY BLUME
On Censorship

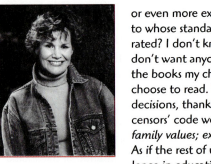

*F*ear has always made people anxious, and we are living in fearful times. Censorship grows out of fear, and because fear is contagious, some parents are easily swayed. Book banning satisfies a need for parents to feel in control of their children's lives. This fear is often disguised as moral outrage. They want to believe that if their children don't read about something, their children won't know about it. And if they don't know about it, it won't happen.

Today it's not only *Sex, Swear Words* and *Lack of Moral Tone*—it is *Evil,* which according to the censors, can be found lurking everywhere. The *Harry Potter* books, as well as stories about Halloween and miscellaneous witches and devils, are all suspect for promoting Satanism. *Romeo and Juliet* is under fire for promoting suicide; Madeleine L'Engle's *A Wrinkle in Time,* for promoting New Age-ism. If the censors had their way, it would be goodbye to Shakespeare as well as science fiction. There's not an *ism* you can think of that's not bringing some book to the battlefield.

Books that make kids laugh often come under suspicion; so do books that encourage kids to think or question authority. Books that don't hit the reader over the head with moral lessons are considered dangerous. My book, *Blubber,* was banned in Montgomery County, Maryland, for lack of *moral tone,* but in New Zealand it is used in teacher-training classes to help explain classroom dynamics.

Censors don't want children exposed to ideas different from their own. If every individual with an agenda had his or her way, the shelves in the school library would be close to empty. I worry about this loss to young people. If no one speaks out for them, if they don't speak out for themselves, all they'll get for required reading will be the most bland books available. And instead of finding the information they need at the library, instead of finding the novels that illuminate life, they will find only those materials to which nobody could possibly object.

Some people would like to rate books in schools and libraries the way they rate movies: G, PG, R, X,

or even more explicitly. But according to whose standards would the books be rated? I don't know about you, but I don't want anyone rating my books or the books my children or grandchildren choose to read. We can make our own decisions, thank you. Be wary of the censors' code words—*family friendly; family values; excellence in education.* As if the rest of us don't want excellence in education, as if we don't have our own family values, as if libraries haven't always been family-friendly places!

And the demands are not all coming from the religious right. No . . . the urge to decide not only what's right for their kids but for all kids has caught on with others across the political spectrum. Each year *Huckleberry Finn* is challenged and sometimes removed from the classroom because, to some, its language, which includes racial epithets, is offensive. Better to acknowledge the language, bring it out in the open, and discuss why the book remains important than to ban it. Teachers and parents can talk with their students and children about any book considered controversial.

I am encouraged that many teachers and parents are doing this. I regularly receive letters from young people who are studying censorship in their classes. And in many communities across the country, students from elementary through high school are becoming active (along with caring adults) in the fight to maintain their right to read and their right to choose books. They are speaking before school boards, and more often than not, when they do, the books in question are returned to the shelves.

Only when readers of all ages become active, only when readers are willing to stand up to the censors, will they get the message that they have every right to decide what their child should read, but not what all children should read.

have unbridled discretion" in determining obscenity and that *Carnal Knowledge* had nothing that fell "within either of the two examples given in *Miller.*"

The history of litigation and court decisions about obscenity and its definition are hardly models of clarity or consistency. Anyone interested in more details of this frustrating but fascinating story should read that marvelous book by Felice Flanery Lewis, *Literature, Obscenity and Law.*

Court Decisions about Teaching and School Libraries

If the implications of court decisions about obscenity are a bit vague, decisions about teaching and school libraries are not notably better. Courts are notoriously leery of decisions involving schools and libraries, lest they be regarded as a national school board, but a few decisions, not unsurprisingly ambiguous, are worth noting about school libraries.

The U.S. Supreme Court had ruled in *Tinker v. the Des Moines (Iowa) School District* (393 U.S. 503) in 1969:

> First Amendment rights, applied in light of the special characteristics of the school environment, are available to teachers and students. It can hardly be argued that either students or teachers shed their constitutional rights to freedom of speech or expression at the schoolhouse gate.

But courts, federal or state, seemed unwilling to extend those rights to the school library in *Presidents Council, District 25 v. Community School Board No. 25* (457 F. 2d 289) in 1972. A New York City school board voted 5–3 in 1971 to remove all copies of Piri Thomas's *Down These Mean Streets* from junior high libraries because of its offensive nature and language. The U.S. Court of Appeals, Second Circuit, held for the school board. The book, so the Court decided, had dubious literary or educational merit, and because the state had delegated the selection of school materials to local school boards and there was no evidence of basic constitutional impingement by the board, the Court saw no merit in the opposing view.

Presidents Council was cited for several years thereafter as the definitive decision, but because it was not a Supreme Court decision, it served as precedent only for judges so inclined.

A different decision prevailed in *Minarcini v. Strongsville (Ohio) City School District* (541 F. 2d 577) in 1977. The school board refused to allow a teacher to use Heller's *Catch-22* or Vonnegut's *God Bless You, Mr. Rosewater,* ordered Vonnegut's *Cat's Cradle* and Heller's novel removed from the library, and proclaimed that students and teachers were not to discuss these books in class. The U.S. District Court found for the school board, but on appeal to the U.S. Circuit Court of Appeals, the three-member panel reversed the lower court. Judge Edwards focused on the main issues of the case in eloquent words widely quoted and much admired by school librarians:

> A library is a storehouse of knowledge. When created for a public school it is an important privilege created by the state for the benefit of the students in the school. That privilege is not subject to being withdrawn by succeeding school boards whose

members might desire to "winnow" the library for books the content of which occasioned their displeasure or disapproval. Of course, a copy of a book may wear out. Some books may become obsolete. Shelf space alone may at some point require some selection of books to be retained and books to be disposed of. No such rationale is involved in this case.

The opinion of the Court that library books gained a tenure of sorts and could not easily be culled by a school board was at odds with the parallel U.S. Circuit Court in *Presidents Council,* but again, the Ohio decision served as precedent only if judges in other federal district courts (or federal appeals courts) wished to so use it.

A year later in *Right to Read Defense Committee of Chelsea (Massachusetts) v. School Committee of the City of Chelsea* (454 F. Supp. 703) in the U.S. District Court for Massachusetts, another decision supported the rights of students and libraries. The librarian of Chelsea High School ordered and made available a paperback anthology, *Male and Female under Eighteen,* containing a poem by a student, "The City to the Young Girl," which had, as the judge wrote, "street language." A parent felt the language was "offensive" and called the board chairman, who was also the editor of the local paper. The chair-editor concluded that the poem was "filthy" and contained "offensive" language and should be removed from the library. He scheduled an emergency meeting of the school committee to consider the subject of "objectionable, salacious and obscene material being made available in books in the High School Library" and wrote an article for his newspaper about the matter, concluding with these words:

> Quite frankly, I want a complete review of how it was possible for such garbage to even get on bookshelves where 14-year-old high school ninth graders could obtain them.

The superintendent urged caution and noted that the book could not be removed from the library without a formal review, but the chair was adamant. When the librarian argued that the poem was not obscene, the chair-editor wrote in his newspaper:

> [I am] shocked and extremely disappointed to have our high school librarian claim there is nothing lewd, lascivious, filthy, suggestive, licentious, pornographic or obscene about this particular poem in this book of many poems.

The school committee claimed "an unconstrained authority to remove books from the shelves of the school library." Although the judge agreed that "local authorities are, and must continue to be, the principal policymakers in the public schools," he was more swayed by the reasoning in *Minarcini* than in *Presidents Council.* He wrote:

> The Committee was under no obligation to purchase *Male and Female* for the High School Library, but it did. . . . The Committee claims an absolute right to remove *City* from the shelves of the school library. It has no such right, and compelling policy considerations argue against any public authority having such an unreviewable power of censorship. There is more at issue here than the poem *City.* If this work may be removed by a committee hostile to its language and theme, then the precedent is set for removal of any other work. The prospect of successive school committees "sanitizing"

the school library of views divergent from its own is alarming, whether they do it book by book or one page at a time.

What is at stake here is the right to read and be exposed to controversial thoughts and language—a valuable right subject to First Amendment protection.

What proved to be a most significant decision about school libraries began in September 1975 when three members of the Island Trees (New York) School Board attended a conference sponsored by the conservative Parents of New York—United (PONY-U). After examining lists of books deemed "objectionable" by PONY-U, the three returned home, checked their district's school libraries, and found several suspect works—Bernard Malamud's *The Fixer*, Vonnegut's *Slaughterhouse-Five*, Desmond Morris's *The Naked Ape*, Piri Thomas's *Down These Mean Streets*, Langston Hughes's edition of *Best Short Stories of Negro Writers*, Oliver LaFarge's *Laughing Boy*, Richard Wright's *Black Boy*, Alice Childress's *A Hero Ain't Nothin' But a Sandwich*, Eldridge Cleaver's *Soul on Ice*, and *Go Ask Alice*. In February 1976, the board gave "unofficial direction" that the books be removed from the library and delivered to the board for their reading.

Once the word was out, the board issued a press release attempting to justify its actions, calling the books "anti-American, anti-Christian, anti-Semitic, and just plain filthy" and argued:

It is our duty, our moral obligation, to protect the children in our schools from this moral danger as surely as from physical or medical dangers.

When the board appointed a review committee—four members of the school staff and four parents—the board politely listened to the report suggesting that five books should be returned to the shelves and that two should be removed (*The Naked Ape* and *Down These Mean Streets*) and then ignored their own chosen committee. (The board did return one book to the shelves, *Laughing Boy*, and placed *Black Boy* on a restricted shelf available only with parental permission.) Stephen Pico, a student, and others brought suit against the board, claiming that their rights under the First Amendment had been denied by the board.

The U.S. District Court heard the case in 1979 and granted a summary judgment to the board. The court held that the state had vested school boards with broad discretion to formulate educational policy, and the selection or rejection of books was clearly within their power. The court found no merit in the First Amendment claims of Pico, et al. A three-judge panel of the U.S. Court of Appeals for the Second Circuit (638 F. 2d 404) reversed the District Court's decision 2–1 and remanded the case for trial. The case then, although not directly, wended its way to the U.S. Supreme Court, the first such case ever to be heard at that level.

In a strange and badly fragmented decision—and for that reason it is unclear how certainly it will serve as precedent—Justice Brennan delivered the plurality (*not* majority) opinion in *Board of Education, Island Trees Union Free School District v. Pico* (102 S. Ct. 2799). He immediately emphasized the "limited nature" of the question before the court, for "precedents have long recognized certain constitutional limits upon the power of the State to control even the curriculum and classroom," and he further noted that *Island Trees* did not involve textbooks "or indeed any books that Island Trees students would be required to read." The case concerned only the removal, not the acquisition, of library books. He concluded the first section of his opinion by pointing out that the case concerned two questions:

> First, does the First Amendment impose *any* limitations upon the discretion of petitioners to remove library books from the Island Trees High School and Junior High School? Second, if so, do the affidavits and other evidential materials before the District Court, construed most favorably to respondents, raise a genuine issue of fact whether petitioners might have exceeded those limitations?

Brennan proceeded to find for *Pico* (and ultimately for the library and the books):

> . . . we think that the First Amendment rights of students may be directly and sharply implicated by the removal of books from the shelves of a school library.
>
> Petitioners emphasized the inculcative function of secondary education, and argue that they must be allowed *unfettered* discretion "to transmit community values" through the Island Trees schools. But that sweeping claim overlooks the unique role of the school library. . . . Petitioners might well defend their claim of absolute discretion in matters of *curriculum* by reliance upon their duty to inculcate community values. But we think that petitioners' reliance upon that duty is misplaced where, as here, they attempt to extend their claim of absolute discretion beyond the compulsory environment of the classroom, into the school library and the regime of voluntary inquiry that there holds sway.
>
> Petitioners rightly possess significant discretion to determine the content of their school libraries. But that discretion may not be exercised in a narrowly partisan or political manner. . . . Our Constitution does not permit the official suppression of ideas. Thus whether petitioners' removal of books from their school libraries denied respondents their First Amendment rights depends upon the motivation behind petitioners' actions. If petitioners *intended* by their removal decision to deny respondents access to ideas with which petitioners disagreed, and if this intent was the decisive factor in petitioners' decision, then petitioners have exercised their discretion in violation of the Constitution.

Four pages follow before Justice Blackmun's generally concurring opinion and Justices Burger, Rehnquist, Powell, and O'Connor offered their stinging dissents, but it is clear that school librarians won something, although precisely what and how much will need to be resolved by future court decisions.

It is equally clear that secondary teachers lost something in *Island Trees*. In an understandable ploy, the American Library Association, the New York Library Association, and the Freedom to Read Foundation submitted an *Amicus Curiae* brief, which sought to distinguish between the functions of the school classroom and the school library, a distinction that worked to the advantage of the school librarian but certainly not to that of the classroom teacher. Apparently, Brennan bought the argument as readers can see, comparing Brennan's words with those from the following brief:

> This case, however, is about a library, not a school's curriculum. This is an extremely important distinction for the evaluation of the First Amendment interests at stake here.

The school board below banned books from a library. Thus, this case does not present an issue concerning the board's control of curriculum, i.e., what is taught in the classroom. We freely concede that the school board has the right and duty to supervise the general content of the school's course of study.

Whether these words will cause serious disagreements between teachers and librarians remains to be seen. Certainly, that phrase, "we freely concede," has rankled a number of English teachers who recognized that *Island Trees* was a serious setback for intellectual freedom in the classroom, a point that was taken up in *Hazelwood* (108 S. Ct. 562, 1988) and later in *Virgil* (862 F. 2d 1517, 11th Cir., 1989).

Anyone who assumed that *Pico* quieted the waters of school censorship must have been surprised by five court decisions from 1986 through 1989. These decisions might have been expected to clear up the censorial waters; instead, they made the waters murkier.

On July 7, 1986, the U.S. Supreme Court announced its decision in *Bethel School District v. Fraser* (106 S. Ct. 3159, 1986) upholding school officials in Spanaway, Washington, who had suspended a student for using sexual metaphors in describing the political potency of a candidate for student government. Writing the majority opinion in the 7–2 decision, Chief Justice Burger said, "Surely it is a highly appropriate function of public school education to prohibit the use of vulgar and offensive terms in public discourse. . . . schools must teach by example the shared values of a civilized social order." To some people's surprise, Justice Brennan agreed with Justice Burger that the student's speech had been disruptive, although Brennan refused to label the speech indecent or obscene.

That decision worried many educators, but a lower court decision on October 24, 1986, frightened more teachers. *Mozert v. Hawkins County (Tennessee) Public Schools* (579 F. Supp. 1051, 1984) began in September 1983 when the school board of Hawkins County refused a request by parents to remove three books in the Holt, Rinehart and Winston reading series from the sixth-, seventh-, and eighth-grade program. The parents formed Citizens Organized for Better Schools and ultimately brought suit against the school board. U.S. District Judge Thomas Hull dismissed the lawsuit, but on appeal before the Sixth Circuit of the Court of Appeals, a panel of three judges remanded the case back to Judge Hull.

Not all the testimony in the trial during the summer of 1986 concerned humanism, particularly secular humanism, but so it seemed at times. Vicki Frost, one of the parents who initiated the suit, said that the Holt series taught "satanism, feminism, evolution, telepathy, internationalism, and other beliefs that come under the heading of secular humanism." Later she explained why parents objected to any mention of the Renaissance by saying that "a central idea of the Renaissance was a belief in the dignity and worth of human beings," presumably establishing that teaching the Renaissance was little more than teaching secular humanism.

Judge Hull ruled in favor of the parents on October 24, 1986, but the U.S. Sixth Circuit Court of Appeals overturned Hull's decision. Worse yet for the fundamentalist parents, the U.S. Supreme Court refused to hear an appeal of the Court of Appeals' ruling in February 1988. Beverly LaHaye, leader of the Concerned Women for America, who had filed the original suit in 1983 and whose group had helped finance the legal fees for the parents, said, "School boards now have the authority to trample the religious freedom of all children." Other people, notably educators, were grateful to the court for giving them the right to teach.

While *Mozert* worked its way through the courts, an even more troublesome and considerably louder suit was heard in Alabama. Judge Brevard W. Hand had earlier helped devise a suit defending the right of Alabama to permit a moment of silence for prayer in the public schools. The U.S. Supreme Court overturned Judge Hand's decision, so he devised another suit, *Smith v. School Commissioners of Mobile County, Alabama* (655 F. Supp. 939, 1987), alleging that social studies, history, and home economics textbooks in the Mobile public schools unconstitutionally promoted the "religious belief system" of secular humanism, as Judge Hand wrote in his March 4, 1987, decision maintaining that forty-four texts violated the rights of parents.

The decision was both silly and certain, but those who feared the bogeyman of secular humanism celebrated for a few weeks. Then, late in August 1987, the Eleventh U.S. Circuit Court of Appeals reversed Judge Hand's decision. The Court of Appeals did not address the question of whether secular humanism was a religion, but it did agree that the forty-four texts did not promote secular humanism. Phyllis Schlafly said she was not surprised by the ruling, but it mattered little because the decision would be appealed to the U.S. Supreme Court. Oddly enough for a case that began so loudly, the plaintiffs were mute, the date for the appeal quietly passed, and all was silence.

The fourth case, *Hazelwood School District v. Kuhlmeier* (108 S. Ct. 562, 1988), will trouble many educators, although nominally the case was concerned with school journalism and the publication of a school newspaper. The case began in 1983 when the principal of a high school in Hazelwood, Missouri, objected to two stories in the school newspaper dealing with teenage pregnancy and divorce's effects on young people.

Associate Justice Byron White wrote the majority opinion in the 5–3 decision announcing that educators (i.e., administrators) are entitled to exercise great control over student expression. Although the case presumably dealt only with a school newspaper, White's words—inadvertently or not—went further. White wrote:

> The policy of school officials toward [the school newspaper] was reflected in Hazelwood School Board Policy 348.51 and the Hazelwood East Curriculum Guide. Board Policy 348.51 provided that "school-sponsored publications are developed within the adopted curriculum and its educational activities."

After commenting on needed school standards and the right of administrators to set standards, White added:

> This standard is consistent with our oft-expressed view that the education of the nation's youth is primarily the responsibility of parents, teachers, and state and local school officials, and not of federal judges.

The three court decisions, which came less than a week apart, supported a Florida school board's banning of a humanities textbook, a California principal's seizure of an "April Fool's" edition of a school newspaper, and a Nebraska school district's decision not to provide meeting space to a student Bible Club.

The Florida decision was particularly troubling and hinted that parallel decisions citing *Hazelwood* as precedent might be on the way. *Virgil v. School Board of Columbia County, Florida* (862 F. 2d 1517, 11th Cir., 1989) concerned a challenge to a school board's decision to stop using a humanities text in a high school class because it contained Chaucer's "The Miller's Tale" and Aristophanes's *Lysistrata,* two works to which parents had objected. After a formal complaint had been filed in April 1986, the school board appointed an advisory committee and then ignored that committee when it recommended keeping the text. Parents filed an action against the school board.

In the district court decision in January 1988, Judge Black agreed with the parents that the school board had overestimated the potential harm to students of Chaucer or Aristophanes, but she concluded that the board had the power as announced in *Hazelwood* to decide as it had.

The parents appealed to the Eleventh Circuit Court of Appeals, which, as in the district court, fell back on *Hazelwood* for precedent for curricular decisions, not merely those concerned with school newspapers. As Judge Anderson wrote in his decision of January 1989:

> In applying the *Hazelwood* standard to the instant case, two considerations are particularly significant. First, we conclude that the Board decisions at issue were curricular decisions. The materials removed were part of the textbook used in a regularly scheduled course of study in the school. . . . The second consideration that is significant in applying the *Hazelwood* standard to this case is that the motivation for the Board's removal of the readings has been stipulated to be related to the explicit sexuality and excessively vulgar language in the selections. It is clear from *Hazelwood* and other cases that this is a legitimate concern.

Judge Anderson found that the school board had acted appropriately, although in the last paragraph he and the court distanced themselves from the folly of the board's decision to ban two classics.

> We decide today only that the Board's removal of these works from the curriculum did not violate the Constitution. Of course, we do not endorse the Board's decision. Like the district court, we seriously question how young persons just below the age of majority can be harmed by these masterpieces of Western literature. However, having concluded that there is no constitutional violation, our role is not to second-guess the wisdom of the Board's action.

Florida teachers must have been touched by those words.

Joan DelFattore's *What Johnny Shouldn't Read: Textbook Censorship in America* is a recent scholarly and readable work that admirably covers major court decisions involving teachers and librarians.

Extralegal Decisions

Most censorship episodes do not result in legal hearings and court decisions. Teachers or librarians come under attack and unofficial rumor-mongering charges are lodged

ee the "Starter Bibliography" at the end of this chapter for sources to help mitigate the negative effects of censorship.

because someone objects and labels the offending work "obscene" or "filthy" or "pornographic." The case is heard in the court of public opinion, sometimes before the school board, with few legal niceties prevailing. The censors (and too often the school board) almost never operate under any definitions of obscenity that a court would recognize, but their interpretations of the issues are operationally effective for their purposes. The book may not always be judged as a whole book (although individual parts may be juicily analyzed), and the entire procedure may be arbitrary and capricious. The decision, once announced, rapidly disposes of the offending book and frequently the teacher or librarian to boot, a variation of old-fashioned Western justice at work. Extralegal trials need not be cluttered with trivia such as accuracy or reasoning or fairness or justice. Many of the censorship incidents described earlier in this chapter were handled extralegally.

Why would librarians or teachers allow their books and teaching materials to be so treated? Court cases cost a great deal of money, and unless a particular case is likely to create precedent, many lawyers discourage educators from going to the courts. Court cases, even more important, cause friction within the community and—surprising to many neophyte teachers and librarians—cause almost equal friction among a school's faculty. A teacher or librarian who assumes that all fellow teachers will automatically support a case for academic freedom or intellectual freedom is a fool. Many educators, to misuse the word, have little sympathy for troublemakers or their causes. Others are frightened at the prospect of possibly antagonizing their superiors. Others "know their place" in the universe. Others are morally offended by anything stronger than *darn* and may regard most of modern literature (and old literature) as inherently immoral and therefore objectionable to high school students' use. Others find additional or different reasons aplenty for staying out of the fray. And that, more likely than not, is the reason most censorship episodes do not turn into court cases.

A New Kind of Censorship

N. R. Kleinfield's article, "The Elderly Man and the Sea? Test Sanitizes Literary Texts," in the June 2, 2002, *New York Times* revealed a certain kind of censorship and hinted at one far more important and pervasive. He told how Jeanne Heifetz was skimming through a familiar quotation on the New York State Regents Examination in English and discovered that words were missing. She checked and indeed the missing words were missing. And there were several quotations that were cut or rewritten.

For example, a quotation from a speech by the United Nations Secretary General was given thus:

Polls show strong American support for the organization at the grass-roots level.

But the original quotation was this:

Polls show strong American support for the organization at the grass-roots level regard-less of what is said and done on Capitol Hill.

Surely a major change in meaning took place between quotations one and two. But another alteration in the speech by the United Nations Secretary General was even more puzzling. At one point, he praised "the fine California wine and seafood," but that was altered so that he praised only "the fine California seafood." Presumably, the mere mention of wine on a test might prove offensive or disturbing to a student.

When the Education Department's Assistant Commissioner for Curriculum, Instruction, and Assessment was asked about the alterations in various passages, she responded, "We do shorten the passages and alter the passages to make them suitable for testing situations." She extended her remarks by explaining that the changes were made to satisfy the sensitivity guidelines used by the department so no student will be "uncomfortable in a testing situation."[29] If the meaning of all those words remained unclear or ambiguous, one thing was clear—passages were rewritten or cut to ensure that no student would be "uncomfortable" while taking a test. It turned out that students could be made "uncomfortable" because of race or ethnic background or place of origin (or where a student may now live). As John Leo wrote in his "Heck Hath No Fury" column in the June 17, 2002, *U.S. New and World Report:*

The New York sensitivity review guidelines ban "language, content, or context that is not accessible to one or more racial or ethnic groups."

Translation: Keep everything bland and down the middle.[30]

Leo also noted that New York University professor Diane Ravitch was preparing a book on the subject, and several months later *The Language Police: How Pressure Groups Restrict What Students Learn* appeared.[31]

Ravitch's book is a detailed commentary and analysis of this new censorship, which is practiced by textbook publishers, school boards, and bias and sensitivity committees. Committee members go through texts to weed out anything that might somehow or somewhere offend or disturb someone for some reason. Text publishers, or any sort of publisher dealing with public schools, have no wish to offend anyone, and "publishers found that the best way to avoid controversy is to eliminate anything that might cause controversy."[32] In many ways, the guidelines of the sensitivity and bias committees are censorship guidelines.

But this is a different sort of censorship than teachers or librarians usually encounter. Censors—as we usually know them—object to the rude, the violent, the disturbing, the offensive, and they want it removed. In this case, people we would expect to be on the side of teachers and librarians already censor what is offensive or violent or rude. As Ravitch noted, "This language censorship and thought control should be repugnant to those who care about freedom of thought,"[33] but clearly the language police do not care about freedom of thought. Protection and condescension are the aim of their notion of education.

What does Ravitch advocate?

We can stop censorship. We must recognize that the censorship that is now so widespread in education represents a systemic breakdown of our ability to educate the next generation and to transmit to them a full and open range of ideas about important issues in the world. By avoiding controversy, we teach them to avoid dealing with reality. By expurgating literature, we teach them that words are meaningless and fungible.[34]

At the very least, teachers and librarians ought to know Ravitch's Appendix 1, "A Glossary of Banned Words, Usages, Stereotypes, and Topics." Ravitch lists words and expressions that have offended the bias and sensitivity people, beginning with *able-bodied,* which has been "banned as offensive, replace with *person who is non-disabled*." *Birth defect* is apparently offensive and should be replaced with *people with congenital disabilities*. *Courageous* is banned as patronizing when referring to a person with disabilities. *Fairy* is banned because it suggests homosexuality and should be replaced with *elf*.

And so it goes.

What to Do Before and After the Censors Arrive

Certain steps should be taken by librarians and teachers, preferably acting in concert, to prepare for censorship.

Before the Censors Arrive

Teachers and librarians should have some knowledge about the history of censorship and why citizens would wish to censor (see the books and articles listed in the Starter Bibliography on Censorship). They should keep up-to-date with censorship problems and court decisions and what books are coming under attack for what reason. That means they should read the *Newsletter on Intellectual Freedom, School Library Journal, English Journal, Journal of Youth Services in Libraries,* and *Voice of Youth Advocates,* along with other articles cited in the bibliography that concludes each issue of the *Newsletter.* A lot of work? Of course, but better than facing a censor totally ignorant of the world of censorship.

They should develop clear and succinct statements, devoid of any educational or library or literary jargon, on why they teach literature or stock books. These statements ought to be made easily available to the public, partly to demonstrate educators' literacy—always an impressive beginning for an argument—and to make parents feel that someone intelligent works in the school, partly because teachers and librarians have a duty to communicate to the public what is going on and why it goes on.

They need to develop and publicize procedures for book selection in the library or the classroom. Most parents have not the foggiest notion of how educators go about selecting books, more or less assuming it comes about through sticking pins in a book catalogue. It might be wise to consider asking some parents to assist teachers and librarians in selection, partly to let parents learn how difficult the matter is, partly to use their ideas (which might prove surprisingly helpful).

They need to develop procedures for handling censorship, should it occur. The National Council of Teachers of English monographs *The Students' Right to Read* and *The Students' Right to Know* should prove helpful, as should the American Library Association's *Intellectual Freedom Manual,* both for general principles and for specific suggestions. Whether adopted from any of these sources or created afresh, the procedure should include a form to be completed by anyone who objects to any teaching material or library book and a clearly defined way in which the matter will be handled after completion of the form. (Will it go to a committee? How many are on the committee? Are people outside the school on the committee? How many teachers? How many administrators?) The procedural rules must be openly available for anyone to consult, the procedures must apply to everyone (no exceptions should be allowed, no matter whether the complainant is the local drunk or the school board president), every complainant must be treated courteously and promptly, and the procedures must be approved by the school board. If the board does not approve the document, it has no legal standing. If the school board is not periodically reminded of the procedures—say, every couple of years—it may forget its obligation. Given the fact that many school boards change membership slightly each year and may change their entire composition within five or six years, teachers and librarians should take it upon themselves to remind the board. Otherwise, an entirely new board may wonder why it should support something it neither created nor particularly approves of.

Teachers who assign long works (other than texts) for common reading should write rationales, statements aimed at parents but open to anyone, explaining why the teacher chose *1984,* or *Silas Marner, Manchild in the Promised Land,* or *Hamlet* for class

Authors have found that one way to fight censorship is to get young people thinking about it by including issues of free speech and censorship either as a primary or secondary theme in books that young people are likely to read.

reading and discussion. Rationales should answer the following, although they should be written as informal essays, devoid of any educational jargon, not answers to essay tests: (1) Why would the teacher use this book with this class at this time? (2) What specific objectives—not couched in behavioral terms unless the teachers are anxious to alienate parents—literary or pedagogical, is the teacher aiming at? (3) How will this book meet those objectives? (4) What problems of style, tone, theme, or subject matter exist, and how will the teacher face them? Answering those questions should force teachers to take a fresh look at the book and think more carefully about the possibilities and problems inherent in the book. Rationales are *not* designed to protect the teacher by showing careful advance preparation before teaching, although clearly such rationales would be valuable should censorship strike. Rather, rationales should be written for public information easily available to anyone interested as part of the professional responsibility of teachers. Diane Shugert offers a number of sample rationales in the fall 1983 *Connecticut English Journal* and in "How to Write a Rationale in Defense of a Book" in James Davis's *Dealing with Censorship*.

Educators should woo the public to gain support for intellectual and academic freedom. Any community has its readers and former teachers interested in students' freedom to read. Finding them ahead of time is part of teachers' and librarians' jobs. Waiting until censorship strikes is too late. Pat Scales's ideas about working with parents in the November 1983 *Calendar* (distributed by the Children's Book Council) are most helpful. Scales was talking to a parent who helped in Scales's school library and who had picked up copies of Maureen Daly's *Seventeenth Summer* and Ann Head's *Mr. and Mrs. Bo Jo Jones* and wondered about students reading books with such provocative covers. Scales asked the mother to read the books before forming an opinion. From that experience came a program called "Communicate Through Literature" with monthly meetings to discuss with parents the reading that young adults do.

Also, we should not forget about discussing the topic of censorship with our current students. See Focus Box 12.1 and the photos on p. 395 for one way to bring up the subject. Today's students could easily be the parents who in a few years will be on the school board or on the library's board of trustees.

Followup discussions are more important than the reading itself. In fact, Suzann Holland has criticized the authors of some of the books listed in Focus Box 12.1 for not keeping up with changing conditions. For example, she could not find books in which authors have "tackled the censorship of music and movies, freedom of assembly, or Internet filters." While acknowledging the possibilities for censorship in virtually all communities, she warns that "the fuse won't always be found in the local Bible study group." Nor will the censors be fundamentalists who act without plans. She was disappointed that in so many books, "the censors stumble badly in their arguments and appear far less intelligent than those trying to prevent such instances of "protection."[35]

Her philosophy of getting young people to explore situations of censorship before they get involved in the emotions of any particular case is similar to that of the American Library Association, which in the last full week of September sponsors an annual "Banned Books Week." See Focus Box 12.2 for ALA's "Banned Books" website, along with other websites that provide materials to support booksellers, librarians, and teachers in countering the negative effects of censorship. ALA provides posters and other items appropriate for use with children, young adults, or adults.

Educators should be prepared to take on the usual arguments of censors—for example, that educators are playing word games when we insist that we select and some parents try to censor. There is a distinction between *selection* and *censorship*, no matter how many people deliberately or inadvertently misuse or confuse the two. The classic distinction was drawn by Lester Asheim in 1952:

> Selection begins with a presumption in favor of liberty of thought; censorship with a presumption in favor of thought control. Selection's approach to the book is positive, seeking its values in the book as a book, and in the book as a whole. Censorship's approach is negative, seeking for vulnerable characteristics wherever they can be found anywhere in the book, or even outside it. Selection seeks to promote the right of the reader to read; censorship seeks to protect not the right—but the reader himself from the fancied effects of his reading. The selector has faith in the intelligence of the reader; the censor has faith only in his own.
>
> In other words, selection is democratic while censorship is authoritarian, and in our democracy we have traditionally tended to put our trust in the selector rather than in the censor.[36]

Finally, teachers and librarians should know the organizations that are most helpful if censorship does strike. Diane Shugert's "A Body of Well-Instructed Men and

Be the Judge. Be the Jury: Tinker vs. DesMoines by Doreen Rappaport. HarperCollins, 1993. This trial is probably the single most influential U.S. Supreme Court decision on students' First Amendment rights.

The Day They Came to Arrest the Book by Nat Hentoff. Delacorte, 1982. Parents object to *Adventures of Huckleberry Finn* because the book is, according to them, racist and sexist. Hentoff advances the cases for both sides.

Fahrenheit 451 by Ray Bradbury. Ballantine, 1953. Although Bradbury's classic story of book burning was published as an adult novel, it is now read by more teenagers than adults. Ironically, a recent "school edition" was published minus the swear words.

The Landry News by Andrew Clements, illustrated by Salvatore Murdocca. Simon & Schuster, 1999. A burned-out teacher is "inspired" to start a class-sponsored newspaper after one of his students writes a critical article about his teaching for the town paper. At last the fifth graders are excited about something, but then the principal decides to use the newspaper as a reason to fire the teacher. Everyone learns something.

The Last Book in the Universe by Rodman Philbrick. Blue Sky Press, 2000. One of the issues in this dystopian science fiction for middle-school readers is the importance of story.

The Last Safe Place on Earth by Richard Peck. Delacorte, 1995. Walden Woods seems like the perfect place to live until a group dedicated to protecting young people from evil books decides to raid libraries.

Lemony Snicket: The Unauthorized Autobiography. HarperCollins, 2002. As part of the madcap adventures in this best-selling children's book, three pages are devoted to a letter from Vice Principal Nero thanking Mr. and Mrs. Spats for sending him the article from *The Daily Punctilio,* which explained "the danger of allowing young people to read certain books." He fired Ms. K. thus saving the children from reading such books as *Ramon Quimby, Age 8; Matilda;* and *Ivan Lachrymose: Lake Explorer.*

Maudie and Me and the Dirty Book by Betty Miles. Knopf, 1980. Eleven-year-old Kate chooses to read a book to first graders that describes a dog giving birth to puppies. Someone objects on the opinion page of the local newspaper and the project of older children reading to first graders almost gets cancelled.

Memoirs of a Bookbat by Kathryn Lasky. Harcourt, 1994. Lasky's book does a good job of showing how censorship can cause dissension within families. Fourteen-year-old Harper runs away to live with her grandmother because she does not agree with her parents' campaign against books and schools that do not espouse their "brand" of traditional values.

Nothing but the Truth: A Documentary Novel by Avi. Orchard, 1991; Scholastic, 2003. No one dreams that what starts out as a fairly simple teacher/student confrontation over free speech will give both Miss Narwin and ninth-grader Philip Malloy their 15 minutes of fame.

A Small Civil War by John Neufeld. Fawcett/Ballantine, 1982; Revised edition, Atheneum, 1996. Neufeld's book is set in a small Iowa town where controversy rages over the appropriateness of teaching John Steinbeck's *The Grapes of Wrath.* People on both sides of the issue become so outraged that hostilities expand far beyond the original quarrel.

Strike by Barbara Corcoran. Atheneum, 1983. Corcoran adds two countermelodies to the basic tune of a father-son debate about the boy's life and plans—a strike by teachers and a group anxious to go through libraries looking for filth.

The Trials of Molly Sheldon by Julian F. Thompson. Holt, 1995. The family store where Molly works becomes the site of protests by a group objecting to rental films, as well as books and magazines. Thompson relies on irony as he develops a comparison to the Salem witch trials and what Molly goes through.

The Year They Burned the Book by Nancy Garden. Farrar, Straus & Girouox, 1999. Jamie is editor of the school newspaper and a supporter of sex education in schools. Her editorial touches some raw nerves and the fight is on.

*T*he idea behind Banned Book
Week is to get readers, both young and
old, to think about the issue of censorship before they get involved in the
emotions of a particular case.

Women: Organizations Active for Intellectual Freedom," in James Davis's *Dealing with Censorship,* has a long list of such groups. Following are six national groups every educator ought to know:

The American Civil Liberties Union, 132 W. 43rd St., New York, NY 10036

The Freedom to Read Foundation, 50 E. Huron St., Chicago, IL 60611

The National Coalition Against Censorship, 2 W. 64th St., New York, NY 10023

People for the American Way, 2000 M St., N.W., Washington, DC 20036

SLATE (Support for the Learning and Teaching of English), National Council of Teachers of English, 1111 Kenyon Road, Urbana, IL 61801

The Standing Committee on Censorship, c/o National Council of Teachers of English, 1111 Kenyon Road, Urbana, IL 61801

After the Censors Arrive

Teachers and librarians should begin by refusing to panic—easier said than done, but essential. Censors always have one advantage. They can determine the time and the place for the attack. No matter how well prepared the teacher or the librarian, only the censor can say *when.*

Educators should not be too surprised or appalled to discover that not all their fellow teachers or librarians rush in with immediate support. If teachers and librarians assume they represent the entire cause by themselves, they are far better off and considerably less likely to be instantly disillusioned.

Educators ought to urge (or even require that) potential censors talk first to the teacher or librarian in question before completing the complaint form, not to stall the objectors but to assure everyone of fair play all around. Teachers or librarians may discover what others have before, that objectors sometimes simply want to be heard and their complaints treated with dignity and dispatch. Sometimes, teachers and librarians may even be able to talk calmly—once the need to battle has died down—with the objectors and to reason with them, which is not exactly the same as convincing them that the teachers or librarians are necessarily right. The objectors may even see why the offending work was assigned or recommended, sometimes even seeing the difficulty in choosing a book for a class or an individual. Many teachers and librarians, although by no means all, agree that if parents ask that their child not be required to read a certain book, educators must agree to find a substitute book. If a substitute book is to be found and if it is to meet a different fate than the first book, parents must help in selecting the new book. Most objectors deeply care about their children's education, and they under-stand why the substitute book should not be easier or shorter (thus rewarding the stu-dent) or harder and longer (thus unduly punishing the student). Finding another book approximately as long and as difficult as the original choice is no easy matter, but par-ents who demand substitutes must help, lest the teacher offend once more.

Librarians and teachers must treat objectors with every possible courtesy. Objec-tors should be expected to complete the school's forms detailing the objection, but the forms should be easily accessible and politely distributed. The complaint form should *never* be used to stall objectors. If it is so long that objectors get discouraged, the school may win one battle, but it will have produced one more disgruntled citizen, and at school bond time one irritated citizen and friends are quite enough to harm the cause of education.

Last, a committee (spelled out in detail before the censorship) meets to look at and discuss the complaint. After considering the problem but before arriving at a decision, the committee must meet with the teacher or librarian in question *and* the objectors to hear their cases. The committee then makes its decision and forwards it to the highest administrator in the school, who forwards it to the superintendent, who then forwards it to the school board. That body, already aware of the policy and procedures much ear-lier adopted to handle such matters, considers this objection and makes its decision, probably after at least one open meeting.

In no case and at no level should the actions of the educators or administrators or the school be viewed as pro forma. They should be considered as thoughtful actions to resolve a problem, not as an attempt to create newer and bigger ones. Objectors should feel that they have been listened to and courtesy has been extended them at all levels and all stages.

Concluding Comments

We believe that the school—classroom or library—must be a center of intellectual fer-ment in the community. This implies not that schools should be radical, but that they should be one place where freedom to think and inquire is protected, where ideas of all sorts can be considered, analyzed, investigated, and discussed, and their conse-quences thought through. We believe librarians and English teachers must protect these freedoms, not merely in the abstract but in the practical, day-by-day world of the school and library. To protect those freedoms, we must fight censorship, for without them no education worthy of the name is possible.

[1]Colin Campbell, "Book Banning in America," *New York Times Book Review,* December 20, 1981, p. 1.

[2]Kelly Pearce, "Twain's 'Sawyer' Is Wrong for Mesa." *Arizona Republic,* September 3, 1999, p. 5-1, 4.

[3]*Newsletter on Intellectual Freedom* 42 (July 1993): 105–106.

[4]*Newsletter on Intellectual Freedom* 45 (November 1966): 198.

[5]*Newsletter on Intellectual Freedom* 46 (July 1997): 96.

[6]Samuel C. Monson, "Representative American Phonetic Alphabets," Columbia University, Unpublished Ph.D. Dissertation, 1953.

[7]Comstock's life and work have been the subject of many books and articles. Heywood Broun and Margaret Leech's *Anthony Comstock: Roundsman of the Lord* (Albert and Charles Boni, 1927) is amusing and nasty and still worth reading. A brief overview of Comstock's life can be found in Robert Brenner's introduction to the reprinting of *Traps for the Young* (Harvard University Press, 1967), pp. vii-xxxi. See also Paul S. Boyer's *Purity in Print: The Vice-Society Movement and Book Censorship in America* (Scribner, 1968) and Robert W. Haney's *Comstockery in America: Patterns of Censorship and Control* (Beacon Press, 1960).

[8]"Fiction in Public Libraries," *American Library Journal* 1 (March 1877): 278.

[9]"What Books Do They Read?" *Common School Education* 4 (April 1890): 146–147.

[10]"Unexpurgated Shakespeare," *Journal of Education* 37 (April 13, 1883): 232.

[11]Elizabeth Thurston, "Common Novels in Public Libraries," *Library Journal* 19 (December 1894): 17–18.

[12]*Library Journal* 21 (December 1896): 144.

[13]Richard Jones, "The Moral and Literary Responsibilities of Librarians in Selecting Books for a Public Library," *NEA Journal of Proceedings and Addresses* (Chicago: University of Chicago Press), 1897, p. 102.

[14]*Library Journal* 24 (August 1899): 479.

[15]*Public Libraries* 8 (March 1903): 114–115.

[16]Arthur E. Bostwick, *The American Public Library* (Appleton, 1910), pp. 130–131.

[17]Evaline Harrington, "Why Treasure Island?" *English Journal* 9 (May 1920): 267–268.

[18]"Standards in Selecting Fiction," *Library Journal* 67 (March 1932): 243.

[19]Louise Kingsbury and Lance Gurwell, "The Sin Fighters: Grappling with Gomorrah at the Grass Roots," *Utah Holiday* 12 (April 1983): 46.

[20]Lee Grant, "Shoot-Out in Texas," "Calendar" section, *Los Angeles Times,* December 25, 1983, p. 21.

[21]*Phoenix Gazette,* June 10, 1981, p. SE-6.

[22]*Arizona English Bulletin* 11 (February 1969): 37.

[23]Diane Shugert, "Censorship in Connecticut," *Connecticut English Journal* 9 (Spring 1978): 59–61.

[24]Kathleen Beck, "Censorship and Celluloid," *Voice of Youth Advocates* 18 (June 1995): 73–76.

[25]Ken Donelson, "Censorship in the 1970's: Some Ways to Handle It When It Comes (And It Will)," *English Journal* 63 (February 1974): 47–51.

[26]"Protest Groups Exert Strong Impact," *Publishers Weekly* 216 (October 29, 1979): 42–44.

[27]"Sixty Seven Targers of the Textbook Protestors," *Missouri English Bulletin* 38 (May 1980): 27–32.

[28]M. E. Kerr, "On Gay Books," *Literature for Today's Young Adults* by Alleen Pace Nilsen and Kenneth L. Donelson (Longman, 2001), p. 293.

[29]*New York Times,* June 2, 2002, p. 30.

[30]*U. S. News and World Report,* p. 53.

[31]Diane Ravitch, *The Language Police: How Pressure Groups Restrict What Students Learn* (Knopf, 2003).

[32]Ravitch, p. 24.

[33]Ravitch, p. 48.

[34]Ravitch, p. 165.

[35]Suzann Holland, "Censorship in Young Adult Fiction: What's Out There and What Should Be," VOYA 25:3 (August 2000): 176–177.

[36]Lester Asheim, "Not Censorship but Selection," *Wilson Library Bulletin* 28 (September 1953): 67. See also Asheim's later article, "Selection and Censorship: A Reappraisal," *Wilson Library Bulletin* 58 (November 1983): 180–184. Julia Turnquist Bradley's "Censoring the School Library: Do Students Have the Right to Read," *Connecticut Law Review* 10 (Spring 1978): 747–775, also draws a distinction between selection and censorship.

Biliographical Sources

McCoy, Ralph E. *Freedom of the Press: An Annotated Bibliography.* Carbondale, IL: Southern Illinois University Press, 1968.

McCoy, Ralph E. *Freedom of the Press: A Bibliocyclopedia Ten-Year Supplement.* Carbondale, IL: Southern Illinois University, 1979.

Newsletter on Intellectual Freedom. A bimonthly edited by Judith Krug with a sizable bibliography at the end of each issue. Available from the American Library Association (ALA), 50 East Huron St., Chicago, IL 60611.

Three Basic Policy Statements and Recommended Procedures

Burress, Lee and Edward B. Jenkinson. *The Students' Right to Know.* Urbana, IL: National Council of Teachers of English (NCTE), 1982.

Burress, Lee and Edward B. Jenkinson. *The Students' Right to Read,* 3rd ed. Urbana, IL: National Council of English, 1982. NCTE's official policy on censors and fighting censors.

Intellectual Freedom Manual, 6th ed. Chicago: American Library Association, 2002. ALA's official policy statement along with a mass of helpful material.

Court Cases

Bosmajian, Haig A., ed. *Censorship, Libraries, and the Law.* New York: Neal-Schuman, 1983. Censorship cases involving secondary schools.

Bosmajian, Haig A. *The first Amendment in the Classroom,* 5 volumes. New York: Neal-Schuman.
No. 1. *The Freedom to Read,* 1987.
No. 2. *Freedom of Religion,* 1987.
No. 3. *Freedom of Expression,* 1988.
No. 4. *Academic Freedom,* 1989.
No. 5. *The Freedom to Publish,* 1989.

de Grazia, Edward, ed. *Censorship Landmarks.* New York; R. R. Bowker, 1969.

Hall, Kermit L., ed. *The Oxford Companion to the Supreme Court.* New York: Oxford University Press, 1993. Invaluable.

Schwartz, Bernard. *A History of the Supreme Court.* New York; Oxford University Press, 1993. A valuable and relatively brief history.

Summaries of Censorship Incidents

Wachsberger, Ken, general editor of *Banned Books,* four volumes, each with its own editor, all from New York: Facts on File, 1998, Each volume summarizes the attempted censorship of an incredible number of books and why those books came under attack.

Nicholas J. Karolides, *Literature Suppressed on Political Grounds.*
Dawn B. Sova, *Literature Suppressed on Social Grounds.*
Dawn B. Sova, *Literature Suppressed on Sexual Grounds.*
Margaret Bald, *Literature Suppressed on Religious Grounds.*

Nicholas J. Karolides, Margaret Bald, and Dawn B. Sova's *100 Banned Books: Censorship Histories of World Literature.* New York: Checkmark Books, 1999. Summarizes the contents of the four volumes above and is highly recommended. Helpful and often frightening.

Books

Ahrens, Nyla H. "Censorship and the Teaching of English: A Questionnaire Survey of a Selected Sample of Secondary Teachers of English." Dissertation, Teachers College, Columbia University. 1965. The first national survey of school censorship and what it does to kids and teachers and schools.

Ayers, Stephen Michael. *The Selection Process of the National Endowment for the Arts Theatre Program.* New York: Peter Lang, 1992.

Beahm, George, ed. *War of Words: The Censorship Debate.* New York: Andrews and McMeel, 1993.

Beale, Howard K. *Are Americans Teachers Free? An Analysis of Restraints upon the Freedom of Teaching in American Schools.* New York: Scribner, 1936.

Beale, Howard K. *A History of the Freedom of Teaching in American Schools.* New York: Scribner, 1941.

Black, Gregory D. *The Catholic Crusade Against the Movies, 1940–1975.* New York: Cambridge University Press, 1998.

Bolton, Richard. *Culture Wars.* New York: New Press, 1992. On the National Endowment for the Arts and its problems, then and now and tomorrow.

Boyer, Paul S. *Purity in Print: Book Censorship in America from the Gilded Age to the Computer Age,* 2nd ed. Madison: University of Wisconsin Press, 2002. The best account of the censorial plague in America by a great historian.

Brinkley, Ellen H. *Caught off Guard: Teachers Rethinking Censorship and Controversies.* Boston: Allyn and Bacon, 1999.

Broun, Heywood and Margaret Leech. *Anthony Comstock: Roundsman of the Lord.* New York: Boni, 1927.

Brown, Jean, ed. *Preserving Intellectual Freedom: Fighting Censorship in Our Schools.* Urbana, IL: National Council of Teachers of English, 1994. A rich collection.

Bryson, Joseph and Elizabeth W. Detty. *The Legal Aspects of Censorship of Public School Library and Instructional Materials.* Charlottesville, VA: Michie, 1982.

Burress, Lee. *Battle of the Books: Literary Censorship in the Public School, 1950–1985.* Metuchen, NJ: Scarecrow Press, 1989.

Burt, Richard. *The Administration of Aesthetics: Censorship, Political Criticism, and the Public Sphere.* Minneapolis: University of Minnesota Press, 1994.

Busha, Charles H. *Freedom Versus Suppression and Censorship: With a Study of the Attitudes of Midwestern Public Librarians.* Littleton, CO: Libraries Unlimited, 1972.

Campbell, Patricia. J. *Sex Education Books for Young Adults, 1892–1979.* New York: R. R. Bowker, 1979.

Carmilly-Weinberger, Moshe. *Fear of Art: Censorship and Freedom of Expression in Art.* New York: R. R. Bowker, 1986.

Carrier, Esther. *Fiction in Public Libraries, 1876–1900.* New York: Scarecrow Press, 1965.

Carrier, Esther. *Fiction in Public Libraries, 1900–1950.* New York: Scarecrow Press, 1985. Excellent surveys of librarians as censors.

Censorship Litigation and the Schools. Chicago: American Library Association, 1983.

Cleaton, Irene and Allen Cleaton. *Books and Battles, American Literature, 1920–1930.* Boston: Houghton Mifflin, 1937.

Cline, Victor B., ed. *Where Do You Draw the Line?* Provo, UT: Brigham Young University Press, 1974. Conservative points of view on censorship.

Clor, Harry M. *Obscenity and Public Morality: Censorship in a Liberal Society.* Chicago: University of Chicago Press, 1969.

Collier, Jeremy. *A Short View of the Immorality and Profaneness of the English Stage.* 1698. One of the earliest attacks on drama advancing all the usual arguments.

Comstock, Anthony. *Frauds Exposed, or How the People Are Deceived and Robbed, and Youth Corrupted. Being a Full Exposure of Various Schemes Operated Through the Mails and Unearthed by the Author in a Seven Years' Service as a Special Agent of the Post Office Department and Secretary and Chief Agent of the New York Society for the Suppression of Vice.* New York: J. Howard Brown, 1880.

Comstock, Anthony. *Morals, Not Art of Literature v. Laws and Briefs.* New York: Society for the Suppression of Vice, 1914.

Comstock, Anthony. *Morals Versus Art.* New York; Ogilvie, 1888.

Comstock, Anthony. *Obscene Publications and Immoral Articles of Mail.* New York: Ogilvie, 1888.

Comstock, Anthony. *Traps for the Young.* New York: Funk and Wagnalls, 1883; reprinted by Harvard University Press, 1967 and edited and introduced by Robert Bremner. Comstock's basic argument against all sorts of evils—light literature, classic literature, the theatre, gambling, and on and on.

Connolly, L. W. *The Censorship of English Drama, 1737–1824.* San Marino, CA: Huntington Library, 1976. The 1737 Licensing Act, which drove Henry Fielding off the stage and into writing novels.

Craig, Alec. *Suppressed Books: A History of the Conception of Literary Obscenity.* Cleveland: World Book, 1963.

Curry, Ann. *The Limits of Tolerance: Censorship and Intellectual Freedom in Public Libraries.* Lanham, MD: Scarecrow Press, 1997.

Davis, James E., ed. *Dealing with Censorship.* Urbana, IL: National Council of Teachers of English, 1979. More or less liberal articles on censorship.

DelFattore, Joan. *What Johnny Shouldn't Read: Textbook Censorship in America.* New Haven: Yale University Press, 1992. Court cases involving textbooks and schools. Basic to any study of school censorship and wonderfully readable.

De Grazia, Edward. *Girls Lean Backward Everywhere: The Law of Obscenity and the Assault on Genius.* New York: Random House, 1992. On movie censorship.

De Grazia, Edward and Roger K. Newman. *Banned Films: Movies, Censors, and the First Amendment.* New York: R. R. Bowker, 1982.

Donnerstein, Edward, Daniel Linz, and Steven Penrod. *The Question of Pornography: Research Findings and Policy Implications.* New York: Free Press, 1987. Sometimes tough going but rewarding on a topic frequently misunderstood and often misused.

Downs, Robert B. *The First Freedom.* Chicago: American Library Association, 1960.

Edwards, June. *Opposing Censorship in the Public Schools: Religion, Morality, and Literature.* Mahwah, NJ: Erlbaum, 1998.

Ehrlich, J. W., ed. *Howl of the Censor.* San Francisco: Nourse, 1961. On the trial of Allen Ginsberg's poem, "Howl," in San Francisco in 1957.

Eldridge, Larry D. *A Distant Heritage: The Growth of Free Speech in Early America.* New York: New York University Press, 1993.

Ernst, Morris L. and Alan U. Schwartz. *Censorship: The Search for the Obscene.* New York: Macmillan, 1964.

Fiske, Marjorie. *Book Selection and Censorship: The Search for the Obscene.* Berkeley: University of California Press, 1968.

Foerstel, Herbert N. *Banned in the U.S.A.: A Reference Guide to Book Censorship in Schools and Public Libraries,* rev. ed. Westport, CT: Greenwood Press, 2002.

Foerstel, Herbert N. *Banned in the Media: A Reference Guide to Censorship in the Press, Motion Pictures, Broadcasting, and the Internet,* Westport, CT: Greenwood Press, 1998.

Fryer, Peter. *Mrs. Grundy: Studies in English Prudery.* New York: London House and Maxwell, 1964. Mrs. Grundy was a character referred to in the first scene of Thomas Morton's play, *Speed the Plow* (1798), who constantly judged the morality and actions of everyone else. She's become the prototype of a particularly disagreeable woman with a rigid moral code, i.e., a censor.

Gardiner, Harold C. *Catholic Viewpoint on Censorship,* rev. ed. New York: Image, 1961.

Gardner, Gerald. *The Censorship Papers: Movie Censorship Letters from the Hays Office, 1934–1968.* New York: Dodd, Mead, 1987.

Garrison, Dee, *Apostles of Culture: The Public Librarian and American Society.* New York: Free Press. 1961.

Garry, Patrick. *An Amerian Paradox: Censorship in a Nation of Free Speech.* Westport, CT: Praeger, 1993.

Geller, Evelyn. *Forbidden Books in American Public Libraries, 1876–1939: A Study in Cultural Change.* Westport, CT: Greenwood Press, 1984. See Louise Robbins for a continuation of the story.

Glasser, Ira. *Visions of Liberty: The Bill of Rights for All Americans.* Boston: Little, Brown, 1991.

Green, Jonathan. *Encyclopedia of Censorship.* New York: Facts on File, 1990.

Haight, Anne Lyons. *Banned Books,* 4th ed. New York: R. R. Bowker, 1978.

Haney, Robert W. *Comstockery in America: Patterns of Censorship and Control.* Boston: Beacon, 1960.

Heins, Marjorie. *Not in Front of the Children: "Indecency," Censorship, and the Innocence of Youth.* New York: Heel and Wang, 2001. First-rate work, about censorship and how it affects the lives of young people.

Heins, Marjorie. *Sex, Sin, and Blasphemy: A Guide to America's Censorship Wars.* New York: New Press, 1993.

Hefley, James C. *Textbooks on Trial.* Wheaton, IL: Victor Books, 1976. A defense of Mel and Norma Gabler's work.

Hentoff, Nat. *The First Freedom: The Tumultuous History of Free Speech in America.* New York: Delacorte, 1980.

Hentoff, Nat. *Free Speech for Me—But Not for Thee: How the American Left and Right Relentlessly Censor Each Other.* New York: HarperCollins, 1992.

Hentoff, Nat. *Living the Bill of Rights: How to Be an Authentic American.* New York: HarperCollins, 1999.

Hofstader, Richard. *Anti-Intellectualism in American Life.* New York: Knopf, 1963. One of the basic books in American studies. A standard, deservedly so.

Homstad, Wayne. *Anatomy of a Book Controversy.* Bloomington, IN: Phi Delta Kappa Educational Foundation, 1995.

Hull, Mary E. *Censorship in America: A Reference Handbook.* Santa Barbara, CA: Oxford, ABC-CLIO, 1999.

Hutchinson, E. R. *Tropic of Cancer on Trial.* New York: Grove, 1968.

Jenkinson, Edward B. *Censors in the Classroom: The Mind Benders.* Carbondale, IL: Southern Illinois University Press, 1979.

Jenkinson, Edward B. *The Schoolbook Protest Movement: 40 Questions and Answers.* Indianapolis: Phi Delta Kappa Educational Foundation, 1986.

Jones, Barbara M. *Libraries, Access, and Intellectual Freedom: Developing Policies for Public and Academic Libraries.* Chicago: American Library Association, 1999.

Karolides, Nicholas, ed. *Censored Books II: Critical Viewpoints, 1985–2000.* Lanham, MD: Scarecrow Press, 2002. Rationales for books under attack, 1985–2000.

Karolides, Nicholas; Lee Burress; and John Kean, eds. *Censored Books: Critical Viewpoints.* Metuchen, NJ: Scarecrow Press, 1993. Rationales for books under attack between 1950 and 1985.

Kendrick, Walter. *The Secret Museum: Pornography in Modern Culture.* New York: Viking, 1987.

Kronhausen, Eberhard and Phyllis Kronhausen. *Pornography and the Law: The Psychology of Erotic Realism and Hard Core Pornography,* rev. ed. New York: Ballantine, 1964.

Kuh, Richard. H. *Foolish Figleaves? Pornography in and out of Court.* New York: Macmillan, 1967.

Lawrence, D. H. *Sex, Literature, and Censorship.* New York: Twayne, 1953.

Lehr, Susan, ed. *Battling Dragons: Issues and Controversy in Children's Literature.* Portsmouth, NH: Heinemann, 1995.

Levine, Judith. *Harmful to Minors: The Perils of Protecting Children from Sex.* Minneapolis: University of Minnesota Press, 2002.

Levy, Leonard W. *Blasphemy: Verbal Offense Against the Sacred—from Moses to Salmon Rushdie.* New York: Knopf, 1993.

Lewis, Felice Flanery. *Literature, Obscenity and Law.* Carbondale, IL: Southern Illinois University Press, 1976. The best book on legal battles involving obscenity.

Lyons, Charles. *The New Censors and the Culture Wars.* Philadelphia: Temple University Press, 1997.

Martin, Olga J. *Hollywood's Movie Commandments: A Handbook for Motion Picture And Reviewers.* New York: Wilson, 1937.

McCormick, John and Mairi McCormick, eds. *Versions of Censorship.* Garden City: New York: Doubleday Anchor, 1962. Fine collection of classic documents.

McCoy, Ralph E. *Banned in Boston: The Development of Literary Censorship in Massachusetts.* Urbana: University of Illinois Press, 1956.

McDonald, Frances Beck. *Censorship and Intellectual Freedom: A Survey of School Librarians' Attitudes and Moral Reasoning.* Metuchen, NJ: Scarecrow Press, 1993.

Mill, John Stuart. "On Liberty" (1859) from *Selected Writings of John Stuart Mill.* New York: New American Library, 1968.

Milton, John. *Areopagitica* (1644). The place to begin any study of censorship.

Moffett, James. *Storm in the Mountains: A Case Study of Censorship: Conflict and Consciousness.* Carbondale, IL: Southern Illinois University Press, 1988. The aftermath of the Kanawha County, WV, textbook bannings in the mid-seventies. For a brief overview of the squabble, see "A Brief Chronology of the West Virginia Textbook Crisis" in the February 1975 *Arizona English Bulletin.*

Nelson, Jack and Gene Roberts, Jr. *The Censors and the Schools.* Boston: Little, Brown, 1963.

Nilsen, Alleen Pace, ed. *Censorship in Children's Literature,* special issue of *Para*Doxa: Studies in World Genres* 2 (Fall 1996).

Noble, William. *Bookbanning in America. Who Bans Books—and Why?* Middlebury, VT: Paul S. Erikson, 1990.

Norwick, Kenneth P. *Lobbying for Freedom: Censorship.* New York: St. Martins, 1975.

Oboler, Eli, ed. *Censorship and Education.* New York: H. W. Wilson, 1981.

Oboler, Eli. *The Fear of the Word: Censorship and Sex.* Metuchen, NJ: Scarecrow Press, 1974.

Ochoa, Anna S., ed. *Academic Freedom to Teach and to Learn: Every Teacher's Issue.* Washington, DC: National Education Association, 1990.

O'Neill, Robert M. *Classrooms in the Crossfire: The Rights and Interests of Students, Parents, Teachers, Administrators, Librarians, and the Community.* Bloomington: Indiana University Press, 1981.

Paul, James C. N. and Murray L. Schwartz. *Federal Censorship: Obscenity in the Mail.* New York: Free Press, 1961.

Perrin, Noel. *Dr. Bowdler's Legacy: A History of Expurgated Books in England and America.* New York: Atheneum, 1969. Dr. Thomas Bowdler (1754–1825), an Edinburgh M.D., published his 10-volume *Family Shakespeare* in 1818, "in which nothing is added to the original text; but those words and expressions are omitted which cannot with propriety be read aloud in a family." His major gift to English was the word *bowdlerize,* i.e., to expurgate in a prudish manner.

Pipkin, Gloria and ReLeah Cosssett Lent. *At the Schoolhouse Gate: Lessons in Intellectual Freedom.* Portsmouth, NH: Heinemann, 2002.

Pivar, David J. *Purity Crusades, Sexual Morality and Social Control, 1868–1900.* Westport, CT: Greenwood Press, 1973.

Plato. *The Republic,* especially Book 2. 5th century B.C.

Pope, Michael. *Sex and the Undecided Librarian: A Study of Librarians' Opinions on Sexually Oriented Literature.* Metuchen, NJ: Scarecrow Press, 1974.

Rabban, David M. *Free Speech in Its Forgotten Years.* New York: Cambridge University Press, 1997. Free speech between the Civil War and WWII.

Rauch, Jonathan. *Kindly Inquisitors: The New Attacks on Free Speech.* Chicago: University Press, 1993.

Rehnquist, William H. *The Supreme Court: How It Was, How It Is.* New York: Morrow, 1987.

Reichman, Henry. *Censorship and Selection: Issues and Answers for Schools,* rev. ed., Chicago: American Library Association, 1993.

Rembar, Charles. *The End of Obscenity: The Trials of Lady Chatterley, Tropic of Cancer, and Fanny Hill.* New York: Random House, 1968. Proof that lawyers can write.

Riley, Gail Blasser. *Censorship.* New York: Facts on File, 1998.

Robbins, Jan C. *Student Press and the Hazelwood Decision.* Indianapolis: Phi Delta Kappa Educational Foundation, 1988.

Robbins, Louise S. *Censorship and the American Library: The American Library Association's Response to Threats to Intellectual Freedom, 1939–1968.* Westport, CT: Greenwood Press, 1996. A follow-up to Evelyn Geller's work.

Robbins, Louise S. *The Dismissal of Miss Ruth Brown: Civil Rights, Censorship, and the American Librarian.* Norman, OK: University of Oklahoma Press, 2000. Ruth Brown was head public librarian at Barletsville, OK, when she was attacked for circulating allegedly communist publications and lost her job in 1950.

Robbins, Natalie. *Alien Ink: The FBI's War on Freedom of Expression.* New York: Morrow, 1992.

Scales, Pat. *Teaching Banned Books: 12 Guides for Young Readers.* Chicago: American Library Association, 2001. Specific and helpful materials for teaching Cole's *The Goats,* Lowry's *The Giver,* and ten more books. A delight to read.

Schumach, Murray. *The Face on the Cutting Room Floor: The Story of Movie and Television Censorship.* New York: Morrow, 1964.

Selth, Jefferson P. *Ambition, Discrimination, and Censorship in Libraries.* Jefferson, NC: McFarland, 1993.

Simmons, John.S., ed. *Censorship: A Threat to Reading, Learning, Thinking.* Newark, DE: International Reading Association, 1994.

Simmons, John S. and Eliza T. Desang. *School Censorship in the Twenty-First Century: A Guide for Teachers and School Library Media Specialists.* Newark, DE: International Reading Association, 2001.

Skinner, James M. *The Cross and the Cinema: The Legion of Decency and the National Catholic Office for Motion Pictures, 1933–1970.* Westport, CT: Praeger, 1993.

Smolla, Rodney A. *Free Speech in an Open Society.* New York: Knopf, 1992.

Steinle, Pamela Hunt. *In Cold Fear: The Catcher in the Rye: Censorship Controversies and Postwar American Character.* Columbus: Ohio State University Press, 2000. The most censored book in America, what happened, why it happened, and what it all led to.

Strossen, Nadine. *Defending Pornography: Free Speech, Sex, and the Fight for Women's Rights.* New York: Scribner, 1995.

Symons, Ann K. and Charles Harmon. *Protecting the Right to Read: A How-to-Do-It Manual for School and Public Libraries.* New York: Neal-Schuman, 1995.

Taylor, John Tinnon. *Early Opposition to the English Novel: The Popular Reaction from 1760 to 1830.* New York: King's Crown Press, 1943.

Theiner, George, ed. *They Shoot Writers, Don't They?* London: Faber and Faber, 1984.

Theoharis, Athan G. *A Culture of Secrecy: The Government Versus the People's Right to Know.* Lawrence, KS: University of Kansas Press, 1998.

Thomas, Donald A. *A Long Time Burning: The History of Literary Censorship in England.* New York: Praeger, 1969. The standard work in the field. The appendices are a marvel in their own way.

Thompson, Anthony Hugh. *Censorship in Public Libraries in the United Kingdom during the Twentieth Century.* New York: R. R. Bowker, 1975.

Wallace, Jonathan and Mark Mangan. *Sex, Laws, and Cyberspace: Freedom and Censorship on the Frontiers of the Online.* New York: Holt, 1996.

Walsh, Frank. *Sin and Censorship: The Catholic Church and the Motion Picture Industry.* New Haven: Yale University Press, 1996.

West, Mark. *Children, Culture, and Controversy.* Hamden, CT: Archon, 1988.

West, Mark. *Trust Your Children: Voices against Censorship in Children's Literature.* New York: Neal-Schuman, 1988. YA authors speak on censorship.

Westin, Alan E. *The Miracle Case: The Supreme Court and the Movies.* University, AL: University of Alabama Press, 1961.

Wiegand, Wayne A., ed. "The Library Bill of Rights," entire Summer 1996 issue of *Library Trends.*

Zeigler, Joseph Wesley. *Arts in Crisis: The National Endowment for the Arts Versus America.* New York: A Cappella Books, 1994.

Zeisler, William, ed. *Censorship: 500 Years of Conflict.* New York: Oxford University Press, 1984.

Selected Articles about Censorship

"A Brief Chronology of the West Virginia Textbook Crisis." *Arizona English Bulletin* 17 (February 1975): 203–212.

Agee, Jane. "There It Was, That One Sex Scene: English Teachers on Censorship." *English Journal* 89 (November 1999): 61–69.

"Are Libraries Fair: Pre-Selection Censorship in a Time of Resurgent Conservatism." *Newsletter on Intellectual Freedom* 31 (September 1982): 151, 181–188, Comments by syndicated columnist Cal Thomas and *Village Voice* columnist Nat Hentoff. Thirty years old and still much worth reading.

Asheim, Lester. "Not Censorship, but Selection." *Wilson Library Bulletin* 28 (September 1953): 63–67. The most widely cited article on the distinction between these two terms.

Baker, Mary Gordon. "A Teacher's Right to Know Versus a Student's Right to Privacy." *Journal of Law and Education* 16 (Winter 1987): 71–91.

Bernays, Anne. "I Don't Want to Read a Novel Passed by a Board of Good Taste," *Chronicle of Higher Education* 37 (March 6, 1991): B–1, 3.

Booth, Wayne. "Censorship and the Values of Fiction." *English Journal* 53 (March 1964): 155–164. Almost forty years old and still the best article in the field.

Bradley, Julia Turnquist. "Censoring the School Library: Do Students Have a Right to Read?" *Connecticut Law Review* 10 (Spring 1978): 746–775.

Broderick, Dorothy. "Serendipity at Work." *Show-Me Libraries* 35 (February 1984): 13–14.

Broz, William. "Hope and Irony: *Annie on My Mind.*" *English Journal* 90 (July 2001): 47–53.

Burger, Robert H. "The Kanawha County Textbook Controversies: A Study of Communication and Power." *Library Quarterly* 48 (April 1982): 584–589.

Burress, Lee A. "How Censorship Affects the School." *Wisconsin Council of Teachers of English, Special Bulletin 8* (October 1963): 1–23.

Clark, Todd, ed. "The Question of Academic Freedom." *Social Education* 39 (April 1975): 202–252.

Click, J. William and Lillian Lodge Kopenhaver. "Few Changes Since *Hazelwood.*" *School Press Review* 65 (Winter 1990): 12–27.

Delp, Vaughn N. "The Far Right and Me: It's Not So Far Away and It's Not So Right." *Arizona English Bulletin* 37 (Fall 1994): 71–76,

Donelson, Kenneth L. "Shoddy and Pernicious Books and Youthful Piety: Literary and Moral Censorship, Then and Now." *Library Quarterly* 51 (January 1981): 4–19.

Farrell, Edmund. "Literature in Crisis." *English Journal* 70 (January 1981): 13–18.

Feiwell, Jean. "Killing Books Softly: Reviewers as Censors." *School Library Journal* 36 (September 1990): 155–162,

Fizgerald, Frances. "A Disagreement in Baileyville." *New Yorker* 59 (January 16, 1984): 47–90.

Garden, Nancy. "*Annie* on Trial: How It Feels to Be the Author of a Challenged Book." *Voice of Youth Advocates* 19 (June 1996): 79–82, 84.

Geller, Evelyn. "Intellectual Freedom: Eternal Principle or Unanticipated Consequence?" *Library Journal* 99 (May 15, 1974): 1364–1367.

Glatthorn, Allan A. "Censorship and the Classroom Teacher." *English Journal* 66 (February 1977): 12–15.

Greenlee, Edwin D. "Recommended Adolescent Literature: Avoiding Those Hidden 'Secrets.'" *English Journal* 81 (April 1992): 23–24. See also the responses to this article in the same issue, pp. 25–30 and Terry Davis' "The Author of *Vision Quest* Responds to 'Hidden Secrets,'" *English Journal* 81 (September 1992): 87–89.

Groves, Cy. "Book Censorship: Six Misunderstandings." *Alberta English '71* 11 (Fall 1971): 5–7. Reprinted in *Arizona English Bulletin* 37 (Fall 1994): 19–20.

Heins, Marjorie. "Not in Front of the Children: Indecency, Censorship, and the Innocence of Youth." *Newsletter on Intellectual Freedom* 57 (September 2002): 187, 224-228.

Hentoff, Nat. "Any Writer Who Follows Anyone Else's Guidelines Ought to Be in Advertising." *School Library Journal* 24 (November 1977): 27–29.

Hentoff, Nat. "When Nice People Burn Books." *Progressive* 47 (February 1983): 42-44.

Hillocks, George, Jr. "Books and Bombs: Ideological Conflicts and the School—A Case

Study of the Kanawha County Book Protests." *School Review* 86 (August 1978): 632–654.

Janeczko, Paul. "How Students Can Help Educate the Censors." *Arizona English Bulletin* 17 (February 1975): 78–80.

Kingsbury, Louise and Lance Gurwell "The Sin Fighters: Grappling with Gomorah at the Grass Roots." *Utah Holiday* 12 (April 1983): 42–61, About censors and what they believe "secular humanism" is.

Koertge, Ron. "Sex and the Single Kid." *Los Angeles Times Book Review*, March 21, 1993, pp. 1, 11.

Krug, Judith. "Intellectual Freedom: A History of the Library Bill of Rights." *American Libraries* 3 (January 1972): 80–83 and 3 (February 1973): 183–184.

Lacks, Cissy. "The Teacher's Nightmare: Getting Fired for Good Teaching." *English Journal* 86 (February 1997): 29–33.

Lent, ReLeah and Gloria Pipkin. "We Keep Pedaling." *ALAN Review* 28 (Winter 2001): 9–11.

Leo, John. "Heck Hath No Fury." *U.S. News and World Report*, June 17, 2002, p. 53. Sensitivity guidelines for selecting school materials become censorship.

Martin, William. "The Guardians Who Slumbereth Not." *Texas Monthly* 10 (November 1982): 145–150. On Mel and Norma Gabler.

Martinson, David L. "*Hazelwood:* The End of the 'Hidden Curriculum' Charade." *Clearing House* 75 (February/March 1992): 131–136.

Mazer, Norma Fox. "Silent Censorship." *School Library Journal* 42 (August 1966): 42.

McGraw, William Corbin. "Pollyanna Rides Again." *Saturday Review* 41 (March 22, 1958): 37–38. A classic—and funny as well.

Meyer, Randy. "Annie's Day in Court: The Decision from the Bench." *School Library Journal* 42 (April 1996): 22–25. A report of the court case involving Nancy Garden's *Annie on My Mind* and Kansas District Judge G. T. Van Bebber's decision that the administrators of Olathe, KS, High School had "unconstitutionally removed the novel from the school library."

Moffett, James. "Hidden Impediments in Improving English Teaching." *Phi Delta Kappan* 67 (September 1985): 50–56.

O'Brien, Mrs. Dermod. "The Pernicious Habit of Reading." *Parent's Review* (England) 38 (March 1927): 151–157. It's no exaggeration to say that the author fears all consequences of reading, particularly if young people enjoy reading.

Peck, Richard. "The Genteel Unshelving of a Book." *School Library Journal* 32 (May 1986): 37–39.

Pipkin, Gloria. "Challenging the Conventional Wisdom on Censorship." *ALAN Review* 20 (Winter 1993): 35–37.

"Rationales for Commonly Challenged Taught Books." *Connecticut English Journal* 15 (Fall, 1983): entire issue.

Russo, Elaine M. "Prior Restraint and the High School 'Free Press': The Implications of *Hazelwood v. Kuhlmeir.*" *Journal of Law and Education* 18 (Winter 1989): 1–21.

Severy, Bruce. "Scenario of a Book Burning." *Arizona English Bulletin* 17 (February 1975): 68–74. The 1973 burning of Vonnegut's *Slaughterhouse-Five.*

Shafer, Robert E. "Censorship in Tucson's Flowing Wells School District Makes for a Nationally Publicized Non-Event." *Arizona English Bulletin* 37 (Fall 1994): 51–57.

Simmons, John. "What Teachers Under Fire Need from Their Principals." *ALAN Review* 20 (Winter 1993): 22–25.

Small, Robert C. (Jr.). "Censorship as We Enter 2000, or the Millennium, or Just Next Year." *Journal of Youth Services Libraries* 13 (Winter 2000): 19–23.

Stielow, Frederick J. "Censorship in the Early Professionalization of American Libraries, 1876 to 1929." *Journal of Library History* 18 (Winter 1983): 37–54.

Strike, Kenneth A. "A Field Guide of Censors: Toward a Concept of Censorship in Public Schools." *Teachers College Record* 87 (Winter 1985): 239–258.

Sutton, Roger. "What Mean We, White Man?" *Voice of Youth Advocates* 15 (August 1992): 155–158.

Tyack, David B. and Thomas James. " Moral Majorities and the School Curriculum: Historical Perspectives and the Legalization of Virtue." *Teachers College Record* 86 (Summer 1985): 513–537.

Vonnegut, Kurt. "Why Are You Banning My Book?" *American School Board Journal* 168 (October 1981): 35.

Watson, Jerry and Bill C. Snider. "Educating the Potential Self-Censor." *School Media Quarterly* 9 (Summer 1981): 272–276,

Weiss, M. Jerry. "Rumbles! Bangs! Crashes! The Roar of Censorship." *ALAN Review* 29 (Spring/Summer 2002): 54–57.

West, Celeste. "The Secret Garden of Censorship: Ourselves." *Library Journal* 108 (September 1983): 1651–1653.

Whaley, Elizabeth Gates. "What Happens When You Put the Manchild in the Promised Land? An Experiment with Censorship." *English Journal* 63 (May 1974): 61–65.

Zeeman, Kenneth L. "Grappling with Grendel or What We Did When the Censors Came." *English Journal* 86 (February 1997): 46–49.

Glossary of Literary Terms
Illustrated by YA Literature

Allegory: An extended metaphor or comparison in which characters, events, or objects are equated with meaning outside of the story. Allegorical stories can be enjoyed on a surface level as well as on a second or deeper level. For example, William Golding's *Lord of the Flies* is on the surface an adventure story, while on the allegorical level it is a warning against lawlessness and how easy it is for people to be corrupted by power.

Allusion: A figure of speech that refers to something likely to be familiar to readers because of their knowledge of history, literature, or popular culture. Allusions are efficient communication because good readers can turn a single reference into an extended idea. For example, Robert Cormier's title *I Am the Cheese* might remind a reader of the old nursery song and game "The Farmer in the Dell." This alludes to the family's newly given surname of *Farmer* and to the closing lines of the song: "The cheese stands alone" and "The rat takes the cheese."

Antagonist: The character (or sometimes event) that opposes the protagonist.

Archetypes: Images, patterns, or symbols that are part of the collective unconscious. Archetypal images are stronger and more durable than stereotypes. The Innocent setting out on a journey is an archetype especially common in YA literature, and so are generational conflicts in which young people struggle to gain their independence from adults.

Backdrop setting: A context of time and place that is like a stage setting in that it does not play an essential or unique part in the plot. The most common backdrop setting is that of a high school because school is the everyday business of teenagers. The fact that there are only so many ways to describe stairways, restrooms, lockers, cafeterias, classrooms, and parking lots gives a sameness to books for this age group.

Characterization: Whatever an author does to help readers know and identify with the characters in a story. Common techniques include providing physical descriptions, letting readers know what the characters say and what others say to and about them, showing the characters in action, showing how others relate to them, and revealing what they are thinking. See also **dynamic** and **static characters.**

Deconstruction: The idea that literature is constructed from words, which only approximately represent thoughts or actions. Once we realize this about a piece of literature, then we are able to undo the construct, that is, to examine and pull out different possible meanings. Deconstructing a piece of literature is taking it apart in different ways. Writers can also deconstruct events before they put them in their novels; for example, Virginia Euwer Wolff's *Bat 6* and Karen Hesse's *Witness* are told and retold by various characters who each have a unique point of view.

Dénouement: Literally, the untying of the knots at the end of a story. The purpose of the denouement is to let the reader down after the excitement of the climax. Orson Scott Card softens the ending of *The Lost Boys: A Novel* by alluding to an afterlife when he writes that on the Christmas Eve when Stevie was abducted and murdered, they lost one other thing: their nicknames. No one made a conscious decision, it was just that they were part of a set, and it didn't seem right to use only some of them. "But someday they would use all those names when *Doorman* [Stevie] met them on the other side."

Dialect: Using characters' individual speech patterns to set them apart from mainstream speakers. A dialect might be illustrated through wording as when Hal Borland wrote in *When the Legends Die,* "The Ute people have lived many generations, many grandmothers, in that land," or it might be through "different" grammar and pronunciation as when such African American writers as Ntozake Shange, Maya Angelou, Virginia Hamilton, Toni Morrison, and Walter Dean Myers use black dialect for a variety of purposes, including the communication of pride in ethnic heritage. For the most part, difficulties in spelling and reading make authors rely sparingly on dialect.

Didacticism: Preachiness, as when an obvious moral or a lesson is tacked onto a story. Actually, most people who write for young readers want to teach lessons or impart some kind of wisdom or understanding. When something is described as didactic, it is being criticized for having a lesson so obvious that it detracts from the story.

Dynamic character: One who undergoes some change during the story. A dynamic character usually plays a major role in a story because an author needs considerable space in which to show how the character changes.

Escape literature: That which requires a minimum of intellectual energy so that readers can relax and enjoy the story with little or no intention of gaining insights or learning new information.

Euphemism: The use of circumlocution or an indirect kind of speech, usually to avoid giving offense. The word is cognate with *euphonious* meaning "pleasing to the ear." Modern writers usually prefer direct speech, but Margaret Craven's title *I Heard the Owl Call My Name* is more intriguing than a bald statement such as "I knew I was going to die," while Hemingway's title *For Whom the Bell Tolls* is both more euphemistic and euphonious than "the one who has died."

Figurative language: Intentional use of language in such a way that additional meanings are given to what would be expected in standard usage. Metaphors, symbolism, and allusions are figures of speech based on semantics or meaning. Other figurative speech is based on such phonological aspects as alliteration (the repetition of consonants), assonance (the repetition of vowels), rhyme (the repeating of sounds), and rhythm and cadence (the patterning of sounds).

Foreshadowing: The dropping of hints to prepare readers for what is ahead. The purpose is not to give away the ending but to increase excitement and suspense and to keep readers from feeling manipulated. For example, readers would feel cheated if the problems in a realistic novel are suddenly solved by a group of aliens when there had been no foreshadowing that the story was science fiction.

Formula literature: That which is almost entirely predictable because it consists of variations on a limited number of plots and themes. To some extent, this description fits most literature; the difference is a matter of degree. Many of the situation comedies, crime shows, and adventure shows on television are formula pieces, as are many of the mysteries, romances, and even horror stories that young people—and adults—enjoy reading.

In media res: Latin for "in the midst of things." This device of bringing the reader directly into the middle of a story is usually followed by flashbacks to fill in the missing details.

Integral setting: The time and place that an author has created so that it will play an important part in the story. In protagonist-against-nature stories, historical fiction pieces, and regional stories, the settings are often integrated into the plots.

Intertextuality: A term created by Julia Kristeva, who pointed out that writers build their new texts on all that they have absorbed and transformed from their life's reading. When readers compare the similarities among the styles or the topics of various writers, they are doing intertextual analysis. Sharon Creech did intertextual writing in *Love That Dog* when she had her young protagonist become so enchanted with the poetry written by Walter Dean Myers that he begins writing poetry himself.

Literature with a Capital L: That which has a degree of excellence not found in the mass of material that is printed every day. Such literature rewards study not only because of its content but also because of its style, universality, permanence, and the congeniality of the ideas expressed.

Magical realism: A kind of magic that happens without genies or good fairies to grant the protagonist's wishes. The magic is all the more startling because of the way it creeps up on the reader as part of what is being read as a realistic story. Francesca Lia Block is usually praised for the way she brings magical elements into her stories. However, some critics suggested it was too jarring when in *Missing Angel Juan,* Witch Baby found herself in a diner filled with the kind of humanoids usually reserved for science fiction.

Metaphor: Figurative language in which basically dissimilar things are likened to each other. A metaphor can consist of only a word or a phrase (a *head* of lettuce or the *outskirts* of a city), or it can be a series of interwoven ideas running through an entire book as when Walter Dean Myers in *Fallen Angels* compares the Vietnam war to various aspects of movies or television.

Mode: A broad term describing the way authors treat their material as comedy, romance, irony, satire, and tragedy. Together these modes make up the story of everyone's life, and in literature as in life, they are interrelated, flowing one into the other.

Narrative hook: A device that authors use to entice readers into a story; for example, a catchy title as in Douglas Adams's *The Hitchhiker's Guide to the Galaxy,* a question as in Richard Peck's *Are You in the House Alone?,* or an intriguing first few sentences as in Paul Zindel's *The Pigman,* when John says, "Now Lorraine can blame all the other things on me, but she was the one who picked out the Pigman's phone number. If you ask me, I think he would have died anyway. Maybe we speeded things up a little, but you really can't say we murdered him . . . Not murdered him."

Open endings: Those that leave readers not knowing what happens to the characters. Alice Childress in *A Hero Ain't Nothin' But a Sandwich* did not want to predict either that Benjie would become a confirmed drug addict or that he would go straight because she wanted readers to think about the fact that boys in his situation turn both ways. Books with open endings are good for group discussions because they inspire involved readers to consider the options.

Personification: The giving of human characteristics to something that is not human. For example, Maya Angelou in *All God's Children Need Traveling Shoes* writes, "July and August of 1962 stretched out like fat men yawning after a sumptuous dinner. They had every right to gloat, for they had eaten me up. Gobbled me down. Consumed my spirit, not in a wild rush, but slowly, with the obscene patience of certain victors."

Plot: The skeleton on which the other aspects of a story hang. Plots are made from the challenges, conflicts, and problems faced by the main characters. The most exciting plots are the ones in which the action is continually rising, building suspense, and finally leading to some sort of a climax. Episodic plots are accounts of a series of events as with such memoirs as James Herriot's *All Creatures Great and Small* and Anita Lobel's *No Pretty Pictures.*

Point of view: The vantage point and the distance from which the author decides to tell the story. The point of view that gives the author the most freedom is the one called omniscient or "all knowing," in which authors can plant themselves anywhere in the story, including inside characters' minds. With first-person point of view, the author speaks through the voice of a particular character. While this has the advantage of sounding authentic and personal, only one character's thoughts and observations can be given. Some authors get around this limitation by writing different chapters through the voices of different characters. Third-person point of view is more objective and is used for nonfiction as well as for many fictional stories. In YA books, the third-person narrator is often a character in the story who is writing about another "more interesting" or "more extreme" character.

Protagonists: The main characters in stories, the ones with which readers identify. Novels for young readers usually include only one or two protagonists because the stories are shorter and less complex than something like Leo Tolstoy's *War and Peace.* Protagonist-against-another is the kind of plot in which two people are in conflict with each other as are Louise and Caroline in Katherine Paterson's *Jacob Have I Loved* and Rambo and the sheriff in David Morrell's *First Blood.* Protagonist-against-nature stories are often accounts of true adventures such as Piers Paul Read's *Alive: The Story of the Andes Survivors,* Thor Heyerdahl's *The "RA" Expeditions,* and Steve Callahan's *Adrift: Seventy-Six Days Lost at Sea.* Protagonist-against-self is a common plot in young adult literature because so many stories recount rites of passage in which the protagonist comes to a new understanding or level of maturity. In Paula Fox's *One-Eyed Cat,* the conflict takes place inside the mind and heart of 11-year-old Ned, who has to come to terms with the fact that when he tried out his new gun, he partially blinded his neighbor's cat. Protagonist-against-society stories often feature members of minority groups whose personal struggles relate to tensions between their ethnic groups and the larger society. Examples include Chaim Potok's *My Name Is Asher Lev* and *The Chosen,* Gary Soto's *Baseball in April* and *Jesse,* Louise Erdrich's *Love Medicine,* and Marie Lee's *Finding My Voice.*

Setting: The context of time and place. Setting is more important in some genres than in others. Fantasies are usually set in the far past or in some place where people have never been, while most science fiction stories are set in the future or in outer space. See also **Backdrop** and **Integral Settings.**

Static character: One whose personality and actions stay basically the same throughout the story. Because in young adult literature the focus is on the young protagonist, most adult characters (parents, teachers, friends, etc.) are portrayed as static.

Stereotype: Literally a printing process through which an image is created over and over again. When reviewers say that an author's characters are stereotypes, they are probably making a negative criticism. However, at least some characters must be stereotyped because stories would fall under their own weight if authors had to start from scratch in developing each character. For the sake of efficiency, many background characters are stereotypes. To solve the problem of always having the same people stereotyped, contemporary authors are making an effort to feature as main characters many of those who have previously been ignored or relegated to stereotypes.

Stock characters: Stereotyped characters that authors can use in the way that shoppers pluck items from the well-stocked shelves of grocery stores. While a laughingstock is an object of ridicule, other stock characters include villains, tramps, bad boys, and little princesses.

Style: The way a story is written in contrast to what it is about. No two authors have exactly the same style because with writing, just as with appearance, behavior, and personal belongings, style consists of the unique blending of all the choices each individual makes. From situation to situation, these choices may differ, but they are enough alike that the styles of particular authors, such as Kurt Vonnegut, Jr., Richard Brautigan, and E. L. Doctorow are recognizable from book to book. Style is also influenced by the nature of the story being told. For example, Ursula K. Le Guin used a different style when she wrote the realistic *Very Far Away From Anywhere Else* from the one she used when she wrote her fantasy *A Wizard of Earthsea.* Nevertheless, in both books she relied on the particular writing techniques that she likes and is skilled at using. J. D. Salinger's *The Catcher in the Rye* has had such an influence on the style of writing about young protagonists that every year promotional materials or reviews compare two or three new books to *Catcher.*

Symbol: An item that is itself but also stands for something else. An example is the title of Linda Sue Park's *A Single Shard,* in which the one piece of the master's pottery that Tree-Ear manages to deliver to the emperor symbolizes the great challenge that the boy faced on his journey.

Theme: A central idea that ties a story together and answers such questions as what the story means and what there is to think about when it is all over. Some authors are explicit in developing a theme, even expressing part of it in the title as did Maya Angelou with *All God's Children Need Traveling Shoes* and Virginia Euwer Wolff with *Make Lemonade.* Books may have more than one theme, but usually the secondary themes are less important to the story.

Tone: The author's attitude toward the subject and the readers. Biblical language may lend weight and dignity to a book as with James Herriot's title *All Creatures Great and Small* or Claude Brown's *Manchild in the Promised Land.* Exaggeration or hyperbole may communicate a flip tone as in Ellen Conford's title *If This Is Love, I'll Take Spaghetti* and Ron Koertge's *Where the Kissing Never Stops.*

Book Selection Guides

The following sources are designed to aid professionals in the selection and evaluation of books and other materials for young adults. We attempted to include sources with widely varying emphases, but, in addition to these sources—most of which appear at regular intervals—many specialized lists are prepared by committees and individuals in response to current and/or local needs. Readers are advised to check on the availability of such lists with librarians and teachers. Also, publications for adults such as *The New York Times Book Review* and the *Smithsonian Magazine* give attention to books for children and teenagers, especially in the weeks prior to Christmas when people are looking for gift ideas. More information can be found on these journals by typing the name into an Internet search engine.

The ALAN Review (Assembly on Literature for Adolescents). National Council of Teachers of English. Order from NCTE, 1111 W. Kenyon Road, Urbana, IL 61801. Subscribers need not be members of NCTE.

> Since 1973, this publication, which is devoted entirely to adolescent literature, has appeared three times a year. Current editors are James Blasingame, Jr., from Arizona State University, and Lori Atkins Goodson, from Manhattan, Kansas. Each issue contains approximately fifty "Clip and File" reviews written by ALAN members who are mostly secondary school teachers or librarians. Also included are feature articles, news announcements, and occasional reviews of professional books.

Booklist. American Library Association, 50 E. Huron St., Chicago, IL 60611. Website: www.ala.org

> Reviews, which constitute a recommendation for library purchase, are written by professional staff members, who also attach a *YA* designation to selected adult titles. Hazel Rochman is the current YA editor, while Michael Cart writes a "Carte Blanche" column. The "Books for Youth" section is divided for older, middle, and young readers. Exceptional books are given starred reviews and sometimes special features. For example, the starred review of Sonya Sones's *Stop Pretending: What Happened When My Big Sister Went Crazy* (HarperCollins, 1999) was accompanied by a "Read-alikes" box on "Mental Illness and the Sibling Connection" that gave annotations for seven other recommended books. An end-of-the-year "Editors' Choice" issue is especially useful as are the lists of "Best Books" compiled by various committees affiliated with the American Library Association. Check the website for several lists related to young adults.

Books for the Teen Age. Published annually by Office of Young Adult Services, New York Public Library. Order from Office of Branch Libraries: New York Public Library, 455 Fifth Avenue, New York, NY 10016.

> The over 1,000 recommendations in this booklet come from the young adult librarians in the eighty branches of the New York Public Library. Annotations are minimal, grouping is by subject with titles and authors indexed. Young adults are invited to enter an art contest for each year's cover.

Books for You: An Annotated Booklist for Senior High, Your Reading: An Annotated Booklist for Middle School Junior High, and *High Interest—Easy Reading: An Annotated Booklist for Middle School and Senior High School.* National Council of Teachers of English, 1111 Kenyon Road, Urbana, IL 61801.

> Committees of English teachers put these books together every few years. They are written for direct use by students and contain concise annotations for between 200 and 1,000 recommended books organized under such categories as "Growing Up," "Issues of Our Time," and "Sports."

Bulletin of the Center for Children's Books. University of Illinois Press, 1324 S. Oak Street, Champaign, IL 61820. Website: http://edfu.lis.uiuc.edu/puboff/bccb

> This is the journal founded by Zena Sutherland and published by the University of Chicago Press. When Chicago's Graduate Library School closed, the *Bulletin* moved to the University of Illinois. In each issue, staff members review approximately 60 new books, with approximately 20 being identified as appropriate for grades 9–12. Reviews are coded with *R* standing for "recommended," *Ad* for "additional title if topic is needed," *M* for "marginal," and *NR* for "not recommended." The website reprints starred reviews and each month features a theme-based list of a dozen recommended titles.

Children's Literature in Education: An International Quarterly. Kluwer Academic/Human Sciences Press, 233 Spring St., New York, NY 10013-1578.

> In this British/American cooperative effort, the editors show a preference for substantive analysis rather than pedagogical advice or quick once-overs. A good proportion of the articles are about YA authors and their works. The table of contents is printed online and access is given to selected articles.

English Journal. National Council of Teachers of English, 1111 Kenyon Rd., Urbana, Illinois 61801. Editorial correspondence to Louann Reid, English Department, Colorado State University, 1773 Campus Delivery, Fort Collins, CO 80523-1773.

> This is the largest journal published by NCTE with its audience being mainly high school English teachers. It appears six times a year and frequently has articles about young adult literature. Don Gallo edits a regular column on YA literature.

Horn Book Magazine. Horn Book, Inc., 11 Beacon St., Suite 1000, Boston, MA 02108. Website: http://www.hbook.com

Since 1924, the *Horn Book Magazine* has been devoted to the critical analysis of children's literature. Many of the articles are written by noted authors, while the book reviews are staff written. Since Roger Sutton, a former YA librarian, became editor, more attention has been given to young adult literature. Big names in YA literature who are either regular contributors or reviewers include Betty Carter, Tim Wynne-Jones, Peter D. Sieruta, and Patty Campbell. *Horn Book* co-sponsors the Boston Globe-Horn Book Awards and also prints a yearly "Fanfare" list of best books.

Journal of Adolescent and Adult Literacy. International Reading Association, 800 Barksdale Rd., Box 8139, Newark, DE 19711–8139.

The audience is high school reading teachers. Although most of the articles are reports on research in the teaching of reading, some articles focus on reading interests and literature. James Blasingame edits a regular review column on young adult literature.

Kirkus Reviews. Kirkus Service, Inc., 200 Park Avenue South, New York, NY 10003.

Kirkus reviews are approximately 200 words long and are relied on throughout the publishing industry. The big advantage is timeliness and completeness made possible by twice-a-month issues.

The New Advocate. Christopher-Gordon Publishers Inc., 480 Washington St., Norwood MA 02062.

Published five times a year, the purpose of this new journal is to encourage teachers to work with literature. Violet J. Harris at the University of Illinois at Urbana-Champagne is the editor.

Publishers Weekly. 245 W. 17th St., New York, NY 10011. Website:http://www.publishers weekly.com

While the focus is on the general world of adult book publishing, much of the information is relevant to anyone working with books; for example, what will company mergers mean to readers, what are the current best sellers, and who are the prize winners. Staff members write the reviews, which include some for children ages 12-up.

School Library Journal. Editorial correspondence to *SLJ* Editor Evan St. Lifer, 360 Park Avenue, South., New York, NY 10011; subscription correspondence to P.O. Box 16388 North Hollywood, CA 91695-6388. Website: http://www.slj.com

SLJ is the most comprehensive of the review media trying in monthly installments to review all books published for young people. Advertisements and feature articles provide good information along with the reviews, which are written by a panel of 400 librarians. A starred review and/or inclusion on the December best books list signifies an exceptional book.

Voices From the Middle. National Council of Teachers of English. Order from NCTE, 1111 W. Kenyon Road, Urbana, IL 61801. Editor is Kylene Beers, University of Houston, TX.

This relatively new quarterly is sponsored by the National Council of Teachers of English for teachers in middle schools and junior high schools. It regularly includes information about YA lit appropriate for tweeners.

VOYA (Voice of Youth Advocates). Scarecrow Press, Inc. 4720A Boston Way, Lanham, MD 20706.

Published every other month, this is a journal prepared mainly for librarians who work with teenagers. It was founded in 1978 by Mary K. Chelton and Dorothy Broderick and is now edited by Cathi Dunn MacRae. Besides reviewing new books, it consistently has good articles on current trends in literature and youth services in libraries. The editors and contributors do an especially good job with fantasy and science fiction.

YALS (Young Adult Library Services) is sponsored by the American Library Association, 50 E. Huron St., Chicago, IL 60611. Website: http://www.ala.org

In its history, this journal has been called *Top of the News* (before 1987) and *JOYS: Journal of Youth Services* (between 1987 and 2002). In its earlier forms, it covered both children's and YA literature as well as research and developments of interest to librarians. *YALS* now appears biannually and is sent to all YA librarians who belong to ALA. Its focus is strictly YA. A recent issue, for example, had as its theme, *Go Graphic!*

APPENDIX

Some Outstanding Books and Articles about YA Literature

Books

Histories of Young Adult Literature

Avery, Gillian. *Behold the Child: American Children and Their Books, 1621–1922.* London: Bodley House, 1994.

Avery, Gillian. *Childhood's Pattern: A Study of the Heroes and Heroines of Childhood's Fiction, 1770–1950.* London: Hodder and Stoughton, 1975.

Axe, John. *All about Collecting Boys' Series Books.* Grantsville, MD: Hobby House Press, 2002.

Axe, John. *All about Collecting Girls' Series Books.* Grantsville, MD: Hobby House Press, 2002.

Billman, Carol. *The Secret of the Stratemeyer Syndicate: Nancy Drew, the Hardy Boys, and the Million Dollar Fiction Factory.* New York: Ungar, 1986.

Blanck, Jacob. *Peter Parley to Penrod: A Bibliographical Description of the Best-Loved American Juvenile Books.* New York: R. R. Bowker, 1956.

Cadogan, Mary and Patricia Craig. *You're a Brick, Angela! A New Look at Girls' Fiction from 1839 to 1975.* London: Victor Gollancz, 1976. Delightful and funny and extraordinarily rich.

Campbell, Patricia. *Sex Education Books for Young Adults, 1892–1979.* New York: R. R. Bowker, 1979. Accurate and funny. Most of us can only envy Campbell's prose.

Carrier, Esther Jane. *Fiction in Public Libraries. 1876–1900.* New York: Scarecrow Press, 1965.

Cart, Michael. *From Romance to Realism: 50 Years of Growth and Change in Young Adult Literature.* New York: HarperCollins, 1996.

Cech, John, ed. *American Writers for Children, 1900–1960. Dictionary of American Biography,* Vol. 22. Detroit: Gale Research, 1983.

Children's Fiction, 1876–1984. 2 vols. New York: R. R. Bowker, 1984.

Crouch, Marcus. *The Nesbit Tradition: The Children's Novel in England, 1945–1970.* London: Ernest Benn, 1972.

Crouch, Marcus. *Treasure Seekers and Borrowers: Children's Books in Britain, 1900–1960.* London: Library Association, 1962.

Darling, Richard. *The Rise of Children's Book Reviewing in America: 1865–1881.* New York: R. R. Bowker, 1968. A seminal book.

Darton, F. J. Harvey. *Children's Books in England: Five Centuries of Social Use,* 2nd ed. First published in 1932. Helpful, though a bit stuffy.

Deane, Paul. *Mirrors of American Culture: Children's Fiction Series in the Twentieth Century.* Metuchen, NJ: Scarecrow Press, 1991.

Demers, Patricia. *A Garland from the Golden Age: An Anthology of Children's Literature from 1850 to 1900.* Toronto: Oxford University Press, 1983.

Dyer, Carolyn Stewart and Nancy Tillman Romalov, eds. *Rediscovering Nancy Drew.* Iowa City: University of Iowa Press, 1995. Papers from the 1993 Nancy Drew Conference.

Egoff, Sheila. *The Republic of Childhood: A Critical Guide to Canadian Children's Literature,* 2nd ed. Toronto: Oxford University Press, 1975.

Egoff, Sheila. *Worlds Within: Children's Fantasy from the Middle Ages.* Chicago: American Library Association, 1988.

Estes, Glenn E., ed. *American Writers for Children before 1900. Dictionary of Literary Biography,* Vol. 42. Detroit: Gale Research, 1985.

Foster, Shirley and Judy Simmons, eds. *What Katy Read: Feminist Re-Readings of "Classic" Stories for Girls.* Iowa City: University of Iowa Press, 1995.

Girls' Series Books: A Checklist of Hardback Books Published 1900–1975. Minneapolis: Children's Literature Research Collection, University of Minnesota Library, 1978. Basic for any study of early girls' books. Much like Hudson's work, below.

Gorham, Deborah. *The Victorian Girl and the Feminine Ideal.* Bloomington: Indiana University Press, 1982.

Griswold, Jerry. *Audacious Kids: Coming of Age in America's Classic Childrens' Books.* New York: Oxford University Press, 1992. Audacious indeed, and more.

Helbig, Althea K. and Agnes Perkins. *Dictionary of American Children's Fiction, 1859–1959.* Westport, CT: Greenwood Press, 1985.

Howarth, Patrick. *Play Up and Play the Game: The Heroes of Popular Fiction.* London: Eyre Methuen, 1973.

Hudson, Harry K. *A Bibliography of Hard-Cover Boys' Books,* rev. ed. Tampa, FL: Data Print, 1977. Basic for any study of early boys' books—and great fun to skim through.

Hurlimann, Bettina. *Three Centuries of Children's Books in Europe.* Trans. and ed. Brian W. Anderson. Cleveland: World Book, 1968.

Inness, Sherrie A., ed. *Nancy Drew and Company: Culture, Gender, and Girls' Series.* Bowling Green, OH: Bowling Green State University Popular Press, 1999.

Jackson, Mary V. *Engines of Instruction, Mischief, and Magic: Children's Literature in England from Its Beginnings to 1839.* Lincoln: University of Nebraska Press, 1989.

Johannssen, Albert. *The House of Beadle and Adams and Its Dime and Nickel Novels: The Story of a Vanished Literature,* 3 vols. Norman: University of Oklahoma Press, 1950–1952.

Johnson, Deidre. *Edward Stratemeyer and the Stratemeyer Syndicate.* New York: Twayne, 1993. Anyone working on early young adult literature owes a debt to Johnson.

Johnson, Deidre, ed. *Stratemeyer Pseudonyms and Series Books: An Annotated Checklist of Stratemeyer and Stratemeyer Syndicate Publications.* Westport, CT: Greenwood Press, 1982. A mammoth book on a mammoth topic. And what a help it is.

Jones, Daryl. *The Dime Novel Western.* Bowling Green, OH: Bowling Green State University Popular Press, 1978.

Kensinger, Faye Riter. *Children of the Series and How They Grew.* Bowling Green, OH: Bowling Green State University Popular Press, 1987.

Kiefer, Monica. *American Children Through Their Books, 1700–1835.* Philadelphia: University of Pennsylvania Press, 1948.

Kilgour, Raymond L. *Lee and Shepard: Publishers for the People.* Hamden, CT: Shoe String Press, 1965.

Kloes, Christine A. *After Alice: A Hundred Years of Children's Reading in Britain.* London: Library Association, 1977. Published for an exhibition at the Victoria and Albert Museum of Childhood, 1977–1978.

MacLeod, Anne Scott. *A Moral Tale: Children's Fiction and American Culture, 1820–1860* Hamden, CT: Archon Books, 1975.

McFarlane, Leslie. *Ghost of the Hardy Boys: An Autobiography of Leslie McFarlane.* New York: Two Continents, 1976.

Mason, Bobbie Ann. *The Girl Sleuth: A Feminist Guide.* Old Westbury, NY: Feminist Press, 1975. Delightful and perceptive.

Meigs, Cornelia, et al. *A Critical History of Children's Literature,* rev. ed. New York: Macmillan, 1969. Encyclopedic and sometimes most helpful.

Michaels, Carolyn Clugston. *Children's Book Collecting.* Hamden, CT: Shoe String Press, 1993.

Mitchell, Sally. *The New Girl: Girls' Culture in England 1880–1915.* New York: Columbia University Press, 1995.

Mott, Frank Luther. *Golden Multitudes: The Story of Best Sellers in the United States.* New York: Macmillan, 1947.

Nye, Russel. *The Unembarrassed Muse: The Popular Arts in America.* New York: Dial, 1970. One of a few truly basic books in our field (and several other fields to boot).

Papashvily, Helen Waite. *All the Happy Endings.* New York: Harper and Brothers, 1956.

Pattee, Fred Lewis. *The Feminist Fifties.* New York; Appleton, 1940.

Reynolds, Kimberley. *Girls Only? Gender and Popular Children's Fiction in Britain, 1880–1910.* Philadelphia: Tempe University Press, 1990.

Richardson, Selma K., ed. *Research about Nineteenth-Century Children and Books.* Urbana-Champagne, IL: University of Illinois Graduate School of Library Science, 1980.

Rosenbach, A. S. W. *Early American Children's Books.* 1933. New York: Krause Reprints, 1966.

Rowbotham, Judith. *Good Girls Make Good Wives: Guidance for Girls in Victorian England.* Oxford, England: Basil Blackwell, 1989.

Salmon, Edward. *Juvenile Literature as It Is.* London: Drane, 1888. One of half a dozen—or fewer—significant books in the field. Impossible to overrate.

Sloane, William. *Children's Books in England and America in the Seventeenth Century.* New York: Columbia University Press, 1955.

Smith, Henry Nash. *Virgin Land: The American West as Symbol and Myth.* Cambridge, MA: Harvard University Press, 1950.

Thwaite, Mary F. *From Primer to Pleasure in Reading: An Introduction to the History of Children's Books in England from the Invention of Printing to 1914.* Boston: Horn Book, 1972.

Townsend, John Rowe. *25 Years of British Children's Books.* London: National Book League, 1977. A sixty-page pamphlet worth searching for.

Townsend, John Rowe. *Written for Children: An Outline of English-Language Children's Literature,* 3rd ed. Philadelphia: Lippincott, 1988. Perhaps Townsend's finest work.

Wishy, Bernard. *The Child and the Republic: The Dawning of Modern American Child Nurture.* Philadelphia: University of Pennsylvania Press, 1968.

Criticism of Young Adult Literature

Barron, Neal, ed. *Fantasy and Horror: A Critical and Historical Guide to Literature, Illustration, Film, TV, Radio and the Internet.* Lanham, MD: Scarecrow Press, 1999.

Bauer, Marion Dane. *What's Your Story? A Young Person's Guide to Writing Fiction.* New York: Clarion, 1992.

Broderick, Dorothy. *Images of the Black in Children's Fiction.* New York: R. R. Bowker, 1973.

Cameron, Eleanor. *The Green and Burning Tree: On the Writing and Enjoyment of Children's Books.* New York: Dutton, 1993.

Carter, Betty and Richard Abrahamson. *Nonfiction for Young Adults: From Delight to Wisdom.* Phoenix: Oryx Press, 1990.

Chambers, Aidan. *Introducing Books to Children,* 2nd ed. Boston: Horn Book, 1983.

Chambers, Aidan. *The Reluctant Reader.* London: Pergamon, 1969. This reads better the older it gets. Practical and sympathetic ideas about getting at hard-to-reach students.

Children's Literature Review. Detroit: Gale Research, 1973.

Christian-Smith, Linda K. *Becoming a Woman through Romance.* New York: Rutledge, 1990.

Contemporary Literary Criticism. Detroit: Gale Research, 1973.

Day, Frances Ann. *Lesbian and Gay Voices: An Annotated Bibliography and Guide to Literature for Children and Young Adults.* Westport, CT: Greenwood Press, 2000.

Dixon, Bob. *Catching Them Young: Political Ideas in Children's Fiction.* London: Pluto Press, 1977.

Dixon, Bob. *Catching Them Young: Sex, Race, and Class in Children's Fiction.* London: Pluto Press, 1977.

Dresong, Eliza T. *Radical Change: Books for Youth in a Digital Age.* New York: H. W. Wilson, 1999.

Egoff, Sheila A. *Thursday's Child: Trends and Patterns in Contemporary Children's Literature.* Chicago: American Library Association, 1981.

Ettinger, John R. and Diana L. Spirt, eds. *Choosing Books for Young People, Vol. 2: A Guide to Criticism and Bibliography, 1976–1984.* Chicago: American Library Association, 1982.

Eyre, Frank. *British Children's Books in the Twentieth Century.* New York: Dutton, 1971.

Fisher, Margery. *The Bright Face of Danger.* London: Hodder and Hodder, 1986.

Fox, Geoff et al., eds. *Writers, Critics, and Children.* New York: Agathon, 1976. Articles from *Children's Literature in Education.*

Harrison, Barbara and Gregory Maguire, eds. *Innocence and Experience: Essays and Conversations on Children's Literature.* New York: Lothrop, Lee and Shepard, 1987.

Hazard, Paul. *Books, Children and Men,* trans. Marguerite Mitchell. Boston: Horn Book, 1944. A seminal book impossible to overrate.

Hearnes, Betsy, ed. *The Zena Sutherland Lectures.* New York: Clarion, 1993.

Hearne, Betsy and Marilyn Kaye, eds. *Celebrating Children's Books: Essays on Children's Literature in Honor of Zena Sutherland.* New York: Lothrop, Lee and Shepard, 1981.

Hendrickson, Linnae. *Children's Literature: A Guide to the Criticism.* Boston: G. K. Hall, 1987.

Horning, Kathleen. *From Cover to Cover: Evaluating and Reviewing Children's Books.* New York: HarperCollins, 1997.

Howard, Elizabeth F. *America as Story: Historical Fiction for the Secondary Schools.* Chicago: American Library Association, 1988.

Hunt, Peter. *Criticism, Theory, and Children's Literature.* Oxford: Basil Blackwell, 1991.

Hunt, Peter. *An Introduction to Children's Literature.* New York: Oxford University Press, 1994.

Hunter, Mollie. *The Pied Piper Syndrome and Other Essays.* New York: HarperCollins, 1992.

Hunter, Mollie. *Talent Is Not Enough: Mollie Hunter on Writing for Children.* New York: Harper and Row, 1976.

Inglis, Fred. *The Promise of Happiness: Value and Meaning in Children's Fiction.* Cambridge: Cambridge University Press, 1981.

Kelly, Patricia P. and Robert C. Small, eds. *Two Decades of the ALAN Review.* Urbana, IL: National Council of Teachers of English, 1999.

Kohn, Rita, compiler. *Once Upon . . . a Time for Young People and Their Books: An Annotated Resource Guide.* Metuchen, NJ: Scarecrow Press, 1986.

Lentz, Millicent and Ramona M. Mahood, eds. *Young Adult Literature: Background and Criticism.* Chicago: American Library Association, 1980.

Lesnick-Oberstein, Karin. *Children's Literature: Criticism and the Fictional Child.* Oxford: Clarendon Press, 1994.

Lukens, Rebecca.J. *A Critical Handbook of Children's Literature.* Glenview, IL: Scott, Foresman, 1976.

Lynn, Ruth Nadelman. *Fantasy Literature for Children and Young Adults.* New York: R. R. Bowker, 1989.

MacCann, Donnarae and Gloria Woodward, eds. *The Black American in Books for Children: Readings on Racism.* Metuchen, NJ: Scarecrow Press, 1972.

MacCann, Donnarae. *White Supremacy in Children's Literature: Characteristics of African-Americans, 1830–1900.* New York: Garland, 1998.

McCallum, Robyn. *Ideologies of Identities in Adolescent Fiction: The Dialogic Construction of Subjectivity.* New York: Garland, 1999.

Moore, John Noell. *Interpreting Young Adult Literature: Literary Theory in the Secondary Classsroom.* Portsmouth, NH: Boynton/Cook, 1997.

Nikolajeva, Maria. *Aspects and Issues in the History of Children's Literature.* Westport, CT: Greenwood Press, 1995.

Nikolajeva, Maria. *Children's Literature Coming of Age: Towards a New Aesthetic.* New York: Garland, 1996.

Nikolajeva, Maria. *From Mythic to Linear: Time in Children's Literature.* Lanham, MD: Scarecrow Press, 2000

Nikolajeva, Maria. *The Rhetoric of Character in Children's Literature.* Lanham MD: Scarecrow Press, 2002.

Peck, Richard. *Love and Death at the Mall: Teaching and Writing for the Literate Young.* New York: Delacorte, 1994.

Petitt, Dorothy. "A Study of the Qualities of Literary Excellence Which Characterize Selected Fiction for Younger Adolescents." Ph.D. Dissertation, University of Minnesota, 1961.

Probst, Robert. E. *Adolescent Literature: Response and Analysis.* Columbus, OH: Charles E, Merrill, 1984.

Rochman, Hazel. *Against Borders: Promoting Books for a Multiracial World.* Chicago: American Library Association, 1993.

Rohn, Suzanne. *Children's Literature: An Annotated Bibliography of the History and Criticism.* New York: Garland, 1981.

Saxby, Maurice. *Books in the Life of a Child: Bridges to Literature and Learning.* South Melbourne, Australia: Macmillan Educational, 1997.

Shields, Nancy E. *Index to Literary Criticism for Young Adults.* Metuchen, NJ: Scarecrow Press, 1988.

Sloan, Glenda. *The Child as Critic.* New York: Teachers College Press, 1975. Northrop Frye's theories applied to YA literature.

Soter, Anna. *Young Adult Literature and New Literary Theory.* New York: Teachers College Press, 1999.

Stanford, Barbara Dodds and Karima Amin. *Black Literature for High School Students.* Urbana, IL: National Council of Teachers of English, 1978.

Stensland, Anna Lee. *Literature by and about American Indians: An Annotated Bibliography* 2nd ed. Urbana, IL: National Council of Teachers of English, 1970.

Street, Douglas, ed. *Children's Novels and the Movies.* New York: Ungar, 1984.

Sullivan, C. W. *Science Fiction for Young Readers.* Westport, CT: Greenwood Press, 1993.

Sullivan, Edward T. *The Holocaust in Literature for Youth: A Guide and Resource Book.* Lanham, MD: Scarecrow Press, 1999.

Sutherland, Zena, ed. *The Arbuthnot Lecture, 1970–1979.* Chicago: American Library Association, 1980.

Tucker, Nicholas, ed. *Suitable for Children? Controversies in Children's Literature.* Berkeley: University of California Press, 1976.

Yolen, Jane. *Touch Magic: Fantasy, Faerie, and Folklore in the Literature of Childhood.* New York: Philomel, 1981.

Libraries and Young Adult Literature

Bodart, Joni. *Booktalking and School Visiting for Young Adult Audiences.* New York: H. W. Wilson, 1980.

Bodart, Joni. *Booktalk 2: Booktalking for All Ages and Audiences.* New York: H.W. Wilson, 1985.

Books for the Teen Age. New York Public Library, published annually.

Campbell, Patricia. *Two Pioneers of Young Adult Library Service.* Lanham, MD: Scarecrow Press, 1999. Mabel Williams and Margaret A. Edwards.

Carr, Jo, ed. *Beyond Fact: Nonfiction for Children and Young People.* Chicago: American Library Association, 1982,

Edwards, Margaret A. *The Fair Garden and the Swarm of Beasts: The Library and the Young Adult,* rev. ed. New York: Hawthorn, 1974. The problems but mostly the joys of working in a library with young people.

Eiss, Harry, ed. *Literature for Young People on War and Peace: An Annotated Bibliography.* New York: Greenwood, 1989.

Field, Carolyn W., ed. *Special Collections in Children's Literature.* Chicago: American Library Association, 1982.

Gillespie, John T. *More Juniorplots: A Guide for Teachers and Librarians.* New York: R. R. Bowker, 1977.

Gillespie, John T. and Diana L. Lembo. *Juniorplots: A Book Talk Manual for Teachers and Librarians.* New York: R. R. Bowker, 1967.

Gillespie, John T. and Corinne Naden. *Juniorplots 3: A Book Talk Guide for Use with Readers Ages 12–16.* New York: R. R. Bowker, 1987.

Gillespie, John T. and Corrine Naden. *The Newbery Companion: Booktalk and Related Materials for Newbery Medal and Honor Books.* Englewood, CO: Libraries Unlimited, 1996.

Gillespie, John T. and Corinne Naden. *Seniorplots: A Book Talk Guide for Use with Readers Ages 15–18.* New York: R. R. Bowker, 1989.

Heller, Frieda M. and Lou LaBrant. *The Librarian and the Teacher of English.* Chicago: American Library Association, 1938.

Hinckley, Karen and Barbara Hinckley. *America's Best Sellers: A Reader's Guide to Popular Fiction.* Bloomington: Indiana University Press, 1989.

Marshall, Margaret R. *Libraries and Literature for Teenagers.* London: Deutsch, 1975.

Rochman, Hazel. *Tales of Love and Terror: Booktalking the Classics, Old and New.* Chicago: American Library Association, 1987.

Roe, Ernest. *Teachers, Librarians, and Children: A Study of Librarians in Education.* Hamden, CT: P. Archon Books, 1965. Superb and maybe the best of the lot.

Rosenberg, Betty. *Genreflecting: A Guide to Reading Interests in Genre Fiction,* 2nd ed. Littleton, CO: Libraries Unlimited, 1987.

Spencer, Pam. *What Do Young Adults Read Next? A Reader's Guide to Fiction for Young Adults.* Detroit: Gale Research, 1994. Invaluable.

Taylor, Desmond. *The Juvenile Novels of World War II: An Annotated Bibliography.* Westport, CT: Greenwood Press, 1994.

English Classrooms and Young Adult Literature

Barnhouse, Rebecca. *Recasting the Part: The Middle Ages in Young Adult Literature.* Westport, CT: Heinemann, 2000.

Beach, Richard. *A Teacher's Introduction to Reader-Response Theories.* Urbana, IL: National Council of Teachers of English, 1993.

Beach, Richard and James Marshall. *Teaching Literature in the Secondary School.* San Diego: Harcourt Brace Jovanovich, 1991

Brown, Jean A. and Elaine C. Stephens. *Teaching Young Adult Literature: Sharing the Connection.* Belmont, CA: Wadsworth, 1995.

Burton, Dwight L. *Literature Study in the High Schools.* New York: Holt, 1970. For many teachers and librarians this was THE book that introduced them to YA books.

Carlsen, G. Robert. *Books and the Teen-Age Reader,* 2nd ed. New York: Harper and Row, 1980.

Chambers, Aidan. *Booktalk: Occasional Writing on Literature and Children.* New York: Harper and Row, 1985.

Corcoran, Bill and Emrys Evans, eds. *Readers, Texts, Teachers.* Upper Montclair, NJ: Boynton/Cook, 1987.

Crowley, Sharon. *A Teacher's Introduction to Deconstruction.* Urbana, IL: National Council of Teachers of English, 1989.

Dunning, A. Stephen. "A Definition of the Role of the Junior Novel Based on Analyses of Thirty Selected Novels." Ph. D. Dissertation, Florida State University, 1959.

Elliott, Joan B. and Mary M. Dupuis, eds. *Young Adult Literature in the Classroom: Reading It, Teaching It, Loving It.* Newark, DE: International Reading Association, 2002.

Evans, Tricia. *Teaching English.* London: Croom Helm, 1982.

Fader, Daniel. *The New Hooked on Books.* New York: Berkley, 1976. First published in 1966 and revised in 1968. Fader's book (and his across-the-country pep talks) made teachers and librarians take YA books seriously.

Farrell, Edmund and James R. Squire, eds. *Transactions with Literature: A Fifty-Year Perspective.* Urbana, IL: National Council of Teachers of English, 1990. Essays honoring the work of Louise M. Rosenblatt.

Hertz, Sarah and Donald R. Gallo. *From Hinton to Hamlet: Building Bridges between Young Adult Literature and the Classics.* Westport, CT: Greenwood Press, 1996.

Issac, Megan Lynn. *Heirs to Shakespeare: Reinventing the Bard in Young Adult Literature.* Westport, CT: Heinemann, 2000.

Marshall, James D., Peter Smagorinsky, and Michael W. Smith. *The Language of Interpretation: Patterns of Discourse in Discussions of Literature.* NCTE Research Report No. 27. Urbana, IL: National Council of Teachers of English, 1995.

Monseau, Virginia R. and Gary M. Salvner, eds. *Reading Their World: The Young Adult Novel in the Classroom.* Portsmouth, NH: Boynton/Cook, 1992.

Moran, Charles and Elizabeth F. Penfield, eds. *Conversations: Contemporary Critical Theory and the Teaching of Literature.* Urbana, IL: National Council of Teachers of English, 1990.

Ohanion, Susan. *Who's in Charge? A Teacher Speaks Her Mind.* Portsmouth, NH: Boynton/Cook, 1994. Brilliant and witty.

Peck, David. *Novels of Initiation: A Guidebook for Teaching Literature to Adolescents.* New York: Teachers College Press, 1989.

Probst, Robert E. *Response and Analysis: Teaching Literature in Junior and Senior High School.* Portsmouth, NH: Boynton/Cook, 1988. One of the best books in our field.

Protherough, Robert, Judith Atkinson, and John Fawcett. *The Effective Teaching of English.* London: Longman, 1989.

Purves, Alan C., Theresa Rogers, and Anna O. Soter. *How Porcupines Make Love II: Teaching a Response-Centered Curriculum.* New York: Longman, 1990.

Richter, David H., ed. *The Critical Tradition: Classic Texts and Contemporary Trends.* New York: Bedford Books, St, Martin's Press, 1989. From Plato to Wordsworth to Eliot to Langer.

Rosenblatt, Louise M. *Literature as Exploration,* 4th ed. New York: Modern Language Association, 1983.

Sample, Hazel. *Pitfalls for Readers of Fiction.* Chicago: National Council of Teachers of English, 1940. Too little read and known. A classic.

Scholes, Robert. *Textual Power: Literary Theory and the Teaching of English.* New Haven: Yale University Press, 1985.

Smagorinsky, Peter and Melissa E. Whiting. *How English Teachers Get Taught: Methods of Teaching the Methods Class.* Urbana, IL: National Council of Teachers of English, 1995.

Somers, Albert B. and Janet Evans Worthington. *Candles and Mirrors: Response Guides for Teaching Novels and Plays in Grades Six through Twelve.* Littleton, CO: Libraries Unlimited, 1984.

Stringer, Sharon A. *Conflict and Connection: The Psychology of Young Adult Literature.* Westport, CT: Heinemann, 1997.

Thomson, Jack. *Understanding Teenagers' Reading: Reading Processes and the Teaching of Literature.* Norwood, Australia: Australian Association for the Teaching of English, 1987.

Zitlow, Connie. *Lost Masterworks of Young Adult Literature.* Lanham, MD: Scarecrow Press, 2002.

Authors of Young Adult Literature

Bodart, Joni Richards. *100 World-Class Thin Books, or What to Read When Your Book Report Is Due Tomorrow.* Englewood, CO: Libraries Unlimited, 1993.

Chevalier, Tracy. *Twentieth Century Children's Writers,* 3rd ed. New York: St. Martin's Press, 1989.

Commire, Anne, ed. *Something about the Author.* Detroit: Gale Research, 1971.

Commire, Anne, ed. *Yesterday's Authors of Books for Children.* Detroit: Gale Research, 1977. Lives of those who died before 1961.

de Montreville, Doris and Elizabeth D. Crawford, eds. *Fourth Book of Junior Authors and Illustrators.* New York: H. W. Wilson, 1978.

de Montreville, Doris and Donna Hill, eds. *Third Book of Junior Authors.* New York: H. W. Wilson, 1972.

Doyle, Brian. *The Who's Who of Children's Literature.* New York: Schocken, 1968.

Drew, Bernard A. *The 100 Most Popular Young Adult Authors: Biographical Sketches and Bibliographies.* Englewood, CO: Libraries Unlimited, 1996.

Estes, Glenn E., ed. *American Writers for Children Since 1960: Fiction. Dictionary of Literary Biography,* Vol. 52. Detroit: Gale Research, 1986.

Estes, Glenn E., ed. *American Writers for Children Since 1960: Poets, Illustrators, and Nonfiction Authors. Dictionary of Literary Biography,* Vol. 61. Detroit: Gale Research, 1987.

Fuller, Muriel, ed. *More Junior Authors.* New York: H. W. Wilson, 1963.

Gallo, Donald R., ed. *Authors' Insights: Turning Teenagers into Readers and Writers*. Portsmouth, NH: Boynton/Cook, 1992.

Gallo, Donald R., ed., *Speaking for Ourselves: Autobiographical Sketches by Notable Authors of Books for Young Adults*. Urbana, IL: National Council of Teaches of English, 1990. In this and a 1993 sequel, nearly 200 YA authors introduce themselves.

Green, Roger L. *Teller of Tales: British Authors of Children's Books from 1800 to 1964,* rev. ed. New York: Watts, 1965.

Haviland, Virginia, ed. *The Openhearted Audience: Ten Authors Talk about Writing for Children*. Washington, DC: Library of Congress, 1980.

Helbig, Alethea K. and Agnes Regan Perkins, eds. *Dictionary of American Children's Fiction, 1960–1984*. Westport, CT: Greenwood Press, 1986.

Helbig, Alethea K. and Agnes Regan Perkins, eds. *Dictionary of British Children's Fiction*. Westport, CT: Greenwood Press, 1989.

Hipple, Ted, ed. *Writers for Young Adults*: 3 Vols. New York: Scribner, 1997. Vol 4, 2000.

Holtze, Sally Holmes, ed. *Fifth Book of Junior Authors and Illustrators*. New York: H. W. Wilson, 1987.

Hopkins, Lee Bennett. *Pauses: Autobiographical Reflections of 101 Creators of Children's Books*. New York: 1995.

Huffman, Miriam and Eva Samuels, eds. *Authors and Artists for Young Adults*. Detroit: Gale Research, 1989.

Jones, Cornelia and Olivia R. Way. *British Children's Authors: Interviews at Home*. Chicago: American Library Association, 1976.

Kirkpatrick, D. L., ed. *Twentieth-Century Children's Writers,* 3rd ed. New York: Macmillan, 1990.

Kunitz, Stanley J. and Howard Haycraft, eds. *The Junior Book of Authors,* 2nd ed. rev. New York: H. W. Wilson, 1951.

Pendegast, Tom and Sara Pendergast, eds. *The St. James Guide to Young Adult Writers*. Detroit: St. James, 1999.

Rees, David. *The Marble in the Water: Essays on Contemporary Writers of Fiction for Children and Young Adults*. Boston: Horn Book, 1980.

Rees, David. *Painted Desert, Green Shade: Essays on Contemporary Writers of Fiction for Children and Young Adults*. Boston: Horn Book, 1984.

Rees, David. *What Do Draculas Do? Essays on Contemporary Writers of Fiction for Children and Young Adults*. Metuchen, NJ: Scarecrow Press, 1990.

Rockman, Connie C., ed. *Eighth Book of Junior Authors and Illustrators*. New York: H. W. Wilson, 2000.

Roginski, Jim. *Behind the Covers: Interviews with Authors and Illustrators of Books for Children and Young Adults*. Littleton, CO: Libraries Unlimited, 1985. Vol. 2, 1989.

Sarkissian, Adele, ed. *Writers for Young Adults: Biographies Master Index*. Detroit: Gale Research, 1984.

Townsend, John Rowe. *A Sense of Story: Essays on Contemporary Writers for Children*. Philadelphia: Lippincott, 1971.

Ward, Martha E. and Dorothy A. Marquardt, eds. *Authors of Books for Young People,* 3rd ed. Metuchen, NJ: Scarecrow Press, 1990.

Weiss, M. Jerry, ed. *From Writers to Students: The Pleasures and Pains of Writing.* Newark, DE: International Reading Association, 1979.

Wintle, Justin and Emma Fisher, eds. *The Pied Pipers: Interviews with the Influential Creators of Children's Literature.* New York: Paddington Press, 1974.

Books of Readings about Young Adult Literature

Broderick, Dorothy M., ed. *The VOYA Reader.* Metuchen, NJ: Scarecrow Press, 1990. Articles from the *Voice of Youth Advocate.*

Egoff, Sheila; G. T. Stubbs; and L. F. Ashley, eds. *Only Connect: Readings in Children's Literature,* 2nd ed. New York: Oxford University Press, 1980.

Fox, Geoff, et al., eds. *Writers, Critics, and Children: Articles from Children's Literature in Education.* New York: Agathon Press, 1976.

Haviland, Virginia, ed. *Children and Literature: Views and Reviews.* Glenview, IL: Scott, Foresman, 1973.

Salway, Lance, ed. *A Peculiar Gift: Nineteenth Century Writings on Books for Children.* London: Kestrel, 1976.

Varlejs, Jana, ed. *Young Adult Literature in the Seventies: A Selection of Readings.* Metuchen, NJ: Scarecrow Press, 1978.

Articles

History and Young Adult Literature

Ashford, Richard K. "Tomboys and Saints: Girls' Stories of the Late Nineteenth Century." *School Library Journal* 26 (January 1980): 23–28.

Cantwell, Robert. "A Sneering Laugh with the Bases Loaded." *Sports Illustrated* 16 (April 23, 1962): 67–70, 73–76. Baseball novels for boys, especially by Barbour and Heyliger.

Carlsen, G. Robert. "Forty Years with Books and Teen-Age Readers." *Arizona English Bulletin* 18 (April 1976): 1–5. From 1939 to 1976 in YA literature.

Crandall, John C. "Patriotism and Humanitarian Reform in Children's Literature: 1825–1860." *American Quarterly* 21 (Spring 1969): 1–22.

Edwards, Margaret A. "The Rise of Teen-Age Reading." *Saturday Review of Literature* 37 (November 13, 1954): 88–89, 95.

Evans, Walter. "The All-American Boys: A Study of Boys' Sports Fiction." *Journal of Popular Culture* 6 (Summer 1972): 104–121. Formulas underlying books by Barbour and various series.

Evans, Walter. "For It Was Indeed He." *Fortune* 9 (April 1934): 86–89, 193–194, 204, 206, 208–209. An important, influential, and biased article on Stratemeyer's Literary Syndicate.

Geller, Evelyn. "The Librarian as Censor." *Library Journal* 101 (June 1, 1976): 1255–1258. Social control as censorship in library selection.

Geller, Evelyn. "Tom Sawyer, Tom Bailey, and the Bad-Boy Genre." *Wilson Library Bulletin* 52 (November 1976): 245–250.

Green, Samuel S. "Sensational Fiction in Publlic Libraries." *Library Journal* 4 (September/October 1879): 345–355. Extraordinarily forward-looking intelligent comments about young adults and their books. The entire issue is worth reading, particularly papers by T. W. Higginson (pp. 357–359), William Atkinson (pp. 359–362), and Mellen Chamberlain (pp. 362–366).

Hutchinson, Margaret. "Fifty Years of Young Adult Reading, 1921–1971." *Top of the News* 29 (November 1973): 24–53.

Kelly, R. Gordon. "American Children's Literature" An Historiographical Review." *American Literary Realism, 1870–1910* 6 (Spring 1973): 89–107.

Lapides, Linda F. "A Decade of Teen-Age Reading in Baltimore, 1960–1970." *Top of the News* 27 (Spring 1971): 278–291.

MacLeod, Anne. "For the Good of the Country: Cultural Values in American Juvenile Fiction, 1825–1860," *Children's Literature in Education* 5 (1976): 40–51.

Morrison, Lilllian. "Fifty Years of 'Books for the Teen Age.'" *School Library Journal* 26 (December 1979): 44–50.

Radnor, Rebecca. "You're Being Paged Loudly in the Kitchen: Teen-Age Literature of the Forties and Fifties." *Journal of Popular Culture* 11 (Spring 1978): 789–799.

Repplier, Agnes. "Little Pharisees in Fiction." *Scribner's Magazine* 20 (December 1896): 718–724. The didactic and joyless goody-goody school of YA fiction in the last half of the nineteenth century.

Trensky, Anne. "The Bad Boy in Nineteenth-Century American Fiction." *Georgia Review* 27 (Winter 1973): 503–517.

Criticism and Young Adult Literature

Abrahamson, Jane. "Still Playing It Safe: Restricted Realism in Teen Novels." *School Library Journal* 22 (May 1976): 38–39.

Abrahamson, Richard F. "Collected Wisdom: The Best Articles Ever Written on Young Adult Literature and Teen Reading." *English Journal* 86 (March 1997): 50–54. A great place to start reading on YA literature.

"Adolescent Literature." *English in Texas* 13 (Winter 1981): entire issue.

"Adolescent Literature, Adolescent Reading, and the English Class." *Arizona English Bulletin* 14 (April 1972): entire issue.

"Adolescent Literature Revisited after Four Years." *Arizona English Bulletin* 18 (April 1976): entire issue.

Alexander, Lloyd. "Fools, Heroes, and Jackasses." *School Library Journal* 42 (March 1996): 114–116.

Anderson, Philip M. and Mitchell Katcher. "YA Literature as Cannon Fodder: Book Choices for Writing about Literature." *ALAN Review* 20 (Fall 1992): 35–38.

Aronson, Marc. "The Betrayal of Teenagers: How Book Awards Fail America's Most Important Readers." *School Library Journal* 42 (March 1996): 23–25.

Aronson, Marc. "The Myths of Teenage Readers." *Publishing Research Quarterly* 16 (Fall 2000): 4–9.

Aronson, Marc. "Teenagers and Reading: A Generational Neurosis." *Journal of Youth Services in Libraries* 12 (Winter 1997): 29–30.

Breen, Karen, et al. "One Hundred Books That Shaped the Century." *School Library Journal* 46 (January 2000): 50–58. Annotated list of significant children's and young adult books.

Broderick, Dorothy. "How to Write a Fiction Annotation." *Voice of Youth Advocates* 15 (February 1993): 333.

Broderick, Dorothy. "Reviewing Young Adult Books: The VOYA Editor Speaks Out." *Publishing Research Quarterly* 8 (Spring 1992): 34–40.

Brubaker, James M. "'Are You There, Margaret? It's Me, God.' Religious Contexts in Recent Adolescent Fiction." *English Journal* 72 (September 1983): 82–86.

Campbell, Patty. "Perplexing Young Adult Books: A Retrospective." *Wilson Library Bulletin* 62 (April 1988): 20, 22, 24, 26. Campbell looks back on ten years of her YA column.

Campbell, Patty. "The Sand in the Oyster: YA and OP." *Horn Book Magazine* 73 (September/October 1997): 543–548.

Carlsen, G. Robert. "For Everything There Is a Season." *Top of the News* 21 (January 1965): 103–110. Stages in reading growth.

Carlsen, G. Robert. "The Interest Rate Is Rising." *English Journal* 59 (May 1970): 655–659.

Cart, Michael. "Of Risk and Revelation: The Current State of Young Adult Literature." *Journal of Youth Services in Libraries* 8 (Winter 1995): 151–164.

Carver, Nancy Lynn. "Stereotypes of American Indians in Adolescent Literature." *English Journal* 77 (September 1988): 25–32.

Chambers, Aidan. "All of a Tremble to See His Danger." *Top of the News* 42 (Summer 1986): 405–422. The 1986 May Hill Arbuthnot Lecture.

Chambers, Aidan. "The Difference of Literature: Writing Now for the Future of Young Readers." *Children's Literature in Education* 24 (March 1993): 1–18.

Chance, Rosemary. "Familiar Fairy Tale Picture Books Transformed into Teen Novels." *ALAN Review* 30 (Winter 2003): 66–69.

Chelton, Mary K. "Unrestricted Body Parts and Predictable Bliss." *Library Journal* 116 (July 1991): 44–49.

Corbett, Linda; "Not Wise the Thought—A Grave for Arthur." *ALAN Review* 21 (Fall 1993): 45–48.

Early, Margaret J. "Stages of Growth in Literary Appreciation." *English Journal* 49 (March 1960): 161–167. A seminal article.

Edwards, Margaret A. "A Time When It's Best to Read and Let Read." *Wilson Library Bulletin* 35 (September 1960): 43–47. Myths of buying books for young adults demolished.

Endicott, Alba. "Females Also Come of Age." *English Journal* 81 (April 1992): 42–47.

Engdahl, Sylvia. "Do Teenage Novels Fill a Need?" *English Journal* 64 (February 1975): 48–52.

Evans, Dilys. "The YA Cover Story." *Publishers Weekly* 232 (July 24, 1987): 112–115. Differences between hardcover and paperback covers on YA novels.

Evans, W. D. Emrys. "The Welsh *Mabinogion:* Tellings and Retellings." *Children's Literature in Education* 9 (Spring 1978): 17–33.

Fox, Paula. "On Language." *School Library Journal* 41 (March 1995): 122–126.

Freedman, Russell. "Bring 'em Back Alive: Writing History and Biography for Young People." *School Library Journal* 40 (March 1994): 139–141.

Gale, David. "The Business of Books." *School Library Journal* 42 (July 1996): 18–21. How publishers take a YA manuscript and turn it into a book. Helpful article.

Garfield, Leon. "Historical Fiction for Our Global Times." *Horn Book Magazine* 64 (November/December 1988): 736–742.

Gauch, Patricia. "Good Stuff in Adolescent Fiction." *Top of the News* 40 (Winter 1984): 125–129.

Gebhard, Ann O. "The Emerging Self: Young-Adult and Class Novels of the Black Experience." *English Journal* 82 (September 1993): 50–54.

Glasgow, Jacqueline N. "Reconciling Memories of Internment Camp Experiences During WWII in Children's and Young Adult Literature." *ALAN Review* 29 (Fall 2002): 41–45.

Greenlee, Edwin D. "Recommended Adolescent Literature Avoiding Those Hidden 'Secrets.'" *English Journal* 81 (April 1992): 23–24. See also response to Greenlee, same issue, pp. 25–30.

Grenz, Dagmar. "Literature for Young People and the Novel of Adolescence," in Maria Nikolajeva, ed. *Aspects and Issues in the History of Children's Literature.* Westport, CT: Greenwood Press, 1995.

Hamilton, Greg. "Mapping a History of Adolesence and Literature for Adolescents." *ALAN Review* 29 (Winter 2002): 57–62.

Hamilton, Virginia. "Everything of Value: Moral Realism in the Literature of Children." *Journal of Youth Services in Libraries* 6 (Summer 1993): 363–367.

Hancklel, Frances and John Cunningham. "Can Young Gays Find Happiness in YA Books?" *Wilson Library Bulletin* 50 (March 1976): 528–534.

Head, Patricia. "Robert Cormier and the Postmodernist Possibilities of Young Adult Fiction." *Children's Literature Association Quarterly* 21 (Spring 1996): 28–33.

Hedley, Kathy N. "Freedom's Journeys through *Shuttered Windows* (1938), *Words by Heart* (1968), and *True North* (1996)." *ALAN Review* 29 (Fall 2002): 26–28.

Hentoff, Nat. "Fiction for Teen-Agers." *Wilson Library Bulletin* 43 (November 1968): 261–264. On the shortcomings of YA fiction.

Hentoff, Nat. "Tell It as It Is." *New York Times Book Review,* May 7, 1967, pp. 3, 51.

Hinton, S. E. "Teen-Agers Are for Real." *New York Times Book Review,* August 27, 1967, pp. 26–29. Brief and excellent.

Hipple, Ted. "Articles about Young Adult Literature: A List." *ALAN Review* 29 (Winter 2002): 63–68. Along with Abrahamson above, a helpful start in reading some of the best articles in the field.

Hipple, Ted and Amy B. Maupin. "What's Good about the Best?" *English Journal* 90 (January 2001): 40–42.

Hipps, G. Melvin. "Adolescent Literature: Once More to the Defense." *Virginia English Bulletin* 23 (Spring 1973): 44–50. Thirty years old and still one of the best rationales for adolescent literature.

Hollindale, Peter. "The Adolescent Novel of Ideas." *Children's Literature in Education* 26 (March 1995): 83–95.

Hughes-Hassell, Sandra and Sandy L. Guild. "The Urban Experience in Recent Young Adult Novels." *ALAN Review* 29 (Spring-Summr 2002): 35–39.

Hunt, Caroline. "Young Adult Literature Evades the Theorists." *Children's Literature Association Quarterly* 21 (Spring 1996): 4–11.

Huntwork, Mary M. "Why Girls Flock to Sweet Valley High." *School Library Journal* 36 (March 1990): 137–140.

"Is Adolescent Literature Worth Studying?" *Connecticut English Journal* 10 (Fall 1978): Two opposing positions—Robert P. Scaramella, "Con: At the Risk of Seeming Stuffy," pp. 57–58; Robert C. Small, Jr., "Pro: Means and Ends," pp. 59–63.

Janeczko, Paul B. "Seven Myths about Adolescent Literature." *Arizona English Bulletin* 18 (April 1976): 11–12.

Kaye, Marilyn. "In Defense of Formula Fiction: Or, They Don't Write Schlock the Way They Used to." *Top of the News* 37 (Fall 1980): 87–90.

Klein, Norma. "More Realism for Children." *Top of the News* 31 (April 1975): 307–312.

Knickerbocker, Joan L. and James Rycik. "Growing into Literature: Adolescents' Literary Interpretation and Appreciation." *Journal of Adolescent and Adult Literacy* 46 (November 2002): 196–208.

Kraus, W. Keith. "Cinderella in Trouble: Still Dreaming and Losing." *School Library Journal* 21 (January 1975): 18–22. Pregnancy in YA novels from Felsen's *Two and the Town* (1952) to Neufeld's *For All the Wrong Reasons* (1973).

Kraus, W. Keith. "From Steppin' Stebbins to Soul Brothers: Racial Strife in Adolescent Literature." *Arizona English Bulletin* 18 (April 1976): 154–160.

LeMieux, A. C. "The Problem Novel in a Conservative Age." *ALAN Review* 25 (Spring 1998): 4–6.

Lenz, Millicent. "Varieties of Loneliness: Alienation in Contemporary Young People's Fiction." *Journal of Popular Culture* 13 (Spring 1980): 672–688.

"Living with Adolescent Literature." *Connecticut English Journal* 12 (Fall 1980): entire issue.

Louie, Belinda and Douglas Louie. "Empowerment through Young Adult Literature." *English Journal* 81 (April 1992): 53–56.

Martinec, Barbara. "Popular—But Not Just a Part of the Crowd: Implications of Formula Fiction for Teenagers." *Engish Journal* 60 (March 1971): 339–344. Formulaic elements in six YA novels.

Matthews, Dorothy. "An Adolescent's Glimpse of the Faces of Eve: A Study of the Images of Women in Selected Popular Junior Novels." *Illinois English Bulletin* 60 (May 1973): 1–14.

Matthews, Dorothy. "Writing about Adolescent Literature: Current Approaches and Future Directions." *Arizona English Bulletin* 18 (April 1976): 216–219.

McDowell, Myles. "Fiction for Children and Adults: Some Essential Differences." *Children's Literature in Education* 4 (March 1973): 48–63.

Meek, Margaret. "Prologomena for a Study of Children's Literature, or Guess What's in My Head," in Michael Benton, ed. *Approaches to Research in Children's Literature.* Southampton: University of Southampton, 1980, pp. 29–39.

Meltzer, Milton. "Where Do All the Prizes Go? The Case for Nonfiction." *Horn Book Magazine* 52 (February 1976): 17–23.

Merla, Patrick. " 'What Is Real?' Asked the Rabbit One Day." *Saturday Review* 55 (November 4, 1972): 43–49. The rise of YA realism and adult fantasy.

Mertz, Maia Pank and David A. England. "The Legitimacy of American Adolescent Fiction." *School Library Journal* 30 (October 1983): 119–123.

Myracle, Lauren. "Molding the Minds of the Young: The History of Bibliotherapy as Applied to Children and Adolescents." *ALAN Review* 22 (Winter 1995): 36–40.

Nicholson, George. "The Young Adult Novel: History and Development." *CBC Features* 47 (Fall-Winter 1994). Not the easiest article to find but worth the search. An adaptation was printed in the 5th edition of *Literature for Today's Young Adults,* pp. 8–9.

Nixon, Julia H. and Robert C. Small, Jr. "Christianity in American Adolescent Realistic Fiction from 1945 to 1981." *ALAN Review* 12 (Spring 1985): 9–12, 53.

Noble, Susanne. " 'Why Don't We Ever Read Anything Happy?' YA Literature and The Optimistic Ending." *ALAN Review* 26 (Fall 1998): 46–50.

Peck, Richard. "Huck Finns of Both Sexes: Protagonists and Peer Leaders in Young-Adult Books." *Horn Book Magazine* 69 (September/October 1993): 554–558.

Peck, Richard. "In the Country of Teenage Fiction." *American Libraries* 4 (April 1973): 204–207.

Peck, Richard. "Some Thoughts on Adolescent Literature." *News from ALAN* 3 (September-October 1975): 4–7.

Peck, Richard. "Young Adult Books." *Horn Book Magazine* 62 (September/October 1986): 618–621.

Peck, Richard and Patsy H. Perritt. "British Publishers Enter the Young Adult Age." *Journal of Youth Services in Libraries* 1 (Spring 1988): 292–304. Useful survey of British YA publishers.

Phelps, William Lyon. "The Virtue of the Second-Rate." *English Journal* 16 (January 1927): 10–14. A marvelous article, worth anyone's time.

Pierce, Tamora. "Fantasy: Why Kids Read It, Why Kids Need It." *School Library Journal* 39 (October 1993): 50–51.

Poe, Elizabeth Ann, Barbara G. Samuels, and Betty Carter. "Twenty-Five Years of Research in Young Adult Literature: Past Perspectives and Future Directives." *Journal of Youth Services in Libraries* 28 (November 1981): 25–28.

Popkin, Zelda F. "The Finer Things in Life." *Harpers* 164 (April 1932): 606–611. Contrasts between what young adults like to read and what parents and other adults want kids to read. Obligatory reading.

Probst, Robert. "Reader Response Theory and the Problem of Meaning." *Publishing Research Quarterly* 8 (Spring 1992): 64–73.

Reed, W. Michael and Jeanne M. Gerlach. "Literary Merit and the Adolescent Novel." *ALAN Review* 21 (Fall 1993): 51–56.

Root, Sheldon L. "The New Realism—Some Personal Reflections." *Language Arts* 54 (January 1977): 19–24.

Ross, Catherine Sheldrick. "Young Adult Realism: Conventions, Narrators, and Readers." *Library Quarterly* 55 (April 1985): 174–191.

Salvner, Gary M. "Lessons and Lives: Why Young Adult Literature Matters." *ALAN Review* 28 (Spring/Summer 2001): 9–13.

Silver, Linda R. "Criticism, Reviewing, and the Library Review Media." *Top of the News* 35 (Winter 1979): 123–130. The entire issue on reviewing YA books is fine, particularly "What Makes a Good Review? Ten Experts Speak" (pp. 146–152) and Patty Campbell's "Only Puddings Like the Kiss of Death" (pp. 161–162).

Small, Robert C. Jr. "The Literary Value of the Young Adult Novel." *Journal of Youth Services in Libraries* 5 (Spring 1992): 277–285.

Spencer, Pam. "Winners in Their Own Right." *School Library Journal* 36 (July 1990): 23–27.

Stoehr, Shelley. "Controversial Issues in the Lives of Contemporary Young Adults." *ALAN Review* 24 (Winter 1997): 3–5.

Sutton, Roger. "Forever Yours: An Interview with Judy Blume." *School Library Journal* 42 (June 1996): 24–27.

Sutton, Roger. "The Critical Myth: Realistic YA Novels." *School Library Journal* 29 (November 1982): 33–35.

Townsend, John Rowe. "Didacticism in Modern Dress." *Horn Book Magazine* 43 (April 1967): 159–164. Townsend argues that nineteenth-century didacticism is remarkably like didacticism in modern YA novels.

Townsend, John Rowe. "Standards of Criticism for Children's Literature." *Top of the News* 27 (June 1971): 383–387.

VanderStaay, Steven. "Young-Adult Literature: A Writer Strikes the Genre." *English Journal* 81 (April 1992): 48–52.

Wigutoff, Sharon. "Junior Fiction: A Feminist Critique." *The Lion and the Unicorn* 5 (1981): 4–18.

Wilson, David E. "The Open Library: YA Books for Gay Teens." *English Journal* 73 (November 1984): 60–63.

Using Young Adult Literature in Libraries and Classrooms

Abrahamson, Dick and Eleanor Tyson. "What Every English Teacher Should Know about Free Reading." *ALAN Review* 14 (Fall 1986): 54–58, 69.

Asher, Sanfy. "Life, Live Theater, and the Lively Classroom." *ALAN Review* 21 (Spring 1994): 2–8.

Barnes, Walter. "The Use of Modern Fiction in the High School Class in Literature." *Education* 39 (March 1919): 436–447.

Beers, Kylene and Robert Probst. "Classroom Talk about Literature or the Social Dimensions of a Solitary Act." *Voices from the Middle* 5 (April 1968): 16–20.

Breck, Emma J. "The Efficient High-School Library." *English Journal* 5 (January 1916): 10–14. Still worth our time, old or not.

Broderick, Dorothy. "Serving Young Adults: Why Do We Do What We Do?" *Voice of Youth Advocates* 12 (October 1989): 203–206.

Bushman, John H. "The Reading/Writing Connection: The Role of Young Adult Literature." *ALAN Review* 20 (Fall 1992): 42–46.

Bushman, John H. "Young Adult Literature in the Classroom—Or Is It?" *English Journal* 86 (March 1997): 35–40.

Carroll, Pamela Sissi. "Today's Teens, Their Problems, and Their Literature: Revisiting G. Robert Carlsen's *Books and the Teenage Reader* Thirty Years Later." *English Journal* 86 (March 1997): 25–34.

Carter, Betty. "Adult Books for Young Adults." *English Journal* 86 (March 1997): 63–68.

Chelton, Mary K. "Booktalking: You Can Do It." *School Library Journal* 22 (April 1976): 39–43.

Cosgrove, Helen W. "The Stimulation of Outside Reading among High-School Pupils." *NEA Journal of Proceedings and Addresses.* Washington DC: NEA, 1922, pp. 1032–1037.

Hale Lisa A. and Chris Crowe. " 'I Hate Reading if I Don't Have To': Results from a Longitudinal Study of High School Students' Reading Interest." *ALAN Review* 28 (Spring/Summer 2001): 49–57.

Hopkins, Dianne McAfee. "Challenges to Materials in Secondary School Library Media Centers: Results of a National Study." *Journal of Youth Services in Libraries* 4 (Winter 1991): 131–140.

Janeczko, Paul. B. "Seven Myths about Teaching Poetry, or, How I Stopped Chasing Foul Balls." *ALAN Review* 14 (Spring 1987): 13–16.

Johannessen, Larry. "Young Adult Literature and the Vietnam War." *English Journal* 82 (September 1993): 43–49.

Lesesne, Teri S. "Developing Lifetime Readers: Suggestions from Fifty Years of Research." *English Journal* 80 (October 1991): 61–64.

McGee, Tim. "The Adolescent Novel in AP English: A Response to Patricia Spencer." *English Journal* 81 (April 1992): 57–58.

Mearns, Hughes. "Bo Peep, Old Woman, and Slow Mandy: Being Three Theories of Reading." *New Republic* 48 (November 10, 1926): 344–346.

Nelms, Ben F. "Reading for Pleasure in Junior High School." *English Journal* 55 (September 1966): 676–681.

Pace, Barbara G. "Resistance and Response: Deconstructing Community Standards in a Literature Class." *Journal of Adolescent and Adult Literacy* 46 (February 2003): 408–412.

Peck, Richard. "Ten Questions to Ask about a Novel." *ALAN Newsletter* 5 (Spring 1978): 1.

Probst, Robert E. "Adolescent Literature and the English Curriculum." *English Journal* 76 (March 1987): 26–30.

Probst, Robert E. "Literature as Invitation." *Voices from the Middle* 8 (December 2000): 8–15.

Probst, Robert E. "Mom, Wolfman, and Me: Adolescent Literature, Critical Theory, and the English Classroom." *English Journal* 75 (October 1986): 33–39.

Probst, Robert E. "Three Relationships in the Teaching of Literature." *English Journal* 75 (January 1986): 60–68.

Rakow, Susan R. "Young Adult Literature for Honors Students." *English Journal* 80 (January 1991): 48–51.

Reid, Suzanne and Sharon Stringer. "Ethical Dilemmas in Teaching Problem Novels: The Psychological Impact of Troubling YA Literature on Adolescent Readers in the Classroom." *ALAN Review* 24 (Winter 1997): 16–18.

Robertson, Sandra L. "Text Rendering: Beginning Literary Response." *English Journal* 79 (January 1990): 80–84.

Ross, Catherine Sheldrick. " 'If They Read Nancy Drew, So What?' Series Book Readers Talk Back." *Library and Information Science Research* 17 (Summer 1995): 201–236. Too little known and deserving of wide readership.

Scharf, Peter. "Moral Development and Literature for Adolescents." *Top of the News* 33 (Winter 1977): 131–136. Kohlberg's six stages of moral judgment applied to YA books.

Scoggin, Margaret C. "Do Young People Want Books?" *Wilson Library Bulletin for Librarians* 11 (September 1936): 17–20, 24.

Schontz, Marilyn Louise. "Selected Research Related to Children's and Young Adult Services in Public Libraries." *Top of the News* 38 (Winter 1982): 125–142.

Small, Robert C., Jr. "The Junior Novel and the Art of Literature." *English Journal* 66 (October 1977): 56–59.

Small, Robert C., Jr. "Teaching the Junior Novel." *English Journal* 61 (February 1972): 222–229.

Stallworth, B. Jean. "The Young Adult Literature Course: Facilitating the Integration of Young Adult Literature into the High School English Classroom." *ALAN Review* 26 (Fall 1998): 25–30.

Stotsky, Sandra. "Is the Holocaust the Chief Contribution of the Jewish People to World Civilization and History? A Survey of Leading Literature Anthologies and Reading Instructional Textbooks." *English Journal* 85 (February 1996): 52–59.

Stover, Lois T. "What's New in Young Adult Literature for High School Students." *English Journal* 86 (March 1997): 55–62.

Thurber, Samuel. "An Address to Teachers of English." *Education* 28 (May 1898): 515–526. The best writer of his time, and one of the best English teachers of any time, on getting young people excited about reading and literature.

Tuccillo, Diane P. "Getting Teens Hooked on Reading: What Public Librarians Can Do for Teachers Today." *ALAN Review* 30 (Winter 2003): 63–65.

Tuccillo, Diane P. "Leading Them to Books—for Life." *Publishing Research Quarterly* 8 (Spring 1992): 14–22.

Vogel, Mark and Anna Creadick. "Family Values and the New Adolescent Novel." *English Journal* 82 (September 1993): 37–42.

Vogel, Mark and Don Zancanella. "The Story World of Adolescents in and out of the Classroom." *English Journal* 80 (October 1991): 54–60.

Wilde, Ann and Alan B. Teasley. "The High School Connection: Young Adult Literature in the High School." *ALAN Review* 26 (Fall 1998): 42–45.

APPENDIX

A Brief Bibliography on Films Generally and on Transformations of Print into Film

NOTE: See our website for complete lists of suggested films to accompany each chapter.

Films

Burmester, David. "Mainstreaming Media: 101 Ways to Use Media in the English Classroom." *English Journal* 72 (February 1983): 109–111. Practical suggestions on using film and other media in class.

Costanzo, William V. *Reading the Movies: Twelve Great Films and How to Teach Them.* Urbana, IL: National Council of Teachers of English, 1992. Good throughout, but particularly good on copyright.

Gilmore, Hugh. "What Film Teaching Is Not." *Media and Methods* 7 (September 1970): 41. Succinct and still accurate.

Johnson, Ron and Jan Bone. *Understanding the Film.* Skokie, IL: National Textbook, 1976.

Knight, Arthur. *The Liveliest Art: A Panoramic History of the Movies.* New York: Macmillan, 1957. The easiest place to begin understanding the history of movies.

Kuhns, William. *Movies in America.* Dayton, OH: Pflaum, 1972.

Langman, Larry. *Cinema and the School.* Dayton, OH: Pflaum, 1976.

Maltin, Leonard. *Movie and Video Guide.* Signet annually. Ubiquitous and always helpful, Maltin's paperback is loaded with all kinds of information, and the list of mail order sources early in the book is the best of its kind. It's also a great browsing book.

Maynard, Richard. *The Celluloid Curriculum: How to Use Movies in the Classroom.* New York: Hayden, 1971.

Murch, Walter. "Restoring the Touch of Genius to a Classic." *New York Times* ("Art and Leisure" section), September 9, 1999, pp. 1, 16–17.

Murray, Edward. *Ten Film Classics: A Re-Viewing.* New York: Ungar, 1995.

Ross, Lillian. *Picture.* New York: Rinehart, 1952. The making of John Huston's *The Red Badge of Courage.*

Sarris, Andrew. *"You Ain't Heard Nothin' Yet"; The American Talking Film.* New York: Oxford University Press, 1998.

Selby, Stuart Alan. *The Study of Film as an Art Form in American Secondary Schools.* New York: Arno, 1978. First published in 1963.

Street, Douglas, ed. *Children's Novels and the Movies.* New York: Unger, 1983.

Teasley, Alan B. and Ann Wilder. *Reel Conversations: Reading Films with Young Adults.* Portsmouth, NH: Boynton/Cook, 1996.

Wallace, Amy. "How Does the Panel That Judges U.S. Films Rate?" *Los Angeles Times,* July 18, 1999, pp. A–1, 28–30. Valuable information on what kind of people are on the rating board and how they go about determining ratings.

Transforming Print into Film

Bluestone, George. *Novels into Film.* Baltimore: Johns Hopkins University Press, 1957. The pioneer study.

Boyum, Joy Gould. *Double Exposure: Fiction into Film.* New York: Universe, 1985.

Butler, Teri Payne. "Books to Film." *Horn Book Magazine* 71 (May/June 1995): 305–313.

Culkin, John. "4 Voyages of the Caine." *Media and Methods* 3 (October 1966): 21–28. One of the great early discussions of turning books into film and plays—Herman Wouk's novel, *The Caine Mutiny* (1951); Wouk's play, *The Caine Mutiny Court Martial* (1954); the movie, *The Caine Mutiny* (1954); and the TV play, *The Caine Mutiny Court Martial* (1955).

Giddings, Robert, Keith Selby, and Chris Wensley. *Screening the Novel: The Theory and Practice of Literary Dramatization.* Barnstable, England: Macmillan, 1990.

Lupack, Barbara, ed. *Vision/Re-Vision: Adapting Contemporary American Fiction by Women to Film.* Bowling Green: OH: Bowling Green State University Popular Press, 1996.

Marlin, Janet. "If It's in the Book, It Doesn't Mean It's in the Movie." *New York Times,* February 28, 1992; p. B-1.

McDougal, Stuart Y. *Made into Movies: From Literature to Film.* New York: Holt, Rinehart, and Winston, 1985.

McFarlane, Brian. *Novel to Film: An Introduction to the Theory of Adaptation.* Oxford: Clarendon Press, 1996.

Seigel, Janet. "From Page to Screen: Where the Author Fits In." *Top of the News* 40 (Spring, 1984): 277–283.

Suhor, Charles. "Film/Literature Comparison." *Media and Methods* 12 (December 1975): 56–59.

Acknowledgments

(p. 2) Photo taken by A. P. Nilsen, Courtesy of Elaine Meyers, Phoenix Public Library.

(p. 4) Photo courtesy of Patty Campbell.

(p. 7) Photo courtesy of Ted Hipple.

(p. 10) Photo taken by A. P. Nilsen.

(p. 11) Photo taken by A. P. Nilsen.

(p. 12) Photo taken by A. P. Nilsen.

(p. 13) Photo taken by A. P. Nilsen, courtesy of Diana Lee Messana, Amanda Smith, Jennifer Hamby, Rosemary Luiks.

(p. 14) Photo taken by A. P. Nilsen.

(p. 28) Jacket cover from *Hole in My Life* by Jack Gantos, reprinted by permission of Farrar, Straus and Giroux, LLC: Copyright © 2002 by Jack Gantos.

(p. 29) Jacket cover from *19 Varieties of Gazelle: Poems of the Middle East* by Naomi Shihab Nye, © 2002, reprinted by permission of Greenwillow/HarperCollins.

(p. 38) Photo taken by A. P. Nilsen.

(p. 50) Jacket cover from *Othello: A Novel* by Julius Lester, © 1995, reprinted by permission of Scholastic.

(p. 50) Jacket cover from *Sirena* by Donna Jo Napoli, © 1998, reprinted by permission of Scholastic.

(p. 52) Photo by A. P. Nilsen, courtesy of Ken Donelson.

(p. 59) Photo courtesy of Tempe Historical Museum.

(p. 66) Photo by A. P. Nilsen, courtesy of Ken Donelson.

(p. 70) Photo courtesy of Virginia Euwer Wolff.

(p. 74) Photo courtesy of A. P. Nilsen.

(p. 78) Cover photo from *The Gospel According to Larry* by Janet Tashjian. Jacket Design © 2001 by Henry Holt and Company. Reprinted by permission of Henry Holt & Co., LLC.

(p. 79) Jacket cover from *Paint Me Like I Am* by Writer's Corp, © 2003, reprinted by permission of HarperCollins.

(p. 82) Photo by Marion Etlinger, courtesy of Joyce Carol Oates.

(p. 83) Jacket cover from *MIIB Men in Black: The Movie Storybook*, © 2002, reprinted by permission from HarperCollins.

(p. 83) Jacket cover from *Blue Avenger and the Theory of Everything* by Norma Howe, © 2002, reprinted by permission of Fresh 'N Brite/Carus Publishing Co.

(p. 92) Photo taken by A. P. Nilsen, courtesy of Britton Nilsen.

(p. 100) Photos by A. P. Nilsen, art work by ASU students.

(p. 101) Photos by A. P. Nilsen, art work by ASU students.

(p. 114) Photo courtesy of Paul Fleischman.

(p. 115) Photo by A. P. Nilsen, art work by ASU students.

(p. 116) Photos by A. P. Nilsen.

(p. 118) Jacket cover from *Every Time A Rainbow Dies* by Rita Williams-Garcia, © 2001, reprinted by permission of Amistad/Harper-Collins.

(p. 118) Jacket cover from *All American Girl* by Meg Cabot, © 2002, reprinted by permission of Morrow/HarperCollins.

(p. 122) Jacket cover from *Big Mouth & Ugly Girl* by Joyce Carol Oates. © 2002, reprinted by permission of HarperCollins.

(p. 128) Jacket cover from *Esperanza Rising* by Pam Munoz Ryan, © 2001, reprinted by permission of Scholastic.

(p. 135) *Reprinted by permission of Farrar Straus and Giroux, LLC:* Jacket design from TRUE CONFESSIONS OF A HEARTLESS GIRL by Martha Brooks. Copyright © 2002 by Marth Brooks.

(p. 145) Photos taken by A. P. Nilsen, courtesy of ASU students Merrily Pancoast, Rosemary Luiks, Ryan Smith, and Joseph McCormac.

(p. 151) Photo taken by A. P. Nilsen, courtesy of ASU students Nicole Perkins and Christine Williams.

(p. 155) Photo taken by A. P. Nilsen, courtesy of Kami Nilsen.

(p. 156) Photo taken by A. P. Nilsen

(p. 158) Photo taken by A. P. Nilsen, courtesy of Aaron Levy.

(p. 163) Photo courtesy of Helen and Jerry Weiss.

(p. 169) Jacket cover of *Surviving the Applewhites* by Stephanie S. Tolan, © 2002, reprinted by permissions of HarperCollins.

(p. 176) Photo courtesy of Cornelia Funke.

(p. 178) Jacket cover of *Down the Yukon* by Will Hobbs © 2002, reprinted by permisson of HarperCollins, 2002.

(p. 183) Photo courtesy of Dan Gutman.

(p. 184) Jacket cover of *The Crazy Horse Electric Game* by Chris Crutcher © 1991, reprinted by permission of Greenwillow/HarperCollins.

(p. 191) Photo by A. P. Nilsen, courtesy of ASU students in Young Adult Literature class.

(p. 194) Jacket cover of *Scary Stories 3: More Tales to Chill Your Bones* by Alvin Schartz, Drawings by Stephen Gammell © 1986, reprinted by permission of HarperCollins.

(p. 202) Photo taken by Robin McKinley, courtesy of Peter Dickinson.

(p. 207) Photo taken by A. P. Nilsen.

(p. 209) Photo taken by A. P. Nilsen, courtesy of ASU student Elizabeth L. Moreau.

(p. 215) Photo taken by A. P. Nilsen, reprinted courtesy of Mesa, Arizona Public Library.

(p. 221) Jacket cover of *The House of the Scorpion* by Nancy Farmer © 2002, reprinted courtesy of Simon & Schuster/Atheneum.

(p. 226) Photo courtesy of Chris Crowe.

(p. 228) Jacket cover of *The Kite Rider* by Geraldine McCaughrean © 2002, reprinted courtesy of HarperCollins.

(p. 231) Photo courtesy of Karen Cushman.

(p. 232) Jacket cover of *Rodzina* by Karen Cushman © 2003, reprinted courtesy of Houghton Mifflin.

(p. 243) Photo taken by Marguss Tantalo, teacher at Gilbert Junior High School in Gilbert, Arizona, reprinted courtesy of Samantha Edge, Alexea Tafoya, and Angela Jordan.

(p. 246) Jacket cover from *War and the Pity of War* ed. by Neil Philip, © 1998, reprinted by permission of Clarion.

(p. 252) Jacket cover from *Don't Know Much About the Presidents* by Kenneth C. Davis © 2002, reprinted by permission of HarperCollins.

(p. 256) Photo taken by A. P. Nilsen, courtesy of Jack Gantos.

(p. 264) Cover from *AN AMERICAN PLAGUE: The True and Terrifying Story of the Yellow Fever Epidemic of 1793* by Jim Murphy. Jacket illustration copyright © 2003 by Leslie Evans. Reprinted by permission of Clarion Books/ Houghton Mifflin Company. All rights reserved.

(p. 278) Photos taken by A. P. Nilsen.

(p. 280) Cover from *This Our Dark Country: The American Settlers of Liberia* by Catherine Reef. Copyright © 2002 by Catherine Reef. Reprinted by permission of Clarion Books/Houghton Mifflin Company. All rights reserved.

(p. 289) Photo taken by A. P. Nilsen.

(p. 293) Photo courtesy of Vivian Vande Velde.

(p. 304) Photo taken by Harold Farmer, courtesy of Nancy Farmer.

(p. 311) Photos taken by A. P. Nilsen.

(p. 313) Photos taken by A. P. Nilsen, courtesy of Phoenix Public Library and Mesa Public Library in Arizona.

(p. 317) Photo taken by A. P. Nilsen.

(p. 324) Photo taken by A. P. Nilsen, courtesy of Mary J. Wong.

(p. 338) Photo taken by A. P. Nilsen.

(p. 340) Photo taken by A. P. Nilsen, courtesy of Jerry Brimhall, teacher at Gilbert Junior High School in Arizona.

(p. 341-343) "Ten Questions" courtesy of Richard Peck.

(p. 351) Photo taken by A. P. Nilsen.

(p. 352) Photo courtesy of Gail Carson Levine.

(p. 354) Photo taken by A. P. Nilsen, courtesy of Mel Glenn.

(p. 357) Photos taken by A. P. Nilsen, courtesy of Scott Levigne and Jim Blasingame.

(p. 362) Photos taken by A. P. Nilsen.

(p. 364) Photo taken by A. P. Nilsen, courtesy of Marilyn Wurzburger, Arizona State University Special Collections Librarian.

(p. 373) Photo taken by A. P. Nilsen.

(p. 380) Photo taken by Sigrid Estrada, courtesy of Judy Blume.

(p. 388) Photo taken by A. P. Nilsen.

(p. 392) Photo of *Nothing But the Truth: A Documentary Novel* by Avi © 1991, new edition 2003, reprinted by permission of Orchard/Scholastic.

(p. 392) Photo of *Lemony Snicket: The Unauthorized Autobiography* by Lemony Snicket © 2002, reprinted by permission of HarperCollins.

(p. 395) Photo taken by A. P. Nilsen.

Author Index

Bridgers, Sue Ellen, 22, 24, 25, 42, 133, 290, 294, 331
Brin, David, 218
Brindell, Dennis Fradin, 271
Brokaw, Tom, 272
Brönte, Charlotte,
Bronte, Emily, 161, 347
Brooks, Bruce, 7, 21, 22, 23, 30, 134, 136, 137, 331
Brooks, Hindi, 152, 154
Brooks, Kevin, 164
Brooks, Martha, 16, 339
Brooks, Noah, 56
Brown, Claude, 72, 254, 373, 409
Brown, Dee, 254
Brown, Joanne, 294
Browning, Robert, 63, 106, 147
Brozo, William G., 37
Bruchac, Joseph, 196, 241
Brunvand, Jan Harold, 162
Brynie, Faith Hickman, 276
Buck, Pearl S., 71
Buckley, Christopher, 219
Bugbee, Emma, 57
Bugliosi, Vincent, 274
Bunting, Eve, 96
Burnett, Francis Hodgson, 132
Burns, Ken, 186
Burns, Olive Ann, 23, 28, 31, 140
Burress, Lee, 363, 367
Burroughs, Edgar Rice, 59
Bush, Valerie Chow, 107
Butcher, Grace, 150
Butcher, Nancy, 212
Butler, Charles, 196
Byars, Betsy, 103
Byatt, A. S., 206

Cabot, Meg, 141
Cadnum, Michael, 229, 230
Calabro, Marian, 236
Callahan, John, 274
Callahan, Stephen, 268, 408
Cameron, Steve, 275
Campanella, Roy, 73
Campbell, Joseph, 98
Canfield, Jack, 275
Capote, Truman, 255
Caputo, Philip, 249
Card, Orson Scott, 15, 23, 28, 87, 195, 214, 216, 405
Carlson, Lori M., 143, 302
Carroll, Lewis, 100
Carroll, Michael Thomas, 296
Carroll, Pamela Sissi, 294, 326
Carroll, Rebecca, 272
Carson, John F., 182

Cart, Michael, 123–124, 140, 212, 261, 339
Carter, Betty, 252
Carter, Jennifer, 179
Carter, Peter, 237
Carvel, Marlene, 148
Carver, Raymond, 329, 335
Cary, Lorene, 272
Castlemon, Harry (né Charles Austin Fosdick), 156
Cather, Willa, 102, 237, 270
Cavanna, Betty, 68, 73
Chabon, Michael, 203
Chaiet, Donna, 277
Chamberlain, Wilt, 274
Chambers, Aidan, 7, 16, 133, 139, 240
Chambers, Robert W., 63
Chan, Jeffery Paul, 302
Chandler, Raymond, 188, 219, 293
Chang, Ina, 272
Chatwin, Bruce, 269
Chaucer, 63, 386–387
Chbosky, Stephen,
Chekhov, Anton, 335
Cheripko, Jan, 125, 181, 184
Cherryh, C. J., 203
Chesler, Ellen, 270
Childress, Alice, 24, 26, 30, 31, 126, 134, 292, 332, 358, 383, 407
Chin, Frank, 298–299, 302
Christie, Agatha, 187, 188
Chute, Marchette, 57
Cisneros, Sandra, 15, 23, 28, 301
Clancy, Tom, 88, 93
Clare, Bell,
Clark, Walter Van Tilburg, 335
Clarke, Arthur C., 213, 214–215
Cleary, Beverly, 40, 100, 105
Cleaver, Bill, 27
Cleaver, Eldridge, 72, 126, 254, 383
Cleaver, Vera, 27
Clement-Davies, David, 208
Clements, Andrew, 394
Clements, Bruce, 235
Clifton, Lucille, 150
Clinton, Catherine, 150
Clinton, Cathryn, 241
Cohen, Richard, 263
Cohen-Sandler, Roni, 37
Cohn, Rachel, 137, 166
Colbert, David, 266
Cole, Brock, 7, 19, 21, 22, 42, 310, 374
Colfer, Eoin, 164, 203, 208
Collier, Christopher, 227, 230, 373
Collier, James Lincoln, 230, 373

Coman, Carolyn, 17, 124, 137
Commire, Anne, 126
Compton, Ann Eliot, 138
Comstock, Anthony, 365, 369
Conford, Ellen, 105, 409
Confucius, 364
Conniff, Richard, 263
Conrad, Joseph, 335, 358
Coolidge, Susan (né Sarah Chauncey Woolsey), 47, 56
Cooney, Caroline B., 20, 112
Cooper, Michael L., 272
Coover, Robert,
Cope, Bill, 81
Corcoran, Barbara, 394
Cormier, Robert, 3–4, 7, 8, 10, 13, 17, 21, 22, 23, 24, 25, 26, 28, 31, 42, 75, 103, 119, 123, 133, 135, 142, 190, 196, 262, 294, 310, 331, 332, 341, 351, 356, 358, 360, 361, 373, 374, 405
Corrigan, Eireann, 113
Cosby, Bill, 168
Coville, Bruce, 127, 133, 203, 339
Crane, Milton, 335
Crane, Stephen, 236, 329, 365–366
Craughwell, Thomas J., 162
Craven, Margaret, 132, 406
Crawford, Christina, 273
Creech, Sharon, 17, 135–136, 137, 144, 148, 406
Crew, Linda, 129
Crispin, Edmund (né Bruce Montgomery), 188
Crompton, Vicki, 37
Crowe, Chris, 180, 225, 226, 230, 261, 294
Crum, Shutta, 86
Crutcher, Chris, 4, 7, 8, 11, 19, 22, 29, 32, 127, 136, 139, 181, 183–184, 339, 374
Cummings, Priscilla, 130
Curry, Jane Louise, 203
Cushman, Karen, 7, 19, 230, 231

Dahl, Roald, 45, 100, 270
Daly, Maureen, 57, 68, 73, 335, 393
Daniels, Harvey, 346
Danneberg, Julie, 266
Dante, 358
Danziger, Paula, 105, 163
David, Kati, 243
Davidow, Joie, 302
Davis, James, 367, 375, 392, 393
Davis, Jenny, 22
Davis, Terry, 7, 139, 182
Day, Frances Ann, 296

Dean, Carolee, 127, 143
Deans, Sis, 125, 181
Deaver, Julia Reece, 112
Deland, Margaret, 62
DelFattore, Joan, 387
Dell, Ethel M., 63
Denenberg, Barry, 249, 271
Denton, Sally, 237
Dessen, Sarah, 112, 113
Deuker, Carl, 181
Devaney, John, 242
Dias, Patrick, 149
Dick, Philip, 217, 218
Dickens, Charles, 103, 161, 220
Dickinson, Peter, 9, 21, 30, 31, 196, 202, 203, 210, 220
Dickson, Paul, 162
Dillard, Annie, 251, 268
Ditko, Steve, 91
Dixon, Ann, 261
Doctorow, E. L., 235, 254, 408
Doherty, Berlie, 9, 20, 21, 31, 34
Donne, John, 147
Donnelly, Jennifer, 16
Donovan, John, 367
Dostoyevsky, Fyodor, 70, 267, 332, 347, 358
Douglas, Lloyd, 132
Dove, Rita, 150, 272
Dowd, Olympia, 266
Doyle, Arthur Conan, 59, 188
Dresang, Eliza T., 77
Dressel, Janice Hartwick, 297
Druett, Joan, 179
Duder, Tessa, 181
Du Jardin, Rosamund, 68
Dumbach, Annette E., 240
Duncan, Lois, 24, 25, 197, 374
Dunning, Stephen, 149, 150, 349
DuPrau, Jeanne, 212
Dyer, Daniel, 270

Eaton, Jeanette, 60
Eckert, Allan W.,
Edelman, Bernard, 249
Edelson, Paula, 277
Eleveld, Mark, 144
Eliot, George,
Eliot, T. S., 152, 329
Elkind, David, 36
Ellis, Edward S., 65
Ellis, Sarah, 196
Ellison, Ralph, 72
Emerson, Ralph Waldo, 225
Emery, Anne, 57
Erdoes, Richard, 302
Erdrich, Louise, 408

Erskine, Albert, 335
Euripides, 358

Facklam, Howard, 280
Facklam, Margaret, 280
Fargo, Lucile Foster,
Farjeon, Eleanor, 150
Farley, Walter, 68
Farmer, Nancy, 16, 29, 34, 42, 220, 293, 321
Fast, Howard, 230, 308
Faulkner, William, 42, 72, 298, 335, 347, 358
Feiler, Bruce, 268
Felsen, Henry Gregor, 57, 68
Ferris, Jean, 127
Filipovic, Zlata, 241
Finders, Margaret J., 36
Fine, Anne, 125
Finley, Martha Finley (née Martha Farquharson), 56
Finney, Jack, 216
Fitzgerald F. Scott, 42, 182, 335, 356, 358, 367
Fleischman, Paul, 17, 80, 114, 115, 124, 129, 137, 151, 160, 241
Fleischman, Sid, 8, 16, 18, 29, 114
Fleming, Candace, 271
Fleming, Ian, 72, 189
Fletcher, Lucille, 153
Fletcher, Ralph, 349
Fletcher, Susan, 51
Flowers, Pam, 261
Flynn, Robert, 235, 237
Fogelman, Eva, 245
Foon, Dennis, 222
Forde, Jasper, 203
Forman, James, 240, 358
Fox, Paula, 19, 23, 26, 32, 42, 332, 374, 408
Fradin, Judith Bloom, 271
Francis, H. D., 182
Francis, Robert, 150
Frank, Anne, 242–243, 358
Frank, E. R., 119, 125
Frank, Rudolph, 238
Franklin, Benjamin, 163, 271
Franklin, Jon, 260
Fraustino, Lisa Rowe, 127
Fredericks, Mariah, 140
Freedman, Russell, 186, 252, 261, 270, 281
Freedom, Benedict, 72
Freedom, Nancy, 72
Freeman, Mary E., 335
French, Paul (né Isaac Asimov), 216
Freymann-Weyr, Garret, 16, 140, 288

Friedlander, Mark P.,
Friedman, Ina R., 245
Fritz, Jean, 266
Frost, Helen, 160
Frost, Robert, 329
Frye, Northrop, 98, 111
Fugard, Athol, 153, 329
Funke, Cornelia, 175, 176

Gaiman, Neil, 195, 316
Gaines, Ernest J., 8, 27, 31
Gallagher, Tess, 150
Gallo, Don, 9, 157, 160, 181, 339, 348, 351
Ganeri, Anita, 266
Gantos, Jack, 8, 45, 166, 256, 267, 347
Garbarino, James, 36
Garden, Nancy, 7, 19, 23, 308, 373, 394
Gardner, John, 373
Garfield, Leon, 231–232
Garner, Alan, 204, 332
Gaskins, Pearl Fuyo, 107
Gates, Henry Louis, Jr., 272
Gatti, Anne, 51
Gauch, Patricia Lee, 228
Gay, John, 358
Gay, Kathlyn, 253
Genge, N. E., 218
George, Jean, 136
Giblin, James Cross, 261, 284–282
Gibson, William, 153, 218
Gies, Miep, 242
Gill, Brendan, 168
Giovanni, Nikki, 107, 272
Gipson, Fred, 132
Glasser, Ronald J., 249
Glenn, Mel, 147, 148, 149, 348, 354
Godfrey, Neale S., 264
Goethe, Johann Wolfgang von, 358
Gogol, Nikolai, 335
Going, K. L., 16, 125
Golding, William, 73, 341, 373, 405
Goldsmith, Oliver, 61
Goodall, Jane, 268
Goodman, Alison, 80, 212
Goodwin, Doris Kearns, 186
Gordimer, Nadine, 358
Gordon, Patricia Neale, 153
Gordon, Ruth, 150
Gottfried, Ted, 277
Goudge, Elizabeth, 72
Gould, Jean, 152
Gould, Stephen Jay, 186, 251
Goulden, Joseph C., 162
Grafton, Sue, 189

Critics and Commentators Index

Subject Index

Title Index

Abbreviations for publishers have been used in this index, as follows: American Library Association, ALA; Farrar, Straus, Giroux, Farrar; Harcourt, Brace, Jovanovich, Harcourt; Houghton Mifflin, Houghton; International Reading Association, IRA; Little Brown, Little; Lothrop, Lee, and Shepard, Lothrop; National Council of Teachers of English, NCTE, Random House, Random; and Simon and Schuster, S&S.

piled by Paul B. Janeczko (Candlewick, 2002), 349

Seek by Paul Fleischman (Marcato/Cricket, 2001), 17, 114, 115, 124, 160

Seize the Night by Dean Koontz (Bantam, 1998), 212

Send Me Down a Miracle by Han Nolan (Harcourt, 1996), 135

Sending of Dragons, A by Jane Yolen (Delacorte, 1987), 210

Separate Battle: Women and the Civil War, A by Ina Chang (Lodestar, 1991), 272

Separate Peace, A by John Knowles (Macmillan, 1961), 57, 105, 290

Serpico by Peter Maas (Viking, 1973), 254

17: A Novel in Prose Poems by Liz Rosenberg (Cricket, 2002), 148

Seventeenth Summer by Maureen Daly (1942), 57, 68, 393

70,000 to One by Quentin Reynolds (Random, 1946), 73

Sex Education by Jenny Davis (Orchard, 1988), 22

Shabanu: Daughter of the Wind by Suzanne Fisher Staples (Knopf, 1989), 21, 34, 321

Shadow Boxer by Chris Lynch (HarperCollins, 1993), 20, 181

Shadow Catcher: The Life and Work of Edward S. Curtis by Laurie Lawlor (Walker, 1994), 271

Shadow Spinner by Susan Fletcher (S&S/Atheneum, 1998), 51

Shakespeare Bats Cleanup by Ron Koertge (Candlewick, 2003), 144

Shakespeare: His Work and His World by Michael Rosen (Candlewick, 2001), 266

Shakespeare Scribe, The by Gary Blackwood (Dutton, 2000), 230

Shakespeare Stealer, The by Gary Blackwood (Dutton, 1998), 230

Shaman's Nephew: A Life in the Far North, The by Simon Tookoome and Sheldon Oberman (Stoddart, 2000), 265

Shane by Jack Schaefer (1949), 234

Shared Heart: Portraits and Stories Celebrating Lesbian, Gay, and Bisexual Young People, The by Adam Mastoon (HarperCollins, 1997), 277

Shattering the German Night: The Story of the White Rose by Annette E. Dumbach and Jud Newborn (Little, 1986), 240

Shield Ring, The by Rosemary Sutcliff (Oxford Univ. Press, 1957), 233

Shining Company, The by Rosemary Sutcliff (Farrar, 1990), 21, 31, 233

Shipwreck at the Bottom of the World: The Extraordinary True Story of Shackleton and the Endurance by Jennifer Armstrong (Crown, 1998), 287

Shizuko's Daughter by Kyoko Mori (Holt, 1993), 321

Shoeless Joe and Me by Dan Gutman (HarperCollins, 2002), 183

Shoes: Their History in Words and Pictures by Charlotte and David Yue (Houghton, 1997), 266

Shootist, The by Glendon Swarthout (Doubleday, 1974), 235

Short Circuits: Thirteen Shocking Stories by Outstanding Writers for Young Adults edited by Donald R. Gallo (Delacorte, 1992), 339

Short Life of Sophie Scholl, The by Hermann Vinke (Harper & Row, 1980), 240

Short Stories in the Classroom edited by Carole L. Hamilton and Peter Kratzke (NCTE, 1999), 335

Short Story Masterpieces edited by Robert Penn Warren and Albert Erskine (Dell, 1954), 335

Shrapnel in the Heart: Letters and Remembrances from the Vietnam Veterans Memorial by Laura Palmer (Random, 1987), 249

Shuttered Windows by Florence Crannell Means (1938), 57

Side Effects by Woody Allen (Random, 1989), 168

Sight, The by David Clement-Davies (Pan Macmillan, 2001), 208

Sigmund Freud: Pioneer of the Mind by Catherine Reef (Clarion, 2001), 280

Silas Marner by George Eliot (1861), 63, 332, 368, 391

Silver Kiss, The by Annette Curtis Klause (Delacorte, 1990), 7, 21, 30, 31, 32, 142, 195

Silver Treasure: Myths and Legends of the World, The by Geraldine McCaughrean (S&S, 1997), 51

Sin Eater, The by Gary Schmidt (Dutton, 1996), 134

Sing Down the Moon by Scott O'Dell (Houghton, 1970), 233

Singing the Dogstar Blues by Alison Goodman (Viking, 2003), 80, 212

Single Shard, A by Linda Sue Park (Clarion, 2001), 229, 254, 410

Sinister Pig, The by Tony Hillerman (HarperCollins, 2003), 190

Sir Walter Ralegh and the Quest for El Dorado by Mark Aronson (Clarion, 1999), 280

Sirena by Donna Jo Nalpoli (Scholastic, 1998), 50, 51

Sisterhood of the Traveling Pants, The by Ann Brashares (Delacorte, 2001), 17, 105, 139

Situated Literacies: Reading and Writing in Context edited by David Barton (Routledge, 1999), 81

Sixteen: Short Stories by Outstanding Writers for Young Adults edited by Donald R. Gallo (Delacorte, 1984), 339, 348

Skeleton Man by Joseph Bruchac (HarperCollins, 2001), 196

Skellig by David Almond (Delacorte, 1999), 8, 196

Skin Deep by Lois Ruby (Scholastic, 1994), 246

Sky So Big and Black, The by John Barnes (TOR, 2002), 212

Slap Your Sides by M. E. Kerr (HarperCollins, 2002), 241

Slaughterhouse-Five by Kurt Vonnegut, Jr. (Delacorte, 1966), 373, 383

Slave Dancer, The by Paula Fox (Bradbury, 1972), 26, 374

Slot Machine by Chris Lynch (HarperCollins, 1995), 181

Small Avalanches and Other Stories by Joyce Carol Oates (HarperTrophy, 2003), 82, 394

Small Civil War, A by John Neufeld (Fawcett/Ballantine, 1982, revised edition, Atheneum, 1996), 394

Smithsonian Book of the First Ladies: Their Lives, Times and Issue, The edited by Edith Mayo (Holt, 1996), 270

Smoky, the Cowhorse by Will James (1926), 56